JESSE

JESSE

THE LIFE AND PILGRIMAGE
OF JESSE JACKSON

MARSHALL FRADY

RANDOM HOUSE

NEW YORK

All rights reserved under International and Pan-American
Copyright Conventions. Published in the United States
by Random House, Inc., New York, and simultaneously in Canada
by Random House of Canada Limited, Toronto.

This work was originally published in hardcover
by Random House, Inc., in 1996.

A portion of this work was originally
published in *The New Yorker*.

Library of Congress Cataloging-in-Publication Data is available.

ISBN 0-679-77845-4

Random House website address: http://www.randomhouse.com/

Printed in the United States of America on acid-free paper

2 4 6 8 9 7 5 3

First Paperback Edition

Book design by Jo Anne Metsch

for Barbara

. . . a Black Prince, Potentate of his people, new Poombah of Polemic . . . he was the mightiest victim of injustice in America, and he was also the mightiest narcissist in the land. Every beard, dropout . . . and plain simple individualist paid him homage. The mightiest of the black psyches and most filigreed of the white psyches were ready to roar him home. . . . What a tangle of ribbons he carried on his lance, enough cross-purposes to be the knight-resplendent of television . . . at once a saint and a monster to any mind that looked for category.

—NORMAN MAILER,
on Muhammad Ali, 1971

KERNER: . . . you think everybody has no secret or one big big secret, they are what they seem or they are the opposite. You look at me and think: *Which is he? Plus or minus?* . . . you insist on laboratory standards for reality, while I insist on its artfulness. So it is with us all, we're not so one-or-the-other.

—TOM STOPPARD,
Hapgood

"The past is never dead. It's not even past."

—WILLIAM FAULKNER,
Intruder in the Dust

FOREWORD

ANY SERIOUS CONSIDERATION of any black figure in America must begin from one elemental and encompassing circumstance: however familiar and even tiresomely repeated a proposition by now, it nevertheless remains the case that the fundamental American crisis is still that of race. Well before Alexis de Tocqueville, as early as Thomas Jefferson, the recognition was already emerging that the American political adventure, begun in such largeness of possibility, may have also from its very inception—the instant the first black man in chains set his foot on this continent's shore—held the dark seeds of its ultimate undoing. That aboriginal crime has been with us ever since, accounting for successive convulsive travails of which the Civil War was merely the most seismic and bloody. But its effects have also proliferated and complicated down through the generations—not only in both black and white society but, more, in the black and white psyche. And to such a myriad and diffused extent that those conditions and attitudes no longer seem to have any connection to the primal crime that began them. The result is that now we, and particularly those of us who are white, have no real sense of how we continue to be entailed in the lasting consequences of that original great Cain-Act, the systematic brutalization of a whole people.

Since the transformations worked by the Martin Luther King phase of the civil rights movement, America's racial travail has evolved into a merely more subtle complex of tensions. While most of the laws and institutions of racism have nominally been abolished, and our popular culture, from beauty pageants to television sitcoms, would seem substantially integrated now, virtually every social duress in this country—poverty, hunger, crime, drugs, family disintegration, generational imprisonment in the underclass—is still the lot of a hugely disproportionate mass of African-Americans. And who can seriously question that, only some thirty years after the conditionings of three centuries of slavery and its slightly abstracted sequel of segregation, it is history's lingering legacy of racism—in whatever less overt forms, less measurable and so less engageable by law and regulation, but no less pervasive and intractable—that is still acting to lock blacks into those conditions? We remain—in where blacks can live, what they subsist on, the quality of their lives, what future they can expect—still largely divided into two Americas, racially drawn, estranged from each other.

Even among African-Americans who have managed to escape the undertows of the past and enter the comfortable preserves of the middle class, there can be heard, for the very reason that they have presumably made it into the American promise, the most bitter angers of alienation. Most critically, in our inner cities, there steadily expands a kind of Third World country within the United States, a population of inner exiles empty of any sense of possibilities or any connection to the rest of the national community—millions of those whom James Baldwin once described as "the most dangerous creation of any society . . . that man who has nothing to lose." The enormous combustible potential of such a situation is obvious, and it is fearful to ponder what might ensue if the distraction and anesthesia of drugs were ever actually removed from these masses of the unhoping. But just how distant most whites are now from any sense of source for the consequences they behold was indicated when, in the midst of the upheaval in Los Angeles in the spring of 1992, a local white television newscaster kept insisting, with a blankly grave and pale peer into the camera, "This has nothing to do with civil rights or any of that. This is just about hoodlums and lawlessness."

Yet the black youths who were seen on that first day of flames and wreckage pulling a white driver from his truck and then battering him with a methodical brutality were not *born* with rocks uplifted in their hands. Nor, for that matter, were the white policemen born holding the clubs with which they, just as methodically, battered Rodney King. The legacy of slavery, in its almost measureless ramifications, has continued to brutalize us all. And racism endures as the one endemic American dilemma that could yet rupture this always precarious democracy.

In the middle of Jesse Jackson's first presidential campaign, on a summer evening in 1984, James Baldwin told journalists Bob Faw and Nancy Skelton, "Now here comes Jess. Young man out of the civil rights movement, out of the pain . . . and the Republic refuses, really, to recognize [him]. How he comes here before us we don't really know. But we do know this: that his presence presents the American Republic with questions and choices it has spent all its history until this hour trying to avoid. . . . And nothing will ever again be what it was before."

ACKNOWLEDGMENTS

THESE ARE THE people whose craft and wisdom and patience critically helped this book to happen, and surely account for much of whatever is best in it:

John Bennet and Josselyn Simpson at *The New Yorker*, and its past editor Robert Gottlieb. Of course, Frank Curtis, of Rembar & Curtis. Also, strategically, David Fanning and Michael Sullivan at *Frontline*, and particularly Mark Zwonitzer and Tom Lennon of the Lennon Documentary Group; most particularly Mark Zwonitzer, whose research and interviews for his *Frontline* documentary on Jackson have additionally much enriched this story. In their own various other ways, Jack Pratt, Alan W. Wolfson, Ermes Muzio, James and Riccardo Gandolfo. But preeminently, the heroically intrepid David Rosenthal of Random House and, with her exquisite editorial sorceries, Ruth Fecych.

Finally, she who has borne all the long haul of time this work has taken, with a steady belief in it, consistent urgings beyond the flat lagging lulls, and all with a natural sweetness and goodness of heart still wondrous to me to find in such a beauty, which is one reason why I love her—my wife, Barbara Ann Gandolfo.

CONTENTS

PART

ONE

A MYSTERY OF CHARACTER

I

The Man First Encountered

IT WAS BACK in the late sixties, when, as a beginning journalist in the Atlanta bureau of *Newsweek*, I was covering the latter days of the civil rights movement—still a rather raw provincial not that long emerged out of a white southern small-town upbringing, abruptly plopped into the midst of that stunning moral pageantry—that I came across a young assistant to Martin Luther King, Jr., named Jesse Jackson, himself out of a small South Carolina town. I saw him only fleetingly—perhaps once or twice in the Atlanta headquarters of King's Southern Christian Leadership Conference (SCLC); at a mass meeting somewhere; then at SCLC's final, doomed enterprise of Resurrection City on Washington's Mall, a shacky encampment that was part of SCLC's soon-to-be-vanishing Poor People's Campaign. But from those occasional, passing encounters, a memory lasted of a strapping, somewhat oversized youth, unusually grave and self-contained, always wearing a flat glower of some private purpose but also with a kind of buccaneer's dash about him—and who, though a newly attached and clearly reverential acolyte of King's, seemed almost radioactive with a tense urgency of his own. Already then he carried a certain glamour of portent that prompted other journalists besides me to speculate that, of all King's aides, he just might turn out to be the successor.

Over the following decades, one was sporadically aware, from press mentions and television glimpses, of Jackson pitching about on the margins of the nation's life for some fulfillment of that large expectation, which he had now made plain was no less his own. Decamping from SCLC after King's death, he had formed, in his adoptive hometown of Chicago, an organization that he had ambitiously titled People United to Save Humanity, or PUSH—an eclectic sort of social ministry, occupied mostly in campaigning for economic racial equity but eventually ranging, around the mid-seventies, to widely acclaimed rallies, conducted by Jackson in black schools across the nation, for educational rigor and self-reliance. Despite those initial anticipations for him, he still seemed adrift, a still auspicious but curiously unclassifiable, free-form black evangel not yet come into his true definition—all this while passing through a series of mutations in dashikis, fuming Afros, clerical gowns, safari suits, as if trying to dial himself into his right public persona. Then, after a revival-like sweep of mass meetings through the South on a voter-registration crusade in 1983, came his two successive presidential campaigns—guerrilla adventures that wound up far outreaching all prior projections. In the long and bitter history of racial schism in America since slavery, these campaigns amounted to the first genuinely serious presidential runs by a black candidate ever. And a specific part of that drama, after what had seemed a muddled and brackish stasis since the simple brave hopes of King's time, was the possibility that—deriving from what was perhaps the most important victory of King's movement in the sixties, the claiming of the vote—Jackson's candidacy could bring a rematerialization of that moral vision and movement, in the form of the political arrival of blacks in America on a national scale.

Yet at the center of the phenomenon of those two campaigns, the ambiguity of Jackson himself—what he was actually about, what he meant to be, "What does he want?"—had only magnified. In attempting to transfer the movement's moral gospel into an actual presidential competition, he had become a much larger, more clamorously argued enigma. That may have accounted, in part, for much of the disquiet about him: no one was certain exactly who he was. He had been careering about with increasing conspicuousness in our national experience since the early seventies, to the point where polls indicated he had become one of the most recognizable public figures in the land, but a kind of familiar stranger whose exact nature remained unclear. One journalist remarked that he "seems to have several personalities which fit together only very loosely, as if events have come too quickly and fame crowded too closely." It was as if, out of some pell-mell impatience to realize his early promise, he had simply gone for too much, wanted to be too many things, and this left him with varied identities, like overlaid images from multiple photographic exposures— not just a preacher, not just a politician, not just a social activist, not only a militant young black Joshua to his people but also a tribune for white farmers and striking union workers, while expanding his circuit-riding movement ministry to expeditions to the Middle East and Africa and Latin America, and in the course of all this, becoming a star of sorts in the nation's pop firmament of the diversely famed. His profusion of involvements once moved an aide to slip him a note, *The most you can is not the best you can.* And an early associate later lamented, "Jesse has got to grow up. He has got to make up his mind what he wants to do, what he wants to be." In his multiplicity of images, though, he had come to be characterized as everything from, in the words of George Bush once, "a Chicago hustler," to "the moral voice of our time," as Andrew Young declared after Jackson's first presidential campaign.

But he had, at the least, traveled an awesome distance from that early discipleship to King, and almost unimaginably far from his abject beginnings as an illegitimate black child in the poorest quarter of Greenville, South Carolina. All of this, then—and especially my own fancy that he might hold a possibility for some continuation of that immense moral drama of the sixties, which had been a Damascus Road experience in more lives than mine—was why, in late 1988, I set out on this book.

It was on a dimly misting autumn morning in Chicago, several weeks after Jackson's spectacular oration at the Democratic convention in Atlanta, that, after only intermittently glancing him in the depthless window of television, I saw him in person for the first time since those now remote movement days. He had briefly returned from trooping about the country in behalf of the Dukakis-Bentsen ticket to conduct his regular Saturday-morning service at his PUSH headquarters in a former synagogue on the corner of a frumpish street on Chicago's South Side—an auditorium, beyond its vast dull-cream fluted pillars and tall windows of colored glass, now rather anonymously bare and seeming a bit cavernous for the congregation scattered about. But the podium itself was thronged with assorted attendants and guests, and presently, a flourish of organ tones brought Jackson striding onstage.

Television's trick mirror commonly exaggerates presence, so that the real person, when encountered, usually seems strangely dwindled and prosaic, but Jackson surprisingly matched the size of the familiar image of him on TV. A commandingly tall figure, straight-backed, with a strutful, pouter pigeon's bulge to his chest, he was attired, with the sober nattiness of a Beverly Hills investment broker, in a charcoal-gray suit traced with faint pinstripes, a glimmering red-and-black-banded tie on an ice-blue shirt, with a crimson handkerchief brimming from his breast pocket. He had about him a high-collared flair of the cavalier: that swashbuckler's carriage I remembered from the sixties now gone a little heftier. But he had lost none of the bearing of some dramatic personal portent. I was struck again by how much his look—his broad, flattish face; his wide, helmetlike brow above far-spaced and slightly bulby eyes with a vaguely split focus; his Zapata mustache curling over a small pouch of a mouth—seemed to hold some elusive resemblance to King himself. He wore the same masklike expression of a grave, almost Oriental imperturbability, with the same level, still gaze that gave King the peculiar effect of at once intently occupying the moment but also being removed some far distance beyond it. He had not acquired that similarity of mien by coincidence; he once explained the unwavering solemnness he was already maintaining in the sixties, "Smiling wouldn't have looked like a leader was supposed to look." Now, after his entrance this morning, his face remained emotionless as the spirited ovation continued around him, and when the congregation finally swung into singing and clapping out a song, "You Gotta Keep Reachin'," Jackson, while clapping along, stood looking over the audience and the stage around him with a swift proprietary appraisal. When he noticed several journalists in the front row below him, he widened his eyes, gave a quick cock of his head, and with one of his curiously flat, squeezed grins under his mustache, hiked high one long thumb curving far backward like an ibex's horn, as if in acknowledgment of some secret complicity between them.

Finally taking the pulpit, he commenced, also much in the manner of King, in a slow, subdued, idly browsing voice, as if moseying around for what he would actually wind up talking about, with his hands lying loosely cupped on the sides of the pulpit, now and then stroking back and forth along its edges with a little hip-nudge under his coattail at the delivery of a phrase, not unlike someone playing a pinball machine. "We moving into the latter stages of this campaign now. Sometimes we may have . . . may have *narrow* choices. But we *do* always have choices. We struggled long and paid in suffering to win the right to those choices, and we, we"—shuffling up these lines, looping them out with softly hesitant hangs of suspense as if fly casting—"we *do* have choices now!" He then rolled his head around to see how he was beginning to register on those assembled about him, and meeting with assenting hums and nods, he went on, "But we going on beyond November. The race goes not to the swift but to the patient and long-enduring, to those who persist and tire not. Going on *beyond* November!" He now turned all the way around in the pulpit to look at those seated directly behind him, as a happily expectant murmuration arose in the auditorium, along with a few whoops. Swinging back to the congregation, he shouted, "The best is yet to come!" He had found the frequency now. "We going to outwork, outwalk, outtalk, outfast, and out*last* them all. The best is yet to come!" He took a step back from the pulpit, spread both hands down wide and flat against the side pockets of his snugly buttoned coat with his elbows winged out. "I may not be on this ticket, but I am still *on the scene*! I can't *wait* to get back up outta bed every morning, I don't need no alarm clock to wake me up—I'm driven by *purpose*."

Not inappropriately, Jackson made these pronouncements under an admonition still inscribed in large letters high over the former synagogue's podium: *Know Before Whom Thou Standest.* And that was precisely what perplexed a considerable number of people across the nation about the tall, theatrically apostolic figure now booming away below it.

Traveling with Jesse

THAT SATURDAY-MORNING service at PUSH was the beginning of what would turn out to be, though I hardly suspected it then, six years of tracking about with Jackson in a kind of migratory, open-ended tournament of talking. Jackson carried on a continuous discourse of recollections and reflections not unlike those one-actor stage monologues from the life of Mark Twain or Teddy Roosevelt, but with the principal himself providing the performance — a free-floating disquisition that was not necessarily connected to his surroundings at the moment, whether traveling from his mother's kitchen down in Greenville to snow-dusted streets in Moscow, from back roads twining through Missouri farmland to a gilded antechamber of Saddam Hussein's presidential palace in Baghdad, where he was waiting to continue negotiations for the release of hostages held after Iraq's invasion of Kuwait. Jackson would keep up this marathon soliloquizing even while stampeding up and down stairways from one engagement to another: "It's been a constant struggle of spirit over flesh — but I got to go into this meeting here right now," and then, after a suspension of a few hours or even sometimes a few weeks, would pick it back up virtually in midsentence, as if only a moment's interruption had intervened, ". . . I was saying, constant struggle of spirit over flesh, but Jesus went through it, Dr. King went through it, constant war inside you against temptations of your baser nature. . . ."

Jackson had, of course, already become fabled for an inextinguishable loquacity verging on logorrhea — the columnist Mike Royko once observed, "He looks on a defenseless ear the way William (Refrigerator) Perry eyes a roast chicken" — and his compulsion to expound was not daunted by hopeless language differences. Riding into Paris early one morning after a flight from Gabon at the end of a tour through sub-Saharan Africa, he began propounding to a Gabonese general sitting in the front seat, a chunky man in a funereally dark civilian suit, about how the splendors of Paris passing by them had been created largely from the wealth of French colonies, when he suddenly seemed to realize he was getting no response, and leaned forward to nudge the general's shoulder, "That right, what I'm saying?" The general turned and smiled uncertainly: "*Je ne parle pas anglais.*" Jackson paused only an instant: "Hunh? Oh. Yeah, but you get my drift, don't you?" And declaimed on. Often, at the end of a long and manically scrambling day in Armenia or Zimbabwe or Seattle or the West Bank, the last sound to be heard in the hotel corridor late at night was Jackson still hoarsely bleating away in his room to an aide or on the phone to someone in Chicago or Los Angeles or even Tokyo—and one would be awakened early the next morning by the same urgent, muffled callioping, producing the impression that he had been at it throughout the night. More than once he brought to mind William Faulkner's fancy, in his Nobel Prize speech, about the last red evening at the end of time in which there would still be the lone sound of man's inexhaustible voice clamoring away in nothingness. Before long, there were moments when one re-garded Jackson's approach, eyes brightening and mouth already opening to begin expatiating some more, with something close to woe. On one flight from Paris back to the United States, in the Gulfstream executive jet furnished by Gabon's president, Jackson kept up an exuberant oratorio of reminiscences and random musings until I finally retreated into the rear compartment and feigned sleep for several hours, dimly aware of his wandering back several times to check on whether maybe we could resume.

I soon suspected that, in my case, his volubility was additionally invigorated by a certain fascination with the happenstance of my having grown up, almost the same age as he, in a town only twenty-six miles away from Greenville that much mirrored his own hometown—that, in the South Carolina of the fifties, we had grown up in parallel, as it were, but in two utterly separate worlds—mine the comfortably insulated sedateness of a modest middle-class white neighborhood where my father was a Southern Baptist minister. More than that, I had eventually attended the college in Greenville—Furman University—whose oak-bowered men's campus had once sprawled just across the street from a huddled row of houses where Jackson was raised. His grandmother had taken in laundry for several fraternities, and Jackson, as a boy, had dreamed of being a student at Furman himself one day. He is now fond of constantly discovering in life around him what he calls "the poetries of time"—far-flung correspondences, synchronicities large and small, wide circles being closed with unexpected irony—and this particular little convergence seemed to afford him an exorbitant and lasting relish. At dinner with Armenian officials one evening in Yerevan, he reported to everyone around the table with a zesty drollness, "Frady here, he was raised in Anderson, just a few miles from where I was raised in Greenville. I grew up right beside the university there, Furman. Always wanted to go to school there. But couldn't in those days, of course. Frady, though, *he* comes over and goes to Furman. Our family, we used to iron his shirts—twenty cents apiece. Used to park his car at the football games. He'd go to the library there—I couldn't go." What he did not go on to say, though he had not neglected to imply it on a number of other occasions, was, *But here we are, he's running around following me after I've run for president two times, reporting on what I'm doing now. . . .*

Still, there was a deeper and more difficult matter involved, of which I was perhaps more uncomfortably conscious than Jackson in all his eager expansiveness. For a white journalist undertaking to tell his life, there was inevitably the question of whether it's possible for any white to understand fully what it means, how it feels, to have grown up black in this society—if there would not always be some last, impassable barrier to really knowing that central reality about Jackson. In the past, he had remarked to white reporters, "The fundamental character of racism in America is so congenital, it's impossible for white folks to perceive reality. I don't know how capable you are of getting my story right, your world is so different from mine." When I once asked him about this, he replied in somewhat cryptic metaphor, "Well, you know, we used to say back home, hogs grow up on the hill and hogs grow down in the valley, they different, *taste* different, 'cause they lived different. Or it's the difference between flyin' someplace and takin' a train: you go slower, you notice more, so you *know* more than somebody flyin' in a jet. But it's mostly whether it's just sympathy or empathy. Can be done, but it's awfully difficult." Nevertheless, I was hardly unaware of the strong claims, continuing since the furor over William Styron's *Confessions of Nat Turner,* that no one who has grown up white in America can ever presume, whether in a novelized "meditation on history" or a journalistic account, to enter into and describe the life of a black American with any fully dimensioned realization: that there are inherent limits to any white writer's understanding beyond which he properly should not venture. But that claim supposed special reaches of human experience sacrosanct to those who have dwelt there, and in that notion there seemed to me implicitly some final defeat and despair, in itself a denial that all of us are, in the end, of one nature, of one heart.

Even so, for any white who would write closely about a black personality, there is without doubt much to make one's way through. Racism comes in many forms, some quite polite and unthinking, often sublimated into a spectrum of secondary, at-one-or-two-remove reactions, but it is essentially the feeling, conscious or instinctive, malign or even genial, that there is some natural, fundamental difference in those of another ethnic origin which means that they are not really us. And no one growing up white in this society, however earnest and of goodwill, should presume he has escaped the infinitely varied and discreet conditionings of its atmospheric racism. For instance, on arriving late at the terminal for Jackson's flight to Africa on the jet provided him by Gabon's president, I noticed a youngish black man, in a crisp white shirt and black tie, standing beside the laden luggage trolley, and I was pushing my bags toward him, saying, "Could you put these on there, too, for me?" when I noticed a Jackson aide vigorously cross-flagging his hands at me. He pulled me aside to mutter, "No, no, man, that's the *Gabonian ambassador*." To the degree that any whites of some sensitivity of conscience recognize their own implication in the weather of racism in the general society—and those whites happen to know, from the inside, how truly pervasive it is in white culture, from the daily talk of cabdrivers and salesclerks and neighbors and professional colleagues and their own friends and even family—then those whites tend to carry at least vague ghosts of guilt, and a concomitant urge to compensate, to atone. Jackson himself, actually, has never been oblivious to that sensitivity, and he would not abstain from employing it occasionally in attempts to morally shanghai one with such casual remarks as "We had such bad luck in the past with white writers, you know, betraying us, messing us over, just don't know sometimes whether we ought to trust any of them. . . ." Yet however much a ploy, one knew he happened to be more than a little right.

A further concern about perspective, though, was that, having covered the civil rights movement from which Jackson emerged, I was left, like most other white journalists, with a certain romanticism about that time and its figures: it was an experience that has since assumed, for many of us, an almost mythic magnitude, as if we were briefly involved, if only as reporters, in a momentous passion play of the human spirit, and through the duller accumulation of years, some central part of us has remained emotionally imprisoned in the simple, lyric sentiments, or sentimentalisms, of that high moral theater.

The effort then was to try to move past all that somehow—the doubtlessly persisting inflections of racism, dim guilts because of that, and the lasting romanticisms from the movement—and to cross over the shadowy, complexly mined border zone into that other country of being black in America, to try, as a white stranger in that unfamiliar land, to understand this singular black American, along with everything else he's become, simply as a man.

II
The Gift and the Hunger

IN THE FALL of 1991, shortly before announcing that he would not be undertaking a third presidential run, Jackson appeared with an assortment of other potential and declared contenders before a conclave of the Democratic National Committee in Los Angeles, and more or less abducted the entire occasion with a passionate address that some political journalists there pronounced one of the most powerful they had ever heard him deliver. It happened to be less than a year after the Gulf War, and Jackson cited to this convocation of party curators assembled at the Biltmore Hotel the legions of veterans now adrift and destitute in American society. "If we really love our troops," he rumbled, "and love them genuinely, beyond wearing yellow ribbons and symbolic expressions—if we really *love* our troops—then we will love them when they are no longer troops, we will love them when *they come back home.* They deserve—if we really *do* love them—not a Canadian health-care plan or a British health-care plan, they deserve the *congressional* health-care plan—the same plan that those who sent them *off* to war have got. If we love them, provide for loan guarantees so they can get homes. If we love them, guarantee their children a college education. If we *really* love our troops." He went on, "Neither race, class, sex, or religion should stand between our children and the best education America has to offer. It costs less now to go to Yale than to go to jail—because we have not made the judgment to invest in the *frontside* of our children's lives. All across this nation, these decadent and retarded values. Our children are being *abandoned, neglected.* We must rescue them!" He appealed, "Ultimately, those who have the *moral* imperative will outlast those driven by political calculation. If we take the high ground, we will win—and *deserve* to win."

He then described his recent visit to Hamlet, North Carolina, where, several days earlier, twenty-five workers had perished in a fire in a chicken-processing plant. "Imperial Foods—ran away from the North and unions that kept filing objections to doors locked from the outside. They moved their plant to the New South, to a nonunion workforce, black and white. Eleven years, not one inspection. The workers mostly women, making four twenty-five an hour. No health insurance. Then a fire. Doors locked on the outside by managers afraid some worker might steal a chicken. Twenty-five killed, seventy injured. Women, mostly *women*—who never make conferences like this in big hotels, can't afford it, don't even know when we meet. Women who have only two five-minute breaks a day to use the bathroom. Women who work on those lines until their hands freeze and they don't even realize at first if they've lost a finger. One of them told me, she was crying, 'So glad *somebody* came to our town, 'cause we way off to the side of the road down here.' Well, I'd remind all of you, so was Nazareth, so was Selma. God has done great things in small towns. She said, 'Reverend, I got three children and I ain't got no husband, but I really don't want to be on welfare.' Said, in her own ungrammatical but profound way"—and he suddenly took on her voice, high, hurried, blurring—" 'They makes us pluck a hunnerd chicken wings a minute, and' "—Jackson hunched over, his hands tightly milling in circles at his waist, strangely as if beginning now to assume her form—" 'and us can't stop. And then we gits that, that *carpal* thing in our hands and wrisses, and we can't ben' 'em' "—he twisted his hands in front of him into claws—" 'and then, then they fires us, and us can't 'dress our grievances no mo'. And we can't get no mo' jobs, 'cause if we tawk back here, they blackballs us. And . . . and we can't work nohow 'cause our wrisses hurt' "—he moved one hand slowly up his arm and held his elbow, briefly bowing his head to one side—" 'and then we put on welfare. And they calls us lazy bitches then.' "

Jackson paused for a long moment. Some members of the audience now were wet-eyed. Then he shook his head and began flagging his finger around the assembly, with a little outward roll of his lower jaw and his own voice now squeezed into a struggling whisper, "We must *rescue* those women." Applause began to stir, gathered louder, and he now shouted as the full force of that feeling filled him, "We must *rescue* those women! *We must rescue them!* They must *not* be abandoned!" And over the long explosion of applause, he cried out again, "Party, we need to go to Hamlet! We need to take *America* to Hamlet today, we need to let *all* the Hamlets of America know we stand with them! We cannot lead where we do not *go*. *We got to go to Hamlet!*"

It was one of those addresses of Jackson's that once moved cultural essayist Stanley Crouch to declare him a "moral poet" who "can reach levels of such lyricism that the body politic itself seems some sort of poem still being born in heroic proportions." Afterward, as he was leaving the Bilt-more, Jackson was approached by a Clinton campaign aide, Harold Ickes. "You have such a gift," Ickes told him, "you've just got this *gift*."

Jackson replied, "Well, why don't you *use* that gift? Why don't you just bring me on in? You can keep on tryin' to cut me out if you want, but I'm not goin' away. You can try to go around me, try to go under me—sho can't go *over* me, you know that. So why don't you just bring me in?"

IN A CERTAIN sense, most of Jackson's life has been occupied in a labor to deploy that gift to get inside. And over the course of that exertion, few have managed to rise quite so high from so far outside the main society of America.

He began, in fact, as a multidimensioned outsider to that society—born not only black but illegitimate, and in the most impoverished pocket of the black community of his hometown of Greenville. But ever since sensing early in his youth that he bore an uncommon personal promise far beyond the bounds of what he had been born into, his obsession has been to re-create himself into someone with a meaning large enough to answer that early sense of his possibilities—that is, quite simply, to belong to that wider society in which he found himself outcast by making himself into a moral hero in its life.

That extraordinary undertaking of Jackson's is what this story is about. It's not often one encounters a figure who, from such meager beginnings, has so consciously set about constructing himself to such a grandiose mea-sure—and who, even more rarely, has seemed to hold from the start the actual, natural, imposing stuff for it, however rough and rudimentary. But his compulsion to cast himself as the central player in some unfolding his-toric moral saga can at times approach a high reel of hubris. Asked once if he actually considered himself in a line of moral succession from Gandhi and King, Jackson hesitated not an instant in replying, solemnly, "It's what I aspire to." Stanley Crouch has suggested that Jackson "will be forever doomed by his determination to mythologize his life," and in that urgency, above almost all else, he lusts for drama always around him—that is when living is, to him, most real, most vivid, and he can scarcely bear the long monotone intervals of its absence. "There's something in him that says: if you're going to live, make it dramatic," says a former assistant, Bernard Lafayette. "For Jesse, Shakespeare couldn't have been more right. This life is a stage."

But one perverse irony of Jackson's life is that he wound up curiously misplaced in time for his grand aspiration. Absent the great moral dra-maturgy of King's day, Jackson was left to struggle in the vague spiritual flats of a more prosaic and middling season to find his apotheosis, his mountaintop. As a consequence, he finally resorted to the expedient of seeking his fulfillment as a prophetic successor to King, not outside the system, which has been the classic position of social prophets, but inside it, as a contender in the processes of political power itself—a prospect that much more riskily seductive for someone with Jackson's huge hunger to belong.

IN THAT POLITICAL gambit, he fared far more impressively, as it turned out, than even he imagined he would. While at first he seemed to his party's custodial establishment—and to many journalists—little more than a kind of picaresque adventurer, he showed in his two freebooting campaigns a primal popular vitality that, like some unmeasurable fifth force of political physics, disrupted all the equations of the orthodox sophistication about what was possible for him. In 1984, when he came steaming virtually out of nowhere as a black social gospelteer with no past governmental experience to make his first foray into the Democratic presidential primaries, his effort was generally dismissed as a venture of the most whimsical implausibility. But it's important to remember now that against that standard presumption and despite certain staggering gaucheries he committed near the start, Jackson managed to collect 21 percent of the total primary and caucus votes, including 80 percent of the black vote—some 3.5 million votes altogether—and out of the initial gallery of eight candidates, he pushed past five all the way to the convention, behind only Gary Hart and Walter Mondale. It was, at the least, an arresting showing for a black candidate supposedly engaged in only a historically diverting gesture. New York's governor Mario Cuomo declared, "When they write the history of this [primary campaign], the longest chapter will be on Jackson. The man didn't have two cents. He didn't have one television or radio ad. And look what he did." At the convention in San Francisco, he delivered an organ-pealing oration, watched by a huge television audience, from which he emerged as an incandescently dramatic new protagonist in the nation's political theater.

Even so, most political seers concluded that Jackson would amount to no more than what columnist George Will termed "a comet hitting the earth's atmosphere, burning brightly but fatally and soon to be a small cinder." Yet in the presidential primary campaigns four years later, in 1988, Jackson expanded his popular vote to some 7 million, exceeded only by Governor Michael Dukakis's 10 million, and more votes, as Jackson afterward never tired of pointing out, "than any other second-place primary finisher in history." This time, his count included 12 percent of the whites who voted—three times the number he had drawn in 1984. At one point, about midway through the primaries, when he unexpectedly won the Michigan caucuses, he was for a dizzying moment actually considered the front-runner for the nomination. Overall, he placed first in fourteen primaries and caucuses and second in thirty-six others, among them such overwhelmingly white states as Maine and Minnesota. Against initial projections that he could hope this time to amass only about 550 delegates—perhaps 700 at the most—he went into the convention in Atlanta with over 1,200 delegates, approaching a third of the total, and more than any other runner-up for the Democratic nomination before him. And he produced in Atlanta another oratorical sensation.

That a freelance black activist initially regarded as only a flamboyant political novelty, and setting out with the sparest resources and staff, could proceed so far on not much more than the sheer heats of his populist Pentecostalisms and the voltages of his public presence, was arguably one of the most remarkable political assertions within recent memory—a feat of imagination and audacity over the heaviest tilt of circumstances. Not the least of his achievements in this was that after Frederick Douglass became the first black presidential candidate in a major party, receiving a single vote at the 1888 Republican convention, Jackson with the surprising seriousness of his campaigns had finally broken a long-abiding barrier by beginning to dispel in white minds, and those of blacks as well, the simple unthinkability of a black in the country's highest office—whose historic beneficiary, it began to seem in 1995, could well be Colin Powell. From having been reckoned in 1984 only a provocative curiosity, Jackson emerged after 1988 as a figure who would have been considered among the more auspicious contenders for the nomination in 1992—if he had been almost anyone other than Jesse Jackson. Instead, to the party's management, he loomed like some ominous Robber Bridegroom, boding incalculable havoc for the party's prospects in its competition with the Republicans for the country's supposed conservative mainstream.

In one respect, Jackson was simply another of those unruly populist outriders who, periodically, have come ransacking from obscure reaches to intrude themselves into the central political process of choosing the president of the Republic—such formidable irregulars as William Jennings Bryan, Huey Long, and even in his own dowdy and surly fashion, George Wallace. Populism itself, originally a folk-combustion of radically egalitarian, country-Jacobin militancy after the Civil War, constituted perhaps the only truly indigenous American revolutionary proposition since 1776, and while always consummately a movement of outsiders, it has continued to flare intermittently through our politics for well over a century, though by the 1990s, the term "populist"—along with that of "outsider," for that matter—had come into a rather promiscuously loose currency. But it's fair to say that none of the other notable populist tribunes preceding Jackson—not Bryan, not Long, and surely not Ross Perot—had ever journeyed from so far outside. And Jackson presented something of a singular new variation, as an ad hoc black social evangel in a corporate, technotronic age, of that old and rowdy American political impulse.

To warnings from Democratic regulars—many of them permanently traumatized by the defeat of past liberal candidacies at the hands of silent-majority politics from Nixon to Reagan—that Jackson remained hopelessly alien to the nation's presumed Reaganite mainstream, Jackson returned, "If that's the mainstream of people's thinking in America, it's 'cause of the absence of anything else around that's dynamic and alive. It's mainstream by default—passive mainstream, negative mainstream. What leadership's all about is bringing into being something that wasn't there before. That'll always sort of radically change the chemistry of a situation." Jackson proposed, in short, to summon forth a mainstream of his own. It would be composed of a collection of minorities across the social spectrum—a "Rainbow Coalition" of not only his already massive black support but also struggling working families, liberal urbanites, Hispanics, women's rights groups, college students, environmentalists. While demographically diverse, this new popular front, said Jackson, would have a common mood of discontent with the "empty materialism" lasting from the Reagan years, an impatience with the mere maintenance politics of both the Bush presidency and the Democratic leadership, and a readiness for adventure again in "humanizing this society and our policies around the world." All this potential majority of combined minorities needed, he insisted, was the one indispensable, the sine qua non, that had been lacking since Robert Kennedy: a galvanizing figure to bring it all together, to catalyze it into being. "What makes it sort of interesting," Jackson said with a small smile, "is that nobody ever figured on that person being black."

"We're Up Against an American Original"

FROM THE BEGINNING of his presidential campaigns, it was always a misperception to take Jackson as simply a political being. He was impelled all along by purposes that were finally far more deeply extrapolitical. Jackson differed strikingly from every other past presidential contender who had arrived at anything like a similar consequence in that he was embarked not so much on a political enterprise as a sort of political evangelism—one deriving from the essentially religious social vision that had animated King. He readily acknowledged, "What I'm doing is carrying the moral vision of the civil rights movement into the context of conventional politics. But this thing goes way beyond politics, it's *larger* than politics." He would proclaim at his rallies, "This ain't no ordinary campaign, it's about finding the light!" What he had in mind, in fact, was nothing less than trying to re-create the popular consciousness, and thereby conscience, of the country—"not just changing or broadening the party but changing the culture"—all aimed toward shaping a transracial, transclass, egalitarian common American neighborhood fulfilling the old Peaceable Kingdom dream of the movement. It may have been a rather ethereally romantic notion, but Jackson has always been nothing if not a moral romantic.

Yet Jackson's ambition billowed well beyond that. "I'm just somebody from Greenville," he once happily proposed on a flight from Angola to Paris, where he was to meet with President François Mitterrand, "trying to change the world." In 1989, after passing a day in the cold desolations of Armenia, forging among survivors of a recent earthquake with huge hugs and reverberating prayers, he began to fret on the drive back to Yerevan about being pressed, by *Washington Post* editor Ben Bradlee among others, to run for mayor of Washington: "Seems like I'm always havin' to rassle with these attempts of people to assign me and confine me to runnin' this or that piece of real estate. But what I been doin' today, who's gonna be doin' this? *This?* I mean, I have the opportunity now to be part of the conscience of mankind."

Indeed, there are times when Jackson seems to suggest that his line of moral succession extends significantly further back than even King or Gandhi. "Press, lot of politicians, they keep saying, 'By what authority does he speak? He's not elected to anything. He's just driven by ego, by political ambition, wants to overthrow the government, *something's wrong with him.*' While on the other hand, there're the people, and a whole lot of the people, who believe, *In him I see the fulfillment.*" Jackson once proudly reported the observations of his driver in Washington, just after Jackson had delivered a funeral eulogy: "He said, 'Reverend, I know your secret, know why them people flip out over you. Lot of stuff people like me be feeling and wanting to say, you be *saying* all that stuff.'" Jackson paused portentously. "Man, if that's not one way of saying the Word has become flesh and incarnate dwelling amongst you—idn't it?"

Such professions made Jackson probably the oddest figure ever to have counted so seriously as a presidential candidate. At the least, it's safe to surmise, few before him were ever to be heard freely describing their actions as "clearly a product of God's mission for me" or talking about "redemptive suffering" and "national defense through just loving your neighbors" and "governing by Jesus' Great Commission." Precisely in that incongruity lay one of the hazards of entering into a presidential candidacy to define himself an apostle to the national conscience. In seeking to translate an essentially religious social militancy, coming directly out of King's radical moral vision, into the earthly commerce of politics, Jackson was essaying a dubious transfer between two probably fundamentally alien mediums—endeavoring to move matters of the spirit into the machineries of Caesar, as it were. For one thing, the American citizenry itself has always tended to feel a bit queasy about visionaries aspiring to high offices of authority in its government. But a particular treachery of that extension for Jackson was that it changed the terms of everything: once he entered that elementally different game, Jackson gave himself over to being defined solely by its notably less than spiritual measurements. In one respect, it was an intriguing exercise he was undertaking. But its great danger—and the outcome of that risk has yet to be decided—was that it could compromise and, worse, trivialize him in that larger meaning to which he had always actually aspired: that he might in the end survive neither as an authentic social apostle nor a credible political figure—both could be lost.

Simply owing to his propensity for histrionic self-dramatizing, many journalists covering his campaigns came to entertain the most choleric cynicisms about him. If no man is a hero to his valet, even less is any political aspirant to a journalist who's long had him under close scrutiny, and particularly one flourishing the large moral claims for himself braved by Jackson—that almost ensures dyspeptic reactions. Accordingly, he was soon being characterized as megalomaniacally self-obsessed, a towering humbug, a voracious opportunist—antipathies only intensified by Jackson's tireless, almost abject desperation for media notice: "*Assiduous* courting," remembers Ben Bradlee with a droll smile, "and he was absolutely bald, shameless about it." It was like an eagerness, out of his old feeling of being an outsider, to have his sense of his significance register in the general eye, to be *recognized*. He has simply seemed to *need* too greatly. But that urgency produced, instead, a virtual allergy among the press. At the same time, the public glare accompanying his presidential candidacy exposed certain awkward matters left from his long, feverish climb out of obscurity—his tale of bearing on his shirt the blood of the slain King, questions about how he had managed to subsidize his one-man operation so widely for so long—those misgivings then compounded by his "Hymie-town" comments during his first campaign and his subsequent reluctance to separate himself from the supportive invective of Louis Farrakhan. The deprecations of Jackson reached a point where journalist Henry Fairlie was prompted to suggest, in *The New Republic* in 1984, "It is a historical fact that many of the most important struggles to establish some vital principle have been led by . . . not the most savory or principled characters on the scene," and "seldom led by men with unstained hands and hearts."

But more widely, something about the very nature of Jackson's popular effect—spontaneous, explosive, uncontainable—unsettled many as holding a reckless ambivalence of possibilities, at once for the more humane reordering of the American community he preached but also for darker demagogic mischiefs. Bert Lance, the Georgia banker and political pasha who has been a longtime, if somewhat improbable, confidant of Jackson's, reflects, "There are a lot of people that don't think you ought to have that ability to create that sort of public excitement." Eleanor Holmes Norton, the black political activist who is the District of Columbia's representative in Congress, once compared Jackson to Huey Long as a figure who aroused in the country both dreams of breathtaking possibilities and nightmare prospects of upheaval. Along with that, Jackson's own gusty extravagance of nature seemed to affront certain sensibilities in the way that custom, caution, the tight and orderly of spirit—the communicants of the received respectability—are always accosted and alarmed by the advent of a turbulently original vitality, a larger life. One of his campaign advisers in 1988 observed, "His opponents and a lot of people in the press just start with a suspicion toward him, and much of that suspicion is the suspicion of passion generally." Such figures, to the extent they quicken the country's sense of possibilities, excite as well uncommon dismays, and even hates. Reporting on the 1988 arrest of a Missouri white couple who had threatened to assassinate Jackson, *Newsweek* remarked that "racial tensions are only one reason. . . . He is also more electrifying than most politicians. Historically, assassination attempts have tended to be directed at public figures who connected emotionally (both positively and negatively) with the American people."

In any event, as unexpectedly successful and even historic as his presidential exploit turned out, Jackson paid a profound toll for it in the mistrusts and dislikes he incited, including skepticisms roused about his past. While King himself could serve as an instruction on the deeply conflicting forms in which apostles often appear to us in their own time, to many journalists and others of the mainline political sensibility there seemed far less of the apostle than the self-prospector about Jackson. On the whole, cynicisms about him have come to accumulate into a kind of forbidding attitudinal barrier through which no slight effort is required to pass in order to apprehend him anew.

But that is the effort now ahead. And for that, we will be traveling into a mystery.

CLAIMING A GREAT complexity of contradictions in a party one is trying to explain may be an indication one has not yet quite figured out one's subject. In the case of Jackson, one is presented with a personality of such deeply contrary properties that he might almost best be described in terms of quantum physics. While all human personality is probably, at bottom, in a kind of chaos, and only compelled into coherence by the necessity to act in the outer world, it has traditionally been the endeavor of biography in all its forms to impose a more or less Newtonian pattern of linear intelligibility on this turmoil of an individual's nature. But in *Hapgood*, Tom Stoppard's quantum-mechanics version of a spy drama, one character declares, "We're not so one-or-the-other. . . . We're all doubles." In Jackson's case, it's more like multiples. The problem is, we're simply not accustomed to understanding character in that myriad sense.

But Jackson has always been a far more labyrinthine affair than is apparent in his image as a political or social or even racial figure. He could be almost as much a literary character as a journalistic one—a tumultuously mixed piece of work altogether. In his long labor to fashion himself into some form of hero, he has wound up a creature of the most hugely uneven parts—a combination of the prodigiously gifted, the naive, the splendidly aspiring, the rankly boorish. He once apprised a black female reporter, "One of the many things I don't like about you, you are disrespectful and have no grace. . . . I'm going to have a ball helping you make a fool of yourself." While discussing the distinction between ethnicity and ethics with a young black scholar and his fiancée, he startled them both by asserting, "Now, say I was going to rape Marcelle here—wouldn't be ethnicity but *ethics* that would hold me back." A former campaign adviser, Richard Hatcher, declares, "He can be hugely insensitive. *Hugely* insensitive. He can do and say things, almost without thinking, that are just *terrible*."

Yet he will also sometimes lose himself in great swells of compassion. On his visit to Armenia after the earthquake, he was being conducted through the chill barren rooms of one hospital amid a steady whimpering of children in makeshift beds, alongside which were grouped heavily wrapped women, their mothers and grandmothers, one of whom, telling him through an interpreter that almost everyone else in her family was now gone, began weeping. Jackson pulled her into an enveloping hug, murmuring, "Okay, honey, gonna be awright, love you very much now," his own voice breaking slightly, and continued to hold her against him with one hand stroking her back, "*Love* you, honey," the woman answering in an effort at English, "Luffou." And as he approached the other women he could not refrain from taking them one by one into his hands, stroking their backs and shoulders and holding them in long silences as they cried against him, kissing one grandmotherly woman on the top of her gray hair as his own eyes blurred with tears. Later, in the town of Spitak, which looked as if it had been blasted by carpet-bombing, he addressed a small crowd that had filtered out of the wreckage to collect around him in a dusty wind-smacked street in a savagely cold dusk—leading them in his familiar campaign cry, "Keep hope alive!" which they chorused back, "Kep hop aliff!"—and returning finally to his car, he saw out the window, just as the car was pulling away, scatters of other people hurrying down the street to the site, and stammered, "Wait, wait, I gotta tell 'im to hold up here a minute, they comin' from everwhichaway, I gotta—" and flung open the door before the car had come to a stop, plunging back out into the growing crowd with double-clutching handshakes and grabbing hugs, shouting, "Keep hope alive, now! *Love* yawl!" until full dark.

It has been suggested more than once that, while Jackson does clearly love people in the mass, he can seem somewhat impatient with them in the particular—or as one acquaintance put it, "Lot of times it's like he's got a greater feeling for the body politic than the bodies *in* the politic." His manner of dealing with his own staff can resemble the imperiousness of one of the more fearsome of the sixteenth-century czars, he unnoticing of their tribulations in his service, railing at them in abrupt public tirades for delinquencies, curtly and coldly discarding them when terminally miffed or suspecting disaffection. A former press secretary even claimed that, at moments of exasperation during his 1988 campaign, he would trample on her feet and one time slugged her in the back. To an associate's proposal once that he promote one of his oldest and most dutiful assistants, he snapped, "He ain't got the sense to take care of his own affairs, why should I put him in a position where I got to count on him to take care of mine?" A former aide says, "He could destroy your feelings in the snap of a finger, and save you from suicide in the next second." Another old compatriot who was especially close to him reports, "He can be this wonderfully warm and generous person, but if he feels you have turned on him or you are no longer very useful to him, he can be vicious and utterly ruthless. A coldness comes over him that is absolutely like a chill wind that goes through you."

But then, on an early Sunday morning in 1987, after visiting Bill Cosby's ailing mother in a hospital in Los Angeles, Jackson was proceeding back down the corridor amid a sizable retinue of attendants, hastening to catch a plane, when a man fell in walking beside him. "Excuse me, Reverend Jackson, but my wife's in intensive care, she may not make it. Could you stop in to see her for a minute, maybe say a prayer?" Walking steadily on, Jackson said, "What's wrong with her?" and the man, keeping pace beside him, explained that, since surgery to remove a blood clot from her brain, she had been lying virtually comatose for the past two weeks, the only indications of any consciousness an occasional faint stirring of her right hand and a dull blinking of her eyes. An aide behind them pleaded to Jackson, "Reverend, we can't do this, it's the only plane today," but Jackson, without looking around, asked the woman's name, asked about the rest of her family—she was a forty-four-year-old mother of two—and striding on past the elevator doors, he followed the man to the intensive care unit where, leaving his dismayed entourage outside, he swooped in with the man to his wife's bedside. She was lying motionless, her eyes closed, her head muffled in bandages, her sister and a nurse standing beside her. Jackson leaned over: "Ronnie? Ronnie, it's Jesse Jackson. Take my hand, Ronnie." He clasped her still, slight hand in his and motioned to the others by the bed to form a circle and join hands. He then began praying: "Lord, you are the God that parted the Red Sea. You're the God that saved Daniel in the lion's den. We need a miracle here now, Lord. Touch this room. Touch this woman. Give strength to this family. . . ." By the time he finished, as the man's brother later recounted the episode, "my brother was sobbing loudly," and when Jackson pronounced *Amen*, "Ronnie opened her eyes. The circle broke up, but Jackson did not leave. He took my brother in his large arms and held him until he stopped crying." Weeks later, though "we could not tell what part of the event she had remembered and what part she had heard from others," the man's brother reported, "after she had recovered her strength, Ronnie told the story over and over again. 'Jesse Jackson came to visit me.' " The family happened to be Jewish, and the man's brother confessed that, after Jackson's convivial hug of Arafat in 1979 and then his "Hymie-town" remarks in 1984 and subsequent reluctance to denounce the invective of Louis Farrakhan, "even now I waver, searching for some definitive statement that will set my mind at ease about Jesse and Israel, Jesse and the Jews. I haven't found it yet, and I am still disturbed. But I was not the one who was held crying in his arms."

A number of months after that incident, when Jackson was in the midst of his primary campaign in California, he was briefly taken aside by another man who asked if he would say a prayer into a tape recorder that the man could then play over the phone for his brother, who was dying of leukemia in a New York hospital. Jackson said, "I'm not gonna be saying a prayer for your brother in a tape recorder. Give me his phone number." Early the next morning, Jackson called the man's brother in his hospital room, and spent a full hour talking and praying with him, wholly out of sight or knowledge of the media waiting for him downstairs in the hotel's lobby.

But in such impromptu acts he can also be a curious commixture of the genuine and the feigned. During the last weeks of 1988's general election campaign, a birthday party was given for Jackson by one of his Los Angeles benefactors at his villalike home in the high slopes of Brentwood, at which the Democratic nominee, Michael Dukakis, was expected to appear. At one point a troop of neighborhood children, all of them white, drawn by the fanfare in the courtyard, wandered in and instantly clustered around Jackson, who began leading them, clapping and singing, through a battle song from the movement, "This little light o' mine, I'm gonna let it shine," turning once to murmur gleefully to a reporter with him, "This's a little *deeper* than politics here, see?" When word presently rustled through the gathering that Dukakis was about to arrive, Jackson kept on clapping with the children through another freedom hymn from the sixties—only pausing for a moment when he spied, at the edges of the crowd, the bow-swell of reporters and camera crews rippling through the shadows under the palm trees in advance of Dukakis. With that, Jackson leaned down closer to the children and resumed his clapping and singing with them with a distinctly more robust animation, all the while slipping his eyes over to see if the scene had been noticed yet by the television folk accumulating there. Noticed it soon was, and Jackson went on leading the children through "Down by the Riverside" in a brilliance of camera lights. From what had begun as a spontaneous and warmly authentic little happening, Jackson had moved, in barely an instant and with a strangely effortless shift, into a slyly counterfeit performance.

More than a few close observers who are neither unthoughtful nor ill-willed have found him at times an insufferably sanctimonious swaggerer—he once actually had himself brought onstage at a PUSH gala to the splendoring paean of "Jesus Christ, Superstar"—who is often disposed to the most byzantine paranoias about machinations against him. Yet he seems to have a peculiar capacity for suddenly becoming wondrously larger than all his unlikabilities—as in his address to the Democratic National Committee in Los Angeles about the chicken-plant fire in Hamlet, North Carolina, as in his exertions in Iraq in the fall of 1990 to bargain for the release of Americans and other foreign nationals. One former aide, an affable goliath of a man who left a post as a union organizer to serve as Jackson's bodyguard and general factotum, only to find himself regularly stormed at for such irritations as late-appearing tailors and failing to bring along Jackson's suitbag for television appearances, began rumbling privately about quitting but admitted that "the only reason I don't, he's the best we got out there—only *real* one out there. With all his faults, he's bigger than he is, know what I mean? That's the only reason I put up with it all."

One afternoon in 1993, on a visit to Los Angeles shortly before the verdict was announced in the second trial of the policemen involved in the beating of Rodney King, Jackson decided to take a walk through a housing project that lay deep within the terrain of the previous spring's rioting. He had just begun making his way along its narrow scabby streets, between dumpy barrackslike apartments pocked with holes, in the swampish heat of the dull afternoon, when a young mother rushed up to him, her T-shirt drooping off one shoulder, two small children fastened by their fists to her long gauzy skirt, and after he had kissed her, "Hey, now, darlin'," and enfolded her in a hug, she cried out to the others swiftly gathering around them, "Can you believe it? I can't believe it! Everything's gonna be awright now! We needed the Lord to come by here, and here he is!" Jackson chortled. "I'm not the Lord, honey," and she sang out, "Well, you'll do!" He proceeded along the project's lanes as more figures dimly appeared behind ragged screen doors, emerged from dark doorways with muddy stares of unbelieving wonder at Jackson's abrupt materialization among them, calls ringing out around his progress, "What's happenin' out here? . . . C'mere, lookahere, it's Jesse Jackson out here!" One man, bumbling out of his door, yelled to the door next to it, "Evelyn! C'mon out here, Evelyn, it's Jesse Jackson. Naw, it *is*!" Jackson eventually came upon the young mother's father, a short thick man who seized Jackson's hand in both of his and gazed up at him, tears filling his eyes: "Reverend, I been waitin' on you for thirty-something years. I *knowed* you be comin' someday. Oh, man, I'm so glad to see you, *so* glad to see you!" He could no longer speak through his weeping, and Jackson wrapped an arm around him, "God bless you, my bruthah." To the journalists who had finally caught up with him, Jackson declared, to the visible elation of the throng now surrounding him, "There's *humanity* here! Let's break the stereotype. Watts? But these young children you see here dream dreams untold—this's Watts. Here's a young mother takes her Bible and her children to Bible class every Sunday—Watts. Here's her father, a veteran of foreign wars—Watts. There're people here who *are* workin'—Watts." Before leaving, he stooped down to lead the profusion of children who had been straggling after him through his now accustomed refrain: "I am somebody. . . . Respect me. . . . Never neglect me. . . . For I am somebody. . . . I want to learn. . . . 'Cause my mind is a pearl. . . . I can do anything . . . in the whole world! . . . For I *am* . . . *somebody*!" It was, all in all, an uncanny visitation. Its eventual effects will probably never be known—indeed, Jackson has been regularly belabored over the years for an absence of any demonstrable, substantive results of his ministry. But in the end, he operates in the interior regions of the heart, where pride and hope happen, which makes any sequence of effect between his efforts and their consequences virtually impossible to trace, to statistically measure and quantify; those consequences would only later brim forth into life seemingly sourceless, like artesian wells.

When Jackson sets out on expeditions abroad, he commonly meets with tumults of enthusiasm that remarkably mirror the popular fanfares of his street appearances and rallies back in the United States—from earthquake-wrecked Armenian towns to Zambian villages to the back lanes of West Bank communities, one hears the same cries of "Jes-see! Jes-see! Jes-see!" Through television's new, global nerve system of consciousness, creating a certain communalization of experience over the whole planet, Jackson has been translated into a kind of international populist tribune. His address at the 1988 Democratic convention was watched in Gabon, live, at four o'clock in the morning, and a U.S. embassy official in Libreville recalls, "It was very strange to look out at that hour and see houses all over the city with this dim blue light glowing in their windows." In Moscow in 1989, the editor of a liberal journal declared, "The popularity of Mr. Jackson is here so very great. We are a country of 285 million population, and not all of them are reading American publication each day. But from television, popularity of Mr. Jackson even among our peasants is popularity of man who is so widely known among so-called simple people, for how he is for simple people." One morning, in the northern bush of Zimbabwe, as Jackson was walking down a dirt trail leading to Victoria Falls, he passed three men hunkering in the shade under low scrubby trees, and one of them, staring, stood in a slow motion of gradual astonished realization as Jackson went by, lifting his arm to point and inquiring in a thin treble of one in Jackson's party, "Is this . . . is this the great Reverend Jesse Jackson?"

In truth, he may have come to be regarded with more esteem abroad than in the United States, and not only popularly. His passages from nation to nation are attended by government receptions of the highest ceremony. All of this has prompted some to suggest that Jackson might ultimately find his greatest enlargement in such a global extension of his ministry. While in the Soviet Union in 1989, he managed to negotiate the release of four Jewish citizens refused permission to immigrate—"refuseniks"—and then met with a delegation of others one evening to give them the news. "But only the four will be allowed to go?" said a woman. "No more? What about the others? It's like a small gift, a special gift for you." This response put on Jackson's face a flatness of irritation. "Well, I would hope it's a gift for you, too. And for them," he said. The woman replied, "Yes, of course, but there're still so many who haven't been made presents to anybody. And it's a shame they should give a present of four long-term refuseniks to some great people visiting." Her reaction seemed to disconcert Jackson. "Indeed it is a shame," he said dryly, "but would you rather the four of 'em stay here? Every little victory counts, dudn't it?" But the woman persisted in her protests, as if through a simple repetition of plaints and arguments she could, through Jackson, cling a little longer to a larger world of freedom before having to go back out into the black cold of the Moscow winter night. Finally Jackson said, "Look, let me make an observation, and I don't want it to sound presumptuous, okay? But sometimes we struggle for so long without anything happening that we become cynical. We start a self-defeating process of resentment, denigrating the possibilities. But this government's own professions before the whole world lately on liberalization and human rights have obligated them in a way they never been before. So we're in a position to raise with them the concerns of people like yawl in a right compellin' way now. Follow? That's why we were able to get permission today for the four people to leave. I'm tellin' you, *believe me*, things are happenin' *never* happened here before, and it's just the beginnin', you watch. So don't give up now, after all you been through. You've come very close to shore, so don't stop swimmin' now." Before the delegation left, Jackson gathered them in a circle of joined hands for a prayer: ". . . People everywhere, Lord, will not rest until human rights reign for people anywhere over this world. And let something we do or say make a difference in the lives of these who have come here to us this evening. Give them the assurance, Lord, that they are *not* alone and forgotten, and the inner strength to hold on until the morning comes. Bless them. And hold them safe in the hollow of your almighty hand. . . ."

Jackson then left for a formal dinner at the U.S. embassy. About midway through the evening, he was beckoned from his table and given word that a call had finally gotten through to a Leningrad relative of one of the four refuseniks granted permission to leave. In an alcove at the far end of an enormous salon, Jackson took the phone from an embassy deputy. "Mr. Feldstein?" he boomed. "This's Jesse Jackson. What? Yes, Jesse Jackson. How are you, friend? Good to hear your voice. Mr. Feldstein, we have been able to get an agreement today from the Soviet government to release Mrs. Feldstein. That's right. What? Yes, I am, that Jesse Jackson. So I want you to tell your family now there in Leningrad that your prayers have not been in vain, and that all of you have many friends in the United States who will be very glad to—hello?—" Lifting the phone away for a moment, Jackson whispered gravely to those standing around him, "Started cryin'. He's cryin'." He spoke again into the phone, "No, that's okay, friend, I understand, it's awright. I love you very much. And give Mrs. Feldstein our love. And yawl keep hope alive over there in Leningrad, okay?"

JACKSON'S CAPACITY FOR both a magnificence of spirit and an appalling crassness evokes, for many who happened to know them both, something of the *monstre sacré* quality of Lyndon Johnson. Not only does he have Johnson's sort of engulfing physical loom but also, says Roger Wilkins, an old Jackson friend who served in Johnson's Justice Department, the same "*huge* appetites, just"—and Wilkins emits several terrific, buffalolike grunts—"so much alike, it's eerie. And both of 'em the kind of person who, if you stay too close to them, will burn you up. Jesse'll call you up at any hour, while you're sitting talking to your daughter or listening to Miles Davis or Beethoven or having a romantic interlude with your wife, and he can't figure out why you aren't right that instant thinking about what he's thinking about. 'You weren't asleep, were you?' 'No, Jesse, I've been sitting up here just waiting for your call.' Late one night, my wife answered the phone in the other room, and I heard her just raising hell with some 'Mr. Jackson.' I wondered who in the world she was talking to, because always with Jesse, it was Jesse or Reverend. So who was this Mr. Jackson she was bawling out? Then I heard her say, 'And don't you *ever* call here at an hour like this again!' And I knew." As with Johnson, claims Wilkins, "the characteristics that make Jesse a great man are the very characteristics that drive people crazy. It's the same package."

"There are deep and interesting questions there, why Jackson's smallness seems inseparable from his bigness," says Mark Steitz, an adviser Jackson inherited from Gary Hart for his 1988 campaign. Steitz, who has a master's in economics from Yale, suggests some sturdy, overgrown pixie with pale thinning hair and is untiringly ebullient in analysis, his eyes repeatedly flaring wide in delights of recognition. "Jackson really does wake up every day and figures, 'Well, what can I do next? God hasn't finished with me yet.' But to get up every morning believing that, that very thought gives you permission to do a lot of things that offend and even frighten people. But lacking that thought, it's very hard to get many of the grandest things in this world done. And somehow inextricably involved in being big in imagination and big in action and in forcing things is trying to protect yourself at that level—and you should not underestimate the incredible amount of back-stabbing and bushwhacking he's gone through. So there's that imagination and deep hunger for bigness, and when things go bad, there's a very fast tunneling side of the intellect, and you're pulled into these intricate little fights in which you can lose the big picture—only, being pulled into those little fights is part and parcel of it. Taking yourself seriously enough to believe you're dealing in matters of serious truth tends to create problems in dealing with the pettiness in the world, problems which, oddly, are often solved by out-pettying the pettiest. You say, but *ah*, that's awfully ugly, there's strychnine there—and it's one of the reasons most of the rest of us back off from certain megalomanias that we know in our own souls. But somehow power, and a lot of good power, incorporates that protective strychnine, and you just have to finally strip it out or at least find ways of controlling it. You take people like Jackson, though, who approach the world at 180 miles an hour, making big decisions fast, and with a greatness in their understanding of their own experience, they've always got a conflict, because being honest and true to their experience is something that leads to impolite understandings. But if you try to get behind Jesse Jackson's eyes and look out at the world from there, what he does and what he says make more sense than you could ever imagine."

Jackson reportedly once strode onto the set of a live TV newscast in Chicago that was featuring one of his most persistent detractors and, snatching a microphone, gazed icily at the man while announcing, "He has one simple problem. I am tall, black, and international—and he is short, white, and local." But under all his bravado, he remains exorbitantly sensitive to hurt, still brims into tears as readily as when he was a nine-year-old boy, "just allows his feelings to get injured too easily," Bert Lance found. A black pastor in Brooklyn remembers that, when Jackson first began exerting himself nationally, "the black elite leadership held him in some disregard—here he was coming on as their peer, and a real rival in how he could connect to the people, but his background was not theirs, he'd been raised with his father gone, all that—and their slights made him shed some big tears." A longtime assistant of his says, "People that he loves can hurt him, and he will cry in a minute"; when his call for a boycott of a city promotional festival in Chicago went unheeded even by the pastor who was closest to him, the assistant reports, "I saw him sit there and just *cry*, unashamedly." Disparagements from other quarters, like his old colleagues in SCLC, have left him in a spiritual misery. "In spite of the fact that all of us have criticized him," says Andrew Young, "and the criticisms have been more distorted in reportage than we made them, he still calls you up to try and explain himself." At the same time, he tends to operate from an initial, improbably almost Anne Frank–like faith in the essential goodness of most people. Even in his negotiations with the political crustaceans of Mayor Richard Daley's regime in Chicago, recounts one of his seminary mentors, "Jesse would say, 'Now when we go in to talk to this person, assume that if conditions were different, this person would act differently. If you assume at the beginning a cynical attitude toward him, that everybody like him is dumb and out there only for his own gain, well, they'll seem like that is how they react to you. If you start by confrontation, that'll prevent any movement of your relationship and so the situation. Just assume the best about him, that he's not just a narrow, self-centered person, assume an underlying mutuality between you—that he's wonderful. He has all kinds of pressures on him, but he's a human being, and if you provide him with alternatives, he'll act in ways that fulfill your hopes, too.' " No doubt for that reason, says John Johnson, the black publishing magnate, "Jesse has an ability to push people further along than they ever thought they wanted to go, without them even knowing they've gone that far." But on the whole, in the windy swoop of his ambitions, he seems given to curiously naive presumptions about what can happen in this world, a kind of hopeful innocence of enthusiasms that at times lends him an air of poignant vulnerability. "He has a real belief that all good things are possible, that all children can do what he's done," says the former chaplain at the North Carolina college he attended, "a belief that is sometimes almost heartbreaking."

Indeed, he is constantly reconnoitering the distances he has traveled from the shabby streets of his beginnings in the black quarter in Greenville. At the birthday party for him in Brentwood, he looked over the shimmering assembly of L.A.'s liberal haut monde eddying under the palms, and presently remarked to the reporter with him, "Bunch of purty folks here, I'd say. Long way from Haynie Street in Greenville, ain't it?" Yet he seemed to feel vaguely displaced among the political glitterati swimming about him, passing long intervals standing off by himself. It was only when he found himself surrounded by the pack of neighborhood children that he clearly appeared at ease at last, and he kept them closely collected around him for most of the rest of the evening, as if for shelter or refuge. For that matter, wherever Jackson appears, he will pull protectively around him whatever children he spies nearby—even when he's speaking, no child within arm's reach is safe from being suddenly swept against him, they wearing a startled expression of sheepishly proud captivity in his huge hands as he orates on above them. Mark Steitz says, "I've watched him be in a disastrous situation, in the lousiest mood, and then have his day completely turned around by a child that walked by. People look at me as if I'm crazy on this, but you find me one photograph of a child crying with him. It's a spirit in him, the spirit of the child and he connect, and he's re-ordered and moves fluidly on."

But his moods, says Steitz, "dolphin up and down, and when he does not have room for you in his spirit, you might as well move on away, because anything you do is only going to piss him off." Exuberant or morose, though, he finally keeps the innermost part of himself closed off, an interior isolation in which he travails alone with his most elemental furies, almost never admitting anyone else to that center of him. A former assistant of Jackson's recalls that, during a staff donnybrook once over whose position was operatively closest to Jackson's, Jackson himself burst into the room to announce, "Nobody is close to me but the people *I* know are. And I'm the *only one* who knows who's close to me. If anybody's saying they're close to me, they're lyin'. Because *only I know.*" The campus minister at the college he attended now suggests, "Jesse's been in the public eye since he was twenty-four by not doing too much other than being himself. He himself is the institution, and that's awfully lonely. The peril of growing up in the public eye is that you have to go through the kinds of crises all of us are prone to have, only in the public view. But people who have become institutions in themselves sometimes fear that if they become human persons who cry, who have pain, who are indecisive, if they show that side of themselves, then perhaps people, even closest friends, will not regard them in the same way they did before." That resolute self-barricading has extended even to a grim resistance to disclosing himself in an autobiography that a succession of editors have mightily labored since the early seventies to get from him. One of those editors recounts, "His approach was, they want to know what I'm saying, what difference does it make about my personal life? He was clearly reluctant to talk, not so much about his personal life, but his personal take on his personal life. We finally said, well, we'll take the manuscript like it is—which had been put together by a writer he'd approved—but we'd just like you to put some meat on it. And I've never in all my years of publishing known an author, after we'd finally accepted a manuscript, to say, 'Well, you may accept it, but I don't. I don't think this is me.' " Another editor submits, "My bet is that, as a black child of poverty in the Old South, there is something daunting to him about being codified out there in that other world on the other side of the tracks, codified by his own word with his own name on it, that scares him in a way probably not entirely explainable by him. If he does finally put the period at the end of that sentence, he has committed an act that becomes something bigger than he is, that will outlive him. It's all right if somebody else does it, you can always disown that. But it's probably terrifying to be defined that way by *himself*—it becomes a little inescapable then."

BUT THE MOST profound complication in Jackson's nature may finally have to do with the matter of race itself. In Jackson's effort to expand his political ministry to a wider national constituency, perhaps the most formidable divide he was attempting to cross was simply that of the different, inverse perspectives through which white and black America perceive each other: in many deep and inimical ways, they are not to each other what they are to themselves. Jackson once offered his own ruminations on those separate perspectives while riding through his old Greenville neighborhood: "Thing that amazed me when we first ran for president was how white people, especially in the national press, immediately expected from us an absolute equanimity about the past—total forgiveness and forgetting, no matter what'd been done. As if somehow, if you went through all that maiming and you still have any anger, any hurt, you just not a swell person. You know, *this black don't like white people*. It's like, say, I hit you, knock some of your teeth out, and then I explain to you why you not hurtin'—wadn't *that* much of a hit, and anyway, it's all over with now. And one of my people says, '*Surely* you can understand that, I agree with Reverend Jackson, but let's vote on it, that's democracy—well, two against one, see? You couldn't possibly be hurtin'.' " Such sensitivities to implicit affronts in white attitudes around him are the sort of secret second sight that has immemorially been both the privilege and extra duress of a disdained minority—the outsider—in a society. Roger Wilkins allows, "People don't understand it when I say that white people are culturally disadvantaged. But if you're black and smart and you care, you know more about this country than white people do—know stuff that most white people deny. White people do things to me every day that they don't know they do, or why, and would even deny that they do it." But while Jackson's campaign proposed to pass nonetheless across that perceptual gap between the races, one sensed after only a short time with him that it was a crossing Jackson himself had still to complete. He insists, "Now I believe in this redemption stuff. *All* have sinned and come short of the glory of God, so none of us is in a position not to forgive anybody else. If I were of an unforgiving or unredemptive nature, I couldn't relate to white people at all." Yet for all of Jackson's lyricisms about creating a common transracial American community, he still holds old private brines of racial aggrievement. That disparity is one of the reasons Stanley Crouch has averred, "[In] the space between what Jesse Jackson is and what he is saying, we are again eyeball to eyeball with the tragic dimensions of the man."

That he has continued to identify so passionately with the pains of the black past in America has had mixed effects. On the one hand, it brought him the mass black support that has served as his one great unchallengeable strength. And in his presidential enterprise, he unquestionably prospered on the deference accorded him by press and political competitors because he was black, and because of the enormous enthusiasm he inspired in the black community. On the other hand, as one political analyst noted at the time, "constant legitimacy tests are applied to him that are just not applied to others." But most important, the fervent racial identification that bonded Jackson to black America, which was the strength that made everything possible for him in the beginning, produced a kind of schizophrenia. He seemed unable to disenthrall himself from the racial pains of his own past, and reluctant to risk any disenchantment among the black constituency that was his one great asset, to stretch himself enough to truly embrace the wider popular coalition he hoped to form.

In one sense, there would seem a certain perversity at work, in itself testimony to backdrafts of racism, that it should have been required that Jackson abstract himself out of his racial identity to be acceptable to America at large. Be that as it may, some submerged smolder of racial resentment that Jackson seems to carry in his message and manner stirs an answering unease in many white Americans. Indeed, the very inflections of his voice discomfort many white sensibilities. For whatever reason, Jackson has never undertaken to "whiten" his enunciation into the reassuringly colorless precisions of other black figures. His voice still holds the thick croker-sack textures, the juke-rock churns of the poolhall street corners and muddy alleyways of his origins.

But for all of Jackson's marveling over the long way he's come, what soon strikes one after spending any time with him is how thoroughly he feels himself, despite the celebrity and consequence he's acquired, still to be constitutionally an outsider. It remains his fundamental sense of himself, the central condition of his life—as if he were a kind of American version of Ishmael, that older half brother of Isaac, dispossessed and left to wander endlessly as an unreconciled outcast.

AN ADVISER TRIED to explain to a baffled Dukakis after Jackson had defeated him in the Michigan caucuses to become at that point the actual leader among primary candidates, "We're up against an American original." That aide was more right than perhaps he knew. Jackson may in fact be the most original figure, all things considered, ever to have reached such an importance in the nation's civic life. "He goes in there to find out from himself what he is and to give it expression," says an old associate from his Chicago days, Larry Shaw, "but to the outsider, you cannot put him in any classification. What he is, there's no title or description of it in the dictionary. What in the world is this thing? Who is this masked man?" There have really been no precedents for him; no past references quite contain or explain him. He seems finally uncategorizable: a singularity. Jackson himself seems not always certain exactly who and what he has become, where he is actually headed. While he was riding once down some back road in Nigeria, he lapsed into one of his occasional mystical musings: "It's been like moving through this kind of slow chain-combustion of dreams, one after another. Dreams infinitely within dreams, that keep on exploding one out of the other, on and on. So that, anybody ask me, 'Did you ever dream ten years ago you'd be where you are today?' the answer is no, because where I was ten years ago came out of a dream years before that, and that one out of a dream years before that. And they keep coming, *boom, boom, boom.* . . . What's happening to me now, back when I started I didn't even *know* to dream for it, just like now I don't even know to dream for what's *gonna* happen. It'll just come—*boom.*"

But in becoming someone now so distant from the world of his beginnings, he has in a sense turned himself into yet another kind of outcast, in exile from his own sources; in meeting with heads of state from Margaret Thatcher to Yitzhak Rabin to Hosni Mubarak, he sometimes seemed not wholly sure how much he really belongs in such august circumstances. Nevertheless, the old urgency that has propelled him this far propels him on. Bob Beckel, who was Walter Mondale's campaign manager in 1984 and has since operated as a political consultant in Washington, declares, "He'll never stop. You can still see it in his eyes. He'll never stop." Jackson himself confesses, "I *can't* quit. I can't turn loose of it. It won't turn loose of me."

He is now about the only figure remaining from the classic days of the civil rights movement—the last survivor—who is still actively at it, who has not wandered off into other occupations. In the same way, he has become one of the few remaining voices of any force in the land still unabashedly campaigning, like the Last Believer, for the old, liberal conscience in American politics—to the point where he has come to be regarded by many as a kind of orotund anachronism.

But more than once in the past, Jackson has seemed to disappear from sight and relevance on the far side of the moon—almost nothing heard from him, beginning to be forgotten—only to come swinging back around again, in some slightly altered but larger form. "You just can never count him out," says Roger Wilkins. "For one thing, Jesse is very, very, very smart. Number two, he is the most persistent sumbitch in the world. And number three, he's got more energy than three locomotives." Journalist David Halberstam says, "He just keeps on growing. And that's why, if you try to measure Jackson by what's behind him, you're going to miss him every time." Asked not long after Clinton's election if it might be possible that Jackson's day had passed, one of his seminary teachers said, "He's still alive, isn't he?"

For his part, Jackson avows, "This campaign we on is eternal. It's not captive to the schedules of political seasons or election cycles." In truth, he seems strangely to move in his own, separate field of time. "This is not a right-time and right-place person in anything like the ordinary sense," says Mark Steitz. "This is somebody who's played ball for a long, long time, not just in politics but in the public spiritual dialogue. He talks about how history's clocks and moral clocks work on a very different time than political clocks and calendar time and certainly media clocks. To him, time is a very variable and relative thing. Something that you think'll take four years may only take three weeks—or take a decade, or a generation. So who knows what segment of time he's in now?"

John White, the canny Texas politico who was the Democratic party chairman during the Carter years, observed shortly before his death in 1995, "Jesse represents something to a large part of the population that is very important, and to dismiss that is a big mistake by any politician or president—and I'm thinking of Clinton." Bob Beckel once advised a high deputy in the Clinton White House, which was summarily discounting Jackson's pertinence, "You guys better understand something. You may think that time has passed him by. But just go out there on the street with him someday. Just walk around with the guy out there for a while." Another longtime Jackson observer declares, "There's no way to begin to really understand Jesse Jackson without getting out on the road with him. Watch him among those people, all sorts of people out there across the country. That's where he comes into his true reality. And that's still his possibility, make no doubt about it, can still be his future, too."

■ ■ ■
Carrying the Gospel

IT WAS DURING the closing days of the 1988 presidential contest, as Jackson was beating about the country for the Dukakis campaign, that I passed my first extended stretch of time with him. I did not yet realize that this political enterprise of his was a kind of illusory scenario—what Jackson had originally meant to be only a means to a much larger mission. But he now seemed to have become intensely involved in that means almost for its own sake.

I found him, with some surprise, still smarting over not having been selected Dukakis's running mate, a disgruntlement that struck me as a trifle implausible in assumption. Nevertheless, as he was lofted from one rally to the next, slumped in his shirtsleeves in the cramped front cabin of the jet, his bulky hands folded over his paunch and his stockinged feet plopped on the seat facing him, he continued to grump. "They said, 'Jackson, we thank you for registering all those new voters. Thank you for bringing issues to the campaign. Thank you for the excitement, for rousing people. Thank you for a historic breakthrough. *But*'"—and he snapped his head down to the side, as if just hit by a crick in the neck, and then slowly rolled his eyes back around to peer up from under his brow, dropping his voice to a soft husking—"'but can't put you on the ticket. No, can't do *that*.' Even though we came just a heartbeat away from being the party's presidential nominee. All without being accountable to those who have imputed to themselves custodianship of our country's destiny. Hard thing for them to let into their heads, that we did that."

Whenever Jackson said "we," it set one mentally scurrying back and forth for the reference—himself? blacks in general? his whole constituency of supporters?—until one realized his "we's" were always in a sort of indeterminate flux of application among all three, between the collective and himself personally, which to him usually came to the same thing anyway. But many journalists found that usage yet another of his irksome affectations;

one columnist, emerging from a hotel room session with him, protested, "He sat there all that time holding forth without once saying 'I'—just 'we' this and 'we' that, like he was some head of state or something."

For his part, the news media was "enmeshed in that whole system" that churlishly persisted in discounting his importance. He remarked, in the low toneless murmur he reserves for reciting particularly scandalous grievances, "Real national stuff, you know, s'pose to be for the *big* boys. They'd say, 'Well, we know he knows something about civil rights, but what's he know about the budget? About banking, interest rates? NATO, national defense? Couldn't know about those things. Mean, couldn't actually be wantin' to be the *president*. So what's he *really* want? Tha-tha-that's," he stammered in urgent umbrage, "that's a contemptuous question, 'What's he really want?' Disrespectful question. Didn't ask it about the other candidates. It has an underlying assumption of racial limitation. And then they say"—and Jackson's voice lifted into a thin, rapid, mincing mimicry—"*What's he mean by this 'Respect me,' what's he mean by this respect thing, what's he talking about?* That became more of a problem for them than almost anything else—defense, budget, foreign affairs issues. *What's he really want for respect? How we ought to handle that?* became the only question for them, *How can we handle Jackson?* Nothin' but flat racist, all that talk." As he was rummaging out these complaints, we were flying through the night somewhere over Illinois, and he twisted impatiently in his seat to glower for a moment at his reflection in the dark oval window. "Hell, I don't ask that they necessarily agree with me on the issues. But I do ask that they take me legitimately."

Even while privately fuming over all these perceived disrespects, Jackson had barnstormed on through the general election campaign lustily enough to become strangely like a fifth, shadow player in the race—somewhat suggesting that extra, unaccountable figure that appeared in Nebuchadnezzar's furnace with Shadrach, Meshach, and Abednego. When I mentioned this analogy to Jackson, he did not find it disagreeable: "Yeah, and that figure was an angel of deliverance, you know." But beyond dutifully commending Dukakis, his service to the ticket consisted mostly of walloping away at Bush and Quayle with his own gonging scriptural allusions: "They both rich young rulers, looking down on the disadvantaged with contempt. There is no fairness in them. They a barren fig tree, there is no fruit of hope to be taken from them." Quayle, predictably, afforded him particularly extravagant sport, raillery of almost a schoolyard roughness: "Our national bird is the eagle, it's not the frail quail. Bush may be coldhearted on the issues in America, but Quayle don't even *comprehend* the issues. Flat don't know what's going on. Can you imagine Bush now talking about how he's gonna put Quayle in charge of crisis management? Quayle *is* a crisis that needs *to be* managed." But his fulminations against Bush—"something dangerous and mean-spirited about him, this disdainful rich man with no mercy for the poor and homeless"—were of a rather hyperbolic and sometimes startling stridor. Citing Bush's derogations of the American Civil Liberties Union (ACLU), Jackson blared, "When you attack lovers of civil liberties and freedom, Mr. Bush, you in an ugly tradition. You join the tradition of Pharaoh, Mr. Bush, you in the tradition of Herod, and Hoover, and Hitler. All them attacked civil liberties, too." One of Jackson's advisers later observed, "When he gets into these historical references he does tend toward the Fox-TV version, the most vivid and violent, what you'd call the high-ratings version of history."

As for the campaign of Dukakis, Jackson dispensed approving testimonials of noticeably milder vigor. "They say he doesn't have passion," Jackson declared, "but that's a new extraconstitutional requirement, this passion business. It's the *people* s'pose to have the passion, anyway. The presidents have the priorities. The Abolitionists and slaves and Frederick Douglass, *they* had the passion; Lincoln had the priorities and the emancipation pen. In the nineteen-sixties, Jack Kennedy and Lyndon Johnson never led one demonstration, they didn't inspire *us*, we inspired *them*, *we* had the passion and gave them the priorities for the Public Accommodations and Voting Rights Acts. Now, it's working mothers needing day care who got the passion, poor folks needing health care got the passion, workers lost their jobs abroad and family farmers overwhelmed by giant conglomerates, they the ones got the passion. Don't be worryin' about Dukakis's passion—*we* got that. Dukakis's got the priorities. This campaign's not about the passion of Dukakis, anyway, it's about the *lack* of *com*-passion of one George Bush!"

But the disparity between Dukakis and Jackson in "the passion quotient," or "the passion factor," became a special discomfort for Dukakis's own people, and Dukakis himself had clearly shown by now a wariness about wandering into any close proximity to Jackson that might tempt comparison to his own taut, neatly stapled manner. Actually, the same uneasiness about being in Jackson's immediate vicinity seemed shared by other Democratic worthies then. While Senator Al Gore was still in the primary campaign, Jackson managed to dragoon him into a joint appearance before the press, throughout which Gore, shorter than Jackson, was observed by someone behind both men "virtually shaking as he kept trying to balance on his toes." Jackson reported that he had once appealed to Georgia senator Sam Nunn and Virginia's Charles Robb, when they were both prospective presidential candidates, " 'Look, guys, we' "—in this instance, his "we" plainly meaning himself—" 'we take yawl to our churches and meeting halls in the black community. But yawl got a reluctance, seems, to take us to your First Baptist churches and Kiwanis Clubs, and us *share* platforms together.' All I was asking them for," Jackson explained, "was equal access. If they'd give me that much, just an entrée into their crowd, I'd handle the rest of it myself." I suggested that might have been exactly why they were reluctant, out of a suspicion they would then be swallowed up by his performance. For a moment Jackson savoringly mulled over the implication that any public association with them would therefore require of him deferential restraints, and he then mumbled, "Well, that'd be like askin' . . . mean, can't ask a home-run hitter to *bunt*."

Late in the campaign, there was a large rally for Dukakis in downtown Chicago, in an auditorium that resembled a restored opera house from the Gilded Age, its plump tiers of ornate galleries banked up to a vaulted ceiling—a fustian elegance that was filled that evening with a brawling reunion of the remains of the city's once-fearsome Democratic guard. But Jackson was the only one among the several other former primary contenders collected on the platform who was not asked to speak, and his presence even went unmentioned by Dukakis when he addressed the crowd. A few days later, while we were waiting at a small airfield in Iowa for his plane to be reserviced, Jackson abruptly turned to announce, "Other night in Chicago, that clinched it for me, the man's pettiness. Word got to us beforehand that he didn't even want us to be there. I sent word back, 'Look, you can't tell me that. Chicago's where I live, it's my town, I'm *comin'*.' But then didn't even recognize me sittin' there. That just wasn't"—and he leaned in closer, with a dolorous glare of his round, widely spaced eyes, and his voice sank to a heavy whisper—"wasn't actin' right. Because it was my home, you know? It's where I'm *from*. That wasn't *kind*."

But on the day of the election, when Jackson arrived late that afternoon for a rally at a college in Duluth, he was first taken into a back office to return a call that had come in a few minutes before from Dukakis's headquarters, and emerged to stride with a visibly reenergized briskness toward the rally awaiting him in the college gym. He was greeted with a storm of cheering—"*Jes-see! Jes-see! Jes-see!*"—to which, after bounding up onto the platform, he began flinging the hiked crescent of his thumb back over his head as if cranking the ovation on, grinning with the tip of his tongue dabbed out between his teeth in delight. But his speech was a bit short, and when he finished, he called out, "Governor Dukakis is asking me to alter my schedule to go to Milwaukee. So I must hurry, now—"

Back outside, as he toppled into the front seat of his car, a somewhat rumpled and thistle-haired student leaned his head in the window across from Jackson. "Reverend Jackson, just want to say you're the most inspiring man I know." Jackson pitched himself across the seat to shake the youth's hand. "Thank you, love you, buddy, hang in there." Turning back to his aide, Jackson said, "Where's your telephone? Need to find out— Got your phone? Don't? Shit. Well, everybody in the cars? We got to go here."

His car then plunged off for the airport. "Seems like the vote in the inner cities is runnin' way below what they were expecting," Jackson said. "They ignored all those places through the whole campaign. Now, Santa Claus running into heavy weather, and he calls for Rudolph. Understand what I'm sayin'?" Over the following months, Jackson would return again and again, with baroque elaborations, to this rather improbable analogy to describe his own situation: "Why, Rudolph's nose was so red, you know, he was up there in front of the sleigh, catching all the wind and snow. Out front of everybody else. Rest of them other reindeer, they couldn't pull that sleigh. Dancer, Prancer, Blitzen, those quality of politicians, they can always hide behind nice résumés and try to exploit the gravity of averageness. But there is no greatness in averageness. It took Rudolph to pull that sleigh. But Santa Claus didn't give him no equity for that. All Rudolph wanted was equity, even treatment, which was the one thing Santa couldn't give him. These themes keep on coming up out of the Rudolph story, see? For instance, take those selves, make them little and call them elves, half people, building all those toys on minimum wage, no credit, no union—" After a point, one began to wonder if Gene Autry had ever realized all he was actually singing about with that Christmas ditty of his. "In the final analysis, it's the double burden that makes you love the hero, because Rudolph had to do more than the other reindeer to get his recognition. Rudolph pulling the most weight. But Santa says, 'Well, we thank you, Rudolph.' 'Course, no promotion, no equity, no vice presidential nomination. But don't worry—your name will go down in history.' "

Jackson's plane landed at Milwaukee into a frenetic despair among the party workers waiting for him at the airport. "Nobody's coming out," wailed one, "there's no enthusiasm." A haphazardly assembled caravan of taxis then swept Jackson and his entourage through a deepening dusk to the campaign headquarters downtown. There, before a clutch of reporters in a cramped and grubby room, in a chalky wash of television lights, Jackson spoke into a thicket of microphones. "I urge everybody within the sound of my voice to vote these remaining hours. The polls are open until eight o'clock. Vote! Keep hope alive!" But it was, given the hour, a somewhat forlorn last bugling. Jackson was then led out through a dim blur of back rooms and hallways that were filled with a shadowy milling of other local party operatives who seemed suddenly oblivious to the Dukakis campaign collapsing across the country as they called out after Jackson, *"Jes-see! Jes-see! Jes-see!"*

The Jacksonian Physics of Reality

IN FACT, EVEN as he was hauling on through those final weeks, Jackson had already moved himself out of that particular political period and back into his own, larger field of time. The arrangement he had won at the Atlanta convention for funds and a personal jet to course about the country for the Democratic ticket had enabled him simply to resume his own never-ending, custom-styled populist apostleship.

Jackson maintains, "I don't go off by myself and sit down with a blank legal pad and start working out a blueprint for what I'm gonna do next. The flow of events fills up that page for me." One longtime adviser notes, "He's brilliant at politics in the moment, politics as it's moving—fast-break politics, if you will. If he can create fluid motion, then he can act and innovate with the best of them." Indeed, he seems to think only in movement, in action—is not at home apprehending things from stillness. It's as if, to Jackson, sheer momentum itself creates and defines. Says Roger Wilkins, "He feels that if he keeps going and keeps going and keeps going, after a while some good things are going to happen." From the instant he awakes every morning, usually before dawn and immediately pouncing to the phone, until, some twenty hours later and often three thousand miles away, he subsides back into sleep, he lives in constant, headlong movement, as if, should he cease moving, he would disappear. During unavoidable intervals of arrested animation, as when flying to his next destination, he will, even in the middle of an interview, sometimes drop off into an apparently solid sleep for some few minutes, but then come bouncingly awake again. Says a longtime assistant, "Most the time when he seems to be dozing, he's composing," and if no listener is immediately at hand when he resurfaces from a nap, he will look wildly about for something to write on, often reduced to snatching the air-sickness bag from the seat pocket in front of him and sketching out notes under its instruction, "After Use, Fold Toward You."

This guerrilla's urge has impelled him on despite a persistent siege of ailments—sickle-cell-trait exhaustions, bronchial infections, recurrent passes of pneumonia, all resulting, as he casts it, from "sins against my finitude"—and despite a distinct dread of flying.

As he has pitched on through the years without pause, he has come to know the country probably more familiarly than anyone quite has before him. "Anyplace you go," says a former aide, "he knows its embodied history." The aide reports he was once sitting with Jackson in the Cincinnati train terminal, waiting to be picked up for a rally, and after glancing around, Jackson began to discourse, "You know about this building? You ever noticed how many black people there are in Cincinnati? This terminal was the cheapest ticket out of the South. If you had the money, you could make it to New York or Chicago or Detroit, but this stop right here was the cheapest." And Jackson went on talking about the terminal and the families of black poor from the South who had arrived here as their own sort of Ellis Island port into the Promised Land of the North, until, the aide remembers, all the multitudes of that exodus over past decades seemed evoked once again, dimly thronging through the high ringing spaces around them. "His knowledge of this country," says the aide, "its physical history, is utterly breathtaking."

But with his ceaseless moving about, space itself—all physical delineations and distinctions of place—has somehow collapsed and merged into one great everywhere. "I don't know how he does it," says an eminent black educator who often counseled Jackson in college. "I look on television, and there he is in Egypt, shaking somebody's hand. Then I bump into him that night in a hotel in New York." The former chaplain at Jackson's college, A. Knighton Stanley, exclaims, "Who can get off a plane from the Middle East and fly to Decatur, Georgia, without being disoriented one whit by it? And he's really *in* Decatur when he gets there, you know?" Stanley relates that an Ethiopian high school student working in a Capitol Hill office once remarked to him, "I don't understand it. He is everywhere. *He is everywhere.*" For this almost supernatural ubiquity, he was once termed, by *The New York Times*'s Alessandra Stanley, the "Zelig" of public life in America. But it's as if all the world has become as immediately intimate to him as his front yard. "What is that line? . . . 'I am the cat, and all places are alike to me,' " says Mark Steitz. "He takes himself to an airport in another city the way the rest of us would walk into another room. I'm thinking this afternoon about going out to Bethesda to the supermarket; he's thinking this afternoon about flying to Baghdad."

At the same time, after so many years of heaving from one public occasion to another, it's as if what has happened to his sense of space has also happened to him inwardly, psychically. As he passes through his endless succession of appearances in church sanctuaries and union meeting halls and school assemblies, he maintains a continual exposition that is curiously heedless of whether he's addressing just another person in the car with him or a rally of thousands. This imperviousness to the nature of his audiences prompts one to wonder if any real line of demarcation exists for

Jackson, any inner sense of difference between the personal and the mass moment, if they have not become, for him, more or less indistinguishable. If, in fact, he has any private personality left.

Most of all, in the process of his everlasting movement through the years, time itself seems to have dissolved for him in its ordinary, linear sense. One political observer has described him as appearing to live almost wholly in the present tense, in a succession of separate moments each holding its own reality. He seems to exist in a fuguelike simultaneity of past and present like some Joycean implosion of time—so that, on any given day, he is dwelling in the years of his beginnings in Greenville, in his passage through the movement, in his laboring through the seventies to deliver himself out of his peripheral significance into the notability he gained in the eighties, all this together with an anticipation of the prospects ahead of him. It's as if he lives in a kind of time-loop that is expanding in detail and circumstance with each of its recirclings, but essentially always coming back around.

The Testament

AFTER THE CONVENTION in Atlanta, as he traveled from rally to rally to speak for the Democratic ticket, one got a sense that he was, in fact, reenacting a campaign that was going on independent of the incidental vicissitudes of any particular election. It had become the principal exertion in that lifelong compulsion of his to enlarge himself into a hero, the public self of this eternal campaign his only real self. In the small cabin of his jet as it was streaking through a late night from Chicago to New York after a batteringly long day of rallies, he sat slouched back in his seat, the only sign of fatigue a look to his mouth and eyes of having subtly gotten smaller and rounder and farther apart in his broad face. He began quietly talking about how most other politicians will retreat back into private life after a campaign defeat or just the natural expiration of their public careers: "They all go back home sooner or later. That's the difference between me and them. I have no home to go back home to. This *is* my home."

As he journeyed through those autumn weeks, he presented once more the slightly surreal vision of a solitary black social evangel forging through an Inner American panorama of settings, his burly voice baying over assemblies of plain folk in Iowa courthouse squares and Indiana factory neighborhoods, weather-chapped farm families gathered in country schoolyards and midwestern youths with wheat-bright hair crowding the bleachers of college gyms—for many of them, as one journalist noted, he

was "one of the few black men they had ever seen up close." At these rallies, Jackson continued to deliver those populist preachments that make
up his central political testament, during which he at times took on a striking resemblance to the Ben Shahn sketch of King's round, bullish head
orating with mouth thrown wide in a roar of power from the back of his
thick-packed neck: "More millionaires on top but ten million more in
poverty, almost forty million Americans with no health insurance. Something about that's not right. More working women in poverty, more children in poverty, expansion of malnutrition—something not *right* about
that! Makes no difference whether you black, brown, or white, when your
child's hungry it hurts the same. When there's no heat in the house, we all
cold. When they close down your factory or foreclose on your farm, and
comes time they pull the plug and the lights go out, we all—we *awwlll*—
look amazingly *similar* sitting there in the dark. Yet you hear folks who
don't have dental care or health care, can't buy enough groceries or pay
their 'lectric bill, hear 'em talking 'bout they somehow got something in
common with Reagan and Bush, say, 'Me 'n' Bush, we both for the flag,
against crime, believe in prayer. Both us is *con-serv-a-tive.*' Naw. Naw—
one of yawl is rich, and one of yawl is *po'.*"

And he would move then into that incantation repeated throughout his
past campaigns, which nevertheless still brought rising swells of clapping
as he rolled through it once more. Standing stiffly erect, his hands
clamped against his flanks, he merely tilted back and forth on his heels as
he released, as if from terrifically pent-up compressions, each heavy-
tolling line: "Most poor people not black, they white, mostly female and
young. Most poor people are not on welfare, they work. They work every
day! Get up every morning, catch the *early* bus. Never seen by Bush. Most
the poor *not* lazy, Mr. Bush, don't be *unkind* to them, they're the common
people, work *every day*! They're family farmers struggling to keep their
land. They drive cabs, sweep the streets, collect our garbage. Go down in
mines to dig our coal, clean the motels you sleep in, serve your table at
restaurants—*they work every day*! They care for the sick in our hospitals,
wash the bodies of those in pain and with fever. Clean their bedpans. No
job is beneath them! And yet, yet, when *they* get sick, they cannot lie in
that bed they make up every day! People down in the admissions room
dying 'cause they cannot afford to go up and lie in that bed that's waiting
empty for somebody wealthy or with insurance to get sick. That is not
right, America, we got to be a better nation than that! A nation's judged by
how it treats the *least* of those in its midst. Let me tell you something"—he
held his two forefingers pointed at each other just below his chest and
tightly circled them together as if briskly unspooling his phrases—"when

members of Congress get sick, they go to Walter Reed. When members of the Supreme Court or the president get sick, *they* go to Walter Reed. And if government-supported health care is good enough for Congress and the Supreme Court and the White House, then it's good enough for your house and my house, it's good enough for *everybody* in this democracy! . . ."

Jackson took this populist pentecostalism equally to ballroom banquets and black churches, university amphitheaters and coal miners' union halls—one hazard being that his themes were occasionally a bit awry to his locales. The exhortation he would deliver to inner-city black youths about the social crisis of unwed mothers he would deliver, with the same energy, to a gathering of Minnesota dairy farmers, occasioning a vague momentary puzzlement: "If dogs can raise their puppies and cats can raise their kittens, then young men old enough to make babies must surely raise those babies that they make!" To one rally of farmers in north-central Missouri, he orated on the long struggle of the movement in the South to achieve the Voting Rights Act, then extended that act's implications, a bit inventively, to "enabling farmers to vote without having to pay the poll tax." But as Jackson explained once, "I operate according to the parable of the sower. Throw that seed out everywhere. Some of it falls on rocky ground, some the wind blows back in your face, but a lot of it falls on fertile ground and germinates. And what germinates is sufficient so as not to miss what hit the rocks and wind."

He suggested at times a kind of populist John the Baptist storming across the wide expanses of the Republic. Landing in the Michigan interior on a snow-blowing Sunday morning, he was driven past bare sweeps of shorn cornfields and on into Saginaw, to an auditorium that was like an unfinished airplane hangar, its high vaults of exposed girders and scaffolding the starkly stenciled architecture of countless other civic arenas where much of the nation's public life takes place, with no one knows what desolations visited on it by such enclosing drabness. Jackson's voice clangored in electronic amplification, "More people working in poverty! Corporations taking manufacturing jobs overseas, not for better labor but cheaper labor. Number one exporter from Taiwan last year was *not* Taiwan, it was General Electric! Asia's not taking jobs from us, the multinationals are taking jobs *to them*." And somehow, even in the huge bleary spaces of this arena, an aliveness began to gutter, shouts and applause gusting over the crowd as Jackson spoke on. "And the loss of factory jobs overseas can't be offset with service jobs here. Far more security and pride and stability in making cars than making hamburgers—but the workers who used to make our cars now making french fries and fish sandwiches, for minimum wage!"

He landed in Eau Claire, Wisconsin, on another cold morning, with only a dull yellow lurk of light lying along the flat horizon, and paused inside the small terminal to greet an elderly couple, a dumpling-plump matron with her grasshopper-slight husband tilted uncertainly on a cane beside her, the woman whooping, "Well, you have certainly made my day, Jesse Jackson!" and Jackson chortling back, "Mercy, mercy," as he leaned down to give her a loud-spanking kiss. He and his entourage were then carried, in a stale and lumbering bus, out into the vacant and wintry countryside, crossing over the Chippewa River, and finally, after turning onto a thinly tapering road, began to pass cars parked along both sides until, nearing the dairy farm where he was to speak, cars and trucks and vans and station wagons were crammed and tucked into every possible cranny of space around the farmhouse's muddy side yard and cattle lots. "Don't worry," Jackson assured a reporter who questioned just how spirited a reception could be expected at such an unlikely site, "we gonna make something happen here." Packed inside a vast shed behind the house was a surprisingly large multitude—young couples, the wives in bulky denim jackets with heads wrapped in scarves, the husbands in rumpled khakis stuffed into buckled rubber boots, holding twisty and whimpering children; older couples with weather-crinkled faces that had acquired over the years a dull similarity of almost brother and sister, the men with hands shoved in nylon quilted jackets zippered up to their chins, little felt hats atop their heads. Jackson towered over them from the back of a pickup truck, his tie stripped off in one concession to the setting; in a musk of hay dust, his voice blared over the shed, "Republicans trying to play Halloween with this campaign, but Halloween's 'bout over with—time they took off their mask! After eight years of Republicans in the White House, condominiums for the few, and hallways and alleyways for the millions homeless. Take off the mask! Gone from a creditor nation to a debtor nation, a fundamental shift in who we are in the world, banks failing—got to take off that mask, now! Farm prices down thirty percent, consumer prices *up* thirty percent. It's not the rural farmer taking advantage of the urban consumer, it's the *corporate barracuda* taking advantage of them both! Take the mask off, not playing Halloween any longer! . . ." Yodeling cheers broke out around him in the shed. "A kinder, gentler nation, yeah. Kinder and gentler for the corporations and merger-maniacs and megaconglomerates swallowing up the family farmer and taking factory jobs overseas. Urban America looks like it's been bombed out, rural America abandoned like a plague's hit. Family farms gone, jobs out, drugs in, profits up, wages down, workers abandoned. And yet they playing us off one against the other, trying to make us think we different kinds of people, playing those ole race games with us when we *need* each other. . . ." Listening to all this, the older men with weather-cured faces at last withdrew their thick blunt hands from their jacket pockets and smote them together in heavy deliberate applause. "Always some kind of scheme by the economic aristocracy to try confounding democracy. But lemme tell you, if the family farmer and urban worker, black and white, the good-hearted common people all over this country, if we should ever—watch out!—*get together*, then we sure 'nough *would* see a kinder, gentler nation; a fairer, freer, juster, stronger America all way round."

Afterward, he had to grapple his way through a churn of enthusiasts that had the loud holiday brawl of a county-fair midway, pulling himself from hug to double-clutching handshake on toward the bus, where he was waved aboard with a last uproar of cheering. He then discovered that, somewhere in his passage through the crowd, he had lost his tie, which an aide found a moment later outside, trampled in the mud. It was a loss that hardly distressed Jackson. As the bus pulled back down the road, he stalked up and down the aisle, still on updrafts of elation from the heat of his rhetoric and the crowd's response. "What'd I tell you?" he stopped to remind the reporter who'd questioned what reception they could expect at this spot. "Fired up! Ain't gonna take it no more!" and he gave a gleeful waggle of his hips, piston-pumping his thumbs upward.

In all these rallies, Jackson was constantly infusing into his egalitarian evangelisms an extra, crackling vigor from the Scriptures—a combination that makes up, in fact, his own novel political catechism: what could be called "gospel populism." "Can you imagine Jesus, for instance—he was preaching one day, big crowd, and a woman sick with an issue of blood came up behind him and reached out to touch his robe to be healed—can you imagine Jesus turning around and taking out a clipboard and saying to her, 'Wait a minute, first we got to fill out this form. Le'see, now. How long you been sick? You sure you *really* sick? What's your name and address? Got any children? Say you have—well, you married? And who you work for? How much you make? And when you get well, just what is your payment plan going to be?' No, Jesus just looked upon her suffering and *healed* her. When somebody's sick, the only moral question is not where is your money but where is your *pain*." Some of the political parables Jackson improvised from the Scriptures were more innovative. In an imaginative reconstruction of the Christmas story to apply to the homeless, he declared, "Jesus wasn't sent through Herod's house, he wasn't the innkeeper's son. God sent Jesus through a poor, *homeless* couple. Father with a skill who couldn't find a job. Didn't have the right to vote. Innkeeper wouldn't let them in 'cause they couldn't pay. . . ." Not precisely the case, of course, the inn simply being full, and Mary and Joseph merely having journeyed from their home in Nazareth, where Joseph worked as a carpenter, to Bethlehem to pay their taxes. Unconfined by such textual punctilios, though, Jackson went on about "the wise men, middle-class businessmen who owned their own farms, owned their own sheep, but chose God over their sheep, fled their sheep to bring gifts to this homeless couple," thereby effectively consolidating the Magi and the shepherds into a single delegation of conscientious burghers. But so fond was he of this political reformulation of the story, he would repeat it on well past Christmas, until an aide finally asked him in late February, "Reverend, what's for Easter?"

At a luncheon gathering of the Hollywood Radio and Television Society at the Beverly Wilshire Hotel, Jackson repaired to the Bible for a spirited apologia for the tradition of liberalism, while at the same time performing his customary semantic riffs on the word itself: "The three wise men — liberals! Took their gifts to the homeless. Liberals *liberate* — that's what the word means. Liberation is inherently a *liberal* process. Moses, Jesus, they were the liberals, and Pharaoh, Herod, Pilate, ole Nero, they were the conservatives. Conservatives want to conserve it all like it is. Liberals liberate and expand what is into what it ought to be." This scriptural exegesis on liberalism Jackson expanded on at other rallies: "When Jesus said to feed the hungry, clothe the naked, comfort the afflicted, those were *liberal* values. 'Come unto me, all ye who are weary and heavy laden, and I will give you rest' — that's liberal! Grace — that's a liberal dynamic, no such thing as conservative grace, grace is by definition a *liberatin'* business." ("And by the way, yawl," he would sometimes add, deadpan, "when Jesus came into Jerusalem the last time, he did *not* ride no *elephant* into Jerusalem. It was a donkey. Hear what I'm sayin'?")

Jackson even brought dire religious intonations into mock-sorrowful reproofs of Bush for ridiculing liberals — chiding him for that in a kind of gently appalled, patiently instructive recital that was not altogether fair or precisely true, but in which Jackson progressed from historical judgments to sounding like some political Elijah confronting a Republican King Ahab: "When Mr. Bush, in his ugly-spirited way, attacks the liberal militants of the sixties —" Actually, Bush had opposed the 1964 Civil Rights Act. "Well, those who perished back then for the right to vote were on the *right* side of history, Mr. Bush, and those who hated them were wrong. Viola Liuzzo, white mother from Detroit, came down to Selma to help in the struggle, shotgunned to death on a dark highway. Mr. Bush, Viola Liuzzo was right, and those who murdered her were *wrong*." And this litany of rebuke would mount on a gradual welling of cheers and clapping. "Schwerner, Goodman, and Chaney, two Jews and a black, killed in Mississippi, bulldozed-over with their eyes wide open, they were *right*, Mr. Bush, and those who killed them"—he hung for an instant, and then uttered with an almost pained softness—"were *wrong*," to a great concussion of applause, shouts, *Please tell it!* "Martin Luther King, John F. Kennedy, those three little girls blown up in a Birmingham church, Mr. Bush, *they were right*, and those who took their lives, they *were wrong*!" The ovation now was deafening. Fair or not, the effect of these progressive regretful reproaches was devastating—Jackson loosed into full forensic political combat can be a fearsome affair—and from these delicately savage admonitions he would then proceed into warnings of a vaguely cosmic balefulness: "When you unkind to the homeless, disparaging them as derelicts, you on treacherous moral ground, Mr. Bush. 'Cause there is another power. The moral arc of the universe is long," he would echo from King's oratory, "but it bends toward justice. Those who cannot defend themselves, they got a silent partner, they got . . . got *another* power. And when you, when you attack liberals, good-hearted folks, lovers of civil liberties, Mr. Bush—Mr. Bush, watch out! You tamperin' with another power! They once said we were nothing from nowhere going nowhere, we never could win"—this "we," again, carrying multiple references, his own campaigns not least among them—"but Mr. Bush, there was *another* power. You may be riding high today, Mr. Bush. But there *is* another power!"

One afternoon, as we were riding to an airport after a rally, Jackson allowed, "I do believe that I am able to exegete the Scriptures in ways that make sense to people. The gospel is truth through personality. It's like, you know, Jesus went about doing good, speaking the truth to folks." At random moments over those campaign weeks, he offered other such expositions, when the spirit moved, on his gospel populism. After a day of swooping about New York, on our way to Queens for a last rally, I sensed a sudden stillness behind me in the backseat, and turned to find Jackson had nodded off amid the bawl of sirens around us. But then, as we were passing along an avenue in Brooklyn beside the East River, I heard him abruptly mumble, "The new Rome." He was now looking out his window at lower Manhattan's massed bluffs of corporate towers. "The new Rome," he pronounced again—a proposition he subsequently amplified on, in that way of his of circling back to a matter again and again, an hour or sometimes a week later, to parse it out further: Jackson does not so much address a question as, with successive passes of commentary, eventually surround it and consume it. "Must realize," he continued as we were riding through a frosty night somewhere in the back stretches of Missouri, "that the first reaction to the words of Jesus was terror from the politics of the day. Rome, Herod, you know, got so much power, so much sophistication—mean,

Rome be *civilized*, now. But if Rome is decadent, *transform* Rome. Jesus was constantly challenging that government in the service of the people. Wadn't he? You hear very few of these vigorous popular preachers on television today, though, preaching land reclamation and debt restructuring for farmers, fair wages, social justice, equal rights for women—can't recall hearing any of 'em talking those things." I submitted that most electronic gospelteers were actually engaged in their own sort of social evangelism, it was just from a direction contrary to his, such as inveighing against the feminist movement by citing Paul's admonition to women to subjugate themselves to the leadership of men. Jackson snorted. "Well, that's a—a text used out of *context*. Which is a *pretext*." Another of his spry little verbal ripples, I observed. He muttered, "Thank y'very much, but it's also true. That's why it ripples good. But," he went on, "if you had an active movement in the white churches, with that evangelism connected to the daily realities of how folks actually live— Yeah, we're with the flag and we're with the prayer business, but what about also paying workers right, what about health care for the poor? Same kind of revolution as happened in black churches in the sixties, I mean, it would change politics overnight! And, leading something like that, you could become the transistor, the connection point, between today and tomorrow. That right? Mean, that's sort of what we been trying to do. To take what soul and spirit is left in the traditional church and translate that into the relevant current agenda. With slavery, for instance—" We now happened to be walking through the teeming Los Angeles airport, and now and then someone would swerve over to greet him. "With slavery, many in the church finally came around to saying, 'They God's children—' "

"Reverend Jackson? Seen you often on television but never had the chance to shake your hand."

"Thank you, friend, good to see you." He returned immediately to "Church said, 'They God's children, not s'pose to be slaves. God ain't pleased.' That's my political principle. Is God pleased? On every question, I proceed from that. Reaganomics, corporate welfare, giant military, supporting friendly dictators—might be convenient, might make us feel good, might be comfortable, might be expedient, might be profitable, might even seem political. But God *ain't pleased*! The problem in the end is not really—"

"Reverend Jackson, want you to know I voted for you. So did my wife here, we both did."

"Hi, dear! Gimme a hug, then. Ummm-*hummmmh*! God bless yawl, so long, now— Problem is not really any particular individuals or personalities, but powers and principalities, like the Scriptures say. The structure of society has *got* to be challenged. So the need is leaders who see the role of government"—this as he was sprawled awkwardly in the undersized middle seat of a van taking him to catch a flight to Baltimore—"see the role of government as that of the Great Commission. 'Love ye one another, even as I have loved you.' Which drives right into 'Treat others as you would have them treat you. Of all these things I have told you, the law rests on this: love one another as I've loved you.' *That.* The gospel happens to be the most revolutionary manifesto in history. Man, *think* about it. When you start dealing in terms like forgiveness and redemption and treating the least of these like they were you yourself, that's saying something that goes way beyond left-wing or right-wing. Homeboy, that's *witnessing!*"

I asked, as we were pulling into the airport, if there were not, however, something unnaturally awry about aspiring to effect an essentially spiritual ethic through the offices of civil power. "Why?" he barked. "How come? We certainly do not want to entrust the political process to administrators who have holes in their souls. Anyway, if it's moral, it's going to be political sooner or later. People will always respond when somebody shows up in town who represents that thing that will feed the hungry and clothe the naked and set the captives free and make the crooked ways straight. . . ."

In fact, for all his lusty defenses of liberalism throughout the campaign, Jackson took to protesting, "The issue is not conservative or liberal at all. It's moral center. My momma, now, she's not left-wing—wanting to use a rest room downtown, that's not left-wing, My momma's about moral center. I never been left-wing. Somebody has simply imposed on us a dialectic and terminology taken from their own concept of left and right. I challenge anybody to define what is my, quote, liberal agenda. Debt reduction in Latin America, hemispheric energy plan, reducing the budget deficit, reducing military buildup, reinvesting from arms into America's infrastructure, fair prices for farmers and workers, war on drugs, integrity on Wall Street—all that ain't liberal or conservative, that's *center.* Emancipatin' human beings, whether it's Jesus or Gandhi or Martin, that's not left-wing or right-wing, that's the moral center." Jackson, by his account, presented this argument to Senators Robb and Nunn in a private meeting not long after his primary campaign, complaining to them, "You guys keep on talking about me being on the left and all that. But look, I don't represent the left *or* the right," notifying them then, "I represent the *moral center.*" How they received this piece of news from Jackson one can only surmise.

But "the people are responding," Jackson kept insisting, "because they know I address those longings they got. Everywhere I go, they always giving me notes, hand 'em to me at airports, slip 'em under my door at the hotel, 'Please say something about this. . . .' They can't turn to the government, can't turn to Congress, 'cause those folks are already too locked into the arrangement." He liked to recount how, "when I speak at these big Democratic banquets, five-hundred-dollar-a-plate deals, I say, 'Maybe instead of a thousand Democrats here at five hundred dollars a head, we ought to have fifty thousand people at ten dollars a head. Can we really use means like this to win leadership of those who set our tables tonight, who'll change our beds in the morning, who drove us here from the airport? Can they see any real distinction between us gathered here for a five-hundred-dollar meal and those we tell them we're battling against in their behalf? Somehow in this process, the humble people, the disregarded common people, have lost their place at our table.' And you know, while I'm saying all this at one of these banquets, the janitors and maids and cooks will come to the doors along the sides to listen, and I'll say, 'They standing over there right now, and they're welcome here, too. They know instinctively what all you must know. If I'm welcome, *they* welcome.' See, it's all *those* people—workers, the poor, family farmers—they the life of this continuing movement, 'cause they know I argue their case."

During the last week of the campaign, Jackson landed one afternoon at a little wind-slapped airfield near Columbia, Missouri, and set out in a van, with a few reporters and a farmer named Roger Allison, for a rally at Allison's parents' farm about forty miles away, the van trailed by a sizable caravan of cars with a state patrol escort. Allison, a heftily built man with a cornbread-plain face, was a veteran supporter of Jackson's, going back to the formation of what seemed Jackson's unlikeliest alliance—with beleaguered farmers—during the troubled season of foreclosures in 1983. "People felt a little hopeless and apathetic until Reverend Jackson started coming out and firing us up," Allison told the reporters in the van. Before Jackson's 1984 campaign even began, according to Carolyn Kazdin, one of his advisers, "we were coming in on a plane to a farm area where we couldn't get the local police to provide security. And these farmers said, Ah shit, we'll provide the security. So we're coming into this airstrip out in the middle of nowhere, and we've got a hundred tractors around it. The pilot's circling, looking for the airstrip, and he sees this thing lined with tractors: 'What the hell's going on down there?'" Actually, in those tense and harrowed times, it was an alliance not without certain incendiary potentials: one of Jackson's first farm audiences, in Great Bend, Kansas, was composed mostly of members of the Posse Comitatus, a kind of reactionary vigilante agrarian equivalent of the Weathermen in the sixties. Then, at a protest rally in 1984, farmers arrived wearing paper sacks over their heads, and Jackson learned only afterward that it was a precaution to avoid being identified by farm bureau officials: "I looked out there, all these guys in hoods. Sort of a little moment there." Allison, sitting beside Jackson, chuckled at the recollection, and Jackson clapped him on the knee. "But our people have always had more in common than other folks supposed—right, doc? We've both felt locked out. Exploited and discarded. People saying about the family farmer exactly what they say about unemployed urban blacks, 'Something's wrong with them. If they worked hard like me, wouldn't be in all that trouble.' Fact, more you get into this thing, more you realize that black comes in many shades. We've found out we kin. Even got common religious values," Jackson ranged on. "What they sing in church here, we were singing the same songs down in Greenville, South Carolina," and he then posed the somewhat hopeful fancy, "Very similar cultures, actually. Similar music—Charlie Pride, Ray Charles . . ." From his first reachings out to family farmers in 1984, "he loved to get into overalls," says Carolyn Kazdin. "I'd tell him that we were going to do some farm stuff, and he'd say, 'Can I wear my overalls?' Excited like a little kid. Someone would go to Sears and buy him a new pair of overalls, and when he was speaking at the rally you could still see the creases and the tags and strings hanging off." Once, in Des Moines, "I arranged for him to milk these cows, and called AP and told them they could get this picture. He didn't stage it, I did. For him, it was real. At five o'clock in the morning, he got up to milk that goddamn cow, and he was in heaven." Eventually, Jackson had begun organizing his own sort of cultural exchanges, having black mayors and the congregations of black churches travel out to farm rallies, bringing farmers in to services at black churches. "By coming together like that, we began seeing our common ground. We both in a struggle against an economic aristocracy. For farmers, it's a whole exploitative macrosystem subsidized by the government, a new, corporate feudalism, big corporate dealers taking over family farmland, then shipping what they grow to Third World countries."

"Reverend Jackson's expanded our consciousness out here about a hundred and fifty percent," Allison declared to the reporters. "I have absolutely no interest now in having what I raise go to agribusiness exporters like Cargill to bust farmers in Thailand. We just never thought about those things before. And I have a relationship now with the civil rights movement in St. Louis and Kansas City, whereas I was afraid to even think that way before."

At one point, Allison called Jackson's attention to a distant farmhouse, all its windows darkened in the dimming afternoon, and mentioned the name of its occupant, whom Jackson knew. "He's still living out there," said Allison, "but he's about to go under. He won't hardly ever leave that house now, just sits out there."

"Well, I'll call him tonight," said Jackson, "see what we can do to maybe he'p him, cheer him up some. Big, strong guy," Jackson told the reporters, "'bout a size-twenty neck. Big ole slumped shoulders. He looks like every stereotype you ever . . . mean, he makes Archie Bunker look like he's from Oxford University. For him now to be just *broken*—" And this melancholy case moved Jackson into the wholesale and slightly exorbitant lamentation, "Rural poverty, *godamighty*! People everywhere out here are just *suffering*. Cold, hungry, just *die*!"

"Well, ole boy back there," said Allison, "whether he makes it or not, he'll at least know what happened to him. His whole outlook has changed quite a bit. Lot of people," Allison said to the reporters, "their lives have been changed for the rest of their lives by what Reverend Jackson's had to say."

"See," said Jackson, suddenly pitching forward in his seat, "it's as much a new alliance of cultures as it is black and white." Once again, he eagerly recited the diverse constituencies that would make up his envisioned populist majority, not only those same "common folks" of George Wallace's litanies—"cabdrivers, truck drivers, waitresses, plant workers"—but also Jackson's more cosmopolitan and ecumenical overlay: "environmentalists, peace activists, women's rights groups." Jackson seemed to compose this coalition in the air by simply sounding its various components, tossing his hands inward as if assembling an invisible salad. "*Cultures* coming together. City and country. Workers and college students. Young and elderly. *That's* our country's future. We not dividing our politics, we *renewing* 'em, we *delivering* the country from its past schisms—"

As Jackson went on invoking these large prospects, the caravan of cars trailed behind us in the deepening dusk, rippling through a gentle lilting of hills with police lights winking, the occasional approaching car quickly pulling to the other side of the road out of the apparent assumption it was some late funeral cortege. "I don't know how long it'll take, but I know it's just a matter of these pieces coming together. And all of a sudden there's a big opening to people who, historically, been conditioned to be afraid of me. That's why this flower keeps on unfolding. Why a new majority is dawning."

As Jackson enthused on, it was curiously as if a subtle amnesia had infiltrated the van, in which one forgot that a presidential race also happened to be under way across the country. "You never quite know when these social births are going to take place. Fact, fact, it's like that concept 'in the fullness of time.' That whole dialectic of a man and a woman and their fullness of time. It's some combination of the fullness of man's time and the fullness of God's time, in some explosive convergence for which you can be the agent. When the moment comes, when the moment is pregnant, and you ready, it can't be stopped."

But I asked Jackson if, after all the benevolent social exertions of government since Roosevelt, Republican presidencies since Nixon had not reflected a popular backwash of moral exhaustion and disillusionment with the idea of governmental intercession to rectify inequities—a disaffection with the very kind of governmental altruism that he was preaching: if, in short, the country had not simply wearied of trying to do good. "Not atall," said Jackson. "The nation will respond because it *needs* to do good. Everybody wants to be good, even those who are often not good. The rich and powerful want, when they die, somewhere in their obituary that they cared for the poor, built a wing of the church. Even the rich tyrant will say, 'I'm gonna relate to you poor folks, I'll build some houses for you, I'm not just powerful and smart, see. I'm good. In addition to getting profits, I do extras, I'm *good.*' Conscience. Never underestimate the force of that, the desire to be good. That's why right is might in the long run. You may be powerful but never be good, but if you're good, you can't *help* but be powerful. 'Cause there's a *power* in goodness—great, great power. Political strength comes out of moral authority. That's why my biggest threat when I began in '84 was that I came out of a movement whose strength was its moral right. Not money, not organization, not status, not cunning—simply its *moral right*. And that became very difficult for our opponents to counter."

Now, nearing the rally at the Allisons' farm, Jackson continued, "People have an amazing capacity to rise to the occasion once the reality is laid out there for them. Whenever America sees the *real* deal, actually sees a wrong—like the homeless, like the famine in Ethiopia, like South Africa's racist system—they'll say, 'Naw, now, naw, we not goin' with *that.*' You can get enough numbers of weapons systems to make America stronger, but I'm convinced the way to win friends and elections both is, you get enough *people* wanting to make America *better*. That's our strongest national defense. Besides, people ought to love each other just because it's a good feeling. What's happening where we going now, way out here in the middle of nowhere, is that you gonna find people working on that. Working on being better people. Now I think that . . . that's a big deal. And all the powers and maneuverings of the system can*not* defeat that."

The van finally pulled off the highway and up a short, steep drive to the Allison farmhouse, where a substantial crowd was gathered over the side yard under a low, cold, smoky sky, everyone heavily muffled against icy smackings of wind. Jackson addressed them from a flatbed trailer, his voice electronically ringing from amplifiers set atop hay bales—"Don't let anybody ever set us against each other again. Our strongest defense starts in our hearts. Love one another, that's what'll keep America strong"—in what amounted more or less to a continuation of his discourse in the van. In the stunning cold, though, it wound up a somewhat abbreviated speech, and after finishing, Jackson expeditiously retreated into the house, into a warm kitchen with steamed windows and rich savors of fried chicken and coffee and yeasty baked bread. Much of the crowd piled in after him, quickly filling the kitchen and small adjoining parlor, and Jackson, finding everybody so densely crammed about him, could not resist addressing them again, in an extensive postscript to his speech. Standing behind the oilcloth-covered kitchen table with a yellow plastic bowl of apples set in its precise center, he seemed to bulk overlarge in the snug room, his head near the ceiling, his voice too big and reverberant—again a curious apparition, this powerful black presence amid a homey congregation of white farm folk. But over the squealing of several babies, his pulpiteering was accompanied, in one cross-cultural interechoing, by an underchorus of *"All right," "Amen," "Say it," "Praise God," "Yes,"* in Baptist Wednesday-night-prayer-meeting fashion. He concluded with "Now, we do have all these rights in America, but we also have the very basic right to eat homemade rolls and chicken," and he promptly settled himself at the table to go about that with a two-handed gusto. When he was done, he stood and announced he wanted to conduct a parting prayer, and everyone joined hands in a line that twined through the rooms. "Father," he called out over the bowed heads, "we all live in the same world. We are all the sheep of your pasture. All over this world tonight, may we study war no more. May all the world know that peace you promised, when the lions and lambs lie down to rest together. . . ." After his "Amen," he boomed, "Friends, we got to go to St. Louis now!"

Back in the van, traveling through full darkness, Jackson began effusing, again with that odd little instant shift into removed assessment, "People in that house, you see how they changing their lives? Groups like that responding to me, they breaking through ancient cultural barriers. Those folks back there are reaching out across every conceivable line—race lines, class lines, background. That's what I mean about, you have to call this authentic, as opposed to political, *beyond* political. It's, it's"—and he breathed—"*so* real."

WITH ALL HIS ebullience that evening about the racial conciliations he assumed he was bringing to pass, it was only some days later that I ventured to ask him if he was also aware of how profoundly he continued to affront no neglible number of other whites—how much they still perceived him as devious, opportunistic, subversive; if, in the end, it might not turn out to be precisely the matter of race that would cause his whole apostolic mission to miscarry. To this suggestion, Jackson blinked several times, and pondered dourly for a long moment. I suddenly had an obscure sense that the question had somehow hurt him. "Well, it's a cynical view of life," he finally proposed softly, "that white people aren't capable of moving beyond that. I know that truth has a penetrating power. I've seen too many white people respond to truth in a wholesome way to assume it doesn't. Like when I spoke to this rally of GE workers in Cicero, two white ladies walked up afterward, kind of edged closer and closer, and finally one reached out to me and I reached out to her and we embraced, and she started to weep. She said" — and relating this, Jackson's voice again sank to a low whisper of marvelment — "said, 'Our husbands are standing over there, they're a little ashamed to come over here. But we need our jobs so bad, *please* don't let them close this plant. At our age, we can't get no retraining, we ain't got no place else to go. Know this is kind of strange coming from us, but you 'bout the only hope we got left.' " Jackson seemed to have momentarily moved himself in telling this story, and he paused to clear his throat. "I mean, when I decided to run for president, I know some white people said, 'He's crazy, he's dangerous, he's stunting around, he's an egomaniac,' but other white people said, 'Well, now, wait a minute here. He's making sense. I think I'm for him.' That number, by 1988, had tripled. So I'm not pessimistic about what can happen in time, about white people's ability in some inherent way to respond to what is good for them and *who* is good for them."

In truth, as Jackson made his way about in public, passing through hotel lobbies and restaurants, he was approached by what seemed a surprisingly large number of white admirers who eagerly announced they had voted for him. Proceeding through the Los Angeles airport, he encountered a covey of white matrons who instantly flurried around him, one burbling, "We *all* voted for you," and Jackson enfolded them in a collective hug, "Yawl so *spe-shulll*. Bless you," and they chimed back, "God bless *you*!" A minute or two later, another white lady slipped up to him — a slight, pale woman, a little frowzy of hair — and thinly sang, "I just got to shake your hand, I'm so proud to meet you. You're a great man," and Jackson replied, "Awright, dear, thank you, now." A moment later, she reappeared with her husband and small son. "I just had to bring them over, it's not every day we get to meet a great leader," and she gently eased her son, with her palm on his back, toward Jackson. He beamed down on the boy, who was perhaps five. "Hi, baby! Wanna give me a hug?" and reached down for him, "C'm'ere on up, 's how you do that thing." But the boy proved one of the few children to instantly recoil from Jackson's huge outstretched hands, twisting away and scampering a few steps off, his back turned to the whole scene. "Say, he's a little scared and everything," offered Jackson. "Probably just woke up or something." He took a step forward and leaned farther down toward the boy. "Hey, mister. You ain't no baby, you a big fella now, aren't you?" But the boy could not be charmed even into facing Jackson. "A little shy," mumbled Jackson, to no one in particular. But he still did not want to give it up, and with a kind of casually resolute amble pursued the equally resolute dodgings of the boy. "Hey, buddy, c'mon, gimme a hug, now." When Jackson at last stalked him around a column, the boy scuttled about fifty yards away. "Gettin' away from here, ain't he?" Jackson chuckled, a bit flatly. "Guess that's one I ain't quite got yet." The mother said, "I don't know what's wrong with him, he always gets so excited seeing you on television." Her husband declared, "Well, I hope we're going to get the chance to vote for you again. We've voted for you both times you've run." They bustled off to retrieve their son, and I remarked to Jackson that if all the whites had voted for him who were now professing they had, the puzzlement was why he hadn't won. "Good many of them probably did," he said. "Some of 'em would have but couldn't quite bring themselves this time. Next time, though . . ."

But whatever cross-racial concords Jackson's campaigns may have elicited, certain cultural statics still lingered. When his party was picked up late one night at the Des Moines airport, to be transported some fifty miles to the little country town of Greenfield, which Jackson had chosen as his campaign headquarters for the 1988 Iowa caucuses, the driver of one van, a young businessman, politely confided to the journalists riding with him, "There're still a lot of people around who just don't know exactly how to take his style of speaking. It's a little too much like a revival meeting. People out here don't think their politicians ought to . . . well, *be* like that. Sort of preaching, the way he does."

Nevertheless, at the rally the next morning in Greenfield's courthouse square, the reception was loudly convivial and neighborly. It was a gray morning, under a dim sky seeming to hold an imminence of snow, and Jackson, wearing a neat, crisp, pale-cream raincoat, spoke from a platform rigged over the courthouse steps, his amplified voice racketing over the square to frequent cheers from the crowd, almost totally white, spread over the lawn all the way to the sidewalk. When he had finished, a woman standing amid a herd of children near the platform called up to Jackson, "They want you to talk about your grandmother's quilt!" It was a little personal fable of Jackson's, related by him in his oration at the 1988 Democratic convention in San Francisco, which they had obviously also heard here in Greenfield more than once before. "Grandmamma's quilt!" said Jackson. "Awright, yawl come closer," and he bent down on one knee at the edge of the platform, "All yawl c'mon up here real close, now." And to the children collected below him in a small pond of rapt uplifted faces, he told the story again. "One winter when I was a little boy, living in this humble little house without any heat, we couldn't afford a blanket. So my grandmother had to make us a quilt, or else we'd've froze. All we had, though, were pieces of old cloth, wool, gabardine, croker sack. But my grandmother gathered together all those patches and pieces, and when she finished sewing them together, it made a big quilt that covered us and kept us warm." The children gazed up at him transfixed. "And that's like America. It's not a blanket made out of just one cloth. It's a great quilt made out of many patches—urban patch, rural patch, poor patch, afflu- ent patch, black patch, white patch, different-colored patches—all held together by common threads, threads of fairness, understanding, toler- ance, concern. Just like my grandmother sewed that quilt together with love and caring." The children applauded, the whole crowd applauded, and Jackson stood back up and led the children—his voice now worn and raspy—through his familiar refrain, they shrilling each phrase after him like a Sunday school class repeating verses of Scripture after their teacher: "Save the farmers! Save the workers! Save the children! Save the teach- ers!" and finally, what could be his own, personal, fundamental text, "I *am* somebody! If my mind can conceive it—and my heart can believe it—I *know* I can achieve it!"

Before leaving, Jackson took a stroll along the square's surrounding gallery of aged, faded brick buildings—Turner's Department Store, Mather Pharmacy, Farm Credit Services, Sears Authorized Catalogue Sales—passing nothing but white faces, fresh and simple and wholesome as hominy, Jackson greeting them with "Hey, there, sweetie! . . . Good to see you, ole buddy! . . . How you doin', dear?" They chorused greetings back with a cordiality most notable, as was the entire reception that morn- ing in Greenfield, in that it seemed everyone was utterly oblivious of Jack- son's race—an unmindfulness that would perhaps constitute the ultimate, simple, unsensational arrival of any true racial conciliation in this country. Jackson stepped at last into Toad's Cafe, a narrow eatery of minimal decor, and leaned across the counter to buss a waitress. The proprietor came bar- reling out of the kitchen in a baggy apron and, arms akimbo, bawled to Jackson, "Where were you this morning? I was gonna fix your grits for you." Jackson said, "Got tied up. Next time, next time." The proprietor snuffled: "Tied up. Well, anyway, we got your—" and before he could fin- ish, a portly woman appeared beside him and held out to Jackson a huge jar of orange juice. "Aw, mercy me," said Jackson. "Missed m'grits but got m'juice. Put it in a sack for me, honey, I got to get on down the road." He flung one arm high, "Bye-bye, everybody, love you all, be back 'fore long," and headed for the door with a low, throaty cackling of gratification. Back outside, he suddenly stopped and turned to me: "You remember all those purty people at that party few weeks back in Beverly Hills? Hunh? Now, these people here—these *real* people, ain't they?"

JACKSON DELIGHTED IN the crowds of that popular processional of his through the fall of 1988 no less than they seemed to delight in him. What soon struck one was how, though he was no longer an active contender himself, he yet drew such large and effusive turnouts almost everywhere he went and touched off combustions of enthusiasm that seemed strangely impervious to his final failure in the primaries. It was as if, to those throngs that still collected to hear him, he had indeed passed beyond ordinary politics into some sort of pop legend. At the least, he had by then entered that dimension as a public personality in which he had come to be commonly referred to by masses around the country simply by his first name—a kind of casual folk intimacy achieved by few politicians. Arriving for a rally at a college coliseum or a city auditorium, his car would ease through a press of people calling out, "Hey, Jesse! . . . Get 'em, Jesse! . . . Love you, Jesse!" their hands scrambling toward him through the car window when he lowered it, he briefly clasping their fingers and calling back, "Bless you, love you." He would climb out of his car into a heat lightning of flashbulbs as these faithful converged around him with wails and squeals. To then follow him inside to the rally was to experience secondhand something of what must be the heady flush of a rock star's entrance—first, hurrying with his shoal of attendants down a back corridor, then passing through the hushed, hidden, barnlike glooms of backstage, Jackson now nattily shooting his cuffs and slipping his hand inside his jacket to smooth down his tie, giving a quick little side-twist of his head to settle his neck more comfortably in his high collar . . . and then walking out into, all at once, a sudden vast openness and blaze of light and blast of cheering like an almost physically felt gale of electricity: the sensation for Jackson must have been, each time, like a kind of psychic rebirth.

Indeed, it seemed to give him a capability for an almost endless self-regalvanization. Reports one of his advisers then, Robert Borosage, whenever Jackson appeared to be flagging from exhaustion, "we'd run him into a black church for a rally, and you could just see him reviving, getting bigger and bigger, and he could then go for three or four more days on that energy."

One night in an overcrammed black church in St. Louis, with people overflowing into the aisles and up against the walls, he bellowed away in a hoarsely cracking voice, his face glittering with sweat, "What kind of sick need is it not to prefer the whole personhood of a woman? *God* obviously had a high regard for women, he didn't send his only begotten son through a whirlwind or have him wash up on no beach—sent him through a *woman!* But we got people who look on women, if they work, call them unfit mothers, and if they don't work, call them lazy—" An answering murmuration rose from the women in the congregation, *Thank you, thank you.* . . . "If a woman does work, she makes only sixty-two cents on a dollar of what a man makes. But a woman can't buy a dollar's worth of bread for only sixty-two cents—" *Yes, Jesse!* "Can't buy a dollar's worth of milk or medicine, or heatin' oil to keep her babies warm, for only sixty-two cents!" *Oh, Jesse! Go, Jesse!* "Women who work must be *paid right* so they can raise our *children* right!" As he waited, his face shellacked with sweat, for the tumult in the church to subside, a hand discreetly slipped a glass of water up to him, from which he took a quick sip, and then a handkerchief was handed to him, which he swabbed across his forehead and above his mouth. "But 'course, don't hear much from Mr. Bush 'bout that, 'bout helping working mothers with fair pay and day care and— Listen! Better Head Start and day care and prenatal care on the *front*side of life than welfare, jail care, and *des*pair on the *back*side of life! But those Republicans, all they wanna talk about is Willie Horton gettin' let out of jail—" More cries arose from the congregation, *All right, tell 'em 'bout it!* "Fight crime, yes! *Yes,* Willie Horton ought to been in jail. But Oliver North"—and instantly a howl began gathering—"and Poindexter"—and there was a rumble of stomping feet now under ecstatic shouts, *C'mon, Jesse, talk it, son!*—"and McFarlane ought to be right there in the same jail with him! And when they got there, they ought to found Nixon already sittin' there waitin' on 'em!" This set off a thundering in the church that lasted a full minute. When Jackson had at last finished, and began making his way through a mobbing of admirers, he seemed transported into the dazed, spinning euphoria of a child amid a lavish Christmas-morning bounty— with an open grin, his tongue-tip pressed between his teeth, springing his widespread hand suddenly forward for a great slap of a shake, including to reporters who'd been with him for days. Heading down a stairway with a huge wake of people tumbling after him, he suddenly halted at the bottom, immediately arresting with a tremendous jostle the entire procession behind him, and announced, "Wait a minute. This ain't my raincoat, got on somebody else's coat here." As an aide left to retrieve his, he regarded the host of people dammed up the stairway above him and happily called up to them, "I can see the headlines tomorrow, yawl. 'Jesse Jackson arrested in St. Louis for stealing raincoat in church,' " and gave a relishing snicker.

One morning he appeared for an outdoor rally at the University of California at Los Angeles, and as he walked toward the rally site, rifflings of applause began to spread ahead of him through the vast crowd sprawled over a plaza under eucalyptus trees in the cool, pale sunlight. A voice rang from the public address system, "All right, everybody! It's time! It's time!" and a roar swelled over the plaza. "The greatest freedom fighter in America—Jesse Jackson!" He skipped up onto the small stage, tall and chesty in his sleek suit. "Got some notes here," he began, withdrawing a folded sheaf of papers from his inside coat pocket. "But I don't need to use any notes," and he stuffed the papers back into his pocket. "I got *convictions*, I know what I'm talking about—" And the roar rose again from the throng. It was more like some festival of mutual celebration than a rally. Jackson finished with "America is bigger than one race, it's bigger than one religion, it's bigger than one class," And he then posed his own somewhat millennial ambition "to keep America expanding, to take America beyond racism, beyond prejudice, beyond anti-Semitism, beyond sexism, beyond *all* hatred, beyond fear, beyond poverty, beyond war," which brought yet again that mass chant, surging in a great surf of voices over the plaza, *Jes-see! Jes-see! Jes-see! . . .*

THE INTERPLAY OF energies that pulsed between Jackson and his crowds was of a kind, in fact, that I had encountered, in over twenty years of reporting, with only two other, and otherwise radically unlike, political figures: George Wallace and, in his last years, Robert Kennedy—and this even though, as *The Washington Post*'s Paul Taylor noted, during Wallace's and Kennedy's time "the political seas would have been heaving no matter who ran," while Jackson's campaigning "was waged on calm waters." I was to hear explanations of Jackson's popular effect, from both supporters and unenchanted observers, that one once heard so often about Wallace: "It's just that he's so much more *alive* than the others. People at least feel there's something real up there in front of them. . . ." More, the popular exhilarations through which Jackson moved during those final weeks of his own alter-campaign called to mind an observation offered years ago by then senator John Tunney of California about Robert Kennedy: "His sense of politics was physical, in that he knew you had to throw yourself out there among the people again and again, to be directly heard and seen and touched and sort of handled and pushed around by them. Because the malaise in the country is people feeling isolated and alone in a disappearance of any large, embracing sense of community, feeling decisions about their lives are being made by faceless strangers and processes beyond their control. So there's a huge hunger to connect to an actual physical presence—a tribal leader, really, with that kind of personal relationship between him and the people—who can give them a sense of meaning and value as a community again. They need to feel that he has almost recklessly, with a willingness to take extraordinary risks, given himself over completely to that, and to what he believes in, which answers what they believe in. It's something almost primitive, mystic."

Jackson himself would not infrequently expound on this relationship in his own case, albeit with his tendency to move toward the unabashedly operatic. "It's a covenant. Somehow all these people, workers, students, farmers, they seem to feel, for some reason that I do not fully comprehend"— and he confided this again in a husky murmur of awed reverence—"they feel they have a stock in me. Whether they'll ever even vote for me, they still feel that whatever it is I represent, it's something they are shareholders in. I sense all those expectations, and I'm obligated to respond. Everywhere I go, they expect so much of me, they pull out of me my energy and spirit, just . . . *pull it out of me.* When I get up to speak, I see in their faces this, this *belief.* That I can make a difference for them. And that makes *me* believe I *can* make a difference. And they then respond to that belief in *me.* It goes back and forth between us like that."

There are even times during Jackson's speeches when he seems to be laboring to actually merge himself somehow with the people assembled before him. "I am of you," he will cry. "I *am* you." At stray moments, Jackson would offer musings on how he reaches the high pitch of personal communion thrumming between him and his crowds—describing it with, once more, that curious detachment of one who has moved himself out of the happening to observe it and to narrate it as if he were also a spectator of what he was doing. "Truth, like electricity, is all around us, but we have very few conduits for it. What you do is plug into the socket of the people, they give you that electricity, and you give them heat and light. Lot of people say, you know, 'He's a great speaker.' Well, speaking is a result of feeling, of *thinking*—you *thought* of what to say. So when people say, 'He sho does talk good,' ain't just talkin', it's a *brain*, I got a brain that sends messages to my jaw muscles, I be feeling and *thinking* what I'm saying. I work, and work, and work to say that thing right, spin that thing just right, so when people hear it, they"—and he blew out a soft whoosh of breath, *Whew!* while yanking upright in his seat, wide-eyed, as if himself from a sudden shock of voltage—"it's like that. I struggle hard to conceive it as a *live* thing."

One of those who have nominally assisted Jackson in preparing his speeches in the past is Mark Steitz, and he recalls the evolution of one of Jackson's now trademark phrases. "It began from thinking about the idea of hope and the need for optimism. He makes a note: 'Hope reborn.' Not quite it, but getting there. Finally then, 'Keep hope alive.' *Wham!* One damage of this century is the overprofessionalization in dozens of human endeavors that has led people to confuse obscurity with genius. But what you learn from Jackson is that when something comes to you very simply, very clearly and directly, you're getting better—you're not just finding a more clever way of saying it, you're *understanding* it better. It's not merely packaging, it has extraordinary moral and intellectual content, just the process itself of getting to that right phrase. 'Keep hope alive!' "

Jackson's particular predilection for rhyming—he has become something like the High Sultan of Assonance and Alliteration of American political discourse—has invited not a few derisions that he conducts campaigns of jingles. One Herblock cartoon of Jackson during the 1988 primaries carried the caption, "Drugs are bad. Crime is messy. Don't be sad, vote for Jessy." Even one of his former college teachers complained, "If he keeps on quoting that 'hope in the brains, not dope in the veins' kind of stuff, he's gonna run the risk of being trivial. That gets on people's nerves after a while. It's like he didn't think about the thing long enough, he's trivializing the issue." But it is Jackson's instinct, according to several advisers, that rhyme elicits implicit kinships between ideas and between values, a sense of accordant or contrary relationship realized in shared sounds. As one former adviser explains, "He has an understanding that the link between words and ideas is a deep and meaningful one, and he goes after that until—'I got it! I got it!'—he has that sense of *clasp.*"

But it is not always that premeditated a process. After an especially skinprickling oration of Jackson's, says Bert Lance, "I'd kid him, 'Just where did you *get* that? Who's your writer?' And he'd always say, 'The spirit. The spirit.' " Steitz recounts that, once while they were campaigning in Iowa, "we got locked into this little tiny airport, two hours late for one thing and gonna have to cancel another one. Everything's fucked up, not even a phone that works. Jackson is so mad, he can't see. There had been a meeting two days before in Chicago, where he'd gone on and on about how sick and tired he was of, whenever something went wrong and he'd ask somebody about it, they'd say, 'Well, I tried, but he lied, so we died.' So now I walk over to him where he's steaming in a corner—I'm still a little tentative, because this is a very angry man—but I say, 'Reverend?' He growls, 'Yeah!' I say, 'You know that "I tried, he lied, we died" business? Did you just think that up on the spot, or had you been carrying that around for a while waiting to use?' He looks at me and his face turns into a happy four-year-old's. And he whispers, 'Steitz, when I get the idea, the words, they just *come*!' "

In fact, says Steitz, most often the actual creation of a speech "is happening *exactly* in the course of his giving it. That's why he doesn't really have a speechwriter. Never has, never will. You'll draft all sorts of ideas, come up with an outline, and then you watch him moving that into a full speech—watch him, as he would say, Jesse-ize it." One old associate of Jackson's says, "He's going to rephrase everything, it don't make no difference whether Jesus, Moses, or God said it, Jesse has to Jesse-ize it." As a result, says Steitz, "writing for him is like throwing wet, wet clothes into a dryer. You turn it on, and the whole thing rattles, makes an awful noise, you're convinced it's going to break—BANG! BANG! Then it's going just a little quieter, Bang-Bang-Bang. And finally—*Whoo, whoo.*"

At another point as he was trooping from rally to rally through that autumn of the 1988 presidential campaign, Jackson enlarged on the matter of the spontaneous workings of the spirit in connecting to people in his speeches. "When I first came back home from the seminary, I was asked to speak at church, and my grandmother and some of the older folk came up afterward, 'That was a nice speech, young man, very nice speech.' They meant the words were. Words came out nice. That's what it was . . . was a speech. But as you go on and begin to really catch hold of it, you start hearing them say, 'Well, now. You spoke to my soul. You burned me this morning.' Got to do more than *speak*. You can get informed listening to a newsman or weatherman. You got to be moving toward the heart of the matter, got to burn people's souls. You got to get *inside* of people. That's where it all is. And you can't get inside of them unless you open *yourself* up to be gotten inside *of*. Follow what I'm saying? The key to other people's heart is finding the key to yours. Got to give to receive, got to open up to get inside somebody else."

Several weeks later, after the election, as we were flying to Africa, he resumed these reflections: "You always searching for where the people are. I come to a town, I be talking to the driver on the way in from the airport, talk with the maids at the hotel, the cooks, sometimes even their children. If you speaking from their concerns, you pretty much on track. 'Cause they live their lives on the ground, they have the depth. What's good for them is pretty much what's good for the whole world, you can usually count on that. They *are* the base, the bottom line. An', an', an' "—he stammered in eagerness—"and they do have an ungrammatical profundity, they do have a way in their pealing tones—they be saying something, you know? And I like to capture that and turn it into the music that's really there, find those common, universal chords in it. Because, get right down to it, most people's lives is not about ideology, left-wing, right-wing, any o' that—they hurt, hope, rejoice mostly about the same personal things. Feel good when their children are growing up right, don't want broken hearts because their children went astray. Best fuel for your engine is the spirit-fuel of folks struggling for those simple, decent, basic things in life. When you stay in touch with that music, that rhythm, you speak with authenticity. Because you're *into* it. I couldn't get up there and talk if I hadn't been fighting to keep close to that. Keeps you real. Keeps you out of the abstract. It's what gives color to your language. Gives the bass note to your soul. Deep speaks to deep. The real speaks to the real."

Robert Borosage says, "When Jackson's at a podium, you will often see his fingers at first going like this"—and Borosage flutters his fingers—"on the side of the lectern. It's like he's getting the psychic currents from the crowd." Steitz describes it as "a conversation. He's thinking, he's actually in a deep dialogue with the people that has real moral, intellectual, emotional substance. In that dialogue, he has the most extraordinary focus groups every time he speaks that anybody could have. His concentration is on what the listeners are hearing—he spends so much time in a speech *listening* to the audience. He doesn't consider he's speaking alone, but listening inside and looking out around to see what's connecting to people, making them nod, making them light up, and then speaking from that. Most politicians spend huge amounts of time looking at people in the media to figure out what makes them light up, what makes them start scribbling. In this media age, a lot of politicians are very good at figuring out what interests the interested. What Jackson is great at figuring out is what interests the uninterested." At the same time, this live communion with his audience seems to lend him an uncanny ability to rouse himself again and again for the delivery of an address as if it were the first time he was delivering it, "sometimes making it come so alive," one journalist noted in 1988, that even to a reporter who'd been covering him for weeks, "it seemed he was actually hearing it for the first time." That capacity for an almost indefinite repetition of genuine passion would be not the least of his fortitudes.

JACKSON KEPT UP his own ancillary and separate campaigning even through Election Day of 1988. As soon as the polls opened in Chicago, he voted at his neighborhood polling place, arriving amid a fleet of reporters, and, glancing around at the other voters already gathered there, he declared, "It's a good sign when you got a long line!"—first thing in the morning, hitting the ground rhyming, as it were. But throughout the rest of the day, while the nation was making the determination of who would be its next president, Jackson was flying to lead rallies across the Midwest. In the course of this tour, he began to receive flickering indications of the decision taking shape across the country, the first projections that Bush might be the overwhelming winner, but he noted these reports with what seemed only a curiously incidental interest, as if it were all merely some parenthetical happening. At one of his last rallies, held in a black church, Jackson clamped both hands to the sides of the pulpit and reared back to deliver a deep-bellied bay: "I see something, yawl!"

"What you see?" came shouts from the congregation.

"I see the hungry fed, the homeless sheltered, the sick ministered to, the low lifted up. *See* something, yawl!"

"What you see, Jesse?" a heavier rolling of shouts answered.

"See red, yellow, black, brown, and white, all precious in God's sight, all comin' together. *See something,* yawl!"

"What you see, Jesse?"

"I see joy in the morning! I see *victory.* So hold your head high. Let your hope expand so the children can feel it like the risin' sun. When the sun comes out in the springtime, flowers blossom, eggs crack open, chickens start talking that chicken talk—*hope* is alive! Everything in the universe starts to stir when there is hope in the air! We got too much experience, already seen too much, to ever be pessimistic, we *know* there is honey in the rock, we *know* that joy cometh in the morning!"

IV
"You Belong and Yet You Don't"

SHORTLY AFTER THE election, as we were sitting at the kitchen table in his mother's home down in Greenville, I asked Jackson how, without the high national theater of a presidential campaign, he would now contrive to avoid slipping into a kind of indistinct limbo. "Same way I always have," he declared. "*Testify!* Be *witnessin'*." Through the following weeks, he continued traveling about the country, exhorting assemblies of farmers and students and striking union members almost as if the election had never taken place, in what political writer Andrew Kopkind called "a kind of generic political campaign that may at any time assume electoral form" again. Privately, he kept proposing that, despite what seemed sizable indications to the contrary, the campaign had opened up a new political day in the nation. "It's changed America's way of looking at things. Set the agenda for the country, really. Even Bush ran on some of my message—kinder, gentler nation, day care, gettin' drugs out of our society. All that came out of our campaign." Almost obsessively, he celebrated what he took to be his hard-won legitimacy as an apostle to the nation's conscience through his own presidential primary efforts. "I got seven million votes," he kept repeating. "Seven *million*. Nobody else out there now—no senator, no congressman, no governor, certainly no DNC member—can bring to the table seven million people who voted for them. That's a compelling, objective number—not just a theory or rhetoric, but a compelling *happening*." He was constantly noting how he had finally come to be taken seriously, with whatever reluctance, by major political players. "Once people began to respond, they began to come our way to get validation. Pressures shifted to them to support me. They were trying to catch up with their people."

Beyond that, he elaborated at another point, "I speak now with heads of state in Africa, Latin America, all over the world, and when I have these discussions, the question foreign policy circles never ask about me anymore is, 'By what authority?' They may have some debate with my ideas, but truth is, so far, most of my ideas have been prevailing. On Central America, talking to the Palestinians, sanctions against South Africa—every position we were attacked on in the past has now become center policy. Who's made the adjustment? What was extreme is now mainstream. Can't be radical advocating those things anymore. Getting to where, way history is moving, you have to work harder and harder to stay radical for long, have to really sweat away at it, you know? There's a new center now, and we're in the *heart* of that center. It is," he intoned, "a strange and rewarding gratification to see policies that we were labeled radical for preaching now become the moral center of national politics and U.S. policy. Seldom does a person live to see that happen. And the press, not many of them writing any columns anymore about *He's stupid, he ain't got no head on him.* None of that now. They can't say, *He does not understand policy.* They now say, in fact, I know more about Third World policy, for instance, than the secretary of state does. Mean, they have just come to *assume* that. So those would seem to me credentials—anybody else out there can match 'em, I can't think of who right off."

But in the end, for all his exuberant professions of having acquired at last a national authenticity with his presidential campaigns, he still insisted that his meaning reached beyond the domain of ordinary politics. "The basis of *my* strength and credibility is not any office or position, but my relationship with the people. Somebody'll say, 'You know, I got X number of constituents in my district, that's why I got authority.' But all you are is elected to an office from that district, that's all. Some people been elected like thirty-four times, but they still don't have a following. He's occupying that *office*, he holds that seat, but he's not head of all those people. Follow what I'm saying? And the masses of the people, who are *un*structured and so not depending on people and processes they don't see or know, they have responded to what they saw in me. Other guys had the positions, but they didn't have the following. Officials in government think they got power, but they only got the *portfolio* of office. Can say, I'm chairman or senator or secretary of whatever, supported by friends, everybody's polite to me—I run around and everyplace I go, somebody meets me at the airport, and every time I speak, somebody gives me a plaque. Well, see just how *fast* all that airport-reception and plaque-giving business stops when you out of office."

It was a kind of political ontology of Jackson's—antistructural, antisystem, even antipolitical, in a sense—that seemed an odd attitude for someone who'd pursued the system's paramount office. "Elected officials most of 'em, get locked into an arrangement that distracts them from serving the real interests of the nation," he contended. "In terms of the relationship between political office and the realities of any given society, the views actually get *narrower* as you go toward the top. Guys at the top, they got big positions but small perspectives. What you find up there as the strategic overview is really just a broad collection of individual myopias. Most of their lives are invested in getting reelected, campaigning in their districts, their caucuses, trying to get on some committee with limited responsibility. Cross-fertilizing, increasing their own stature. That's the system they locked into, and unless they play by its limited rules, they will be denied promotion. And while they accept that trade-off, the people are moving on down the street." This syndrome, Jackson averred, claimed black politicians no less quickly than whites. "Often our leaders have emerged from the movement, from the struggle, from the bush, and gotten elected to some governmental office. And they wind up before long 'bout as conservative and cautious as what they replaced. While they still mouthin' righteous principles, their real preoccupation is reelection or heading some committee or election to a higher office. The system's got 'em. Happens all the time. They trade off their street power, their people power, for security in the tokens and technicalities of importance."

During Jackson's passage through southern Africa not long after the election, a visit to the compound of a Yoruba king in the Nigerian interior moved him, on the way back to Lagos, to another of his mystic ruminations, which he managed to apply to his own situation. "You know, it's like Tillich said, 'God is the ground of my being.' I asked the king back there where his power and authority came from. He said it all came to him from the earth, from the ground of his people up to him. The people are the ground of his being. A leader with that kind of authority is a little different from some general or government official in charge of distributing the flour and grits. He has *another* authority, because he moves people. It's more than just political or official, it's love-and-justice power. The people are the ground of his power. That's *another* kind of power. Sometimes it's hard for other folks to quite figure that out. Party officials, government figures, the pundits, they have sort of a hard time gettin' that."

BUT FOR ALL Jackson's brave assertions after the campaign that he had arrived at last—that the sun of his significance had reached its highest point yet—he privately seemed still unreassured. Despite all that had remarkably transpired with him since his ragged beginnings in Greenville, despite his celebrity now, despite the deference accorded him by other political eminences, despite his own sense of having finally attained a singular national importance—he continued to dwell in the odd counter-feeling, if anything more profound than ever, that he did not really belong at all. That he remained immutably an outsider. It was a brooding that somehow imparted a sense that one could expend all one's life in spectacular exertions to answer old aggrievements that are in actuality forever unanswerable.

In his meeting with Senators Nunn and Robb shortly after his own primary campaign, Jackson had essayed one tentative approach to that "in-club," as he put it, that continued "to keep me shut out." As he later recounted, "I told them we were being mentioned together in news articles about every day, but I'd not talked to them two hours in my whole life. Said, 'Look, you guys are all the time speaking about me. I never speak about you, but you guys are always knocking me, giving this and that analysis of my motives. But it's an analysis not born of your primary experience. You guys, see, what you don't understand,' I told them, 'is that I happened to grow up in a certain kind of community acquainted with *pain*.' "

Over the course of his trips abroad after the election, he kept reflecting on the sense of displacement that has endured within his people ever since their abduction from Africa into captive servitude in America. "Racism's still the X factor in American society, in ways that aren't even consciously hostile. It's still holding us in bondage, but it's elusive, because it's so embedded in the soul of our culture—almost like, you know, born and bred into iniquity. Even *we* are kind of resistant to acknowledging it, because it's such a heavy thing, all these old images—cursed descendants of Ham, dirty people, naive, childlike. Sociologically, just can't adjust. Color we had, must be different. Talk different. All of us supposed to have soul, have rhythm—I've seen blacks in wheelchairs trying to roll with it, didn't even have any legs, but you black, *you got to dance*. We've grown up surrounded by these depersonalizing images, an I-it relationship rather than I-thou. Low expectations. When I was at the hospital waiting for our last baby to be born, there was a white guy there, too, walking around in circles. Had a cigarette—*I* had a cigarette, and I don't even smoke. Both of us with our wives in there. Time came, we put on these little backless robes, and we went down that hall together holding hands. They brought 'em out—white baby, black baby. And I thought, that white baby has not come out with a chemistry book in its hand. And my baby did not come out with track shoes on. Whatever's happened to them since—if his baby turned out a physics professor and mine turned out only a high school runner—it would not be the way God sent 'em here. It's the mythology of the society. African-Americans supposed to play ball. Universities take 'em in when they can't read and write, drop academic standards and say, 'It's all right, got to make allowances for *these*.' "

Jackson went on, "In so many ways, *so many ways,* have we been bred into insecurity. Even had our memory of our past obliterated, that connection that can give you a feeling of who you are, and from that a feeling of purpose. That was mostly just erased out of the mind of the black community, that memory and connection. So a lot of our cultural activities now are, like, desperate attempts to grab something to hold on to—to grab back a piece of Africa, wear a dashiki, listen to African music. Reaching back for *something,* you know something is back there, you trying to grab some sorta piece of it. Meanwhile, you still livin' in America, where Du Bois, you know, talked about the burden of double-consciousness of being black in America. How you're ever feeling your two-ness. You belong and yet you don't. You free but yet you're not. It's your place, but yet you kept separated from it. You there but yet you ain't. Still, though it's more difficult trying to make it under that double-role and double-burden, once you survive it, you have double-muscles. But it's like we have almost to be superior just to be equal."

Somewhile later, during a long night ride through the out-country of Soviet Armenia, Jackson, talking quietly in the darkness of the backseat, receded through the years to ponder again his own boyhood, "There's a Scripture that talks about a ship that wrecked because its stern broke. And the Bible says, 'And they made it on broken pieces to dry land.' Sometimes it seems it's really you against the whole world around you. And you have to make it on whatever broken pieces you got."

TWO

THE LONG CIRCLE HOME

V

Outsider

BACK IN 1941, Greenville, South Carolina, was a quiet little hilly city, part of the region's semifeudal complex of textile-mill communities, set in the mild weathers of the state's Piedmont uplands, where the land begins lifting toward the distant, faint immensities of the Blue Ridge Mountains. It had much the quality of Thomas Wolfe's Asheville, only some fifty miles up the road across the North Carolina line, with worn brick buildings idly congregated along its sloping central streets, the look of an autumn town, musing and somehow isolated in its high cool airs. Over the following decades, it would mostly remain serenely abstracted out of the swelterings of racial conflict taking place in the lower deeps of the South. About 10 percent of its inhabitants then were black, almost all of them confined to drab and cluttered precincts on the weedy backsides of town. There, in one of the poorer quarters of plank houses and smoky dirt lanes, in a dim room with a small wire heater glowing in a corner, Jesse Jackson was born on the chill afternoon of October 8, delivered by a white doctor who was a friend of the family his grandmother worked for. Bundled in a rough blanket, he was placed beside his mother in the metal-frame bed.

His family lineage, to the extent it can be traced, vanishes after three generations into that vast obscurity of most of the black past in the South stretching from Reconstruction into the long deep night of slavery. On the south fringes of Greenville lies what remains of a cemetery where some of his antecedents are buried, a bedraggled plot under a scatter of oaks, flush against a wire-fenced yard of parked trucks and right across from a Race-Trac filling station and a Waffle House, unnoticeable to the traffic beating along the road beside it, and about as effaced of memory as that whole multitudinous lost family history before him. It has long been overgrown in waist-high grasses and prickly underbrush, the ground underneath lumpy and rutted with the vestiges of some graves marked only by simple rubbles of rocks and shriveled waddings of paled artificial flowers. In this

barrenness, one small arch-topped tablet, when the brush is pushed away
from it, reads:

Rev. Jesse
Robinson
APR 5 1865
JAN 23 1923

It is the only marker from those generations preceding him still standing
in the graveyard's grassy ruin.

But from the fraction of his genealogy that is known, Jackson could be
said to present, simply in the varied ancestries converging in him, a kind
of essential American story. One of his grandfathers was half Cherokee;
one of his great-grandmothers, who'd been a slave, was also part Cherokee;
and a great-grandfather had been an Irish plantation owner who was sheriff of Greenville County before the Civil War. One can see in Jackson,
when his normally acorn-brown skin takes on a grayish dullness in deep
cold, a faint dappling of freckles under his eyes and across his nose. He is
himself a kind of walking Rainbow Coalition. "We are a hybrid people,"
he has proposed of African-Americans generally. "We are of African roots,
with a little Irish, German, Indian. We are made up of America's many waters. Which makes us a new people, a true American people."

But those lines of descent contained in the cemetery on Greenville's
outskirts lay on the unlegitimized side of his lineage, forever removed
from the household in which he was raised. Jackson has long been telling
high school assemblies of black youths in the nation's inner cities, "You
say, 'But Reverend Jackson, you don't understand what it's really like.' I *do*
understand. I was born to a teenage mother, who was born to a teenage
mother. How do I understand? I never slept under the same roof with my
natural father one night in my life. *I understand.*"

His mother's mother was a short, stout, brisk, round-faced woman
named Matilda—commonly called Tibby—who for years had set out in
the gray early morning from her dumpy neighborhood to work as a maid
in the household of a white family of the town's gentry. In this, she had followed, in the immemorial pattern of southern communities, her own
mother, Cora, who had long served as the live-in maid for another white
family—"a sort of regal woman," a son in that family still remembers,
though when asked where Tibby and Cora's other daughter had stayed
during that time he says, "You know, I never really knew that," only that
Cora "would always hug them hard" whenever they dropped by to see her.
Tibby herself remained illiterate, but was of a fiercely industrious and

pious temper, and almost grimly ambitious for her single child, Helen, born to her as an "outside" baby back in the fleeting frivolities of her own girlhood, when she was thirteen. The father was, as one woman then close to Tibby puts it, "of questionable race," from a grocer's family in a little nearby community who "were all light, with copper-colored hair." But Tibby's mother, says another old friend, "just raised hell when that thing happened." Tibby was later married to a man who, says the friend, "didn't treat her real good and finally left off for somewhere," but Helen had assumed, until her teens, that he was her father. "When she found out he wasn't, she got very upset, real angry," the friend recalls.

Despite the troublesome happenstance of her birth, though, Helen turned out to be a blessing to her mother. By her teens, she had grown into a luminously pretty girl, the lead majorette at her high school and a dancer of such dazzling verve that she was invited to tour with a show produced by a local impresario. Most of all, she was graced with a lush and vibrant coloratura soprano voice that, by the time she was sixteen, had attracted offers of scholarships from five music colleges. While the embarrassment of how she'd arrived in the world had left her "a right private kind of person," according to a woman who grew up with her, "she was a flat-out prima donna. Always had the main role in any musical at the school, was the main soloist in the choir at Springfield church, all that sort of stuff. I know for a truth she could have gone on to Broadway. Oh, yeah. That girl had a *beautiful* future." But it was just at the highest flare of her promise, when she was sixteen, that she gave herself over to a feverish liaison with a married man in his mid-thirties who lived next door with his wife and three stepchildren.

His name was Noah Robinson, and he was an imposing figure in Greenville's black community—of an autocratic tallness, built with a puma's sleek, heavy brawn, his skin the hue of rich amber. In one photograph taken from the time he was a boxer, he poses with a somber glower behind lifted gloves, long legs braced to pounce. He had fought several bouts in Philadelphia, later in Greenville's aged and grimy Textile Hall, under the name of K.O. Robinson, winning eighteen of his nineteen bouts, sixteen by knockout. "He had straight hair," recollects a man who grew up in the neighborhood, "was a real flashy-lookin' figure." His baronial panache owed much to his relatively prosperous position as a cotton grader for a white-owned firm in town, John J. Ryan and Sons. Operating from their office over the railroad depot, Noah Robinson would test the quality of cotton for purchase by running the fibers between his fingers. "I was the only one they had who could do it," he declared in later years, "and then they'd send it out all over the world."

But some ten years after his marriage to a decorous widow with three children, he had not sired any children of his own. Finally Helen, the little girl next door whom he had watched grow into a lambent loveliness, gave him to understand that she would bear a child for him. "She *was* the prettiest little *sweet* thing," attests an old acquaintance of hers. Jackson himself would describe the transaction years later with a peculiar bluntness: "My father wanted a man-child of his own. His wife would not give him any children. So he went next door."

But just as Tibby's pregnancy with Helen sixteen years earlier had desolated her mother, now Helen's own pregnancy devastated and embittered Tibby herself. "Here the girl was right on the verge of being able to go off on one of those music scholarships, and suddenly she lets happen to her exactly what happened to her mother," says one longtime friend of Helen's. "Mizz Matilda went just about crazy there for a while." The situation, when it became more widely known, also appalled the churchly proprieties in the community. One lady tartly remarks, "It's lucky Noah Robinson came along in the age he did. Nowadays, he'd be a pedophile." Another community matron recalls, "It was a bodacious scandal. Mean, here was this prominent married man everybody admired, find out he's been going with this little teenage girl." Over thirty years later, a family member was still fuming, anonymously, to a Jackson biographer, "The whole thing is one unholy mess that should never have happened." Indeed, the congregation at the church where Helen had performed as the premier soloist—Springfield Baptist, in a slightly finer neighborhood near downtown—exiled her from their midst for a time, until she stood before them one Sunday with her newborn son in her arms, proclaimed, "I have sinned," and apologized to them all. But a church member then recounts, "They never did really forgive her. That's why she finally left and went to this much humbler little church, though it was a much longer walk there for her."

In his speeches now, Jackson will sometimes blurt out, as if still out of a brute hurt blind to any delicacies of embarrassment, "When I was in my mother's belly, no father to give me a last name, they called me a bastard and rejected me." There was even a certain furtive stealth to the very process of his birth, which transpired right beside the house where Robinson's family was still living. "No, no, no crying out in labor or anything they could hear next door," says a neighbor from that time. "Kept it quiet. Like a cat. Didn't even want the other neighbors to know what was actually happening. They couldn't help but see you moving around back and forth boiling a lot of water, but you'd say, 'For coffee.' After a while they'd say, 'Awful lot of coffee drinkin' goin' on in there.' You'd say, 'Havin' a meetin', havin' a social,' anything but what it actually was." Helen Jackson now re-members hearing the voices of children passing by in the street while "I prayed and said, 'How can this happen to me?' I was kind of fearful of it. He was the first baby that I had ever seen born, the first baby I had ever held in my arms. Because I was reared alone. I was thinking, *Will this be over in time to get myself ready to go to college?* I was just in that state of mind, you know. But my mother told me, 'What is your responsibility is yours.'" Even so, once the baby was delivered, it was quietly arranged, be-tween Tibby and Robinson, that the boy would at least be acknowledged as his to the extent of giving him the first name Jesse, for Robinson's father, and Robinson's middle name, Louis. The boy's last name would be, like Helen's, Tibby's own—Burns, from her one brief marriage.

Helen, her glamorous hopes for a singing career having evaporated, ab-sorbed herself in raising her son with a concentration so devout, one of Jackson's schoolteachers recalls, that "he was always made to feel he was a gift from God to his mother." For that matter, Jackson would sometimes in his campaign speeches conjure forth a version of the Nativity transmogri-fied into a kind of parable of his own origins: "I know why Jesus was so sen-sitive to the poor and lowly—he was born to a poor couple. Innkeeper told 'em they didn't have enough money to pay, she'd have to have that baby outdoors. In the *wintertime.* But if that innkeeper had had any idea just who that happened to be *in* her belly, she could have had the baby in *his* bed. But in fact, that was *every* woman's baby—every pregnant woman has got one of God's children in her belly!" Recollecting the circumstances of his own case during one wandering, late-night reverie during a flight over the Atlantic, Jackson remarked suddenly in a thinly rising whine of mock incredulity, "But teenage mother? Having a baby? No husband? No job? And you mean you want to go ahead and *have* that baby? Even *raise* it? Why, that's just not realistic, that's naive. That's self-centered. What kind of life can that baby ever expect to have?" In fact, that was precisely the ar-gument a doctor made in urging Helen to have an abortion, and she had not finally decided to bear her child until enheartened to do so by her minister.

It's almost certainly owing to that intimate consideration that Jackson's private sentiments on abortion seem notably more equivocal than his pub-lic professions of support for the option. In casual conversation, he will submit, "In a sense, the whole issue of abortion is a consequence of an ab-sence of self-esteem, self-worth. Connect what I'm saying? But the prob-lem now is, we got this turmoil of extremes. One group saying, *I love babies so much, if we can't provide for them or they're unwanted, don't let 'em come into the world.* The other group saying, *I love babies so much, they must come into the world even if they have to starve.* All of 'em using the language of love." In this explanation, Jackson grew progressively more heated. "We must have the right of self-determination, of course, the right to make judgments, but we must also live with the consequences of our judgments. And there are *moral* judgments upon *that.* What I'm saying is, abortion, if one is pregnant based upon incest, or there're medically extenuating circumstances jeopardizing the health of the mother, there's some moral core to that, that's a life to protect life. If, however, there is not that moral rationale, only convenience or keeping your situation from getting messed up, it's a very weak argument morally. Freedom to make a choice, it must be a moral choice. Choice to do *what,* exactly, what *act,* that's the issue. And this is a question going to the moral heart of the universe. It's about human life, man. *Human life.*"

FOR ALL THE awkward disreputability of his own birth, from the instant of his appearance Jesse was extravagantly cherished by both women in that meager, solitary, manless household—especially, despite her initial distress, his grandmother. Jackson would later relate, "When she heard Mama had had me, she ran all the way home from where she was working. *Ran. All the way.*" During the short period that Robinson remained next door, says a woman who was a close neighbor, "Mizz Matilda more than once would go out in the evening after he got home from work, and yell in his window, 'We *hurtin'* over here! You bring this baby *some milk!*' "

In his presidential campaigns, Jackson often recited such instances from his boyhood as "Thanksgiving Day, we couldn't eat turkey at three o'clock because Mama was off cooking some other family's turkey. Around six P.M., we'd meet her at the bottom of the hill, carrying back the leftovers from that white family's table." But it is the testimony of others close to them then that, as one woman says, "Whenever you hear Jesse talking about his mother, how all she struggled to take care of them, he's really talking about his grandmother. She was the *woman* in that house. Helen was never as strong as her." A later friend of Jackson's, Calvin Morris, attests, "I think he loved his grandmother more than anything else in the world. He could be very dismissive of his mother. Things she would say would irritate him and he would snap at her. Sometimes Mizz Helen would come to hear him speak and when she'd be introduced, Jesse would sit there with this cold look on his face. But he poured his love into his grandmother. He talked about her all the time in his sermons, where he rarely ever talked about his mom. In fact, his mother had had to struggle for the affection of the son because so much of it went to her mother." Helen Jackson was to admit years later, "He'd go to Mama before he would go to me, and I'd tell Mama sometimes, 'Mama, you should be ashamed.'

She'd say, 'Why? I'm not ashamed.'" Indeed, says Morris, "she absolutely loved her grandson. It was unconditional. He was *her* boy. And every time I'd see him with her when he was a big man, all the stuff that had grown up around him would pull away, and he was a little boy, the little grandson with her again." Morris, who had grown up fatherless like Jackson, says, "Grandmothers saw in us those things we did not yet see in ourselves. And in many ways, they believed them so strongly that we came to believe them ourselves." If her daughter had failed her, Tibby determined that her grandson would not. Jackson remembers that his grandmother would bring back to him from the home where she was working "all these magazines and paperback books that the family, when they were through reading them, would give her to put in the garbage can. *National Geographic*, textbooks, little fiction and nonfiction books—couldn't read a word herself, but she'd bring them back for me, you know, these cultural things used by the wealthy and refined. All she knew was, *their* sons read those books. So I ought to read 'em, too. She never stopped dreaming for me."

In the fuguelike simultaneity of past and present through which Jackson constantly moves, a memory of her early warmth returned to him, in an unexpected gust, during a visit in 1989 to a children's hospital in the earthquake wreckage of Soviet Armenia. Volunteer nurses, most of them elderly women, crowded around him, weeping, and he wrapped them in massive hugs, as tears finally blurred his own eyes. "I kept seeing my grandmother in their faces," he said afterward, in a faltering voice. "Hardly any family left, livin' in ruins, jobless, and, by some standards, futureless. Yet the human spirit had not left them. Like, it's tough, but they not lookin' for a window to jump out of. They are about all that's left of their community, they are its strength." The next morning on the plane back to Moscow, he was still dwelling in that emotional recurrence from his past, leaning forward in his seat and, his eyes closed, rubbing his brow with spread fingertips: "Old women cryin'," he mumbled, "it just wears you out. Will wear you *out*."

An Afternoon Drive into the Past

ON THE SATURDAY after the 1988 presidential election, Jackson returned by private plane to Greenville for a community commemoration of his mother's sixty-fifth birthday. But he set out directly from the airport on a long ride through the neighborhoods of his growing up—revisiting those locales, in the bronze light of the late-autumn afternoon, out of his endless compulsion to reconnoiter how far he's come. "I keep thinking about the odds," he said as his driver, who, along with the car, was furnished by a local funeral home, carried him into the old streets, "the responsibility I have now against what I was expected then to be doing at this stage of life. . . ."

Once, during a visit to Nigeria, Jackson rode through a crowded thicket of shanties and muddy cinder-block houses, then came to a crossroads marketplace of ragtag stalls that was filled with an uproarious churning of people amid blowing smoke and dust. And again in that polyphony of time and place in which Jackson exists, he exclaimed, "*Look at this.* This is the American South in the fifties. Those tin roofs on those houses, those cement blocks in those front yards? I grew up here. And this open market . . . I grew up running across this barefooted on Saturday mornings." Now, in Greenville, as we drove around the setting of Jackson's boyhood, I saw that much of it had begun to be surrounded by and digested into glassy, geometric office complexes, with occasional open sweeps of grass where clusters of houses had simply disappeared. But as Jackson rode through what was left—stragglings of scrubby houses among empty lots overwhelmed by kudzu—it was as if he were seeing that old neighborhood of over forty years ago still whole, undiminished—indeed, he seemed actually to pass back into those years, in a way that oddly reminded me of, in *Our Town*, Emily's ghost returning to her youth, to spy on its long-vanished moments once more. "Constant flashbacks," he muttered. "Amazing what keeps living in memory."

Back then, it had been a dingy warren of flimsy little houses, with plank porch railings ranked with rusted coffee cans that, in the summer, held rufflings of geraniums and caladiums. Each house was perched on a tiny, grassless, rutted yard, some scattered with wood chips and upturned washtubs and old tires and bluish puddles of pitched-out dishwater, others whisked clean with strawbrooms and enclosed by spindly fences assembled out of scraps of boards and wire, with walkways bordered by bits of brick and cement block and broken bottles set in neat parallel lines in the dirt. As Jackson directed the driver through a series of turns, he declared, "Man, some of these houses are exactly *the same* as when I was born!" Still in his black topcoat, he was sitting with an upright alertness in the front seat, his head swinging busily back and forth to survey both sides of the street. He suddenly announced in a low, excited murmur, "That one right there, right up there—" The car paused before a small, bleak frame house, its windows dim in the November dusk, and Jackson, tapping his forefinger against the closed window, whispered, "I lived there right after I was born, right there in that house." He gazed out at it for a long moment. "You know, people'd always ask why is Jesse Jackson running for the White House. They never seen the house I'm running from. Three rooms, tin-top roof, no hot or cold running water, slop jar by the bed, bathroom in the backyard in the wintertime. Wood over the windows, wallpaper put up not for decoration but to keep the wind out. . . . In ways, it seems like a century ago." He motioned the driver on. "Yet I remain connected to all this. By continuing to live in those experiences here, you have high-octane gas in your tank—keep those experiences flowing through your soul, it gives you authenticity. You not talking about something defined by some sociologist. My speech at the Atlanta convention, when I said, 'I understand,' that's why people were crying. 'He's well known, been on TV and all that, he be up there with all them big people now, but he still understands. Ain't just talkin' this stuff he don't understand—*he understands.*' "

As we wound on through the neighborhood's gallery of frail, scrappy dwellings, we passed now and then brief rows of neat, brick homes. "See down there, those nicer houses?" said Jackson. "While we were terribly poor, the black neighborhoods were economically integrated. Had to be, the better-off didn't have anywhere else they could go. So you could live in our class but have the benefits of being among all kinds of classes." This concentrated social mixture within the black community provided Jackson his first tantalizing intimation of possibilities for himself beyond the abject lot into which he had been born. "Teachers down there, see. Then, right back here," he said as we turned a corner, "behind our house, in this alley, a whole other subculture—people back in there selling bootleg liquor, fight on the weekend, go to jail. So you could see, like, don't live like *this*"—and he nodded toward the dirt alleyway—"but aspire to *that*"—and he pitched his thumb back toward the brick homes behind us.

We turned up another roughly paved lane, named Haynie Street, and Jackson pointed to a narrow, white-shingled house ahead of us set above a steeply sloping yard. "Now that's where I was born, that house right there, lived there till—" He suddenly snapped forward, his face close to the windshield: "That looks like . . . sho is, that's Mr. Clinkscales. They been here ever since we left." He applied several soft slaps against the driver's arm: "Turn up in here by the house just a minute." At the top of the driveway, an elderly and wizened man paused in his passage from a backyard shed to a screen side door of the house to stare blankly at the car pulling up below him. Jackson unloaded himself out of the car and, bellowing, "Mr. Clinkscales!" went striding up the driveway. Clinkscales stood perfectly motionless with his hand on the knob of the screen door—a fragile, papery figure, with the tieless collar of his rusty white shirt buttoned up around his neck—and watched Jackson approaching him with startled befuddlement. He at last replied, "How you do, sir," with a faintly tremulous uncertainty.

"It's Jesse," Jackson had to inform him, "Jesse Jackson here." He laid one hand on Clinkscales's shoulder and gently patted and stroked it, as if to re-assure the old man in his discombobulation. "How you doin', buddy?" he said softly.

"Oh, I'm doin' fairly well," Clinkscales thinly allowed. Then, his watery eyes puckering into a squint, he inquired mysteriously, "Aren't you in At-lanta?"

The source of this question was obviously too obscure to pursue. "Come back for Momma's birthday," Jackson simply said. "Where's ole Freddie Jean?"

"They gone to town," said Clinkscales.

"Well, tell her I came by to give her a holler, okay?"

"I certainly will," said Clinkscales, in a voice as dry and light as lint. "I certainly will."

He stood transfixed by the screen door, dazed and gaping as Jackson walked back down the driveway toward the car. But up and down the street now, people had begun spilling out onto their front porches, calling to each other from house to house, "Hey, it's Jesse Jackson! Jesse Jackson's here!" which quickly brought more people filtering out of backyards, run-ning from far corners, at his amazing appearance among them in the quiet of this late Saturday afternoon. A number of them collected around his car as it began easing back down the street, calling in to him, "Look a-*heeeere*. . . . How you doin', Reverend? . . . All right, *sah*! . . ." Jackson reached out to brushingly clasp their hands, "Love yuh, buddy, hang in there. Good to see you, baby. . . ." One small girl skipped along right by his window, gazing in at him and gleefully piping to herself in a rapid trill, *JesseJacksonJesseJacksonJesseJackson*, all the way down until the car turned at the corner.

Several streets over, arriving at a cul-de-sac, his car was blocked by an-other car swiftly pulling up alongside. Two teenage girls scrambled out, one of them carrying a baby. "*Now* we caught," mumbled Jackson, not al-together uncheerfully, and opening the door, he hauled himself out again, blaring, "How yawl doin', now? Hi, baby."

The girl with the baby said, "We saw you drive by back there and just had to follow you."

Jackson cuddled the back of the baby's head in one huge cupped hand: "Look at this, ain't this something? How 'bout this precious little thing!"

The girl sang out, "That's *mine*!"

Jackson said, "This's the *real* point, now," and leaned down to lightly nuzzle the baby, sumptuously groaning, "Mmmm-ummmmh." He then enveloped the girl and her infant together in one wholesale hug. "Love you, honey. And take care of this baby, hunh?"

The girl, released, beamed raptly up at Jackson, her eyes dazzling, as if she had just received some magnificent blessing. She could not have been much younger, in fact, than Jackson's own mother when he had been born to her.

"Just Good Ole Little Jesse"

HE HAD GROWN into a child with large, darkly glistening, watchful eyes in a broad, grave face the color of cocoa, with fine, downy curling hair. "He was the most beautiful little boy," says a neighbor from that time. But his normally solemn expression would give way, whenever he managed to lure the affectionate notice of elders around him, to an elfin grin. "He'd charm me so, I couldn't stand it," declared Alma Smiley one morning in 1994. A thin, zestful lady, clad in slacks, she sat with her sister Barbara Mitchell in the den of her house right across the street from the one to which Helen and her mother had moved with Jesse a few years after he was born. "He'd come to the edge of that porch and look over at me, and give me that little smile I can still see in him sometimes today—that little sly conning look. Not old enough to know he was flirting, but that's what it was—"

Alma's sister Barbara interjects, "And she was awfully pretty then, too."

"Yeah, sit up there and just *charm* me, that sweet little devil. Bat those eyes. Knowing I was gonna grab him. Oh, I used to eat 'im up, have to run over and just *bite* 'im. Looked like a shiny little apple you can't help but bite. Every day, I'd get hold of him and take a bite, and he *knew* I would, knew I couldn't resist him."

In time, he took to scampering everywhere about the neighborhood, wherever he spied other people gathered, with a hectic eagerness that soon brought him the nickname Bo Diddley. "I cannot say that I ever remember him being shy," says another neighbor, Wilfred Walker, who was then a teacher in Greenville's black high school. "Other kids would come by, older kids, for help in their schoolwork or to use the encyclopedia, but even though he was much smaller, he seemed so unusually sure of himself." One of Helen's oldest friends, Vivian Taylor, an English teacher at the high school, says, "He was an uncommonly nervy little fellow. Never abashed atall. He thought a whole lot of himself right off the bat. You know, people always saying he was so cute—he completely concurred in that." He also tended to be a frenetically impulsive child, somewhat willful. "Terribly assertive—aggressive, you might say—for a little boy," recalls his high school literature teacher, Julius Kilgore, who knew the Burns household then. "I mean, he'd decide what he wanted and go right after it, without waiting for anybody's permission."

But the single memory of him from that early season of his boyhood most savored by Barbara Mitchell "was when I'd look out the window around suppertime and see him coming down the street all by himself—nobody else around, just him swinging along down the street in the dark, happy. Just Jesse, master of his kingdom. Even the dogs and cats around here knew him. Good ole little Jesse. That sight used to give *me* such a happiness for some reason."

But around the age of eight or nine, she says, "Jesse became sort of more distant, like he'd withdrawn into himself a little." Julius Kilgore reflects, "He had always been a right sensitive little boy, seemed almost overfull of feeling," given to flashing from one mood to another, others report, not only sudden flurries of temper but quick to cry, a propensity for tears that has, in fact, stayed very much with him. And for some time, a recurring singsong chant from other children had followed him in his wanderings about the neighborhood: "Jesse ain't got no daddy, Jesse ain't got no daddy." His neighbor Wilfred Walker acknowledges that "so many other kids around here were scarred then," but it was the common, unspoken staunchness, says a childhood friend, Owen Perkins, that "we tried to be little men. We couldn't be caught crying." Helen Jackson now offers, "If there was anything, it was kept on the inside. I really didn't know if he was confused. Possibly he was at times. Things happened that he didn't understand. Maybe things happened that *I* didn't understand." Even so, those harrying chants from other children, declares Vivian Taylor, "besmirched Jesse upon his sense of himself." Says another boyhood friend, "They hit him deep, hit home. Normally those were fightin' words." But Jesse reacted not by flinging himself at the boys hooting those tormenting calls but by bursting into tears, and retreating into a lonely brooding. "He started kind of staying to himself, to keep away from being hurt by all that stuff," says Barbara Mitchell. "And in doing that," she adds, "he stayed distant enough to observe more than most other children. So he knew just about *everything* that was happening."

Many years after the ordeal of those boyhood taunts, Jackson would freely declare, "That's why I have always been able to identify with those the rest of society labels as bastards, as outcasts and moral refuse. I know people saying you're nothing and nobody and can never be anything. I understand when you have no real last name. I understand. Because our very genes cry out for confirmation."

Actually, by the time Jesse was three, his mother was married—to a quiet, stolid, deliberate man named Charles Jackson, recalled by an acquaintance as "a hardworking, no-nonsense sort of fella," whom Helen had met while he was a shoeshine attendant in a barbershop downtown, shortly before his induction into the army. "My very first memory is of waking up in Mama's arms," says Jackson, "and her showing me a picture of a group of soldiers in uniform, and pointing to one and telling me, 'This is your daddy. He's coming home from the army on furlough for a few weeks.'"

Helen herself, her aspirations for a singing career forever relinquished with Jesse's birth, had begun training to be a beautician. "She was never gonna be workin' as a maid for some white family, like her mother and grandmama had," says one woman who asked to remain nameless. "Not Helen. She was too pretty for that. I mean, what we called 'bitch in the kitchen' beautiful. Her complexion, not a blemish, didn't really need to wear makeup. No wife was gonna want a woman who looked like that workin' in her house. Besides, Helen was never someone to cook anyway. Mostly, Helen was pretty much occupied in lookin' out after Helen, usually seemed to me."

When Charles Jackson was finally discharged from the army, at the end of World War Two, he returned to Greenville to work as a janitor in various office buildings downtown, supplementing that sparse income with miscellaneous other jobs—hanging wallpaper, painting houses, occasional yard work in white neighborhoods. He would later recount that, up until Jesse was five or six years old, he was still "calling me daddy, following me around, tugging at my knee." But before long, he and Helen had a child of their own, a son who was named Charles Jackson, Jr., and with that, Jesse was moved, with his grandmother, to a shacky shotgun dwelling around the corner, where he was to live, his last name remaining hers, until he was about thirteen years old. He grew up through that time, then, in the additional dispossession of being relegated to live apart from his mother and her household. "Of course that hurt him," says Barbara Mitchell, "but it was just more in all the rest of it, *so much* hurt he had to make his way through. Early on, though, he became the type of person wouldn't have a pity party with himself. Just go off somewhere alone and maybe shed a tear or two, and then come back more strong-hearted than ever. But can you imagine, boy like that, living in that situation for so long?"

At the least, it hardly ended the chants of derision flurrying at him from playgrounds and sidewalks, *"Your daddy ain't none of your daddy. You ain't nothing but a nobody. . . ."* Jackson does not recall specifically when he was informed that he was not, in fact, the son of the man he had supposed was his father. But somewhere between the ages of six and nine he finally became aware that his natural father was Noah Robinson.

The Lost Father

FOR THE ABBREVIATED time Robinson and his family had remained next door on Haynie Street after Jesse's birth, the atmosphere around the two houses waxed increasingly stormy. Once, a neighbor relates, Noah essayed to discreetly arrange for the delivery of a crib to Helen, but instead it wound up being delivered to his own house while he was at work. That evening, when Robinson returned home, according to the neighbor, after a protracted furor audible up and down the street, "his wife took a gun and shot right through the Burns house next door." Robinson's wife, usually a meticulously composed lady, "got awfully tense about Noah paying any attention to Jesse," continues the neighbor. "But how do you think she'd feel about his spending any time on that boy, with that beautiful mother of his? It was right about then she decided she'd give Noah Robinson some children after all, quick as she could." The first—a son, given his father's first name, Noah, and middle name of Robinson's beneficent employer, Ryan—was born some ten months after Jesse, and was followed by, ultimately, two more.

Robinson also soon removed his family to another black section of Greenville far enough from Haynie Street to reassure his wife—a more spacious residence, half its cost paid by his white employer, under whose special favor he was continuing to thrive. It was a neighborhood about as glum as the one he'd left, but the house sat in its midst as if in its own isolated pocket of well-being—a relatively stately edifice with a fieldstone base halfway up to neat board siding, and a fieldstone chimney, all reposing on a cedar-shaded corner lot, a creek trickling through its ample backyard. Once his family was settled there, Robinson built a low brick wall along the front sidewalk with manorial square pillars spaced along its length, and had affixed high on the fieldstone chimney a large, wrought-iron monogram, R. It was a place that had, in a sense, been ironically provided to Robinson by cotton wealth—what had once enslaved the South's blacks now generously endowing one of their descendants—and to the rest of Greenville's black community, it seemed an estate, however reduced in scale. "Maybe it doesn't look all that big driving by there now, but it sure did if you didn't have anything," a resident of his old neighborhood still remembers. "When we'd go over there to look at it, we used to think it was a mansion."

It also awed one small boy as that. Venturing occasionally into the neighborhood, where his grandmother's half sisters happened to live, Jesse would often wander over to stand, for as long as an hour, at the edge of Robinson's place, with that scrolled R on its chimney, gazing past the brick wall at the grounds within. At times, he would see the oldest of Robinson's sons, Noah Jr.—a boy with finer features and fairer skin than he—playing in the backyard in the bountiful orchard that the father of them both had planted there, trees of red and yellow apples, cherry trees, pear and peach trees, a fence along the creek massed with vines of white and purple grapes; for Jesse, it was like beholding some alter image of himself, of who he might have been, inhabiting his own denied place and patrimony. He has since confided that, whenever he learned the Robinson family was leaving on the train—in a double-bedroom Pullman compartment paid for by Robinson's employer—for another of their vacations, he would cry that he was being left behind; for some time he even longed to live in their household with them. Once or twice he slipped into the yard and peered through a window to see what he could glimpse of that other, fabulous life taking place inside—assuming, that early in his consciousness, the classic posture of the outsider.

Most of all, for Jesse, dwelling with his grandmother in a makeshift family arrangement in which he was also a kind of outsider, the person of Noah Robinson, that remote and mysterious figure of his true father from whom he was irrevocably separated, took on a mythic aura. "He almost worshiped Robinson," says Jesse's childhood friend Owen Perkins, "completely idolized the man." As the lore in the black community had it, Robinson had, in several astounding instances that testified to his unique status in Greenville, actually walloped whites who'd intolerably offended his proud sense of the distinctive worth he'd won—an abusive cabdriver once, even an officer of his firm, who'd committed the folly of prankishly poking him in his rear. Many years later, when he was in his eighties, Robinson would concede, not without some satisfaction still, "It was known that I wouldn't take anything off anybody." And Jackson says, "I grew up hearing all these things about my father. Great boxer. Tall, upright, industrious. But," as he remembers that boyhood captivation now, "you can't cry about what you don't have. Because you just don't *have* what you don't have."

Once, when Noah Jr. noticed Jesse staring at him from the far edge of the backyard, he waved to him, and Jesse after a moment waved slowly back as if across some immense, dreamlike distance, and then, with a whirl, ran and was gone. "Noah was smart," says his brother, George, "and he sensed something close to this other boy." Noah Jr. would later narrate to an early Jackson biographer, Barbara Reynolds, that when he was around seven, after a woman on a playground had pointed out the same boy to him and told him, "He's your brother," he had run home to tell his father, and brought him back to the playground to show him the boy: "The expression on my father's face told me that the lady was right." Shortly thereafter, says the younger son, George, "My father took us aside, and told us that Jesse was our brother. I was amazed, because my first thought was, if he's our brother, why isn't he living with us?"

In fact, Robinson's wife had maintained a testy resistance to any association between her family and Jesse, instructing Noah Jr. that he was never to play with him, and Noah Jr. would later recount lying awake some evenings hearing the voices of his mother and father crackling in argument over her adamancy on the matter. Nevertheless, Robinson managed to indulge himself in an intermittent, furtive contact with the boy. Now and then, he would stop his car and get out to watch Jesse playing in some schoolyard or side lot, and to any other adult who might be looking on, he sometimes could not resist remarking, with a kind of bluff proprietary gratification, "That's one of mine." Joe Mathis, a high school football coach who took an early interest in Jesse, says, "My own father'd left me to grow up by myself, too. So when Robinson'd come round where Jesse was and be always good to say, 'Yeah, that's mine,' I just didn't like hearing him say that. It kicked back into my own feelings." Occasionally, Robinson would beckon Jesse over, and they would lightly, briefly chat, Jesse addressing him as Didi. At some point, Jesse had learned that there had been several preachers in Robinson's family past, including Robinson's own father, for whom Jesse was named, and his twin brother Jacob. Each calling the other "Blessed Buddy," they had often preached together as a lustily animated duo, one beginning the line of Scripture, "I *am* the *way*—" and the other picking it up, "and the *truth* and the *light!*" The two of them, standing side by side, bulky shouldered in identical dour suits, stare out of an old ashen photograph with a direct, faintly imperious boldness. In his later years, Robinson liked to declare that "Jesse uses his hands when he's preaching just like his granddaddy Jesse." But in one of their sidewalk encounters during Jesse's boyhood, when Jesse startled him by suddenly proclaiming that he was going to be a preacher himself someday, too, Robinson gave a guffaw and discounted the likelihood of anything like that ever coming to pass. He would, though, when Jesse told him, "I need some money for school, some money for clothes," usually smuggle him some pocket change. Beyond that, on Thanksgivings and Easters when Charles Jackson happened to be out of work, gift baskets would be delivered, with no card, to Jesse's house. (That they were accepted says something of Charles Jackson's grim self-constraint and patient resignation.)

But beyond these few perfunctory and glancing attentions, Robinson would venture no further risk of his wife's resentment. "In general, he never really paid Jesse much notice," says Mathis, and it remains the common impression of those in Greenville's black community who knew Jesse then that, as one woman states it, "He always gave Noah Robinson more love than Robinson came close to giving him." Even Noah Jr. would later accede, "Jesse loved our father, but he felt totally rejected." On the whole, says Barbara Mitchell, "you can hardly count all the ways he was made to feel he wasn't really wanted. That 'I am somebody'—that kept his sanity, that came to him way before he ever heard of Martin Luther King. Whenever I see Jesse now and give him a big ole hug, it's different from all these other hugs he's getting all the time—he knows what it's from. That I *know*."

Robinson was to remain only an incidental bystander to the progress of his unclaimed first son until, during his high school years, Jesse began to acquire, as an athlete and lively student leader, a certain measure of notability among Greenville's black population. "Right when he started getting all that popularity is when Noah began showing up with considerable more frequency," says Vivian Taylor. Jesse had, by now, taken on an unmistakable resemblance to Robinson—the tall and haughty carriage, the high-domed forehead, "handsome, fluent, a snazzy dresser, just like Noah," says Julius Kilgore, and another of his teachers declares, "There was no way you could look at him and not know immediately he was Noah Robinson's son. His appearance fairly shouted out the fact." Noah Robinson could not be restrained now even by his wife from widely advertising about, "That boy's the very spitting image of me."

From that point on, through the years of his amplifying renown, it was as if Jesse found himself, in a way, finally born into that full family he had always hungered for: he had made something like that family actually happen at last. When he did indeed become a preacher and delivered his first sermon in Greenville, in his mother's church, both Charles Jackson and Noah were there, remembers Vivian Taylor, "both of them sitting down at the front. Jesse got up behind the pulpit, and for about three or five minutes, he didn't say a thing. Just stood there crying, looking down at his stepfather and Noah both sitting there below him."

In the course of Jackson's 1984 presidential campaign, Robinson turned up at a rally for him in Greenville. Before speaking, Jesse introduced him—"This is my father"—and when he made an appeal for contributions, remembers someone who was there, "Noah was the first to give a thousand dollars." At the same time, though, says an old friend of Helen's, "When Noah began developing that closer relationship with Jesse, it just about tore Helen up. After the way things'd been all those early years, suddenly it was like he was trying to steal him, you know?"

Despite that, over time Jackson himself would take to claiming the idyllic memory of an amiable closeness between the two families—that he would often visit Robinson at his office and accompany him on his rounds about town, and even, in his most improbably lyric reminiscence of all, that one Christmas he walked downtown between his stepfather and Robinson, holding both their hands. For that matter, the Robinson family blithely maintains now, in what seems to have become a common compact to construct a retroactive respectability for the situation, that the two families often ate together, even Robinson's wife proposing, "We made a point of seeing Jesse back then as often as we could," and the younger son,

George, averring that "Jesse's mother and father would drop him off at our house maybe two or three days a week, and we'd all play together."

But, says Alma Smiley, "that story now about how they were all just one big happy expanded family? That's one big happy expanded lie. Robinson never did a damn thing for that boy when he was growing up. There's no way he can ever make up now for how that little boy was treated. It just broke your heart to see it." When Jackson was in college, he brought a friend, Calvin Morris, later to be an aide of his, back to Greenville and "took me to his father's house, Noah Robinson's house. He wanted me to see the beautiful modern brick house and meet his father. He still identified with his dad. I thought how much Jesse was like him. Big in stature, with obvious presence, a sense of himself. He was very proud of his dad at that level." But around that same time, says Morris, "when we talked about us being children of mothers who did not marry our fathers, I was amazed at the vehemence, the depth of feeling that came out of him as he described it. Jesse, you know, when he is angry or upset, his whole face changes, gets tight and hardens, his eyes get smaller. It had a kind of anguish, and a braggadocio, that yes, this was my background, I was put down because of it and people made fun of me, but I'm really about something and I'm going to show those people. And as I remember it, he cried." Even in later years, it seemed, at best, a somewhat erratic conciliation that he and his father had contrived. In 1973, when Jackson returned to Greenville for his first city-sponsored homecoming fete, Noah Jr. thought to dispatch his father out of town to save him the shame of not having been invited to any of the festivities. And during Jackson's 1988 campaign for the presidential nomination, on the night he won South Carolina's Democratic caucus, a celebration was held for him in the auditorium of a technical college in Greenville, but as Jackson forged elatedly through that evening of climactic triumph, Noah Robinson never appeared.

At the age of eighty-six, Robinson and his wife were still living in the house they had moved to in 1958—a yet more handsome residence, lying at the end of a cul-de-sac, in a wide, sprucely tended yard. When I visited them there one morning, Mrs. Robinson conducted me with a studious courteousness through their screened side porch into a wood-paneled den, where I found Robinson, beset the past seven years with Parkinson's disease, sitting with a green flannel bathrobe wrapped over his faded blue-checked pajamas, an aluminum walker beside him, and surrounded by a profusion of photographs of his children and grandchildren, the largest, over a central mantel, being a portrait of him with Jesse and his other sons. Now under the advance of age and illness, he presented a gangling, bony effigy of the formidable figure he had once been, and when he spoke, his voice was a high, winding, thickly straining bleat, the words somewhat smeared. Nevertheless, his handshake was a commanding clutch of an almost brutal energy, as if all the past assurance and power of his manhood had now retreated into his immense hands.

Above his metal-frame glasses, he had Jackson's high, curving forehead, and when talking, Jackson's manner of prodding and nudging the knee of his listener. "I saw him near 'bout every day when he was growing up," he first took care to profess, as his wife, a bespectacled lady of a light tan tint, sat primly erect in a straight-backed chair wearing a faint, steady smile. "He calls me Mom now" was about the only observation she offered. "He's very kind and good and respectful to us."

But I noticed Robinson's eyes blear over when he reported that he had always been aware, when Jesse was small, that he was the boy's hero. "That's right. And still are," and he grinned widely. "Every time he sees me now," he said in his tapering wheeze of a voice, "he puts that big hug on me, picks me right up, tells me he loves me. If he came through that door right now"—he fumbled up one hand to point—"that's the first thing he'd do. That's right. He always loves to see me." I realized then that Robinson was weeping. "I just love to see *him*. I love him still. I couldn't of ever been ashamed of him. How could anybody? Could you have been?" He again nudged my knee. "Only thing I'm ashamed of is how it happened, and I didn't tell her—" He nodded toward his wife, whose expression stayed unwaveringly pleasant behind the twin reflections in her glasses of the daylit window behind him.

But, Robinson finally declared, over all the years of Jesse's ever-widening fame, the one moment he has been proudest of him "was the first day I saw him. They let me into the house about a month after he was born to look at him. And I cried, I was so proud." Once again he was weeping. He seemed full only of the brimming sentimentalism of a wondering pride, and some vague unutterable sorrowing. "He loves us now just like his family," he said. "Couldn't love us any more, don't think." When I rose to leave, he said, still wet-eyed, "I hope you'll come back again with Jesse. I hope you'll learn to love us, too."

"What I Got to Do Next"

THAT SATURDAY OF Jackson's return to Greenville, right after the 1988 presidential elections, for his mother's birthday banquet, he continued riding about the sites of his beginnings in the waning autumn light. We passed at one point a small collection of office buildings at the edge of downtown, and Jackson said, "Over there's the lawyers' building, where my stepfather used to be a janitor. Clean up the lawyers' offices in the evening, you know. I'd help him—he taught me to be a janitor. But he finally got a job over there in the Post Office Building—see that big building? That was really a big deal for him." Jackson recalled with a certain wryness. "When he was working at the lawyers' building, he was just a janitor. But when he began working over there in the Post Office Building, after having to fill out all those application forms, he became a 'custodian,' you understand. *Goodgodamighty* here now, a *custodian*."

By 1954, in fact, Charles Jackson was faring well enough to move his family at last out of the shabby, muddy quarters around Haynie Street to a newly constructed housing project, bringing along not only Jesse but Matilda Burns, whom he installed in an apartment right beside theirs. We presently headed there, dipping down through a low tunnel of trees and then up into a compound of buildings that now, over thirty years later, still had a neatly diagrammed look: straight-stenciled streets running between repeating rows of boxy little two-story brick apartment sections. "Fieldcrest Village!" Jackson announced. "When we moved here from where we'd been, it was like the Promised Land. *Brick*, man! Handles the weather a little different from those houses where you have to use wallpaper to keep the wind out. Solid floor, solid roof, hot and cold running water . . ." A couple of months later, as he was riding in Moscow past great dreary bluffs of apartment complexes in a thickly milling snowfall, his experience in that housing project in Greenville returned to him: "These projects here not really all that different from ours in Greenville, just bigger. 'Course, no private homes here like in Greenville, with spacious lawns and all that, but poverty and wealth is relative, lot of it's in the mind. To us, when we first moved into that project, considering what we were coming from, we thought we were stepping up toward the middle class, you know? I mean, had us a *doorbell*. Mailbox, too. Oh, yeah—" With the recollection of that forlornly inflated excitement he began bumping forth little chuckles. "Telephone, straight line, no party line. Pantry, stove. Closets for the first time. An *upstairs*, I'm talkin' about. Even had us a little backyard. Hear what I'm sayin'? Yessir, *movin' on up*! And that ain't all. Had us"—and his voice was suddenly squeezed by a clutch of laughter—"had us a *color* television set. That's right. Color television! Black-and-white TV with one of those tinted cellophane sheets over the screen. Yeah, man. All of us sittin' there"—his voice could barely wobble on through whoops of his peculiar lugubrious mirth—"we all sittin' there watchin'—watchin' our color television!" He swiped a hand at the tears in his eyes, still jostled by laughter. "Movin' on up! In the *middle* class now . . ."

It seemed at least, though he was still living with his grandmother in the apartment next door, the closest Jesse had yet come to being part of a conventional family. But it was not until three years later, when he was sixteen—about the same time that Noah Robinson began evincing a particular interest in him, "trying to play all these nice tunes all of a sudden," as Joe Mathis describes it—that Charles Jackson went to Helen's minister to report that he had at last decided that he wanted Jesse to have the same last name as his own son. "Well, *adopt* him, then," the minister pronounced.

Over the years, Jesse had addressed him only as Charlie Henry, like everyone else, and by general account, Charles Jackson had always observed a scrupulous deference to Jesse's reverence for Noah Robinson. "Charlie Henry was a lot wiser than a lot of people realized," says Jesse's childhood friend Owen Perkins. "He handled that situation with Noah awfully well. He never really tried to make it a father-son relationship with Jesse, just that of a man who'd married his mother. So he didn't treat Jesse as a father usually would have, would never tell him to do this, do that." His reserve also owed, says Perkins, to "his recognizing early on that something about Jesse was different. He sensed he was gonna be some sort of leader, and seemed to have this strange kind of respect at a distance for him."

But when he finally elected, much at Helen's urging, to adopt Jesse, it produced some discomfiture, including spirited complaints from Noah Robinson. By now, Helen had transferred to Jesse something of her own long aggrievement with his natural father. "He'd been led to believe," as Noah Jr. later styled it, "that Daddy was a ruthless ladies' man that took advantage of his innocent little mother and then ran off and abandoned him." At any rate, this new development left Jesse, according to Mathis, "doing nothing but worrying day and night about the shame of how his family was so mixed up." He took his dismay to one of his teachers, Xanthene Norris, informing her, though with a curiously diffident detachment, "My stepfather wants to adopt me, but my father's got a big problem about that. My father, I appreciate the money he brings me, but I could do without it. One I love is my mother." She asked him if he didn't also love Charlie Henry. "Well," Jesse merely replied, "I don't know any other father."

When the day of the court proceeding arrived, remembers Owen Perkins, "Jesse was very matter-of-fact about it. That's the way he was— whatever came along, he'd learned to take it in stride. Just said, 'I'm going down to the courthouse, getting my name changed to Jackson.' That was it. Just, this is what I got to do next." But even after Charles Jackson had effected the legality of becoming his official father, Jesse continued to call him Charlie Henry.

By the time the adoption was at last transacted, Charles Jackson had been working for some while in the Post Office Building—a granite and marble edifice in a WPA style of modified Mesopotamian-monumental on a hill above railroad tracks and feed warehouses—and as we rode past it that late-November afternoon, Jackson mentioned, "Judge Haynsworth had his office in there, up on the third floor. The whole building's named for him now. But my stepfather used to clean up Judge Haynsworth's office there."

Years later, in 1969, Judge Clement F. Haynsworth, then serving on the United States Court of Appeals for the Fourth Circuit, would be nominated by President Nixon for a seat on the Supreme Court but would be rejected by the Senate over questions, not so much of his bland remoteness from the elemental social tensions of the times, as of the impropriety of his ruling in cases involving personal financial interests. But Haynsworth—a short, plumpish, shy, fastidiously formal man, with a permanent pinkish blush on his droopy cheeks and a soft stammer of gentle abashment—was to remain, until his death in 1989, a central fixture of what passed for Greenville's gentility. An insulated, ceremonious society contained within a sanctum of kingly homes and deeply shadowed streets, it was an order of life that was not unlike Haynsworth's own greenhouse in his backyard, its cloudy panes enclosing a luxuriance of camellias and orchids and roses, from which fresh bouquets, arranged at midmorning, were sent by chauffeur to a neighbor's drawing room several blocks away. In any case, it was a culture that—beyond Jesse's grandmother's daily excursions into it over the years, and Charles Jackson's nightly tidyings of Judge Haynsworth's office—could not have seemed more unreachably distant from the precincts of Greenville in which Jesse was raised.

The Final Dispossession

HE HAD, FINALLY, grown up in a sense of a multiple dispossession—not only discarded by his natural father and more or less displaced in his own family, but he soon discovered himself also one of a subject people discounted and disdained by the larger society around them. The most barbarous face of that racial order occasionally glared in such instances as the night in 1947, recounted by Rebecca West in her classic New Yorker piece, "Opera in Greenville," and still lingering in the communal memory of Greenville's blacks during Jesse's boyhood, when an epileptic black youth named Willie Earl was lynched at a slaughterpen out near the county line by a gang of cabdrivers for fatally knifing one of their fellows, all of them subsequently acquitted. But the pattern of racial rule ordinarily prevailed in more quietly diffused and systematic ways. On our ride around Greenville that afternoon, we happened to pass, not far from the magisterial building where Judge Haynsworth had his chambers, a sprawling cemetery, tombstones thronged over several acres, and Jackson remarked in a quick, flat voice, "This's the downtown graveyard. For whites only, of course." As we continued touring what had been the intricate geographies of segregation in this small southern city, Jackson kept up a running commentary in almost stealthy whispers, again as if he were traveling back undercover through that past. "See, now, all this neighborhood was white. . . ." We were driving by a street of small tidy homes with small tidy lawns. "Basically, white textile-mill employees, these were, all up these streets here. Blacks could not stay back here *at all*. There was a dividing line—Berlin Wall had nothing on the dividing line here. You came over here into this other country only to rake leaves or cut grass. But right over there across the road, look—look—all those houses, see up in there? Drama of it is, all that was *black*. See how close blacks and whites actually lived together along here? Practically within voice call of each other. Some places, whites' backyard was actually contiguous to ours." That intimate adjacency of two societies so alien and isolated from each other seemed to hold an abstract fascination for Jackson now, viewing it from the distance of over thirty years. "Mean, we were not permitted to sit on each other's front porches, but we could sit on each other's *back* porches. That was so southern, black-white relations then. So close but still absolutely separate. Not like the big cities in the North; segregation down here was *personal*, man."

We came to an intersection back in his old neighborhood around Haynie Street, and Jackson said, "For instance, up there on that corner was this little store that had a white owner. I used to play with his son when I was about six, riding bikes and all that, and we'd go into his daddy's store sometimes and give this little whistle, you know, askin' him to give us a couple of Mary Janes—those flat, like, suckers, 'member those? One afternoon, I went in, in some sort of big hurry, said, 'Jack, got to be somewhere, give me a Mary Jane,' and when he didn't answer right away, I gave a whistle. *Man!* He whipped around, grabbed his forty-five off a shelf, snatched me by the arm, and put that pistol right up by my head. Said, 'Goddammit, you ever whistle at me again, little nigger, I'll blow your head off.' Two things I remember about that," Jackson went on quietly. "One was knowing immediately I couldn't tell my stepfather, because he'd come and probably kill the guy. Also, couldn't tell my mother, because she'd be upset about what I did in the first place, that I'd acted that *familiar* toward the guy. Gettin' too common with him. There're boundaries here. Get too common with a dog, it'll lick your face. Can't get too *common* with them, she'd always told me. But the other thing, what got me most, was how the other people there in the store, all of 'em black, pretended they hadn't even noticed it. *That* was really the trauma: the power of somebody white to do whatever they wanted to a black child *right in the middle* of other blacks, and get completely away with it, not even questioned—that I never really got over, it's stayed with me to this day."

We rode past other sites of humiliations visited on him and his people that had largely formed him for the rest of his life. "People up in this alley here, nothing to get by on but a little bootleggin', I could look right out my window and see 'em runnin' from the police. Before long I learned to run, too, and hide under the house at any sight of a police car. Even white firemen, rent collectors—they came in here as agents of white authority, of an occupying power, and we'd hide from 'em all. Yeah. People I knew—ole Red, ole Mutt, daddies and older brothers of friends of mine—we'd see 'em taken off in a patrol car, and then I'd see 'em on the chain gang, their families tryin' to bring food to 'em. . . ." Almost forty years later, during his 1984 presidential campaign, while riding somewhere in the Virginia countryside with a long cavalcade of cars trailing after him, he happened to see a prison crew working on the side of the highway and told his driver, "Wait a minute, stop, stop, tell 'em to stop back there!" With the whole procession slowing to a halt, he got out and spoke to the astonished guard with his shotgun, and then stood chatting with the prisoners with an instant, easy familiarity, for something like fifteen minutes, his entourage—reporters, aides, Secret Service—stretched out along the road waiting.

Now, riding through the streets of his origins, it was as if the incidents he recounted were happening to him again—as, in fact, they always are, in endlessly cycling repetition. "Now, this street here . . . one of my first memories is sitting on the front steps of our house on this street, waiting to go for my first day of school. I could see this school several blocks up the street with green grass around it and flags in front and all that—I thought that was the school Mama was talking about. So when we started walking and got to that school, I made a break for it. But Mama said, 'That's not the one. You can't go there. It's another one.' We kept walking. It was a school much farther away, I found out, and it wasn't at all what I— I'll show you." He gave the driver directions through rambling streets, under large, yellowing oaks. "Would walk along here going to school," said Jackson. "Lot of this was a white neighborhood then—hostile territory, mysterious, an-

other world. Walked past that white church over there every morning that
I couldn't attend. Had to cross some very dangerous thoroughfares, actually. White kids would pass us in school buses, yell things. We didn't have
no school buses then, just had to walk it." We finally pulled up at a corner
where a low, plain brick building was deposited on a large plot of bare
ground. "This was it," said Jackson, "the other school, the one for us. The
one that didn't have any grass. They didn't plant any. Didn't mean for grass
to grow here, or children to grow either. Only place for recreation was slid-
ing on the sand on the sidewalk along here. Books and desks, all old, battered leftovers passed down to us from white schools."

As we headed back toward Haynie Street, we rode past a high stretch of
open field, and Jackson said, "Of course, this is where Furman University
used to be, the men's campus, before they moved it all out of town. All up
on this hill, dorms and classrooms, just across the street from us. Oh, man,
did I *dream* about going to school there one day. One thing really excited
me about Furman was that ROTC. Tell you, to see those Furman guys
down there on a field looked big as an air base, doing their maneuvers, I
mean with *tanks* and all, I couldn't hardly wait. Also, that Frank Selvy,
man, he was my idol then," he went on, referring to a nationally famed
Furman basketball player of the mid-fifties who once scored a hundred
points in a single game. "Oh, yeah, I was gonna go to *Frank Selvy's* school.
Which, of course," he added in a softer voice, "I could not attend, I realized eventually. Though we lived just across the street, and my grandmother did the washing and ironing for all you other students up
there. . . ." (About a month later, in Africa, as we were sitting around talking one morning in the government guesthouse in Lagos, he abruptly continued, as if only a few seconds had elapsed since that observation in
Greenville, "I mean, how come you can go to Furman and I can't? Hunh?
Why was that? You know, given the basic characteristics of Jesus, *he*
couldn't have attended Furman, either. Wrong complexion, not the right
schooling, family poor. Ain't that right? Naw, couldn't of let Jesus in Furman, either.")

A block beyond Furman's former campus, we turned into another narrow street, and I recognized, down a wooded hill, the shape of Sirrine Stadium, where Furman had continued to play its football games after it had
relocated, its worn cement bleachers encircled by a rusted chain-link
fence muffled in honeysuckle vines. "Yeah, when the white people would
come to the football game on Saturday afternoons," Jackson was saying,
"we'd park the overflow of cars in the yards along here, watch 'em for
twenty-five cents. Couldn't get in to watch the game, though, 'less you
were selling peanuts and Co'-Cola. Which I did, too. Some of those peo-

ple, try to shortchange an eleven-year-old boy, or even grab one of your Cokes and peanuts without payin'. Can you believe that? It was only down there at that end of the stadium, up on the side of that hill, where blacks could sit." And I suddenly recalled, for the first time in all these years, students at the games, possibly even including myself, referring to that hillside beyond the goalposts as "the crows' section." This was one little reminiscence, however, I could not quite bring myself to mention to Jackson.

Dusk had begun settling over the town as the car finally descended a long drive into the wide, leafy sweeps of a park. Along its edges were the discreet little window-glows of expensive homes. "This is Cleveland Park now," said Jackson. "We couldn't use this park. *Public* park, too." Gazing out his window now, Jackson talked on in a barely audible voice, as if from the far distances of that past into which he had again receded. "Softball fields along here, right over there. But we couldn't play softball in them. After we moved to the project, bus would come along here every day, and we'd look out the window at the white kids playing softball. But we couldn't play ball there." A moment later, he pointed out his window and murmured, "Over there, that was the swimming pool, which they did finally desegregate. So blacks could swim in it. But then they put seals in it. That's right, *seals*. Black seals, brought 'em from the zoo. When that didn't work—some blacks just jumped on in there with the seals anyway—they turned it into a garden. Filled it up and covered it over with dirt. Yeah. See where all those flowers are now? That was the pool. Beautified that problem, was how they took care of that one."

The road then began lifting out of the park and curving past a palisade of high fences. "Because we rode the bus by here after they built the project," said Jackson, "whites began puttin' up all these fences so we couldn't look over into their backyards." That uninterrupted battery of tall backyard walls somehow looked familiar to me, and I then remembered once seeing them everywhere in the white neighborhoods of South African towns.

We finally started back toward his mother's house. For any white who'd grown up in the comfortable languors of a small southern town like Greenville, it was still stunning to hear of those mortifications encountered at every turn by the unseen, second population. "You know," Jackson said, "it's amazing that there're so *few* blacks now who are openly and verbally hostile, given their experience. There're some whites who still can have the audacity to be unrelenting and unforgiving in their expectations of what black attitudes ought to be these days. But given the scars on our souls, what amazes me is how *freed up* most blacks actually are about those experiences."

At one point, on a wide boulevard running from downtown along the edges of his old neighborhood, we passed the Ramada Inn; its marquee, illuminated now in the twilight, bore the message "Happy Birthday Helen Jackson." Jackson said, "That's where the thing's gonna be for Mama tonight. Right there at the end of Haynie Street, actually."

The Sheltering Triangle

FOR ALL THE pervasive degradations of Greenville's small-town system of apartheid, within the black population itself, Jackson passed his boyhood mostly enclosed in a kind of rigorous communal care. "This was really the most meddlesome community," says Julius Kilgore. "Absolutely everybody thought they had a right to look after absolutely everybody else's child." Jackson describes it now as "a love triangle. Mother, grandmother here—teacher over here—and church over here. Within that love triangle, I was protected, got a sense of security and worth. Even mean ole segregation couldn't break in on me and steal my soul. It protected me long enough until I was able to break out and survive on my own. When it's working, that's what that thing really does."

His explanation of all this happened to come weeks later, in installments between appointments and flight departures during his passage through southern Africa (the closing of yet another, much vaster circle, as he kept pointing out). "Grandmama, Mama always made me feel I was somebody special, told me I was the Lord's gift to them, you know, always saying, 'You're gonna be somebody. Just hold on.' Then came the first day of school—yeah, in that other building on the corner with no grass—but my mother took me in to my teacher and told her, 'He's in your care.' Teacher said, 'Don't you worry, Mizz Jackson, we'll take good care of him.' Principal came in, said, 'It's all right, Mizz Jackson, he'll be all right here.' " It produced an impression of a collective watchful attention focused upon him that a small boy of Jackson's particularly solitary and uncertain circumstances would have found hugely gratifying.

So telling was the effect of that collaborative concern of his elders, in fact, that he has been preaching its importance ever since in his circuit-riding social ministry. "Parents, teachers got to be in it together. If the teacher assigns homework, parent must have the child at home to *do* the homework. Report card time, you must go *to* the school and pick up that report card. Four times a year. I mean, *pick it up!*" And he slapped his hands, becoming greatly exercised while propounding all this one morning in Lagos. Stalking up and down along a long table fairly shouting, he went on, "If a child can go to school thirty-five weeks a year, you can go four times a year to get his report card. You check on your investment stock that much. And your child's the *biggest stock* you got! It's the *parents'* responsibility to get their child educated, and they pay teachers to assist them—teachers are parents' aides, not the other way around. But there must be a thing between the *two* of you. Understand what I'm sayin'? Because your child then knows he can't play the two of you off against each other. Because children are masters of deceit—your little loved one also happens to be a little rascal."

Once, he related, at an assembly of parents at his younger daughter's school, "this black mother was just berating a white teacher, 'I *know* my son is doing better than you say,' gettin' louder and louder, with her son standin' there beside her, 'bout ten years old, keepin' real quiet. Teacher said, 'Well, whenever I give the class homework, your son comes back saying he couldn't do it because his parents are too poor to buy him pencils and paper.' 'He's lyin'!' black mother says. 'He's a damn lie!' I mean, almost hollerin', 'We always worked!' 'Well, now, I didn't know that,' teacher said. 'Course, what the little fella'd been doing, he'd been comin' home and telling his mother how this white teacher was not kind to him. Ten years old but already caught on to how to play that ole race game, play on the stereotypes. So the teacher's over here, feeling guilty, and the parents are over here, feeling hostile, and meanwhile little fella's in the middle, having himself a big holiday. Right about then, the father stepped into the discussion. Looked down at his boy and said, 'Now, your teacher here, she won't be havin' that problem with you no more, will she?' Little voice, 'No sir.' 'I say, *will she?*' 'Nossir, nossir, nossir!' " Jackson clapped his hands again. "Teacher, parents closing that gap! And when they close that gap, homeboy's in a cross fire. Harsh? Eagles are harsh on eaglets until they can fly. And closing that gap is finally a matter of saving that child, saving future heartache—on Christmas mornings, shall you be coming downstairs to open gifts around the tree, or shall you be going over to the jail to take yo' chile a cake and cigarettes?"

In his own case, says Jackson, "My mother would tell my teachers, 'Now, if I miss PTA meetings sometimes because I'm working at a job, I'll see you at church on Sunday.' What it was, see, was a transfer of moral authority from my mother to that teacher. And the teacher had *earned* that authority by the way she behaved with my mother at church. There was respect between them."

It was in that third element of the triangle of care around him that the whole arrangement seemed consolidated, confirmed, consecrated. In his mother's church, Long Branch Baptist—a simple wooden tabernacle with a stand of weeping willows clustered along a deep gulch behind it—the small sanctuary would be crammed on Sundays with a congregation of maids, yardmen, teachers, cooks, mill laborers, their massed voices rolling through old swooping hymns, in thrilling release from the oppressive gravities of the world outside. In all the black churches of Greenville, for that matter, a hearty and full-blown democracy operated on Sunday mornings wholly removed from the strictures of their members' weekday lives. "My teacher, for instance, was a college-trained woman, and my mother was not," says Jackson. "But at the church, Mother sang in the choir. She was the star there. It was a different sort of reality at Long Branch Baptist every Sunday." In fact, those Sunday-morning church services afforded Jackson his first, Eden-like sense of a democratic Blessed Community, ordered not by money or professional station but, simply, moral properties. "Only measure was character," says Jackson. "Here, Deacon Foster, who might be only a janitor at the school, he can be chairman of the deacon board and sit on the front row, while the principal of the school, who might be an ole drinkin' sinner, *he* gonna have to sit ten rows back and keep quiet. It's Deacon Foster, guy who can say the most fervent prayers, who got the status *here.* Different kind of reality."

And somehow a more momentous one as well. At a young age, children in the church would be called down front before the congregation—Jesse among them once—for a special service dedicating them to the Lord. And then, each Sunday, came the moment when the preacher—the Reverend D. S. Sample, a deep black, solidly packed figure, with a basslike face above his bow tie, and a white glisten of hair—would commence to pump into his sermon, pouncing back and forth behind the pulpit in his black robe with an accelerating urgency, flourishing a white handkerchief like a speedway flag with which he was urging himself on. And gradually his great belling voice, to an accompanying percussion of clapping and shouts, *Amen, Thass right, Awright now, Tell it!,* lifted his congregation beyond all the base frets of their daily lot and into the grand, ancient, scriptural dramaturgies of bondage, suffering, endurance, mercy, deliverance, redemption; spirited them back there again with Joseph in Egypt, Moses before Pharaoh, Herod and John the Baptist, the compassion and crucifixion of Jesus. Jackson says now, "That revolutionary gospel I learned at Long Branch Baptist, I've found no higher truths. The values preached back there by Reverend D. S. Sample are still just as real over all the rest of the world." By the time he was ten, Jesse had begun showing up at Sample's house on Thursday afternoons, while Sample was closed off in a room working on that Sunday's sermon, hanging about until he finally invited him in, whereupon Jesse proceeded to press him through a discussion of the Bible until suppertime.

He also was noticing how the greater reality of those Sundays would be translated back into the everyday lives of those close around him. "We never had much at all, of course," says Jackson, "but Mama was always helpin' out folks who needed it, would fill out papers for them to get their welfare checks, buy their groceries and have 'em delivered to 'em. Like she did for this old man who lived near us, Mr. Dave, who was illiterate, and had trouble gettin' around. She'd explain to me why she was doin' all that—need to look out for other folks just like they were one of our own. Straight from that gospel preached at Long Branch. I remember, then, one Christmas, Mama was sick and out of work, and so was my stepfather, had only a little pickup job painting. I knew I wouldn't be gettin' nothing much that Christmas. Fact, we didn't even have hardly enough money for food. Christmas Eve night, time came to go to the church for the Christmas play, where members would exchange gifts and all that. My father was feeling awfully low and discouraged, said we shouldn't be going, we couldn't give any gifts to anybody. But Mama said, 'We can at least go sing in the choir. Can at least add to the congregation.' When we got back to the house that night after church, there were six bags of groceries sittin' on the front porch. Delivery man had left 'em, we figured, like he did sometimes for people weren't at home when he came. We took the groceries into the house and stored 'em away—meats, chicken, flour, lard, fruit, cookies, I mean all *kinda* stuff. Day or two went by, nobody called for them. All that food, 'bout the only food we had in the house, and Mama wouldn't let us touch any of it. She said, 'They don't belong to us, it's somebody else's groceries.' Finally, the old man, Mr. Dave, dropped by, asked if we'd gotten his order. Mama said, 'Oh, yes, we weren't sure exactly who they were for, but we been holding them for you.' He said, 'They for yawl. Knew you were sick and Charlie's been out of work. Figured you could use 'em. Just a little something I wanted to do after all the help you been to me for so long.' He was illiterate, see, couldn't leave any kind of note. Said, 'I thought yawl would just know.' Mama started crying. My father was different about showing his feelings, but he had to go out the room for a minute or two. Now, you think any child can ever forget an experience like that? All it meant? Isn't in some way changed forever by it? And man, did we *feast* there for several days! Still the greatest Christmas I've ever had."

Yet even as he grew up within the warmth of Greenville's black community, he found himself having to answer to its exacting expectations. "First day in the sixth grade, I'll never forget it. Teacher was Mizz Shelton, and she began writing these long words on the blackboard we never even heard of before. We all looked around and started whispering to each other, 'She got the wrong class. She thinks we the *eighth*-grade class.' Somebody finally called out, 'Uh, Mizz Shelton? Those are eighth-grade words. We only the sixth grade here.' She turned around. 'I know what grade you are. I work here. I know what grade I'm teaching. And you'll learn every one of these words, and a lot more like 'em 'fore this year is over. I will *not* teach down to you. One of you little brats just might be mayor or governor or even president someday, and I'm gonna make sure you'll be ready.' And she turned back and went right on writing." At that time, says Jackson, her proposition prompted no glows of possibility in him. "Aim to be governor? Even aim to be mayor, when in Greenville then, there wasn't a single African American on the board of education, in the police department, the fire department? And aim to be president— my *God*!"

Nevertheless, says Jackson, such suggestions inevitably took. "I was taught that even a society of limitations did not have the power to limit your capacity to dream. I was never taught to adjust. My mother, she just never learned to teach me to be inferior." His mother's application to his development may have been additionally energized by her own foreclosed cultural aspirations. "Mama was very articulate even though she had not finished high school. She was always into self-improvement and culture and things like that. When I got to high school, she told me I was to join the choir. I was playing football by then, and I told her, 'Mama, look, I'm a football player. Those others're *choir*boys. You know—'s *different*.' 'I understand,' she said. 'I know what you are. But if you that uncertain about your manhood, a football uniform won't do a thing for you. When you come out of high school, you gonna have learned how to "Hallelujah Chorus" and "Give Thanks Unto Thee," you not just gonna learn James Brown and The Drifters.' So I got to be able to talk about all that a capella and allegretto, 'Hallelujah Chorus,' all of that—only at Mama's insistence."

When he speaks now to assemblies of black youths in schools around the country, Jackson will relate, "Mama made me take French in high school, though I could see absolutely no use for it. Neither could my friends. Guys on the football team said, 'Look, man, in the first place, mamas don't know everything.' Said, 'After all, you don't have none of us on the football team speak French. Chances awfully high you ain't ever gonna have no neighbors who speak French. Yo' mama can't speak French *herself*. Man, *fake that thing*.' So I schemed, managed to finesse it all the way through high school, through college, graduation. Before long, started working with Dr. Martin Luther King. Then—you never know what the future holds, can't see around the curve to it—Dr. King was murdered, and in time more leadership fell to me. Years later, I get a call one day from Washington, saying six ambassadors from the Sahel region of Africa want to come to Chicago to talk to me about getting help for the drought and famine there. Six African ambassadors, comin' to *my home*. 'Member, I'm the adopted one, you know, from the slums, and these African ambassadors are comin' to ask *me* for *help*. My mind started thinking about history, really a *great* sense of the moment. Day comes, I look out the window, these ambassadors are gettin' out of their cars in front of my house, comin' up the walk to my front door, I go out to meet 'em, and every one of 'em—get this, now—every *one* of 'em is speakin' *French*. There I am, can't even understand them, talk to them in their own language. *Caught!* Managed all those years to slide by my mama, slide by my teachers, even got my diploma, but the law finally caught me. What is that law? Sooner or later, you *will* reap what you sow. You got to study those books, my friend!"

In fact, the strenuous disciplines in which he was reared left him forever after obsessed with the traditional rectitudes of grit, pluck, industry, pertinacity—those staunch verities that, as he saw it, provided his deliverance from the claim of the futility and abjectness of the community enclosing him. Indeed, there is a curiously old-fashioned, McGuffey-reader didacticism to his plain-spun ethic of diligence and probity. "My values come out of a conservative Christian orientation," he insists. "Probably surprise a lot of people to know I think that way, but it's what I really believe, deep down in my soul. Way back when liberals were dismissing drugs as just a personal habit, I was already saying it's the number one threat to our national security. When I was arguing that our youth was suffering from lack of discipline and growing decadence in our culture, many liberals, quote-unquote, were wafflin' on those issues." In fact, like his public advocacy of a woman's right to abortion, his eventual support of homosexuals' rights did not come to him easily. He confides, "That's one I've had a lot of trouble gettin' next to, want to know the truth," and in one address to a gay group in the early eighties, the best he could muster was to reassure them, "We have a lot of gay people playing the organ in black churches." His inherent cultural conservatism extends as well to the matter of corporal punishment in schools, which during his own boyhood was regularly applied by his teachers' rulers and the principal's strap: "That was something I only learned was an issue years later. I wouldn't have even understood what the phrase meant, 'corporal punishment,' much less thought to question it. Teachers *got* to teach by moral authority." Education itself, he contends, "must be value-oriented. We cannot have a value-free education, without vision, without ethics. Absolutely not! Must be a commitment to a thing called character in education." That would seem a rather slippery principle, actually, placing him not that far from the impulses of the fundamentalist right regarding schools. Nevertheless, he asserts, "The great teachers know that the lectern is a pulpit. That's why they sometimes call it 'The Ministry of Education.' It's a divine calling, like ministry of the gospels."

In his own ministry to gatherings of high school students, he even preaches the sort of sober sexual restraint that one might hear commended in a sermon from Billy Graham in his stadium crusades. "You say, 'But Reverend Jackson, the new thing is, sex is a thrill.' Le'me tell you, it *always* was. But we not an amoeba or paramecium, we have more than one cell, and we can have more than one thrill. We must broaden the basis of our thrill syndrome. Sex is a thrill, but so is having breakfast in the morning a thrill, graduating is a thrill, going to college is a thrill. Becoming mayor, becoming governor," he goes on to rising applause from the students, "becoming president, your *whole life* can be a thrill!" His notions of the morally worthy can seem at times to take on an almost Victorian stodginess. While he was taping a pilot version of his first, syndicated television program, he kept posing, to a deputation of rap performers defending their lyrics with arguments of artistic freedom, such questions as "But do you see any relationship between freedom and responsibility? You accept any responsibility for the impact of what you say?" Even during his 1989 visit to the Soviet Union, he went about dispensing admonitions like "Keep expanding your freedoms, by all means, but do not then use those freedoms to be decadent."

On the whole, the sedulous didacticisms of his upbringing left him, for the rest of his life, with a rather ponderous high seriousness of nature. A confidant during his presidential campaigns, Richard Hatcher, then mayor of Gary, Indiana, reports, "I was around him a lot, midnight meetings and all that, and there was *never* small talk. Just unbelievable." A former professor of his, remarking on the same unrelenting gravity of Jackson's deportment, says, "I don't know, there *must* be chitchat at least in his family," but Jackson's wife, Jackie, plaintively declares, "He just can't quit being so *serious* all the time. Can't tell a joke, no sense of humor. Always so . . . so *heaaav-vvy.*"

About the only indulgences he came to openly permit himself were a certain effulgence in his apparel and, until restrained by a troublesome incipience of the gout, smacking down sizable helpings of rich southern-cooked food—barbecued ribs, macaroni and cheese, home-churned peach ice cream—announcing, when such fare was spread before him, "Gon' do some *serious* eatin' now." Even while on the move in his presidential campaigns, he would have delivered to his plane boxed dinners of fried chicken, turnip greens, gravied biscuits, which he set to, right after takeoff, with elbows winged out and both hands churning; arriving for a rally at a church, he would first dive down to the basement recreation area, while the choir could already be heard cascading away upstairs, and whoop into the kitchen, "Gimme a roll, got to preach!" On one of his not infrequent stays in a hospital to recover from fatigue, he greeted a breakfast table put before him with a snort, "Poached eggs. White folks' food," and grappled out from under his bed an oil-spotted brown paper sack holding a sweet-potato pudding. An adviser during his 1988 campaign says, "The nastiest look I ever got from Jackson was early one morning in Philadelphia when he had ordered fried chicken for breakfast, and I told him, 'Why don't you just gargle with butter?' "

Other than that, his austerities of conduct, for the most part, approach the Savonarolan. His antipathy to tobacco is such that he will instantly rail balefully about anyone detectably smoking anywhere near his vicinity. On a trip to Israel in 1994, he journeyed down to Hebron to speak to a huge convocation of Palestinians in a civic hall there, many of the men thronged in their half of the chamber exuberantly smoking, and he opened his address by intoning, "First, let us put out our cigarettes," which brought furious applause from some of the older, head-swaddled women on the other side of the room. A book editor remembers that, while he was laboring with Jackson once on a projected autobiography, "the second day I started smoking right heavily, and he finally said, 'We're going to pray for you.' And he actually offered up this little prayer: 'Dear Lord, please look down on this thy servant, and let this terrible habit of smoking be banished from Cork Smith's life.' I was absolutely kind of strangely touched, you know? It was probably a good half hour before, the way the discussion was going, I had to light up another one."

He just as scrupulously abjures any spirits more assertive than a mild wine, and that only now and then, and in widely spaced sips. Part of his abstemiousness with alcohol seems a profound wariness about losing his constant, sure fix of control and locus in the complex flux of reality around him. A dinner one evening with Armenian officials in Yerevan in 1989 turned into an occasion of much mutual glass-clinking, and as the banquet romped on, one reason for Jackson's usually assiduous abstinence gradually became evident. The dinner's host, Armenia's Communist party chairman, a smoothly combed badger of a man in a glossy suit, began by enthusing, "You know that our Armenian cognac is very famous around the world, so it is impossible to avoid drinking cognac tonight!" But he presently noticed Jackson's hesitant dabs of a taste from his glass after each toast, and, himself already well radiant of face, remarked pointedly, "I think whether you are going to really take Armenian cognac tonight or not," motioning a waiter over to Jackson. As he watched his glass being refilled, Jackson pleaded wanly, "But Mr. Chairman, I, I *do not drink*. . . ." Nevertheless, he took an obliging swallow: he rather suggested some lumpishly innocent country revivalist who'd found himself captured by eccentric accident as the honored subject of a roaring high-state cocktail reception. Poured yet another glass, he gave a yelp, "Mr. Chairman, you tryin' to *knock me out*." But impressed into more partakings of the Armenian national nectar than he would have ever been ordinarily inclined to, Jackson finally allowed, "Well, this brandy now, it *does* keep hope alive," and released a loud blare of laughter. The chairman's attention was at length diverted by the late arrival of another member of Jackson's party, a brightly attractive black woman who was a columnist for *The Washington Post*, Dorothy Gilliam, and he began repeatedly leaning far over his plate to grin down the table at her with vigorous, saluting bobs of his head. When Jackson at one point observed to the chairman, "I'm kinda convinced you're a capitalist, Mr. Chairman, way you look," the chairman riposted, "It is because we want to be able to arouse the rapport with the lady," and among the guffaws this set off, he again peered down the table at Ms. Gilliam, lifting his glass to her with his wide, flat grin. It became, after a while, something like a vaudeville interchange between Jackson and the chairman, its focus fixed several feet away where Ms. Gilliam was seated, with Jackson acting as prompter and facilitator. The chairman presented another toast to Jackson for "the promise of bringing more men of your quality into politics," and Jackson returned, "And more *Washington Post* columnists?" This brought gleeful nods of assent from the chairman, and Ms. Gilliam called down the table, a bit crisply, "Thank you, Reverend Jackson. Thanks a lot." Jackson said to the chairman, "Oh, *maaan*, now see? You embarrassin' her," and dipped his head to snicker behind his hand like a larking schoolboy. About then, small dishes of a hazelnutlike dessert were brought in, and as they were being served, the chairman apprised Jackson, "This is what we call 'Greek nuts.' For a man, very useful," and in the explosion of laughter around the table, Jackson, looking with a level solemnness at the chairman, replied, "I'd say some of us here not especially needin' any of this right now."

The dinner finished with the chairman once more pressing Jackson, "I would anyway like you to try one more glass of our national drink," and

Jackson protested in a squalling voice, *"Tellin'* you, I got to *stay away* from this cognac. I have any more, I'm gonna be standin' on top of this table givin' a speech until sunrise tomorrow—*talkin' it."* As it happened, when he returned at last to his room, he was up discoursing to his aides and making long-distance calls until nearly daylight.

VI

The Heroic Obsession

CONSIDERABLY MORE than simply an instinct for earnest self-discipline was acquired by Jackson while growing up within the segregations of Greenville. Those industrious vigors imparted to him by the triangle of care around him came in time to serve a much more expansive impulse: to transcend the constrictions of his origin by, as it were, translating himself into a kind of super-reality—not unlike the spiritual exaltation of those Sunday-morning church services at Long Branch Baptist—as a figure of surpassingly larger dimension than the situation he was born into. "We never thought back then of any of us going great places outside our own community," says Julius Kilgore, his high school English teacher. "But what mattered to Jesse more than anything else in the world, he wanted to rise above the level he found himself in—and we didn't realize how far above it he wanted that to be. It was way beyond what we thought then white folks thought about us."

Perhaps more than anyone else, it was his grandmother, Tibby, who persevered in imparting to him an assurance that he was blessed with some larger promise. Years later, she was still explaining to whomever would listen, "I've always known he was special. I could always tell. Jesse can see. *Jesse can see.*"

Yet it finally remains something of a mystery exactly how Jackson, an illegitimate, poor black youth in Greenville's racial caste system, came to contract his sense of some special portent, what eventually magnified into a compulsion to re-create himself on a scale answering that early sense of his auspicious but balked possibilities. It became the ultimate dream for the outsider of making himself into nothing less than a moral hero in the society where he and his people had long been scorned. The very size of that ambition was, in a way, a measure of the emptiness he felt in his life. One of his high school acquaintances puts it simply: "What he went after was what he needed to be." Roger Wilkins, the eminent journalist and essayist who has long been a close friend of Jackson's, says, "I've seen it in a lot of black people. It's a special compulsion of our particular brand of outsider, an old, deep strain that came out of our oppression. It was almost like it was dirty just to use your education to go out and earn money. You're supposed to get out and *serve*. As long as the rest of our people are stuck, we're all stuck. So I don't think Jesse is unusual in his drive in that sense. I think what *is* unusual about him is that he is a gargantuan human being. I mean, everything has always been outsized in Jesse, including that drive. He's wanted to be . . . well, almost everything that matters."

COLIN WILSON'S 1956 work, *The Outsider*—an adventurous interpretation of such seemingly disparate cultural protagonists as T. E. Lawrence and Hermann Hesse, Ernest Hemingway and George Fox, which produced something of a critical sensation when it appeared—set forth what Wilson discerned, in his otherwise diverse subjects, as a common psychic type: the prodigally gifted but displaced loner who undertakes to compensate for his alienation from the world around him by resorting to extraordinary, and often tragic, exertions to reinvent himself in heroic proportions. As Wilson explains it, each began as "the anonymous Man Outside" but could not reconcile himself to "the circumstances of his birth as the inevitable boundaries of himself (as most of us do)," and who then, "by sheer spiritual force, escaped one set of circumstances and moved into another and higher set."

From the first, says Wilson, "the Outsider's chief desire is *to cease to be an Outsider.*" But his initial ordeal is that, because "he sees too deep and too much" and is constitutionally "not one to take life lightly," he soon finds he cannot bear existence in the prosaic world, accepted by everyone else, of "not living but drifting," a society, moreover, which "has impressed his insignificance on him." Within that society, his obsession becomes "absolute freedom or absolute bondage," but for the Outsider, freedom has a special meaning: it is "to be 'possessed' by a Will to power, to more life," says Wilson, "because that is the means by which he can get to know his unknown possibilities. . . . *Freedom lies in finding a course of action that gives expression to that part of him.*"

In the beginning, Wilson posits, what makes for the Outsider's "lostness" is that "he is not sure who he is." Wilson cites the example of George Fox, founder of the Society of Friends, who was "aware of himself as a dynamo of energy and willpower before he was seventeen; but he had no idea of *what to drive* with his energy," a youth who was "serious-minded, inwardly tormented." But the Outsider eventually realizes that "his salvation lies in discovering his deepest purpose, and then throwing himself

into it," says Wilson; otherwise, "he will always be an outcast and a misfit."
It thus becomes the ever-impelling imperative for the Outsider "to find a
course of action in which he is *most himself,* that is, in which he achieves
his maximum self-expression," and his desperation then is "to discover
how to lend a hand to the forces inside him. . . . With his whole being, he
wants to establish contact with the 'power within him,' and he knows that,
to do this, he must arouse his will to some important purpose."

In short, the Outsider's answer to his sense of exile in that baser world in
which he finds himself stranded is to "seek out the heroic." He can thereby
"set the seal of respectability on his life," says Wilson, "by claiming to be
[an] idealist, a dreamer of dreams." Accordingly, his most impressive feats
come from his belief that he is serving a reality far higher than the common
one around him. Wilson observes, "Let the Outsider accept without further
hesitation: I am different from other men because I have been destined to
something greater; let him see himself in the role of . . . pre-destined
prophet or world-betterer, and half [his] problems have been solved."

With that, says Wilson, outsiders become "play actors of their own
ideal . . . incorrigible self-dramatizers." Yet in virtually every case exam-
ined by Wilson, the Outsider continued to struggle under the disparity,
sometimes ultimately disastrous, of "an unfortunate lack of conscious direction where his own unusual powers are concerned." The tragedy, declares Wilson, is that *these men did not understand themselves.*" Often,
even to the end of a theatrically tumultuous life, the Outsider "is aware of
his strength, but he has no idea how to use it. . . . he is still a child."

JACKSON REMEMBERS THAT, even during his earliest feelings of denial
and aloneness, he sensed that he was headed for a life larger than that of
the society in which he found himself pent. "It didn't really come to me all
at once," he says. "It began more like this low burn that just kept on growing." For one thing, he was surrounded by "an expectation that I would do
something," he says. "I can't explain it, but I was always aware that there
was this exceptional, high-expectation factor for me." Part of the reason, he
proposes, was that even though he was the cast-off child of Noah Robinson, the mere fact that Robinson had fathered him "meant something very
important to people in the community"—and obviously, for all the hurt of
his rejection, also to him. More, "every social level in the community," he
says, "seemed to feel they had this special stake in me—the poorest element, because I was born among them, but also the middle-class, the respectable church folks, because they'd helped train me up."

What invited their special solicitude was that, even as a small boy, he
seemed to have a particularly effusive aliveness. He had always been un-

commonly enterprising, taking on his first job when he was only six, helping one of his grandmother's kin deliver stove wood in a pickup truck from a wood yard where, by one account, he wound up managing the hiring and payment collections by the time he was eleven; at twelve, he was caddying at Greenville's country club, and at one time or another, worked as a curb-hop at drive-in eateries and waited tables at the airport where people sat to watch the planes take off and land.

Most arresting of all, it was as if he had been born rampantly voluble. Throughout his childhood, actually, he struggled with a thick stammer, but despite that, says Kilgore, "just as soon as he began talking, this amazing flair of phrase appeared, like some supernatural gift. If he felt it, he would express it—to anybody, white or black—with the most surprising, well, *ambitiousness* of language, I would say. It was really the most extraordinary thing. It sounded sometimes like there was actually some little man in there inside of him talking."

It was principally for that reason, says Vivian Taylor, that "it soon became clear, at least to me, that Jesse was someone a little more than ordinary." She delivered these reflections on a Saturday morning in Greenville, after I had arrived at her tiny brick home to find she had forgotten our appointment—she appearing behind her front screened door, a strappingly tall figure in a bagging peach rayon housegown and slippers. "Well, come on in anyway, I guess," she said, and admitted me out of the hot midmorning into her cramped, dim, somewhat stale front room. She was the daughter of the Reverend D. S. Sample, the preacher at Long Branch church. Now in her eighties, she sat heaped in an easy chair, atop its crocheted spread, with her bare shins glinting below her knee-high gown, a Bible laid on a file box beside her, while she smoked a cigarette with sideways slurps. Immediately behind her was a murky dinette, its table laden with a profusion of condiments, a syrup bottle, a jar of Cremora, bottles of steak sauce. But she proceeded to talk about Jesse's beginnings in the unexpected, stately tongue of some secret, local sibyl, her stiff black-and-silver hair swept up in sprayed tufts. "Jesse," she pronounced, in a grotto-deep voice, "was prodigious from his inception. Just in the way he talked, he would seek words you never hear *used* by children, never heard coming out of their mouths. For instance, 'Pastor so-and-so *stirred* himself to *mount* into the pulpit.' I distinctly remember him saying that once, couldn't have been more than six or seven years old. It was almost abnormal, understand what I'm saying, how he would use words. From his very start, he was already producing these . . . these oratorical wonders."

At the same time, she went on, "He was always much more *noticing* than the average child, despite his deprivations. Maybe *because* of his deprivations. Anyway, they did not put one single dent in his aspirations, because he recognized himself that he was gifted. Oh, yeah. You could see in his manner, just the way he carried himself, he *knew* he was special."

Around the age of nine, he was reading the newspaper to illiterate grownups, and when the first small boxed black-and-white television sets began infiltrating into the neighborhood, he took to dropping by those same houses to read out the titles and datelines of the newsreel broadcasts—announcing to these, his first audiences, crowded into musty rooms in the shadowy glow of what would prove the medium of his own apotheosis one day, the headlines of spectacular commotions and pageantries, delivering his recital with a gusto that would prompt those collected around him to marvel, "This boy gonna *be* something"—as well as to drop dimes and quarters into the paper cup he always thought to bring with him. Such tributes from his elders, however perfunctory, produced in him great flushes of self-consequence. Before he had even reached adolescence, he proclaimed to Noah Robinson at one of their chance encounters, "I'm a born leader!"

But these anticipations of his were still only a vague, formless excitement, floating unconnected and apart from the daily bleak flatness of life for Greenville's black community. Its claustrophobia of spirit remained unstirred even by the Supreme Court's 1954 school desegregation order, Jackson recalls; it registered only as some remote, imponderable event, with little more immediate meaning than rumors of a sun flare. More momentous were the two occasions when Jackie Robinson passed through Greenville—the first time, in the fifties, when he was scheduled to perform in an exhibition game in town, which was rained out, and he never got off the train. Then, in 1960, he returned to speak at an NAACP conference, and at the airport, waiting for his plane with a delegation from the conference, he took a seat beside a local minister's wife in the whites-only section when she was ordered by a white policeman to move herself elsewhere. That incident shortly provoked a protest march of some thousand black Greenville citizens to the airport, led by the woman's husband, the Reverend James Hall, a young minister just recently arrived at Springfield Church. It was the first demonstration Greenville had experienced, a fantastical occurrence in those days. "Greenville was a strange place," Hall remembers, "a beautiful town, but isolated, and mostly white. They felt comfortable that demonstrations would never break out there." But Greenville's blacks were no less stunned than the white population. Jackson's own parents, he recalls, were scandalized. "It was like 'Why he want to raise up a fuss like that? Just what's he think he's doing? His business is s'pose to be preaching the gospel.' I could tell it sort of frightened them, you know, specially my stepfather."

What made Hall's audacious initiative so portentous was that, in the South then, ministers were about the only figures of true import and authority, free of dependence on whites, left to the black community, and this small elect presided over their people's lives rather in the manner of the tribal high priests of the Old Testament. Accordingly, when Jesse was somewhat older, he informed Noah Robinson, in what had apparently become a strangely insistent pattern of periodically bearing him such brave announcements, that he had been visited by a dream: "I dreamed," he declared, "I was a preacher, leading people through the rivers of the waters." Actually, says one of his friends then, Leroy Greggs, that enlightenment was at least partly derived from the fact that "we'd known for a long time, since we'd gone out to pick peaches and pole beans, that we didn't want to be doing anything like that line of work regular." But in his own church, he had emerged as a vigorously assertive youth, regularly faring forth to state Sunday school conferences and returning to present reports to the congregation with billowings of phrase in which the lisping stammer that had marked him since his childhood began miraculously to disappear. "Church was like my laboratory," he says, "my first actual public stage where I began to develop and practice my speaking powers with more and more confidence. After a while, got to where you couldn't hardly hold me back." He soon found that, while listening to other preachers in church, "I'd sit there watching them, but all I was really seeing was myself up there in that pulpit." When Jesse was fifteen, says Owen Perkins, the two of them were sitting in Jesse's backyard one late-August dusk after football practice, "and he suddenly confided to me that he had made a career decision. Said, 'I want to be a minister. That's what I'm gonna be.' "

First Glory

BUT AROUND THAT time, he was turning out to be a virtuoso in other public performances as well, most conspicuously in sports. In grade school, he had been oversized not only in his hunger for notice but in his sheer physical bulk, looming over his classmates and, by the sixth grade, over his teacher, too. "He just about gained his full height when he was thirteen," says Leroy Greggs, and Perkins recalls that "when he was fourteen, he had a size fourteen shoe. That's right. Was like his feet just kept gettin' larger and larger, keeping up with his age-count." His high school coach, Joe Mathis, says with a chortle, "It was almost like a handicap, size of his feet. He kept having trouble finding shoes big and wide enough for 'em. He was a little embarrassed about it. Once he wanted to see if maybe he could get his feet to fit into something like a size five, and I told him, 'Man, you gonna look *really* silly now, goin' 'round with a size five shoe on.' " Though still a bit blunderously cumbersome when he reached Sterling High, he made the football team as a freshman, playing with eighteen-year-olds. "Didn't surprise me atall," says Perkins. "In the ninth grade he could already throw the ball one hundred yards." He went on to become a star quarterback, as well as pitcher on the school's baseball team—the bravura positions, as it happened, in both sports. Pitching, he averaged seventeen strikeouts a game, but he also "definitely had a bat," remembers Greggs. "He batted cleanup, and would hit it like a *rocket*, I mean *tremendous* home runs. He cleaned those bases a lot."

But it was in his performances in the Thursday-night football games (Friday nights were reserved for Greenville's white high school games) that Jackson came into his first true public magnification—before thundering stands under the flaring field lights of Furman's Sirrine Stadium, where he had once parked cars for the college's Saturday games and peddled peanuts and Cokes to the white spectators. "He'd run it himself a lot," recalls Mathis, "had these big, long, strong, determined strides." But, says Owen Perkins, "Jesse being unusually big for a quarterback, other quarterbacks were faster, maybe more elusive. What set him apart, he was smarter." It had always been Mathis's strategy anyway to design his whole team's offense around the quarterback, an arrangement Jesse did not find uncongenial, and over all the coming years, he ceaselessly reinvoked his quarterbacking style as a metaphor for how he has actually played his progress through life. "We were calling audibles back then," says Mathis, "and he was so big, he could stand up over that line and look over the field in front of him and read in a split second the other team's defense, then call the play from the line to hit the weak spot. Yeah, he was always liable to improvise like that, call an audible at the last second. Every trip, every trip. And could follow through on fakes, with those long arms of his, like a magician. When he was out there on that field, he seemed to feel he could do everything. Could remember anything up in that head," and Mathis taps two fingers from both hands against his temples. "Now, sometimes his *ego* would get to him. I'm the big man, I got to shine, I can run the show. I said, 'Unh-unh, we don't play like that. *I* run the show. You do what I say or you sit over here near me,' " and Mathis lowers his head with a chuckle: "*Oh, boy . . .*"

In one game, Jackson shifted himself to fullback for a while and ran for three touchdowns. He became, in fact, something of a local sensation. Before long, his swashbuckling play had attracted the curiosity of Greenville's papers, the morning *News* and afternoon *Piedmont*. The *Piedmont*'s sports editor, Dan Foster, recollects, "He wasn't just a good player. He was a terrific player, or we wouldn't have heard of him." Jackson wryly told him later, says Foster, "that I was putting his picture in the paper when the papers weren't even using black ink." A photographer sent to his games by the *News*, Benny Granger, would notify Jesse on particularly chill evenings of his wish to get back to the paper as soon as possible, and Jesse on his first plays would take the ball himself and obligingly gallop straight toward Granger's flashbulb on as many successive swings as needed, until Granger signaled him an okay. But it wasn't as if he ever required such promptings, recalls Foster: "He seemed to be attracted to a flashbulb like a moth to a light."

During those years of his first, local glory, he developed into a glad young prince of Greenville's black community. "People'd come flockin' around him wherever he showed up," says Mathis. Lofty and erect, he had now a kind of cleanly graven handsomeness "and a simply *beaming* personality," remembers Xanthene Norris, his eleventh-grade French teacher. He had taken to dressing with a dandy's studied spiffiness, journeying all the way downtown to get his shoes shined, and appearing at weddings arrayed in a tuxedo jacket and vanilla-white trousers as if he were the bridegroom. He even came to school appareled in suits and ties. "It was always a little amazing," says Ms. Norris, "seeing him walk into class in a starched dress shirt and tie." Snappy, ebullient, he was called J.J. by some friends, Bo by others, from his childhood nickname of Bo Diddley. He arrived each day fragrant from a mixture of colognes, "a different combination every day," says Leroy Greggs. "Would mix Palmolive aftershave, Mennen, Old Spice, Aqua-Velva. He said he wanted, every time he saw a girl, to have a different smell."

In fact, "along with everything else outstanding about him then," reports one of his classmates, "Jesse was also right strong on those doves. A real dove hunter, might say." Mathis attests that it "got to where I had to warn him about that, 'cause those girls were already spillin' all over themselves to get hold of him." Nevertheless, Greggs recalls, "Jesse was gonna come to a party to have a good time, that's all there was to it." He still relishes a remembered vision of him at the weekend parties held in a neighborhood park's dank little concrete canteen, bare of all but a water fountain and a record player, when "he'd get out there and really strut his stuff. They'd be playin' that Everly Brothers song—'Bye Bye Love'—and I can still see that head of his bobbin' up and down all happy. He wouldn't of necessarily come there with any girl, but he'd sho leave with one." He came to be stricken by one in particular, a lead majorette and performing dancer, like his mother, who was named Ann Avery. Recalls Greggs, "She was a real high-stepper. Yeah. Jesse, he had a real nose-job for Ann Avery, I'm tellin' you. For a while there, Ann Avery more or less consumed all his time." One reason may have been that she happened to persist in resisting any final enchantment with him; she now suggests, "It was probably because my grandmother, when she met him, just approved of him too much." But that confoundment did not distract him for long. "He was," as one fellow student recollects, "a phenomenon."

He had also become famous for a certain rampaging glibness. Greggs recounts that, the times he double-dated with him, "he had enough conversation for all four of us. He could talk a hole through a billy goat." Greggs, who was two classes ahead of Jesse, coached a neighborhood softball team, and he relates that, when Jesse was playing first base for him, "he'd throw that needle into the other team, I mean, *all game long*. Other team'd get a little behind, and he'd start hollerin' stuff like—we had an air base outside town then—like, 'Yawl need to just go ahead and recruit somebody from the *air force*.' Kept it up, got so caught up in it, I'd finally have to shift him out to right field just to keep his mind on the game." That instant and profuse loquacity he deployed indiscriminately, in both rowdy and more sober moments alike. "He figured he could maneuver himself out of any fight with his powers of talk," says Mathis, "and damn if he didn't always manage to do it." His teacher, Julius Kilgore, declares that "sometimes now when I see him talking on television, I flash back to that quickness of his at Sterling, like when I'd ask him something about Chaucer, and even though I strongly suspected it was something he was only faintly acquainted with, he'd come back with this very assured and elaborate answer, which, remarkably enough, seemed about right most of the time. I didn't realize until a little later that he had sort of subtly changed the *terms* of my question, you know."

On the whole, Jackson still bore the buoyancy of his boyhood that Barbara Mitchell remembered from when she'd see him walking down the street in the dark all by himself—"just Jesse, master of his kingdom." Leroy Greggs observes, "He had a very wide combination of people he could connect with. He didn't carry himself as an intellectual, somebody serious, unless you knew him. He could mix with *anybody*." That included a rougher company of youths who roosted on what was known merely as "the corner," a huddle of pool halls, barbershops, package stores, cafés, where he became not negligibly practiced in blackjack, shooting craps, eight-ball.

Yet he remained, in the end, one of that small body at Sterling referred to as "the good boys"—the presumed inheritors of the community's churchly respectability. Leroy Greggs's softball team happened to be composed of a fairly raunchy collection of stray souls, he admits, and before one especially critical game, "Jesse ups and gathers them around him, and prays a prayer that had everybody in tears. And most of those guys were *thugs*. But you'd see that spirituality come out in him at times like that. . . . That was one night we kept 'em all sober at least until the game was over with—and we won it, eight to four." Owen Perkins declares, "Jesse was always, underneath everything, a very serious, very earnest kind of young person. You felt he was always carrying around deep in him these heavy thoughts, unusually heavy for somebody his age. I remember he told me once, 'It's all right being one of the boys now. But I'm just waitin'. One day, I'm gonna be one of the *men.*' " Diligently observant of the proprieties, still disciplined by his upbringing, he struck his teachers as, in Ms. Norris's words, "almost abnormally conscientious" in his schoolwork, would ask for his classroom assignments in advance of team trips out of town, and board the bus with a sack of textbooks. Jackson himself would later confide, "I was afraid to fail. An all-around excellence in sports and academics, being a first-string athlete and an honor student, could protect you from feeling certain forms of rejection. People don't laugh at you when you get A's. When you make A's, people have to hang around you. With D's, they don't."

But it was a labor for him. In his literature classes, Kilgore did find him "almost a prodigy at character analysis, the psychological implications in a story. And also when we'd talk about figures of speech. He could interpret poetry quite well—the Romantics, the Elizabethan poets." But Xanthene Norris stipulates, "He was not that brilliant a student. He was perhaps a good B student, just a little above average. He didn't have all that much natural ability. But he worked terribly hard at it."

He proved, at the least, ferociously competitive. "Because he could convince about anybody to do what he wanted them to do," says fellow student Horace Nash, "he more or less *ran* Sterling." Though consistently elected an officer of his class, even voted state president of the Future Teachers of America, he was still "always the candidate," Ms. Norris later told biographer Barbara Reynolds. "Whatever office was available, Jesse would be there signing his name. He seemed to be saying, 'Whether you elect me or not, I'm going to run.' " She now reflects, "He was so aggressive, he didn't mind walking over somebody for what he wanted—or simply didn't notice he had. He'd always apologize afterward, of course. But he just went totally after that thing, whatever he decided he needed to have." That impulse backfired at times: when he ran for student-body president his senior year, his friend Owen Perkins was elected instead, Jesse was selected merely business manager, and eventually another student was even voted Most Likely to Succeed. "Students had started complaining," says Ms. Norris. "They were tired of him running over them, trying to take everything himself."

In that obsession, according to Julius Kilgore, "Jesse was still in a way pretty much that sensitive little boy he'd always been. If he didn't do as well as he thought he should have done, he'd get really disturbed. Or if he was challenged in class, his feelings would brim over. The criticism was usually about how he'd constantly volunteer his own interpretation—'Aw, let somebody else talk! You not the only person knows what this means.'" Once, Kilgore relates, while his class was reading aloud passages from *Macbeth*, one student delivered the line, "The King is dead, the King is dead," in what affronted Jesse as an unforgivably mechanical monotone, and he demanded of the student, "If you went into a room and found a person dead, would you come out and say it like that?" miming then with a mockingly exaggerated flatness the student's reading. "Well," says Kilgore, "the boy flared right back at him, really hot. Which astonished and greatly upset Jesse. That was one of the times he became actually tearful and I had to step in to defend him." Helen Jackson admits, "When he gets his fill, he will cry some." In his senior year, he was awarded a football scholarship to the University of Illinois, but at his class's graduation ceremony, the names of other students who had won scholarships were called out without any mention of him, "and he was just so hurt," his mother relates. "After they marched, he came down to talk with us and said, 'I wonder why they didn't call my name?' And he started crying. We said, 'Ah, you know, people forget.' '*But they should have called my name*, that I won that.'"

The Other Son

STILL, IT WAS during those high school years of his first stardom that he had begun to win a closer attention from Noah Robinson. Robinson's youngest son, George, readily avows, "Jesse was my hero, a great athlete. I wasn't even marginal, wasn't even average. But Jesse had always had a need to excel at everything, and because of that, he *did*. I looked at him in awe, you know. I'd say, 'Look at my brother doing that, God, *look at him.*'"

Noah Jr., who was a year behind Jesse—a slighter, trimmer version of him, with a more sharply focused face—was also considered "one of the good boys" at Sterling. "Truth is," says Xanthene Norris, "Noah probably had more native smartness than Jesse, was naturally brighter"; as it happened, he wound up graduating third in his class, where Jesse had graduated only tenth. But Noah came to her once, recounts Ms. Norris, to complain that "his mother was always pushing him to match Jesse. Fact was, he told me, 'My mother hates his guts.' Said she kept telling him, 'You

gotta be as good as Jesse, can't let him outdo you. If he can get into the National Honor Society, you sure should be able to.' " One woman in the
community now remarks, "What do you suppose that did to that boy, being
always thrown into having to compete against somebody like Jesse?" and
she then proposes, "Noah Jr.'s the real tragedy in the whole thing, you ask
me. He was wanted in the first place by Robinson's wife only to keep her
husband, because of Jesse—not really wanted for himself. Because of that,
he came into the world with a veil over his face. It explains all that's happened to him since."

Noah Jr. went on to earn an M.B.A. from Wharton Business School,
built a management consulting business in Philadelphia, and was even
once named an Outstanding Young Man of the Year. A sleek and jaunty
chap with a donnish goatee, he was to lead a somewhat fitful life, eventually occupying himself in motley entrepreneurial gambits that began to attract increasing legal perusal. Yet even then he would freely proclaim,
"I've had thirty different operations. Whenever I saw an opportunity, I
grabbed it." In 1973, recalls Xanthene Norris, when Jackson returned to
Greenville for his first homecoming fete, "that very morning I got this mysterious big package in the mail, delivered with no name on it. I had no
idea who'd sent it, until I opened it up—it was full of clippings and articles, all about Noah. That's all. Just these clippings about what he'd been
doing, too, over the years. With this big event for Jesse going on all over
town, it was like he'd just wanted to let me know, 'Hey, here I am, too.' "

Over the years, Jackson did sporadically reach out to pull him into some
more brotherly association—that small boy he had waved to outside their
mutual father's backyard—but it became a strangely contrary pattern of alternately embracing and repudiating him, a cacophonous relationship in
which more than a few saw Cain-and-Abel tensions at work. Shortly after
Noah had graduated from Wharton, Jackson, then directing SCLC's
Operation Breadbasket offensive in Chicago for economic integration,
brought him up to join his staff and soon assigned him head of a Breadbasket auxiliary division. But before long, office workers were witnessing
raucous rows between them. George Robinson presents it, a little uncomfortably, as a case of "two headstrong individuals, both highly intelligent,
but each wanting to go his own way. Noah wasn't a great athlete, but he
had a real sharp mind for business. Very, very quick." But Robinson then
finds himself obliged to admit, "Noah was about making as much money
as he could possibly make, while Jesse was about helping people. Noah
wanted to help himself. And he was very good at it." One of Jackson's seminary professors in Chicago who later worked in Breadbasket with both
brothers now offers, "Noah certainly had sheer native ability, very able—

clearly there were genes there. A very sharp, well-educated operator. But I don't know what more he was. That's the tragedy. How could you live with a person like Jesse, with the obvious differences in the being of those two people? We know enough about the unconscious to know that you aren't in control of your feelings in that sort of thing."

Perhaps the climactic mortification for Noah came when SCLC's Ralph Abernathy, who regarded him as "a chronic troublemaker," as he later wrote, after being advised by Jesse, "I can't do anything with him" but "he'll listen to his daddy," accordingly called Noah Robinson, Sr., over from Greenville for an admonitory session with his namesake in the SCLC offices in Atlanta. "When Noah saw his father walk through the door," Abernathy narrated, "he wilted like a morning glory." After the door was shut on the two of them, Abernathy and other staffers heard Noah Sr. bellowing castigations "the likes of which we had never heard before," during which Noah Jr.'s voice arose not once. When the door at last opened again, as Abernathy tells it in cartoon-panel fashion, Noah Jr. slipped hurriedly out with the chastened docility of some seven-year-old child, Noah Sr. still glowering behind him as he wiped his brow with a handkerchief.

After a year with Jackson at Breadbasket, Noah Jr. concluded he had to quit, denouncing his older half brother as "a paper tiger who thinks power is made of press releases" but attributing his departure mainly to "Jesse's insecurity" about his own success in developing marketing possibilities for black business: "The closest Jesse ever came to telling me how he felt was one day when he said that I had become an emotional liability to him." Then, when Jackson in turn left SCLC to mount his own movement in Chicago, Noah Jr. was briefly installed at Breadbasket to replace him, and Jackson produced the carefully deliberated comment that Noah reminded him of "a snake an old woman took in from the cold, all battered and on its last leg," which, after the woman had nursed it back to strength, "bit her. When the woman asked why, the snake said, 'Well, after all, I'm still a snake.'" For his part, Noah averred that Jackson "has intelligence, drive, ruthlessness, and vindictiveness, and can be as terrifying as Al Capone."

Nevertheless, in 1975, after five years of their not exchanging a syllable, Jackson phoned to ask that Noah Jr. come by his office. As Noah subsequently related that visit, "He said, 'I can't be preaching brotherhood and family, and not have a relationship with my own brother.' He and I damn near came to tears." In fact, Noah had continued to prosper from Jackson's campaign to compel large companies toward more black inclusion, he being granted a Kentucky Fried Chicken franchise and the first Coca-Cola distributorship ever allocated to a black. But by 1988, he was again publicly decrying his brother's character: "It's a *fear* that fuels his drive."

Long prospecting on his own by then, he became the subject of a rather phantasmagorical murder investigation—an old antagonist of his had been shot through the head after he was summoned late one night to a phone booth in a Greenville shopping center owned by Noah—that investigation also involving connections to drug dealers and to a Chicago street gang allegedly contracted as terrorists by Libya. His younger brother, George—himself a thoroughly genial, gentle-spoken, unassuming soul—labors doughtily to explain, "Noah was the kind of person that liked to help black youths, when they came out of prison, get back into society," but by employing an uncommon number of them in his variegated enterprises, former gang members heavily among them, "he got involved in trying to do things for people that he shouldn't have been doing." When Jackson had landed in Greenville for his mother's birthday banquet that weekend after the 1988 presidential election, a press conference with local reporters beside his plane instantly ended when one asked, "What about Noah Robinson, Reverend Jackson?" and without even indicating he had heard the question, Jackson pushed on toward the terminal; one sensed Noah had become a tribulation that he had simply resigned himself to having to endure in perpetuity. In 1992, already serving sentences on two felony convictions for defrauding the IRS and accessory to attempted murder, Noah was convicted of drug-racketeering, murder, and attempted murder—convictions that were overturned on appeal. He is still serving time in a federal penitentiary in Oxford, Wisconsin, on the first attempted murder conviction while awaiting retrial on the three latter charges. With Noah finally removed into that confinement, Jackson began phoning Noah Robinson, Sr., and his wife with a renewed frequency, commiserating with them over the misfortune that had overtaken his half brother and reassuring them about the prospects for a parole before too long.

DURING HIS HIGH school years, Jackson would later insist to reporters, "I never lacked for anything. I was the star quarterback and made the honor roll as a student. I could get about any girl I liked. I was a leader." Indeed, the taunting calls that had pursued him through his childhood—*Jesse ain't got no daddy, you ain't nothing but a nobody*—were now, for the most part, far behind him, but never completely—hauntings from his origins continued to trail after him, undispellable despite all his feats. Walking past a front porch where some women were sitting with their coffee, he heard one tell the others, "There goes Noah's bastard, thinking he's better than everybody else." Xanthene Norris says, "If he was aggressive, it was because nobody could have come through all those wounds *without* being aggressive. He never got over being sensitive about it, but he tried to cover it up. He wouldn't tell you if something had pained him. But you could see the hurt in his eyes." As Vivian Taylor puts it, "He could have become undone by what he experienced as a child. But he made himself opaque—so you couldn't see through to that." Julius Kilgore recalls that "something came up once, some disappointment I tried to cheer him up about, and his only response was, he was the first person from whom I ever heard the prayer of St. Francis of Assisi—it just rolled right out of his mouth": "Lord, make me an instrument of your peace. Where there is hatred, let me sow love. Where there is injury, pardon. . . . Grant that I may not so much seek to be consoled as to console. . . . For it is in giving that we receive, it is in pardoning that we are pardoned."

Joe Mathis says, "Yeah, he was introverted somewhat, kind of self-conscious. But I saw that hole in him, like the one I had." Mathis, now long retired, retains a chipper shrewdness; he is a stocky, bunchily built man, with round eyes in a round blunt sturdy head, who, the morning we talked, was wearing khaki shorts with white socks pulled up high above tan dress shoes. Raised by his grandparents on a small farm in Georgia, he reports, "I never saw my father but once in my life, when I was five years old. So I knew something about hurt myself, the absence of a father for a boy growing up—hurt like, *God,* I don't know inside. Ah, well, long time ago, nothin' to do about it now." But recognizing that same emptiness in Jesse, Mathis says, "That boy came to be like my son. I made a point every day of being with him. We would do a lot of *meetin'*, you know, always havin' these *meetin's* about things."

Jackson himself, while riding one recent summer afternoon from La Guardia Airport into Manhattan, fell to describing an auspicious youth, not unevocative of him in those days, whom he'd lately encountered: "He's bright, he's handsome, can talk, could lead demonstrations. He's young, but he's really got that thing. Only, he needs a father with an arm around him, and a foot to his ass to kick him on into that next level. When he comes out the other end, he'll be tough, with that commitment and discipline of his consciousness so he'll be able to explode it on people." Asked then who served as that sort of father for him, Jackson said, "In my most formative years, it was Coach Mathis. He was *the* guy in town, could give you this real affirmation of your selfhood. Told you when you did well, don't be be arrogant, win with grace, and when you lose, don't cry too long."

In their constant meetings, says Mathis, he also tutored Jesse in "angling the truth just right. Lot of truth lies in how you angle it." He inscribed in Jesse's yearbook, "To the victors go the spoils." Most of all, he persistently reassured Jesse that "you can be anything you take in mind to be," that fate had marked him as an "heir apparent to great things."

An Anger Rising

YET ALL THE exhilarating intimations of his special promise seemed finally canceled by the intractable confinements of segregation. Greenville High was then the city's all-white upper school for youths generally from those more privileged families where maids like Jackson's grandmother worked, and Leroy Greggs remembers that "we'd always want to play the guys on their basketball team. They'd always get the huge headlines, while we got little bitty ones, if any at all." One afternoon, while he and Jesse were shooting baskets on Greenville High's outdoor court, several players on the school's basketball team, who'd been shooting goals at the other end, invited them into a pickup game. A few moments later, the school's basketball coach appeared, yelling, "If you nigguhs don't get yo' asses away from here, I'm gonna call the police. *Get!*" Jesse began shouting back, "But they *invited* us to play, we were *invited,*" until, says Greggs, "I had to start pulling him away. Tears were welling up in his eyes, he was biting his lip—I could see he was fixin' to get into his mode. Had we stayed, as he was insistin' we do, there'd've been a real confrontation."

Jesse happened to have a counterpart of sorts at Greenville High, a much-acclaimed quarterback and heavy-clubbing catcher named Dickie Dietz, and between them there developed, as Jackson now likes to cast it, a "media parallel" of dueling headlines in the local papers. But the possibility of any direct contest between them was forever foreclosed by the town's implacable racial divisions. "I always wanted to play against Dickie Dietz," says Jackson, "but I knew I never could. It was one more way the system acted to contradict your qualifications." (Years later, he would claim that, at major league tryouts held in Greenville, he pitched against Dietz and struck him out three times, but that Dietz was offered a hundred-thousand-dollar contract and he one for only ten thousand dollars—a story that, under closer scrutiny, proved a trifle evanescent in some particulars. Dan Foster, who covered the tryout, does recall that Jesse "was very impressive," but Dietz would later insist to reporters he only remembered some black pitcher who, far from striking him out three times, merely hit him once in the back with the ball, "hard." Joe Mathis, who had instructed Jesse in "angling" a matter toward its higher truth, now submits, "Well, Jesse, you know, always a little space there"—he lifts his hands to measure an open gap in front of his face—"little space there between what happened and how he'll tell it. Gives himself a little latitude, you know, to go on a little further with it." Dan Foster suggests, "Maybe he has a euphemistic memory." But when news reports of Dietz's own account appeared in 1987, just as Jackson was moving into his first presidential primary endeavor, Foster was sitting at home with his wife. It was Christmas Day, he relates, "and the phone rings. 'Mr. Foster, I'm so-and-so with Reverend Jackson. Are you gonna be home in an hour? Jesse wants to call you.' *Christmas Day.* I said, 'If I weren't I would be if he's gonna call.' So he called, said he and his wife were just sitting there, Christmas Day, talking about people they really just wanted to call. So forth and so on. Then he had a little aside. 'You remember when I tried out? Well, I told them I pitched to Dickie Dietz. And what happened was, a couple of papers called Dietz, and Dietz said he didn't remember, just there was a black pitcher threw behind him.' He said, 'You know, Dick's one of my heroes, and I don't want to have a bad relationship with him.' Said, 'Ask Dick to give me a call.' So I called Dick—he was in Myrtle Beach—and I said, 'Dietz, Jesse Jackson wants you to call him.' He said, 'You're kidding me.' I said, 'No, here's the number.' Then I went over to my brother's, and two hours later, a call came over there. 'Reverend Jackson would like to talk to you.' Jesse came on and said, 'Dan, son, Dick called me, and we've had the greatest Christmas we ever had. We talked for half an hour. I'm going to make him director of the Small Business Administration.' ")

But beyond the secondary discrimination of being precluded from contending with white athletes on the same field, the demeanings were usually more direct and primal. On his senior-class trip to the state capital in Columbia, Jesse found when they arrived that "they wouldn't even let us take a class picture on the lawn. Not talking about inside the building where the governor and all the legislators were, but not even out there on the *lawn.*" In truth, for all his proud bravado in high school, it would probably be impossible to measure the inner depredations left in black youths like Jesse from having grown up in the racial exclusions of an overwhelmingly dominant white society. As he now recalls it, "It was like we were some reject people kept under rule in an occupied zone. Mean, why'd we have to sit in the back of the bus? I once asked my mother. 'White kids are going to the front of the bus'—you want to sit where the other kids sit, you know, right up there by the driver, that you-can-see-what's-happenin'-in-the-front-seat-type thing. Mama said, 'They're the same, son. Back of the bus is goin' where the front is goin'.' Tryin' to spare you the pain as long as possible. 'Besides, if they have a bus wreck, those in the back won't get hurt.' But why we have to use the back door of cafés? Couldn't sit at the lunch counters downtown? Couldn't go to the theaters downtown,

couldn't go to a white church? Hunh? Why was that? Why all the bus drivers, department store clerks, supermarket clerks, all the firemen and
policemen and judges, all were white? Why *we* couldn't be firemen and
policemen? 'Member one white cop locked up a black man for lookin' at
a white woman over a hundred feet away from him, charged him with
reckless eyeballin'. We weren't even allowed to stand in front of the department store display windows when they were changing the clothes on
the white dummies. And why no blacks on television? Movies only about
white characters? Why no blacks in Congress or the Senate or the state
capitol? Mean, *why?* You felt the whole society was out just to *erase* you."
Years later, says Jackson, while he was watching a performance of *Sizwe
Banzi Is Dead* in New York, the audience around him broke into laughter
at "that part about blacks going downtown to look at their reflections in
store windows, but I suddenly had tears filling up in my eyes. Because we
used to do that when I was growing up, because we hardly ever actually
saw our faces."

Just how deep the inner desolations worked by segregation went was revealed by the peculiarly exorbitant excitement with which, a few years
later at college, Jackson and his fellow black students received word of a
U.N. study of racial comparisons. "The big preoccupation for us at school
was whether we were actually inferior or not. We'd sit around discussing
books by Margaret Mead and others. Any anthropological study showing
us not to be inferior was very important stuff to us. So when this UNESCO
report came out stating that, scientifically, people of African descent were
not inherently inferior, *man!* That was a big thing. We took that paper and
quoted from it, went around giving speeches on it everywhere. I mean, the
United Nations said it. It was *validated*—we were *not* inferior!" There was
the same almost poignant extravagance to his rejoicing over comments in
a television address around that time by President Kennedy: "He came on,
said, 'What's happening to Negroes in America is not only not right under
the law, it is also morally wrong.' Greatgodamighty, man—*morally* wrong!
I choked up, started just *quivering*. I'd never heard a white politician in my
life before say something like that, talk about the moral foundations of our
society. He took it into another dimension with that," and stirred again by
the recollection even these many years later, Jackson smacks his hands and
lets loose a light, amazed whistle, "*Morally* wrong. My *God!*"

But while Jackson was in high school, what became especially unen-
durable about Greenville's racial order was its bluff, indifferent affront to
his growing sense of his own possibilities. "It can make you uncontrollably
angry," he reflects. "But once you're angry, you can't see clear. So it becomes a mind game. They'll hang you every now and then, but mostly

they do it with mind games. So you learn to play under pressure." One of his fortitudes for that game seemed an uncanny imperviousness to any intimidation by whites. "The taint we had as black people just never seemed to matter to him," Vivian Taylor observes, and Owen Perkins still marvels that "somehow, he'd never been trapped in that old mentality of slavery. Whereas, I was—didn't *think* I was, but was, until King. But he seemed totally unafraid of white people, way before King." In fact, another friend, Horace Nash, would later tell reporters, "He actually looked down on white people, and in those days that was unusual. He used to make up jokes about whites, how foolish and stupid they were." Jackson himself would propound over the following years, "Grasshoppers have a strange complex. They wallow in the grass, they change color with the grass. They're scared of shoes. They panic when they hear lawn mowers. But *giants* do not wallow in the grass. Do not run from shoes, or panic when they hear lawn mowers. Giants stand *tall*, and *act* tall."

His singular absence of abashment before whites Jackson now ascribes partly to the happenstance that "I was bicultural. I grew up working in white sections of town, so I knew how whites lived and felt and thought." A white surgeon in Greenville, Dr. Larry McCalla, the son in one of the households where Jesse's grandmother had served as a maid, returned from medical school on a holiday in 1953 and set out one morning for a stretch of golf at the country club, picking up a caddy in the clubhouse. But it was not until he reached the tenth fairway that the caddy, a hulking boy not yet in his teens but impeccably polite and cordial, at last chose to introduce himself: "I'm Jesse Burns. My grandmother is Matilda Burns, she's worked for yawl." McCalla now says, "I was a little surprised, actually, that he'd waited all that long, through nine holes, before he let me know who he was. Proud, I guess, but I suppose he had to be. But he made a very favorable impression, very friendly."

Nevertheless, Jesse would occasionally engage in furtive retaliations for the abasements he had long borne. While working as a waiter in the dining room of the Poinsett, a patrician hotel downtown, he says, "I'd serve people sometimes who'd just be so *mean*, but I soon found if I kept serving them with a genteel efficiency, you could melt 'em after a while, they'd start letting their guard down." But it's testimony to his submerged fury that he would also resort, he later reported, to quick little spits in the soup of those same white customers before emerging from the kitchen and delicately placing the bowl before them. "Hardly call it even, though. Spit in their soup while they burn our churches." That particular reminiscence some thought suspiciously similar to an episode in Richard Wright's *Black Boy*, when a cook in a Chicago diner spits in the soup he is preparing, and

Jesse would eventually claim, "I never did that, really." Whatever the case, the story left Greenville's white citizenry permanently incensed. When Jackson returned for a rally during his first presidential campaign, he spied Dr. McCalla in the crowd while he was making an appeal for thousand-dollar contributions, and motioned him—"Larry, come on up here!"—to stand by him on the stage, whereupon he impressed him into pledging a donation of his own. "I'm not sure I ever got around to actually writing the check," says McCalla, "you know how those things go." But before the sun was down that evening, he was under a bombardment of outraged calls from his fellow white townsmen: "What in *God's name* did you mean, Larry? Pledging a thousand dollars to Jesse Jackson? When he spit in that soup at the Poinsett?"

But Jesse's only open protest so far—the first of his life—occurred when he was around fifteen, right after the final triumph of the Montgomery bus boycott. He and Owen Perkins caught a Greenville city bus one afternoon after school—"Jesse thought we ought to test what'd happened in Montgomery," says Perkins—and, sitting up front by the driver with their school note-tablets to transcribe, if challenged, the driver's name and remarks, the two of them proceeded to ride that bus and then, getting transfer slips, a succession of others all over town. "It was a very dangerous thing to do then, I guess," says Perkins, "this was still, like, around 1956, you know. But we didn't really know how dangerous it was. We'd just chat to each other now and then, but mostly we were staring out the windows. We were seeing neighborhoods of Greenville we'd never seen before. Nothing happened, except we got to really know the whole town for the first time since we'd been living there." Boarding one bus, Perkins was dismayed to see his mother sitting in the back, "but after we sat down in the front, she just looked at us down that long aisle and gave me a nod—this little nod of approval and blessing."

From then on, Jesse would regularly seat himself near the front of the bus, and finally, on his way to work at the Poinsett one afternoon, the driver reprimanded him, and he snapped back a curt retort. "That driver," recalls Julius Kilgore, "was reportedly a Klansman, name something like Whitfield, and the whole black community was a little afraid of him. But it was all over school the next day: 'Jesse stood up to Mr. Whitfield! Talked back to *Mr. Whitfield!*' "

Then, in 1959, Jesse left for his first year of college in the remote and supposedly more open clime of the University of Illinois. He returned to Greenville for the Christmas break. A train bore him, nattily clad in gray slacks and navy blue Bugle Boy blazer, back down into the piney country of his origin, which he had left for the first time in his life only a few months earlier but which now, despite everything he had undergone there, seemed strangely dear. "I mean, I was some kind of excited," Jackson recollects. "It was the longest I'd ever been away from home, and it felt awfully good to be going back, even for that little bit of time." But while there, he was required to compose an address assigned him in his speech class, for delivery at an oratorical contest in a month or so. "I had to write it and memorize it, and had this list of about two dozen books I needed to prepare and document it. Had something to do with patriotism, as I remember." Once back in Greenville, by simple conditioned instinct, he first sought out the books on his list not at the city's main public library but at the McBee Avenue Colored Branch. None of them were to be found there, but the librarian sent him on, with an explanatory note, to the white library downtown—telling him, "The lady there is my friend, she'll handle this for me"—and took the precaution of phoning ahead for him. It was one of Greenville's balmy winter days, Jackson remembers, and though the central library was some dozen blocks away, "I jogged the whole distance, I was so happy and eager." But when he entered—through the rear entrance—he discovered several policemen collected around the librarian's desk, quietly talking to her. She took his note, then glanced over his list of books, and informed him that none were available there at the moment: "It'll take us at least six days to get these books." Aghast, Jackson pleaded, "My God, *six days*? Couldn't I just go back in the shelves and look for them, way back in the stacks where nobody would even see me? There's nobody here but us." She replied, "No, you can't do that." Jackson said, "But it'd just be me by myself—" and she snipped, "I knew what you meant. You simply cannot have the books now. That's the way it is." One of the policemen then interjected, "You heard what she said."

"And I knew what *that* meant," recounts Jackson some thirty-five years later. He walked back out through the library's rear door and then around to the front of the building. "I just stared up at that 'Greenville Public Library,' and tears came to my eyes. I said to myself, 'That thing says *public*, and my father is a veteran and pays taxes. I'm going to use this library.' " On the long walk back to his house, continues Jackson, "I was still cryin', I was so angry and humiliated. I knew I was on an academic and athletic par with white students in Greenville, but I couldn't go to Furman or Clemson, like them, because I was black. But now I'd gone to the University of Illinois, and if I could compete at Illinois, I sure could compete at Furman or Clemson. Yet Furman, Clemson students could use that library, even the town's white high school students could use it—but *I* couldn't. It was like my mind couldn't fit into the socket in the wall. I knew I was really being abused, like they'd gone out of their way to do it. It *still* hurts, like I *still* can't believe it." What it meant, says Jackson, was "that after being away from home so long, I had to break off my Christmas vacation four days early, leave all my friends, to go back to Illinois to get that speech done. Because I knew if I stepped back in there the first day classes reopened and said I didn't have my speech prepared because I couldn't get the books, to those white students I would have failed—in their eyes I'd have fallen into the stereotype of black and low expectations. I'd of gone to *New York* to get them books. But," Jackson adds, "what I intuitively learned in that experience was, instead of exploding, 'stead of being a catalyst of the sort that's destroyed in the process, just to take on a disciplined rage. If you *im*plode, you can turn your pain to power. So I imploded when that thing happened. Just this very private, deep-down resolution. I remember riding that train back to Atlanta and then to Nashville and on up to Chicago and taking a bus on to Urbana, thinking the whole way, *That library's public. And when I get back home this summer, it's gonna go public for real. I'm gonna use that library.* It wasn't any matter of Gandhi or Dr. King then, it was just my own private pride and self-respect."

THAT OBSTINATE SELF-REGARD had finally been transmitted to him, to no small degree, by his mother and stepfather. "Despite everything, they'd always had this great sense of personal dignity," says Jackson. "It was maybe their most important gift to me." One of his first shocks of a closer knowledge of his stepfather came when he was still a small boy—a moment, Jackson now declares, that "when I was running for president kept crossing my mind over and over and over again": Charles Jackson was then out of work, "having to do odd jobs of manual labor," and Jesse was helping him rake leaves one morning in the yard of a German immigrant family recently moved into Greenville; at one point, Jesse asked him, "Why those people don't talk like other folks do here?" and then was astonished to see his stepfather, pausing to lean on his rake against a tree, "start cryin'. I'd never seen him cry before. He told me, 'It's 'cause they German. I went over to Europe to fight a war to save this country from the government they had over there in their country. Now, they come over here, and can go right away into any restaurant they want. Can get a good job downtown, pretty soon can vote. But I can't. I still can't do any of those things. But don't *you* get downhearted about none of that, boy, it's gonna get better one of these days." And Jackson still recounts with huge delight the Sunday afternoon, when he was older, that his stepfather took him and his half brother, Charles Jr., to the bank building downtown where Charles Jackson was then working as a janitor: after first pointing out how "he'd sometimes find money left in the trash baskets to trap him, test him"—he was showing them how to operate the floor-buffing machine when "his boss came in with some of his buddies, called to him, 'You, Charlie, c'mere.' Father said, 'Be there in a minute.' Boss called him again—showing off for his buddies, you know—said if he didn't come right away, he'd kick him. Father said, 'Well, you might do that,' and took this bunch of keys off his belt and handed them to the guy, 'So you better takes this job back before I get in trouble, 'cause if you *do* try kicking me, you'll have only one leg left after it.' And he took me and my brother with him on out the door." As it turned out, the effect of that burst of indignation from his stepfather, says Jackson, was that "not only did his boss insist he stay on, but gave him a strong recommendation when the post office job opened up."

But later, as the civil rights movement began gathering over the South and Jackson made his first ventures into student activism—in which, he says, "I was simply carrying out my momma and daddy's sense of dignity"—his parents found, as commonly happens with values passed between generations, that dignity unexpectedly taking a form in their son that was deeply discomfiting to them. "While they had this powerful sense of pride, that didn't translate for them into marches and getting arrested." Tensions began to smolder especially between Jesse and his stepfather. "His thing was fear. Somebody gonna get killed." But a year after his rebuff at the city library, Jesse did in fact return there—twice. The first time, he and five other students, all of whom had been tutored in nonviolent confrontation by Greenville's young ministerial provocateur, the Reverend James Hall, were advised when they appeared on the library's front steps that they would be arrested should they proceed any farther, "and so," says Jackson, "we left." Incredulous, Hall wailed to Jesse, "But that's the *whole point!*" Shortly thereafter, remembers Helen Jackson, "Jesse came in and said, 'Mama, now I know you watch the news, and I'll probably go to jail this afternoon.' I said, 'You *what?*' He said, 'Go to jail. So I probably won't be back home on time, because they'll probably lock us up.' I said, 'Lock *who?*' He said, 'And if they do, don't get upset, I'll be home early as I can.'" On that mild Saturday afternoon in July, Jesse showed up at the library again, with seven other students, five of them girls, and they staged a forty-minute sit-in inside, were duly arrested, charged with disorderly conduct, and held for some forty-five minutes before being released on bail posted by Hall. Their jubilant emergence from the jail was filmed by a local television-news camera. Helen Jackson saw it on the small TV set in her home beauty shop, "and I just dropped my irons. The first time I ever saw him on television, he's coming out of jail. I said, 'What will I do from here?' My husband said, 'Ah, you'll be all right. If he's not home within the next half hour or so, I'll go over there and see what's the matter.' "

By that time, Charles Jackson's financial circumstances had improved to the degree that he had been able to move his family into an old but more commodious residence on a corner in one of the more substantial black neighborhoods—an eight-room, two-story wooden house, painted green, with a galleried front porch and an immense magnolia in the front yard. Returning there late that Saturday afternoon after his release from jail, Jesse was in the kitchen making a sandwich, as he tells it, while Charles Jackson was sitting in the adjoining den watching television. "Then he came into the kitchen, said, 'How things been, son?' Very calm, you know. 'Just fine,' I said. Then he said, still just as quiet and level, 'I work hard for this family, you agree? Your mother, too, doing those ladies' hair? Well,' he said, 'I just been watchin' yawl down there at the jail talkin' 'bout not being able to use the library, not being able to eat downtown. See that 'frigerator? Enough food in there for you? You ever had to go without a meal around here? Got enough clothes to wear? Thing is, when you out there talkin' 'bout you got to go to jail 'cause you can't get enough to read or eat someplace, that's sort of a *reflection* on me and your momma. Know you full of a lot of ideas about what all you think ain't right and all, but I don't want you bringing that trouble around here. I don't think you ever quite thought how it could affect this family. So if you can't adjust to the situation here, maybe you ought to just go away on from here."

Over time, Jackson managed to construe for himself an explanation for that chilling rebuke: "It was very painful for him, see, to have to say that to me. It was really his love for me, because of his fear of the consequences of what I'd begun doing. After all, people were getting shot in those days, homes bombed." He also offers one of his vaguely mystical reflections to account for the episode: "It's the points of pain in life, you know? They lie along the borderlines, points of pain, along the outer limits. At birth, the pain indicates something new and great is happening. When a society or a person is growing, the points of pain are the points of transition into a new life. Can't happen without the pain."

From the sit-in at the library, students continued to demonstrate through that summer in Greenville—"We hit the lunch counters, hit the swimming pools, hit the rec parks," says Hall—but without Jesse: he felt compelled now to comply with his parents' demands that he refrain from joining in any more public confrontations. They had warned him about Hall: "That young fellow over there ain't about nothing but causin' trouble." Nevertheless, when youths would assemble at Hall's house for planning sessions before setting out on another mass protest, "Jesse would slip away and come to our meetings," Hall relates, "just to be at least that much a part of it. We would sit and talk about the theology of the movement, the philosophy of nonviolence and what Gandhi and Martin Luther King were about, and Jesus as liberator. Those were very exciting discussions then, just when the movement was starting to break out everywhere, and Jesse was very forthright in his suggestions, he'd get really excited in those talks. He wanted awfully bad to go along with us, you could see it in his restlessness. He was torn, no doubt about it. But he didn't want to be disobedient and disrespectful to his parents." When the rest of them, then, gathered to head out, including Hall and his wife, Jesse was reduced to staying behind in Hall's house, "baby-sitting my daughters, who were very small then, playing with them," until everyone returned. It left him, says Hall, the most distressed he had ever seen him.

Even so, Hall soon detected the urgency forming in Jesse that "he had to go across the grain of what his mother and father were saying to him. That he had to make some determination whether or not he was going to pursue the purpose for which he was beginning to feel he was born, or be caught up in a system that would never let him be fulfilled."

A Separate Peace

THROUGH THE FOLLOWING years, arguments continued to flash between Jesse and his stepfather about the movement into which Jesse had pitched himself. In that reach for a final, widest legitimacy, he had made himself something of an alien again in his own household. To Jesse's suggestions that his stepfather rightfully belonged, like himself, marching alongside Martin Luther King, Charles Jackson replied with cynicisms about King not that different from what could be heard around the dinner table in many white homes at the time. "He'd say, 'Ah, he's just marchin' to be seen. Just wants to be out there marchin' for something, is all.' Or, on Vietnam, you could give him seven reasons why King said he was against the war, but he'd say, 'What's any preacher know about the Vietnam War?' I'd come back, 'Well, just gave you seven reasons he said he was against it, he didn't say he was just *guessing*.' But seemed like he just had to attack him. *Had* to, 'cause he couldn't afford what it would mean, at that point in his life, supporting what King was doing."

Even so, in the last years before Charles Jackson's death, in 1979, "he became very proud when I started appearing on magazine covers, *Jet*, *Time*," says Jackson. "He'd show those magazines when they came through the post office to the people he was working for—'Yawl ain't ever talked to no president or been on the front of no magazine around here.' " For Jackson, at least, it was as if it were only in the grace of his widening popular advent that, in a way as with Noah Robinson earlier, he and his stepfather, for the first time since Charles Jackson had taken over his household, reached a kind of closeness at last. With Jackson, it became in time something like a love retroactively realized, as he would later tell high school convocations of black youths: "Your daddy, just because he's bowing and scraping, he ain't doing that because he loves to bow and scrape but because he loves you enough for you to walk across on his back. He's using his body as a human bridge for you to go across."

By 1979, Charles Jackson had acquired the thick, satisfied stoutness of any placid suburban burgher, respectably mustached and graying, given to wearing soft golfing sweaters. He died suddenly, stricken while sitting in the sauna of an exercise club. Among those attending the funeral in Greenville was a trio of ladies from Jackson's PUSH ministry in Chicago, and the three of them followed Jackson and his own family now, Jackie and their five children, on to the burial service, with a seemingly endless caravan of cars twining behind them into the cemetery. Some fifteen years afterward, collected around the dining room table in Jackson's Chicago home, the three women recalled, in an interplaying chorus of still faintly uneasy wonder, Jackson's startling, abandoned, almost berserk grieving— the only time they had ever seen him utterly out of control.

"When his daddy passed, *oh, God!*"

"They put him in a mausoleum, and I thought Reverend was going to get in there with him—"

"He was trying to crawl up there *on* the casket. He was *screaming*. You talk about weeping and wailing and calling. *Daddy! Daddy!*"

"You could hear him over the whole graveyard. You could hear him in the cars, there were so many cars, wrapped around and around—"

"I kept trying to tell Jackie, 'Jackie, go *get* Jesse.' The media was out there. I said, 'Don't let them see Jesse crying like this.' She said, 'I can't move. I can't do anything with him.' Said, 'I don't think I can take this—'"

"I can still see him trying to get up there on that casket. I can still hear him, I mean, just screaming out . . . *Daddy!*"

VII
Beginning the Quest to Belong

NOT ONLY DID Jackson's growing fame seem to close somehow his boy-hood distances from both his stepfather and Noah Robinson, but over time he found it winning him a measure of favor from his hometown itself. Re-turning there once in the seventies, he phoned Dan Foster at the *Piedmont* to tell him, "I've got laryngitis or something, and you know there's not a single black doctor practicing in this town," and Foster said, "Jesse, despite our superficial differences, you realize how much alike we are inside? You want me to get you an appointment with a doctor? I'm playing tennis with one this afternoon." As Foster relates it now, "I told this doctor, 'Leslie, I don't know how much experience you've had treating *Time* cover subjects, but—' and Leslie very considerately said, 'Have him over at my office in the morning an hour before opening time.'"

For that matter, when Jesse set out for college at the University of Illinois in 1959, he did so as the recipient of surprising solicitudes on the part of that white order of Greenville from which he'd long felt irrevocably outcast. He had been admitted to Illinois, in the first place, through the intercession of Furman University's football coach, Bob King, who, having witnessed a few of Jackson's Thursday-night performances in the college's stadium, arranged for Illinois, where he'd earlier coached, to offer Jackson a scholarship. "It was prima facie at that time that no blacks were going to be playing football at any of the predominately white southern colleges," says Foster. Jesse at one point dropped by Foster's office at the *Piedmont* for counsel: "He told me he also had this offer of a baseball contract, you know, and he asked me, 'I just wonder what you think I ought to do?' I told him, 'Look, take the football thing'—if his pitching arm was that good, it'd still be good in four years, and if it wasn't, he'd sure as hell have him a good college education." Foster en-couraged him in that direction because, he says, "You can look at people and there's intelligence in their face. I didn't think I was necessarily dealing with the guy who was going to be the best orator at two Democratic national conventions, but there was just something different, something promising, about Jesse." Finally, Judge Clement F. Haynsworth himself called him into his chambers and, his plump pear-shaped face flushing pink behind his spectacles, pronounced a gently stammerous blessing upon him—to the effect that he had proved himself a worthy boy, a source of pride to his parents, and if he kept his head clear and bent to his books, he would fare fine.

It had, in fact, become Jesse's own eagerness now to escape the South's racial travailings—"It felt awfully good just to be getting away from all that tension"—and in the cool, quiescent refuge of that distant northern campus, to apply himself to his own self-improvement rather than to any social militancy. As it would turn out, he was to swing back and forth in a fretful ambivalence between those two urges until the end of his college years—alternately lurching out into a swirl of public activism and then contracting back once again into earnest attentions to the personal life. At Urbana, he immediately enclosed himself in a private world of studying, football, social sporting; he joined a black fraternity, Omega Psi Phi. Out of his old avidity to belong, he seemed to be devoutly pursuing his image of that full, easy normalcy of life that had been denied him from his birth; delivered to this campus in "the legendary liberalism of the North," as he recalls his anticipation, he would at last begin to enter into the main story of American society. At Illinois, he curiously now kept most of his past to himself. "I never had any inkling there'd been any difficulty in his background at all," says another black freshman on the football team, Michael Summers. "Never a mention of it from him. All I knew, his family always saw to it that he had plenty of home-cooked food, like sweet-potato pies, he always had lots of stuff like that in his room that came from home." In all, Summers remembers, "he was just another big, rawboned dude with an assured sense of himself," and by Summers's testimony, still voluble: "I mean, he really *loved* to talk. He was a master at that."

An additional exhilaration about being at Illinois, Jackson says, was that "we were always aware in Greenville that the best and brightest of us would probably be the breakthrough crowd, the generation that'd open the system up. It was just in the air then. And I felt I was gonna be one of them. What made it especially sweet, I was at a *Big Ten* school, where people actually looked *down* on Furman and Clemson. I thought that proved I was more than qualified for those colleges in the South that wouldn't let me in." All that was now required, he assumed, was the diligence and enterprise in which he'd been tutored in those exacting classrooms back in Greenville. "I thought," he says, "that I was doing everything right."

Soon, though, misgivings gathered. When he reported for his first day of football practice, one coach pointed to a small group of other blacks on the field and notified him, "Now you're like those guys over there." Jackson says, "I'd just left that Greenville–Sterling High dual system thing, you know. But the mere thought of playing before thousands, ten games a year, in that uniform with Illinois's colors and a number, I mean, that was *important to me*." His wife, Jackie, now offers, "He was a black boy coming from the South with the greatest expectations. I'm not going to suggest to you that he was the greatest football player ever, but you could not find a football player who had as much excitement, as much desire, as Jesse Jackson did." While he once quarterbacked the freshman team to a victory over the varsity in an intramural scrimmage, he was soon shunted from quarterback to accessory positions. "They switched him first to halfback," says Michael Summers, "and then they moved him up front somewhere on the line. It was a long, long way from quarterback, the glamour position." Jackson would afterward maintain that "they told me blacks could not be quarterbacks," even in the Big Ten. But Illinois's starting quarterback also happened to be black. Summers, who arrived at Illinois from the Chicago suburb of Evanston, suggests, "It was really his accent. He had that southern accent, a little bit slower speech pattern and thick drawl even to me, and they told him it threw people off their rhythm." Even so, Summers reflects, "a necessary evil would have been all we'd've been perceived by some of them. Like, 'Hey, if we're going to win, we need them, but we don't have to like them, they smell bad,' all that. I had a buddy from Louisiana, came there as a running back. After the middle of his sophomore year, he told the coaches, 'I didn't come all the way up here from Louisiana to get the same kind of treatment. I'd rather go back home and take my chances there than deal with this northern version of the same thing I left in the South.' And he quit, went back home."

Jackson would later relate that "while the white guys were out there partying with girls on weekends, the blacks sat in their dorms drinking Coke and playing cards." Further, leaflets were once slipped into the mailboxes of the black athletes on campus, warning them they were at Illinois only to play ball and "not to socialize" with the white coeds. When some black athletes complained to the athletic director about this admonition, says Jackson, he stunned them by recommending they heed it: "said, 'It's not important, things like this happen, we must not let the press know and bring a bad image to our school.' "

Steadily, almost casually, similar humiliations accumulated like whiffs of old, familiar sulfurs. Black students were not allowed into a concert by the Count Basie band, while, Jackson says, at a party his fraternity gave the next weekend, "all we had for music was those little ole scratchy forty-fives." Before long, a cold realization settled over him. "All that time I'd been imagining that Illinois had to be different from places down South, it wasn't atall. I wasn't prepared to handle that—I was going to the land of Lincoln, you know, the Promised Land of the North. But it was the same thing as South Carolina, just way off somewhere else." Indeed, when he returned to Illinois during the Christmas break to complete his speech, after the Greenville library had refused him the books he needed, he was walking to the university's library when he heard, from white students arriving back on campus, yells of "Nigger! Nigger, your ass is grass, and we're the lawn mower." Jackson says, "It was the first time I'd ever really heard that expression. Never heard it down in Greenville, never heard it before, until I was walking across that campus back in Illinois." But when he at last completed his speech, he delivered it to his class, composed mostly of seniors, and they voted him one of the three students to be sent to an annual state oratorical competition. Jackson was so elated, he dispatched a telegram to his mother. The professor, however, relegated him to being an alternate. Then, when one of the other students withdrew, Jackson wound up speaking anyway. But while two of the judges accorded him close to the 9.0 perfect mark, Jackson says, the third dropped him almost five points lower, with the notation, "Negro dialect."

Only a few months into his freshman year, he had drifted into a deepening dislocation. His classwork began to falter. Feeling himself now merely one of an isolated minority on the campus, surrounded by a light contempt and not infrequent derision, he floundered on in a distress that was all the more harrowing because "I was supposed to be one of those representing our race there, carrying that responsibility. Couldn't hardly bear the idea of failing and being ashamed and disappointing, embarrassing your people." He still managed to present a brave front, recalls Summers: "I thought he was completely confident and comfortable about himself. But you know, we all cover up someplace. He was doing what he had to do. There wasn't a fallback position, didn't have Dad waiting there, 'Well, you can come work in the family business.' He had to make it." But that year at Illinois, which had begun in such hope, had turned into an ordeal, Jackson now confesses, that "came close to breaking my spirit."

Toward the end of classes in the spring, he approached Summers with a request that he return some books for him to the library. "It was a minor thing," says Summers, "but it was the way in which he asked—the quick laugh, the hesitancy. I didn't know what it was, just there was something different about him, not his normal bravado. Instead, a kind of reaching out for help that showed me, for the only time, a lack of security in him. Although I wasn't aware of it, he was preparing to go back home. And so it was almost like a pleading: 'I'm a little unanchored now in terms of what

I'm doing or where I'm going or how I'm going to even do when I get there. Can you at least help me with this one part of it? Take these books back for me?' With a kind of melancholy at this disconnecting taking place."

Finally defeated in his first real frontal attempt to move into the society at large, he forsook Illinois at the end of that freshman year—with a despairing suspicion that the racism in which he'd grown up in Greenville was in fact the mentality, in whatever blander attenuations, of the rest of the nation as well, along with a wariness, for the rest of his life, about "letting yourself get overwhelmed and lost in the majority mainstream." Retreating to the familiar ground of the South, he chose "the sanctuary," as he describes it, of North Carolina Agricultural & Technical College, a mostly black institution in Greensboro.

Actually, it happened that some in the family of his mother's father—this man's mother and two of his sisters—had lived across the street from A & T, and had even taken Helen in for a while during her teenage pregnancy to shelter her from the scandal in Greenville, and, Jackson says, "It had always been Mama's first choice for me to go to school there." But when he presented himself there to enroll, at summer's end in 1960, a procedural difficulty developed. The school's president at the time, Dr. Samuel Proctor, recalls, "I was sitting in my office and the public relations director came bursting in, round little fella with a round face, named Ellis Corbett, came rushing in all in a big huff and sweat and puffing: 'Doc! Doc! We got a fella downstairs who spent a year at Illinois trying to get on the football team, and now he wants to be a star here. But they're giving him a hard time down there in the registrar's office.' Said, 'Doc, don't let those jackasses turn him down, it will be a big mistake.' " Proctor chuckles. "The first day Jesse's on campus, and the P.R. man is rushing to my office like lightning just struck the barn—I mean, the first time he'd ever *seen* him. That's the way Jesse was. Corbett, his little fat self bouncin' in excited, 'Doc, you know how these registrars are, all they want is to keep the paper clean. Man, you've got a *bigger* picture here to deal with!' I said, 'What is it that's so striking about this guy?' He said, 'Doc, just don't let them turn him down. You'll find out.' So I said, 'All right, go down and tell the registrar that I said to let him in, and then come here and tell me the details and we'll work them out.' "

It was a considerably more modest campus than Illinois—a few low, stark, redbrick buildings distributed over rough-grassed grounds under old oaks and magnolias, the site of an army camp during World War Two, with all the men students quartered in a single, block-long dorm of bare concrete floors and cinder-block rooms. Even though four A & T students had, the winter before, begun a series of lunch-counter sit-ins that would eventually spread over the South, for Jackson, it was as if he had simply re-turned to a version of the snugly insulated Elysium of his high school days. He eagerly immersed himself in his studies, became an honor student, and soon turned into a celebrity quarterback again (though, as some team-mates later recollected, with rather a careful self-containment when it came to blocking for other runners). Fellow student Robert Patterson, who was one of the leaders of the sit-in demonstrations, recollects that "Jesse Jackson may have been one of the very few college students then who'd play religious songs in his room. You'd pass by and hear gospel music com-ing out of his room, Mahalia Jackson and the Soul Stirrers. That was some-thing kind of unheard-of, especially with Jesse being a football star and all." Before long, he had emerged as a social bravo on campus, jaunty in narrow-brim hats and plaid sport jackets, an ebullient fraternity fellow. Journeying to a general convention of Omega Psi Phi, he got himself elected to a national post bearing the majestic nomenclature of Second Vice-Grand Basileus—after disposing of a challenge from the floor by one of his opponent's supporters, a young Virginian named Douglas Wilder. In time, he was elected president of A & T's student body.

"Yeah, Jesse was big in stature and big in ideas," remembers Dr. Proctor, "and big in aggressiveness." Indeed, his open, earnest ambitiousness did not go unremarked by Proctor. "He had an idea that he wanted to be close to the president," says Proctor with a slow smile, and though Jesse had few aspects of the ministerial about him then, when Proctor, who was himself a minister, delivered a message in chapel, "he would come up afterward and say, 'Doctor, I needed that sermon today. I wish I could get more of that.'" After a while, on trips to academic meetings out of town, Proctor frequently found he had Jesse riding along in the car with him. "He would stay close to my secretary to find out when I would be going."

Still, though, he scrupulously avoided any involvement in the student sit-ins sporadically under way in Greensboro.

Then, after taking a semester off for surgery in Greenville on a knee in-jured in football, he returned to the A & T campus in 1961, and came upon a vibrantly attractive and blithe-spirited coed, five foot two but as extrava-gantly energetic as he, named Jacqueline Lavinia Brown—called, by everyone, Jackie.

A Courtship

HER OWN CHILDHOOD had been, if anything, even more unsettled than his. She had been born to a sixteen-year-old migrant farm worker in Fort

Pierce, Florida, who picked beans and tomatoes for fifteen cents an hour from Florida to Virginia, and whose own mother "was what you would call a lady of the evening," she reports. She recalled her progression to that campus in Greensboro many years later while sitting in the front parlor of her Washington home—a woman still of lavish enthusiasms, with a flaring grin and a lusty, belting voice seeming too big and brawling to come from so small if still plush a figure. She never came to know her father, Jackie says, only that he was a Rastafarian. She and her mother, Gertrude, were soon taken in by a woman next door, herself not much older than Gertrude, who became for Jackie thereafter "my aunt," and who, says Jackie, "soon decided that she wanted me to live with her for the rest of my life." When Jackie was about six, her mother married a military service-man in Virginia and left to live with him in Newport News, but "my aunt determined she was going to keep me for herself. My mother had a little fight with her, because she wanted me to come to Virginia. But she couldn't do anything about it. My aunt was the moving force." Her name was Juanita, and she effectively raised Jackie until her death when Jackie was twelve. In the sandy flats of that migrant community of haphazard shanties under high thin pines hung with rags of moss, Jackie grew up in the loose and vagrant freedoms of an earthily natural girlhood. Already an unconfinable spirit, she scuttled everywhere about the dirt tracks of the neighborhood happily barefooted: "I never wore shoes there. I have never liked shoes since."

Juanita was a short woman, "dark complected," says Jackie, "with very negroid features"; she weighed a solid three hundred pounds and was fear-some with her fists: "I mean, she used to fight *physically.*" When Jackie was once whipped at school by a teacher—"I always talked too much"—the next morning Juanita walked her to the school and "she beat the teacher." Jackie reminisces now, "She was a tough woman. Had enormous respect in the community. And she was very good to me." It was from this stumpy and lumberous guardian—dark, homely, balefully combative, simple, indefatigable in this one elemental affection given to her—that Jackie first discovered, she says, "a true love and pride of womanhood. It was through her that I really first began to want to be a great woman." She still periodically travels down to Fort Pierce to place memorial wreaths on her grave.

Juanita also happened to be the area's bootlegger, keeping her half-pint bottles of moonshine buried under the dirt floor of a chicken coop in the backyard. From the age of six, says Jackie, "I was one of those she singled out to run the bottles." When men dropped by in the middle of the night to make a purchase, Jackie would be awakened to go out, barefooted, into the moldy reek and alarmed fluster of the chicken coop to dig up a bottle: "I'd rinse it off in the yard, run some water over my feet, and bring it back in for the customer."

When she was a little older, she began serving as a lookout as well, perched in a mango tree, for neighborhood youths slipping into the tin-sheeted garage below for quick scuffles of copulation, dropping a mango on the roof with a heavy clang at anyone's approach. In the course of this sentry work, she became herself smitten, around the age of eleven, with one of the boys frequenting the garage. "His name was Charles Dewberry," she declares, "and he was my hero. I *loved* Charles Dewberry. Somehow I'd come to see men as powerful, believable, supposed to be able to think and do things. And so with Charles Dewberry. Once when I wanted a puppy, Charles Dewberry told me if I got some dog defecation that's turned white and buried it six inches in the ground, and if I'd go back the next night, the puppy would be there. So the first time I saw a dog near the place where I'd buried the defecation, I chased it, 'cause I *knew* that dog was mine. And that dog turned and bit the shit out of me."

Her adoration of Charles Dewberry managed to survive this incidental disillusionment. She finally demanded that he take her into the garage, too. "I had no real idea what they were actually doing in there. All I knew was that they seemed to like each other, and I wanted Charles Dewberry to show that he liked me, too. I told Charles Dewberry I wasn't gonna be his lookout girl anymore until he did the same thing with me. You should have seen his face. But he took me into the garage and told me to lie down and when he got on top of me to say, 'Ooch, ouch, ooch, ouch,' like the other girls did. There was no sex, of course, just, 'Ooch, ouch.' And that *was* sex, I thought, that's all it was"—an assumption that lasted, she insists, over all the years up to her encounter with Jesse at A & T. But for the rest of her life, she declares, "I loved that boy. Charles Dewberry."

With Juanita's death, though, Jackie moved at last to Newport News, Virginia, to live with her mother, and there she found herself, after the easy barefooted freedoms of Fort Pierce, clapped into a rigorous drilling in the decorums of comportment. "I had to stop cursing, and take ballet and piano lessons. I had to walk around the house with books on my head. Sitting, you cross your ankles! Fold your hands, place them to the side, keep your back erect, don't bow your head, look straight in the eyes of the people you're speaking with! I'd get so many whippings for all these niceties. My mother kept polishing me and polishing me." Such cultural ambitions would seem somehow improbable from one so long a migrant farm laborer, but even in the migrant community of Fort Pierce, reports Jackie, there was a sort of fierce respect for the respectable: "When drunkards saw the teachers on the street, or even the barbers, they'd try to straighten themselves up and say good morning," and if someone saw a child behaving rudely, "they'd pick them up and say, 'Don't act like that,' or say, 'Take your hat off.' " Indeed, for virtually all black Americans at that time, there was little more than that value of a self-dignity allowed to them. In Newport News now, says Jackie, all excursions beyond her home were restricted to her Catholic church and her school. "I had to be home from school at three-thirty. Had to go to church. I won all sorts of Bible verse contests there. I knew damn near all the hundred Psalms — every Psalm." She even came to believe for a time that she wanted to be a nun.

Then, when the moment drew close for her departure for college at A & T, for the first time since her girlhood in Fort Pierce, "it was the greatest freedom I'd ever imagined. I was walking out of my mother's door, and she wouldn't know where I was. It was like, I can *talk* again." Before leaving, she sewed a wardrobe for herself, from fabric she had bought at Woolworth's, and she landed on A & T's campus somewhat sensationally, "in the most provocative clothes," she cheerfully recounts, "all very tight. I had the greatest body in the world — thirty-seven, twenty-two, thirty-six — and I mean, they *fit*." This ensemble ran toward parrot-bright colors, and her long, glassy-black hair she streaked with a single orange blaze. At the same time, she took to scurrying about the campus, as she had in Fort Pierce, barefooted. "If I was in a hurry, I'd just put my shoes in my bag and run, because I run better without shoes"; when she neared her destination, "I'd slip on my little stockings, put my heels on — do it anywhere, by a car, run into a room — and then walk on to the place."

Rather rapidly, "I acquired a tremendous reputation," as she puts it. "I was invited to all the parties. I was unattached, unavailable, but very outspoken — a very exciting person! Everybody looked up to me because I was the *whomsoever*." Sitting amid the heavily Victorian decor of her front room now, over thirty years later, she shines with glee again at the memory. "Everybody knew me, would say, 'Hi, Jackie! Hi, Jackie!' Oh, yes, I was some kind of cute during that time. But, ah, time," she groans, "time, *time* . . ."

Yet she remained, in a way, still whimsically innocent. "I didn't have boyfriends, didn't have sex. I've always had the big bosom, the little waist, the butt — always had that. But I never knew what to do with it," and she laughs, a rich-throated cackle. And neither, she adds, "did I know what to do with my seriousness," and for all her florid siren's wardrobe, she still wanted most of all to be a nun: "It was the only way I knew I could say I had values. I was very serious about wanting to go into the convent." But then, she says, "the nuns came out with that 'Dominique, dah deet, dah deet' thing," which somehow signified to her that "the cloister and all that was a little too tight, [and] they were getting ready to fly on up here into the world." Soon, she says, "I was less interested in being told and instructed, and started looking deeper into things for myself. Also, America in the sixties was about to begin to live. Everything prior to that had been on paper. Now America began to think, We're gonna have to *live* what we been preaching." From that, she shortly developed into a spirited leftist militant on campus, an enthusiast of Castro's then two-year-old revolution. "I was very much into international affairs. I wanted to go somewhere in that."

Late one rainy afternoon, she took a stroll to the canteen, where the football players, after practice, would ritualistically line up on both sides of the walkway right outside, "so you had to pass through them. They'd shout, 'Hey, whatcha doin' this evenin'?' It wasn't what they'd say today, but it was still offensive," and she goes into dialect, " 'Ah shuah like the way you wawk! *Mmm-hmmh.* Look a'dat. Saint Peter must be dead, 'cause an *angel* just fell out of heaven!' " Passing through such observations from the gallery of players that evening, says Jackie, "I had my strut anyway. Most of the girls would complain you couldn't go to the canteen because of the football boys there, but I didn't walk through that line gently—I mean, like, hell, I gave them a *number*, I played with them, and went on." Then she heard a voice bay out, "Hey, girl! I'm gonna *marry* you." She turned, as she tells it now, "with that 'marry you.' Looked around, you know, like"—and she performs a quick, wide-eyed, accosted gape of startled curiosity; it was her first sight of Jesse—"Those were the first words I ever heard from Jesse Jackson. To be perfectly honest with you, I stepped into a puddle when I turned to see who'd said this. Ruined my black suede pumps. But I just kept on walking, I moved on." Her immediate impression was "he was just trying to outdo the other guys, because I was a very popular girl. I had an attitude that I didn't care about them," and, she asserts, not only might Jesse have found that bewitching, "they *all* found it bewitching. I had many callers and pursuers. But his comment stood out. It stood out."

After that, "I started running from that moment on every time I saw him. I don't know *why* he made me so nervous, but he did." She regarded him, from a distance still, as "a bit too full of himself. He was always wearing his fraternity sweater, and I saw him as one of the others in the fraternities. They thought themselves better than the rest of the students, had some small, class-bullshit thing, and to hell with them. I did not like people who did that, a group of people defining themselves as more special than all the little people." She surmises now that "he saw that I had a disdain." But when he again came across her as she was walking to an evening tutorial class and finally introduced himself, "he was extremely courteous; asked,

'May I walk with you?'" He later took her to eat at a café, and at the table—where they were to divide between them a fifty-cent bologna sandwich—"he pulled out the seat for me, I mean, he was Johnny-on-the-spot. After we got married, now I wait for him to hold that seat, he's shaking hands with the waiter and everybody else he can reach, I fall on the floor. But then, he was extremely polite. He was very interested." As for herself, Jackie says, "I still didn't take him seriously. But I *liked* him. He was trying very hard to be nice to me, and I wanted to be nice to him." More, she remembers, "I felt an innocence in him. I was innocent, too, probably stupider than he was, but I really sensed his naïveté."

They were both sociology majors, with Jackie pursuing a second major in psychology, but when they began keeping company, Jesse was appalled by her political ardors, which were far more effusively radical than anything he, the campus gallant, had ever thought of entertaining. "Every time I saw Jesse, I'd say, 'Hey, man, look what's happening!' Fidel Castro, I thought he was just incredible, he was like the new world order—oh, I would have *kissed* him. But Jesse was very cautious, reserved. 'Fidel Castro? Communist? I mean, *really*—you shouldn't go around talking like this, you may get in trouble, you should stay out of these things.' I was going to get thrown out of school, that was his concern." When she nevertheless elected to write a paper suggesting that Red China should be admitted as an observer to the U.N., "Well, it was like, 'You've gone too far now, you're really gonna be put out of school, especially if you argue this in class.'"

On the whole, he initially struck her as close to insufferably stilted, careful, reverential of the prevailing proprieties—she not fully knowing yet of his huge urgencies for legitimacy. "He was going to church every Sunday," she recites, and soon he began undertaking to haul her along with him. "I'd gone to church every Sunday in Virginia because my mother forced it on me, and here I am in college with this new freedom, and this man is talking about making me go to church again? A football player, supposed to drink beer, be foolish, *bad* on campus? He should really be a right-wing Christian. Every Sunday morning he's calling, 'You going to church?' Got to where, when the phone rang, I'd tell my roommate, 'If it's Jesse, tell him I'm not here.'"

About two evenings a week, he would bring a small detachment from his fraternity to her dorm and "they would stand under my window and sing those hit songs of that day—'Mr. Postman, look and see if there's a letter there for me'—Smokey Robinson songs." His mother would occasionally drive up from Greenville "with a trunkful of pies," says Jackie, "and she would leave him with five dollars. He would share one of his sweet-potato pies with me, and give me a dollar of his money—but tell me,

'Now, you're not to use this to buy cigarettes from the canteen.' I mean, he would *organize* that dollar, understand what I'm saying?" The sensation increased that he was assuming a pronounced proprietary manner toward her. "He decided that he would watch me. He went to work in the office at the school, and he would come back to *share* with me my grades. Told me I had to do better, that I had to be in my classes. He'd say, 'You have Humanities at eight-thirty in the morning, and I stopped by your class and you weren't there,' which I thought was just a little too much. I didn't want to tell him that 'I go late to avoid you.' "

While he seemed to grow progressively more serious, says Jackie, "I never got serious—I got angry. I felt he was trying to take a father's role over me, almost." At the approach of each weekend, a list would be posted in the women's dorm of those invited to fraternity parties, "and my name would hit that list every time," says Jackie. Suddenly, though, she discovered her name had disappeared from that weekly posting, and she finally inquired of one fraternity member if he knew why. "He told me, 'You better see Jesse. Aren't yawl involved?' I said, 'No! He's just a friend.' But no one believed that, because he had notified the guys that I *was* involved with him." She then hotly confronted him, protesting that "he was undercutting me, undermining me. I said, 'I'm not going with you, you're not my boyfriend,' " to which, she reports, "he merely sat there calmly and said, 'I understand that,' " but then proceeded to advise her on how a lady should appropriately behave, and that her frisking through a round of fraternity parties every weekend "I don't think is healthy for you." Nonetheless, she demanded he go back to his friends and inform them that she was not under any claim by him. As a result, she reappeared on the list—but only as invited, by him, to his own fraternity's party.

"Well, that's the only one I can go to now, so I went," she says. "All the guys there invited me to dance, 'cause I loved to dance," and with a liveliness, by her own proud testimony, tending toward the Dionysian: "Whenever the music began, the guy would swing me around, and, *oh,* I'd fall all over him, I mean, I'd cut loose, I had *all* the moves." If nobody happened to step forth to ask her onto the floor, "I'd ask a guy for a dance. During that time, you didn't do that. But my feeling, if it's a dance, you *dance.*" Finally, Jesse took her aside and admonished her to "sit and wait to be asked to dance. He felt I was bein' a little too, uh, aggressive." As one recourse for containing her, he would now and then take her onto the floor himself, "but I still did my dance. And he'd say, 'Why don't you cool it, why don't you calm down?' "

In time, she allows, "I grew to hate him. Like, hey, wait, you're doing something to me that I don't want to happen to me. But he just quietly started taking over my life." She bubbles into another rich, incredulous laugh. "It's interesting how he does that. I see him doing people like that today, and I want to tell him, 'Don't, just don't do it. . . .' "

Eventually, he asked her to accompany him to "what he told me was a surprise birthday party for a fraternity friend of his," says Jackie, "a guy named DeCarlos, who was the most popular Omega. Of course, to be invited to that made me feel just the belle of the ball. I even had my mother send me a very expensive dress that we'd had on layaway a very long time." Only later, Jackie declares, did she realize that Jesse had tried to give her to understand that it would be the occasion when "he was gonna introduce me to the splendors of sex." As she recounts that night, he picked her up at the dorm with a manner about him of almost excruciatingly exquisite courtliness, and on their arrival at the house, deposited the two of them on a sofa in a downstairs room, where they proceeded to chat while she noticed a persistent traffic of people up and down the stairs to the floor above. "I sat there beside him, had my little black dress on, gorgeous," and after a while, she says, "he's trying to reach, trying to—and I said, 'Oh, no, don't touch my hair,' because I had it all twisted and teased up into a sixties beehive. He said, 'Oh, no, you can get comfortable,' " supposing her disconcerted by the procession continuing on the stairs, " 'that's just Brother So-and-so.' "

But, says Jackie, "people kept passing back and forth, and I kept waiting for the cake, for the surprise. But see, *I* was supposed to be the party." For all his past corsairing, he now seemed strangely awkward and lumpish. "There were other girls there, but they all seemed busy upstairs, and as they'd then come down to say good night, we're still sitting on that sofa. This looks bad for him, you understand. He was supposed to have enough conversation for this kind of situation. One of the guys came down and said, 'Man, you not doin' so well, hunh?' " It was at that point, says Jackie, that "I asked, 'Well, when is this guy DeCarlos coming? It's getting late, I've got to get back to the dorm.' " By now, says Jackie, "he's very frustrated, and he says, 'Well, I guess we'll just go.' I said, 'You mean you're not having the *party*?' You know, I'd been sitting there, and these people moving back and forth, all these little comments, and then they were leaving, and I *still* didn't get it. That I'd been duped.

"So when my husband took me to this party that never happened," she continues, "after he did that to me, that was it for him. I figured it was a trick." It was only then that he found himself obliged to explain exactly what was meant to transpire that evening. "I told my roommate, and she said, 'Jackie, Jesse is your boyfriend, and you're supposed to do these things.' " She had, by now, actually been unable to resist a brimming fondness for him—they had both, in fact, become taken by a large and thrumming restlessness each sensed in the nature of the other. "I knew when I met him that he was going to be the most exciting person in this country one day," Jackie now professes, "and that I would be the second most interesting person in the country." But the implication in her roommate's exhortation was "that something was wrong with me," says Jackie. "*I* felt something was wrong with me. So I had to take the test, had to get this initiation over with, knew I had to do it." The one, unsuspected complication was that she still supposed, she contends, that it all amounted to only the prone idle shuffle and accompanying vocal effects of that business in the garage in her aunt's backyard down in Fort Pierce: "I thought it'd just be Charles Dewberry again."

The transaction at last took place, "not at a motel, oh, no," from which, she points out, blacks were then still excluded, but at "a black brothel"—an old, drably weathered, hulking wooden-frame building, like a derelict boardinghouse, on the frowsy edge of town. When they entered, "it was very dim inside," she remembers. "Very dim. There was a lady sitting there in a little room, and you gave her five dollars. They had made many rooms in the house, and it was big to me. It was scary. It was without champagne glasses and all that." But, she declares, it did not even occur to her to expect any more glamorous an aura to attend this occasion: "Not at all. Because I wasn't living then in *today*, I was still living yesterday—from the chicken coop, remember? I transferred Charles Dewberry in the garage now to Jesse Jackson here." Accordingly, she says, "I acted as if I had done this before. Until we finished. And I said, 'Why did we do that?' I told him, 'I got nothing from that. I think it's a waste of time.' He looked at me as if—" and she produces a mock stare of stricken astonishment. "As a male who'd had girlfriends, I know I must have thrown him to say, like, you didn't perform well or something, that you didn't knock me down," and the unbelieving, exasperated distress on his face, she merrily suggests, has never in a sense entirely passed away in his regard of her.

But what finally and conclusively committed her to him, she admits, "was his patience with me. And as I said, I *liked* him." And from that point on it was as if a kind of compact formed between them: "I was one of the people around the chicken coop, and I never wanted to be. But one day . . . you *will* make it out of the chicken coop, because you're special. And at A & T I found that he, too, had the same circumstance, from how he grew up in Greenville. We had this tree where we'd meet and talk all the time," Jackie relates, "how he wanted to work in the movement some way. We didn't talk about how we would have a Cadillac and live in a house on a hill. It was about where we were going to go: one day we would go to Africa, one day see the Great Wall of China. We were talking about the exciting things we were going to experience." Then, under that tree one evening, says Jackie, "he suddenly told me, 'I'm a bastard.' And I said, 'I'm one, too. Isn't everyone?' See, I thought most other people were, too." He wanted her to know this about him, Jackie reflects, "because there was still some tension in South Carolina as a result of his birth, some things not resolved that created some pain in him. But I made that pain insignificant. I let him know that who his father is or was made no difference to me.

"So we both wanted to get out, to *go*," Jackie continues. "We felt we were at A & T to obtain something much greater than the small towns and communities we'd left, to make a difference in the world. And then to bring that big something back to those communities, to create a new community. That's what we agreed on. We were very serious young people, we thought we were part of a bigger idea about society. And we went together. As we then grew, from A & T to Chicago, we *were* going. But we were going with a people, because every black person is responsible for every other black person. We could not go by ourselves, we had to go with our people. And I was going with my aunt 'Nita. And with my mother, who kept saying tó me, 'Girl, go! Go, go, go!' And I *did* go." She pauses for a moment, sitting on the edge of her Victorian couch now after the long sweep of her years with Jesse since that dim five-dollar room in the black bordello in Greensboro. "Now you've made me very sad," she murmurs. "I wasn't supposed to be here. . . ." She then pulls herself upright, her back erect, her head lifted. "But it's a story for my people—to get out, to go. And I *am* so *happy* to be black and fifty and where I am at this day and in this time. Because I know where we came from." At the Democratic convention in 1988, she relates, "When he said that 'people see me running, but they don't see what I'm running from,' it was the most jolting thing, because I didn't know he was going to be saying that publicly. After that, I heard nothing else that he said. Because I was thinking about South Carolina, and about Fort Pierce, Florida, and about racism and having a skin that's dark in this country, and yet here we are, pleading with you to let us help make America better. I sat there, and nobody knows how hard I had to fight back tears."

SOMETIME IN THE late fall of 1962, Xanthene Norris, Jesse's high school French teacher back in Greenville, was surprised to get a call from him, in which, after announcing that he was getting married, he began to reminisce about the many private talks they'd had at Sterling, including discussions about his relations with girls. "He'd tell me back then, 'I wouldn't have sex with a girl I wouldn't marry,' " recalls Ms. Norris, "and he said on the phone now, 'You remember that thing we used to talk about?' I knew then that he'd gotten caught." But Jackie maintains that she wound up pregnant by a deliberate design of his, to hasten her into marrying him and starting a family of his own: "It was the only way he could have gotten me, and he knew it."

The wedding was set for New Year's Eve, in his stepfather's home in Greenville, and that Monday twilight in December turned out unusually warm, almost like a summer dusk. Up until only a minute or two before the ceremony, while Jackie waited in the wedding dress she had made herself—an eggshell silk gown, circumspectly tailored with a high waist—Jesse remained upstairs, working on a speech with several friends for another oratorical contest in a few days. "I hated that group," Jackie recalls. "They were always huddling. My husband comes from a generation of men huddling." Jackson at last came downstairs, in a grave dark-blue suit, "completely self-possessed," remembers his boyhood friend Owen Perkins; it was that same bearing of an even, considered deliberation, recalled by Perkins from their youth, of simply proceeding with "this next thing I'm going to do." And in Helen Jackson's small, wallpapered front parlor—thronged with an accumulation of ornate furnishings, "She had her real sho nuff stuff in there," says another friend, which now had been shoved aside to allow some space for the ceremony—Jesse and Jackie were married by the preacher from Long Branch Baptist, the Reverend D. S. Sample.

Making His Own Family

OVER THE FOLLOWING years, despite the disorderly winds of the public life in which he came mostly to dwell, Jackson yet managed to create, with Jackie, a remarkably sturdy home and family for himself, as if in a kind of resolute compensation for the ragged irregularity of his own boyhood as an illegitimate child living in another man's precariously poor household. Jackson now proudly recites, "Over thirty years. One wife. Five children. Broke the cycle. Stability, security."

Six months after he and Jackie were married, their first child was born, a daughter they named Santita, and over the next twelve years, there followed three sons and then another daughter, who was named for Jackie. "He wanted a family quickly," Jackie recounts, "but we were having babies so fast, my friends were saying that Jesse was gonna have babies coming out of the chimney. Once Martin Luther King came over to our place, and he saw that I was pregnant again. He said, 'Jesse, boy, I'm going to have to give you a raise so you can buy you a *television set*. So you can find something *else* to do.' " Their five children were raised for the most part in the Chicago house to which Jackson moved the family in 1970. Located on a narrow, quiet street of ample brick and stucco homes, close together under heavy trees, in a mellow neighborhood on the city's South Side, just beyond the end of Lake Shore Drive, it was a spacious white mortar dwelling with Tudor trim and stained-glass windows, of even more expansive dimensions than that corner residence with the *R* on the chimney down in Greenville—on its own chimney now a *J* in scrolled script, with two stone lions perched with heraldic stone tablets atop each end of its gable roof.

Inside, its commodious rooms were filled with a chaotic clutter, its creaking floors steadily laden over time, from Jackie's gusto for accumulating antiques, with heavy, dark, Victorian furniture and rococo cut-glass ornaments, a red velvet rope like those in opera house lobbies running up one side of the stairs, with giant fluted lampshades swathed in plastic sitting on the floor, the white lace cloth draped over the long dining room table scattered with hatboxes, an empty champagne bottle, a capless bottle of corn syrup. In this general dishabille, assorted visitors were usually milling about in an insistent shrilling of telephones. For his children, growing up amid this amiably pandemonious disarray through the years of Jackson's improvisational activism, their father's exact business was no less a puzzlement than it proved for others trying to precisely parse him. The middle son, Jonathan, recalls, "Kids'd be talking, you know, one says, 'My father's a doctor,' others say, 'My father's a teacher, a policeman, a lawyer.' When they ask you what your father does, what can you tell them? I couldn't say he was a reverend because he didn't actually have a church. He goes around talking to people, trying to help them? Frankly, I never knew exactly what to tell them. When they'd ask me what he did, I'd just say, 'He's Jesse Jackson.' " But like many other children of the famed, they found in time they had been born by happenstance into a public exposure whose real extent they could never quite be sure of, or know when uninvited reactions might suddenly blast back at them: "Kid would come up to me," remembers Jonathan, "and say, 'My father says your father is *dead wrong*.' And I didn't even know who his father *was*, much less what it was he thought was wrong with mine. All you can say is, 'I'm sorry to hear that.' But it did bother some."

Nevertheless, Jackson and his wife managed to bring up their five children through the turbulent magnetic field of his celebrity with assiduous care. They came to present—it is at least one matter Jackson's admirers and antagonists generally concur on—one of the most refreshing and commending things about him. Uniformly genial and open young people, unflaggingly polite, they seemed a surpassingly wholesome lot. The country at large discovered them when all five appeared together on the rostrum at the 1988 Democratic convention to deliver testimonials to their father: in their assured and articulate earnestness, their simple brightness of nature, they produced a virtual national carillon of acclaim, and a journalist for *Esquire* was moved to pronounce, "In a little under ten minutes of prime time the Jackson children replaced the Cosbys as America's first black family." They sent an even more profound tide of pride swelling through the nation's black community: as one minister in Flint, Michigan, rejoiced afterward to his congregation, "What a marvelous message to America about the black family that was!"

One long acquaintance of the Jacksons proposes, "Those children are mostly Jackie's handiwork, actually." Jackie herself declares, "They were really raised by a nation," by which she principally means the membership in Jackson's PUSH operation in Chicago. One of those faithful acknowledges, "Those kids had a lot of parents. Everybody looked out after them, drove them to school, picked them up from school," and, says another, "Anybody who saw them doing something bad would whip them." When Jackson himself was at home, his own discipline at times partook of the stern style in which he had been reared: one PUSH member relates that Jesse Jr. one evening kept jumping from a stair landing to the vestibule below despite repeated reprimands from other PUSH members in the house, unaware that Jackson was sitting in the living room right off the vestibule, reading, until, at another cry of "Jesse, I *told* you don't jump *off that stair*," he vaulted out anyway and "landed right in his daddy's arms, and Reverend snatched off his belt. . . ." But even for the long stretches of time that Jackson was away, he would call about every day, "and you never knew when he was going to show up," so that, in a sense, his presence was always palpably impending in the house. At times when something particularly troublesome developed with one of the children, they would often awake in the middle of the night to discover him abruptly materialized from whatever far distances standing over their bed, says one family intimate, quietly saying, "Wanna talk about this thing?"

As the children grew older, says Calvin Morris, "I saw Jesse carrying them, especially the boys, into his campaigns, because he had recognized that he was absent during much of their earlier life, and it had taken its toll. When they got to be of an age, they told him, and it helped, you know, sort of jar him." They came regularly to engage him in spirited, philosophical banter—Jonathan, along with Jackson on one of his visits to his mother in Greenville, conducted in the hallway of her home late one evening an extensive chat with him exploring the social and religious freights of, in this case, tipping. On one flight during the last days of the 1988 presidential campaign, Jackson and Jesse Jr. passed some twenty minutes closely tilted toward each other across the plane's aisle in what appeared some urgent political conferring but which, when overheard in passing, turned out to be a discussion of what was entailed in the concept of the philosopher-king: "He's got to have that combination of power *and* wisdom *and* compassion that comes from understanding things whole," Jackson was saying. "But wisdom part, compassion part, always got more authority than just the power, king part."

As eagerly conscientious as any of them is Yusef, the youngest but largest of the sons, with a heavyweight's massive build. Accompanying his father to Africa in 1989, he passed much of the long night of the flight sprawled across several seats reading through a thesaurus, every so often looking up to inquire about a word: "What's this one, 'aberration'? Would it be correct to say, 'Talking with his mouth full was an aberration of his'?" During Jackson's stay in Gabon, the liaison assigned to his party by President Omar Bongo's office was an African-American woman from New York, still living in Libreville after her divorce from a Gabonese official, and one of her principal preoccupations over those several days became engineering an attachment between Yusef and her teenage sister—a girl who, in about every respect other than the calendar, seemed a good ripe decade older than Yusef. Despite all the woman's strenuous promptings to come with them on outings about the town, Yusef remained cheerfully uncornerable until, after one long lunch at Jackson's hotel, during which Yusef had lightly dodged all her suggestions, the woman finally blurted, "But when you're back at college, don't you ever go out?"

"Nope," replied Yusef.

"You mean, you don't ever go out to dance, or to the movies with a date, or anything like that?"

"Nope."

"But what do you do for fun?" exclaimed the woman.

"I read periodicals," said Yusef.

"What do you mean, periodicals?"

"Like, you know, *The Nation, The Atlantic, Harper's.* You know . . . *periodicals.*"

"No, no, I mean what do you read for fun? *Fun.*"

"That's a lot of fun," declared Yusef. "Sometimes when I'm reading a really good article in my room, I laugh right out loud."

(Actually, Jackson later indicated, Yusef had also turned out to be something of a Lochinvar at his school: "What I mean, he ain't readin' quite all *that* much.")

In an attempt to shelter them from being "burned by too much public light," Jackson's children were educated largely in private schools, including, for his sons, St. Alban's in Washington, where Vice President Al Gore was once a student, and for Little Jackie, private high schools in New England and Maryland. The eldest child, Santita, after studying at Howard University, moved to New York and served for a time in the backup group for Roberta Flack, though it was on the operatic fullness of her own voice that her final aspirations rode. Little Jackie went on, in 1994, to college at her parents' school in Greensboro, as had two of her brothers before her. Still, Jackson, these many years after, as a small boy, lurking alone outside the walled grounds of Noah Robinson's house, seems to carry a special, robust devotion for his three sons. Jesse Jr., born in 1965 while Jackson was in Selma during King's campaign there—"Almost named me Selma," he says, "which I've been mad about his almost doing to me ever since"—has a smallish frame, taken from his mother, but a compacted heftiness, with a puckish sprightliness of expression. The two younger brothers, however, are built with the bulking brawn of piano movers: Jonathan, born in 1966, is an outgoing and languidly droll-humored young man who, after earning an M.B.A. from Kellogg Business School at Northwestern, took a position on the Chicago Board of Trade; Yusef, born in 1970, attended the University of Virginia on a football scholarship, a starting linebacker in his sophomore year, and after graduation and then two years in its law school, went to work in the London branch of an American law firm. All three sons served, off and on, in Jackson's presidential campaigns, scrupulously referring to their father in public as the Reverend. In truth, they were not always spared Jackson's periodic, Lyndon Johnson–style of indiscriminate explosions at his staff. Even so, great gusts of affection still rush back and forth between them; with an unselfconscious openness seldom seen between a father and his grown sons, they regularly wrap each other in immense hugs when meeting or parting in airport lobbies or at curbside taxis, giving each other walloping kisses and shouting, "*Love* yuh!" "Love *you!*" Indeed, it happens with an insistence that suggests, on Jackson's part, an obscure compulsion still for some reassuring affirmation against uneasy shades yet hanging from his past. In Havana with his father for Jackson's session with Castro the Christmas of 1993, Jesse Jr., one empty and raining afternoon while everyone was waiting in the guesthouse, fell to complaining plaintively, "The man's *still* always hugging. I'm a thirty-year-old man myself now. You know? But every time he sees me again, I'll hold out my hand, like, for at least a handshake first, but he blows right through it. Gotta hug me."

On almost all his jaunts abroad, actually, he arranges to carry at least one of his sons with him. During a trip through southern Africa in 1989, he brought both Jonathan and Yusef along, and happening to be in Zimbabwe on Jonathan's birthday, he took them for a celebratory ride that afternoon up the wide sheen of the Zambezi River in a clattering, canopied cruise launch. While they drifted past distant glimpses of a wet rolling of hippopotami, with nyala antelope shadowing through trees along the shore, Jackson began softly chanting in happiness, "Johnny, Johnny, your twenty-third birthday, and *goin' up the Zambezi River!*" and finally undertook to sing, croakingly, in only a vaguely recognizable approximation of the tune "Happy Birthday," "Twenty-three-hee years old—goin' on forty-six. . . ." If Jonathan did seem then to have aged a bit beyond his years, part of it could have been due to the fact that on trips with their father he and his brothers usually wound up occupied from dawn until well past dusk in a skirmishing to tend to his phone traffic and laundry and luggage and the running logistics of his schedule. On their flight from Nigeria to Angola, Jackson even began gently exhorting Yusef about retrieving, from the strapped-in banks of luggage in a front compartment, some saltine crackers and a can of sardines. When Yusef returned from his first effort at it to plead, "I can't reach 'em, they somewhere behind all those bags," Jackson softly suggested, "Why don't you try again, son. See if you can't maybe get back there to them." Yusef dutifully dove back up toward the compartment, and finally, after much wrestling, managed to return, a trifle winded, with at least the sardines. "See now?" said Jackson, holding the can in his palm. He said then, "But you sure those crackers are just completely unreachable?" Yusef moaned, "But the problem is, the bags are heaped up all *around* 'em." Jackson murmured, "Understand. Understand. But since you know what the problem is, maybe if you try it one more time, what I'm saying." Yusef lunged back up the aisle at an almost horizontal forward lean, but after much struggling, the best he could come back with was half a bag of crumpled pretzels. Jackson grunted. "Have to do, I guess. . . ." In Harare, Jonathan and Yusef finally availed themselves of a brief midafternoon hiatus in the schedule to flee the unremitting telephones and volleying directives from Jackson, rushing out of the hotel and into a taxi at the curb, where Yusef dropped spread-armed into the backseat as if shot, and Jonathan, slumping out a window, mumbled to one of their party, "Don't know where we goin', be back in a little while, but don't tell *him*, not *anybody*." On these expeditions abroad with their father, all three sons have acquired a kind of desperate facility for snatching naps at the slightest lull that offers itself, going into an instant deep doze in limousines and in the corners of airport lobbies and even, now and then, during their father's colloquies with government ministers. Jonathan, when he can find an isolated backseat on a plane, will compose himself with one hand slipped inside his shirt and placed over his heart as he sleeps, as if, for such momentary suspensions of the turmoil, to recenter himself with this little gesture of self-comfort.

Jackson has also made a point, in his journeys overseas, of taking his sons along on his meetings with presidents and premiers—figures ranging from Mitterrand to Mugabe to Sadat to Sakharov to the pope. And though by their twenties they had exchanged pleasantries with probably more world eminences than have most secretaries of state in their entire careers, the blurred succession of so many appointments in so many high governmental chambers would leave them, at times, blankly stupefied. During Jackson's sojourn through southern Africa, right before a conference in the Zimbabwean foreign ministry, Jonathan frantically muttered to Jackson, "Dad! Dad! *Where are we?*"

Yet, whenever Jackson summons them to head out with him again, whether to Egypt to meet with Mubarak or just across town for a labor convention, they remain intrepidly game. They clearly revere him. On his visit to Havana in December of 1993, Jackson, somewhat dispirited about his efforts to coax Castro into some substantial conciliatory move toward ending the long estrangement between Cuba and the United States, was sitting by himself one evening in the large common room of the guesthouse, heavily humped in a rocker, strangely still and silent, while Jesse Jr. watched him from the table in the adjoining dining room; suddenly, to the others sitting around him, Jesse Jr. announced, "See that man in there? Look at him. That's a great man."

Jesse Jr. by then had acquired a master's in theology from Chicago Theological Seminary, where Jackson himself had studied after A & T, and a doctorate in law from the University of Illinois. Now married, he had indefinite plans of returning to Chicago someday to run for, probably, Congress (which in 1995, he did, and won). But in the meantime, Jackson had begun conveying to him some of the responsibilities of his own work with the Rainbow Coalition: "He's the one most like me," said Jackson, "fiery, quick temper, impatient," but also compassionate. As Jackson reports with solemn gratification, after dispatching him once to Zambia to speak in his place at the funeral of an exiled African National Congress leader, "They told me he broke down and cried two times in his address. Boy, was I proud of that. It's a good sign if you have the capacity to cry for people, be authentic that way. Good sign."

As to how his three sons and two daughters have managed to navigate a way of their own through the gales of his fame, Jackson says, "They've stayed pretty steady. I've spent a lot of time over the years drilling them on the power of good manners. 'Cause people got long memories. And I know that every bit of rudeness or arrogance they might betray is another hole that enemies will want to bury them in when I'm not around any longer."

Even so, for all his exertions over the years to maintain a household secure from the dislocations in which he grew up, he has not been able to completely exempt his children from one particular duress: the continued harryings of racism. When Jesse Jr. and Jonathan once flew to Miami to meet him on one of his presidential campaign tours, Jackie got a call from Jesse Jr. at the Miami airport: "Mama, I don't know what to do. They have Jonathan pinned up against the wall here." A white woman had complained to the airport police that her purse was inexplicably missing, and they had promptly fallen on Jonathan as he passed by—"'Cause he *looked* like a suspect," snaps Jackie—and had him spread-eagled against a wall, frisking him while they barkingly interrogated him. He was only released when they were satisfied that he was Jackson's son and had just arrived to join his father.

In his move into the august dominion of high finance in Chicago, Jonathan has met with more oblique little affronts. Arriving for lunch with a banking executive, he was kept waiting in the building's lobby by a dubious security officer until the executive himself had to instruct that he be escorted up so he could validate him for the guard. In conversations with young white associates about the subtle baffles of such casual and sometimes even unwitting discriminatory reflexes lingering throughout American society, they would protest to him, "But it's nothing *I've* done," and he would reply, "Yes, but you're still being favored by it, prospering from it. While it's hurting me."

Both Jackson and Jackie took it as a more monstrous instance of abuse, obscurely involving much higher, political machinations, when, in 1993, Jesse Jr. but especially Jonathan happened to be named, by way of accessory substantiating evidence, in the indictment in Chicago of an acquaintance of theirs for trading in drugs—citations occasioned by their phone conversations in which it was supposed they were talking in code, Jonathan in one taped call remarking, "I'll get the killer on that," which, in this case, turned out simply to be the nickname of the barber long used by Jackson and his sons. "Jonathan is decent," states Jackie, "but he knows shit when he sees it." The matter soon officially evaporated, but Jonathan observed one evening about a year later, "What's so insidious about it, that imputation can just stay hanging out there without their ever having to either indict me or retract it. Can you imagine what that can do to my career in the professional world I've gone into?" At the least, it would have been difficult to devise a more intimate, direct, vital assault on Jackson himself—his meaning and message, what seemed his one unassailably admirable aspect of the children he'd raised, what he most personally valued himself—after all these years.

Jackie herself was enraged. "They are seen as Jesse Jackson's sons, and people are constantly trying to slay them. But to do that was the cruelest thing. I'd always thought the family was off-limits, yet my children are subjected to that kind of meanness. I'll never forget the power they used on my child—the most vicious and wrongest thing they could do."

But over the years, in fact, "they've seen the ugliest deals," she asserts. "I don't know how to articulate what they've had to deal with, but they understand it. They have just lifted above all that." Indeed, it would not be the most negligible achievement of how they were reared that they seem to have remained, for the most part, buoyantly hale and unembittered of spirit. For his part, Jonathan has been reduced now to a certain grim wryness: "Have to keep a sense of humor, or you'd go berserk at some point."

But Jackie proclaims, "Oh, that they've made it anyway! That they have *survived*!" Sitting in her front parlor in Washington that summer afternoon in 1994, she reflected, "My children decided, just like me with the chicken coop, to take the negatives and build on them a beautiful road. Sure, we've had a lot of trouble," she allows. "But they've compared us with the other families they've seen, and they've said, 'Hey. We're going to stand *here*.' Many of us who worked through the civil rights movement have had no continuity with our family. I have. I know that I have some continuity here.

"Jesse is going to continue to try," she goes on, momentarily wistful, "and I will continue to assist him. But I know that we won't make it. But," she then announces, "I have something for you! Fidel said, 'History will absolve me.' Well, I've got something coming along for you. I have a bunch of children, and they are extraordinary children, these children I have given light to. I've got a royal group. I have done something that you don't even know about—the establishing, the cementing of the heart, to believe in God and in good, and if it is good, let them slay you, but you stand, because you know what is right." The need she has always sensed and struggled to answer in her children, she says, is "their 'Keep me honest, keep me pure, so I don't have to think about messing anybody up.' Well, I've *kept* them pure. Because the history is that you won't do it. No, you won't do it—*I do it*. And I am sending you now some *fine human men* that white men will learn to respect. I am sending you some children that will be fantastic for the world. Do you hear me? I've set a force into the world!"

In December of 1995, one of those children, Jesse Jr., achieved something his father never has—actual election to a public office, as representative of his old home district in South Side Chicago in the Congress of the United States. While this hardly meant, as many suggested with perhaps no small measure of wishful vigor, that Jackson would now be relinquishing his own lifetime's striving in deference to his son, he was nevertheless virtually giddy with exultation for weeks. In another late-night phone call, he enthused, "Long way from that old neighborhood down there in Greenville, ain't it? Even if it took a generation. But they talk about the Kennedy family. Hell, man! What we got comin' along here is gonna be the Kennedy family of *black* America. Still two more boys, you know, two daughters. And me, Jackie, Mama, Gran'mama. The Jacksons!"

And Jackie Abides

JACKIE HERSELF OVER the decades has arrived at a racial understanding of her own that is somewhat more ambivalently complex and shadowed—mordant, rueful, ironic, finally only tenuously hopeful. To begin with, she offers, "I love my blackness, I love my people, but I am not a racist. There's some kind of fear whites operate under, that if I love black people, I can't love them. During the campaigns, they asked me, 'Are you black first, or are you an American?' Well, first thing, how in hell am I going to jump out of my body? You know, you can't trust me if I don't like me." But she accedes, "It's grim that we have this vague pall hovering over all of us that keeps us from living together fully." When they moved into their new Chicago neighborhood in 1970, a number of white families lived along their street, and Jackie's attitude was "Hey, I'm not going to worry you. I'll do my barbecue and notify you about the smoke, and you can eat your garlic. But we can coexist." What white residents are still there now, she says, "are very shy." One of them, right next door, "was there before I was. She's Jewish. When I came, she put up a fence. Then when Yasser Arafat came into our lives, it must have scared her to death. She didn't raise her fence any higher, no. No—dog came. But I saw her at the dentist's office the other day—we have the same Jewish dentist—and all of a sudden we talked more than we have in twenty-four years." But with most of her white friends now, she has found that "all they want to talk with me about are racial problems, like I'm their racial chaplain or something. My white roofer even, he was telling me how he was trying to understand, and I was having to explain to him. Yes, my *roofer*. I just want my roof repaired—'Why don't we have coffee as we discuss roofs.' But they all want to talk about racism."

She continues, though, more sharply, "Look. Let me tell you something. What is America? America is castoffs. Trash. They dropped a group of motherfuckers here, I'm talkin' about. You got dumped, I got dumped, we all got dumped—it was a new land. But you been tryin' to make me feel that I got dumped the *worsest*. The game is always to pretend that you are a little better. Every white person here is trying to trace back their shit and make it into something, but they been fuckin' here and fuckin' there—Indians, white man, black woman—and that's why *all* of us are a mutation. We're all trash, white trash, black trash; we were sold here to the white trash that Europe itself wanted to get rid of. *I* know who you are. And I know who I am. And," she cries out with a sudden gladness, *"we're somebody.* Guess what? We all made something out of nothing. So how do we take this trash we are, and make something more out of it? Hey, I'm *with* you, we'll do it together. My job is to push you to be the *new* that we are. We're all one family. So what are we going to make of this soup?"

She will often affect a chipper waggishness with white journalists, inquiring at the end of one interview, "Would you like to go with us to the Cheesecake Factory? Or you got some white people you got to see now? That's all right, I need you with important white people, 'cause I don't have access to them."

Even so, her own experiences have left in her deeper brimstone deposits of anger, and she will now and then lapse into moments of simple, unappeasable, fierce fulmination. "I've been taken on the presidential campaigns to every nigger section in America. You must listen to my language and understand what I'm saying. There are no nigger sections in the black community. It's only nigger sections out there, when I leave my community, the nigger sections of white America. Black people understand that, whites will *never*. I watched us go through the Democratic campaigns in the nigger section, and yet before the world I behaved and my husband behaved as if he were a legitimate candidate." But she would sometimes produce scenes, often to Jackson's own despair, once even on the eve of his great advent at the 1984 Democratic convention, when they arrived at their San Francisco hotel: "They said, 'We're not ready.' One of the finest hotels, to tell me your hotel is not ready? When they said that, I understood, I said, 'Then why don't you show me the nigger section.' They ran and got the manager, everybody got very accommodating, said, 'Oh, flowers! Champagne!' I said, 'I don't drink champagne. Just show me to the nigger section. I've been to the nigger section all over America by now, you might as well show me yours, too.' "

After the acquittal of the Los Angeles policemen whom the nation had watched on videotape systematically battering Rodney King, and then the national accolades for King's conciliatory appeal during the subsequent rioting, Jackie sank into a dire mood. "It's like, even though you beat me, you then say, 'You mean you ain't bitter?' My people have a problem when they let you get off on us while you try to deal with your fucking racism and keep telling us, 'Why, you're not bitter!' There's a violation somewhere in that. They keep beating your ass and congratulate you for not being bitter,

I got a serious problem with that. 'Oh, I'll whip your ass and then just feel good 'cause you won't give me up and you'll forgive me.' "

In fact, during such terminal broodings, Jackie even discounts Martin Luther King's ethic of redemptive endurance. "That was before black people integrated and understood you. You like violence. You *like* meanness, you do that for pleasure. You kill the animals. You cut down the trees. You fuck up the environment. For fun. You have just about killed the entire earth. Well, guess what. You can beat me, and I die and I die and I die, but I'm not forgiving you anymore. You cannot keep fucking up the world, and the world forgives you. Martin and I tried integration. Now, I'm with a new generation who went through the integration shit and are saying, 'Hey, I don't like this. How long do I have to get beaten up so you'll understand? I don't think you're so special that I'm going to get my ass whipped forever until you grow up.' " At times, when she feels the oppressiveness of these angers closing in over her again, she simply flees them by fleeing the country. "Now," she says, "you know why I go to Europe a lot."

NEVERTHELESS, SINCE HER marriage to Jackson that warm New Year's Eve dusk in Greenville in 1962, Jackie has persevered for the most part as an uncontainably free-spirited creature. "If you talk about bomb throwers," as Richard Hatcher, long a family intimate, presents it, "Jackie is a real bomb thrower." Jackie herself, never abashed about advertising her own satisfaction with her high-octane nature, declares, "Like somebody said once, *life* happens around me." She is disposed to an instant, clamorously open conviviality. "I love to need people. I love it that you make me necessary and I make you necessary. I feel I only have a few moments on this earth, and I want you to be blessed—quickly! *Quickly!*" She herself lives in a hectic medley of enthusiasms, from salvaging discarded antiques to studying Emerson and Sartre to exploring assorted spiritualist theories to simply talking, rompingly, indefatigably. "Also, I know how to make lox," she announces. "I know how to make Norwegian lox, I know how to make all of them! I know how to make barbecued ribs, too, and I know how to make baked beans and hot dogs and hamburgers."

Her small figure is still sumptuously proportioned, her long face with its twinkling almond eyes has a kind of Ethiopian queenliness, and she has retained her predilection for dressing with a snazzy swankiness, pants suits in billowy bright fabrics, large hoop earrings and many bangles, stiletto heels that, as often as possible, she still plucks off to pad about barefooted. "My feet must be free. Ofttimes when I am penned into these little formal situations like banquets, I know my back must be straight and I must look the part, but under the table, I'll take off my shoes. Because something must express freedom there. I am," she proposes, "progressively old-fashioned." Utterly unlike Jackson in his studious abstention from tobacco and alcohol, she long smoked more or less incessantly and is hardly averse to spirits, from cognac to vodka tonics, of which she partakes with a hearty Elizabethan readiness; when traveling, she keeps a small "medicine bottle" nestled in the bottom of her purse. "They like to say I'm an alcoholic because I have a drink now and then," she once pronounced, "but they also say I'm a lesbian because I'll hold hands in public with a woman friend. I don't care. I just live my life the way I want."

She has remained unsubdued in her political zests, insisting that "to be taken seriously" is still the greatest challenge confronting women. Immediately after she and Jackson were married, she avers, she began pulling him out of his strictly male tribalism: "When he stepped into the world with me, it was '62, the beginning of men and women sitting together, and he came to understand that if men didn't want their pan turned over and their beans spilled, they better participate with us." She has, since then, done a fearsome amount of trooping about the globe on her own as a partisan for concerns — disarmament, peace movements, the destitute of the Third World — that have generally paralleled Jackson's own. And in more than a few instances, repeating the pattern of their political exchanges at A & T, she has prodded him beyond his more cautious instincts. She journeyed ahead of him to the Middle East, to Cuba, to the Nicaragua of the Sandinistas. "I can go places," she says, "that he cannot go" — or, more exactly, will not go at first. In the late seventies, she cites, "I wanted to take a vacation, so I said, 'Why don't I go to Beirut?' I was frustrated that things were going a little slow, and I'd been reading about Lebanon and the problems there. I mentioned this to my husband, and he said, 'Are you *sure* you want to go there?' He asked his friend, Reverend B. W. Smith, to accompany me. After we met with a lot of Palestinian people, I said, 'Long as we're here, why don't we see Mr. Yasser Arafat?' Reverend Smith said, 'Anybody but Arafat. That'll get us in a lot of trouble.' But I went ahead. He was a most moving individual, I thought. When I got back, I went to a board meeting of PUSH, and I was so emphatic that we should become involved in the issue over there, one member got up and placed a motion on the floor never to permit me to go out of the country again." It was also she, years ago in Chicago, who first put Jackson in touch with Louis Farrakhan and his Muslim sect, explaining she was simply impressed by their rectitudinous self-discipline and "the way they have taken over their own lives. They were really trying, and what is it all about but an effort?" In fact, she has fairly regularly prompted Jackson into those extensions that have landed him in his most trouble — and not only Jackson, for that matter. On her return from her visit with the Palestinians in Lebanon in 1979, she met with Andrew Young, then U.S. ambassador to the United Nations, and urged him into the informal contact with a PLO representative that wound up forcing his resignation.

At the least, as she points out, albeit a bit superfluously, "I'm not a robot." But over her years with Jackson, she has evolved a kind of gentle arrangement for unobtrusively looking out for him. As she describes it, "God didn't give him *everything*. What I do, I try to help make people like him. Because sometimes he can be so . . . well, rough. So I try to keep him in touch with people, with the little considerations that matter to them. He already has the gift, but you have to polish it now and then, dust it off. And I'm a great duster!" Even so, she will occasionally confess now to certain despondencies since they first set out, in Greensboro, on their collaborative journey together from their mutually bleak origins. "You know, I've always understood that a man has to do what a man has to do. His life is out there in the world, and I don't condemn him for that. But I just can't live that public life anymore. I've been under such *stress* all these years."

To be sure, their marriage has not proceeded as a wholly serene affair. Much to his consternation, after her row with the hotel when they arrived in San Francisco for the 1984 Democratic convention, she then refused to appear with him on the podium along with the other candidates and their wives at the convention's close, still incensed at how dingily she felt the party's hierarchy had treated him through the campaign. On occasion, they have not been hesitant about flaring at each other before onlookers. During the 1988 Iowa primary campaign, according to his then press secretary, Elizabeth Colton, when Jackie once decided simply not to show up at his side for a statewide circuit, he railed at her from a pay phone in an airport terminal, "You're shitting on me. I need you with me now. You're violating me. We're supposed to be together." Jackie herself relates how the two of them were in South Africa shortly before the release of Nelson Mandela from prison. They arrived for an appointment with President Frederik de Klerk, and after an aide informed them de Klerk was ready to receive them, they were passing through an antechamber to his office, by themselves for a moment, when "he suddenly grabbed my arm, pushed me up against the wall—I mean, my head *banged* against that wall—and he said, 'You keep your mouth *shut* in here.' He'd never done anything physical like that to me before. *Ever*." But, she adds, under particularly tense circumstances, and few could have been more elaborately tense for Jackson than this imminent audience with the high magistrate of apartheid, "my husband gets very nervous, you know." When they were settled before de Klerk, he asked Jackie if she would like tea or coffee, and she, insuppressible still, replied, "Well, my husband told me I wasn't supposed to open my mouth in here, so I don't guess I can tell you, Mr. President. . . ."

More difficult has been the accommodation she's had to develop over the years with the wide swim of rumors about Jackson's romantic careering. One of the old PUSH regulars in Chicago acknowledges, "Nobody else could have stayed with him. And she's struggled. But these are the words that she said: she married with the intention to stay married to Jesse, and she never intended for her children to be raised without a father." Constantly embattled, though, by queries from reporters, she has notified them, "My husband is a public man. He is rarely home, but I give him no ultimatum on when to return. He returns because he wants to, and when he does, I am happy to have him back. I am not a slavemaster over his commitment to me, and neither is he over mine to him. My husband is a big boy. In fact, he's a grown-up man. We're both grown people. Of course I know what happens out there, I'm no *dummy*. I understand other women being attracted to him. But I don't believe in examining the sheets. My portion of him is mine, nobody comes into my house or my bedroom, and I can't spend too much time worrying about other women if I am to develop myself." Even so, according to one of the series of writers enlisted for Jackson's endlessly undelivered autobiography, Jackie once privately complained, "I've covered his ass right down the line on that thing, but do you think he's grateful? Shown any gratitude at all? No. Not one word of thanks from that sonuvabitch." In 1987, when allusions to his purported dalliances proliferated in the press as he approached a second presidential campaign, Jackie finally permitted herself the obscurely ominous remark to one reporter, "I would suggest that he take care. That he take care with what he does in the streets so he won't excite the horses." Early in 1989, when there seemed a likelihood of Jackson's mounting yet another presidential effort in 1992, some of the aides who came along with him on his trip to the then Soviet Union began exchanging murmured misgivings one evening, in the dark of a car transporting them along Moscow's streets, about Jackie's humor on the matter: "All you can do is just hold your breath. . . . Nobody knows if she'll keep on keeping still or if she's not gonna just break loose finally. . . ." But the mind about it that she has maintained, as she apprises reporters, is "Whatever, just don't be bringing it through my door, up my stairs, into our bedroom. Unh-*unh*. I don't want to be hearing about anything from anybody. If my husband has committed adultery, *he* better not tell me, either, and you better not go digging into it, because I won't let you be the one to destroy my family. So long as it's a rumor, it remains a rumor. It's not true until it's true to me."

In the end, every genuine marriage is probably a universe unto itself, its own peculiar truth separate from comparative evaluation by any other marriage whatsoever. At least, that of Jackson and Jackie seems to have endured as its own reality, with its own sort of authenticity in the profound symbiosis between them, described by a friend from their Chicago days as a "yin and yang dynamic." On the whole, Jackie now allows, "That's an interesting affair we've had." She commonly came to refer to Jackson, not only in talking to others but even in her own notes to herself, almost always as merely "my husband." Or, she says, "If I'm angry, it's Reverend Jackson. If I'm happy, it's Jesse." She would often assume a brusque unsentimentality about the modus vivendi the two of them had arrived at. As Bob Faw and Nancy Skelton related in their account of the 1984 campaign, *Thunder in America*, when Jackson once offered on Jackie's birthday to take her out for dinner, she crisply declined, instead cooked him a simple meal and dispatched him to bed, and then set out to enjoy the evening with a few close friends: "Why should we sit there and roll eyes at each other," she said, "Him asking me, What does this taste like? Why would you eat that?"

Yet she and Jackson have continued to hold a snug relish for each other. She will tuck herself under his arm and cuddle against him when they are together. When she reached him from Washington by car phone one afternoon while he was riding about Los Angeles, Jackson momentarily handed the phone to a reporter in the backseat for him to say hello, and she chirruped, "Now, you tell him to hurry on back home, baby needs its milk." Jackson himself declares, "She's grafted onto me." Often while ranging about remote locales, he will suddenly refer to her with a happy fondness. During his trip through southern Africa after the 1988 campaign, while he was waiting one morning in Luanda at a villa for a meeting with Angolan president José Eduardo dos Santos, he ambled about the dining room where his two younger sons were eating breakfast, and presently paused to contemplate an ancient, massive chiffonier against a wall. "Your mother, now, wouldn't she like to have this thing?" he called, with evident delight at the thought. "Never saw an antique she didn't love. Right? She see this thing, would have it shipped over *tomorrow*." He paced around the chiffonier, quietly chortling. "Put it right in the bedroom. No room there, would just put it in the kitchen or dining room someplace. Yeah, yo' mother, couldn't get it anywhere else, would put that sucker right . . . in . . . the . . . *hallway!*"

For her part, Jackie readily professes, "I happen to like him more than I love him. Love can be so temporary an emotion. But to consistently *like* somebody," she proposes, "is very unique, I think." In any event, despite all the tribulations he's afforded her, she insists, "I like him all the time. He keeps my adrenaline up. And flowing and moving around the block and making U-turns. I like who he really is." These many years since that unspoken compact they entered into back in Greensboro, she finds herself still touched by the old unsureness from his boyhood that he has continued to carry deep in his center. "He is actually very modest about himself," she says, and all that he is finally made up of, she declares, is "emotion. Spirit." It has left him with a vulnerability in which, she reports, "he's in a lot of pain about a lot of things. You don't understand the *pain*, because the system—" and her eyes briefly fill with tears. "And I can't do anything about that. That pain . . ." She still sees in him much of that exorbitantly, sometimes poignantly hopeful innocence of his days at A & T. "He's a person who can like you when he knows you're not good, and will spend the time trying to reshape you. He believes he can take little people and pull them into big ones. He thinks you can take evil people and pull them into good ones. Now, I don't totally agree, and I don't think he's very successful at it," she says with a low chuckle, "but God, he does try." The Reverend Willie Barrow, a longtime associate of Jackson's, attests, "People that did Jesse wrong, and I *knew* they did him wrong, he never gave up on them," and Jackie says, "Do you realize how difficult it is to love somebody who's spitefully used you? Do you know how difficult it is to be kind to that person? But do you know what I've seen him do sometimes with that belief in them anyway? He can get that individual to do all sorts of things—*horrible* people, when they're with him, they're so good, they end up with so much respect for him. But if he goes off for a while and doesn't watch them, then, it's move outta the way. That's where I'm around the curve to cover his back."

But, she muses on, "He lifts you up to what is good in you," and then declares, with a deep husky crow of a laugh, "I, too, am a victim. Yeah. He saved me, as he often says, from myself. I would never tell him that. But he's made me better—though I've tried to put on this facade." During the speculation in 1995 as to whether he would make an independent run for the presidency, Jackie declared, "I don't know about him, because he hasn't announced it yet. But I'm always running." Still, she said, "at this age now, I would like a little more tranquillity. I would love for him to slow down. But when I tell him I'm a little too old to go on like this, he tells me, first, to get some exercise. Then, I need some vitamins. Take some exercise and vitamins, and that's supposed to do it. And don't forget to pray. I tell him, I've been doing that. It's not working. He says, 'Continue to do it.' Do I get tired of this man? Yes. Yes! *Yes*. But as you might have noticed, I like antiques, and he's my favorite one."

At the least, she now pronounces, "It's been a life."

VIII
"History Is Upon Us"

A CLOSE ACQUAINTANCE back when they were in college recalls, "Even in those earliest years, Jackie was always a peculiarly strong woman to operate in the context of a Jesse Jackson who already then was on a path toward his own self-actualization." But when Jackson returned with Jackie to the A & T campus after the wedding in Greenville, the actual direction that path would take was still not at all clear. To Dr. Proctor, he seemed then a youth hardly religious of nature, only that "he was the kind of person who was gonna do *something* big. Either sell a lot of real estate or do a lot of surgery or win a lot of law cases. Whatever, was gonna be *big*." One friend then, Calvin Morris, says, "When I first met Jesse, his vision for himself was so huge. He thought globally about himself, saw himself in places that young Negro boys like ourselves had never considered. I mean, I saw myself maybe as a college president, that was the biggest thing. Jesse saw himself as a president *of the United States*! Which was *crazy*! But that's the kind of sense of his own destiny that he had, far in excess of where either of us was right then." As another acquaintance would note, "Not only does Jesse believe in God, but Jesse believes God believes in him." But a student minister at A & T found Jackson "still in search of self, his role in the dramas of history, only he wasn't sure what he should commit to."

At that time, the distant thunder and sheet lightning of the movement had begun playing more widely over the landscapes of the South, and the lunch-counter sit-ins begun a year earlier by A & T students in Greensboro itself had set off a chain combustion of others in some fifty-four cities over nine states. But Jesse, settling himself and Jackie in a narrow little two-story apartment in the married students' compound, devoted himself to tending to his private life, to the making of a home and family of his own.

Years later, out of his everlasting propensity for espying mystical correlations in his life's progress, Jackson would propound about his episode with the Greenville library that Christmas of 1959, "The *mysterium tremendus* of it—the tremendous mystery—was that, while it was in my heart to do what I later did because of what happened to me there, they were planning to do the same thing in Greensboro that February, and they did it. And about two hundred miles from Greenville, across the mountains over in Nashville, that group at Fisk, they were meeting that same Christmas, preparing to sit in, too. Greenville, Nashville, Greensboro—disconnected physically. But an idea whose time had come."

Nevertheless, what remains surprising is that for so long Jackson kept himself carefully apart from that immense moral drama rising around him. One student organizer later recollected to William H. Chafe, a historian of the Greensboro movement, "We needed Jesse as a football player the girls loved, the president of the student council." Yet despite his earlier flurry into activism out of his old angers in Greenville, he now stiffly resisted all efforts by other students to draw him into the sit-in confrontations. It was another instance of the fundamental duality in Jackson that has persisted throughout his life, an endlessly unresolved tension between an innately conservative conventionality and the call of larger revolutionary excitements. Protest demonstrations, says Proctor, were "not his cup of tea then. But do you know how many black people want to see change take place with order? They don't want chaos, they have a stake in this thing. Jesse was just not temperamentally disposed to anything that looked disruptive and out to destroy. He was not a nihilist in any sense. He wanted change to take place in order." Jackson himself recalls, "They were determined to get me to be a part of the demonstrations, kept challenging me, but I expressed absolutely *no* interest in that business. I just wasn't into what they were into. Said, 'Point isn't sitting in, it's standing up.' I kept criticizing the movement from a distance like that."

His abstention was not, however, without an inner fretfulness. He showed up among the thousands at the Washington March in 1963, and heard King's address there. All that while, says Jackie, "he was always thinking about *society*, you know—what was good, what was bad. Always *thinking*." But he seemed finally daunted by the sheer reckless brazenness of outright street protests. "Imagine what a departure that was at that time for those fellas," Proctor points out. "You were snatching the clothes off the emperor." The campus chaplain then, A. Knighton Stanley, surmises, "Jesse was less secure at that time, and his reluctance to go into the movement was that he had been brought up in the southern culture of that day. Who was going to win that thing was not at all a given, and remaining in school mattered a great deal to Jesse." As it was, he had come to A & T after having foundered at another school, and his friend at Illinois, Michael Summers, remembers the trauma of that for Jackson: "Pain, real pain. His family in that little town had invested a lot in him, and to have to go back home and say, 'It didn't work out.' " Now, says Stanley, "here you are, part of your position on campus is that you've gotten this access to the administration, which itself has very mixed feelings about it all, because they're trying to defend their budget in Raleigh with the North Carolina legislature on their backs, threatening. So you wonder how it would be received by the powers that be on campus if you made this commitment, where you're going to stand with them." Jackie recounts, "You were a student, a child, and your stay at school was in jeopardy. You could be expelled. And that would be very disappointing for your family, that you were thrown out of school for this. So there were a lot of heavy decisions to be made."

Jackson himself would later profess, "I get frightened now when I think how close I came to not getting into the movement," explaining, somewhat harshly, "I was brought up in a materialistic, individualistic society, and might never have escaped." He then added one of his customary cosmic construings: "It must've been divine."

How it worked out more terrestrially was that, after demonstrations had expanded, in the fall of 1962, beyond lunch-counter sit-ins into a profusion of demands, including integration of all public facilities and equity in employment, the movement suddenly seemed to sag into a windless lull. "We had gotten down to the dregs of commitment among students," says Stanley, who acted informally as counselor to the campus activists. "We needed somebody to pick the rest of us up so we could keep going." Jackson by now had consented to at least attend a meeting of the campus chapter of CORE, the Congress of Racial Equality, which had largely directed the protest campaign so far, and though he sat through that session mostly wordless, he appeared for a second, at which, he narrates, "Somebody stood up and turned to me and said, 'Jesse Jackson, now you been having so many criticisms about what we doing, just what's *your* point of view? C'mon, tell us what *you* think we ought to be doing?' They sort of lured me on into it that way."

Actually, many of the movement's leaders had also held a certain wary ambivalence about him, already sensing that to bring him into their enterprise would almost surely mean his appropriating it before long. "Oh, yes, no question of that," says Stanley. "There was an understanding that if he came in, he would lead." To assay the implications of that, several of CORE's principals met with Stanley one evening, and their deliberations, conducted with a goodly supply of Southern Comfort, reeled on throughout the night. Stanley—who now pastors a Congregationalist church in Washington, a slender, ashen-haired man with a patrician bearing and patrician face—recounts, "The discussion about Jesse was, do we need him?

Will he stick? But the specific negative in that conversation was that he would take over. Because he took his cues from nobody. There was also some feeling that he hadn't paid his dues, so why should he lead? These students who were now head of the movement had an awfully long-term gut commitment to it, I mean, they were deeply serious, deeply engaged students. And they did not go out as solo performers. We all often dealt with the potential guilt that we were demonstrating to become celebrities, your name in the paper and on television, as over and against the real cause. And there was no little concern in that conversation that Jesse might be particularly susceptible to that. But my position was, if we don't bring him in, then we won't have anything that he'll lead anyway. So what do we have to lose?"

They finally determined to risk it, says Stanley, and "after this evening of Southern Comfort, I was sent as emissary at daybreak to Jesse's house." As soon as his batterings on the door brought Jackson downstairs to let him in, though, "I asked to use his bathroom, and went there immediately, where, on my hands and knees, I got rid of all my Southern Comfort." It was actually some while before he emerged, he calculates, because when he did, he found that Jackie, "who was already full with child," had cooked a breakfast of bacon and eggs and canned biscuits. "Neither of them said a word about why I was in the bathroom so long. They did not embarrass me. And I developed at that moment a very warm place in my heart for them." Over Jackie's breakfast, then, as the daylight brightened in the windows, Stanley presented the invitation agreed on by the others after the past night's consideration, and somewhat surprisingly, for all Jackson's long period of evasion, "I did not have to struggle to get his acceptance," says Stanley. "He was not reticent at all." He did incidentally inquire about the sentiments of the others at the meeting that night, recalls Stanley, "and I don't know if I was honest about it or not."

But Stanley's mission that morning served, for Jackson, as the conclusive, compelling manifestation of all the electricities of special expectation, familiar to him from his boyhood, that he had felt collecting around him again here at A & T. "One thing is," Jackson reflects with gratification still, "people've always seemed to look to me to make something happen, to do something big. They've refused to let me stay small, you know?" And it was the elating sensation of those wider expectations that ultimately abducted him out of his disinclinations and fully into the movement in Greensboro at last. After joining CORE, he and other student leaders were summoned to a conference with an A & T administrator, Dr. L. C. Dowdy, a few hours before a mass march was to set out for downtown. Actually, says Stanley, "Jesse had a tremendous respect for his elders," and he was not insensitive to the fact that "when Dr. Dowdy was making his appeal for his budget before the North Carolina legislature, one of them asked him about how his students were acting up. The newspaper reported what Dr. Dowdy said, and it was absolutely incoherent. It was one of his finer moments. Rather than betray his students and pull the rug out from under them, he just became incoherent." But in his session now with student leaders before the march, says Jackson, "he told us he believed in civil rights just like we did, but said he'd gotten a call from the state capital in Raleigh. 'They told me if I don't do something to stop these demonstrations, we'll lose our accreditation, your diplomas won't be any good.' Said, 'I can't tell yawl to stop demonstrating. But I know yawl've worked awfully hard to have your degrees, your parents sacrificed a lot. So it's up to yawl.' Dropped his little number on us, and left us sitting there." In fact, it was an advisory that registered in all of Jackson's old cautions and sensitivities like an underground detonation. Later that day, at a meeting at the church from which the march was to depart, "we were still debating among ourselves. Students were waiting outside with their toothbrushes, ready to go. And all of a sudden, everybody's turning toward *me*. 'What we ought to do?' Mean, I was still just a junior then, but it was like there was all this pressure upon me from the other students—'You got to say something to them out there, you can explain it.' We went outside," Jackson continues, "at least thirteen hundred students out there. We got up on the church porch, and some others talked before me, while I stood there looking out at all those people. And I felt such a . . . I don't know, we'd just had this serious challenge about our accreditation—felt such a sense of obligation. Felt so *alone* in that crowd. But it was 'Not my will but thine be done.' My will was to go back to the campus. But I couldn't, 'cause I knew, just as a quarterback, you can never choose the path of having no confidence. Came my time to speak, I said, 'History is upon us. This generation's judgment is upon us. Demonstrations without hesitation! Jail without bail! Let's go forward!' And we moved on out."

Thus he began to discover not only the galvanizing clap of rhyming oratory but the powers of his public effect. When a number of students at Bennett, a neighboring women's college, were jailed after a demonstration, he was appointed to serve as marshal for a protest march, and he appealed to A & T athletes to join him: "These big football players, you know, 'Not gonna get involved in that mess, not gonna take this nonviolence shit,' but I said, 'We got to go down there and help out the sisters at Bennett, we can be the *leaders* of this thing.' " Seeing about fifty of the athletes following Jackson across the campus, other students came spilling out of the dorms. "Result was, we had more than two thousand marching downtown that night"—and Jackson was heading the entire multitudinous procession. With that, he was wholly caught up in the high theater of the demonstrations.

They would usually mass in the late afternoon and proceed toward the center of town, and one local reporter then recalls, "Those silent marches, they were kind of weird. They'd be walking very quietly in the semidarkness. Strong, strong in number." Jackson in front, in a narrow-brim hat and a sport jacket, sometimes with CORE president James Farmer beside him, led them on to confrontations at the S & W Cafeteria, Meyer's Tea Room, and the Mayfair Cafeteria, where he once engaged in an exchange with its owner, Boyd Morris, a large, thick, middle-aged man with gray rippling hair, who was blocking the front door. Jackson, his hat cocked back on his head, said, "Can I be admitted?"

Morris answered in a harshly barking voice, "No siree, you cannot be admitted."

"Why?" said Jackson, staring directly at Morris, his face bland.

"I am *not* going to serve you."

"Because of my race?"

"I'm not going to serve you."

"It's because of my race."

"*Move on,*" said Morris, flinging one hand out in a shooing motion. "I'm *not* going to serve you."

"*Why?*" demanded Jackson, with what must have seemed to Morris an infuriatingly obdurate persistence. "Why don't I qualify? I'm human."

"*I'm not going to serve you.*"

Still expressionless, standing motionless, looking with a flat directness into Morris's face, Jackson said, "I don't dislike *you,* Boyd."

"I don't dislike you."

"So why won't you serve me?"

"I'm *not* going to serve demonstrators. Today, tomorrow, or any day."

"If I came back by myself," Jackson haggled on, "would you serve me?"

"*No!* You're a demonstrator."

"I wouldn't be demonstrating."

"You're a demonstrator," Morris simply repeated.

And with that, Jackson turned back to the crowd behind him with a small, knowing, triumphant smile.

AS IT HAPPENED, those demonstrations were taking place roughly coincident with the marches under way in the streets of Birmingham, Alabama—the campaign in Greensboro, at the center of which Jackson now found himself, proceeding like a kind of atmospheric reflection of that dramatic confrontation led by Martin Luther King some four hundred miles away. "Truth is," Jackson contends, "Birmingham had the fire hoses and bombings, but the demonstrations in Greensboro were really bigger." In any case, Jackson was also being closely tutored in the elements of King's vision by several A & T professors, especially by Samuel Proctor, who had been a fellow student of King's at Boston University and remained a counselor to him, a stocky man with a large, calm, heavy face, who became something like Jesse's spiritual Merlin during those Greensboro days. "He kept throwing King up to me," says Jackson, "how King was able to do what he was doin' 'cause he was using these larger concepts of theology and history. 'He's prepared himself for this. He's not down there in Birmingham just talkin', he's *relatin'* those concepts to the whole of society.' " Proctor remembers that "Jesse was very moved by the image of Martin Luther King," and it was not long before he entered into what would prove a central fixation of his life: "He thought somebody like King was the kind of thing he would like to be," says Proctor. "He saw himself as embryonic to something bigger like that." Soon Jackson was exploring for himself how King's "moral dynamics" could be deployed within the folk values of southern culture. During one demonstration outside a cafeteria, he says, "police finally were moving in to arrest us, and we kneeled and started saying the Lord's Prayer. Police all took off their caps and bowed their heads. Can't arrest folks *prayin'*. We finished, they started for us again. We stood up and started singing 'The Star-Spangled Banner.' They stopped, put their hands over their heart. Can't arrest folks singing the national anthem. We were touching something bigger, see, that we both respected. Opening up the moral terms of the situation. Went on for, like, half an hour, until we got tired and let 'em arrest us."

Greensboro itself was once described by a local black as one of the "nice-nasty" towns of the South then, the racial acrimonies of its white community dressed in a studied civility. Its chief of detectives, Captain William Jackson, is recalled even by his adversaries then as, in Stanley's words, "a fair and just man, something of a gentleman. He raised horses, you know. We trusted him more than we did the FBI." In time, a protocol of sorts had set in between marchers and Captain Jackson's police officers, in which, says Stanley, "we'd often tell them what we were going to do when we staged demonstrations," this arrangement producing confrontations described by one witness as "a kind of ballet." But as Jackson inexorably assumed leadership of the movement, says Stanley, "it got hot and heavy, it did reenergize things"—to a point where "it was a little frightening. Because it seemed out of control." Joining the demonstrations before long were "troops from the community," as Stanley phrases it, "and nonviolence was not one of their virtues—as the preachers described them, 'hoodlums and thieves walking in the streets.'" But Jackson seemed remarkably able to manage them with that same capacity noted during his youth in Greenville for connecting across the whole social spectrum; as his friend Leroy Greggs had put it, "He didn't carry himself as an intellectual, he could mix with *anybody*." Now, according to Stanley, "while Jesse was more princely in his carriage than the leadership which had always been there, his communication with the street people was far better than theirs. We were afraid we now had a monster on our hands."

At the same time, Jackson began to acquire a canniness for a certain situational jujitsu—deftly developing a combination of concurrent threats and options to a converging critical point, which he would then use to leverage the whole conflict to a stage beyond all prior expectations—an intricate counterplay that was to greatly serve his progress through the years ahead. At rallies, he would bawl forth such baleful forecasts as "We won't stop until we get all we want! We'll be there tomorrow and tomorrow and tomorrow! We'll *take over* the city of Greensboro!" Having conjured these dire prospects, he would then nimbly step in to act as mediator between the students and Greensboro's white power system to avert what he had invoked, with a settlement advancing the matter further than most had thought possible. This rather isometric exercise also happened to entail his initially striking out on swashbuckling ploys of his own, independent of the rest of the movement's leadership. As he now explains it, "I had my popular base with the students while I kept my position in CORE, had that base there, too, as an option." But his predilection for virtuoso initiatives occasioned the same irritations then as it would throughout his career, confirming the forebodings of the other student leaders who had met that night to discuss bringing him into their campaign. "You can imagine the tension among those guys who had sweated through the movement a long time before him," says Stanley. "Now Jesse was showing up in photos out front, looking good. We began to swear that Jesse was showing up in the *Greensboro Daily News* even when he was not present. He would be in the picture, and we'd say, 'But he wasn't even *there*.'"

Finally, though, on a hot May afternoon in 1963, an illumination far more profound than such tactical gymnastics came to him. The Greensboro police, having run out of jail space along with their customary civility by now, herded some four hundred students into the dilapidated wards of an abandoned polio hospital meant to hold only a hundred and twenty-five occupants, a low, flat, barrackslike construction. Jackson led a march there, and when he arrived, found classmates crammed up in the windows for air, who, as soon as they saw him, wailed out over the teeming police dogs and troopers, "We dyin' from heat in here, man! You got to help us! Don't let us perish in here!" Jackson bellowed back to them over the chain-link fence, past the police with their dogs, "We'll get you out, we'll get you out! They can't stop us! We'll set you free!" and turning to the marchers behind him with barely a pause, his face shining with tears and sweat in the sun, he began delivering himself of a sudden, impromptu oration. . . . Stanley got there after Jackson had begun, but was immediately overwhelmed: "It was a tremendous speech. It wasn't a tirade about the harshness of being in prison without soap and toothpaste and all that. He was talking about the suffering of those inside in the larger context of justice, and what this movement meant in terms of a turning point in the history of the nation. It flowed without forethought. It was poetic. Those of us who were listening, we said, 'My God, this is comparable to Martin Luther King's letter from the Birmingham jail!' " When Jackson had finished, both Stanley and a white friend with him were so awed that "we agreed it needed to be in print, that he must say it again so we could transcribe it and publish it." But when the two of them rushed over to Jackson and told him it was imperative he repeat the speech into a tape recorder as soon as one could be fetched, he only gazed back at them, remembers Stanley, "with a kind of nonplussed amazement. He said, 'What did I say?' He had absolutely no recall of what he had said." It was as if, Stanley suggests, some other force, "some voice and authority beyond himself," even what some might term the Holy Spirit of the original Pentecost, had descended on him and taken him over. In retrospect, Stanley considers it "probably his inaugural speech in getting on to the business of his life."

"I Would Be a Greater Something Than Me"

JACKSON NOW DECLARES that what happened to him there that May afternoon, with his captive fellow students crying to him from the windows of the hospital, amounted to "a revolutionary moment in my life," a kind of epiphany that "threw me into a whole new psychic pattern." Up to then, all his personal aggrievements and desperations had found no "comprehensive language of action," as he terms it, "to confront the general condition that your individual plight was just one part of." Out of that recognition arose his apostolic ambition "to spend my life working as an agent to transform the outer structures of society, and the inner structures of people, to bring about a new heaven and a new earth." Jackie's own sense of it was: "A fire had already been lit from Greenville, but he began to live and became a man in Greensboro. He took on his identity in Greensboro, and from there he moved into what he's been doing ever since." Not long after that afternoon at the polio hospital, she recalls, "he came to me and said, 'It's getting very hostile downtown, and I think I'm going to be arrested. I want you to know about it before you hear about it.' And when it happened—it's still difficult for me to talk about it, because it was a sad time for me. I was very young and very frightened, and I didn't yet have the whole picture of things."

On a smoldering June night, Jackson led a march downtown that flooded the streets around City Hall. "Jesse improvised on us again," says Stanley, "by insisting everyone simply lay down in the middle of this main intersection." A warrant was issued for his arrest on a charge of inciting to riot. That was all it took for the movement's other leaders, whatever their prior feelings about Jackson, instantly to collect around him, and they arranged for his arrest to take place when he came out of a mass meeting scheduled by them for the next day, a Thursday, at a still unfinished mission church. It was another hotly glaring day, and after some fifteen minutes Jackson emerged from the church before a hastily convoked company of print reporters and television cameras—this the first glimpse of him to flicker over wider geographies of the nation: a neat, self-composed youth with a precociously debonair mustache and, already, a certain cinematic incandescence about him, who was notably taller than the officers taking him into custody, a procedure he submitted to with a strangely solemn, wide-eyed stare. Stanley recalls, "There was an uncommon sadness about him. I remember being moved by it. It was not a jubilant moment. His head was down. Look, here was a young man being taken off to jail who, up to that point, had never been in real trouble. Which this was. And that's frightening. I do remember being moved almost to the point of tears by his arrest." Part of Stanley's melancholy owed to a sudden sense that, with his daybreak visit to Jackson's apartment back in the spring, when "Jesse and Jackie had become my friends, the way they had treated me after my night of Southern Comfort," he had somehow precipitated Jesse into this grim moment now. But almost immediately after Jackson was jailed, some ten thousand handbills were distributed over the A & T and Bennett campuses and the black sections of Greensboro, bearing the headline "Your Great Leader Has Been Arrested," and a mass meeting was held that night in another church, attended by about a thousand supporters who cheered denunciations of his arrest from the pulpit. From the church, then, an enormous march stormed on into the center of Greensboro, and from his jail cell Jackson could hear murmurs of its uproar. "What did I feel? Most of all, felt peace. Felt at peace." Before he was released, he managed to sketch a "Letter from a Greensboro Jail," in emulation of King's already famed epistle from Birmingham.

JACKSON'S EXULTATION NOW was that, after pitching about for so long in the indefinite suspensions of a multidispossessed outsider, he had at last found a potential for belonging that answered, with splendor, the abjectness of his origins, that was breathlessly broader than all his conventionally industrious self-calibrations up to now. "It was like," he says, "it took me outside myself." This transporting inspiration, Proctor submits, came to a degree "from the fact that he was a teenage mother's child and was not with his father, and a whole image of failure is presented to such kids. It becomes obvious when students are seeking to overcome the deficits of such humble origins, you can tell they're being driven by that, being impelled. And Jesse was clearly impelled. Whenever I hear his name called now, that's the first image that pops into my mind: a fellow who wanted to prove that people who are born of modest circumstances can, in fact, be great." In only a few years, when Jackson would wind up being taken on by King, Andrew Young would learn of his past. He now observes, "It's clear that Jesse has always been trying to prove himself to the father that rejected him, no doubt of that. But then, Sartre talks about that disorganizing factor in the childhood of great leaders that creates their compulsion to lead." That compulsion in Jackson seemed a consummate instance of the moral-heroic urge as described by, among others, Colin Wilson and Erik Erikson: to submerge oneself in a purpose and meaning far larger than one's individual reality, thereby enlarging oneself to that magnitude. "That's what the Jesus story is all about," Jackson will still assert, paraphrasing a New Testament passage, "He who loses his life in the great truth I offer shall find a greater life."

Accordingly, no criticism has offended Jackson over the years as more vandalistic to his meaning than that ascribing his aspirations simply to the subjective, to the impulsions of ego. "All this 'seizing the power and the glory.' Why couldn't the motivation be service and justice? Why must those who seek human dignity and peace always be driven by some lesser, neurotic, selfish motivation? That stuff comes from people got the sort of mind that can't conceive of anything beyond personal self-interest. It's all they know, all that makes *them* run, so they keep trying to make you that little, too." Indeed, in the coverage of him over the decades, constructions of self-concern have been applied, strangely by almost common reflex, to virtually everything he's done, but while in truth he does remain much captured in self-interests, he has also undeniably seemed always to aspire to escape those cramped preoccupations into the larger life of the noble;

he has indisputably *wanted* to be that. "The reason and authority isn't yourself," he insists, "but 'I am He who sent me. Bigger than *who* I am is *whose* I am.' If you clear on that, you at the center of a much wider whole."

Some might consider that this still amounts to Jackson's ambition performing a kind of altruistic flimflam on itself, an extravagantly liberating sublimation. An editor who early on worked with Jackson on his yet unaccomplished autobiography speculates, "I think Jesse really does believe this cosmic message of his, but whether he's also conned himself along the line on some of it, that's where the really interesting judgment comes in. Where does one stop and where does the other begin?" For that matter, most of the difficulty with the autobiography, the editor says, came from Jackson's militant aversion to having himself explained at all in terms of his personal history. As Jackson himself still complains, "One long drama of that personal, human kind of stuff is just less important, has less merit than the big picture of your mission." After the autobiography was contracted in the late seventies, the editor says, Jackson seemed especially balky on the matter of his illegitimacy. "At the time, it wasn't widely known, and he was worried that it would be used against him. We battled back and forth on that. We insisted that his own life story was an integral part of his ministry, that, in fact, he was his own best subject. But what he wanted was to change the scenario, primarily, of his upbringing. To obscure it and get rid of it, to sort of come in on himself in college somewhere." Another editor who worked with him remembers that the early drafts furnished by Jackson were "all peroration, a lot of talking in ballooning, explications of how things were and how things should be, and how if PUSH went ahead, all things *would* be. A good deal of passion, but it was a kind of impersonal passion. We didn't think it was very good because there wasn't much Jackson in it. But he wanted it to be his testament, to a certain degree his springboard, his 'This I believe' book. While what we wanted was, yeah, put in the 'This I believe' stuff, but let's have a little bit of a plot, too. I said at some point, 'I don't want to cheapen this whole thing, but a little anecdote wouldn't hurt here and there. I mean, if you could just illustrate a point with a story now and then.' His life was sort of in there, but in passing almost. As for getting any closer to his emotions about what his life had been . . . it simply wasn't there." Jackson adamantly continued to resist entering into that personal territory until the publisher at last abandoned the project.

But the grand revelation opened to Jackson in Greensboro—what released him into his social apostleship through the years, even to his presidential adventure—was, he maintains, "the enormous strength I could tap into by giving myself over to God's truths in history," as he puts it. "Surrendering yourself to struggle for your people, for *all* the people, you get bigger than yourself. Choosing to be selfless, you expand your life beyond the ordinary." The ultimate reach of that ambition in Jackson, however— to count in his time on the scale that Gandhi and King counted in theirs— stirs some misgiving even in Proctor now of a final, possibly tragic disproportion of urgency: "It may be hubris, in a way. I don't think anyone should define himself in those terms. You see, you don't know. You can't leave home and say, Mama, good-bye, I'm going off now. Where you going, son? Going to be great. You can say, Mama, I'm going off to serve, or I'm going off to teach or to write or to discover. But greatness is an elusive thing. You have to leave it to come if it comes."

Nevertheless, in the midst of one late-night speech in Chicago during the 1988 campaign, Jackson suddenly cried out in a hoarse howl, as if in longing still these many years since Greensboro, "I see, I see something else *bigger* than me! I would . . . I would be a *greater* something than me!"

Seeking a Medium

HIS ACTUAL COURSE toward that end would still prove erratic. For the rest of his time in Greensboro, with the demonstrations lapping on more quietly but working modest results in desegregating the city, Jackson occupied himself in miscellaneous other political involvements, even joining the state's Young Democrats, and was eventually elected president of the newly formed North Carolina Intercollegiate Council on Human Rights. Once, Stanley recounts, "we rode to Raleigh to talk to these aides in the governor's office about how they could help in integrating Greensboro. These were clandestine conversations, of course. Jesse drove, far too fast for me. When we got to the state capitol, the aides took us on into the governor's office. He was not there. As I went in, I recalled that as a black child growing up in North Carolina, we could only visit the state capitol on particular days, and those days when the legislature was not in session and there were no white children to be found anywhere. But Jesse could not resist going over and sitting in the governor's chair behind his desk. And he said, 'One day, I'm going to sit in this chair.'"

Journalist Ken Bode, then a South Dakota migrant studying at Chapel Hill, had wandered into the civil rights movement himself, and he recalls first meeting Jackson in the back room of a church in the state capital, Raleigh, where some ten students were plotting a demonstration at the Sir Raleigh Hotel, in which most of the state legislature was lodged. "Jesse was the youngest guy in the room," says Bode, "but I remember he was smart, and listened to." At the demonstration at the hotel, "we had the whole state legislature more or less captured," says Bode, "more whites in seersucker suits with sun-toasted faces and farmers' hands than you can imagine. We sang 'We Are Soldiers in the Army,' sang it over and over again, and got duly spat on." But that demonstration happened to provide Jackson with his first portentous personal access to a higher province of power, when Governor Terry Sanford invited some of the marchers, including him and Bode, up to his suite at the top of the hotel. "He sat us down, offered us something soft to drink," says Bode, "and kept us there for an hour or more, talking about what was going on downstairs, what our perspective was, whether we understood what we were provoking in the legislature. 'Those guys from places like Rocky Mount,' he said, 'you fellas have to understand the way they see you.'" During this session, Sanford found Jackson impressive enough in his own understanding to appoint him later as a consultant on a projected series of black forums for state educational television.

Bode, who was also a member of the Young Democrats, was still in Chapel Hill when a delegation was sent to the national Young Democrats convention in Las Vegas, where they put up one of their own, a moderately decent young squire of the state's establishment, for national president. "But civil rights was a big national issue," says Bode, "and here's this guy from North Carolina with all that baggage you carry, running against a guy from Illinois, who had basically big-city, northern states with him." Bode shortly got a call from someone in the delegation, who told him, "We're getting beat up out here. We want you to come to Las Vegas, we'll pay your way, and we want you to bring a Negro and a Jew. You're our northern liberal." Bode phoned Jackson and presented the proposition to him. "I said, 'I'm the northern liberal, I've got the Jew, and you're the Negro. Would you like to go?' He said, sure. With eagerness." Catching a twin-engine propeller flight from Greensboro, they found, when they arrived at their Las Vegas hotel, that all three of them had been stored in one room, something like the delegation's liberal holding tank. But what Bode principally remembers of Jackson from that moment on is "mostly his absence. Jesse just took off. You know, he's always gonna be after absorbing everything he can absorb. We mainly just ran into each other on the floor of the convention. In that setting, though, he was *everywhere*. He did exactly what he was asked and expected to do. Something needs to be done, Jesse just up and goes about it—you only see the tracks later." As it turned out, the North Carolina candidate won the national presidency. As for Jackson, he jubilantly announced to Bode afterward, "I had a wonderful time 'cause I met all these people"—among them, Harold Washington, who would become Chicago's first black mayor, and Willie Brown, in later years the Speaker-prestidigitator of the California Assembly and one of Jackson's own presidential campaign directors.

But even in the midst of these relatively mild political exercises, Jackson also felt compelled at one point, in some deeper restless groping to find his ultimate definition, to make the long drive from Greensboro up to New York in the hope, though he had not called ahead, of meeting Malcolm X. "I just wanted to hear him speak, then maybe talk with him a little while afterward. He just appealed to me, the way he could cut down the enemy with his tongue. That was his excitement for black people then. Martin's liberation was his public movement, opening up the system to blacks. But Malcolm's was more personal; he somehow removed the fear in blacks' personal encounters with whites." But by the time Jackson reached Harlem, Malcolm had already set out on the pilgrimage to Mecca in which he was to undergo his own transfiguration. Jackson thereupon called on Malcolm's attorney, Percy Sutton, who years later would become one of Jackson's most crucial sponsors, and who in that first encounter was intrigued by Jackson as "this overcharged young man up from the South who insisted I tell him everything about Malcolm X."

Approaching his graduation from A & T, Jackson was still casting about, after the momentous possibility disclosed to him in the demonstrations there, for what might be his fulfilling script, his stage. For a time, he had entertained notions of becoming a lawyer. "The models for change I knew then were basically lawyers. King was a minister, but he was special, a category of his own." Proctor recalls, "Lawyer to him meant what Thurgood Marshall was doing. Lawyer to him did *not* mean being in a court trying to get somebody's will or real estate straightened out, or cleaning up a profit. A lawyer for him was being out there up front." But Proctor and a few other professors began pressing King on him as a demonstration of the ministry's greater efficacy for catalyzing social regeneration. "They kept telling me," he remembers, "the seminary would be much broader than law school, because it involved everything—poetry, history, sociology, philosophy—the *whole* picture." Proctor says he pointed out to him, "Martin Luther King, you know, is the pastor of a church. And he's become universal, from a Baptist church, and not even the main one in town. And because he has a greater sense of history and philosophy and ethics, he's going to outdistance all these other guys, and he will outlast any single given protest." Actually, Jackson still did not seem notably inclined to the churchly or spiritual, Proctor attests, but "he wanted to be a reformer, and I had space in my theological construct for that. I told him, 'You don't have to enter the ministry because you want to save people from a burning hell. It may be because you want to see his kingdom come on earth as it is in heaven.' We talked a lot about that." As Proctor recollects those conversations, "Largely the frame of reference was the eighth-century B.C. prophets—Isaiah, Amos, Micah, Hosea—how prophets could be relevant, how theology could be contextual, and you deal with the meaning of God and human experience where you are, not generically and abstractly. And he was fascinated by that kind of role." For Jackson, it was something like the discovery of a complex of moral nerves running from the Scriptures into the moment. Proctor remembers his rising excitement "when he began to understand that you could be a person who was a reading and thinking creature and still have a deep religious sensitivity. He wanted to know all I'd studied in the seminary. He would just ask questions *continually*."

In the end, says Jackson, "I decided to go to the seminary to learn how to do without the law to change society, change it in deeper ways." Many years later, while flying across southern Africa, he amplified on that original rationale that had taken him into the ministry in the course of recalling the anticlerical sentiments he had confronted in marathon sessions over the past with Marxist leaders like Castro, the Sandinistas' Daniel Ortega, Robert Mugabe of Zimbabwe. "Most of those guys had religious backgrounds, you know. What is Marxism anyway but a reaction by guys coming out of very strong Judeo-Christian traditions to the bitter exploitation of people? Now, when they go into that godless-society thing, that's where we part company. 'Cause I see God's hand moving in history. But when they were fighting their revolutions, they found the mainline traditional church fighting *against* them, *for* those ruling powers exploiting the people. And having come through some of that myself, I could kind of understand what they were saying. It was part of my own struggle about going to the seminary. Mean, even the black church had to a great degree a theology that simply accommodated the culture, preaching what was essentially a leftover slave theology. But if the church is only an extension of the culture, it only embellishes and reinforces the culture instead of transforming it. If it can't deal with truths higher than the habits of the society of the day, it's salt that's lost its savor. 'Member 'bout the time I was going to the seminary," Jackson continued, leaning back in his seat and crossing his stockinged feet on the seat facing him, "people'd gotten all agitated about that book, *Is God Dead?* Well, the point at which the church is not moving for justice, not feeding the hongry and clothin' the naked, then in that church, God *is* dead. Your brothers and sisters bein' oppressed because of the color of their skin, people and little chil'run gettin' blown up, and you preach a sermon like it ain't even happenin'? Now"—he suddenly yanked himself upright, stamped both of his feet flat on the floor, slapped his hands—"is God dead in that church? The point is not, is *God* dead, but is he dead *in your life*? . . . So from my own experience," he picked up about an hour later as the plane began angling down in its approach to the Libreville airport, "I could understand what Castro and those guys were talking about. But I was fortunate to have a Martin Luther King as an example of the alternative to the traditional church. Whereas Castro, Mugabe, they never really had a Martin Luther King–type preacher as an alternative to the church authorities, so they could have said, 'I identify with *that* wing of the church.' I mean"—and he scuffled forward in his seat again, cocked his head to one side—"s'pose if all I'd had was Falwell, Pat Robertson—that was *the church*? S'pose to identify with *that*?"

Even so, Jackson's own passage into the ministry was hardly an even progression from one confident resolution to the next. Through the intercession of Stanley and others, he was supplied a scholarship from the Rockefeller Fund for Theological Education, one of twenty-five grants to black students in the United States and Canada to carry them through a year of seminary study, "a trial year for a person who hadn't fully decided for the ministry yet," says Stanley. "Which was appropriate for Jesse, because there were still some uncertainties there." To a number of others, the ministry seemed a bizarrely improbable vocation for Jackson. His teammate at Illinois, Michael Summers, recalls, "I just didn't see him in that arena. I never heard him speak in a fashion that would've led you to believe that. He was one of the guys, a man's man—hardly a prig, not by a long stretch, if you understand what I mean." Even the young pastor in Greenville who had counseled the library demonstrators there, the Reverend James Hall, admits, "The thing that shocked me more than anything was when I heard he was leaning toward the ministry. He'd never indicated he wanted to be a preacher. I just saw him as more arrogant and pushy than the average preacher."

With his Rockefeller Fund scholarship, Jackson initially applied to Duke Divinity School, but both Stanley and Proctor felt he would be settled too comfortably close to all his southern sources. "He was on a demonstration high," says Stanley, "and my fear was that if he was that near Greensboro and others in the movement, he wouldn't focus as a serious seminary student." Proctor reports that "when Duke called me up and talked with me about it, I said, 'I'd really like to see him in a school in a larger urban setting, like New York or Chicago. Yawl are a southern school, trying to prove to black students that you love and care for them,'" which was precisely the sort of indulgent solicitude, Proctor sensed, that was the last thing Jackson's young ego needed at that moment. He told the people at Duke, "I think he needs a place where they've become *accus-*

tomed to black students, and have a whole train of them." Around that same time, Proctor had talked with the dean at Chicago Theological Seminary—a school associated with the Congregational church, on the South Side of the city, near the University of Chicago—about another prospective student, who happened to bear a "IV" at the end of his name, "and the dean said, 'Tell me about this fellow, why does he go around calling himself So-and-so the fourth?' I said, 'Because he *is* the fourth,' and the dean said, 'Let me tell you something. Up here we don't give a damn how many there were, we deal with them one at a time.' So I said, that's where Jesse needs to go."

Principally at Proctor's urging, then, Jackson chose the seminary in Chicago, a decision not without a certain irony, as noted by Michael Summers: "After trying to make it as part of the system up here and thwarted by that system, he went back home to a smaller school, then came back here. Starts something, gets slapped down, goes into the wilderness, so to speak, strengthens himself, then cuts back and tries to do it better—that's how a lot of things have gone in his life."

Coming into Chicago

IN LATE SUMMER of 1964, after graduating from A & T with a degree in sociology, Jackson once again headed north, now with Jackie and their first child, rattling the some six hundred miles up to Chicago in an aged white Corvair pulling a U-Haul laden with their belongings. "Because I was pregnant again and the car had no air-conditioning," says Jackie, "we put a sack of ice in a plastic bag and set it on the floor by me, so when the heat of the car passed in, it blew on the ice. That was our air-conditioning." On arriving at the CTS campus, Jackson unloaded their things into their scantily furnished one-bedroom apartment, its linoleum floors the dull tan of stale chewing gum. When he had finished—stricken by the disparity between the grandeur of his epiphany back in Greensboro and the meagerness of these new surroundings, and perhaps even more desolately, by doubts about that vision of his eventual high destiny—he sat on the edge of the bed and broke into tears.

Now, as if in some after-recoil from the riskier sweep of the potential he had discovered for himself in Greensboro, he undertook to recede into the personal life again. "With Jackie and the baby, I just wanted to get away from that high-level active scene I'd been in, for a few years of study. Stayed lost in those books at first." But he also had to seek some sort of work to supplement his skimpy means for subsistence. His first call was to none other than Chicago's mayor, Richard Daley, after supplying his office with a letter of recommendation from North Carolina's governor, Terry Sanford. He and Daley passed about an hour of affable chatting, which ended with Daley advising him to begin with a political apprenticeship in one of his machine's South Side precincts. Jackson tried that for a few dreary weeks, noticing that white youths also working for Daley soon came by fine jobs downtown, but when he was finally offered only a post as toll collector with the city's transit system, he angrily rejected it. A black friend then at the University of Chicago's Divinity School, Henry Hardy, remarks, "He thought he was going to get something that was more commensurate with his self-concept, if you will. You know, he had come out of school as a star athlete, president of the student body, with a letter from the governor—there were other toll collectors, I'm sure, who never had a letter from a governor. But all of a sudden, somebody punctures you in this way, trying to diminish you. That may have been really an instrumental moment in his life." If nothing else, with the woe Jackson would later come to visit on Daley's blunt brow, the mayor may have had moments to mourn that he had not responded more expansively when Jackson had first come to him as a supplicant.

With one child already and another imminent, Jackson was now close to destitute. But he had begun attending the Baptist church where the mother of Chicago's black publishing baron, John Johnson, founder of *Jet* and *Ebony*, happened to be a steadfast member, and Johnson recalls that one morning "my mother came to me and said, 'Son, there's a young man at our church who needs a job.' I said, 'Mother, I don't have a job,' and she said, 'John, I want him to have a job.' I said, 'Okay, Mother, if you feel that strongly, but the only job I have is loading and unloading trucks.' She said, 'Let me call him and ask if that's all right,' and she called me back and said, 'He said he'll take anything.' I never thought much about what he would be like when Mother said that," Johnson goes on, "but when he arrives, he's a very tall, striking, handsome young man, and when he begins to talk, very articulate. And the first thing I'm saying to myself, I cannot have him loading trucks. I realized that he was special. I thought, well, maybe circulation, where sales are involved."

As a result, Jackson began hustling *Ebony* and *Jet* to newsstand dealers, in the course of which he also, not incidentally, came to be intimately versed in the intricate street terrains of Chicago's inner black neighborhoods. "He was very effective in convincing news dealers to carry our magazines," says Johnson. "I wish he was still here. But when he left to go with King, I gave him my blessings, because he was bigger than anything that was mine to give him at that point." Jackson himself reflects, "Daley saw only a toll collector,

Johnson saw a communicator." More than that, Johnson—a slight, tautly vigorous man who was himself born brutally poor in Arkansas and now enjoys casually mentioning that "the *Reader's Digest* had a little item about 'From Welfare Rolls to Dinner at the White House,' 'cause I've had dinner with every president since Eisenhower"—also quickly recognized in Jackson compulsions kindred to his own. "What impelled him was growing up without a father, and he wanted his mother to be proud of him, he wanted to make all those people in that town respect him, to show that he had the right stuff. That's deep-down. Any of us who had embarrassing things in our childhood want to prove that—it's an extra energy. I understand that, because when my mother brought me north to go to high school, my stepfather wouldn't come. And all her friends said, 'That boy will never amount to anything.' So I wanted to succeed for her, I didn't want her friends to laugh at her. She washed dishes, she was a cleaning woman, you know, a domestic, she never went beyond the third grade. But the thing I feel best about is that she saw thirty years of my success." Sitting in the conference room of mellow polished woods and glass walls on the top floor of his Ramsesian headquarters, Johnson happily reports, "When I built this building, I built an office for her. It's still down there, just the way she left it. She would come here to work every day, and call up her friends—called them in Arkansas, called those in Chicago who had moved up here, too—call them up and say, 'You remember that boy you told me would never amount to anything? Well, I just drove down here with my chauffeur and my maid in a car that that boy bought me. And I'm calling you from my office in his building.' " Johnson would eventually become a vital patron in Jackson's support complex of black Medicis, Jackson taking to addressing him always as "Godfather." Yet Johnson, for some reason, has kept at a certain reserved, civil distance from Jackson despite their profoundly similar pasts. But Jackson would regularly drop by Johnson's office each Christmas, and once conducted a devotional in his conference room that so affected him, he pulled aside one of his *Ebony* editors after Jackson left and told him, "Scrap the March cover. I don't care what it costs. I'm going to put Jesse on the cover. It's what my mother would have wanted me to do."

Though the movement's steady expansion over the South was increasingly occupying the national consciousness, Jackson remained locked in his seminarial studies. Despite that, "other students began to embrace me," says Jackson, "as if waiting for me to bring energy to the student body. Which was strange, since I was just a freshman. But they knew I'd been leading demonstrations down at A & T," one of his fellow seminarians, Steve Davidson, recollects. "There were all these things happening in the culture that made a natural arena for a Jesse Jackson. He was sort of poised to happen." He finally allowed himself a casual involvement, as a part-time organizer, with a loose association of local civil rights groups called the Coordinating Council of Community Organizations, or CCCO, which in time furnished much of the organizational base for King's ultimate move into the city. "He was fuddling around here with some of the churches," recalls Dr. Alvin Pitcher, then a professor at the University of Chicago's Divinity School and one of CCCO's white directors, a lean and grizzled old civil rights campaigner in the city, "and I'd been looking for leadership for the Chicago freedom movement, somebody who could take it somewhere. I was sitting in my back office at CCCO, which had one of those Dutch-window doors, when he came in one day and leaned over that half door, and I looked at him and said to myself: here he is. One glance, that's all, and I said: Here is the man." But, says Jackson, "I held back from getting into that scene again. It wasn't why I'd come up there. I mostly hung close to those books. Until that Sunday of the Selma Bridge."

A *Spring Pilgrimage*

ON THE EVENING of March 7, 1965—only some six months after his arrival at the seminary, and while Jackie was in Greenville with his family, awaiting the birth of their second child—Jackson was sitting by himself in the lounge of their apartment building, watching the late news on television, when he saw the long, unfolding tableau of Alabama troopers, on foot and mounted on horses, trampling with flailing clubs through a toppling column of black marchers in a haze of tear gas. "Was like all those years in Greenville, everything that had built up in me there and then what happened in Greensboro, it all just blew up." That night, he remembers, "I couldn't hardly sleep." Early the next morning, he went barging into the student cafeteria on the ground floor, clambered atop a table, and began baying forth what was, in his words, "a challenge to everybody there. How we'd been studying the costs of discipleship, and now a time had come to validate with our lives what all we'd been studying about. Who was gonna go with me down to Selma?" And, Jackson says, "A whole bunch of 'em took off with me down there. All of 'em white, too." Davidson recalls, "It all came together very quickly. There was a kind of moral imperative to it, and it was like 'Pack your bags!' But that was Jesse's style—boom, boom, boom!"

Early the next morning, with about twenty other students and a third of the faculty following in cars behind them, Jackson set out with seven of his fellow seminarians crowded into a van, festive, Davidson recounts, with "a kind of exhilaration of our righteousness." But as they trailed on down the middle of the country through the first chill edge of spring, drawing ever nearer the dark bourne of Alabama, the mood in the van grew steadily quieter, says Davidson, "more and more introspective," as the stories rose again in their memory of civil rights workers slain in those alien reaches lying ahead of them. For Davidson, as for most others in the van, "this was brand-new terrain. I'd never done anything like this in my life." They had passed on well into the fastness of the South when they stopped for gas, "and a few bubbas began to gather at this gas station," says Davidson. "Jesse, of course, was aware of what was happening." He rapidly notified the others, in a low easy voice, "Right here, we've got to go now," and everyone scrambled back into the van. When they crossed at last into Alabama, "Jesse began encouraging the driver to be very careful," says Davidson, "because the Alabama state cops were on the lookout for any out-of-state cars. Plus the fact we had this not inconspicuous African-American with us, you know." They rode the final miles on to Selma, Davidson admits, "in absolute fear." In fact, the very night of their arrival a white Unitarian activist minister from Boston, James Reeb, was waylaid by a small pack of whites when he emerged from a black café and beaten savagely with clubs and sticks, shortly dying of his injuries.

But through the eighteen-hour drive down from Chicago, Jackson had also carried an anticipation that he was headed for what could turn out to be the most important appointment of his life. Actually, Selma would not be the first time Jackson had personally encountered King. About four months earlier, when he had flown to Atlanta for a fraternity convention, he was walking down the airport concourse when he suddenly saw King approaching him amid a large entourage, and Jackson stopped him to effusively introduce himself, learning with a further flush of excitement that King was setting out for Sweden to accept the Nobel Peace Prize.

Now, as he and the other CTS students entered Selma, they found themselves surrounded by a huge assemblage like some combination national street fair and movement camp meeting. "I mean, there were *thousands* of people milling along the streets, with a lot of other cars arriving at the same time," says Davidson. "We got the van parked, and began to just follow the crowds with this feeling of jubilation as we were welcomed by blacks as well as whites. We were finally directed to a place where we could sleep for the night, somebody's home that was a safe house." But Davidson then adds, "You know, thinking about that experience, it occurs to me: we didn't see Jesse much once we got there."

Amid the Brueghelian panoply of other pilgrims massed there in the March drizzles and pale chill sunshine—sallow young clerics thin as tallow candles; wispy-haired housewives in ponchos; black civil rights circuit riders in denims and Caribbean plantation hats and high buckskin boots; ruddy labor-union regulars bulky in satin union jackets; college students in army fatigue jackets and clay-caked brogans; even a few American Indians, including a Comanche; along with doctors and lawyers and tweed-coated professors, a multitude resembling a mural by some radical Norman Rockwell of the American conscience of that time, or for that matter like some early premonitory manifestation of Jackson's later vision of a Rainbow Coalition, numberlessly collected in a cloudy puttering of exhausts from television trucks, while gaggles of television crews rippled among them and radio reporters wandered about muttering into microphones clamped close to their mouths in intense private discourse to their shoulder-slung tape recorders; church canteens serving this great host soupy scrambled eggs and vapid coffee while helicopters clattered over-head—amid all this, Jackson abruptly materialized in furious motion, plunging about to offer his services to King's staff and even pontificating to random sidewalk gatherings, in what suggested some mysterious frenzy of auditioning. Andrew Young, one of King's principal aides, recalls that his very first glimpse of Jackson came during an all-night-vigil mass meeting, shortly after Jackson arrived, that was under way at Brown Chapel A.M.E. Church, operational center for the Selma movement, which was then sur-rounded by police barricades a block away: "Jesse came up, this big, hand-some, natural leader of a young man, you know, not just as somebody wanting to take part but as leader of the Chicago delegation, saying, 'What do you want *my people* to do?' " He also presented himself during the mass meeting to Ralph Abernathy, King's closest confidant, who would later re-count, "Jesse approached me asking what he could do to help keep the all-night vigil going," and it wasn't long before "he asked if there was anything open on the staff." The next day, Young noted, "everybody else who came down would get in line as one of the troops, but Jesse wouldn't get in line, he would start lining people up. He *immediately* got to the front, automat-ically started directing marchers, functioning, wholly unbidden, as a staff member." At one point, King's aides were startled to discover Jackson vo-ciferously dispensing inspiration and instructions to marchers from the steps of Brown Chapel itself. One reporter afterward observed, "I thought it was strange, when he was not on the SCLC staff and had not been in-cluded in any of the strategy meetings. He just seemed to come from nowhere." In fact, that was about the first sight of him for Davidson since they had arrived: "I mean, he was so *new* there, and now here he's speak-ing on the steps of Brown Chapel, in a kind of impromptu way." At the time, Young admits, "I got a little annoyed, because he was giving orders from the steps of Brown Chapel and nobody really knew who he was," but Jackson soon sought him out to enthuse about a pamphlet Young had written, "telling me what a great pamphlet it was, and that sort of took the edge off." In the meantime, he caught the notice of Roger Wilkins, then head of the Community Relations Service in Johnson's Justice Department. Even though "the movement was full of thrusting young people," says Wilkins, "he became a name around the place. 'Have you seen this kid, Jesse Jackson?' It was our business to know the personalities in the movement, and if there was a new personality, you wanted to know about him. So I got to know this new kid, and my earliest memory is kind of a big guy swaggering, totally himself in self-confidence."

More, it was as if, as soon as he had landed in the drama and spectacle massing in Selma, he had come swarmingly alive, had somehow found himself loosed at last from his long oscillation, lasting since the Greenville library demonstration, between his personal instincts for a cautious conformity and the recklessly grander promise of social militancy he had sensed in Greensboro. Davidson relates, "We didn't see a lot of him in Selma, but when we did see him, he was totally in the flow of things and very elated in a way. You could just feel his tingle of energy, that he had kind of found his place. He was home. It was, for me anyway, the first look at what he would become later on, of what his life would be."

As it developed, his extemporaneous performances of oratory and scampering readiness to execute any chore provided no little puzzled vexation to many of King's aides. "Most of them were battle-tested," says Wilkins. "They had tested themselves against their own fears and defeated them, and had experienced success in pushing back injustice. So like any veterans, they were very close to each other and had a distrust of outsiders." Despite that, Jackson's enterprise soon won the beguiled admiration of Ralph Abernathy. Following Jackson's query on their first meeting about a position on the SCLC staff, Abernathy finally agreed at least to take him in for a talk with King. Conducted into King's presence one morning, Jackson promptly proceeded to exhort him to extend his movement northward to Chicago, a strategic departure already being deliberated by SCLC, and he suggested that he himself could be of considerable assistance there—a prospect that would also happen to create a singularly promising theater for a possible advent of his own. This session with King emboldened Jackson to later bring Davidson in to meet him, too, even though, Davidson remembers, it was clear that Jackson and King "were still very new to one another." King was sitting in a back office of Brown Chapel, at an hour of the afternoon when few others were in the church, and he struck Davidson, in contrast to Jackson himself, as a surprisingly unprepossessing figure, short and chunky, "not an overwhelming presence, really. Rather quiet and humble. But very sincere, very gracious and warm, and he expressed again and again his appreciation that we had come." But according to Abernathy's later account, King remained hesitant about taking on Jackson after so brief, however high-voltage, a contact with him, but Abernathy had been impressed enough to persuade King to consider it seriously. Andrew Young now reflects, "People criticized Jesse for being forward and aggressive, but in fact that was exactly the kind of self-assurance and assertiveness we needed. That's the way we identified staff people. When we went into a town and got involved, we figured that people who had the most energy and courage and vision *would* come to the front. You were looking for aggressive, fearless fools for Christ, as we'd say."

All of these effects and developments took Jackson only two days in Selma to transact. During this time, there was another march to the Edmund Pettus Bridge. But with a federal injunction still in place against any march to Montgomery, and by a last-moment arrangement between King and federal mediator Leroy Collins, the march was halted and, after a prayer, turned back to town. "Jesse was up front someplace," says Davidson, "and I didn't see him." Once, though, Jackson and the Reverend C. T. Vivian, a leader of SCLC's campaign in Selma, were in a march to the courthouse that was broken up by police and "we were trying to get outside of the quartering of police that were roaming the area," says Vivian. "We saw a police car coming, and since we were in a housing project and knew they were on our side, we went up and knocked on a door." As Jackson relates it, "We ran up to one door, and when some children answered, we said, 'Is your mama at home?' When she came down, we begged her to let us in." She opened the door for them, and once they were inside, asked if they were with Dr. King. "We said we were, and then she asked us again, 'Are you *sure* you with Dr. King?' " She then told them, "I know who killed Reeb"—she was a waitress in a restaurant where, the night Reeb was attacked, she had seen a man leave and then come back in several minutes later with a bloody stick. But she would only give the man's name to Dr. King, she told Jackson and Vivian, and they took her to King, who passed the information on to the FBI. The man was arrested, but neither he nor anyone else was ever convicted of Reeb's murder.

Shortly after accomplishing his introductory conference with King, though, and before the Selma March itself set out, Jackson, bleary now with a low-fever flu, left with the other CTS students to drive back to Chicago, and so missed that epic processional, numbering thirty thousand people when starting out. "It seemed that the whole nation was marching to Montgomery," journalist Renata Adler wrote in *The New Yorker*, "every conceivable religious denomination, philosophical viewpoint, labor union, and walk of life." John Doar, chief of the Justice Department's Civil Rights Division, remarked to a student at one point, "You're only likely to see three great parades in a lifetime, and this is one of them." But all of that was to come to pass over a week later. Late in the night of his departure from Selma, Jackson paused in Birmingham to place a call from the phone booth of a gas station to his student quarters in Chicago, and learned that Jackie had given birth, in Greenville, to their second child, a son. But even these tidings, on top of the euphoria of everything else that had transpired in Selma, could not keep him from sinking into an exhausted sleep that lasted for much of the drive back. The van arrived in Chicago in a March witch-wind, and Jackson, back in the spare little apartment he had left only five days before, immediately toppled into bed with pneumonia, which soon brought Jackie back up from Greenville, with their newborn son, Jesse Jr., to care for him.

She found that his encounter with King in Selma had left him "overwhelmed. As of that day, it changed his life. All he wanted to do now was to work closely with Dr. King."

Finding a Footing

ONE CIVIL RIGHTS leader in Chicago at the time remembers that, not long after the Selma March, "I heard that Jesse was going around the city meeting with all the prominent individuals in the movement. He came by to see me, asked a number of questions, you know, sort of saying we've got to have a coalition and all that. After he left, the secretary of my organization, who'd been sitting in on the meeting, said to me, 'You know what Jesse is doing? Jesse is really assessing individuals in the civil rights movement. Because what he's trying to figure out is how he can become the predominant figure here.' And she was correct. He was really just critiquing the situation."

Only a few days after he had returned from Selma, Jackson had thrown himself into the sizable task, while pressing on with his studies at CTS, of trying to cultivate a receptive disposition toward a King mission in Chicago among the city's black ministers that might attract him into a final commitment there. This was a not unforbidding endeavor given those ministers' mistrusts of King and even more byzantine competitiveness with each other, not to mention their almost uniform deference to Mayor Daley's feudal rule.

Jackson first determined to locate an agreeable church and minister to attach himself to. One Sunday night not long after his return from Selma, he was driving along Chicago's Dan Ryan Expressway when he happened to hear on his car radio a broadcast of the evening services from Fellowship Missionary Baptist Church. Its pastor, the Reverend Clay Evans, whom Jackson had glancingly met before, was a sturdy man with a long, massive, somewhat dolorous beagle's face, who had become famed in Chicago's black community for both declaiming and singing his sermons with a whooping, soul-shuddering gusto. For Jackson, as he listened to Evans this lonely Sunday night, it was reminiscent of Reverend Sample back at Long Branch Baptist in Greenville. Shortly after hearing that broadcast, Jackson appeared at Evans's office in the basement of his still-uncompleted church. "He had on beach sandals and these short cut-off pants," relates Evans's secretary at the time, Lucille Loman, "and he came right in and went straight into the pastor's study. I said to myself, Who is this audacious character, where in the world did he come from?" Dropping himself onto a couch with his sandaled feet crossed atop Evans's small coffee table, Jackson announced that after listening to the broadcast of Fellowship's services, he had been moved to come by to offer whatever strengths he owned to help a church with so significant a radio ministry. "Taking over my office like that," Evans marveled years later, "a person doesn't usually act that way when they first come into your office. For somebody I couldn't remember ever meeting before, he relaxed on that couch as if he'd been knowing me for years, made himself very comfortable." Though Jackson's associations with King were still quite tenuous, Evans recalls that "he began to talk about his relationship with Dr. King at some length. He told me he was interested in justice rolling down like water—he quoted the passage on that from Amos—and righteousness like a mighty stream." He also indicated that he would like to preach in Evans's church some Sunday. But even though "Jesse presented himself to me in this rather brash manner," says Evans, "right from that point we seemed to have a kindred spirit." The next Sunday, Jackson joined his church.

For all his bravado, Jackson's haggard personal circumstances soon became evident when he showed up in the church's weekly food line to collect free groceries for his family. "He wasn't making any money then," says Lucille Loman. "But, see, Jesse would also do anything to make a statement. Even in that, he was making a statement that he wasn't too proud to get in that line." And he shortly translated himself into the same sort of conspicuously vigorous presence in the church that he had been when a teenager at Long Branch Baptist. He began working with its youth, taking them off on retreats to Wisconsin and Michigan, and before long, he was conducting the Sunday-morning Scripture reading, "making a major production of it," in the words of his friend Henry Hardy, "you know, 'Well, now, the Scripture is found—' and reading it with this stentorian, thespian, mystic quality."

All this while, he had also begun prompting Evans toward an enthusiasm for a King campaign in Chicago that would address the squalor of its ghettos. He once took Evans to the fetid room inhabited by an invalid black mother subsisting on welfare, who was unable to stir from her wheelchair even to shoo away the rats mingling among her children on the floor. "He'd always thought he knew about poverty," says Jackson, "but he left that room a shaken man." Actually, Evans now amicably reports, "He tricked me into that thing. He had a picture taken of us in that room that was run in *Jet* magazine, and when it came out, he sent it to Dr. King and had Dr. King call me. But he didn't tell me he'd done that. I just thought I was getting this call from Dr. King out of the clear blue sky. It really made me feel good." But, Evans goes on, "Jesse didn't have to do all that. I came from Brownsville, Tennessee, and I knew what injustice was and how white folks treat black folks. I knew racism was here in Chicago, in jobs, in housing, in everything. I had been involved in some civil rights here before Dr. King. But it was on a small scale before I met Jesse, not at the level they were doing it. So it just *suited my spirit* to get involved with them. I joined up with Jesse because it wasn't difficult for me to do." In fact, as Evans recounts it, he had, in a sense, long been waiting for Jackson to appear in his office that morning. "The Lord had given him the mind, had given him the youth and the force, to really do what I wished I could have done. So when I saw Jesse, I just praised the Lord for him. Here was somebody I could join up with that could put things on a larger scale than me and the little group that I was working with then. See what I mean?" At last, Fellowship Baptist issued an invitation to King to speak from its pulpit—at a time, Jackson would proclaim years later, "when Martin couldn't get a pulpit anywhere else in the whole city of Chicago"—and after that, Lucille Loman proudly relates, when King was in the city "Jesse would bring him right into our office there at Fellowship."

Beyond Evans and his church, however, the perspective remained far more daunting. One potentate of Chicago's black ministerial community, Dr. Joseph H. Jackson, who was also president of the National Baptist Convention, the nation's largest black denomination, had come to so detest King that a few years later, when the boulevard in front of his church was renamed for King after his assassination, he shifted the church's address to its side-street entrance. And not only he but "almost all the black establishment in Chicago," says Jesse, "preachers and politicians, were incorporated into Daley's system. Even Harold Washington"—who was elected Chicago's first black mayor eighteen years later—"he was part of the machine then." Many black churches even relied on outright financial subsidies from that machine. "So ministers held a press conference, said Dr. King should not come to Chicago," Jackson says. "It was this big church meeting, preachers and choir singin', 'Must Daley bear the cross alone, and all the world go free?' Actually happened, was on television." Evans recounts, "Most of the preachers fled, didn't want to get too close to Clay Evans or Jesse Jackson. Oh, yeah, we were treated as if we were *plagued.*" Some of Evans's clerical colleagues privately advised him that Jackson was an unsavory and dangerous sort who was "not up to any good," and that he'd best keep a prudent distance from him.

Evans soon discovered his alliance with Jackson and King was not without sterner costs. After his church's old structure had been demolished, Evans had continued to operate from its basement quarters, with the steel girding of the church's new edifice already erected, while he awaited the final grant of a mortgage to complete its construction. Those imminent funds, however, suddenly disappeared, Evans says, "when they found out that I had endorsed Dr. King's coming." The broker who had earlier assured him that he would arrange the financing now retreated from that agreement, explaining simply, "Don't you know that the mayor has the power to stop any building programs in this city?" Once, Evans actually took King along with him to appeal to the broker, but he informed King, "Reverend Evans is not going to get the money if he aligns himself with you. Those are the orders that have been given to me." Everywhere else Evans turned, "the financial institutions had just all clamped down, said they couldn't cooperate with us." In the end, Evans says, the steel skeleton for his new church "stood out there on that ground and rusted for seven years." During that stretch of time, Jackson grew steadily more frantic to rescue Evans and his congregation from the mortifying pass in which his exhortations had stranded them. "I didn't want him to feel that way, because what I did was on my own volition," Evans benignly offers, "but he felt awfully bad about it anyway. And he did not stop. For seven years he was working on it, and finally pulled a coalition together—Jesse did it, I never could have done it—got five churches to take a piece of the guarantee on it, and a bank Jesse worked with, he even had the head over to his house. Plus," Evans adds, "he signed the note along with them. Went on that mortgage for a half-million dollars." It was not until fifteen years later, when the mortgage was at last paid off, that Jackie learned he had committed them to that gallant if potentially catastrophic half-million-dollar obligation.

As Jackson now reviews the social geography confronting him that summer and autumn of 1965, "The ministers were locked into Daley's structure over here," and he tosses out his left hand, "while the real needs of the community were way over here," and he flings out his right hand—he interposing himself as an interlocutor, with his now characteristic nimbleness, to ease "as many ministers as possible into this great gap here in the middle," a position from which they could then more readily respond to King's call for a crusade against the degradation of Chicago's slums. Evans recalls that "he did begin to win some over. He was very persuasive at kind of making them feel guilty, that as men of God they ought to be free." By now, Jackson was also working with SCLC's main deputy in Chicago, James Bevel, perhaps the most intense of King's young adjutants—a close to malarial mystic, with flickering black eyes in a tawny mandarin-like face. He was usually fitted with an arabesquely embroidered skullcap, which, he told reporters, was "a link to our Old Testament heritage." Calvin Morris recalls him as "an awesome mind. Bevel was talking everything. I remember Jesse as a person who had all these great dreams for himself. I remember Bevel because of his ideas." He and Jackson had begun directing the action committee of CCCO, the omnibus consortium of civil rights groups in Chicago that would furnish the organizational traction for King's undertaking there, and for a period Bevel became something like Jackson's mentor in his progress toward a place on SCLC's staff. Along with Evans, Bevel and Jackson gradually, with a certain delicacy of moral importuning, reconditioned sentiments in the black ministerial community for a mobilization by King in Chicago.

At the same time, Jackson was growing more conspicuous around the city through his steadily closer attachment to King. When King would come to reconnoiter the field being prepared there, Jackson would pick him up at the airport in a limousine provided by Evans and drive him into the city "leading a parade of cars flying down the expressway," remembers a local white organizer. "Oh, he was hungry. Hungry." King began to commend him at rallies in Chicago "as this young man he wanted us to work with," recounts the Reverend Addie Wyatt, the lady minister of one of the city's more prestigious black churches, "this very spicy and articulate young man who nobody really knew," and another female pastor remembers him as "this guy who had on coveralls, very good-looking even in those coveralls. But I still didn't think that much about him until he spoke, and that's when I knew he was different. People heard him and they began to rave and rage about it." In fact, one civil rights leader in the city relates how he was sitting beside King on the podium at a mass meeting, waiting to introduce him, "when Jesse got up and started speaking, and he was really in top form. People were enthralled. When he finished, there was rousing, standing applause. And King—you know, if you do a lot of speaking, you can tell the days you have it and when you don't—and King suddenly developed laryngitis. That's right. Immediately after Jesse finished, he turned to me and whispered, 'Bob, you know, I don't think—' told me he had laryngitis. But I knew what it was. That's when I discovered just how *much* charisma Jesse Jackson had."

But among the church leadership, says Reverend Wyatt, "there was real resistance to him at first. You know, 'Here comes this young upstart to tell us what to do, when we've been here all this time.' Then, when he'd start speaking, he'd rhyme all his punch lines"—he was still entranced by that effect of oratorical chiming that he'd discovered back in Greensboro, oblivious to the slightly disconcerted stir it produced in this entirely different sort of audience in a more sober setting—"would rhyme his punch lines to make them all fall in place, and there were a number who were critical of that, too. It personally gave me a sinking feeling to hear that, because you could see that here was something we'd been longing for. I remember saying, 'Leave him alone and let God have his way with him.' Because I felt we had something great coming." And before long, Reverend Wyatt began to notice that "when he'd walk into a crowd of people, they would ask, 'Is that Jesse Jackson?' and others would say"—she repeats it in a whisper—" 'Yes, that's him. That's Jesse Jackson!' "

At last, some six months after his expedition down to Selma, Jackson was brought onto the staff of SCLC—at twenty-four the youngest of King's aides. Though still having to serve only part time while he labored on with his studies at the seminary, he nevertheless showed such ferocious enterprise that, about coincident with King's arrival in Chicago to open his new, northern front, Jackson was selected, largely at Bevel's urgings, to direct the corollary expansion into the city of SCLC's Operation Breadbasket—an economic campaign, patterned on one initiated in Philadelphia some seven years earlier by the Reverend Leon Sullivan, that applied the dual suasions of boycott threats and negotiation offers, a ploy not unfamiliar to Jackson since Greensboro, to bring more blacks into major business concerns in the inner city on levels ranging up to executive. Initially, though, says one owner of a black enterprise then, "Jesse didn't know what the hell he was talking about, because he was just a theology student. So we taught him business. We took him into stores in the neighborhood and showed him how ninety-nine percent of them did not hire the persons they received their money from. How we had products that most of the stores would not accept." Yet there was more: it was also meant in the end to deliver into the hands of the black community its own economic fortunes. It was an effort to be mounted, as almost all meaningful black social movements necessarily were, from the churches, and it was reckoned that Jackson, being still a seminary student with no church of his own, would offer a relatively neutral figure in the ongoing tournament of egos among Chicago's black ministers; as one veteran of that time recalls the computation, with a light laugh, "This guy'd be a threat to nobody." But this secondary project by SCLC in the city was also initially resisted by its black ministers with a fractiousness that sometimes lent to their conduct of ecclesiastical affairs a rowdy Virginia City flair; when Clay Evans, then president of the Baptist Convention of Chicago, began proposing Breadbasket's program to a ministers' conference in one church, the pastor quickly protested its even being brought up, and to Evans's insistence that he could at least raise the matter, "the pastor went into his office," relates Lucille Loman, "and came back with a gun. Everybody scattered like flies," including Evans, Jackson, and a number of CTS students he'd brought along with him. Eventually, though, Jackson and Evans managed to coax most of the clergy into planning sessions with black businessmen, held on the campus of CTS, in which Jackson expounded on the Breadbasket concept by diagramming on a chalkboard the economic colonialism of the black community by white businesses, explaining that a more equitable balance could replace this domination by the simple means of "squeezing a company's vitals, which is its profit margin."

One young black entrepreneur who joined Breadbasket, Larry Shaw, remembers Jackson from that time as "somebody who was still looking up at buildings in Chicago and saying, 'Wow, that's tall buildings!' We were working with a very open and, in worldly ways, unsophisticated person. But he had a power that could only be classified as supernatural."

What Jackson was like in those days is also recollected by George O'Hare, who was then merchandise and sales manager for all Sears, Roebuck stores in Chicago. Now a silver-haired bantam of a figure, rosy of face, he declares, "I was born and raised a white Irish-Catholic racist. Anti-Jewish, anti-Polish, anti-Lithuanian, anti-everything. There were only two kind of people in the world: the Irish and those who wish they were Irish." But somehow, first through chance contacts with Dick Gregory and then Martin Luther King, he found himself gradually entailed in the movement in Chicago. At a church rally one night, "Dr. King asked me, said, 'I've got a young man in Chicago, and I'd like you to do his public relations.' He introduced me to this young fellow in a T-shirt and dungarees and gym shoes: 'This is Jesse Jackson.' The name even sounded funny to me. Dr. King told him, 'George works for Sears, Roebuck and Company.' At the end of the rally, Jesse comes over and says, 'Did you say you worked for Sears?' I said 'Yeah.' He says, 'Can you get me a discount on an air condition?' I said, 'You mean an air conditioner? Sure, I can find one that's been returned, and they'll give you a good deal on it.' Seemed he was living then in an attic apartment with only one window, and his wife was pregnant, and the heat was unbelievable. I told him to come down and see me in the morning, and he said, 'What time?' I said to get there early.

"I always got into my office around seven in the morning. The security guy downstairs says, 'There's a guy upstairs waiting for you in your office.' I went up to my office, and he's sitting there. He'd been there for an hour. I sat down with him, and he started pontificating about the future of this country, the future of the movement, the future of the world, the future of everything. I thought all of a sudden, this twenty-three-year-old man was ninety-nine years old. I didn't know where he came from, but whatever it was, boy, he came out of it already pontificating. I sat there two and a half hours listening to this guy, watching him get excited about what he believed in. He gave me a college education in just a little over two hours.

"We finally went on downstairs onto the floor," O'Hare goes on, "and I introduced him around to the salesmen. At that time none of them knew who the hell Jesse Jackson was. And I tell you, he talked to everybody. 'How are you?' Asked questions the average customer wouldn't ask. 'How long you been here?' I don't think he asked how much money they made, but he came close. They'd never seen anybody like him. He picked himself out a returned air conditioner, and then he started thinking about other things he wanted to get. He looked over and saw the television sets. 'Well, how much are they?' I got back upstairs to my office, and I started getting telephone calls. 'Who was that guy? Who is he? The way he walked around, he somebody special? Is he coming back?'"

During that visit, Jackson had also asked O'Hare to meet with him that night, "and I did. He said, 'I want you to be my public relations promoter.' And I worked for six and a half years around the clock for Jesse Jackson. My three sons thought I was crazy. But you knew you were on the right side of history. After that, most of our conversations are brief. But every time, I can see eyes going out thinking five years from now, twenty years from now."

To the surprise of many, Jackson, operating out of a dumpy cubicle on the second floor of SCLC's ramshackle South Side headquarters, began engineering Breadbasket into a whomping success. Its first confrontation was with a dairy company. Dr. Alvin Pitcher, the professor who was advising him then, recollects that "the guy was up at five-thirty calling the big preachers he wanted to get to a meeting to plan their negotiation strategy, and he came to that meeting with four-by-seven cards with everything he wanted to say. Never anybody better organized in the whole history of my life than he was for that meeting." Three days after a boycott was proclaimed from the pulpits of about a hundred churches, the dairy agreed to open forty-four new or upgraded positions for blacks, a 20 percent increase. Shortly thereafter, the High-Low grocery chain, after squads of picketers marched outside its stores for ten days, committed itself to hiring 183 blacks for positions from delivery boys to department managers. Jewel Tea pledged to find 662 jobs for blacks, and after a fourteen-week campaign, A & P instructed its stores in Chicago's inner-city neighborhoods to admit blacks into 970 of its jobs there, as well as contracting with a black sanitation firm, organized by Jackson, to collect those stores' garbage, and placing much of their advertising in black media. Jackson also pursued contracts for black exterminating companies—"We have a monopoly on rats in the ghetto, and we're gonna have a monopoly on killing 'em"—and in Breadbasket rallies evangelized for the products of black enterprises, Mumbo barbecue sauce, Diamond Sparkle wax, Joe Louis milk. "Now, Joe Louis milk does not come from a Negro cow. Only difference is, your husband can make twelve thousand a year driving a truck for this company. . . . Say it loud: I'm black and I'm proud, and I buy Grove Fresh orange juice. . . . Say it loud: I use King Solomon spray deodorant, and I'm proud. . . . I use Swift Out. Why, it's so strong, if you pour it in your sink it'll open up the sewer down the block. . . ." Eventually, companies doing business in the South Side opened accounts in two black-owned banks there, which increased those banks' deposits from $5 million to $20 million. Altogether, in less than two years, Breadbasket would generate some three thousand jobs for Chicago blacks, according to a report in *Time*, and enlarge the annual income for South Side residents by some $22 million.

But Jackson's parallel urgency through his Breakbasket endeavor was to have its effects reflected in the wider eye of the media. "Oh, he was into media, he was into having press," says George O'Hare. "Jesse Jackson, if you were drinking a bottle of beer and put it next to his face, he would start talking into the bottle."

After one press conference at which no one showed up, says former Jackson aide Bernard Lafayette, "he went home late that night and got into bed and got on the telephone. Jesse, you know, pursued things like a predator. And he called every one of those news agencies we'd invited, and read his statement, word for word, on the telephone. Took a lot of time. But the next day, you would have thought they were all at the news conference. It was covered all over, with quotes from Jesse. Yeah."

But initially, says Hermene Hartman, one of Jackson's early partisans, "nobody would cover anything. We'd go to the *Sun-Times*, the *Tribune*. It was 'Jesse who? Jesse what? Jesse why?' We worked for one full year before we got coverage. One press conference—when we actually got the press out to cover it—the reporters came in and said, 'Does Reverend Jackson have a statement?' I said, 'How on earth can we have a statement when he hasn't made a statement yet? Nobody knows what he's going to say, including him.' I went back to Jesse and I said, 'I think there's something here that we're supposed to have that we don't seem to know about. What's a press statement?' He said, 'I don't know. They asked you, you figure it out.' You talk about naive, making it up as you go. We didn't even know enough to make it up."

Before too very long, though, Jackson was instructing Calvin Morris that Morris would "never do well in terms of the press." Jackson told him, "When people ask you a question, Calvin, you consider what they're asking and take time to frame your answer. You can't do that. When someone asks you a question, you have to have ready what you want to say no matter what they ask you, your answer may have nothing to do with the question they asked, and you have to do it in thirty seconds, because that's all they're going to take."

Jackson's imposing performance inspired SCLC to expand Breadbasket, in 1967, into a national program, though initially under another director. But Jackson now began journeying widely about the country, accompanied often by Richard Thomas, formerly a superintendent at a foundry who, after three months of volunteer work with Breadbasket, "wanted to do that more than I wanted to live. I traveled with him for about nine years." On those first trips, though, "we didn't have any money, didn't have any credit, so we stayed wherever Lucille Loman could get us in, whatever hotel would have us. Single room, double bed. Didn't bother Jesse, though. His idea of a fun evening in those days was to get into bed with the Bible. Said a prayer by the side of the bed and then climbed on in with the Bible. So I started carrying some fiction book to read while he'd read his Bible." But a Brooklyn minister appointed to manage Breadbasket's effort in New York, the Reverend Herb Daughtry, recalls that Jackson soon acquired the brio and élan of "someone who was distinctly in charge. He'd come in and gather us around and begin to talk about what we needed to do, with a knowledge of the terrain and personalities beyond that of many of us who had lived here. He used a phrase I'll never forget—said, 'What we've got to do now is *swing somebody through.*' Said, 'In this city of New York, you've got about eight million people, and the news media is only going to pick up about ten, twelve events. So somebody has got to be *swung through* as the spokesperson who'll command the attention of the media.' Which, of course, while he was here, became Jesse. Nobody can command the attention the way Jesse does. Nobody's light is gonna shine as bright as his."

An Existential Impatience

UP UNTIL HE had been assigned to develop Breadbasket in Chicago, Jackson had been doggedly toiling on with his courses at the seminary. During one of his brief meetings with King in Selma, he had noticed, in King's opened briefcase, two books of theological commentary, one by Reinhold Niebuhr and the other by Paul Tillich, and he remembers his awe that "here in the middle of this big crisis and confrontation going on in Selma, he was still reading, still studying works like that." But King, from his early youth, had set about compiling an intellectual vision for himself through a sedulous, systematic exploration of religion and philosophy, making his way through Plato, Rousseau, Hobbes, Locke, Nietzsche, surveys of Hinduism, Jainism, Islam, as if methodically undertaking to stalk and capture the final meaning, the Truth, of life. And then, largely by the happenstance of a weary black seamstress, late one December afternoon in 1955 in Montgomery, Alabama, refusing a bus driver's demand that she surrender her seat near the front to a white man, he had been conscripted into articulating that intellectual vision into historical action. Jackson, however, seemed congenitally restive with any such phase of scholarly seasoning, with dwelling for very long in the life of the mind. Despite his claims of repeated hankerings—at Illinois, at A & T, now at CTS—to remove himself into calm academic sanctums, he seemed inherently given to action over intellection, the experiential over the cerebral, always impatient to rush into that ultimate definition only found, he sensed, in the welter and heat of actual events. As he has since contended, "It's like sympathy has a role, but empathy has a greater meaning. Knowing *about* has a place, but knowing as in acting—to act, to *be*—is deeper."

His professors at CTS would later recollect him as dazzlingly quick to apprehend and assimilate the broad strokes and spirit of an idea. It was a kind of hurly-burly swoop of comprehension propelled by "an insatiable need to perceive the meaning of everything of consequence going on around him," says Alvin Pitcher, who not only had brought Jackson into CCCO but also taught him a course on Reinhold Niebuhr. "I wouldn't say he was fully formed then, but he was searching." Even when Jackson encountered Pitcher out on the street, he would detain him for a protracted sidewalk discourse on "some question about Niebuhr, asking me to clarify what he meant or what Tillich was talking about. Every time I met him. He was really struggling—but eagerly, oh, eagerly—to understand what was being said by these giants of the theological world. Of course," Pitcher adds with dry smile, "he came to a point where he understood in a sense, in terms of what to do and how to proceed with it, that surpassed his teachers."

Yet he proved rather haphazard and cursory in his actual studies. "It was like he still writes most of his speeches, on the fly, you know," says a fellow student of his then. "It was difficult for him to stay focused on the academic discipline of reading the books and writing the papers and getting the job done in the classroom. He was always more eager to get on with the work at hand out there in the world." He seemed, on the whole, "compared to other mortals, a tremendous vitality," says Pitcher, and "an electrifying chap," said another professor years later. But others of his teachers were less enchanted. One would remember him as "a spectacular guy with spectacular gall." In fact, by his second year at CTS, says Steve Davidson, "the faculty began to divide in their opinion of Jesse. There were those who felt he had been irresponsible as a student, had not completed assignments and had asked for special favors." In one course on Christian ethics, he elected not to write any papers, declaring that he would "speak" his examinations, and he declined even to write out his sermon assignments, which brought him a D in his preaching course. He also missed so many classes that the faculty deliberated asking him to withdraw from the school (and some years later, when he was accorded an honorary degree by CTS, "it damn near blew some of the faculty out of the water," says Davidson). Once, after listening to the reproaches of one professor, Jackson, leaning in the doorway of the professor's office, serenely apprised him, "You have to understand. I'm special."

What made his case rather complicated, though, was that it seemed to more than a few of his teachers that he *was* special. Pitcher insists, "The guy just had the most active mind I'd ever seen," and much of his difficulty then and through the rest of his life, Pitcher asserts, was the peculiar clumsiness of "seeing things so much faster and bigger than almost anybody else he's ever with." But along with that prodigious faculty, the deep mix in his nature that would pattern the rest of his career was then detected by some at CTS: that Jackson's most sabotaging flaw could be not so much an excess of ego as his voracious insecurity. "If you got beyond the oratory and the apparent charisma," says Davidson, "you could begin to see that uncertainty and that groping for direction, for affirmation." Nevertheless, his vagaries as a student met with a measure of indulgence by certain of his teachers, like Ross Snyder, a professor of ethics, who contended to his colleagues that, at that moment of truth in the racial history of America, "any black worth his salt wouldn't just be sitting around in classrooms."

Snyder was the professor at CTS who became perhaps most intrigued with Jackson. He was something of an odd, enigmatic article even in that seminarial preserve, a sort of Blakean ecstatic, most often described by past students and colleagues as a "theological poet"—a stocky man with overgrown brambled eyebrows and a shaggy hummock of white hair. "He was very charismatic," Davidson says. "He liked to plumb the depths of human experience to pull out the meaning of existence, and when he'd be talking about those things, his whole body just came alive. You did get the feeling sometimes that he was just sort of running around in his own inner world there." He was finally obliged by the seminary's president to retire in the mid-seventies—"The story was that Snyder could save everyone but himself," says Davidson—and ended as a melancholy figure, a stroke leaving him only a blur of his prior self for the last several years before his death.

But what had captivated Snyder about Jackson, according to Davidson, was "Jesse's sort of boundless imagination in his sense of the dramatic." As David Maraniss related in a discerning series on Jackson in *The Washington Post* in 1987, Snyder in time came to regard Jackson in actual mythic terms—as a young, emergent black prophet who, from his beginnings as an outcast on the social fringes, had been embarked on a classic "hero's journey" through repudiation and conflict, in which he had become one of those rare figures who had "discovered his truth and his integrity" and gained "an authentic existence" in a life in which he was perpetually "in the act of becoming. . . ."

In any event, Jackson's impulse for engagement over what he calls "the paralysis of analysis" has endured since CTS as the chief aspect of what Snyder and many others have considered his essentially existentialist nature. He has seemed in ceaseless battle against the gravities of precedent: "I couldn't've read history and projected doing in two presidential campaigns what I actually did. History would've told us, hopeless to try, to even dream of anything like that. See? You can*not* go forward by looking backward." And books to Jackson are by and large museums of precedents. "Educated person will decide what he's gonna do by reading a book first. But the creative person doesn't have the book for what he's gonna do, 'cause by definition it hasn't happened yet for there to be any book about it. Creative person, by definition, he creates something out of nothing." Therefore, he maintains, "greatness is not in reading pages full of somebody else's writing. It's acting creatively in a cause that has not yet been fully tried and cultivated. Even a guy like Reagan, say, with whom I had in common about absolutely nothing else, when he decided to meet Gorbachev on nuclear arms reduction, Kissinger-types bitterly argued that it's absurd to expect a guy like Reagan can do anything with Gorbachev, who had about five hundred and ninety-seven volumes of Lenin, whole libraries of history and economics, and yet Reagan, not knowing any of all that stuff Kissinger had learned, not knowing any Russian except maybe 'vodka,' he sits down and gets a historic deal out of Gorbachev. *Made* history, that all those little wannabe Kissingers in the future will spend their lives analyzing. Anyway," Jackson goes on, "many things are much simpler than they're made to appear. Lots of people making their living at universities and in the media by inventing and developing complications—the complication industry. But somebody once asked Duke Ellington, 'How can you write so many different-sounding kinds of songs?' and he said, 'Well, I never went to college and learned I couldn't. Or learned I *shouldn't.*' Way it often is with the great creators. Real leader, once he moves and sets the pace and sends the word out, people say, 'Well, now. *That's* what time of day it is.' "

Nevertheless, when King, on one of his scouting trips to Chicago, finally took Jackson aside and proposed, as Jackson recounts his words, "Come on with me full time, and you'll learn more theology in six months than you would in six years at the seminary," Jackson claims that he was hesitant, and "it was Jackie who persuaded me to do it." Coming from someone who had so diligently fortified himself with scholarship as had King, it seemed a peculiar proposition, but it may have been prompted by the fact that Jackson was already so clearly restless about the relevance of his seminarial studies. Jackson now likes to construct it as "the movement I had been trying to escape when I moved to Chicago *came* to Chicago to claim me." More exactly, his own feverish strivings had not a little helped to bring it there. But only some six months away from graduation, he forsook the seminary to heave himself completely into the civil rights movement at last—at the side of its most fabled and auspicious figure.

IX
The Acolyte

IN HIS SHORT two and a half years with King, there evolved what was probably the single most vital, tortured, exalting, fateful relationship of Jackson's life. Long afterward, Jackson would strangely insist, "King didn't just lean down, you know, and raise me up out of the mire and breathe life and motion into me, like everybody seems to assume. There's not been enough attention to the anatomy of my own development. I was already very active on my own before I ever went with King." In that surprising, faintly churlish assertion, there would seem some defensive need now to validate his own place by abolishing the claim of anyone else, even King, to have been his author. They were, to be sure, different beings in fundamental ways. He had hardly grown up, like King, as the favored son of a fiercely protective father in a comfortably middle-class family of the black community's gentry, amid reverential attentions from the congregation at the church pastored by that father, all of which had left King, from his earliest childhood, with a sense of being at the privileged center of the world around him. In barren contrast, Jackson had had to make himself, and make his place, almost completely out of nothing. Some of King's aides, dubious about Jackson from his first blustery intrusion into their midst, would later tell David Garrow, author of the King biography *Bearing the Cross*, that even after Jackson's arrival on the SCLC staff, he continued to be "really an outsider in a way, striving very hard to be accepted, to be respected," and would "hang around . . . currying favor" with King.

To Andrew Young, it was obvious that "one of the things that Jesse wanted and needed more than anything in the world was the support and approval of Martin Luther King and the rest of us. Growing up as a child seeing your father in another family, there is an irrepressible need for the support from the father that you never got as a child." One of Jackson's closest friends at that time, a white fellow seminarian named David Wallace, recalls that, on a trip together to Atlanta for Jackson's first SCLC staff meeting, "we didn't have any money or hotel reservations, so Dr. King took us home for dinner, and we slept there overnight." That evening, and every other time he found himself with King, Jackson besieged him with an unstoppable pell-mell philosophical discourse "in which he'd ask King a question," says Wallace, "and then answer it himself. Because Jesse thinks while he talks, you know. We were flying once from Atlanta to Savannah for a retreat, and the whole flight down, Jesse is sitting by King, with these books he'd been reading in his lap, Tillich and Niebuhr, and asking King questions about them like some hyper student, and then answering the questions himself as he thought through them in asking them. Until King finally said, 'Well, Jesse, you don't even give me time to answer the question.' " To Wallace, it seemed not only a ravenous impatience "to glean from Dr. King," but "he wanted to show him that he could think, too, he wanted that kind of approval. But it annoyed the hell out of the others around King. Because Jesse just wouldn't *cease*, just *monopolized* King with this endless questioning." Once, King himself, exasperated by Jackson's relentless importunings, curtly told him to leave him alone, and Jackson, with a look of despair, pleaded, "Don't send me away, Doc, don't send me away."

The truth was, he regarded King with an almost abject adoration and awe; Ralph Abernathy would later characterize it as "this deep need" for "a special closeness to whatever seemed holy." But there's little question that King became for Jackson something like the miraculous appearance at last of his own spirit's true, heroic father—a figure in whom he perceived a realization of the grand scale of his own dreams of what he wanted to become, to mean. Abernathy would state flatly, "Jesse wanted to *be* Martin." What particularly enthralled Jackson about King was that he seemed to provide a definitive manifestation of that "higher power than man in the universe" and "high intensity of purpose," as Colin Wilson formulates it in *The Outsider*, which opens up for the lone spirit who feels himself "destined to something greater" the cause and course of action that will "lend a hand to the forces inside him" and enable him to fulfill his own promise.

At that time, after Montgomery and Birmingham and Selma and his majestic sermon at the Washington March, King was already coming to be regarded as the American Gandhi—even if in the improbable form of a middling-sized, slightly pudgy Baptist pastor in staid business suits, his round and faintly Mongolian face, black as asphalt, wearing a bland gaze of placid imperturbability. He always maintained that rather stilted reserve in public as if careful to present, against white southerners' minstrel image of blacks, an unfaltering demeanor of what Matthew Arnold termed "high seriousness." But for all his ponderously sober comportment, his power for moving multitudes largely came from having grown up in the oratorical raptures of black church services like those of Jackson's own boyhood. The genius of his often cumbrous and fustian rhetoric—"For too long have we been trampled under the iron feet of oppression, *too long* bound in the starless midnight of racism"—was that it was the shout of the human spirit rousing itself to slow and stupendous struggle. From all those Sundays of soul-reeling preaching in his father's church, King had acquired an almost physical sense for the protean energy and life of language, in which, as one associate observed to biographer Stephen Oates, "the right word, emotionally and intellectually charged, could reach the whole person and change the relationships of men."

But in a more important respect than oratory did Jackson seem to fashion himself directly out of King. With that swift and ready facility evidenced at the seminary for absorbing whole the ideas of others that illuminated and gave body to intuitions from his own experience, Jackson assumed as his own lifetime's vision King's radical, gospel, moral metaphysic. King proceeded from the essentially religious persuasion that in each human being, black or white, whether deputy sheriff or hardware dealer or governor, there exists, however dimly, a certain natural identification with every other human being; that in the overarching moral design of the universe that ultimately connects us all, we tend to feel that what happens to a fellow human being in some way also happens to us, so that no man can very long continue to debase or abuse another human being without beginning to feel in himself at least some dull answering hurt and stir of shame. Therefore, in the catharsis of a live confrontation with wrong, when an oppressor's violence is met with a forgiving love, he can be vitally touched and even, however partially or momentarily, reborn as a human being, while the society witnessing such a confrontation will be quickened in conscience toward compassion and justice. It may have been a proposition that, as some later suggested, simply presumed too much of the species, but the transformations it worked in the South's old segregationist order seem, in retrospect, nothing short of epochal. And the relative racial amity that, perhaps more astoundingly, followed that transformation would very likely have been impossible without King's nonviolent strategy of sorrow and understanding for one's oppressors. To that elementally Christian perspective he adapted certain other precepts: King himself may never have been a truly original thinker—his was always an interested, didactic pursuit, its ends active—but not unlike Jackson, he had a formidable ability to assimilate and synthesize ideas. Among those animating him were Niebuhr's notion of "collective evil" to explain why men in herds will behave more monstrously than as individuals, Walter Rauschenbusch's "social gospel" calling for "a moral reconstruction of society" to replace "mammonistic capitalism" with a "Christian commonwealth," and Thoreau's proposal that "one honest man" could morally regenerate an entire society. Marx had only produced a "grand illusion" of a moral society, King concluded, "a Christian heresy." But he became most of all captivated by Gandhi and his expansion of Thoreau's principle of individual passive resistance into the massive, patient, nonviolent resistance of a whole subject people, which would exert a moral force that could purge a society of its overt brutalities by posing impossible inconveniences not only to its agencies of authority but to the conscience of its rulers. Thus, King propounded, the universal moral verities evoked by the civil rights movement could, beyond delivering blacks finally into full citizenship, "also redeem the soul of America."

Jackson happened to join King, in fact, just as King was escalating his mission into that of a prophet to the conscience of the entire national community. His evangelism against racism—its denial of that natural connection to other human beings, which then permits any manner of savagery against them—evolved, inevitably, into an evangelism against what he saw as the moral coma of the country's whole corporate, technological order: its separation of individuals from each other in a clamorous void of barbarous materialism; its technician's detachment from the human effects of its interests and policies, with the incalculable vandalism that was being performed on the life not only of America but elsewhere in the world, most garishly in Vietnam. He could not, he testified, protest against the violence in Mississippi without challenging "the greatest purveyor of violence in the world today—my own government." As early as Montgomery, actually, King had begun decrying "the madness of militarism," and after the Kennedy administration launched the Bay of Pigs invasion, developed by the Eisenhower administration to demolish Fidel Castro's still-new guerrilla government in Cuba, King declared, "For some reason, we just don't understand the meaning of the revolution taking part in the world . . . against colonialism, reactionary dictatorship, and systems of exploitation." Such preachments make Jackson's own pronouncements later, for which he was much belabored once he had entered into an outright political candidacy, seem virtually sedate. In his prophetic witness, King wound up pitting himself against the very spirit of the age in America.

His ambition, therefore, when he finally undertook to project his movement beyond the South to Chicago, was, through the same strategy of nonviolent confrontations that had begun to remake the South, to re-create America itself. But his Chicago offensive turned out to be, at best, an inconclusive exercise. It began as a campaign "to bring about the unconditional surrender of forces dedicated to the creation and maintenance of slums," but it encountered a field of resistance far more nebulous than the blunt antagonisms in the South—a spectrum of real estate interests, zoning technicalities, not to mention the Florentine wiles of Mayor Daley, who proved entirely too canny to place himself in any open collision with King, countering instead with his own proclamations of antipoverty measures and craftily applied grants and subsidies throughout the black community. "When it was a battle cry to end the slums, the rats and roaches and all that, Daley agreed to that, oh, yeah," says Robert Lucas, a gristly regular of Chicago's civil rights strife, who was then with CORE. "Daley sent out all his inspectors and people with rat poison, poisoned rats left and right, then had press conferences." When King himself moved into a slum tenement, a brigade of plumbers, electricians, carpenters, painters suddenly descended on the site and rapidly refurbished the entire premises, prompting the quip to circle about the city that King could rescue all of Chicago's slums simply by moving from building to building. "So Daley took that one away from us," says Lucas, "and that's when we decided to march into white neighborhoods for open housing. Because there was no way he was gonna co-opt *that* away from us."

By widening his Chicago mission to a campaign for open housing, King was now taking on the final, most intractable front of American apartheid— its measureless complex of racially segregated residential compounds that fractured the whole national neighborhood by projecting its divisions into the larger pattern of racial isolations in the rest of society, in schools, in employment, proliferating like a fault line through all economic and social classes and which has remained the country's most implacable and bitter racial divide precisely because it is so immediate and intimate to the personal lives of white Americans. Marches into the tidy little streets in white suburban neighborhoods around Chicago, domains of the city's ethnic kaleidoscope of Poles, Lithuanians, Germans, Italians, met with howled imprecations of "You monkeys! . . . Kill 'em! . . . White power!" and barrages of bricks and bottles. SCLC field staffer Stoney Cooks recounts, "They were coming out of houses with a bottle of beer and yelling, 'Get the fuck outta here!' and throwing the bottle of beer at you. Andy Young's car that I had parked, they pushed that sucker into a lake. They burned cars. Bricks, firecrackers. It was horrible." King himself was once hit by a rock, stumbling to one knee. He remarked afterward that, in all his marches in Alabama and Mississippi, "I have never seen so much hatred and hostility on the faces of so many people." But beyond these bedlams on the streets, King was confronted by that impalpable firmament of power and interests that made his exertions in Chicago like trying to engage a vaguely malign smog. "His great strength in the old fight was his ability to dramatize the immorality he opposed," wrote David Halberstam, but in Chicago, it was finally "an immorality with invisible sources."

King's whole endeavor there ended in the ceremonious contrivance of a "summit agreement," contained on a single page of paper, professing cheerful intentions that, along with their amorphous terms, happened to carry no timetable. Robert Lucas was sitting in his office at CORE when "somebody called me and said, 'Do you know they're meeting at the Palmer House about some summit agreement?' I ran the two or three blocks over there, and when I got to the door, King saw me and waved to the policeman to let me in. But the consensus had already been reached, the vote taken. I looked at the thing—just one eight-and-a-half-by-eleven page—and it said *nothing*. No way to enforce, no teeth in it. *Nothing*." Lucas declares, "People are still afraid to say it, but there's no question, King was beaten here." King himself bravely advertised afterward that "the total eradication of housing discrimination has been made possible. Never before has such a far-reaching move been made," but he privately confessed to several journalists that Chicago had confirmed for him the endemic, infinitely resourceful intransigence of racism in the American system. It left him, reported Halberstam at the time, actually "closer to Malcolm than anyone would have predicted five years ago—and much farther from more traditional allies like Whitney Young and Roy Wilkins."

With his confoundment in Chicago, King seemed increasingly oppressed by a sense that he was caught in a kind of terrible race between a progressive deadening of America's heart and the last hope for its "moral reconstruction" into a true, interconnected human community. Flash combustions of despair and rage in Watts, Newark, Harlem, and Detroit, and the emergence of a blankly furious nihilism among new young black Robespierres, had begun to bode a widening withdrawal of faith in King's testament of redemptive, nonviolent resistance, a cynicism that had been setting in even before the Selma March. In the summer of 1964, shortly after three civil rights workers were murdered in Philadelphia, Mississippi, King went on a tour of the state, and at a mass meeting one night in Greenwood, while his voice rolled over the assembly—"We have a power that's greater than all the guns in Mississippi, greater than all the bombs and armies of the world; we have the power of our *souls!*"—an accompanying undertone of low hooting came from several young partisans of the Student Non-Violent Coordinating Committee (SNCC) scattered around the back of the church, "Oh, de *Lawd*! De *Lawd*, now!" At the same time, his outcry against Vietnam, in a period of general popular acceptance of that foreign exploit, had disconcerted many of his own supporters. Not only did it earn him the suspicion and rancor of Lyndon Johnson's Washington, but it scandalized such dependable allies in the past as the worthy *New York Times*. The backfire was so wide and vituperative that King now and then actually collapsed into weeping. Jackson's wife, Jackie, recalls that once, when King visited Chicago while Jackson himself was out of town, she and several others joined him for dinner at Trader Vic's: "I was so excited about going to have one of the fabulous dinners they had there, which I had never seen, and with Dr. King," but at one point "I mentioned to him that he should do more about the Vietnam War, that we have to stay on Vietnam—and he stomped and turned swiftly to me and looked at me in such a fury, it was intimidating. It was the first and only time he shouted at me, spoke to me harshly. He said, 'You don't understand. I have done everything I can for Vietnam. But the press is against me, white people are against me, much of the religious community is against me now over this.'"

But even though King found himself, on all sides, more and more isolated, he was soon proposing, in the summer of 1967, the most expansive and radical venture of his career: a national mass movement called the Poor People's Campaign, which would gather into one monolithic popular force not only of blacks but of all the country's dispossessed and discarded—American Indians, Appalachian whites, Hispanics—a cycloramic populist front that Jackson, some fifteen years later, would seek to repeat with his Rainbow Coalition. It was to be a great, Gandhian crusade to free the destitute of America from their generational ghettos of economic hopelessness through a concerted siege of "major dislocations," he said, of the nation's entire custodial complex, not just its corporate citadels but the central institutions of Washington itself, into which a Poor People's March would converge from all over the country and set up an encampment. What King had in mind was nothing less than the reordering of the economic and power arrangements of the nation, the values and terms on which America worked. Some of its particulars included a possible nationalization of the more vital industries and major services, a multi-billion-dollar Marshall Plan for the inner cities, a guaranteed minimum income for all households. But more generally, he told David Halberstam then, "for years I labored with the idea of reforming the existing institutions of the society" through "a little change here, and a little change there," but "now I feel quite differently. You've got to have a reconstruction of the entire society, a revolution of values." In thus following his moral vision to its final implications, he had become perhaps the most subversive man in the country. What he was contemplating was an altogether different matter from simply according constitutional rights to southern blacks, and considerably more people of consequence besides J. Edgar Hoover now viewed him with distinct alarm. Even among those long close to him, defections multiplied. He passed one night in the Manhattan West Side brownstone of a couple who had persevered as faithful patrons up to now, entreating their support for this last grand hope of his while downing, with a kind of heedless abandon, one orange juice and vodka after another. But he finally departed, desolated by their refusal.

King was passing into that far region of all true prophets: the lonely terrain beyond the conventionally enlightened, the standard civic respectability. One of his private backers, a Chicago business entrepreneur named Cirilo McSween, remembers that after an all-day conference convoked by King at his Ebenezer Baptist Church in Atlanta to try explaining this new initiative to his oldest corps of supporters, several of them were standing outside the church in the warm January evening, discussing all that King had arrayed through that long day's session, and only then did it come over them "what it was really all about. The total seriousness of the thing. He had done all these other social things, but this was the culmination, this was really intense. Because it was embarking on the financial structure of the country." And it was at that moment, as they talked in a hushed rustling of voices in the dark outside the church, all still slightly dazed, that for the first time, says McSween, "we really understood that Martin Luther King was a revolutionary. This was big business, absolutely radical. And it had become very dangerous." But when King himself came outside and stood chatting with them for a few moments on the sidewalk—it also happened to be the evening of his thirty-eighth birthday—"He was very relaxed. Even though," McSween recalls, he suddenly became aware for some reason that "he had no protection at all around him."

But even some on King's staff, including Jackson, were still resisting the Poor People's Campaign as too sweeping and strategically uncertain a commitment. Jackson argued, "Suppose Johnson turns his back on us? What then? Are we just abandoned? How are we supposed to counter a rejection from the White House and Congress? What's the hook if that happens? If we don't get some results, we'll lose face." He urged, instead, some less Armageddon-like undertaking styled more after the tactical, hedgerow battling of Operation Breadbasket for black economic inclusion, such as the threat of a national boycott of General Motors. But "none of us were particularly excited about the Poor People's Campaign," says Young. "Bevel wanted to take on the war in Vietnam. Hosea wanted to build a political base in the South. Everybody had a different agenda." Neither was the staff especially enheartened when King "talked seriously of mounting the kind of campaign that would possibly lead to our being in prison for a year or two. Nobody was that happy about a one- to four-year federal prison term, and we knew that was the sort of thing he was leading us into." King, though, seemed to Young "almost as if he were looking forward to spending a couple of years in jail. It was almost as though the only way he saw of getting a sabbatical was to go to jail."

The persisting dissents from his own staff did not precisely alleviate King's sense of embattled aloneness, his growing fatalistic gloom. And in fact, his Poor People's Campaign may have been, from the start, a hopelessly misbegotten enterprise for the same reasons that his Chicago expedition miscarried: again, but on a national scale now, he was addressing an array of interests far more elusively abstract than the glandular simplicity of Birmingham's Bull Conner or George Wallace's troopers on the Selma Bridge—a muzzy profusion of federal bureaucracies, company executive committees, glib and pleasant policy apologists, among all of which, in the words of a gospel song, "You can't find the one to blame / It's too smart to have a name / It's not flesh and blood we fight with / It's powers and principalities."

Yet strangely, as if in inverse measure to his distress as he watched the preparations for his "last, greatest dream" beginning to falter around him, King's urgency seemed only to reach wider, ranging beyond the nation to embrace, almost deliriously, the world itself. America's disorder, he declared, was "inseparable from an international emergency which involves the poor, the dispossessed, the exploited of the whole world." It was as if he had come to feel weighted with all the planet's grief—famines, massacres, maraudings of war, the slums not only of Chicago but of Cairo and Calcutta and Lima—all the earth's cruelty and anguish. "He felt he should be able to convince Johnson to withdraw from Vietnam," says Young. "He felt he should be able to wipe out poverty. He should be able to stop violence." On Christmas Eve of 1967, only about three and a half months before he was assassinated, King appealed, from his pulpit at Ebenezer Baptist, for a climactic movement to accomplish a wholly new global community beyond class, tribe, race, nation—"a world unity in which all barriers of caste and color are abolished." In the largest sense, King was really just beginning when he wandered out onto his motel room balcony in Memphis that April evening of 1968.

"King Understood Who Jesse Was"

IT WAS, THOUGH, this messianic social vision of King's that was to transfer almost entire into Jackson's own—the understanding from which he was primarily to act throughout the ensuing years. "I mean, he *cloned* himself out of Martin Luther King," says former King aide Bernard Lafayette.

And while Jackson was entranced with King as a personification of his own great aspirations, King, for his part, seemed intrigued by the electricities of special promise that Jackson carried. "King would have seen the energy, the intelligence," says Calvin Morris. "He would have seen some of himself." As it happened, Jackson, at twenty-six, was the same age King had been when he had assumed leadership of the Montgomery bus boycott in 1955, and by Jackson's report, King even had him preach once or twice in his place at Ebenezer, although he was still unordained, "because Martin saw something in me." On one of King's visits to a home in Los Angeles to which he often retired for soul-cooked meals with the family and their friends, a teenage girl in the household can still remember how, after dinner that evening, he began telling the others around the table about "this young man on our staff now named Jesse Jackson, who's really coming up, he's gonna be somebody," confiding to them his amazement at "how incredibly fearless" he seemed to be, "he will just do things others wouldn't think of daring—he must think he's immortal," but confessing as well to some concern that "he's too volatile" and could even risk "the nonviolent character of what we're doing."

Before long, King also developed an uneasiness about Jackson's undisguisable, hugely beating ambition, his proclivity for theatrical posturing. One of King's associates later recollected that "Jesse could never pass a reflective surface without pausing—whether it was a store window or just a shiny car, he'd have to stop a second and check himself out again." And King, for his part, knowing what was quite likely ahead for this bountifully gifted and blurtingly eager young protégé of his, detected in Jackson a disquieting susceptibility to the sirens of consequence and celebrity. As early as their days together in Chicago, it was evident that "King understood who Jesse was," says Jackson's close friend then, Henry Hardy. "Jesse has always been so highly charged a personality, people were sometimes a bit astringent in their appraisals of him. But Dr. King was able to see something there others could not see, because he understood the complexity of the human psyche—and Jesse is a very complex affair." That understanding came to King not least because he was himself so complex a being, and if he had misgivings about the capacity of a temperament like Jackson's to resist the blandishments of pride and glory, it owed not a little to the fact that those beguilements were profoundly familiar to King himself.

Indeed, King was a far more excruciatingly complicated man than all the icon imagery of his subsequent beatification would have it. To hallow someone is usually to hollow him, but the true maze of tensions within

King suggests in what mysteriously mixed forms our prophets actually, personally, come to us in their own time—sometimes even unpleasant as with Gandhi, a rather chillingly and autocratically ascetic sort who, behind his appearance of "extraordinary innocence and benignity," as related in the autobiography of his Indian contemporary Nirad Chaudhuri, could be exquisitely vindictive, with an "insatiable love of power and implacability in its pursuit." Such baser aspects, though, do not so much diminish great moral protagonists like Gandhi or King as somehow lend them, and what they became, a yet greater dimension, far beyond their more commonplace, depthless, mass-cult sanctifications. Not altogether incidentally, for that matter, almost all the accusations later raised against Jackson could also be heard about King during his day: that he was staggeringly self-important; breathtakingly pompous; a brazen and sometimes craven opportunist, as in his final resort to enlisting schoolchildren to continue his Birmingham demonstrations ("I'm worried to death," he had said after his triumph in Montgomery, "that people will be expecting me to pull rabbits out of a hat for the rest of my life"); as well as forlornly inept as an administrator of his organization, even suspiciously derelict in its financial accountings. "They accused Martin of embezzling money, you know," recalls Andrew Young, "as well as of being an egomaniac. You've almost got to expect that anybody who adopts a prophetic position and troubles the waters is going to be maligned."

But the truth, David Halberstam observed at the time, was that "the average reporter . . . suspects King's vanity," that he had been "thrown into a prominence which he did not seek but which he has come to accept, rather likes, and intends to perpetuate," that, in fact, "he has finally come to believe his myth," and "colleagues find him occasionally pretentious." Even his longtime confidant Dr. Samuel Proctor concedes, "I'm not sure that King was not aware of this sense of destiny. Every now and then, I'd hear something drop from his lips. I'll never forget hearing him say"—and Proctor recites in pipe-organ tones—" 'I have wondered how long I should have kept my silence on the Vietnam question.' Kind of like, you know, the whole world has only been waiting for you to break your silence." With increasing frequency, "phrases like that he'd let fall."

But where King markedly differed from Jackson was that he greatly travailed with himself over his fallibilities. Even as a small boy, King had evidenced an exorbitant, and not a little self-impressed, inclination to take upon himself great cargoes of guilt, which impelled him twice, before he was thirteen, to bizarre gestures of suicide—once, when he assumed that his having slipped away one Sunday to watch a downtown parade had somehow accounted for the death that afternoon of his grandmother, he flung himself out of an upstairs window of his home. Later, in organizing the popular confrontations of his movement, he was often left with a woe that he was centrally responsible for whatever suffering attended them. In the summer of 1964, King's SCLC had mounted a series of demonstrations in Florida's little moss-hung antique of a city, St. Augustine—marches that proceeded almost nightly from the black section to the town's square, where, under darkly clacking palms, they would be immediately engulfed in a rampage of violence from whites who'd steadily collected there through the hot sullen twilight. After one particular Walpurgis Night of fury on the square—a maelstrom of baseball bats and shrieked rebel yells, fists and kicks, tire tools and trace chains, even the concrete saucer of a birdbath lofted through the air—the marchers straggled back into the refuge of the black quarter, bleeding, clothes torn, sobs and wails breaking out everywhere, while in the shadows of a front porch they passed, unnoticed by any of them, stood King in his shirtsleeves, absolutely motionless, watching the marchers stumbling by in the dark with a look on his face of aghast astonishment. Later that night, he sat behind the drawn blinds in the front parlor of another house in the black neighborhood, holding a large glass of ice water with a paper napkin wrapped around the bottom, and said in a heavy, weary murmur, "You question sometimes, when something like this tonight happens, *What are we doing to these people? Is it worth it?*" Even so, earlier that evening, when he had watched the ragged and reeling retreat from the square, there had seemed on his face, along with shock at what had befallen these marchers who had set forth at his call, a kind of detached wonder and fascination at this tumultuous clash that had been occasioned by his moral dramaturgy of good and evil—and, at the same time, some deeper alarm at that very captivation in himself.

"I am a troubled soul," he declared more than once. Long before Memphis, he had come to dwell in a kind of private Gethsemane of agonizing over what he felt were betrayals of his high public meaning. Always haunted by a reverence for the austere, he attempted to maintain, in place of Gandhi's fasts and spinning wheels, at least a modesty in his own circumstances, a simple home, plain dark suits; yet he remained chronically infatuated with the iridescences of importance, glossy cars and regal hotels and the company of the rich and eminent. He would frequently deplore what he termed "the evils of sensuality," proposing in one sermon, "Each of us is two selves. And the great burden of life is always to keep that higher self in command. Don't let the lower self take over." But in King's own lapses into that lower self—the accumulating reports after his death of lickerish disportings in hotel rooms seeming at first wildly at odds with simply his nature of stately gravity, until they became too plentiful from too many responsible sources to be reasonably doubted—one sensed an extraordinarily harrowed man, caught in the almost insupportable strain of having to sustain such an enormous mass moral struggle, intermittently resorting to momentary escapes, complete and obliterating, into luxurious sensual carnival.

But for someone of King's extravagant propensity for guilt, it was as if all his despair over such private lapses from the high spirituality of his public apostleship could be expiated only by surrendering himself to a readiness to die. Even in his first rallies in Montgomery, he was already casting himself in the same scenario of crucifixion that he would present, thirteen years later, at the mass meeting in Memphis on the last night of his life— suddenly strangling into tears before a dismayed congregation and crying out, "Lord, I hope no one will have to die as a result of our struggle for freedom here in Montgomery. . . . But if anyone has to die, let it be me." And then, when his home in Montgomery was bombed, "If I had to die tomorrow morning, I would die happy, because I've been to the mountaintop, and I've seen the Promised Land!" For the rest of his life, he would go on repeating that same incantation of fatality, right up to that rainy evening in Memphis.

But what seemed most to energize and sustain King, finally, was the exaltation of another kind of self-extinguishment: to lose and redefine himself in a larger self, a larger reality beyond his particular person—that same urge that Jackson, for his own reasons, had given himself over to in Greensboro. However unlike in their origins and temperaments, in that high aspiration the two of them ultimately converged: they became of a kind. That larger life for them both lay in the great historical truth animating a movement that could, King said, "save the soul of a nation . . . save the whole of mankind." However tormented by private forebodings and sinkings of will, King would hold to that sense of a vaster and more comprehending self, "of a cosmic companionship," as he once described it, with its "greater feeling of security."

BUT IF KING had concerns about the hungers that had propelled Jackson into that same pursuit of a larger meaning, many of his aides regarded Jackson with a decided aversion. Part of their antipathy was that he had obtruded into the relatively preacherly decorums of SCLC a style, from operating on the streets of Chicago, that was more like the raffish swagger of the fire-breathing young partisans of SNCC. It made him "sort of a misfit," one SCLC worker remarked at the time, "an off-brand, yeah." Actually, though, King's staff itself was usually engaged in a more or less general free-for-all of egos. "Reporters since then have taken Jesse in isolation," says Andrew Young, "but *everybody* irritated *everybody*. We basically rounded up all these eccentric types, almost all of them self-styled prophets with a kind of messianism that can be troublesome, but that's what it took. Martin always said, look, normal people don't challenge the law of the land. He said you got to be creatively maladjusted. We need people who'll disturb, who'll trouble the waters. But there was *constant* irritation. *Nobody* got along." Young himself, who had taken boxing lessons as a youth in New Orleans, once slugged Hosea Williams for alleging he was an FBI "plant," and Williams has since acknowledged that some staff meetings featured aides hurling chairs and tables in the near vicinity of each other. "All of them strong egos," says Young. "All of them with his own story. All of them, in some way, maybe subconsciously, wishing that he was Martin Luther King." Jackson's misfortune, says Young, became that of simply "getting out front, where naturally you become the target." Criticisms always collected and focused on anyone who looked as if he were trying to "move toward a leadership position."

That may have been why King's staff was finally most affronted by what seemed the sheer, tireless, undiscourageable, uncontainable appetite of Jackson's ego. "Jesse was just always *on*," Young once complained, "he just didn't *relax*." He was still given to that impulse evidenced during the demonstrations in Greensboro of improvising sudden, dashing ploys of his own; in the midst of King's campaign in Chicago, he appalled the rest of the staff by abruptly announcing, after consulting only his own mood, a march into the city's particularly truculent white suburb of Cicero, and as for the likelihood of wholesale mayhem that might result, he merely observed, "We expect violence." Jackson produced that proclamation, remembers Don Rose, a Chicago publicist serving as adviser to CCCO, one night "when the cameras were on him" at a rally in a West Side church, and "as soon as the cheers went up, I'm surrounded by the press and having to explain this march into Cicero which I had just heard about, start contriving some explanation to protect King." It left the SCLC leadership "in trauma," says Rose. But with that wildcat declaration, Jackson more or less impressed SCLC into reluctantly committing to the march, King himself obliged to affirm, "We're not only going to walk in Cicero, we're going to work there and live there." But Rose acknowledged years afterward, "It brought things to a head much quicker, forced the issue when it was not the goal of the Chicago movement to force it." As it turned out, the march itself never had to take place: simply the unnerving prospect of it raised by Jackson's extemporaneous mention flushed forth one of the few offers of direct negotiations from Daley's regime, and led soon to the summit agreement that at least allowed King to conclude his Chicago enterprise with some semblance of achievement.

It wasn't long, though, before King's staff began to suspect that Jackson was pursuing a secondary script of his own through a symbiosis with King and SCLC. With Operation Breadbasket flourishing now under his direction in Chicago, Jackson strenuously evaded all attempts by SCLC to shift him into its Atlanta office—a move that would have detached him from the small, personal subfranchise of leadership he had begun developing in his new home city, where he sometimes exhorted the businessmen in his expositions on black economic independence, "I don't know if you're ready for a kingdom, but I'm sure ready to be the king." Jackson's insistence on staying in Chicago, Ralph Abernathy later reflected, "was a way of remaining almost independent while at the same time enjoying the benefits of SCLC connections." As Bob Lucas now assays it, "See, Jesse wasn't then, as he is not now, the type of person to follow anybody else. That's not Jesse. He was probably reluctantly a part of SCLC, but that was at least a place to start, you know."

As for King, while he was hardly unaware that Jackson was "engrossed in building his own personal kingdom," one aide later reported, and "challenged Jesse to divorce himself" from it, still, one minister in the Chicago movement declares, "he had a lot of patience with Jesse." According to Young, King once admonished the others on his staff, "You're very lucky you had both a mother and daddy who loved you, and so you don't compulsively need attention. Jesse compulsively needs attention." It was a compulsion, though, of such an imperious fierceness that it once provoked from King, by another account, perhaps the bleakest condemnation he ever uttered about Jackson: "He just simply does not know how to love." At the least, he fretted to aides, "Jesse's just so independent, so ambitious." Don Rose recounts that when *Jet* magazine once carried a photo of Jackson, provided by his Breadbasket office, in which Jackson was standing in a pulpit with a portrait of King affixed below him and a cross hanging high behind him, "King looks at this three-tier picture, and he said, 'Well, at least he had the good grace to place himself below the Savior.' "

But in the end, more than anything else, the awkwardness between King and Jackson suggested that between a father who has, through great strain and daring and endurance, managed to achieve immense things, and a richly but still roughly gifted son who has a blindly lunging haste to fulfill himself in the same way. SCLC staffer Bernard Lafayette remembers that King would try to reassure him, "Just be patient, Jesse. Your time will come." But it became Robert Lucas's impression that Jackson had "some preoccupation of dominating. I think Jesse wanted to be *the* number one black American leader himself someday. Now I don't think Jesse was foolish enough to believe that he could displace King. But he was clearly competing with him anyway." Arriving with King at one mass meeting, Jackson even indulged himself in the delicious presumption, as he afterward told one Breadbasket member, of abstaining from speaking when "he noticed how the young people in the crowd got all excited when they saw him. So he decided he would take a backseat, because he didn't want to take anything away from Dr. King." But more commonly, Don Rose claims, "Jesse's grabbing at the leadership became a big problem for them. King never showed consternation, but Andy Young was visibly perturbed." Actually, Young now insists, "there were times when *everybody* went through a phase where they thought they, well, that Martin Luther King was going too slow, let's put it that way. Martin was so calm, mild-mannered, soft-spoken, extremely logical and analytical about everything, that almost everybody else would get constantly upset— wanna *do sump'm*! Typically, brash young men mistake humility for weakness, and everybody was always doing that to Martin—thought they could one-up him, manipulate him, co-opt him for their own purposes. And he'd never fight back. It was almost as though he felt he had to let us all do that, and somehow in this neurotic mix he could find the final formula for continuing the movement." Even so, at an opening mass rally for King's Chicago campaign, held in Soldier Field, Jackson's own barging ambitiousness "showed itself in a way that really shook us," says Young. "This was supposed to be Dr. King's moment. The only thing was, Jesse was speaking earlier in the program, and he tried to do an imitation of the March on Washington speech. I mean, it was obvious he was trying to do a Dr. King speech himself, not a speech as just a director of the Chicago project. He was trying to give his *own* vision for the movement in the future. It just wasn't *appropriate*."

Yet all this while, when in the immediate company of King, Jackson remained for the most part devoutly deferential, recall a number who saw them together, as near to subdued and abashed as they ever saw him, as if still with that "deep need" cited by Abernathy "for a special closeness" to what seemed holy. Or as one Chicago minister recollects, "like a son with a father that he was very proud of." Cirilo McSween remembers that the last time King came to Chicago, in January of 1968, the weekend before his thirty-ninth birthday and only about three months before his death, he presided at a small meeting "where he was talking about where we had to go, and in that meeting was kind of saying, I don't know when I'll see you again," and afterward, as he stood delivering parting pleasantries to the group while preparing to leave, Jackson took King's topcoat and settled it gently over his shoulders, "just affectionately, you know," says McSween, "put on his overcoat for him, there in front of all of us. It was a moving moment somehow."

That Evening in Memphis

IN THOSE LAST months, King had begun suffering from migraine headaches as he continued to contend with those on his staff, including Jackson, who were still contesting the soundness of the Poor People's Campaign. When he then decided to respond to an entreaty to intercede in a strike by black sanitation workers in Memphis as a kind of preliminary exercise for that larger effort, it distressed Jackson and others as a pointless diversion in what was already a colossally dubious undertaking. "We felt like you just couldn't take on everything," says Young, "and if we went into Memphis, we'd get bogged down there and never get to Washington. But Martin said he couldn't turn his back on those garbage workers." Jackie Jackson relates, "My husband felt that we were talking about economic reparation with the Poor People's Campaign, and here was Martin going on an 'I am a man' thing in Memphis. He and others on the staff felt it was too small, when we were already declining in popularity and attention. Memphis was an isolated area, the media wasn't there, and we were already in a media slump. They had about locked Martin out of the press, and the Memphis garbage workers could only be a small space at best." Jackson, whether or not out of trepidation now about losing that symbiosis with King by which he had so popularly prospered since proposing to him in Selma that he come to Chicago, kept urging him instead "to stick with Chicago," says Jackie, "that he ought to be in Chicago where he'd be dealing with the economic conditions that would be the issue of the next century."

At last, Abernathy and King journeyed to Memphis alone, to lead a march that rapidly devolved into a small riot, a number bloodied by thrown rocks, store windows shattered, their merchandise looted. Afterward, says Young, "I saw a kind of despair in Martin that I had never seen before. A real, deep-seated depression because he felt he was responsible and had miscalculated. He got very, very quiet, and spent almost from Monday to Friday alone. Saw almost nobody. And then he asked us all to come to Atlanta for a meeting that Saturday."

At that meeting, in a study at Ebenezer church, King "just jumped on everybody," says Young. "He said we'd let him down. That we all had our own agendas and constantly left everything up to him. He said, 'I can't take all this on by myself. I need you to take your share of the load.' " Finally came his outburst of exasperation, far more widely retold, with Jackson, who had kept pressing for alterations of the Poor People's Campaign: King had fumed out of the room, with Jackson trailing after him, along with Young. Jackson called from the top of the stairs as King and Abernathy were turning on the landing below, "Doc? Doc?" Young recalls, "Jesse tried to encourage him, but it was a sort of glib thing, you know, 'Don't worry, everything's going to be all right.' " At that, King wheeled and pointed a finger up at Jackson: "Jesse, everything's *not* going to be all right. If things keep going the way they're going now, it's not SCLC but the whole country that's in trouble. I'm not asking, Support me. I don't need this. But if you're so interested in doing your own thing, that you can't do what this organization's structured to do, if you want to carve out your own niche in society, go ahead. But for God's sake, don't bother me!" Jackson was left with a blasted and desolate stare. Young remembers, "It was shocking in the sense that he never talked to anybody like that. Though he'd often been mad at me, nobody had ever seen him mad like that before." (Indeed, shortly afterward, King quietly instructed Abernathy, "Please take care of Jesse.") But Young insists that King's message to Jackson on that stairwell at Ebenezer went far deeper than simply a rebuke. "It was a profound statement on the state of the nation. He said, 'I think this country is in critical condition, and SCLC is one of the few organizations that can help it. But SCLC can't do it unless we're all pulling together. If you're on separate agendas, we're not going to make it.' He saw the problems that we were going into not as his problem, not as Jesse's personal problem, but as America's problem. He felt that the only thing that could save us was us working together to try to redeem the soul of America."

That challenge turned out to be the last substantive words King ever passed on to Jackson, Young acknowledges. "And it, and—" and Young's voice suddenly clogs, and he hangs for several long seconds before finally sobbing out, "And he's never forgotten it."

A FEW DAYS later, King phoned Jackson, when he was back in Chicago, and as Jackie tells it, "asked him to come to Memphis. Martin was trying to get all the staff into Memphis with him, and I remember Reverend on the phone didn't want to go, and Martin was trying to convince him that the Memphis garbage workers' strike and the union situation there tied into the whole economic thing. So after a while, Reverend conceded he would go. He hung up the phone and turned to me and said, 'Martin is upset,' that he sounded so down, he had to go." When Jackson arrived in Memphis, says Jackie, "He called me and said, 'There's something strange here. Martin is extremely depressed.' The staff was there but many of them were still not supportive. 'They're rumbling,' he said, 'they don't want to be here, but we're stuck.' "

But as Abernathy later related, Jackson's own avid assertiveness persevered up to that last night's mass meeting in Memphis. When King at first elected not to appear at the church that evening, Abernathy suggested to him, "Why don't you let Jesse go? He loves to speak." At King's tart reply— "Nobody else can speak for me"—Abernathy asked if he could at least take Jackson along, and King said, "Yes, but you do the speaking." Shortly thereafter, says Jackie, "Reverend called me back and said, 'I'm going to the church tonight. Martin may not come, because he's not feeling well, he's awfully down.' And he said he might speak that night if Martin didn't come. They didn't know about the crowd, because it was raining." But despite the heavy unloading of rain in the hot night, when Abernathy arrived with Jackson at Mason Temple, he found so enormous a throng that he began looking for a telephone to summon King. Jackson quickly offered, "Don't call him. If you don't want to speak, then I'll speak." Abernathy phoned King nonetheless, and when he returned to the podium, Jackson inquired, "Is Doc coming?" At Abernathy's word that he was, Jackson's face glazed over with dejection. But later that night, says Jackie, "he called me back, and told me that Martin had given the most brilliant speech of his life. That he was lifted up and had some mysterious aura around him, and a power as if saying that now everything's going to be all right. That the crowd was tremendously moved, in tears. But he also said he felt that Martin was in a lot of pain." One local minister in the church that night, the Reverend Samuel (Billy) Kyles, remembers that "the fans were on because it was so hot. But they would bang now and then, and each time they did, King gave a start. So they finally shut them off."

Late the next afternoon, according to various accounts, King stepped out onto the balcony of the Lorraine Motel in his shirtsleeves, tucking in his shirttail as he prepared to leave for a southern soul-cooked dinner at a local preacher's home before another mass meeting, and he seemed, in chatting with several aides clustered around a white Cadillac limousine in the parking court below him, suddenly and pointedly solicitous of Jackson. "Tell Jesse to get ready," he boomed down, "he's going to dinner with us." As if instantly evoked forth by that mention, Jackson came battering down the metal stairway to take his place with the others in the courtyard. He had on a casually mod garb of olive turtleneck sweater with a polished brown long leather jacket, and when someone asked why he had not put on a tie, he jubilantly rejoined that he'd always believed all one needed to take to a dinner was a good appetite. King, who'd gone back into his room to get his coat, reappeared on the balcony and Jackson cried out, "Our leader!" King now called down directly to him, "Jesse, I want you to come to dinner with me." In fact, Jackson had already taken the precaution of arranging for that: standing beside King on the balcony was the minister who'd invited King's party to eat at his home, the Reverend Samuel Kyles, and Kyles informed King, "Jesse took care of himself long before you did. Jesse was the instigator of this thing. He already got himself invited." King chuckled. Jackson then happily called up to King to introduce a member of his Operation Breadbasket band in Chicago, a saxophonist and soloist named Ben Branch, whom he'd brought down to perform at that evening's meeting. King, whose joviality in this reconciliation with Jackson was evident to everyone watching, replied, "Oh, yeah, he's my man," and leaned forward with both hands braced on the iron balcony railing. "Ben, I want you to sing 'Precious Lord' for me tonight like you never sung it before. Want you to sing it *real* pretty." King's driver, Solomon Jones, then advised him the evening seemed to be turning cool and he should get his topcoat, and King, saying, "Okay, Jonesy," was straightening up to turn back into his room when there racketed over the courtyard, like a startling slap against the calm of that spring dusk, a single loud shot.

AFTER THE CHAOS that followed from that rifle clap—which split apart the very sky of hope for masses of black Americans, setting off firestorms in cities across the nation, smoke even dimming the sun over the white domes of Washington—it would come to seem that King's death was almost a personal enactment of the death of the nonviolent movement in America, the extinguishment of what had been perhaps the nation's highest moral folk saga since the Civil War. And though King had entered into an apparent decline, after Memphis, in the terrible definition sometimes of violent death, it suddenly appeared that on no one else, save, perhaps, Robert Kennedy, had the last possibilities for averting a final irreconcilable racial schism in the country—and thus for the survival of a true American community—so directly depended. About a month after Memphis, there was a memorial march in Washington—an eclectic accumulation of citizens, white and black and brown, priests and militants and students, that was curiously like a spectral afterimage of Selma, King's last great moment—all of them moving now, eerily voiceless, in a flickering drizzle through streets still scorched and gutted from the rage and flames of a month before. But presently a singing began to rise from them, a ghostlike choiring and clapping of those huge anthems from the simpler, heroic time of Montgomery and Birmingham and St. Augustine that seemed like some labor to somehow call him forth again: the sun momentarily broke through the rain—an unrelenting southern sun—under which the steaming streets shone with a soft silver light, and for an instant his presence seemed actually to be there in the air. He *had* to be in the midst of that procession and that singing, it would be only a second more before one would glimpse him again, that stocky figure striding along in his shirt-sleeves with an impassive gaze of remote and solitary inner communion. But that sense of him was there only for an instant, as brief as a single indrawing and release of breath, and what returned was the awareness of an enormous absence.

The Story of the Blood

AFTER THE RIFLE-CRACK that April twilight in the courtyard outside the Lorraine Motel, among the dazed and pandemonious plunging about of King's aides, Jackson's own first reactions were to become a subject of furious dispute that would harry him throughout the following years. Undisputed is that it was Jackson who first succeeded in getting through to King's wife, Coretta, in Atlanta, who was just returning home from a shopping trip when the phone rang. He delicately told her that King had only been hit in the shoulder. Later, a solitary reporter, waiting in the wanly lit hush outside the hospital morgue where King's body lay, saw Jackson go in with Abernathy and two other King associates, Young and Bernard Lee, for a last, brief visit. But then, late that night, Jackson fled back to Chicago, stretches of which were already burning. The next morning, he appeared on the *Today* show and, later, before a special memorial convocation of Chicago's city council, called by Mayor Daley. "The mayor's office had asked me to come down to city hall for the service," says George Johnson, the cosmetics manufacturer who was one of Jackson's patrons. "I informed Jesse and said, 'You want to go?' He said, 'Yeah.' So I took Jesse down. There was no place for him, and I more or less forced him in. He sat right behind the mayor, and listened to these tributes by the councilmen and all their professions of sorrow and contrition. Jesse got so full he tapped the mayor on the shoulder and told him he wanted to say something. The mayor didn't react at first, so Jesse mentioned it to him again." Jackson, his eyes masked in dark glasses, first appealed for "nonviolence in the homes, on the streets, in the classrooms. . . . I'm challenging the youth today to be nonviolent as the greatest expression of faith they can make in Dr. King, to put your rocks down, put your bottles down." But he delivered these remarks while still wearing, as he had during his *Today* interview, the olive turtleneck sweater from the night before, only it was now blotted with blood that he declared was King's: "I come here with a heavy heart be-cause on my chest is the stain of blood from Dr. King's head. . . . This blood is on the chest and hands of those who would not have welcomed him here yesterday. . . . He went through, literally, a crucifixion. I was there. And I'll be there for the resurrection." But he had also by now, in random brushes with the press, indicated that he was the last person King had spoken to, and once even, as if presenting his own kind of a pietà, that he had actually held King as he was dying.

That night in Memphis, after King's body had been taken away, Jackson was meandering about outside the motel in a pursuing swirl of media, mi-crophones crowding under his chin at his every move, reporters calling after him, "Jesse? Reverend?—"

"I need to see Dr. King," he insisted. Turning to someone passing, he said, "Can I get a ride to see Dr. King?"

"Reverend, could you tell us just what happened, please?"

He swerved away again from the thrusting mikes and tape recorders with a glower, his head lowered in the camera lights. "Can you wait a lit-tle while?"

"Would you tell me just what happened so we can get this film in, please?"

At last, he could not refrain. "People were, some in pandemonium, some in shock, some were hollering, 'Oh, God.' And, uh . . ." He glanced up at an angle, peering into the middle distance above him as if meditating: "And I immediately started running upstairs to where he was. And I caught his head. And I tried to feel his head. And I, I asked him, 'Dr. King, do you hear me? Dr. King, do you hear me?' And he didn't say any-thing. And I tried to—to hold his head. But by then . . ."

IF THE REST of King's troupe of assistants had never been particularly charmed by Jackson to start with, most of those who'd been at the Lor-raine Motel that evening were apoplectic when they learned of his claims. Several insisted Jackson had never come near King's body. One later reported he had instead scurried off at the rifle blast to take shelter behind the motel's swimming pool, another that he had remarked after-ward, "I'm sick, I got to go to Chicago and check into the hospital, this thing's really shot my nerves." Hosea Williams maintained that, after Jackson had demanded that no one talk to the journalists who were swiftly collecting at the scene, he glanced out his motel room to discover Jackson discoursing to several reporters off behind a chain-link fence, and ambled over to hear him explaining how he was the last mortal King had talked to; Williams had clambered halfway up the fence to fall upon Jackson—"I was gonna stomp him into the ground"—before someone pulled him back down.

Over the following years, as King's lieutenants scattered off into their separate and widely diverse destinies, their recollected impressions of Jackson's performance after the shot in Memphis continued to rankle, if anything more rancorously with the rise of Jackson's own star. Especially bitter was James Bevel, who had been Jackson's closest confederate in SCLC, and probably the most mystically ardent of all King's attendants. Andy Young now observes, "Bevel just sort of could never find a home after King died," and he eventually wandered into an involvement with Lyndon LaRouche's esoteric society of zealots. Among the journalists who would later avail themselves of Bevel's broodings for dismissive profiles of Jackson was Gail Sheehy, who quoted him as inveighing that "to prostitute" and "lie about the crucifixion of a prophet within a race" for the sake of "one's own self-aggrandizement" was "the most gruesome crime a man can commit." As it happened, points out Garry Wills, who was actually in Memphis right after the slaying, "SCLC members who have denounced Jackson for his publicity seeking—Hosea Williams, especially, and James Bevel—were very aggressive in their courting of the cameras in the next few days." Williams himself sat in King's room displaying for a camera the contents of King's briefcase. Nevertheless, even King's wife, Coretta, could not bring herself for a long time afterward to speak a word to Jackson.

As for Jackson himself, throughout his later public progress the matter of Memphis was to repeatedly rear up to confront him like an unquiet shade from his past—in the recurrent questioning of journalists, in the derision of his adversaries—and he would attribute such dark imputations to misconstructions of his comments after the episode, to old resentments among the SCLC staff, to the malevolence of his antagonists. Finally, he simply declined to address the issue anymore, out of a reckoning that it had proved bootless anyway and only served to stir the suspicions again. "I *never* respond to it," he snapped to yet another query, from Myra MacPherson of *The Washington Post*, as late as 1988. "It has no useful or redeeming value. To whom does it matter, the continuous rehearsal of that?" About the extent of any particular commentary from him on the event has been his insistence, since meeting for four hours in 1978 with King's convicted assassin, James Earl Ray, that, as he told reporters then, "I do not believe he killed Dr. King. I am absolutely convinced Ray was involved, but was not alone. Others involved are still walking the streets." Once, in a speech in Memphis on the seventh anniversary of King's slaying, he did allow himself to venture so far as to mention that, after the shot, "I turned to my right looking on that hill where there were so many police and firemen. I threw my hands up as I ran toward the steps, screaming, 'Please don't shoot.' As we ran to get his body, some strange things happened—" But then, as if catching himself, he ended, "I have not really felt like talking about it." One of the editors at Viking who had striven to get some sort of publishable autobiography out of Jackson recalls that, "about King's shooting, there he really did clam up. Although I tried. 'Look, if you could tell us what went through your head—' and he said, 'That's such a strong emotional thing for me that I can't, even today, can't quite talk about it.' I said, 'But can you just say a little bit about what you went through when it all happened?' and he'd say, 'Well, we were very upset'—and then go off into a peroration about what King meant to the world." In truth, admitted a Jackson aide in 1987, even his critics "have no idea how it haunts him. It's a drop of poison in his glass." During one late-night phone conversation in 1990, he did blurt out the protest, "Look, I was up there, I was pointing"— obviously referring to the now-familiar photograph of several King assistants ranked on the balcony over King's fallen form and pointing together in the direction of the shot. One of those figures, partly concealed behind a woman, does appear to be Jackson.

It is not impossible, of course, that Jackson himself does not remember precisely what happened in the wildness of those minutes after King was hit. Andy Young observes, "In a moment like that, confused and frantic, you do a lot of weird things you don't recall afterward, you just focus on these little incidental, disconnected details around you." But according to one witness—Reverend Kyles, who was with him on the balcony, just turning to walk down the stairs, at the slam of the rifle shot—"Of course [Jesse] got blood on him" in the turmoil that followed. "We all did," he later told Garry Wills. "There was blood everywhere."

King had been jolted backward to his left. One witness later described seeing him "go up with the shot against the brick wall, and as he went up his arms went out to the sides like he was a man on a cross." Then he lay slumped across the balcony floor with his shoes awkwardly crammed against the railing slats and trying to move "like riding a bicycle," someone later told Jackie, his slightly lifted knees pulling his trouser cuffs above his black ribbed socks, and his left arm outflung where it had fallen from its instinctive grope for the railing as he toppled. At the shot, the people in the courtyard had thrown themselves to the pavement, and Kyles and Abernathy—he had been in the room splashing on aftershave lotion—were the first to reach King. His neck and right jaw were blasted open, blood surging into a massy pool already brimming heavily around his shoulders. A moment later, the balcony was swarming with other people. "We all rushed up there," Young himself now recounts, "including Jesse. That's

232 / J E S S E

just your natural impulse. So yes, I saw Jesse there. It would have been much stranger if he were *not*." Among the tumble of others on the balcony at one moment or another—a deputy sheriff from somewhere, a black South African documentary filmmaker, a reporter for *The New York Times*—was a white Justice Department official, James Laue, who worked for Roger Wilkins in the Community Relations Service and had accompanied King to Memphis, his room right next to King's, and who, after the shot, had rushed out to clumsily swaddle King's head in a towel. Years later, Laue joined Wilkins on the faculty at George Mason University in Fairfax, Virginia, and "I asked him," says Wilkins, "what happened with Jesse. And he said, Jesse was around. He said he didn't know if he was on the balcony right then, he wasn't paying attention to anybody else, but that afterward, yeah, Jesse was there." In the meantime, Kyles had ripped an orange bedspread from one of the twin beds in the room and brought it out to cover King, taking out of King's hand a crushed pack of cigarettes: "King never smoked in public, so I took it out of his hand." At any rate, "several of us handled him," Kyles has since attested, and among that number, he says, was Jackson. Only some five minutes after King was struck, he was lifted onto an ambulance stretcher by Young, another assistant named Chauncy Eskridge, and two policemen, and taken off to the hospital.

Kyles assured Garry Wills years later that he was certain, as Wills wrote, that "Jackson touched the blood and wiped it on his shirt." As for what some took to be Jackson's implication the day after the shooting that the blood on his sweater had come from actually holding King, Young says, "About his cradling Martin's head in his arms, if he did say that, that was wrong." But when several of them returned from the hospital to the motel, says Young, Abernathy brought out from the room a sheet of cardboard from a laundered shirt and bent to begin "scooping the blood into a jar, that's how thick it was, scooping up the blood and crying, 'This is Martin's precious blood. This blood was shed for us.' People did strange things that reflected their own insecurities." And still in his memory, Young now declares these many years later, "I can see Jesse going over and leaning down and placing both his palms down flat in that pool of blood, and then standing up and, like this"—and Young slowly passes both his hands down his chest—"wiping it down the front of his shirt." Young adds, "There's nothing that unusual about it, it's what you'd have done. We Baptists, you know, we believe there's power in the blood—power that's transferrable." As Garry Wills has noted in one of the more thoughtful appraisals of the whole affair, it has immemorially been a deep human urge in such instants of violent martyrdom to dip one's hands into, to preserve on oneself some touch of the blood of a slain prophet or hero.

Roger Wilkins says, "My own judgment is that it was not terrific to be on TV the next morning in those same clothes. It wasn't something I would have done. But on the other hand, given Jesse's sense of drama and his emotionalism . . . you know, anybody who's ever been through a family funeral knows that people do things around the time of the death that later they wish they hadn't done." Actually, it would have hardly been a more extravagant reaction than Jackson's strangely berserk grieving at the death of his stepfather some ten years later. In what Jackie later characterized as "the trauma" for him of King's murder, Jackson had phoned her that night from Memphis, she relates in a slow, hushed voice, "and he said, 'Jackie, Dr. King has been shot. He is dead.' He said, 'There's a lot going on down here, I don't understand any of it.' Then he said again, 'Jackie, *Dr. King is dead.*' He maybe thought he was repeating it to make me understand it, but I think he kept saying it to make himself understand it." She met him at the airport when he got in that night, and she remembers that "his eyes were kind of deep-set. And he was wearing this shirt that was bloodstained. When we got in the car, there was a silence; what had happened was too much to talk about in a car. Then when we were home, he got in the bed with his shoes on and the shirt on, staring at the ceiling. And he just lay in the bed like that off and on, whenever he was back home, for maybe two or three days. And he, usually he likes cologne and all that, but he didn't wash. Seemingly forever he lay in that bed staring at the ceiling with his shoes on and that shirt on. You know, blood, after it dries, it looks funny, and it was a nasty stain, and I knew he shouldn't keep on wearing that shirt looking like that. But he told me, 'I'll never take this shirt off. This is Martin's blood.' "

Yet with a number of others having supported over the years much of Jackson's initial account of his experience that evening, including now even Andrew Young, the puzzle remains why Jackson himself has continued to be so resistant to fully describing what happened. When directly queried about that as late as 1995, he would only offer, "It would just start up a big back-and-forth about it again. What I've always felt, you know, is that I would outlive all those slanders." "He is very rarely reticent when asked a question," says Calvin Morris, "but around that issue, he gets somewhat silent." An early colleague of King's, the Reverend Wyatt Tee Walker, who would later work occasionally with Jackson, suggests, "Jesse probably demurs because it was such a private, mystical something he did, and you can't really explain those sorts of things afterward."

More, one senses that Jackson, in his own considerations of it all afterward, could have come closer than he ever had before to that one emotion that had heretofore most marked his difference from King: a capacity for guilt—in this instance, an almost unbearable mortification at what he came to suspect could have been a macabre eagerness of self-promotion.

IN THE END, though, at least the symbolism of Jackson's story—a transfer of the commission, signified by a kind of anointing with King's very blood—would turn out to be largely the reality. In his eventual massive national activation of the black voting rights won by King in Selma, in his perpetuation of King's vision in the nation's life, in his ascent to become an almost totemic figure for America's black community, he would indeed prove to be probably King's most notable legatee. In that respect, then, Jackson's account right after Memphis, however approximate to the circumstantial particulars it may have been, could also be understood as something like a symbolic assertion of his own sense of the consequences to follow.

As Jackie recalls her own feeling, "At Memphis, we physically lost one individual, but actually we lost many lives there. A portion of my husband's life and many of the members of SCLC, many of us, were left there on that balcony in Memphis. But we could not let the enemies of peace and enemies of our movement win like that. So our time stopped in Memphis and it began in Memphis. All of a sudden, the movement was our responsibility." The very night of the shooting, says C. T. Vivian, King's own staff "went back to the motel and we talked half the night about how to handle this, about the possibilities. What should we do? The whole idea was future movement." For his own part, Vivian admits, while in Atlanta for the funeral, "I spent my time thinking how SCLC could raise twenty million dollars from this. So we could go into an enlarged program that we were never able to do before. I think that's the way Martin would have thought. I was trying to think out of the mind of Martin. And Martin wasn't concerned about being murdered; Martin was concerned about how do we keep the freedom movement going." Jackson's intimate then, David Wallace, states, "Prior to Dr. King's death, he saw himself that he had unusual potential. He knew it, I knew it, a lot of others knew it. But we didn't think it would come in that kind of way. With that kind of shock." Nevertheless, says Calvin Morris, "It wasn't time for a whole lot of grief. I remember Willie Barrow saying to us in the most gruff voice, 'Dry up your tears. It's no time to cry now. We've got to continue the work.' And," Morris adds, "Jesse always senses the moment. And it was an epochal moment. And he was there. And he responded."

Shortly after his address to the Chicago city council, relates Don Rose, the publicist for CCCO, "Jesse calls me and says, 'Can you get me on the weekend talk shows?' Which wasn't hard to do, since they were already falling all over themselves to get to him." Rose arranged appearances on two or three local programs, and the next day, the two of them rode from station to station, sitting in the backseat of "this big car that he had available to him, with a driver." Jackson was attired in a dashiki, recalls Rose, although his blood-smeared sweater "I think he also had with him. He had some kind of tote bag." To Rose, Jackson seemed still unmistakably stunned from the scene in Memphis, "very sober." But as they wound their way from appearance to appearance, Jackson also proceeded to speculate about the possibility now that he might come to assume King's place. "The word used was leadership," says Rose, "nothing crass. But it was, in effect, 'Do you think I could take on King's mantle?' I said, 'You probably can. You know what it's about, and people know who you are.' " They surveyed the landscape of the movement at that moment and the cast of other prospects: "The day of CORE was dying. Snick [SNCC] was falling apart. Roy Wilkins's day was over. Whitney Young was never a charismatic leader." Even at that point, neither Abernathy nor Young seemed really in the running. "He was the only one of them all who had a foot in the establishment and could still communicate with the youth. I said, 'I think you can bridge the gap between black power and civil rights. You bridge that gap as well as the age thing.' I also said something like, 'Of course, you're the only one who has anything like Martin's gifts as a speaker.' Of course, I didn't have to bring that concept to him, because he knew it. By then, that was a given." On the whole, Rose insists, this traveling discussion between the two of them was all "very businesslike. Without being callous at all in a time of crisis, we were dealing with the business at hand," and it became Rose's certainty as they talked that succeeding King was "what he wanted not just on that day but well before. He was just very focused on what he was going to do. He didn't have it all mapped out yet, and he wasn't overly salivating at the prospect, but he saw himself as the logical inheritor. And his questions to me were, 'Don't you agree that I am? Or that I *should* be?' "

Inspiriting indicators shortly began emerging. At Jackson's regular Breadbasket service on the Saturday before King's slaying, only some four hundred people were sitting in the auditorium, but the following Saturday—after King's death on Thursday, and right after Jackson's extensive backseat deliberations with Rose a day or so later—four thousand appeared for the Breadbasket memorial service. When Jackson rose to address them, they erupted "in hysterics," as one reporter described it, "as if King was being reincarnated in that man," and as Jackson began speaking, in "his voice, his intonations," it seemed to that reporter, "it was like he was trying to *be* King." Afterward, as the varied multitude filed out past Jackson—welfare mothers, NAACP officials, community militants—"almost the way you would file by to greet the spouse of someone at a funeral," says Don Rose. And Jackson directly connected with every one of them with a warm personal word, a black-power or standard handshake, in a kind of catholic closeness, a white attorney there later marveled, that could have been brought off at that time "by no one else in Chicago, or perhaps the nation."

"It was like it grew overnight, like wildfire, after Dr. King was killed," remembers Hermene Hartman. "It wasn't another ball game. It was another world. Jesse was the only one now." And, says Calvin Morris, "not only did Jesse's persona grow after Dr. King's death, it zoomed into the stratosphere."

WHATEVER MAY HAVE been its oracular import, though, Jackson's story about Memphis continued to be widely discounted over the years as the contrivance of, in the words of one skeptic, "a compulsive con artist." Nearer the case would be the reconstruction of a compulsively self-dramatizing visionary with an insuppressible inclination toward hyperbole. In fact, Jackson's entire career since then of struggling to accomplish his moral-heroic promise could be considered a perpetuation, in a way, of his Memphis episode. He has always shown a deftness for appropriating a happening, a situation, even the most incidental circumstance, and investing it with the most adventurously amplified symbolic meaning, a process in which there is often at work a certain robust imprecision of particulars. One of Jackson's seminary professors told journalist David Maraniss that "his greatest gift was also his greatest peril," that with his melodramatic imagination, "his ready tongue and vivid language" could "carry a thought beyond what closer scrutiny would justify."

But for Jackson, symbology itself can, in some demi-Eucharistic way, constitute substance, and often of a greater reality than the rudimentary factual specifics of the matter. Accordingly, he is prone to load inordinate freights of morally self-romanticizing symbolism on scenes and events in which he is involved. While traveling about Soviet Armenia after the devastating earthquake in 1989 to arrange for an internationally televised concert to raise relief funds, he stopped in one town where a crowd gathered out of the ruins and thronged around him, and he confided in a murmur when back in his car that he had been visited by a kind of self-mythicizing vision: "When I watched all those people coming toward me, I couldn't help but think, I had this flash, that they'd have in their minds for a long time that—the most surprising source for them—an African American once came to them and reached out to help them when they were in terrible need. And that may become a part of their tradition, of their legends."

In a series of meetings then with Soviet officials, he produced somewhat boggled stares across the table with his expatiations on the millennial implications of the earthquake itself: "There was a providential dimension to its coming when it did. That's the paradox of this disaster. It gives us the opportunity to respond to it across ancient barriers of race, region, ideology, and religion, and from that"—all this a vision, one suddenly suspected, that had simply begun spontaneously combusting wider and wider like a kind of Big Bang in his head as he sat there talking—"to build an infrastructure of people-to-people, joint experiments to develop new medicines together, clean up the environment together, joint ventures into space. If we can rebuild Armenia together, we can rebuild the world together!" Jackson possesses one of the few imaginations that could actually exaggerate the impact of a 6.9 Richter scale shuddering of the earth that had left half a million people homeless. Privately, he even posed metaphysical reverberations: "This tremor has had a profound effect upon Communist leaders here. They can't turn to their system for an answer or solution. Dealing with a natural disaster, you know, you have to deal with who *controls* nature. It's shaken them away from the party and toward God."

Similarly, he attached rather exorbitant moment to his having dragooned Castro into attending church with him one Sunday during his 1984 visit to Cuba: "He had me speak at the university there in Havana, and when I got through, I told him, 'Now I'm gonna go down and speak at the church, I want you to go with me.' He said, 'What? What?' Came along, though. When we got to the church, pastors there stepped out at the door, saw Castro. Eyes went wide. We could see everybody inside twistin' around to look. I said, 'Fidel, that cigar . . .' Then said, 'And that hat . . .' We went walkin' on down the aisle, people started applauding. Pastor in the pulpit introduced Castro to speak, Castro got up there—" and Jackson's voice assumes a rolling, stentorian resonance. " 'Wellll, reverrrunds, gooood to be here,' " and he breaks into a heavy cackle. "Fidel up in that pulpit, *talkin'* it. Sat down there then through the service, had him a *religious* feeling. But you know," Jackson continues, "many of our U.S. media people were there, they saw all that, but refused to *look* at it, know what I mean, to recognize its significance. What excited them in that church and the Cuban Council of Churches was, Castro had not been within a church in thirty years. For them, it broke a sound barrier. Media completely missed the meaning of the whole thing."

Perhaps the main problem with Jackson's perfervid metaphorical sensibility, though, is that it allows almost anything to happen symbolically. Once, when he was forging through the South to decry the Reagan administration's "violations" of the 1965 Voting Rights Act, he finally forced the Justice Department to dispatch the punctiliously conservative custodian of its Civil Rights Division, Bradford Reynolds, to tour sites of alleged transgressions with him, though Reynolds had indicated that he regarded the whole trip as absurd. Nevertheless, at one point Jackson seized Reynolds's hand and pulled him into hymning with him "We Shall Overcome," in which he later placed much hopeful store. But when such symbolic spectacles are possible, all symbology begins to lose meaning.

But a kind of hyperthyroid interpreting, a constant inflation of metaphor and symbol in life, seems innate in Jackson, down to what would appear the most idle commonplaces. During a flight to Angola in 1989, he peered for a long moment at a can of sardines fetched for him, then held it up and, waggling it, commenced to intone, "Now, where we headed right now? And whose did Angola used to be? *Umh-humh.* And now I'm sitting here about to open this can of sardines, and what do I see here on the top of it?" He read out then with a heavy solemnness, "Product of Portugal. What it says right here"—he tapped the lid with a forefinger—"Product of Portugal. Now, now"—and he rolled his eyes about him significantly—"now, how you *explain* things like this? Hunh?"

It was his quickness to descry the mystically symbolic in almost any happenstance that, as much as anything else, was probably operating in the scenario he presented after King was slain. While he was still at the seminary, he reports that one Sunday afternoon, after having watched Malcolm X on a local television talk show the night before, he was lying across the bed in his apartment, napping and "dreaming about Malcolm," when he was suddenly awakened by another student to be told that Malcolm had just been assassinated. "Mean, I had just been *dreaming* about him!" Jackson exclaims. Shortly afterward, he joined a crowd collected outside Elijah Muhammad's mansion near the seminary, and, he says, the police picked him out to briefly question him—"*Me,* out of that whole crowd. Just after Malcolm had been killed." After this enigmatic disclosure, he observes, "Now, I couldn't tell anybody about that without their saying, you know—" But then he goes on to offer the occult proposition that "Martin mentioned me in his last book," that he had also preached Jackie Robinson's funeral, and that "all those strains came together in me somehow."

On his 1989 Africa trip he had what could be regarded as an especially transcendental afternoon while wandering along the edges of Victoria Falls. It was only a few months after his second presidential campaign with his Rainbow Coalition, and he paused to declaim, over the tremendous roar of the falls, "You know, when the slave trade in America finally died out, it ended at this little town in Alabama called Africa Town, not far from Mobile, where the last slave ship landed. About a hundred years later, only about two hundred miles from that spot, Rosa Parks refused to go to the back of the bus. So, from the boat stop to the bus stop, and the emergence of Dr. King . . . and then, during our 1988 campaign, we came to Africa Town for a rally. And as we were driving in, there was this huge rainbow over it. *Huge* rainbow, right in front of us, and we followed it all the way to the church we were speaking at. Now. Here I am back in Africa, on a campaign for a massive American economic and political involvement with the continent of Africa. I'd call that sort of coming around full circle in a right big way, wouldn't you?" In the everlasting thunder and mist along the falls, nature seemed to conspire uncannily in Jackson's fancy with an almost banal symbolism: while expounding on his Rainbow Coalition, he walked among myriad little rainbows hanging everywhere about him, reaching up with gleeful whoops as if to grab them from the air. "The Rainbow! The Rainbow! This is where it began, where it begins again!"

X

The Struggle for Moral Succession

THAT TERM WHICH Jackson had come to apply to his political movement, "Rainbow Coalition," happened to be only one of the phrases and concepts he would appropriate from elsewhere over his labor of self-enlargement after Memphis. The name Rainbow Coalition was first sounded in the announcements in 1968 of the Poor People's Campaign to characterize the multiethnic mass constituency it hoped to convoke.

That haphazardly sprawling crusade, mounted the summer following King's death, became more or less a moment of truth for the continuation of his movement beyond King himself. Its centerpiece was to be the encampment in Washington, along the Reflecting Pool between the Washington Monument and the Lincoln Memorial, of the impoverished from across the country. Called Resurrection City, it was to serve as a staging area for a series of demonstrations in America's capital. But Resurrection City itself finally constituted more a metaphor than anything else, as Calvin Trillin noted at the time. It was situated in the picture-postcard setting of the Mall, where, not quite five years earlier, the vast multitude of the Washington March had assembled, with Lincoln's monumental figure gazing down, as it were, on the magnified and much complicated consequences of his actions a hundred years later. Now with King's own posthumous expansion of the meaning of that day with the Poor People's Campaign, Resurrection City was to bring into absolute focus the dichotomy of power and desperation in America, visibly accosting the nation in its capital with the rank want in which much of its population lived.

Despite the resentments still simmering from Memphis, Abernathy appointed Jackson Resurrection City's "mayor," partly in the expectation that he could contain the more roisterous street youths in the encampment, a number of whom Jackson himself had imported by bus from Chicago. Some of them he designated his deputy marshals, and all of them he notified through a bullhorn after an initial ruction, "Now let's get something straight. I'm a preacher, but I can talk that talk and walk that walk just like you can. I have been named mayor of this camp. I'm going to run things, and I can tell you now that all this down-home and on-the-street hell-raising is over. We are on the Lord's business here, and every one of you is gonna get in line." Amazingly, for a while most of them did.

But from the first, the whole undertaking was staggering through the central distraction of SCLC's simultaneous struggle to reconstruct itself around the void left by King's death. Roger Wilkins, then still with Johnson's Justice Department, recalls, "I was to be the front guy to figure out how we were going to deal with the Poor People's Campaign logistically, but I wasn't getting very precise answers about what their plans were—it was a typical SCLC thing, it was just going to unfold. I went to see Ralph Abernathy to ask, 'What's going to happen?' Might as well have been talking to that cloud over there." Abernathy, a slow, tubby hedgehog of a man with a lugubriously drooping face, had served ever since Montgomery as a kind of Falstaff to King, his Bottom, with a droll rollicking humor and a robustness for the more humble and common delights of life that, many felt, had kept King, with his high somberness of mission, in touch with the earth. Selected by SCLC to succeed King as its leader, Abernathy passed those first few weeks seemingly still in a stupor, while flying about the country trying to salvage both SCLC and the Poor People's Campaign, his days a blur of rushing movement as if, after what happened in Memphis, he could only exist in noise and speed, in a jet-roar's abolishment of time and distance and so reality. He would sit slumped in a front-row seat, a somewhat disreputable-looking figure in soiled denims in a cabin of businessmen, a kind of lost and displaced drowsiness about him. He would obsessively reminisce to whatever reporter might be riding with him, "I was always good at warmin' up audiences for Martin, you know. Was always good at tellin' jokes and bein' humorous for him," and then insist, "This is just something that's been thrust on me, I didn't ask for it. I didn't kill Martin Luther King. But members of my church came up to me the other day and said, 'Just because Dr. King died, we get the impression you want to die now, too.' " In fact, says Roger Wilkins, "the whole upper echelon of SCLC was kind of walking around in circles, bumping into itself. Ralph, Andy, all of them. Andy Young was almost sleepwalking. It was an organization with a gaping hole in its soul." Young admits, "I was even angry at Martin, as if he had something to do with it. *How can you leave us like this?* You know, we were barely making it *with* you. Now, without you, we're done." In the meantime, over two thousand people had collected into Resurrection City, "all these people down there in the mud doing nothing," says Wilkins.

In the end, Resurrection City became a casualty of its very nature as a metaphor, its problem as a stratagem for continuing the movement after King being precisely that it was not movement but emblem, static and so passive. A hastily clapped-together agglomeration of some fifty plyboard shelters in sheets of plastic, it soon devolved, under steadily battering rains, into a slum itself—a microcosmic ghetto of shoe-sucking mud and lassitude and increasing little dog-snaps of violence. Its occupants remained stranded inside its encircling waist-high wooden-slat fence for the same reason they were confined inside their ghettos back home: they had no means to go anywhere else. Meanwhile, Abernathy had installed himself and his staff, including Jackson, in a nearby motel, for the sake, he claimed, of its telephones for directing the campaign, but angry raiding parties from the Mall swept in periodically to protest, while back at Resurrection City, tourists strolling along the Reflecting Pool began pausing to take pictures of the plyboard shacks, which soon brought youths spilling over the ragged wooden fence to waylay them. With SCLC itself still floundering to find a new life without King, Resurrection City was left languishing without that essential kinetic of marches, outward challenges, on which the movement's dynamic had always depended, the very act of demonstrating having served as its own kind of liberation of spirit. And the more the whole project on the Mall seemed deteriorating into outright disaster, the more the suspicion spread that it was all because of the absence of King's genius and personality. It was in the growing sense of that great emptiness that Jackson began to assert himself.

He was still then a somewhat peripheral presence, "a principal secondary figure," says Wilkins, "but not like Ralph or Andy." But with all the others of King's old adjutants seemingly powerless before the apparent irreversible entropy of the entire Poor People's Campaign—the two thousand mired in Resurrection City dwindling soon to five hundred—"all of a sudden," says Wilkins, "here came Jesse. Not to suggest he wasn't grieving as much as anybody else. It's just that Jesse is almost a force of nature. He emerges as the one clear person who figures out something to do, a protest that made sense—taking people to the Agriculture Department and HEW and having sit-ins. 'Let's go and start demanding that those people feed poor people some food.' He did that out of his own head. He was the one guy who had the force and vision for it. He was awfully young, but Jesse invented brash." He began leading marches from Resurrection City, though not much more than token in size, to the Department of Agriculture every day, where he would bouncily hail the official assigned to cope with the demonstrations as "Brother Joe," and the secretary of agriculture himself, Orville Freeman, as "Brother Freeman." He once led a detachment of demonstrators down the serving line at the department's cafeteria, where they racked up a bill of nearly three hundred dollars, which Jackson then announced was owed by the nation to the poor, not by the poor to the nation. An increasingly discomfited Ralph Abernathy shortly replaced him as supervisor of Resurrection City with Hosea Williams. But when eighteen in a march from the encampment were arrested during a demonstration at the Rayburn House Office Building, Jackson hastened to the site and, after a conference with police and congressional stewards, moved all the demonstrators, the media, some three hundred people altogether, into the hearing room of the House Interstate and Foreign Commerce Committee for a rally that fetched the attention of *The New York Times* as "undoubtedly the only revival sermon ever to echo via a bullhorn" through that chamber. Jackson declaimed, "We have been the nation's laborers, its waiters. Our women have raised its presidents on their knees. We have built the highways. We have died in wartime fighting people we were not even mad at. America worked us for three hundred and fifty years without paying us. Now we deserve a job or an income." The *Times* reported all this in a profile of Jackson as its "Man in the News." He was then still only twenty-six.

But all his enterprising solo efforts were hardly enough to save the Poor People's Campaign. Resurrection City might have been vitalized by the demonstrations Jackson led from there if it had not been that their objectives, Washington's bureaucratic agencies, had that same impersonal institutional diffusion that had balked King in Chicago. And while in the South the profusion of statutory technicalities deployed against the movement had almost always singed away like spiderwebs in the moral heat of direct confrontations, Resurrection City became probably the first major civil rights undertaking to succumb to a minor legal nicety—the expiration of its land-use permit. Barely two months after its construction, national guardsmen trampled through its rows of shanties early one morning, flushing out the last few shadowy occupants, then swiftly dismantled it all. So ended the Poor People's Campaign.

The opinion persisted among many afterward that King would have probably carried it all off somehow, and its collapse seemed to confirm that there was really no way to compensate for his absence. Jackson, however, had not ceased his own attempts at it. The day before Resurrection City was to be obliterated, though he was now sick himself with hepatitis and ptomaine poisoning from the camp's tinned food, he addressed the huddle of remaining inhabitants from the back of a flatbed truck—a moment Jackson has cited ever since as one of the most vital in his making—bellowing out to them what was to be repeated through the years as perhaps his most famous litany. As he will still recall for audiences, "It was a rainy morning, and our heads were hanging low, our hearts were heavy. When I looked down from the back of that truck, it was mostly women and children, all colors, a rainbow of them. And they looked up at me for something I could not give them—I couldn't give them any money for a bus ticket back home, nor could I take away the pain in their hearts because Dr. King had been killed. But then I remembered something. That when you've lost every-thing—every *thing*—you still have your humanity and your integrity, you still have your will to be somebody. So I asked all of them standing down there before me, asked them to repeat these words, *I am somebody*. It just came out of me—'I am somebody!' And they came back, *I am somebody!* I went on, they answering back each line, 'I may be poor . . . but I *am* . . . *somebody*. . . . Red, yellow, brown, black, and white . . . we are *all* precious in God's sight.' I could see pride and hope come back into their faces. 'Re-spect me! . . . Never neglect me! . . . For I *am* . . . *somebody!*' It was like, as I went along, the words just formed in front of me, and it began to transform that whole morning."

IN FACT, THAT was a refrain that King had been using since at least the savage summer of 1964 in Mississippi, which had settled a quiet terror over blacks in the state, when he took a long amble through the black quarter of Greenwood one steamy afternoon after a leaden rain, leaning in past the screen doors of barbershops and grocery stores and poolrooms to invite the astonished faces gaping at him to a mass meeting that night. He finally stepped up onto a crude plank bench across from the Red Rooster Night Spot, and in his heavy-swelling voice called out to the small throng that had collected, "You must not allow anybody, *anybody*, to make you feel you are not significant and you do not count. *Every* Negro has worth and dignity, because white, Negro, Chinese, Indian, man or woman or child, doctor or preacher or cotton hand, we are *all* the children of God. You are *somebody*. I want every one of you to say that to yourself—say it out loud, now: *I am somebody*," and as he repeated it several times, he was answered by a rising murmuration from the assembly below him.

But such derivative inspirations of Jackson's have seemed merely an in-stinctive pattern throughout his progress of a ceaseless, omnivorous assim-ilation of whatever seems to him serviceable. His impulse to attach to himself with a magpie's alacrity whatever he feels he needs extends even to bringing along Gideon Bibles from hotel rooms to peruse on his long flights. Somewhat in the same manner, he will also confiscate any inter-esting occasion where he happens to be present. Many years later, after a private session in Luanda with Angola's president José Eduardo dos Santos, Jackson persuaded him to invite into his office the gang of reporters outside and to repeat for them, before a large map of Angola and its immediate neighborhood, his explication of the arrangements then being negotiated for ending the civil war in the country. While dos Santos sportingly began explaining it all again with taps of a pointer on the map, Jackson loomed beside him with a distinct air of somehow being supervisory of this whole diplomatic development, finally leaning in past dos Santos to interpose his own report to the journalists, swiping his hand down the eastern edge of Angola, "and the ANC crowd all in here, see, they'll be leaving from here . . . ," gradually easing himself into dos Santos's presentation until he had effectively taken it over. "I'd like to say, too, Mr. President, that the significance of all this is that the Benguela railroad that runs along here, goes through Zambia over here—see, yawl?—it'll be opened up again," with dos Santos now standing to one side merely contributing occasional hums of concurrence.

Jackson's old confidant, Richard Hatcher, admits, "He will, at about any cost, seize the moment." It became such a notorious trait of Jackson's that the Reverend William Sloan Coffin once felt constrained to offer the defense, "History is always better served by those on the make than by those who have it made." But what has offended many ever since Memphis as Jackson's almost manic opportunism would owe not a little to the fact that—with his early excitements about his possibilities hugely quickened during his time with King—he was left, after King's death, struggling to make himself into a similarly momentous figure in what had become an essentially unmomentous time. It was a dilemma—how to create himself in a vacuum, as it were—of a sort that can tend to induce a certain antic urgency. But that was the peculiar quandary he now found confronting him after the demise of the Poor People's Campaign.

The Media Resort

He had finally plunged himself fully into the saga of the movement only near its end, virtually in its last hours. Even before Memphis, the classic phase of the civil rights struggle that had begun in Montgomery was already heading into a kind of indefinite and distracted twilight like some ultimate version of what had befallen King's Chicago and Poor People's campaigns—scattered, sporadic, transitory scufflings with a murk of bureaucracies over busing, affirmative action, the delinquencies of government social programs, occupied not so much with King's high mission of revolutionizing the heart of the nation as with miscellaneous matters of policy mechanics and administrative engineering. It was the sort of dispersion of purpose in which it seemed impossible for any single leader to emerge into dramatic definition. At the same time, the nation as a whole, after the strains of the immense social initiatives of the preceding decade or so, had begun to surrender to what seemed a deep weariness of spirit and conscience, a withdrawal into a cautious, stale season of inversion that was to be most conclusively announced by the election of Richard Nixon, reaching its climax with the Reagan presidency but extending even to the Gingrich Congress. Essayist Henry Fairlie reflected years later that Jackson had been left to battle against "circumstances that are far more chilling than those confronting Martin Luther King, Jr."

Jackson's singular difficulty then became that of trying to realize himself as a social apostle in a time that happened to be empty of any large passions and drama. Absent a great moral mass conflict like that in which King had come to prominence, Jackson did have available to him one factor King had not: the rapidly expanding mirror of the media, most of all television. Accordingly, it became for him something like a secondary, compensating theater for his realization—though, precisely because of that lack of a larger dramatic social script, he also had to make his own press almost single-handedly out of nothing. "We had a meeting in the basement of a church on the South Side soon after Dr. King's assassination," says Calvin Morris. "We had seen how the images of Selma and Birmingham had galvanized the nation, that being in the national news and local coverage had become very critical. But the discussion took that a step further—to develop ways of *compelling* the media to hear us. That needed to be a central part of who we were. Specifically, of course, it was about the role that Jesse would have to play in that media understanding. I argued, unsuccessfully, that it should be our *programs* that would have the content for the media. But the decision was made to move in ways that would cause media to respond to us." Somewhile later, says Morris, "there was this article about Jesse in *Harper's* that I thought was terrible. Jesse said, 'Calvin, no article is a bad article. It may not be all we want it to be, but it *is* an article in a major publication, and we'll take what we can from it and work from there.'"

Actually, it seemed to a number that Jackson had been custom-fashioned for the hectic new element of television, which was soon forming most other coverage after its own strobing nature. "Jesse was always quick-minded in a way that was different from King," says Samuel Proctor, Jackson's mentor at A & T. "King was ponderous and trained in a very historically oriented sort of way, hesitating until he was really sure about something. Jesse would just cut straight to the center of a matter. Putting things in easily consumable language, codifying things quickly." But the Reverend Wyatt Tee Walker, who served as a consultant to both King and Jackson, submits that "while with King the age of the media hadn't quite come, he commanded its attention because of his great moral prowess. Jesse, on the other hand, comes along half a generation later, a reflection of the era of the media, and somewhere in his psyche is buried the idea that leadership carries with it fame. It does to a degree, but I'm not sure that Jesse has always sorted out the appropriate relationship."

But with Jackson—after Greensboro, after Selma, after his time with King, after what he had already remarkably wrought with Breadbasket, all of which had confirmed for him what he had sensed he held within him since Greenville—it was the desperation of a constitutional outsider to have his true import register in the general public eye. It did not exactly moderate his excitement about his own possible impending apotheosis that, following King's death and the dissolution of the Poor People's Campaign, he found himself the subject of flashes of attention from the press. Only a month after Memphis, *The New York Times* had declared him "probably the most persuasive black leader on the national scene," and a 1969 *Playboy* interview introduced him as King's "fiery heir apparent" (Hugh Hefner soon becoming one of his first major benefactors). Beyond that, he was actually named by the U.S. Jaycees one of the Ten Outstanding Young Men for 1969, along with John D. Rockefeller IV. He was described in a *Life* profile that year as perhaps "the most astute black political leader" in the nation, with one journalist quoted as saying, "Jesse is the man right now." Then, in 1970, he was carried on the cover of a special issue of *Time* on "Black America," which featured a Lou Harris poll showing him already ranking ninth among the twenty-one black figures and organizations most respected by the nation's black community, right after Thurgood Marshall and ahead of Senator Edward Brooke, Adam Clayton Powell, A. Philip Randolph, and Muhammad Ali. "He'd thought he was gonna blow *Time* away by talking about his low beginnings and all," says Larry Shaw, who had now become Jackson's publicity manager. "Oh, he was hot. When he got word then that he was gonna be on the cover of *Time*, he asked me, 'Will you go up there and see to it that I come out all right?' He wanted me to go check out what they'd written. I said, 'Sir, excuse me. I am not going to be able to do that, I don't think.' I mean, how was I gonna go asking *Time* magazine to do this? He said, 'Okay, meet me there.' And he went up there to do it. Who would have that audacity to start with, plus he doesn't know what the hell's he's doing? We meet with the chairman of the board of *Time* magazine, and Jesse says, 'Look, how's the story goin' over here?' Says, 'Look, uh, can Larry here look at my story and see how it reads?' Well, this is probably the first time in his career this man has been asked directly to let somebody look at a story about himself. The color kind of fell out of his face. He says, 'I tell you what I'll show you. You see this stack of paper here? This is how much research we got on you for this story.' Well, *that* impressed Jesse. He says, 'You can't put all that in *Time*, that's bigger than the whole *Time* magazine.' The chairman says, 'But this is all I can do, we can't let your advisers look at the story. We don't go about our practices that way, you know.' Jesse says then, quiet and low like he's just now realizing it, 'You mean I *can't* see it?' The chairman says, 'Maybe I can give you an advance copy,' and Jesse says, 'Yeah, let me have that at least. Least maybe I can fix that before it comes out.'"

"He did come into prime time pretty quickly," notes Robert Beckel, who had to contend with Jackson years later as Walter Mondale's 1984 campaign manager. Beckel suggests that, with the suddenness of King's departure, "I don't think Jackson was quite ready for that. You know, King overshadowed so many people, and I think Jesse was still looking for his own rhythm at that point—in fact, to this day, still is." But one editor relates, "I think just about everybody then realized he was going to become a political force. He was clearly the most charismatic and attractive of all the people who'd been with King. You could feel an energy, something in him that communicated, 'I am going to be the natural successor.'"

That was the suspense, then, that prompted his first shimmer of media notice: that Jackson could turn out to be the catalytic black folk-figure who could revive King's movement, in a form reflecting his own, different, nature. A larger historical difference between King and Jackson was proposed in a thesis in 1971 by a Chicago theological student, William Samuels, which cited Joachim Wach's distinction between the reformer and the prophet, reformers appearing "in times of threatening decay and disintegration" but "not on a level with the founders . . . their creative power does not match that of the originator," though they "somewhat resemble the founders in the power and possibly even in the magneticism of their personality, in their energy and endurance."

But even if Jackson seemed then a bombastic but lesser version of King, the speculation of many was that he could become a kind of bridging figure from King to the new generation's stormier romance of black power and black nationalism. He had about him at least the radical flourish of that new militancy—had not only transmuted himself from his tight look of closely snipped hair and thin dark ties from the sixties into a flaring Afro and giant neck-chain medallions with leather vests and boots, but had also taken on a forensics to match, declaring at one Breadbasket service not long after King's death, "Every once in a while, my jaws get pretty tight about white folks, and I find myself in Whitey's chest beating his heart for him." He would refer to "cracker" policemen for whom "the brothers" had their own recourses worked out, and once ominously warned, in his own variation of Malcolm's *by any means necessary*, "We will be as nonviolent as we can be, and as violent as we must be." In his *Playboy* interview, he partly explained this direr deportment: "Every black man who has won the loyalty of his community has indicated some form of defiance of the white man. Malcolm X is a good example. He could look Whitey straight in the eye and tell he was lying."

But much of the press did not fail to detect that it all finally seemed, rather than an actual message, more an attitude that Jackson was wearing. Samuel Proctor reflects, "He was so young then, but I'll tell you what he did not do. He never finally crossed over to the violent side. He never allowed the 'Burn, baby, burn' syndrome to capture him." What intrigued the media was that Jackson was presenting more a kind of militant non-violence to accommodate and disarm the new mystique of violence by assuming its sounds and manner and gestures, the upraised fist to call for restraint. In all this, he was having to negotiate the trickiest of perceptual lines. "There is nothing Americans love better," says Don Hewitt, producer of *60 Minutes*, "than a nonthreatening black. Bill Cosby, Arthur Ashe, Ed Bradley—they adore them." With other black figures, Hewitt maintains, "it's not that we don't like you because you're black; we don't like you because you scare us." Jackson's novel combination of King and Malcolm even attracted the mild fascination of William F. Buckley, Jr., who termed him "by increasing agreement, successor to Martin Luther King as leader of the moderate-militant black community," and confessed to an admiration for him as "very young, very able, and extraordinarily intelligent" in having "contrived a superb blend of rhetorical intransigence and analytical sobriety," his grim oratory and manner assuring "his followers that there is nothing of the conciliator in his system."

The effect of that dual character was witnessed by Roger Wilkins as early as the day Resurrection City was effaced from Washington's Mall, when, sometime that dusk, "we got word that a crowd was gathering, getting bigger and bigger, at this nearby intersection in the black community." Attorney General Ramsey Clark had been called by a concerned President Johnson, says Wilkins, and "Clark said to me, 'Would you go and do something?' " When Wilkins arrived at the intersection, he found "a mob about ready to torch the damn city. They're saying, 'What the hell did the people get? We didn't get *nothin'*.' In those days, you had the really tough guys, hard guys, just street revolutionaries, and if you were to the right of that, you were in danger of being branded an Uncle Tom and losing your credibility. But in the center of it I see, from a distance, up on a flatbed truck, somebody talking to them. And they're listening. I think at first, this is somebody who's exhorting them on into action. I get closer, and I realize it's Jesse up there. And he is preaching. 'If I *am* somebody, I don't go out and burn up and tear down. People who *are* somebody gather up their strength for another fight for the good of their people. Tearing down the neighborhoods where the people have to shop to get their amenities, that's not the way for a person who is somebody to be.' Now, he's taking a terrific risk, in both limb and reputation. Because you've got a mob there with fire in its eyes that's ready to go out and *do stuff*. And here's Jesse standing up there before them saying, 'Don't—' And he preached the riot out of that crowd. I'll never forget that as long as I live."

Not everyone was beguiled by Jackson's double effect during those days, though. Chicago's old fire-breathing radical activist Bob Lucas is a long, loping, and slow-drawling man who is still given to wistful mentions of Lenin, and he admits that one of the great disappointed hopes of his life was that the Chicago movement did not "turn into a real revolution"—his main plaint about Jackson being that he sabotaged that possibility. During a confrontation in the spring of 1969 over the exclusion of blacks from construction unions, "some of us got tired of writing letters and begging," says Lucas, "so what we decided to do—Jesse was not a part of this—we decided to organize the gangs, which were not then as violent and involved in drugs as they now are. We got together the Black 'P' Stone Nation, the Black Disciples, the Vice Lords, and the purpose of this coalition was to close down all the building going on in the black neighborhoods." When gang members assembled at the first construction site, they were instructed, says Lucas, "to form a nice, orderly picket line. They said, 'For what?' We said, 'To march up and down, see, and pretty soon their conscience is gonna make them negotiate with us.' They said, 'But what is it exactly you want them to do?' We said, 'We want to make 'em negotiate by forcing the workers to leave the job.' They all said then, 'Ohhh. Okay, we see what you want—' " and they went boiling off toward the construction site. Says Lucas, they "didn't really touch anybody, but in a few seconds, you could see all these white guys, you know, headed with their lunch buckets for their cars to get on back to the suburbs, mean, their car keys already *out*."

This stratagem met with such success, says Lucas, that before long "we had only one more to close down"—that being the site where an extension of the University of Illinois was under construction. Stopping the work there, Lucas and other organizers were certain, would finally "break the back" of union resistance to admitting blacks. Only by now, Mayor Daley had gotten an injunction against any further such intimidating protests, so that when Lucas arrived "with maybe three thousand people, mainly the gangs, only a sprinkling of people like me," they found brigades of police on the other side of the fence, heavily armed. "Our strategy was to jump over the fence, challenge the guns, and chase the workers away. We weren't prepared to fight, but we were prepared to die if that's what it took." It may have seemed a hair-raising prospect of imminent mayhem, but it filled Lucas with a revolutionary exultation.

But suddenly Jackson appeared. "And somehow he got the leaders of the Stones, the Vice Lords, the Disciples, got them all together," reports Lucas, still woefully, "and I couldn't believe what I was hearing. He began telling them about the futility of doing this. 'The way to do it is peacefully, what we've got to do is just march around, and I can convince the labor unions to give you guys all the jobs you want'—which he couldn't and never did, of course—but he went on and on, and he convinced them. He *stole the whole thing.*" Not long afterward, Lucas laments, "I looked up and there was Jesse on TV leading a demonstration around the site, and then they prayed and then they disbanded. And I thought to myself, what a hell of a contrast! Instead of people rushing onto a job site and chasing people off, they're walking around and then dropping to their knees and praying. Sure, that was more the way of Martin Luther King, but there are moments that require something other than that. I mean, we'd had a real *revolutionary moment* there. I think had we gone over that fence, that would have broken the closed labor unions, leading to who knows what today. You never really know about moments in history—they come and they go by, they come and they go by. But that was *one!*" Lucas now confesses to the melancholy thought that "the workers are not gonna make any revolution in this country. So blacks have to be the social force." But it was that popular potential in the black community then, Lucas is convinced, that Jackson shorted out.

Years later, after leading a protest rally outside the Los Angeles police headquarters after the beating of Rodney King, Jackson quietly remarked back in his car, "Would've been so easy to raise hate from that crowd. But some of the meanest-lookin' faces down there were the first to bow their heads when I called for prayer. You can't give up that thing that's always made you different, that nonviolent message."

In any case, his compound quality of nonviolent militancy was to become Jackson's special captivation for the media as a possible successor to King. But there were certain elemental liabilities in resorting to the media as a secondary means, in a more monotone time, for achieving himself as a national apostle. In a way wholly different from King and his predecessors in the pre-television age of print, when awareness and memory were slower to take but longer-lasting and somehow more individualized and personally alive, Jackson would come to be formed as a social evangel from TV's nervous system of consciousness, and so to a great degree partake of its nature: its electronic sensibility of the mass reality, instant and impressionistic, those impressions simultaneous and undifferentiated, interchangeable and forever replaceable, amnesial and ephemeral. As one of Jackson's former Chicago aides puts it, "The media giveth and the media taketh away. And they will do it in a millisecond." Jackson's running ordeal, then, became having to constantly register in that fitful and evanescent field of reality or wane away like last season's miniseries or Super Bowl. Spending himself on that forever imminent perishability would persist as one of his most subverting adversities, producing his seemingly frenetic opportunism.

Yet another toll attending his reliance on the media owed simply to the ultimate size of his aspiration: to make himself into a moral apostolic figure not just for the black community but for the entire nation. Already he was allowing, "I'm always presented as a *black* leader speaking on *black* issues. Why can't I be a *moral* leader speaking on *moral* issues?" But one problem in Jackson's recourse to the media for that was, as Roger Wilkins explains, "black leaders in earlier generations labored outside the vision of most white people, although they were widely known in the black community. But Jesse picked service in the whole national eye, and so became a visible American figure who is there for white people to comment about all the time. And because he is perceived as a threat, they visit on him an awful lot of racism that most of the time they keep in the closet. I don't know how he's taken it."

But all of this would become only gradually evident as Jackson set out now, at the end of the Poor People's Campaign, on the next, long stretch of his struggle to reach that moral-heroic promise first intimated to him during his youth in Greenville. Throughout that struggle, though, Jackson had been left by King's death in yet one more critical difficulty, according to Larry Shaw. "Jesse was still without a lot of elderly wisdom, that's what he suffered from the most. King was like a father, and he knew how to be one. As long as he was there, there were certain reins on how far the young man would go. Just King's existence had that influence on him. After he was removed, who took the reins? No one. Jesse had nobody else who was older who he could respect enough to monitor him. So without King, he operates like a person who has no father. Like a child spoiled by everybody else. Crazy in going after things, stubborn in staying with what he wants. *I'm gonna do whatever it takes to get it.*"

X I

Coming Into His Own: The Economic Apostle

WITH KING GONE, Jackson almost immediately began to feel himself impossibly confined within SCLC.

He had by now turned his Operation Breadbasket campaign in Chicago for black economic empowerment into not only the single measurable success left behind by King's efforts there but one of the rare self-sustaining civil rights enterprises in the nation. King adjutant C. T. Vivian declares, "What Jesse was doing with Operation Breadbasket was bigger than anything we'd ever thought of. Remember, none of us had really operated in an urban environment. But Jesse was the first of us to get involved in the urban world in a meaningful way and create a power base there. Didn't even understand how he did it at first." Breadbasket's particular pertinence at that time, acknowledges Andrew Young, was that "while we had changed the legal structure of the country, and the educational system had opened up and the political system was opening up, we really had not found a way to open up the economy. But Jesse was doing just that in Chicago."

He had come up with an ideology for Breadbasket that he called "The Kingdom Theory," a premise actually not that distant from the economic black nationalism propagated by Malcolm and the Muslims. As Jackson presented it in his chalkboard seminars for the ministers enlisted in Breadbasket, "Black people must understand themselves as having the authority of kings, and that their dominions are their communities. They need to be informed of the people who benefit economically from our community but have no real investment in that community. It means seeing then that our money remains within our community instead of quickly entering and leaving at an acute angle. We have the power, nonviolently, just by controlling our appetites, to determine the economic fortunes of our neighborhoods." To do that, Jackson devised a program for a kind of holo-grammic economic regeneration of the inner city, addressed not just to jobs but to the marketing of black products; contracts with black firms for janitorial, extermination, construction, transportation services; utilization of black-owned financial institutions. What has largely been lost in Jackson's story over the years and its accumulating assumptions of administrative waywardness is a recognition of the extent to which he actually brought much of that economic reformation to pass.

Usually acting from word circulating in the black community, he would dispatch a letter to a company's officers, notifying them, "We've gotten complaints about your operation," and enclosing a questionnaire, which he would request they fill out and return, about the percentages of blacks in all their job categories, and their comparative salaries. If the company should decline to perform this chore, a mass rally would be convoked "to let the community know," says an original Breadbasket stalwart, the Reverend Willie Barrow, "that we were calling in, say, Sears for an educational meeting." Before long, there was no need to even utter the words "boycott" or "picket," says Barrow. "We'd just call it 'withdrawal of enthusiasm.' They'd run over us getting here." In time, says Jackson, firms began offering on their own to negotiate accords simply "when they heard our feet coming."

Those negotiations were conducted by Jackson and his ministerial deputations in something of a prayer-meeting style, applying what had become Jackson's dialectic of gospel-egalitarian militancy, all of which corporate officials found not a little discombobulating. "How in the world do you fight the man," one remarked afterward, "when he comes into the room and starts right off with a prayer that God will help you see the light?" As discussions then proceeded, Jackson and his group would pass in a blink from economic formulations into disquisitions on Shadrach, Meshach, and Abednego in the fiery furnace. "One minute they'd be talking about how many truck drivers we had to hire," another company manager reported incredulously, "and the next minute they're talking about man's relation to God." Jackson would finally close negotiating sessions by having everyone stand in a circle with arms interwound while he prayed again, this time for God's redemption of the company president's soul. Some white businessmen began privately referring to Jackson and his preacherly negotiating squads as "the moral Mafia," and indeed, their suasions were sometimes perceived to be not altogether spiritual. One Breadbasket veteran recalls the complaint of a corporation's negotiators "that Jesse was using double-meaning words in a way that they saw as threatening. We all know how Jesse can bend things just a little at times. And he would say things like, if a store was going to be built without any black people in the construction, it probably wouldn't be built at all. Now, to anybody in a management position, they figured Jesse meant he was going to burn the fucker down, right? 'Course, that wouldn't be what Jesse really meant at all. . . ." But neither, the man adds, did Jackson overly exert himself to disabuse them of that impression.

When an agreement was at last reached, the company's executives were required to produce themselves at a press conference, before which they signed a "covenant," as Jackson termed it, that was composed of language—"creative employment and business development aimed at ending the economic indignities and injustices which have ravaged the Negro people physically and spiritually"—which no one supposed had issued from those executives either. Breadbasket would then follow with periodic reviews to gauge whether the companies were complying with their commitments, and when it was found that they weren't, which was not infrequent, demonstrations of "withdrawal of enthusiasm" were revived.

The results of Breadbasket's economic crusade were unquestionably uneven, but the overall statistics were arresting. Within six months after the first rounds of picketing, all major food chains operating in Chicago's black communities had arrived at pacts with Breadbasket. And almost all black businesses allied with it had their sales increase appreciably—for one food producer, from virtually zero to a six-figure volume. A & P alone began carrying the products of some twenty-five black manufacturers. By 1971, *Life* reported, Breadbasket was directly responsible for four thousand new jobs for blacks in Chicago, and for an estimated ten thousand more indirectly.

To be sure, Breadbasket's achievements were accompanied by persistent criticism. Even from black managers in some firms, there were complaints about the desultory and erratic performance of new black employees and contractors, which seemed to fulfill the warning of Leon Sullivan, whose Philadelphia project in the late fifties had been the genesis for Breadbasket's program, that "integration into the job market without preparation only leads to frustration" for blacks "long denied the opportunity to acquire the necessary experience and adequate access to training." There were other misfires. "The food stores said, okay, we'll give our garbage to whoever you say is the garbageman," says Larry Shaw. "Well, there was this man who was supported to the extent he got a hundred-and-some-thousand-dollar garbage truck. We had a big rally as the truck is leaving to go to work. A black man in the garbage business for a change. He went to the stores, they filled up his shiny new garbage truck, everybody proudly riding with him all the way to the dump. And he couldn't get into the dump. The same union that had kept us out of the garbage business also controlled the dumps. So this man went out of business with the stinkingest new garbage truck you'd ever seen. This is a bitter man to this day."

More common were protests that Breadbasket was only serving a small set of middle-class black business prospectors, and was hardly discomforting, in fact was reassuring, to the larger system of economic interests. One tenant-union activist decreed Jackson to be "the Booker T. Washington of the late sixties." In truth, he seemed at times a peculiar amalgam. Several years later, after he had reincarnated Breadbasket's program under the name of PUSH, "Republicans got attached to it," says A. Knighton Stanley, Jackson's old college chaplain at A & T. "PUSH was kind of a Republican thing." While Gerald Ford was president, Stanley visited Jackson at Washington's Sheridan Park Hotel, "this enormous suite, all kinds of rooms, really an apartment. And while I was there, Rockefeller, who was vice president then, called him. His office was offering Jesse grants in connection with PUSH, and they wanted to talk to him about this grant money. So a little while after Jesse hung up, he looked at his watch, said, 'I've got to go on over to the White House.' I thought he was going over to get a check for the grant. But then he revealed that he was going to the White House not to pick up a check but to picket in front of it. He had many issues then, I don't remember what this one was. But I said, 'Why the hell do you want to picket the White House when you can go on inside? You were just talking to them on the phone. Why don't you just walk on in there and talk to them?' He seemed very astonished that there might be some incongruity in the whole thing."

An associate Jackson had inherited from King, Bernard Lafayette, cheerfully concedes that "Jesse didn't have any problem with the whole trickle-down theory—the idea of building larger black businesses in the hopes they would hire more black people. Nothing radical at all, nothing like the people owning the means of production. Why did anybody ever think he was dangerous? They had nothing to fear from Jesse." Jackson himself insisted at the time, "If I thought we were just developing some more black capitalists with the same value system as white capitalists, I would quit this morning. What we want is white folks' technology with black folks' love." But he maintained, "We're in the system whether we like it or not. Look at 125th Street and Seventh Avenue in Harlem. Black orators have forever stood on that corner rappin' about goin' back to Africa, or pickin' up the gun and goin' down to Mississippi. Well, they was on—o-n—that corner, but now in 1971, we still don't *own*—o-w-n—that corner. Chock full o' Nuts does. Some black folks think they can escape the system, talk about blacks who are, quote, 'in' or 'out' of the system. That's a lot of bull. Even to have civil rights without economic justice is to have the right to dive into a swimming pool without water, the right to check into a hotel without the ability to check out."

At any rate, so extensive were Breadbasket's effects in Chicago that, by 1974, the city's black community had developed the most sizable and powerful financial base of any in the United States—a complex that included six banks, three savings-and-loans, two insurance companies. Of the nation's one hundred black-owned enterprises with annual sales of over a million dollars, eighteen were in Chicago, a count second only to New York's, and all eighteen had been demonstrable beneficiaries of Jackson's efforts. Though Breadbasket eventually expanded beyond Chicago to offices in some fifteen other cities, those remained mostly token and tenuous outposts, and it never really took as a national operation. One reason why, says Calvin Morris, was "Jesse recognized that his base in Chicago would be far more powerful than a diffuse base that would in effect be SCLC." But it's fair to say that, in all, in Chicago Jackson's Operation Breadbasket had set off something close to a black economic renaissance, which indeed produced benign ripplings—aid to other young black entrepreneurs, scholarship and emergency-assistance programs—throughout the black community.

IN THE COURSE of his Breadbasket campaigns, Jackson had also rapidly established a small dominion of his own in Chicago, assembling around him a prestigious company of patrons, most of whom had initially been coaxed by King, "I want yawl to be good to this young man," but who soon were captivated by Jackson himself as, in the words of one, "very, *very* young, maybe, but a phenomenon, a prodigy. And always very sure of himself—right or wrong." The Reverend Willie Barrow remembers, "He'd know how to touch all the bases, would tell me, 'Get ahold of John Johnson, let me run this by him,' or 'Get hold of Cirilo McSween.' He worked night and day on those businessmen. He went to their houses, he sat on the floor and played with their children, talked to their wives. He organized their wives, and after that, he organized all their children. The whole family." In turn, under the attentions and solicitudes of these business worthies, his own personal situation improved significantly from that time, just a year or so before, when he had been forced to stand in line for free groceries at Clay Evans's church. His family had then been lodged in a barren apartment, recalls a woman who visited them there, that "was way up in this attic kind of place," with little more than a park picnic table set on its linoleum floor so "you could hardly sit down anywhere. All the children had colds. He didn't even have any family insurance for them." Jackson did not seem all that noticing of this dreary state of affairs, but his backers were so embarrassed for him that they furnished him supplemental funds and insurance, and one of them, a combination undertaker and preacher named A. R. Leak, relocated the family to an apartment on the third floor of a building he owned. Leak, says Jackson's wife, Jackie, "was *the* funeral director *extraordinaire* of Chicago," and the apartment he provided them "was a wonderful place, nine rooms, sunporch in the front and another in the back."

But beyond benefactors like Leak and Johnson and McSween, Jackson had developed a wider community of support, recounts an aide from those days, "with the younger, up-and-coming entrepreneurs and young administrators in the city—remember, this was during the War on Poverty programs. Everything sort of fell in place for him. He's got a burgeoning middle class that's moving up, he's got a political group that wants to move up, he's got ministers, he's got big businessmen—they all sort of come together for him at the same time. Yessir, Jesse was on the move now."

Most of all, he had become a sensation among Chicago's black citizenry at large. Richard Hatcher, then mayor of nearby Gary, Indiana, says, "Chicago had kind of a history of black people in politics who were perceived in the black community as not belonging to the community, figures who'd been made by the Daley machine. And those were really powerful people in that machine. But here was this young man, I mean, it was incredible, he didn't seem intimidated by *anybody*." A woman who was then in her twenties recalls, "We always knew that even if he went into the room with our worst enemy, we weren't afraid that he was going to be bought off at all." He had also quickly attracted the attention of a variety of other, more informal speculators in the city's black neighborhoods, says a Breadbasket staffer, "people constantly pulling at him and trying to make deals, saying, 'Let me help you so you can help me,' because they saw his potential even at that time." But they met with no more success than the city's white power system in attempting to co-opt him.

"Oh, yeah, everybody knew of him," says one of his assistants then. "He was bigger than life, even at that time. He had this sort of a swagger of a come-on, you know. And of course, he was greatly admired by the ladies, which helps tremendously. You look at any important social movement, women have always played a tremendous part in them." Indeed, an extraordinary number of strong, shrewd, intense women seemed to figure crucially in Breadbasket's career from its beginning, one of them being the secretary to the Reverend Clay Evans, Lucille Loman. Still a sharply handsome woman with a grand duchess's tall and courtly bearing, she remembers Jackson then as "always on fire. He was always on fire." But "it was the Martin Luther King history that first drew me to him," she says. "He was nothing but a boy, but he had already met King, had been to

Selma." Another woman relates, "I had taken my daughter to music lessons one Saturday, and when we got back, my husband told me—this was after Dr. King was killed—told me, 'You know, I just heard a young man on the radio, and he really can speak. He reminds me of Dr. King. You've just got to hear him.' " It was that evocative, déjà vu impression, Hatcher maintains, that accounted not a little for Jackson's developing into a popular phenomenon in Chicago: "People really saw him as, this is the next Martin Luther King."

The weekly communal heartbeat for this following of Jackson's were the Breadbasket services, held on Saturday mornings in deference to the Sunday services in the churches of his ministerial allies—three-hour inspirational jubilees "like a combined town meeting and revival," says John Johnson, that were attended by up to two thousand people, sometimes more, and also broadcast to a considerable radio audience over the city, Jackson having persuaded a black-owned station to open up time to him without charge. These services, from their simple beginnings in the cafeteria of Chicago Theological Seminary, had migrated through a series of church sanctuaries and ballrooms and auditoriums, including for a time an old movie palace of a seedy *Arabian Nights* opulence. But whatever the locale, cars would be triple-parked outside by eight-thirty, with the sidewalks around crowded with a clamorous bazaar of vendors selling black literature, African jewelry, amid which wandered funereal-faced young men in crow-black suits and bow ties holding out copies of *Muhammad Speaks* from the stacks under their arms. The thickening swell of those arriving for the service would pass on inside to be conducted to seats by ushers in dashikis, a band on the stage romping through preliminary rills as the auditorium filled. These congregations were a diverse assemblage, about two-thirds women, a dappling of whites, along with contingents of gang members, while there also usually showed up various political nabobs—it was one indication of the speculations already about Jackson's moment by 1969 that George McGovern, Eugene McCarthy, and Nelson Rockefeller had paid calls on Breadbasket. When Adlai Stevenson III, then Illinois's state treasurer, appeared at one service not long after having deposited state funds at Breadbasket's behest into local black banks, he was conscripted by Jackson into helping take up the collection: "Now, Adlai, you go up the center aisle here. . . ." Also dropping by would be such entertainers as Billy Eckstine, Dionne Warwick, Nancy Wilson, Isaac Hayes, Redd Foxx, and with a certain piquant appropriateness, given Jackson's own rather rakish look now, the actor who played "Shaft," Richard Roundtree. Muhammad Ali came by, and a propitious frequent visitor was Quincy Jones, who was to become one of

Jackson's most vital sponsors over the years. Along with these luminaries there regularly appeared presidents and premiers from Ghana, Liberia, Nigeria, Ethiopia, whom Jackson would introduce while attired in denims and tennis shoes. In all, "they were the kind of services where anything could happen on any given Saturday," a former staffer relates. "One Saturday, you'd have Black Panther Bobby Rush surrendering"—Rush having been a fugitive since an early-morning state police raid on an apartment in which Fred Hampton and Mark Clark were slain. "Yeah, Rush actually surrendered at one service. Jesse arranged it, because he had that kind of rapport with the Panthers"; with Rush standing beside him on the podium, Jackson said to the congregation, "You see this man? We're turning him over with no scars, no marks, and we expect to get him back that way," and he then relayed Rush into the hands of two black officers whom he had personally selected for the occasion. "Then the next Saturday, you'd have a young Michael Jackson and his family suddenly walk onstage and perform. Or anybody else who happened to be in town that weekend—you never knew."

At first, actually, "Jesse didn't always know who these people were," says Calvin Morris. "One day Odetta was on the stage, and Jesse leaned to whisper to me, 'Calvin, who *is* that?' " In the beginning, at least, "he was different because he wasn't one of them," says Larry Shaw. "He would be awestruck by them as well, but respected them as human beings. Because he wasn't one of them, they respected him—until he became more as they are, when he began to act more like a star. He was very unsophisticated at first in the ways of the world, but he learned those ways eventually and became more victim of them than victor. He chose to want expensive suits because he liked the way they looked on these rich celebrities. And he lost consciousness of what he was before that." As it seemed to Calvin Morris, "he became a celebrity among celebrities. He was a celebrity with them, they were celebrities together, with their ladies-in-waiting and men-in-waiting. And he loved it."

But throughout these Saturday-morning extravaganzas, Jackson, despite his mod raiment of bell-bottoms and fringed buckskin vests and velour sweaters, maintained an unfaltering, graven seriousness, that righteous comportment in which, as William Buckley once observed, "he never smiles, avoiding affability with total success." When he would finally be presented for that morning's address—an aide announcing, "Ladies and gentlemen! Meet the Reverend Jesse Jackson!"—he would move up to the pulpit, hoist high an open palm, and bugle out over the ovation, "*I am . . . somebody!*" For his part, at least, Jackson had come to be possessed by now of a lordly self-assurance. When he once found himself standing near Chief Justice Earl Warren at a graduation ceremony, he remarked to someone with him, "A few years ago I'd of popped right over there and said, 'Yessuh, Mr. Chief Justice, *suh*,' but no more, brother. Let him come over here." He readily apprised reporters, "I apparently do have an appeal that is special." And now in his Saturday-morning messages, he would proceed from meditations on the tribulations of David in the Old Testament to proclaim of himself, "My head has been anointed with oil. I have confidence today that in spite of what tomorrow holds, that goodness on one hand, and mercy on the other, will follow me *awwlll* the days of my life!"

But while a princely young preacher presiding theatrically over his own homegrown flock, Jackson for a time still happened to be technically unsanctioned for the ministry. "He didn't think nothin' about being ordained," says the Reverend Clay Evans. "He said, 'Aw, that don't make no difference.'" Evans's secretary, Lucille Loman, recalls, "He didn't think it was something he really needed to do. He'd been preaching for so long and been called Reverend that it seemed to him like going back to the seminary. He said, 'Oh, Lucy, I can't be going and . . . that's, like, *childish*.' But I explained to him, 'You just gonna have to get ordained, because you cannot marry people and all those kinds of things if you don't.'" Evans finally admonished him that "God says, 'Jesse, you got to give me the deed, to have and to hold.'" Though Jackson had dropped out of the seminary six months short of a divinity degree, he at last agreed, shortly after King's death, to attend to the formality of getting ordained, in Evans's Fellowship Missionary Baptist Church, which happily required no academic certification for the ceremony. But so conspicuous a presence had he become by then in Chicago's black community that the fabled preacher C. L. Franklin, Aretha's father, delivered his ordination sermon—"We been very close to that family," Jackson allows. What's more, printed in his ordination service program as a "Special Guest List" were: "Mr. and Mrs. Bill Cosby, Mr. and Mrs. Robert Culp, Senator and Mrs. Charles Percy, Miss Eartha Kitt, Mr. Sidney Poitier, Mr. Tony Franciosa, Mr. Marlon Brando," and "Mr. Walter Cronkite." Asked about that "guest list" almost three decades later, Evans chortles and fans his hand in front of his face: "That Jesse! Invited, yeah, but no, no, no, *'course* they weren't there."

Nevertheless, says Lucille Loman, Jackson kept on declaring in his Saturday-morning Breadbasket messages that, ordained or not, his ministry derived out of Luke 4:18: "The Spirit of the Lord is upon me, because he has anointed me to preach the gospel to the poor and to heal the brokenhearted, to preach deliverance to the captives and to set at liberty them that are bruised." And that early, she reports, in his Breadbasket sermons "he was already talking about why he could not be contained in a local parish. Because the world was going to be his parish."

Creating a Personal Empery

GEORGE HARRIS REMEMBERS that "Jesse was like a wild stallion in those days. Abernathy certainly couldn't control him. He was just bigger than everybody and everything else." It was hardly a surprise, then, that after King's death, Jackson began evidencing a pronounced restlessness at being pent within the structures of SCLC. Along with everything else, a great bulk of the monies from Breadbasket's success in Chicago were still being directed down to SCLC headquarters in Atlanta, to the extent that it had become a question of which was actually carrying which. Along with that, says Richard Thomas, "once Dr. King had been killed, it left a vacuum in the leadership in which none of them could compete with Jesse for national press. He was a charismatic figure, and there was little, if any, charisma in Atlanta." The truth is, says Calvin Morris, though Jackson was only twenty-seven, improbably at first "his ambition was to become head of SCLC." At the organization's 1968 convention, which was held in Memphis only a few months after King was slain, he made an impulsive reach for at least a position far higher on its echelons of responsibility, but was brusquely rebuffed by the more circumspect ministerial and professional elders on its board of directors, one of whom complained afterward, "He tried to leapfrog too many people." Then, according to various claims, at the 1970 convention in Atlanta, Jackson again demanded, "At least make me a national vice president if I can't be president," and in 1971, at an executive board meeting in Detroit, he insisted that if he were to remain in SCLC, "I must be given a post that is consistent with my national position." Meanwhile, he grew progressively disdainful of the worthily bumblesome Ralph Abernathy, once snuffling, "Man, I never listen to that nigger." Larry Shaw recalls, "Jesse would give an awards banquet for Abernathy, give him all these speeches and plaques, people applauding, as a way to get him out of the way. He'd just promote him. If he's hungry, give him some more, whatever his heart desires. A great, Solomon-level wisdom in that." But he soon contracted a surliness about even Coretta King. Despite her resentment of what she took to have been Jackson's behavior right after Memphis, she had become dismayed at the prospect of Jackson abandoning SCLC, and she made a game appearance at one of Breadbasket's Saturday-morning services to profess, "After my last visit to Breadbasket, I told my husband that Jesse Jackson will make a tremendous contribution to our society. I hoped then, and I still hope now, that he will remain with SCLC." But at a staff meeting beforehand to plan out the service, Jackson had snappishly remarked, "We'll take care of our business, and then Mrs. King can do her woman-power thing. . . ."

At the same time, within SCLC, exasperation grew over Jackson's indifference to scheduled staff conferences, his refusal to even consider transferring some of his operations down to Atlanta. Especially vexing, his budgetary procedures were even more casual than those of SCLC itself. When SCLC bookkeepers once asked for an accounting of Breadbasket's operational expenses for the year, they received from Chicago, according to Abernathy, "little more than a paper bag full of canceled checks and receipts—and more of the former than the latter." And it was finally not so much a matter of mission as that baser, fiscal contention that would precipitate the separation.

IN 1968, JACKSON had put together in Chicago a promotional festival for black businesses called Black Expo, to which he had managed to attract a galaxy of entertainers. According to George O'Hare, the whole event was organized from Jackson's hospital bed only two weeks prior to its opening. "He'd been hit with his sickle-cell anemia trait. One day he called a meeting, about six or seven people in his hospital room. Said, 'We're going to have a Black Expo.' He gave us our assignments from his bed. In two weeks, the International Amphitheater was full." A triumph that first year, Black Expo became an annual spectacular—politicos, jazz ensembles, hosts of businessmen, including Japanese investors, milling among some five hundred booths that were advertising eventually as many white enterprises as black (Jackson having encouraged white exhibitors, "A strong black economy is the best alternative to the welfare state"). George O'Hare relates, "Jesse called me, said, 'We're going to have a booth on black inventors. Do you think you could get Sears to sponsor the booth?' I said, 'Before I go to Sears, what do you mean, "black inventors"? There are a lot of things in life, but I don't know anybody black in life that ever invented anything except maybe peanut butter, I think I remember hearing once.' So he got Jackie to take me over to this doctor's house, and he had in his basement all these artifacts of inventions from black history. Open-heart surgery, blood plasma, third rail of the trolley, bicycle frame, the shoe clasp that everybody walks around on every day, baby buggy, refrigeration on trucks. I went to my Sears people and told them all this. 'That's not true,' they said. I took our display manager over to this doctor's basement to see. Sears put up a Black Expo booth on black inventors, and we won the contest for best booth." These events took place in a spangling of celebrity visitations—Bill Cosby, Aretha Franklin, the Jackson Five, Roberta Flack, Flip Wilson, B. B. King, Cannonball Adderley, Sammy Davis, Jr. Even Hugh Hefner showed up. There were growing misgivings now among some, like former King adviser Wyatt Tee Walker, about what seemed Jackson's inordinate fondness for "always hanging out with show-business people. It just seemed out of place for what he was supposed to represent." Richard Hatcher admits, "He did like the idea that he could pick up a telephone and call Bill Cosby, and Cosby would answer his call. And he *really* liked the idea of calling you, 'Hey, Hatcher, come on over here, I've got Ossie Davis in the house.' " But with Black Expo soon drawing some 800,000 attendees, even Mayor Daley found himself disposed to decree a Black Expo Week, and to pose, a wide beam on his broad pumpkin's face, exchanging soul-shakes with Jackson for photographers at the event's opening.

Then in 1971, the SCLC office in Atlanta discovered that Jackson had discreetly appropriated the entire affair from SCLC by incorporating it under a separate body composed of his Chicago sponsors. This provoked a full-scale furor among the organization's inner councils. Abernathy and several other SCLC officials flew to Chicago to confront Jackson about this apparent piece of legerdemain, summoning him to a meeting on a snowy Sunday in a motel conference room near O'Hare Airport. Actually, a Jackson adjutant then contends, the incorporation had mostly been the initiative of Jackson's sponsors, who, "as Expo grew and the receipts came in, began saying, 'We send all this money to SCLC, but we've got expenses here, we need money to have at our disposal.' " But when Jackson presented himself at the conference room with a briefcase under his arm, according to several accounts, Abernathy barked at him, "We're not ready to see you yet. Wait outside until you're called." Only after three hours of discussion among themselves and with others behind closed doors did Abernathy's panel of inquisitors at last admit Jackson into the meeting, he by now in a cold, tight rage of humiliation. It ended with Abernathy announcing that Jackson had been suspended for sixty days, with pay, though Abernathy made a point of disclaiming any "fiscal dishonesty" by Jackson, and acknowledged that SCLC itself "has never had a tight structure." Despite those indulgent notations, a friend of Jackson's reports, "he cried over the way he felt SCLC had treated him." And it proved the climactic fracas between Jackson and King's old organization.

What is puzzling in retrospect, actually, is that Jackson, with all his lunging restiveness after King was gone, lingered on in SCLC as long as he did—over three and a half years. In the end, it was bizarrely as if he almost had to be flushed out, but by repudiations which, even more bizarrely, he had himself set up. John Johnson recalls that he pressed Jackson simply to disconnect from SCLC "because it was too small for him, he had moved beyond it. He was already more popular than Abernathy. But they were not going to let him override Abernathy. He said, 'I just can't be on no damned *suspension.*' I said, 'Rev, you were a little out of line, he's *got* to put you on suspension. But being the kind of guy you are, you cannot accept it. So your only choice is to leave and start an organization of your own.'" But Willie Barrow remembers, "Jesse really did not want to leave, and wrestled and wrestled with it; he spent some long sleepless nights. On the inside of Jesse, he was very pained." Says Richard Thomas, "It aged him five years." Jackson kept fretting to others, "It's the organization I grew up with," as if only now realizing that he would, in a sense, be losing yet another home. As it was, though, "you had SCLC board members playing on Dr. Abernathy's insecurity," says a Jackson associate, "and you had people in Chicago playing on Jesse's ego, saying, 'Jesse, you don't need SCLC, you don't have to go through this kind of stuff.'"

Finally, he telegraphed a resignation letter to SCLC, and with the matter so decided, publicly announced, in a jubilation of release at striking out wholly on his own at last, that he would be forming his own organization "to keep myself alive. I need air. *I got to grow.*" He consolidated around him, in a meeting at the Commodore Hotel in New York, an auspicious bevy of backers, among them Quincy Jones, Berry Gordy of Motown Records, and Manhattan borough president Percy Sutton. Then, on Christmas morning, 1971, at a rally inside the dingy and tawdry hulk of another derelict South Side theater, which was so clobberingly cold that, remembers one on the stage with Jackson, "we were all shivering; Lord, it was like *zero,*" Jackson formally proclaimed the creation of his organization: "A new child has been born!" He had named it People United to Save Humanity (only later was that "Save" modified to a slightly more temperate "Serve"), or Operation PUSH. At that inaugural service, "people were crying," says Hermene Hartman, and "Jesse himself was scared. He was still insecure—though the insecurity of Jesse was always internal, never outward. But he was only twenty-eight years old. He hadn't ever done anything like this before."

Though he was decamping from SCLC, he declared that "we ain't taking no money, we don't own nothing." But in fact, he transported with him into PUSH not only all of Breadbasket's files and office equipment but most of its membership, including its entire staff of twenty-five, and all but five of its thirty-five board members. The Saturday-morning services continued, as did their radio broadcasts over the city. On the whole, about all

Jackson left behind him was Breadbasket's name. PUSH itself turned out to be mostly a reconstitution of Breadbasket's program of economic militancy widened into a more general social ministry, an interracial popular movement—explaining it, Jackson made one of his first mentions of a "rainbow coalition"—to extend King's perspectives into all reaches of the nation's life. But it remained an undertaking about as elusive of precise definition as Jackson himself would prove over time. Not exactly a church, not simply a political action body, it was instead more a curious montage of assorted ad-hoc social initiatives with churchly inflections. It was structured into no less than twenty-three subgroups—a minister's division, special projects divisions, youth division. "I had about seven titles myself," says Richard Thomas. "We passed out those titles like rich people." For all its lavish organization, though, PUSH amounted to simply a personal apparatus improvised by Jackson to serve as an organizational extension of his own free-form inspirations.

Its manner of operation, as described by former PUSH staffer Robert Starks—"eclectic, spontaneous, periodic pauses and spurts"—happens to be close to a description of Jackson's own nature. Another former assistant asserts that, with Jackson, it's always the case that "*he* is really the organization, and it flows the way his mind flows. And you become kind of parts of him, you know, you're his finger or his foot, and as he sneezes and moves, so does the organization." Starks says, "He could get a phone call, and change the direction and focus of a whole program in a minute, to incorporate what he thought was a new current in a situation." One assistant finally took the precaution of phoning him at six each morning to make sure Jackson had not come by some "vision" during the night that would totally alter a project elaborately worked out over previous days.

In truth, there issued from him a ceaseless blizzard of inspirations— among them, during that period of a general black cultural awakening, notions for a Black Christmas, then a Black Easter. "He'd dream 'em up every minute," says George O'Hare. "Black Easter. What's a Black Easter? Black Soul Saint. That's the black Santa Claus. Just came out of him all the time, all the time." It seemed at times as if he were striving, with an organization of his own, to create a whole alternative ethos in place of the one in which he had been born alien and outcast. And he would not wait until dawn to transmit these enthusiasms to friends and confederates. "Jesse had no idea of a clock, of time," says the Reverend Claude Wyatt, who copastored a church with his wife, Addie. "He'd just pick up the phone at four in the morning and call and say, 'Listen, Claude, I need to talk to you and Addie. Is she asleep? Wake her up.'" Usually, says Addie Wyatt, "he was just excited about something he wanted to do, he'd say, 'I want the ministers to meet me tomorrow at such-and-such a time, I want to meet with the labor union.' " O'Hare relates, "I got a phone call once at two o'clock in the morning. My wife was next to the phone and picked it up and then said, 'Oh.' And she looked at me: 'This is your friend.' Jesse says, 'Can you come pick up Jackie and take her to the NBC studio in the Merchandise Mart for the *Today* show?' I said sure. 'You got to pick her up at four o'clock,' he said. 'That's in two hours.' I said, 'Jesse. Jesse, why can't you do this?' He said, 'Well, it's the *Today* show. And, you know, you can't teach your wife how to drive a car.' " But as often, these pit-of-the-night calls would be provoked by an unbearable outrage over resistance to one of his ambitious fancies, an indignation "that'd been going over and over in his mind," says Addie Wyatt, "and we'd try to quench that overeagerness and instill the need for patience, we'd talk and pray with him and try to simmer him down."

But he had at least established now a custom-styled personal domain that liberated him to pursue his oldest and largest urges for his own self-realization. Relying only on his own devices, however, his recourses for funding his creation were about as unsystematic and extemporaneous as its guerrilla style of ministry—"hectic and very erratic," says a onetime staffer, "with donations from the Saturday-morning broadcasts, contributors who took memberships, entertainers and businesspeople who'd send money." According to Richard Thomas, "At first, we didn't even have enough money to make a budget. You'd have to go out and raise a dime to get the paper to write the budget on. On Thursday, if we found we were going to have a shortfall of cash for Saturday's payday, Jesse'd make a call to somebody, and a lot of Fridays I'd have to get on a plane and go somewhere out of town to pick up a check, come back, and give it to Lucille Loman, who would then call somebody to open up the bank on Saturday. And they'd cash the check, and we'd make payroll . . . *most* Saturdays. We did that hand-to-mouth for a long time." On the whole, it was an operation that rather resembled the state of the universe on about the second day of creation, much owing, says one later adviser, to the circumstance that "Jackson had been raised in the Martin Luther King school of a kind of organized rolling chaos." In time, says Thomas, "we had access to any number of volunteer accountants, more CPAs than you could shake a stick at. All trying to keep us out of trouble. It was very easy to ask any one of them to come up with a budget. Didn't mean you had *to live* by it, though."

Cirilo McSween, the trim and brisk Chicago businessman who had been SCLC's treasurer, was also now serving as comptroller for Jackson's enterprise. One of McSween's particular values, says Thomas, was that "he was a cornerstone of the black business community, he knew all the right people and they respected him. They knew if he was handling the money, it wasn't going every which way, regardless of what people were saying." More than once, says Thomas, "Cirilo'd go to the airport to check out how many people were leaving with Jesse, because Jesse would take ten people sometimes, depending on what impression he wanted to make where he was going." Hermene Hartman recalls, "It absolutely drove Cirilo nuts. There were times he'd literally stand in front of the plane at the airport and say, 'Yawl ain't all going. We don't have the money for this many. Pick one, 'cause that's the budget. Rest of yawl got to get off.' Jesse would argue with him, 'No, now, I gotta have, David's gotta go. Richard's *gotta* go . . .'"

It was a manner of innovating his means as he went along, largely necessitated by his compulsion to act as an utterly free agent, that nevertheless, when he eventually wandered into closer media scrutinies with his decision to enter into a presidential competition, would retroactively waylay him with the appearance of a venal sort of frenetic hustling, hardly seemly in a putative heir to Martin Luther King, not to mention certain more dubious arrangements. But "he was always raising money," says John Johnson, who supplied him not only with financial assistance but a tutelage in the refinements of soliciting contributions. "Once he had his, like, third assistant call me to get a donation. So I had my fourth assistant call him to tell him no. He called me back, said, 'Godfather, what's going on? You always give me a contribution.' I said, 'But you always ask me. You didn't this time.' He came right down to the office, and I gave him a slightly larger check than usual, and said, 'Rev, if you're smart, you'll do this with everybody.' About a week later, he called me up and said, 'I did what you told me, and I want you to know it works. When I show up personally to ask for a contribution, they'll give it to me every time.'"

Hugh Hefner became a substantial benefactor. George O'Hare says, "Jesse told me one day to go down and get some money from *Playboy*, said to see a guy named Anson Mount there. I had to sneak off from Sears to do this and get back to the office. So without calling ahead, I walked into the place cold turkey, and this black receptionist there says, 'Yes? Mr. Mount? Do you have an appointment?' I said, 'Well, no, the Reverend Jesse Jackson sent me.' She said, 'Jesse sent you?' She ran into the back, and out comes Mount. I walked out with a check for five thousand dollars." Richard Thomas relates, "Lots of Fridays we'd go over to the Playboy mansion, and Hefner'd be either walking around in his bathrobe or sleeping. Bunnies'd be lying around. Actually, it was the dullest place in the world. They had a room down in the basement where you played pinball machines, so me and whoever else was with us would go down and play pinball while Jesse and Hefner talked. They had a cook on duty there twenty-four hours, so we'd have dinner. Then Jesse'd come out smiling, I assumed with a check, because I wouldn't have to go to Memphis or New York or Los Angeles."

Adds Hermene Hartman, "We got so much money from Hefner, some people say Hefner finally left Chicago to keep us from sucking him dry."

The Service Arrangement

BUT FINALLY, AS crucial to sustaining him in his solo operation now was a factor he had discovered even before the beneficences bestowed upon him by his patrons while he was leading Breadbasket. As a teenager in Greenville, when an older friend of his had left for college, Jackson had, unbidden, taken to regularly scuffling under the house of his friend's elderly parents to gather for them coal and wood stored there, for which they would then give him great round pan-baked slabs of cornbread. "People always take care of those who serve them" is how Jackson came to formulate the principle. "Like on the first missionary journey—disciples had no money, didn't have a budget, but Jesus told 'em, 'Go ye amongst the people, take the good news, and be a good servant to them. And the people will keep you in their homes, they'll feed you, they'll befriend you, they won't wanna let you go.' Disciples came back, Jesus asked 'em, 'Well, lack ye anything? You hongry? Got clothes? Got money in your pocket? Lackin' anything now?' They said, 'Nope. Can't say anything we lack.' That's how it works. That's why Jesus said, 'Seek ye first the kingdom of God and his righteousness, and all these things—these *things*—will be added unto you.' Preacher stands up there and inspires the people when they're down, visits 'em when they sick, marries 'em, counsels 'em, preaches their funeral and buries 'em when they dead. In return: free parsonage for the pastor, free food, lights, telephone, car, vacations, educate his children. What they will do for the servant is unlimited. If you serve, people will hoist you up on their shoulders and *keep* you up there."

Jackson had first experienced the full effects of this particular contract, he reports, during the demonstrations in Greensboro, "after I'd come out of jail that time. Jackie and I'd had our first baby, Santita, and when I'd walk down Market Street, people would pull over in their cars and give me money—just *hand it* to you. Or offer to buy groceries for us, mean, couldn't *buy* groceries in Greensboro for people bringin' bags of 'em to us.

Because of service!" The considerations now furnished him for his service with PUSH — a maroon Lincoln Continental with chauffeur, the fifteen-room home on Constance Avenue, and free upkeep of its yard, much of his wardrobe — were simply an extension of the returns on that *natural*, informal contract revealed to him in Greensboro. George Jones, who headed the Joe Louis Milk Company, reports, "We were taking him around one winter to show him the stores where we were having problems, and I noticed he had on a very thin pair of sandals, though there was snow on the ground. I said, 'First thing, let's go in this shoe shop here. We've got to buy you a pair of overshoes.'" Another sponsor, George Johnson, declares, "Didn't even have an overcoat. So we decided to put our arms around him." Jones frankly affirms, "We paid his salary. We took care of whatever bills he had. If he or somebody in his family became ill, we had doctors for them. We got him his house, took care of fixing it up. Carpenters worked gratis, painters worked gratis, carpeters put in carpets gratis. And he wasn't bashful at all if he wanted something specific; he would call one of us up and say, 'I need money for my kids' tuition.' If he needed clothes, a car, a trust fund for his family in case something happened to him, why not? He should live in a decent manner, and we saw to it that he could."

Jackson himself buoyantly observes, "There're all kinds of by-products for the great servants. People *want* you to stay in a comfortable house, want you to wear nice clothes, have a car of your choice — with bulletproof windows. Say, 'We want bodyguards around you.' Somebody will look at all these other things *added unto*, see that chauffeur-driven car and the bodyguards — hey! how come you got all that stuff and they ain't? You must be doin' something shady. But what they don't comprehend, it all comes out of service. It's like some divine law of reciprocity. You cannot hurt somebody without hurtin' yourself, and I cannot help you without helping me. Now, if I'm helping you *just* to help me, it's not the real thing, it won't work 'cause something's missing, spiritually the whole business drops to a lower octave, understand what I'm sayin'. But real service . . . you cast that bread upon the waters, it'll return to you, toasted. With *butter* on it."

If this felicitous interchange left Jackson living in circumstances not exactly as modest as those of King, what were temptations to King would have been outright appetites left in Jackson from his far grimmer origins. "He wanted to drive his own car," says Larry Shaw. "He wanted to have a big house. You'd say, 'You can't own a big house, you're fighting for the poor.' He'd say, 'I didn't say *own* it. I'll just live in it.' So maybe he did better than he ought to have, but who can say what a guy like that ought to have?" But it was a munificent arrangement that, along with his manifold

other resorts to subsidize his freelance social apostleship, hardly met with
a ready appreciation by the gimlet-eyed critical attentions turned on him
later with his presidential exploit.

A Larger Family

FOR A TIME, PUSH had to continue Breadbasket's nomadic career of
wandering from site to site, until Lucille Loman happened to pass a South
Side synagogue with administrative annex that she noticed was for sale,
and she rushed to tell Jackson, "Reverend, that's our building!" Jackson
said, "If it's our building, then go over there and get it," and after she had
negotiated terms with the owners, the financing, says Willie Barrow with a
chuckle, "was turned over to the boys."

For the faithful who then converged there every Saturday morning,
most of whom had followed Jackson from Breadbasket, he had acquired by
now an almost demireligious mystique. One of his original devotees,
Mabel Walker—a small, round, elderly woman in large circular glasses,
who is usually gowned in muumuus—recalls with a dreamy smile, "When
I first met him, he was still just a youngster with a lot of bushy hair, but
they'd bring him out the back way for security, you know, with police and
this crowd waiting there every Saturday just for him to come out that door.
So when he came out, the security guard told him, 'This lady would like
to shake your hand.' And when I got up on him, he had, seemed like, gray
eyes—light eyes—and that was unusual to me. *Piercing* eyes. He just had
something different. He was the most strangest person I had ever met. Special strange. I remember one Saturday when he had finished speaking, we
all started singing and he put his arms out, he had on a robe or dashiki or
something, and he looked to me just like Jesus."

Businessman George Jones attests, "He'd walk out there on that stage
sometimes like, in his stature and appearance, I am *the man*. The whole
audience, two thousand people, would stand, applaud, scream, 'Jesse,
Jesse!' After a point, he thought he *was* the man. He would stand there and
let them applaud a good while before he would quiet them down." It
seemed to his early assistant, Larry Shaw, that "he became more and more
conscious of himself as he grew. He became affected by his audiences.
To many people, he became a little god, they worshiped him. Now, *he*
didn't say he was a god, but he sort of started acting like it. So who do you
blame? All these people coming up to you bowing and wanting to kiss your
ring. He tries to keep his hands in his pockets, but it doesn't stop them
coming. So pretty soon, he starts putting the ring out there, you know. Let

'em kiss your hand." Calvin Morris now proposes, "I reconcile it that Jesse *was* an instrument of the movement for change. But Jesse, and any other of these great men and women in our history, their own pushing becomes merged with whatever the movement is, so most don't see a difference. Now, Jesse in the beginning wouldn't have seen it so much as a personal thing as a way of advancing the movement. But it was my own sense that for a lot of people, and gradually in Jesse's own mind, the movement and his person became one."

FROM HAVING GROWN up as an illegitimate child in another man's household, Jackson now took to casting himself as a "father to a community." His PUSH congregation did, in fact, become something like his own expanded, multitudinous family. The spacious corridor outside his rear corner office at PUSH "would always be just full of people, from wall to wall," reports Lucille Loman. "And the more people out there who wanted to be near him, the better he liked it." In turn, how one PUSH member characterized another—"She has found a place, and her place is Jesse and his family and PUSH"—was more or less true for most of them, actually. "Him and his wife, just like they was my own," says another early follower. "We went to the children's graduations and everything." Beyond that, they would collectively pick out the clothes for him to wear, shop for his family's groceries, even run his bathwater. For that matter, they virtually lived with him in the capacious Tudor-style house that his financial patrons had obtained for him, through a secret land-trust arrangement, in 1970.

It was located in a pleasant upper-middle-class neighborhood in the South Side that had been a habitat of Chicago's merchant squirearchy after the turn of the century, its rooms vast, dusky, and drafty during the winters but during the summers smotheringly hot—Jackson being militantly averse to air-conditioning. Besides an absence of amenities for moderating the climate, when Jackson had first moved in with his family, says Richard Hatcher, "there was no furniture in that house. There was hardly anything to sit on. In the dining room, there were two benches at the table, but not a lot more than that." In time, though, the long, large front sitting room with its dark-wood paneling became outfitted in cherry-red velvet drapes and a cherry-red carpet, with red-and-black French chairs and black leather couches. A Steinway & Sons baby grand piano eventually appeared at one end of the room, atop which there steadily assembled framed photographs of kinfolk and the famed. Still, visitors would find almost all the rooms had the look of a superficial and transitory occupancy, like some boardinghouse in which the family was only tentatively lodging. In the front bay-windowed sunroom, suitcases were scattered about among dusty cactus and banana-leaf plants. And amid the accumulation everywhere of memorabilia from trips and leftover Christmas ornaments and old pamphlets and handout sheets were huge and somewhat floridly melodramatic portraits of Jackson, one looming over the landing of the wide murky stairway to the second floor, another commanding the living room, along with a slightly smaller portrait of César Chávez, done in rust brushstrokes—and autographed by him, "To My Brother Jesse con el mejor de mi Cariño"—hanging in a corner over an oak Victorian desk with carved mythological figures of women-faced cheetahs and a back-coiling griffin, where a fax machine now nests in a chaos of papers.

In 1994, after Jackson had mostly shifted his activities to Washington, three of PUSH's remaining faithful—Mabel Walker, her daughter Aileen, and Lucille Loman—sat about the long dining room table in that house and reminisced a little elegiacally, on a hot still June afternoon with a stale must of mothballs hanging heavily in the uninhabited rooms, about the days when those rooms were filled with a noisy churn of people in a kind of ongoing open reception that somewhat suggested the riotous household in *You Can't Take It with You*. "There'd be people literally everywhere in here, every day," related Aileen. "Some over in a corner having a meeting—always somebody having a meeting in a corner. Others out in the yard. Food was always being brought in, barbecue and fried fish and chicken, whatever. And you never knew whoever was going to drop by. . . ." Once, in the seventies, Sandinista leader Daniel Ortega came by for dinner, Jackson first ushering him and his party out for a game of basketball on the small half-court in his backyard. However courteously he may have conducted himself in that match, usually he did not permit his heavy intensity to relent even in play, going about most other backyard basketball scrimmages with what an aide described as "an outrageous outpouring of fury." Another PUSH regular says, "He wants to win *everything*. He's hurt a lot of people, he's very vicious," and even when playing whist at the dining room table, "if you touch his cards, he's gonna break your hand." But he would always have music whooping through the house, says Aileen, "music, music, music, oh, *God*. We had to have the speakers on in every room, and he'd play Marvin Gaye or Cannonball Adderley, only about four or five that he liked, he didn't want to hear anybody else." Jackie herself chortles at the memory. "It was like a commune from the sixties. People'd come into the city and stay a year at my house. Not only did they come, they always brought somebody. My children were never told that they had to go to bed at a certain hour. They just mingled, and sat under the table and bit people on the foot and leg. My mother called them products of the movement. She said, 'These children, they don't go to bed, they just pass out.' " It would all "just go on and on," says Aileen, "and then he'd say, 'Well, I'm asleep,' and go upstairs to go to bed." But there, he would often continue to receive a train of visitors and conduct meetings, reposing in navy blue silk pajamas, while also making calls, scrawling notes on legal pads spilled across the bed. "He never wanted to be alone," says Calvin Morris. "On the telephone, that's about as much as he'd be alone. He would keep a room full of people until he fell asleep." While he would "have six or seven people in there, holding court," says Hermene Hartman, Jackie, lying beside him, "would take a pillow and cover up her head."

More, not only did his PUSH following largely live with him then, but *in* him, Jackson magically enlarging all their lives over the course of his own expanding circumstances through the seventies. "The things we did in a lifetime we would of never been able to do if it hadn't been for him," vigorously attests one of his most doughtily loyal believers, a diminutive, Yoda-like figure of a woman. "I didn't meet no damn body till he came along. I didn't know no kings or presidents, we wasn't in with no celebrities." The three women sitting at the dining room table in Jackson's now unoccupied house seemed still slightly dazed by the extravagant sweep and dazzle of those times, recalling them in a litany of interchiming nostalgias. "It was like a university without walls," proclaimed Lucille Loman, and Aileen Walker added, "He took me on my first plane ride. It was to Washington, D.C." Now a trim, quietly serious woman who has remained unmarried, she declared, "He was somebody who could make things happen, and you just wanted to be around somebody who made things happen. We went to visit PUSH in Detroit, we went to visit PUSH in Cincinnati—" Her mother, Mabel, warbled, "Got to ride in limousines!" "Yeah," said Aileen, "and the crowds! The cheers!" Lucille Loman went on, "When we were with him on the road, sometimes we'd begin dragging, and then when he'd get up there and those crowds started to holler, the energy would just come into us again—" And Mabel pronounced, "Oh, he made a *great* difference in our lives."

That turned out more abundantly the case for his immediate staff. "The things I was able to see and do with him," says a former aide, "were things not many others ever get to see and do." One younger assistant who served him some years later describes it as "very much a father-son kind of thing. My own father hadn't been around, I didn't know him. And here was someone who was willing to show me the world, who had a big idea in his mind and was asking me to help." But they found it an exhilaration commonly accompanied by the ordeal of, in the words of the same aide, "working hard the whole time and thinking that you're doing the best you can do, while he's always telling you you're not doing your best." In fact, Jackson ruled over the staff of his personal domain at PUSH with a peremptory impatience approaching Caesarean proportions. Asked by a reporter once about his astounding roughness sometimes with his personnel, Jackson asserted, "Shit, I can't keep people's wings flapping forever." It seemed a harshness at garish variance with his other generosities of spirit, in itself testimony, perhaps, to how desperately important to him this creation of his was, but it unsettled many who witnessed it. Willie Barrow, a short, bustling, hefty woman who long functioned as Jackson's second at PUSH, explains with a certain clinical equanimity, "If you can't pull it, you can't work with Jesse. He isn't going to give you much help. He announces some Saturday morning that we're going to organize against Ford, then gets on a plane and goes to Seattle—all he wants to do is articulate what the situation is and lead it, but his team has to put it together. If he sees it, you ought to be able to catch it and move it and make it happen. Grow it. If you can't, Jesse can't deal with you."

What made that fiendishly complicated, though, was Jackson's obsession with reserving to his own person all final decisions in directing the course of his self-conceived enterprise, which left its staff floundering in an organizational void. As a result, an aide reported to one of Jackson's early biographers, "the light that draws people to Jesse can also be very debilitating. He pulls good people working in the movement into his inner circle," but then, owing to his fixation on reposing all responsibility in himself, they would find themselves not infrequently reduced to "carrying his suitcases and answering his doorbell." Neither were they recompensed that bountifully, a consideration that did not seem to particularly trouble Jackson either. When a staffer once began hinting, in a sort of woebegone half jest, for a salary increase, Jackson made as if he'd said "celery," and roundly assured him that more salad greens and even carrots would shortly be supplied him. Another assistant in later years recounts, "I was working hard from morning to evening, but I was making almost nothing, I was going broke. I was hungry all the time, I was skinny. My car got snatched, because my credit went bust—being on the road with him all the time, I had nobody back home to take care of my business. I mean, you know, that becomes a resentment after a while. You haven't been to a dry cleaner for weeks, and you're packing his bags and talking to the press and all that, and you don't have time to tend to any of your own affairs, I mean, barely to stay *clean* much less pay your bills. It's very hard to pay your bills from Zimbabwe. But he never really notices that."

Then, when his oppressive manner finally drove staff members out of PUSH, Jackson viewed it as betrayal and defection, and instantly consigned them to oblivion. This owes, Morris surmises, to the primal hurt of

Jackson's beginnings, "how he came up in Greenville with people laugh-
ing at him. How you re-create yourself from something like that is very critical, and the residues in Jesse are some mean-spiritedness. Still that
fighting, that defensiveness and insecurity. Having been an illegitimate
child, it may feel like abandonment again when a person years later goes
away." In any case, it left not a little wreckage behind him over the years.
"I saw people lose their jobs, I saw marriages break up," admits Hermene
Hartman. "I saw some destruction." Richard Thomas himself eventually
quit. After a meeting at PUSH, with Jackson having left for the airport, he
sat in his office with his wife, who also worked for Jackson, "and I just
started to cry. She asked me what was wrong. I told her I had to resign. I
wrote a resignation out for Alyce Tregay to give to Jesse at the airport before
he caught his plane. He called me then from Los Angeles and asked why I
was leaving him. I couldn't tell him. I just knew I had to go. And I couldn't
just step in and step out at will. The magnetism of the man causes you to
give whatever it is you have when you're around him. So I had to leave totally." Jackson did not talk to Thomas again for some five years.

Even so, many of those who have fled his domination "spend the rest of
their lives," says one such fugitive, "seeking his approval. Every new project of theirs, every new job, they're calling him, needing to seek his blessing, you know. It's real strange." Morris himself served as Jackson's chief
deputy until an abrupt rift between them in 1971, and he now reflects,
"There's a kind of bittersweetness about it, because I still very much appreciate him. I actually love Jesse very much. Those of us who get hooked
are rarely ever unhooked. I'm not quite sure what was broken. But I've not
had whatever it would take to mend it, and he doesn't have the inclination, I don't think, nor, in his own sweep of history, any time in order to
mend it. But I certainly feel very, very, very deeply the loss and the hurt."

Perhaps more than anything else, though, what finally compelled associates like Morris to leave was Jackson's eternally testy wariness about anyone
else assuming any measure of leadership that might subtract from his own
total proprietorship over the public stage he had fashioned for himself with
PUSH. His half brother Noah Robinson, Jr., whom Jackson briefly brought
on at Breadbasket, claimed afterward, "Jesse is just too damn insecure to
gather any supertechnicians around him," and he never appointed a genuine executive manager at PUSH, says Wyatt Tee Walker, because "he
couldn't find anybody who he trusted enough to do that. In this media era,
what is buried deep in his psyche is who is going to get the attention." That,
of course, without the great social drama of King's time, seemed mortal
now to Jackson for any self-fulfillment. Once, Morris says, shortly after Jackson had been appointed national director of Breadbasket, he arranged to

have a photograph taken of him and King together, "knowing it was one of the ways to enhance his credibility," and Morris, who had just been named associate director, asked for a similar picture with King, thinking "I would also be enhanced on a local basis"; but Jackson "was furious. He was seething. He got that tight look, his eyes got small. I think he felt I was trying to usurp, but I really wasn't." Improbably, Jackson constantly had "a concern that he not be overshadowed in any way," says Morris, "which is a paradox, of course. Because I don't know anybody, certainly myself included, who could ever overshadow Jesse Jackson."

But it was almost a mania with him that eventually harried out of PUSH his closest white friend up to that point. David Wallace, a small, thin, dark-haired, intense but quiet-spoken young divine from Pecos, Texas, had been one of the first two students Jackson had encountered when he pulled into a parking lot at CTS after his drive up from the South that summer of 1964—the other being Gary Massoni, also white, who has managed to maintain an association with Jackson ever since. Wallace had by that time served on an American Friends Service Committee project in Tanzania, and on his return to the States, had been involved in civil rights activities, once even making a trip to Montgomery to meet King while he was still preaching there. He and Jackson were lodged on the same floor of the married students' dorm, and he wound up one of those riding down to Selma with Jackson. Before long, a rapport developed between them so deep that, when the two of them were talking, Wallace could often finish a thought Jackson would begin. "There was almost telepathy between them," remembers Richard Thomas, and Hermene Hartman, who was later briefly married to Wallace, says, "If you talked to David, you were talking to Jesse." Wallace had followed Jackson from Breadbasket into PUSH as his principal operational familiar, where he "became the administrator to Jesse's irregular behavior," says Larry Shaw. "Jesse would start something and then leave it, and David would make sure it stayed intact and moving."

But then, in 1973, Wallace abruptly left PUSH and Jackson. He had become, in the words of Hermene Hartman, "another casualty of Jesse. He just flat burned out." Jackie Jackson explains now with some regret, "Things were changing that made it very difficult for David. In the sixties, we could go everyplace together, but during the seventies, we could no longer do that. Black people needed that time to discover themselves, to become independent, to feel we could do it on our own. That caused a certain separation. It should *not* have, but it was a growing process for all of us." Richard Thomas concurs that "it got to be a very sensitive thing to have whites so close to you. It gave some people the excuse to say he was being controlled by whites. One guy brought in to fix up the organization told Jesse he couldn't give David Wallace special treatment." But, says Thomas, "Jesse went overboard with it. He was very tough on David, started picking on him about little stuff. And David couldn't handle it. Jesse broke him down." But more than anything else, what Wallace found he could no longer suffer in Jackson, he says, was that "phobia" cited by Morris about "anybody on his staff overshadowing him," though, insists Wallace, none of them could have ever imagined themselves "in any competition with him" . . . as Jackson quite likely was haunted by knowing he had always secretly been with King.

When Wallace finally quit, Jackson reportedly gave him a severance check of nine dollars. "He refused to talk to him," says Thomas. "He just couldn't understand why David had left him." Hermene Hartman says, "I think they both feel the loss, but they won't admit it to this day. When they're old men sitting on the porch they might come to that realization finally."

Wallace eventually removed himself to eastern Washington State, a lonesome countryside of pastures and evergreen groves about two hours north of Spokane, where, down a dirt back road wandering through deep stands of pines, he lives now in a somewhat bedraggled dwelling with the woman he married after Hermene, she also black, and their three small sons. Here, he has long been uncertainly subsisting on varied low-wage jobs, some as far away as Spokane. His sons are being educated at a private Christian school a few miles from his place, a tiny schoolhouse set out in a wide valley meadow, and he sat in one of its empty rooms one quiet spring midmorning in 1995—a stubby figure in a plaid shirt and broad suspenders and blue jeans, with close-shorn hair and a beard now gone ashen. After talking for several hours about his years with Jackson, he idly inquired, "Who are Jesse's friends now? Does he have any? I hope he does." As for himself, since his departure from PUSH back in 1973, "the only times I've seen him have been on TV." Asked finally if he felt any lingerings of bitterness about Jackson, Wallace said in a quick, flat voice, "No. No. I don't think about him at all anymore."

Who replaced Wallace as Jackson's most intimate white confidant, and has ruggedly persevered in that grueling position ever since, is a onetime college baseball hopeful and then aspiring Church of God minister from Missouri named Frank Watkins—a balding, pallid, bespectacled man, homey as boiled cabbage and of an astringent unsmiling earnestness, who after auditioning futilely in the late sixties for pastorates in six churches, found his way to Jackson's staff in 1971. Watkins transferred to that service the aseptic burn of his religious idealism, contending, "I consider myself still in the ministry," the only difference being that, through Jackson, "I have opportunities that I would not have dreamt of on my own. I'm in proximity to something that is changing American history and world history." An almost excruciatingly sensitive soul under his thin-lipped, vinegary seriousness, Watkins seems an absolute reverse of Jackson—unobtrusive, dedicated to a drudging diligence in obscure back corners, while tenaciously enduring Jackson's regular beratings over the years. "Why Frank even stays, I don't know," says a former Jackson aide. "It's a bizarre kind of love-hate relationship between them, a strange symbiosis. But Frank is part of his brain now. Jackson doesn't always listen to him, which frustrates the hell out of Frank. But Jackson needs him there to hit him with these opinions all the time. And just to hit. He's been battered, to say the least." Another past adviser describes him as "sort of like a deformed turtle, in that he's had to acquire a set of many and weird shells about the Reverend. But when you get past all of that, Frank has an appreciation of him that is quite profound." In fact, Watkins developed a strategic shrewdness that made him probably Jackson's most astute and creative adviser. And it would be Watkins who would largely author the most spectacular venture of Jackson's career.

FROM HIS PERSONAL realm at PUSH, Jackson wheeled about through the seventies in search of a front of engagement that would deliver him into some defining advent at last. His crusade for economic racial equity continued to produce "covenants," now increasingly national in effect, with corporations like Coca-Cola and Heublein, franchises like Burger King and 7-Eleven. When Coca-Cola seemed hesitant at one point, says a PUSH veteran, "Jesse brings up South Africa, and the whole pressure in the negotiation shifts. This is one of the areas where they're most vulnerable, because they've got big Coke operations in South Africa. But Jesse's got a big stick. Bill Cosby. Bill Cosby is one of the major spokesmen for Coke, of course, and he's told Jesse, 'I'll back you.' " At the mention of Cosby's name, Coca-Cola shortly arrived at an accord.

Jackson relates, "Negotiating with these major corporations like Ford, I told them, 'We got a consumer base, consumer power, and a tilt one or two percent in another direction can appreciably alter a margin of profits. On the other hand, we got trainable people, we got people with money who want dealerships.' Sooner or later, they'd see the light. Ford had only thirty minority dealerships when we began talking. Now they got more than two hundred and fifty." Agreements with General Foods, Avon Products, the Joseph P. Schlitz Brewing Company, Quaker Oats, the Miller Brewing Company promised a transfusion of more than $325 million into the economies of black communities across the country. Characteristic was the compact with General Foods, which committed that conglomerate not only to bringing blacks and other minorities into 360 jobs at all levels but to increasing its deposits in black banks by $500,000, directing an additional $20 million of its insurance business to black companies, increasing its advertising in the black press, and contracting with more black-owned advertising agencies, black law firms and medical-supply businesses, and black construction companies for the renovation of its plants.

At the same time, in the course of extracting these agreements, Jackson also continued to compile from their beneficiaries a growing legion of indebted backers, from whom he not incidentally expected a "tithe" back into the organization that had gained them admittance into the corporate firmament: "Absolutely. It's like a tax. You pay taxes to the government for services, don't you?" When preparing to challenge another corporation, he would apprise gatherings of black businessmen, not to the total delight of all of them, "We're all family here, but you have to pay to play. You cannot ride to freedom free in Pharaoh's chariot." Along with exacting that return, a number of the corporations that Jackson constrained into covenants also agreed "to build us into their budgets," as he phrases it. He wound up, then, from this economic ministry, drawing a double tithe.

Nevertheless, for all the incontestably substantial effects in the black community of PUSH's economic campaign, it still remained an interior, intramural effort, mostly inconspicuous to the wider public eye. Whatever its triumphs, they were finally taking place in a rather enclosed and inherently prosaic theater that would not, it was soon evident, convey Jackson into a more dramatic sort of visibility.

XII
"It's Nation Time"

THROUGHOUT THE YEARS of his economic battles, Jackson had also indulged in occasional political extensions. But at first "he didn't realize how important black politics were," according to PUSH redoubtable Alyce Tregay, who was also a lobbyist for black concerns at the state capital in Springfield. "When I first started trying to organize political education, he said no. His focus was almost exclusively economics." While he was still at Breadbasket, he had assented to the formation of a political division, which even held a convention that was attended, like an early rudimentary sketch of his eventual Rainbow Coalition, not only by blacks but by Hispanics and students' and women's groups, but it came to little more than an offhand exercise. Early in the Nixon years, Jackson had also been called by Senator George McGovern to testify before his Committee on Nutrition and Human Needs, and he had proposed there that the federal troops regularly deployed to subdue riots in the nation's ghettos during the summers should be deployed again in the winter months to distribute food and medical care, to which Senator Robert Dole, starchily suspicious of Jackson from the moment of his appearance in a nimbus of hair and neckchain medallion, had rasped, "I don't think your goals are any loftier than the President's."

But such initial incidental passes at political involvement soon introduced into him a new inspiration, and "he just *took off*," says Alyce Tregay. "He went all over the state for voter registration, would talk in the schools about having a diploma in one hand and a voter-registration card in the other." In Chicago, he mobilized PUSH to assist the campaign of a marginal candidate for the state legislature who had only $2,000 in funds, and she was subsequently elected. Before long, he was ranging out to make personal sallies into other campaigns, like that of Richard Hatcher for mayor of Gary, Indiana; Kenneth Gibson's for mayor of Newark. For the re-election campaign of Mayor Carl Stokes in Cleveland, Jackson dispatched a band from PUSH and some six hundred of its younger members into the city, where, at five in the morning on Election Day, they went dinning through the streets of black neighborhoods to rout out residents to vote before the expected intimidations of police surveillance at the polls later in the day. So telling did Jackson's interventions seem that Stokes would declare, after his reelection, "There is a growing feeling among blacks that if you want to run for high political office, you'd better have Jackson's support. Jesse can draw more people than the candidate himself."

He began making excursions into wholly white political contests as well, to which he applied the same deftness of his economic offensives to that one power available to a minority: he organized blacks to vote for Illinois's Republican senatorial candidate, Charles Percy, in 1972 out of the same computation that had moved him to campaign for Republican gubernatorial candidate, Richard Ogilvie, four years earlier—to claim "a balance of power," as he explained in Ogilvie's case, by demonstrating to him that "he needed blacks to counteract the big Democratic vote from Chicago." The spring following Ogilvie's election Jackson led a pilgrimage of some two thousand people to the state capital in Springfield to appeal for legislation to end hunger in the state and, as he posed it to representatives, "to remove the scourge of poverty and destitution from all its people, both black and white." This mini–Great Society proposal of Jackson's for Illinois was speedily answered by a bill from the Republican Speaker of the House that would instead contract state welfare payments by 30 percent, which Jackson, in testimony at a House session and to a reinforcing uproar from welfare mothers and gang members in berets whom Jackson had loaded into the gallery, fulminated against as a design for genocide. The Speaker thereupon withdrew the bill but it was a retraction, as it turned out, that had actually been arranged by Jackson with Ogilvie the day before. Jackson soon followed with a second mass expedition, called "The Hunger Trek," which moved through fifteen cities across Illinois and ended at the state capital, and the legislature's response, once again with Ogilvie's support, was to add state funds for the first time to federal school-lunch subsidies, which assured free lunches for all Illinois schoolchildren who could not pay on their own.

Jackson's stratagem of playing the political margins necessarily required black voters to cast split ballots, and in 1972, to ensure the defeat of Chicago's Democratic state's attorney Edward Hanrahan, whose police had launched the early-morning assault on the Black Panther sleeping quarters in which Hampton and Clark were killed, Jackson not only registered some forty thousand new black voters, by his claim, but instructed them in the art of split-voting: "Take one of those ole brown paper bags, the kind you carry your lunch in and roll your hair up in, and write the candidates' numbers down that I tell you. Anybody that has ever played policy or the numbers knows how to split a ticket. Don't think Democrat or Republican. Go by your number. When you go to a baseball game, you don't worry about the whole section, you just look at your number and go to your seat and sit down. Don't worry, I repeat, about Democrat and Republican, you ain't neither one, you're black and you're trapped. . . ." Hanrahan was subsequently toppled out of office.

Taking on an increasing gusto for these political assertions, Jackson soon became a chronic provocateur in Mayor Daley's Chicago, promoting a strike by black bus drivers, leading rent strikes, for which he was arrested once, and demonstrations protesting the exclusion of blacks from city construction projects, for which he was also arrested. Chicago reporters began to get the postmidnight and predawn calls for which Jackson would become more widely notorious among journalists in later years. Columnist Bob Greene remembered being awakened "very early one Saturday morning" to hear, when he grappled up the phone, "This is Jesse."

"Jesse who?"

"Jesse Jackson. I think we should talk about the school board."

Jackson's main running counterantagonist in these civic militancies was, of course, Mayor Daley himself, though neither of them was beyond striking an occasional accommodation with the other. When a city agency once denied Jackson a permit for a Black Expo parade in the Loop, Jackson went to Daley's office, taking Robert Lucas along with him. "Daley was a guy known for almost never blinking," says Lucas, "but Jesse had this way of joking, you know, and he told the mayor, 'You see I've got Bob Lucas here with me. If I don't get that permit, he may just lie down on your floor here.' Supposed to be a joke, but Daley didn't think it was a joke." Jackson then presented a more persuasive proposition. As Lucas tells it, some "opportunists" in the black community would stage demonstrations in white neighborhoods and then bring to Daley's office offers to desist in exchange for certain considerations, "that kind of hustling. There was one particular guy at that time, called himself a preacher, who was marching in and out of white communities, and beginning to really bother the mayor. Jesse said to Daley, 'Look, you know this guy marching in the white community? I can stop him anytime I want to.' He ended up getting the permit to have his parade."

But generally an almost instinctive distaste and mistrust prevailed between them, and Daley had taken the precaution of smuggling into Jackson's entourage, as one of his bodyguards, an undercover officer who was instructed "to report every move he made," the agent later disclosed. Jackson himself would regularly call on Daley at his office, "and whether Daley would see him or not," says Richard Thomas, "Jesse would hold a press conference right outside the glass doors to Daley's office. If Daley had met with him, he'd tell what they'd talked about, and if Daley hadn't, he'd say, 'Daley won't see me,' and then tell what he'd wanted to tell him. Unheard of. Nobody'd ever done something like that with Richard Daley." In 1970, Jackson had ventured the somewhat pixilated flourish of actually announcing as an independent contender for Daley's office, a gambit quickly called off when it took on almost immediate aspects of eccentric futility. Jackson later insisted it was all meant to mount a court challenge to a local law that virtually precluded any independent candidacies for mayor by requiring 60,000 signatures on a nominating petition, in contrast to 4,200 for Democrats and 2,034 for Republicans. Jackson's attorneys, in fact, filed a federal suit to revoke that statutory restriction, a suit subsequently rejected.

Unable to prevail against Daley locally, Jackson availed himself of larger ground. At the 1972 Democratic convention in Miami Beach that was to nominate George McGovern, he flurried briefly into national view, in a striped cabana shirt under his Afro, as he orchestrated the dislodgment of Daley's Cook County delegation by a troupe of liberal irregulars—though it had emerged, under a credentials committee's questioning earlier, that Jackson himself not only was serenely unacquainted with the requirements for qualifying as a delegate but had never voted in a Democratic primary in Illinois. Hardly daunted by that little awkwardness, though, he took to rambling about the convention floor offering himself to correspondents for interviews, and before the roll-call vote that would approve seating his insurgent delegation, he addressed the convention—producing a precociously majestic oration that was a portent of the epic one he would deliver twelve years later in San Francisco.

That 1972 convention was an omen of other, later scenarios as well. Through the months preceding it, Jackson reported, "when McGovern needed black support, he called twice from Wisconsin, came to Operation PUSH, and personally encouraged me to speak for him in the primaries." But once McGovern had won the nomination, he evinced a certain fastidiousness about any further association with Jackson, and a far more strenuous solicitude for Daley's mood—going so far, on one visit to Chicago for a series of sessions with Daley, as letting it be known, "I have no plans to meet with Jackson." Mightily miffed, Jackson remarked, "Before Miami, he was all for us. Now he's all for Daley." While Jackson finally consented, after intricate negotiations, to make a campaign trip for McGovern to Los Angeles, relates Gary Hart, who was McGovern's campaign manager then, he nevertheless exacted retribution of a kind by taking along with him about twenty of his retainers and lodging them all in an entire wing of the Beverly Wilshire Hotel, where they ran up a bill of DeMillean scale. "And he did not work hard," says Hart. "Two speeches a day, strictly as per agreement."

But in one sense, what had happened after the 1972 Democratic convention only affirmed an already developing disposition of Jackson's. A year before, during that ebullient season of a cultural rebirth of black America that was something like a nationally magnified recurrence a half century later of the Harlem Renaissance, a convocation called the National Black Political Convention assembled tumultuously in Gary, Indiana, and Jackson—having assumed the flair of those times, caballero vest and plumy sideburns—delivered the keynote address to its some eight thousand delegates and visitors: "Let us build a nation for all black families to enjoy as long as the earth has air and the sky has sun. . . . This world is not destined to die. We can save the children—and holler love across the nation!" But, he declaimed, "we are doomed to remain in the hip pocket of the Democratic party and the rumble seat of the Republican party. I do not trust white Republicans or white Democrats. I want a black party!"

Actually, as early as 1969, Jackson had declared that one consideration in his crusade for an economic vitalization of black America was that "one cannot hope to develop a strong black independent political movement without cultivating the economic resources of black people. Where there are independent black entrepreneurs, there is a possibility that they will support independent black candidates." In his ever more extensive peregrinations about the country, he was even talking about—though he himself was still almost a decade too young to be eligible—a black running for president: "Couldn't mess the world up no worse than these sick white cats." By the spring of 1971, in fact, there had begun flickering through his head visions of organizing a third party, composed of both blacks and white liberals, that "would give people a choice between two evils, the Republican and Democratic parties—that snake with two heads"; prospectively titled by him the Liberation Party, it would field a black presidential candidate in 1972 while also pressing the Democratic party to nominate a black as vice president. Jackson's calculations—much invigorated, ironically, by George Wallace's startling success in his wildcat presidential run in 1968—were again a political transfer of PUSH's economic approach of attacking the sensitive critical margins of an operation's fortunes. "With 450,000 more votes in just three states in 1968," Jackson pointed out, "George Wallace would have thrown the election into the U.S. House of Representatives." By raising that same serious possibility with a third-party campaign activating the potential massive black vote, Jackson reckoned the same effect might be worked for blacks, only in the reverse direction, that Wallace had exercised on the politics of the Nixon presidency, as in its Supreme Court appointments and suppression of busing initiatives. "In 1968, two million blacks did not vote and Nixon won by 500,000 votes. There are more unregistered black voters in Chicago than there are black people in Mississippi. We are going to get those people on the books." The result could be to realize at last a prospect that had been lurking in national politics, actually, ever since Selma had produced the Voting Rights Act: "The new party could siphon off more than ten to twelve percent of the vote in a national election, and would be a phenomenon that both major parties would have to consider." That fall of 1971, Jackson set to roaming out across the country to address the college students, black church-folk, peace activists, and women's rights groups who made up an incipient constituency, beyond Democrats and Republicans and Wallace's own following, that he took to calling "the Fourth Force." And now, in his Saturday-morning liturgies with his congregation in Chicago, he began to call out, "What time is it? . . . It's nation time! . . . *Nation time!* . . . Awright, look *out.* . . ."

IN THESE EARLIEST political excitements, Jackson had not lost his more grandiose moral-heroic aspiration—it only seemed now that a medium might be emerging for it. As he posed the possible combination then, "We want to become a unified national independent political force, the conscience of America," and rather broadly announced, "I have grown into the hearts of thousands of nameless, faceless people." By the end of the seventies, in fact, suggestions to that effect were coming from some unexpected sources, such as Pennsylvania's Republican senator John Heinz III, who once introduced Jackson at an awards ceremony as a "moral leader for our time." Jackson himself began sounding at times well-nigh self-messianic: "The truth I represent is capable of transforming anybody."

But during his brief fancy about running for mayor against Daley, Larry Shaw, for one, had cautioned him, "Damn, you don't want to do that. If you did, you wouldn't be Jesse Jackson anymore. You'd have to be whatever Richard Daley is, because of the pressures of that seat. Else, you'd have to mess up the whole concept of mayorhood." Whatever he found amiss in the political order, Shaw told him that "he had to fix it from the position he was in. You see, he had the ability to curse and to bless. And who is that in the village? Who has that power? Jesse Jackson was the medicine man, the shaman, for the village in which he operated. But never the king. And shouldn't ever *want to be* the king."

Now, corresponding with Jackson's growing tantalizations with the expedient of politics, a black Chicago alderman, talking to Jackson biographer Barbara Reynolds, raised what was a kind of early and not unprophetic warning: while Jackson's movement was now "pushing on a lot of fronts," he observed, "politics just doesn't follow the same rules as civil rights."

In one augury of what was to follow, Jackson's initial sortie into the possibilities of a national political apostleship began to invite such skepticisms in press commentaries as Mike Royko's column in the *Chicago Daily News* in 1971: "One of the most dynamic new figures on the political scene today is the Reverend Jessie Jetstream. At a press conference yesterday, the Reverend Jetstream disclosed his latest plans. 'I wish to announce at this time,' he said, 'that I am in orbit. There is no way I can be stopped.' What are you running for? someone asked. 'I have not decided that yet,' the Reverend Jetstream said leaving the room. He returned in a few minutes . . . wearing a tailored jumpsuit with alligator work shoes. . . . 'Since both political parties have ignored us, I am announcing the formation of a third political party. We can't be stopped.' Who will your candidate be? 'I shall run for President.' And your running mate? 'I shall be my own running mate.' . . . Do you have any further announcements? 'Not at this time. The next press conference will be in minutes. Now excuse me, I must change.' "

Searching for a Focus

JACKSON HAD UP to now pitched into political contests only as an accessory player, not as a principal protagonist. As he lurched on through that somewhat unfocused social limbo of the seventies, "what he really ultimately wanted to be," says a deputy of his at that time, "I never knew, and I don't think even he knew." As if to counter his own private uncertainties about his definition with the sheer force of rushing motion, Jackson's perpetual traveling over the country soon reached more than 200,000 miles a year. One tabulation had him, just in the span of one year: directing a march on Standard Oil of Indiana to protest its scarcity of black filling-station dealers; leading other marches for "economic justice" and one for more day-care programs; mounting symposiums on the black consumer and a conference on tax reform; organizing a "Hank Aaron Day" to inspirit the long-hitting Atlanta player in his pursuit of Babe Ruth's record home-run count; in his own progessive movement closer to the nation's inner courts of authority, conferring with President Ford on the interior depres-

sion in black America; campaigning in Chicago for a black superintendent of schools and a black superintendent of police; holding a PUSH version of a Billy Graham Crusade for Christ; and plotting out a marketing
arrangement with a black farm cooperative in Eppes, Alabama. It looked
to some as if he had passed into a kind of St. Vitus' dance of mission.

At the same time, as others besides Royko noted, he continued to go
through a seemingly endless succession of effulgent transformations of appearance, as if that might somehow lead him to some more distinct persona. He would sometimes preach wearing a black clerical gown over a
flamingo-pink turtleneck, and he once met with Nelson Rockefeller clad in
a bankerly suit-with-vest beneath an Afro wide as a sombrero. Other times,
he would be arrayed in paisleyed silk neckerchiefs over thin-striped polo
shirts and felt vests, broad belts and flared slacks and boots, which gave him
the look, with his wide hatchet-blade sideburns, of some matinee-idol pi-
rate, or even of Elvis in his earlier Vegas days; indeed, in photos from that
time, he strangely had Elvis's low-lidded smoky burn—along with a positively glistening, puma-lean, movie-screen handsomeness.

One editor who was discussing with him the possibility of an autobiography remembers, "He looked great—I mean, he was a gorgeous guy,
and the women in the office, when he walked through, there wasn't a normal pulse among them. And he was very aware of that effect." One of Jackson's Chicago business patrons, George Jones, recollects, "He had to fight
them off. I was sitting next to a lady one day while he was speaking, and
she kept crossing her legs and moving around, saying 'Ahh,' she was so enthused. Women'd walk up to me and say, 'Oh, he just *thrilled* me today!'
and I'd say, 'Just go home and take a shower, you'll be all right.'" Larry
Shaw reports, "Some of the women after him were of a status I still can't
mention. And, of course, he was a young man wanting, had tender spots
and could love. He was still saying 'Yes, ma'am' and 'No, ma'am'; his
mother had done a good job raising him to be gentlemanly young man.
But what happens to a guy like that if these women keep asking him to
come to their bedrooms? How many times can you say I'm not supposed
to do that? So it was like the preacher's daughter, you know, she'll turn out
the most dangerous of them all. Was like if you try marijuana or something." Jones admits, "Thing we were trying to do was keep him from
screwing half of the, you know—we knew and were hearing and seeing
some things he was doing that could destroy him. We'd talk to him about
what could happen, 'This will interfere with where you're trying to go and
what you want to be.' He said, 'I don't go after them,' and I said, 'I know
that, they go after you. But watch out, Jesse. Don't get involved, you know
it's not good for you.'" Already, though, there had begun trailing after him
a wide rippling of rumors about amatory musketeering; when he was stay-

ing in New York, the book editor submits, "there did seem to be an awful lot of young women marching in and out of his hotel room." But it also tended to be a common presumption at that time, long before Al Campanis and Jimmy the Greek would come to grief for blurting their own variations on it, that any arresting young black public figure of Jackson's dash and vitality was, as the editor now recalls the attitude, "no different from the athletes sitting in the dugout at a Dodger game with girls hanging over the edge making dates for later in the evening," the editor citing an observation he heard then from boxing savant Ferdie Pacheco that "he didn't think any black athlete in the world could participate without getting laid three or four times a day." In any case, it became a lore about Jackson, from that time when he was coursing about in the relative freedom of a peripheral prospector, that would also ambush him when he moved into presidential contention.

THROUGHOUT THAT PARENTHETICAL and indeterminate decade of the seventies, it became Jackson's wont to show up at the offices of network news producers and newspaper editors in New York and Washington, with no advance alert, to visit for a few minutes. In these chats, recalls one editor, "he had a talent of asking you a question and actually appearing to listen to your reply, making you feel as though what you had to say had some real importance in the world." *The Washington Post's* Ben Bradlee remembers, "Oh, he was a tremendously engaging figure. And maddening. Just bald about what he was doing and what he wanted. He had a great deal of a sort of apparent self-confidence. At least, his ability to find felicitous phrases to convince himself first and then to convince others was enormous. I was interested in whether he was going to be a real leader, and it seemed to me that he was. But just how he would rise, I had no idea then." Others who he assumed would be far more naturally receptive to him were not always that entranced. Roger Wilkins was an editor at the old *Washington Star* when, he says, "One afternoon I'm on deadline, and all of a sudden they call me up, 'Jesse Jackson is downstairs to see you.' When he walked in, I just went off, told him, 'Man, I am *not* your personal flack. I think you do terrific stuff, but it is not my business to put your name in the newspaper. You do something worthwhile, I'll put your name in the paper, but otherwise, don't come bothering me.' I mean, I went into the Harlem patois of my childhood, you know. And he sat there, and his eyes got real wide. Total shock. That's how innocent he was in going about the thing."

In his calls on network producers, though, he usually managed after a few minutes to banter himself onto broadcasts like *Today, Good Morning America,* and *Face the Nation,* and even wound up appearing on *The Joey*

Bishop Show, The Mike Douglas Show, and *The David Frost Show.* He made himself a virtual regular on Phil Donahue's program just as it was beginning to popularly thrive out of the beaverboard obscurities of Dayton, Ohio. In truth, there persisted through those in-between years a media curiosity about him as a swashbuckling young black activist who still carried some suspense of imposing but yet unculminated promise. It was almost as if he were now becoming a star simply of his possibilities.

The School Evangelism

IN THE MEANTIME, for all of Jackson's multifarious exertions, or perhaps because of them, PUSH found itself, around the mid-seventies, financially staggering. An executive board meeting finally arrived at the conclusion that "we were broke," as one member put it plainly. With less than $6,000 in the bank against debts of over $51,000, Jackson was implored to restrain a bit his ceaseless swinging about the country. As it had happened, almost half of Chicago's black-owned businesses had perished in the recession of 1974, and Black Expo at last expired for good along with them. By 1976, PUSH's debt had swelled to $400,000. What's more, the IRS had begun inquiring into its leisurely accounting procedures.

It was during this dolefully overcast period that Jackson, despite his board's entreaties, began to conduct, in numberless high school gyms and auditoriums across the country, rallies for self-respect and self-reliance among black youths. Over the course of his past traveling, he had noticed in schools he visited that "kids walk around not with books under their arms but with radios up against their heads. Children can't read and write, but they can memorize whole albums." Frank Watkins recalls, "They had built a Martin Luther King, Jr., High School in Chicago, a beautiful high school that the reverend had fought very hard to get built and named after King. He drove by there one morning, and saw these kids not in class, but outside shooting craps. He said, 'This is not what Martin Luther King fought and died for.'" Listening to teachers bewailing the vandalism, drugs, teen pregnancies, and dropout rates pandemic in their schools, he began to sense an emergency of enormous, if still unapprehended, magnitude. And he came to determine—an illumination no doubt also partly prompted by the faltering of PUSH's economic campaign—that what remained of its energies should be shifted heavily toward an educational mission.

Initially funded by a Ford Foundation grant, he began touring inner-city schools, addressing assemblies of students who were not unimpressed by him as a figure who, with his militant mien, also connected back into the legendary era of the civil rights movement. He would first demand that the boys in his audience remove their caps. Then he would take the students through the long struggle of the movement to open up American society for blacks. Finally he would ring out, "What does it matter if the doors of opportunity are now wide open if you still too uneducated to find your way through that door? If you too high or too drunk to stagger through it? What does it matter if we won the right to equal schooling if you've lost the will to learn? There is a challenge *beyond* opportunity. The victim is not responsible for being down, but the victim *is* responsible for getting back up. If you can't read or write or do math well, people will pity you, but they won't hire you. We have to *fight* our way up out of poverty, and excellence is our weapon. We must, by the will of our dignity, be more sober, more serious, more determined than our oppressors. It's the only way we will ever break out. If you challenged to play some white suburban team in basketball, you say, 'Bring 'em on!' To those who underestimate you then, say, 'Bring 'em on!' Just 'cause you were born in the slum doesn't mean the slum was born in you, *you can rise above it. . . .*" By this point, many of the students were applauding with tears in their eyes. "To those who say you can only play ball and can't think, say, 'Bring 'em on!' Let the challenges come. You can rise up to where God made and meant you to be. Up to you now! Education and success are not going to kidnap you, you got to get them for yourselves. Up to you now!" Then he would call out over the assembly of students, "Want you to repeat after me: My mind is a pearl. . . . I can learn anything . . . in the whole world! . . . Nobody will save us . . . for us . . . but us!"

These exhortations rapidly evolved into a formal program that was named PUSH for Excellence, or PUSH-Excel. In appeals at the end of his messages that were like tent-meeting altar calls, students were enlisted to sign pledges to study at least two hours a night, and later their parents were enlisted to pledge that they would see to it that their children studied those two hours, with television and radios shut off, and would meet with their teachers to exchange phone numbers, and then personally pick up report cards and test scores.

But it all struck some at first as a rather quaint revivalism for Puritan fortitudes to be coming from a supposed radical black activist—a proselytizing for discipline, industry, moral rectitude—and that was not disagreeable to many conservative parties. The *National Review* even carried an open letter to Jackson from a white former teacher caroling, "For me, there is something in such a man that is akin to that which informed the priests and nuns I knew as a child. . . . You plainly have the good power, Jesse. But unlike me, you have the black power too. In you there becomes possible a sweeping revitalization of the only thing that can still save the children of our ghettos—*black good power*." Not everyone found such testimonials from such sources endearing, however. Jackson's message, said one of his disaffected deputies, "is to relieve the responsibility for institutional racism and put it exclusively on the individual student and the individual parent," by which he had become "an ally of right-wing white America." Roger Wilkins recalls that "a lot of black people were saying, 'What's wrong with Jackson? What's he doing blaming the victim? Why isn't he blaming white people?' "

But it was, of course, consummately an ethic carried directly out of his own upbringing in Greenville, which had left him with an inveterate churchly traditionalism that accounted for such otherwise unlikely propoundments of his as "When we dropped the Bible and the flag, and picked up the brick and the balled-up fist, we lost tremendous symbolic weaponry." To a PUSH convocation in Memphis on the seventh anniversary of King's death, he had proposed, "Somehow, as we try to make external progress, internally we've lost the ability to say our prayers at night. Somehow, little children speaking back to grown folks is part of our culture. Something is missing. I see too many men walking off leaving our women. We are not filling up our churches like our bars. Something is missing!" Now, Jackson declared, an entire generation was being lost in schools "infested with violence, drugs, intercourse without discourse, alcohol and television addiction."

This school evangelism of Jackson's for the old, simple community and family integrities happened to develop, it has since not gone unremarked, long before the concern about "family values" was being energetically retailed by Dan Quayle and the Christian Coalition. Henry Fairlie would later point out that—just as Jackson had, in his economic endeavor to bring blacks into such "mainstream institutions of white 'middle-American' culture as Coca-Cola and Burger King," proved to be "neither *black* nor *radical*" but "all-American in his tastes, his ambitions"—now in his school crusade Jackson turned out to be "the one who spoke of strengthening the family almost in the accents of Reagan," while Reagan was still years away from his national ascendancy. Roger Wilkins asserts, "Way back there before all these Reagan neo-jerks and newborn black conservatives were going around yelling about self-help, and before young Billy Clinton, too, was ever elected and got smart enough to be running around talking to white people about black people by saying blacks gotta be more responsible, here is Jesse already back then, saying, 'You've got to take care of your kids.' " As Bert Lance observes, "People would sort of snort if you said Jesse Jackson's really a social conservative in the personal sense. But after all, he's a fella who *grew up* understanding the need for family values, for education, families staying together, the work ethic—all things that would fit well into the Republican contract now. But we say, well, he can't really believe that because he's leading this and that protest, he's supporting the gay and lesbian movement, he's dealing with the question of AIDS. Because he's saying, 'Well, if you tear down the welfare system, how are you going to replace it?' people say he simply wants to continue deadbeat fathers and paying mothers to have babies. None of that is he about. It's a total miss."

Jackson further expounded in a Sunday *New York Times Magazine* commentary in 1976 that would remarkably rhyme with certain common promulgations two decades later: "Black Americans must begin to accept a larger share of responsibility for their lives. . . . There is a definite welfare mentality in many black communities that derives perhaps from slavery, but that must now be overcome. . . . We don't need to carry chips on our shoulders, fearing we are being treated in a servile manner. . . . In spite of yesterday's agonies, liberation struggles are built on sweat and pain rather than tears and complaints. . . . Many object to my discussing these things in public. But the decadence in black communities—killings, destruction of our own businesses, violence in the schools—is already in the headlines. . . . God knows that I recognize the need for black self-pride. But that must be built on a solid foundation. . . . In the last ten to twenty years, many of us missed the chance to grow up intellectually and chased Superfly instead. . . . We black Americans can rebuild our communities with moral authority. . . . Parents, teachers, superintendents, school boards have all failed to impose discipline. . . . A few years ago, there was a sizable movement for community control of the public schools. But the community-control movement never did seriously address the problem of control of the students by their parents." Finally, Jackson said, "The church is the most stable influence in the black communities," and "black ministers still carry moral authority with our people, except for a hard-core few. Most people want moral authority."

What Jackson seemed to be attempting, in the end, was nothing less than to dispel a mentality lingering from four hundred years of history, at the point of a new generation's emergence, through a labor of simple edification. As Lance Morrow wrote at the time, "It is idiotic to assume that a race so abused by slavery and discrimination in the American past would not arrive at the present much damaged. . . . A lot of the disaster is in the black mind; but, insists Jackson, that mind can salvage itself."

In any event, simply that effort soon brought Jackson another blaze of national media notice, the widest since the flush of speculations in the late sixties about his prospects for becoming King's successor. Don Hewitt, producer of *60 Minutes*, remembers that "Dan Rather did a story on this guy who was on the fringes of the civil rights movement named Jesse Jackson, who was telling black kids, you know, shape up or ship out, that they had to take responsibility for themselves. That ran on a Sunday night, and Monday morning we got a call from Hubert Humphrey asking, Where do I find this guy? That's the moment when he took off like a rocket." More, that 1976 *60 Minutes* piece about Jackson's school ministry happened to be watched as well by Jimmy Carter's secretary of health, education, and welfare, Joseph Califano. Humphrey, who was then dying of cancer, phoned Jackson the next morning, and then called Califano to enthuse, in his fading voice, "You get him down to your office and help him. Will you do that for me?" A week later, an HEW grant of $45,000 was on its way to PUSH-Excel—the first of a sequence of government subsidies and contracts that, along with foundation aid, would total, in 1978 alone, some $2 million, and $4.5 million eventually, with supplementary funding, as PUSH-Excel expanded to some thirty-five schools in nine cities, from local governments in Los Angeles and the states of Ohio, Louisiana, Missouri, South Carolina, New York, Virginia, and Washington. George Johnson, the black cosmetics tycoon, says, "They got that federal money when they really weren't able to handle it. Have to dot every *i*, cross every *t*, you know, and they weren't ready for that. Problem began when they got that money."

Even so, PUSH had wound up wholly resuscitated. And when some 1,200 of its 75,000 members gathered in Cleveland for its eighth national convention, they were addressed by Califano himself.

THE FINAL EFFECTS of PUSH-Excel, though, never acquired any precise clarity. There were reports of enheartening alterations of behavior, for example: in PUSH-Excel schools in Kansas City, Missouri, absenteeism had declined from a daily average of five hundred students to two hundred, and in Los Angeles, from 35 percent on Fridays to under 12 percent. In most schools, supervisors confirmed an appreciable decrease in instances of fighting, thefts, even graffiti, and in some, an equally appreciable increase in students entering advanced courses in English, math, the sciences. Less apparent, however, were any indications of that improved behavior resulting in enhanced scholastic performance. But then, the returns on this school mission were, by its very nature, finally less tangible than those of Jackson's economic projects—and so more subject to ambuscades of skepticism. "You can't just get academic excellence with electrifying speeches," one teachers' union official protested. To be sure, beyond Jackson's oratory, as a program, PUSH-Excel's staffing seemed pitiably flimsy, with little detectable follow-through: it presented, said one journalist, "the question of whether the 'program' can produce anything of substance without the full-time participation of its super-star. The obvious analogy is a rock concert."

To such deprecations, Jackson angrily rejoined, "I play the role of a catalyst. If I bring inspiration and direction, it is the job of the people who work there to develop the actual programs. We're trying to change *attitudes.*" Or, as he would find himself having to insist more than once over his career, "I'm a tree-shaker, not a jelly-maker." It was part of the essential evangelistic nature of all his endeavors that, he once explained—in what could have been a description of his ultimate Dantean hell—"I would go crazy sitting in one limited spot talking more and more to fewer and fewer people." He had not, he said, noted anyone censuring Billy Graham, for instance, for not staying behind after one of his crusades to also baptize and nurture his converts in place of the local churches.

But a cynicism about the true efficacy of his social ministry would nevertheless pursue him through the years. Journalist Ken Bode remembers that "in 1984, the Mondale people would tell me, 'Oh, Jesse Jackson, he has no follow-through. Hundreds of schools he's been to, talking about drugs and alcohol and "pull yourselves up by your bootstraps" and all that, and then he leaves. Just has no follow-through.' I said, 'But Mondale's never been to *one* of those schools. Right?' I mean, give me a fucking break. Jackson *inspires* people—can anyone argue that? He raises them up in spirit. If the local teachers and principals and superintendents can't then follow through on what he's given them, that's where the loss happens."

Rich Barber, one of the editors at Viking, which finally contracted a Jackson autobiography, admits that the prospect of the book had first occurred because "he was talking the language that a lot of whites wanted to hear. You know, you must take responsibility for your own life, your education is important, you are what you learn. Because everybody was realizing by then that very few black kids out there could work—they didn't have the education for it, didn't have the mentoring and role models, and didn't have anything that was going to give them that. So they were doing drugs, rolling and robbing people, and it was only going to get worse, because there was no hope for those kids. So what Jesse was talking about in PUSH, it may have been what we wanted to hear as white people. But it's also what a lot of those black mothers wanted to hear.

"I'll never forget right after Martin Luther King was assassinated, I was coming up Third Avenue late that afternoon on the bus—and what surprised me were all the black mamas on the bus. It was packed, and all of them still in their various work uniforms. Then I realized: they were all going home to save their kids. Because they knew what was going to be happening up where they lived. They could already see their kids out there on the streets. . . . Those mamas were who Jesse was talking to. They're the ones who have to hold that bloody community together, and they were the ones who finally made him important. He's the pretty boy. But he's the one who's talking to their kids. He's their hope."

Becoming Somebody

IF NOTHING ELSE, while most other civil rights activists had peeled off into more personal and parochial orbits, Jackson succeeded in navigating his own way to emerge, at the end of the seventies, as virtually the sole national voice of the black community. In 1983, an ABC poll of black Americans found that he was cited far more than any other figure as their most important leader, by a margin of 43 percent over the second-place Andrew Young. "Most of those names that the press and pollsters had been projecting as the national black leaders didn't even get double-digits," Jackson still relates with satisfaction. "Something was going on with the people that the pundits were more disconnected from than they ever thought they were"—a kind of authoritative analytical astigmatism that, Jackson adds, was to become a curious pattern through the following years.

His popular credibility had reached a point where he was being called on to intercede in labor disputes—a teachers' strike in St. Louis, a firemen's strike in Chicago. In the Chicago strike, he managed to reconcile the contending parties, who'd been at an impasse for a month, after only two days of discussion, applying a canniness acquired over more than a decade of negotiating with corporate powers. Even so, he would not cease to fume that "the next day in the *Tribune* and *Sun-Times*, headline 'Fire Strike Settled,' my name was only mentioned way down in one of the stories, and the other paper didn't mention my name at all. There was no room in their minds for me being a negotiator of a strike of that magnitude—just wasn't in their frame of reference. They would *not* let me out of their journalistic ghetto."

But however much he might still have been disregarded by the media mediators of standard reality, he had at least taken on enough prominence as a black figure to be meeting repeatedly on Capitol Hill with senators like Robert Dole, Edward Kennedy, and Howard Baker, from which he had arrived at the deduction that, as he could not abstain from advertising, "not many politicians can compete with me in the public marketplace. Kennedy has *mystique*, but he doesn't have charisma. You can't earn it, you can't learn it, but if you got it, it can't be taken away, except by God. It's a gift of grace." Then, in 1979, he was among the national eminences — a company that included Common Cause president John Gardner, AFL–CIO president Lane Kirkland, special presidential envoy Sol Linowitz, and the abiding gray grandee of Democratic politics, Clark Clifford — invited to Camp David by President Carter for deliberations on the state of the nation's spirit, from which issued Carter's "malaise" television sermonette, Carter directly quoting from Jackson at one point, "Freedom does not come from the big house or the White House, it comes from your house and my house." Actually, says Jackson, as early as 1977 "Carter was already quoting stuff from me in his speeches."

In the meantime, as he steadily increased in stature and noticeability within the country, he began setting out for excursions abroad. Several years after an initial trip to Liberia in 1972, he was admitted into South Africa, after Secretary of State Cyrus Vance intervened against the buffalo-browed resistance of South African authorities, and while there, he led dustily weltering throngs in Soweto in his familiar incantation, "I may be poor . . . but I'm black and I'm proud. . . . I *am* somebody!"

But far more provocative was his expedition to the Middle East near the end of the decade, which was to hold the delayed flammability of a political time bomb. A sympathy for the Palestinians had long been gathering in America's black community, and trooping through a Palestinian resettlement compound in the West Bank, Jackson declared, "I know this camp. When I smell the stench of open sewers, this is nothing new to me. This is where I grew up." Israeli prime minister Menachem Begin's government, already suspicious of Jackson's sentiments, had refused to see him, but in Nablus, Palestinian youths carried him on their shoulders, shouting, "Jackson! Arafat!" When he then journeyed on to Beirut, there came his casual but, it would turn out, calamitously ill-fated hug of greeting of Yasser Arafat himself. Jackson assistant Bernard Lafayette had cautioned him right before he left, "Jesse, whatever you do, don't get caught hugging Arafat like they do over there. They hug and kiss everybody. But if a picture like that comes out, it'll be exploited and, hey, in terms of mediating and peacemaking, you can forget it. So when you see him coming at you, you're tall and you got a long reach but he's short, so just reach out your long arm and shake his hand." Lafayette recounts, "Well, he agreed to that. But it happened anyway. When he got back, I reprimanded him, 'Exactly what I told you not to do!' He said, 'Well, it couldn't be helped. He just ran right on up to me.'"

But Jackson little suspected what consequences would ensue from that photographed embrace, as his trip now began to escalate into the woozy possibility that he might serendipitously wind up pulling off a diplomatic marvel after the style of Kissinger's shuttle-mediations: he was invited to Cairo for a session with Anwar Sadat, after which Sadat flew him on a presidential jet back to Beirut with an appeal to Arafat to declare a suspension of violent operations against Israel in hopes of inducing Israeli recognition of the PLO, a proposal Jackson then carried on to Damascus to present to Syrian president Hafez al-Assad. For the usual, totally predictable, arabesquely involuted reasons, this enterprise of Jackson's quickly failed. But it served to prime what would be a far more propitious visit of his to Damascus five years later, during his first presidential campaign—in fact, out of this 1979 jaunt to the Middle East would come both the highest and lowest moments of that campaign. In any event, the whole experience left Jackson so elated that he proclaimed, in another instance of what some were now considering an ambition amplifying toward megalomania, "The stone the builders reject can become the cornerstone of great progress. Jesus, Martin Luther King—all stones the builders first rejected. A rejected stone like me could very well become the cornerstone of our global policy."

"It's Time to Move On"

IN RETROSPECT, IT can appear that what Jackson was actually up to through the seventies—in leaving SCLC to create his own personal domain with PUSH, in the base of patronage he steadily built from negotiating corporate "covenants," in his campaigning for black candidates, his expanding political engagements, his endless circuiting about the country to exhort school convocations and other gatherings that were like embryonic forms of his later Rainbow Coalition, in his avid cultivation of the media estate—was a systematic assembling of an eventual national movement of his own. Yet it seemed more a fitful and indefinite lunging about to find his destiny's still-evasive moment of truth during a decade that was itself like some vague and fretful hiatus in history.

Then, with the installation of the Reagan order in Washington, PUSH's improved finances abruptly hit a huge cold front. Almost all the funding support provided during the Carter years was summarily cut off, with a federal audit of PUSH's rather nonchalant bookkeeping even demanding a $56,411 repayment. At the same time, the administration released a report by the American Institutes for Research, commissioned by the Department of Education to assess PUSH-Excel's program, that roundly dismissed its efforts to redeem inner-city schools as by and large meaningless. The author of that analysis happened to be the social theoretician Charles Murray, who was later to propound, in his 1994 book *The Bell Curve*, the genetic inferiority of blacks' learning capacity. The attitude about leaving PUSH-Excel suddenly destitute of funds among the Reagan administration was, as one of its congressional retainers expressed it, "nobody is weeping for poor Jesse." PUSH seemed once again heading into critically, if not terminally, perilous times and, even if he could survive PUSH's collapse, taking Jackson back to a marginal relevance at best.

PUSH nevertheless continued to flex itself politically. In the 1982 Illinois governor's race, it launched a voter-registration drive that nearly supplied Adlai Stevenson III enough votes to overthrow the Republican incumbent, James Thompson. And the next year, though the party machine left behind after Mayor Daley's death in 1977 had kept a hard-knuckled hold on the city's politics, PUSH provided what may have been the decisive organizational brawn in the election of Chicago's first black mayor, Harold Washington. Ironically, Washington's election was to work an effect that Daley had always found beyond his own wiles: to leave Jackson with a sense of displacement in the city that he had made his operational home for almost twenty years. At the victory party for Washington the night he took the Democratic primary, a euphoric Jackson snatched the podium microphone before Washington had come down from his hotel suite and bawlingly led the crowd in the refrain "We want it all! We want it *all!* . . ." until alarmed Washington aides, mindful of the general election still ahead, eased him aside. It was a cry, actually, going back through the history of the movement to at least Selma, when marchers would raise the mass chant, *"Freedom! When do we want it? Now! How much do we want? All of it!"* But it incensed many around Washington, not only for what seemed its reckless risk of alienating the city's white majority, but, says former PUSH operative Robert Starks, who was there that night, "it looked like Jesse's up there trying to take away from Harold when this is Harold's night." When Washington at last appeared onstage, "it was pandemonium," says Starks, "and Jesse, of course, had to move a little back. But he stays within camera shot, you know. And people became angered at that, too." In time, though Washington was facing a fairly innocuous opponent in the general election, "some of his people just plain came up and told Jesse, 'An association with you will make Harold's campaign suffer,'" according to Starks. And all this "left Jesse very hurt. Because a lot of those same people who were telling Washington, 'Get Jesse out of the way,' Jesse had helped and put himself on the line for in the past. But you began hearing them say, 'This town ain't big enough for these two guys. Jesse has got to get out of town.'"

Thus, PUSH's lapse back into financial extremis had corresponded with Jackson's growing sense of dislodgment in Chicago. Another foreboding of that marginality was offered on the night of the general election, when Jackson, as was his custom, simply ambled into the studio of the ABC bureau in Chicago, where a scheduled *Nightline* discussion with Washington about his victory was being prepared, with columnist Bob Greene already seated before the camera as a possible substitute should Washington not show up. When, sure enough, Washington still had not appeared only a few moments to air, the producer quickly notified the control room in New York that Jackson happened to be in the studio, and after only a moment, New York sent back the word, "Keep Greene in the chair."

It was at some point during this time, says Starks, "that Jesse made his decision that he was going to have to shift to some other level"—and with the same apparent, resigned, detached, brisk resolve, whatever his interior pain at being smacked back once again by fortune, that was recalled by one of his boyhood friends in Greenville: "Whatever came along, he'd learned to take it in stride. It was just, this is what I got to do next." Now, says Starks, one day not long after Washington's election, Jackson quietly announced to him, "Doctor, it's time to move on."

WHEN CARTER HAD found himself confronting Ronald Reagan in the 1980 presidential competition, "it was me," Jackson would later state, "that he turned to for carrying the banner to the black community." In that service, Jackson had lustily forged through seventy-two cities in twenty-nine states, and despite Carter's defeat, Jackson's performance proved so effective that, for the 1982 round of congressional races, at the party's behest, he again swung about the country in a voter-registration campaign, and again left behind him wherever he passed a conspicuous increase in the black electorate—a premonitory intimation of what was shortly to follow.

Over the course of all his political foragings through the years, certain large recognitions had unfolded themselves to Jackson. First of all, it seemed clear to him that, even with his widening notability since being discarded by McGovern after the 1972 Democratic convention, he would still remain consigned to the outskirts of any true national pertinence by the nation's power estate. During the Carter years, reports one of Jackson's ministerial advisers who was also a member of the Democratic National Committee, the DNC held a convention in Chicago, "and they really didn't want Jesse to speak. But they couldn't deny him that—so they put him on at the very end of the program, feeling most people would leave before Jesse got there. There was a group of us waiting around outside the meeting room, with a lot of cameras everywhere but nobody shooting the cameras, even though there're all these big shots in the party standing around there talking. All of a sudden the elevator door opens, there's Jesse, and the cameras go *wild*. Some of the party people said, 'See that? All he wants is to get his face on the camera.' I said, 'Well, we've been standing here for two hours, and we have to go ask these TV crews, "Is there anything you'd like us to say?" Then he just steps off the elevator and the cameras go crazy. Is that his fault?' But Jesse was already very discouraged, and then they made him wait and wait and wait in this other room before they brought him on. Finally they called him in to speak at the very end, and you know how biting he can be sometimes . . . he didn't even take up all his time, said, 'I still have one minute left, but I'm through.' "

The reason he would always be kept waiting in an anteroom to the nation's inner chambers of political commerce, Jackson was equally convinced, was simply because he was black. "Always client status, never peer status" is how he recalls his growing resentment then. "The party's blacks were like its Harlem Globetrotters—gave it soul and dynamism, gave it its margins of victory, but never allowed to set policy." Or, in another, slightly humid analogy he offered once, "Like the party's concubines: they make their use of us, then go back to their own family." It was hardly lost on Jackson that, since 1944, the Democratic party had won the presidency only once—Lyndon Johnson's election—with a majority of the white vote. Yet, as he was to protest out of the same glower of aggrievement a few years later when Michael Dukakis rejected him as his vice presidential choice, "Too much to expect that I will go out in the field and be the champion vote picker and bale up those votes and bring 'em back to the big house and get the proper reward. Instead, people who do not pick nearly as many voters and don't carry anything like the same amount of weight among the people, they sit in the big house and make the decisions."

But ever since his boyhood in Greenville, throughout his long progress as an outsider, Jackson had developed a fine sense for detecting crucial gaps in the ruling order of things. And he had come to determine that it is in those openings—between the assumed and the actual, between the structured and the alive, "between the institution and the idea"—that unclaimed power awaits. "Real leadership fills those gaps between what's policy and what's possible, those tremendous gaps of the unknown," he says. "It's in those gaps where the truly significant action occurs. But most elected officials tend to codify, to operate on the line, not in the gaps. People cease to expect them to come home and connect, to have a mass meeting or press conference to address things like: why aren't enough houses being built, how come we don't have an adequate system of health care, why we have drugs goin' up and down the street all the time—those *gaps*.

But that's where a whole lot of dodgin' starts goin' on. Ain't nobody gonna bear the cross. So when somebody steps into the gap and addresses it, he's gonna find favor with the people. 'Cause the people *live* in that gap."

Jackson's own existential alertness for discovering and moving into those margins—and as an outsider, he has in a sense, made his name there—has been the instinct behind what many have taken to be his congenital opportunism. That perception is not slightly owing to the fact, argues an old seminary friend of Jackson's, the Reverend Henry Hardy, that "it's very difficult for this country to accord African-American leadership a full, unqualified respect. You're supposed to belong to certain designated areas, and if you have a larger vision, you're moving out of your bailiwick. But Jesse always said you've got to think quick and run fast. There are certain moments—the Greeks had a word, *kairos*—propitious moments in history that reach out for you to grab. And you must respond, must *seize* that moment. It is in itself an opportunistic situation—and it demands opportunism."

By 1983, he had discerned what he considered a chasm between the nation's prevailing political order and its population of the neglected, the voiceless, the alienated. "Included in that gap, I found, was a real separation between the liberals and the true liberators," he says. "For instance, Harold Washington's campaign for mayor in Chicago, we were gearing up for that victory when we got word that Mondale and Ted Kennedy were coming in to support the opposition in the primary. Mean, here were guys whose careers had been built in large part on the shoulders of black people's struggle for political liberation. About fifty black leaders got together, and we sent a telegram to both Mondale and Kennedy, 'Please don't come in here and interrupt this campaign we got going.' But they came anyway. *They came.*" In fact, to Jackson it soon looked like a collaborative rapport between both liberal and conservative figures in government: "One wants no change, other wants only slow change if got to be any atall. Differ only about degree, not direction. They stay in that circle together for so long, they become completely acclimated just to each other. Their policy interests come together, their tolerances come together. They say"—and his voice dips into a basso profundo, cornmeal-toned imitation—"'Oh, we know why ole Virge is takin' that position. That's just ole Virge.' Pretend to be arguin' and votin' against each other's positions, but never about people's vital life options. They can even sustain socializing together without strain. Have a cloture vote and then all make a mad dash for the golf course together, hurry off to dinner that evening, rush to the airport for another foreign trip together."

Meanwhile, Jackson had also ascertained that "the people feeling locked out of this arrangement were really across all races. I'd been going to conventions and political conferences where blacks and Hispanics and Indians and poor whites'd be protesting, and every year the demonstrators *outside* of the hall would be greater than the number of delegates *inside* of it. Began to have more and more out, fewer and fewer in. Big gap there. And you a leader, you step *into* those gaps. The whole movement was built on operating in those gaps. So I said, 'What we're talking about here is not just blacks, but a . . . a . . . *rainbow coalition.* And all these who feel locked out must become part of that coalition of converging needs.' "

Finally, a certain personal gap between himself and those leaders in "that political in-crowd who always play by their in-crowd rules," as he styled them, had not failed to enter into his contemplations, either. Roger Wilkins asserts, "Of course Jesse has a great sense of self, for which people have crucified him. 'Cause he's been an uppity nigger who doesn't know his place. But he knows his place all right. He looked at all these mediocre white boys running around in Washington with puffed-up titles. And he knows pretty soon that he's smarter than they are. That he's done more than they ever could do a fraction of. Hell, he's going to be in the history books when these suckers are forgotten even by their grandchildren."

The Siren's Song: "Run, Jesse, Run!"

ONE AFTERNOON BACK in 1979, Frank Watkins had fallen into a progressively exhilarated discussion with Jackson assistant Bernard Lafayette about the possibility of Jackson undertaking a run for the presidency. "At first, I didn't know what he was talking about," says Lafayette. "President of what? It didn't click that he was talking about president of *the United States.*" Late that night, which happened to be Halloween, the two of them rushed to Jackson's home to present the notion to him. On the way there, Lafayette enthused, "*Right,* this is the only way he'll ever have enough staff to do everything he thinks of." They found him dozing in his pajamas in his upstairs bedroom, and when they woke him with the proposition, he snorted drowsily. "You guys been out trick-or-treatin' too long. You seen a ghost or something." And pitched himself backward and pulled the covers up over his head, though not unlike a gleeful little boy in doing it.

To be sure, about all past black presidential candidacies had amounted to, as Richard Hatcher says, "was that every four years a Ron Dellums or somebody would announce for president maybe half an hour before the convention opened, knowing that would assure them at least thirty seconds on national television when they would withdraw. Shirley Chisholm made a little more serious run in 1972, but still with no hope whatever of even getting close to the nomination." A Jackson candidacy would have seemed only more astrally implausible, since the presidency of the United States would be the first public office he had ever run for. But shortly after that Halloween-night proposal to Jackson, Watkins phoned Hatcher in nearby Gary, Hatcher relates, "and said he wanted to come over and talk to me. When he got there, he said, 'Look, don't fall off your chair or anything, just hear me out: what about the idea of Jesse running for president?' He was so intense about it, you know, was answering all the obvious questions before I could ask them. Said, 'We'll get the money from the churches. They'll raise the money, and here are the states we've really got a good shot at—' He just went on through the whole thing, it was amazing."

"This was an obsession with Frank," says Lafayette. In fact, in 1979 he had trid to persuade Jackson to run against Carter, "but he wouldn't do it," says Watkins. "He loved Carter. And he didn't want to be responsible for maybe taking him down." Then, in the summer of 1982, in the basement of the PUSH offices, Watkins tapped out on a word processor a ten-page memo assaying a possible Jackson presidential campaign; if Watkins had come to live more largely through Jackson, this would be the most breathtaking enlargement of all, and he now became something like the Merlin of strategy for that possibility. His memo, not incomparable in canniness to the one supplied by Hamilton Jordan to Jimmy Carter while he was still governor of Georgia—both memos largely inspired by the Wallace precedent—posited, in part: "[Jackson] should not run as a 'realistic' candidate with a chance to win" but "must do to the left what George Wallace and Ronald Reagan did to the right, that is, build a potential constituency that must be taken into account," and the way to do that was "to solidify primarily a black political base."

The arithmetic, at least, was powerfully inviting. Since the 1965 Voting Rights Act accomplished by King's Selma campaign, the number of black registered voters had swelled from 6 to 10 million, and they had come to commonly account for one fifth to one fourth of the total Democratic vote in national elections. But some 7 million blacks remained unregistered—and an increase in the next election of only 25 percent in the black vote in eight states that Reagan had won in 1980 would, if his percentage of the white vote held the same, cost him those states—New York and Massachusetts among them—which could well decide the matter. In the South alone, there still remained some 3 million blacks unregistered—in eight of its states, those unregistered numbering more than Reagan's entire margin of victory in 1980.

Yet it seemed to Jackson that "when I looked around, neither the liberals in that political in-crowd nor the party wanted to invest in registering black voters in any really massive numbers, because those voters who would affect conservatives would also affect that liberal-conservative relationship in their little closed society. What I mean, good liberal was not about to commit $100,000 to help register 200,000 more black voters in Georgia to defeat his conservative colleague—'He's a conservative, but he's my friend, and we got to work together.' Hell, could even affect the security of his *own* office, throwing in a big unknown like 200,000 new black voters. So," Jackson says, "I determined I had to lead a major registration drive myself."

In the summer of 1983, he set out on a six-state campaign of political pentecostalism through the South—popular rallies, sometimes forty a week, mostly conducted, like the movement rallies over that region in the sixties, in black churches. Jackson recounts, "I had to do it by just trottin' on out there with no money, had to raise the money from church to church as we went. Go to this town, they'd house and feed us, we'd take up the money in church and next day go to the next place, the next church. Did that for like ten weeks." Additionally sustaining this voter-registration tour, though, was that it happened to coincide with a near-monolithic animus toward the Reagan presidency within the black community. That feeling was owing not simply to the circumstances that, during Reagan's four years in office, the poverty ratio among blacks had risen from 32.5 percent to 35.6 percent—meaning 1.3 million more people in want—and black unemployment had risen from 12.4 percent to 16.2 percent, with even a two-parent family with one parent working having lost $2,000 in annual income. More, there was among southern blacks a deeper, almost visceral antipathy to what they sensed as a dry, heartless indifference in Reagan himself—"no understanding in him," commented one black Mississippi legislator at the time, "no love in the man for any others than his own"—that somehow evoked for them the parched and autocratic piety of the white country-club Bourbons that they had so long had to bear through the segregationist age. Reagan then made the perfect adversarial counterfigure for Jackson's political pulpiteering: "Mr. Reagan keeps asking us all to pray. Well, I believe in prayer; I have come this far by the power of prayer. But then, Mr. Reagan cuts energy assistance to the poor, cuts job training, cuts breakfast and lunch programs for children—and then says to an empty table, 'Let us pray.' Apparently Mr. Reagan is not familiar with the structure of prayer. You thank the Lord for the food you are about to *receive*, not the food that has just *left*. I think we should pray, but not pray for the food that's left. Pray for the man that took the food . . . to leave." An assistant Jackson had brought along with him from PUSH remembers that, at one outdoor rally in Virginia, "he had ten thousand people out there in this field with no loudspeakers. But his voice carries, you know? *It carries*. And hardly a one of 'em left that rally in that field not registered to vote."

As he heaved on across the South—speaking on swampish summer nights in plain brick churches tucked away on dirt back lanes of obscure little inland cities, in solitary pine-plank tabernacles glowing like shuttered lanterns in the moonlit cricket-chittering countrysides of Alabama and Mississippi with all the windows open and cardboard fans fluttering before the packed, dark, polished faces—he would hoarsely peal away, "Our time has come! From the slave ship to the championship, from charity to parity, from the outhouse to the courthouse to the statehouse to the White House—from disgrace to amazing grace—our time has come! In 1980, Reagan won by the margin of our nonparticipation. Won eight southern states by 182,000 votes, while three million blacks there were unregistered. All those rocks, little David, just layin' around. There's a freedom train a-comin'. Only you got to register to ride. Hands that once picked cotton can now pick presidents. Our time has come!" It was, in all, a kind of strenuously elicitive pump priming, and before long, there would begin arising from the congregation a cry, a roaring chant that moved on from rally to rally, *Run, Jesse, run. Run, Jesse, run.* . . .

And in this odyssey of political camp meetings, Jackson began to create, virtually single-handedly, a new mass of voters of his own, beginning with southern blacks but ultimately to encompass other of the system's castoffs, outsiders like himself—"My constituency," he declared, "is the desperate, the damned, the disinherited, the disrespected, and the despised"—that would provide him an opening at last into that otherwise hopelessly closed system of the nation's highest game of power: it would be "a slanting arrival through a side door," Garry Wills wrote, instead of "the long flight of steps one had to climb toward the front door." Almost all in that constituency, Bert Lance reflects, "were looking for a voice to express their situation of exclusion, and to be connected to the main life of this country, not divorced from it—just like Jesse himself always wanted." It was a moment now when they might give that to each other. Though Jackson was to refrain from finally deciding on his candidacy for another six months, exhaustively deliberating on it through all that time, he now more than suggestively proclaimed, for its inductive effects, "There's a fire burning! A black candidacy is an unfolding epic!" Says one of Jackson's eventual campaign advisers, Robert Borosage, "Jackson was operating by his own intuition, and he intuitively understood this vacuum in terms of where the Democratic party candidates were. At the same time, that was combined with the fact that blacks were unregistered in huge numbers, and it was already clear to him that all statistics from voter-registration drives showed one thing: that blacks, or anybody, will register to vote when there's some-body running who excites them. Or who might run if they register. And it worked. It got registered vast numbers of people—got much bigger than anybody had foreseen. He created a new reality. And he was smart enough to move into that reality."

To the Democratic party's management, recalled John White, the Democratic national chairman during the Carter years, "he still seemed a young firebrand with expectations way beyond what was doable." But not a few of them had found unsettling a poll, conducted that summer for po-litical consultant David Garth and confirming an earlier indication in a *Los Angeles Times* poll, that disclosed Jackson already would run third in a primary campaign, behind Walter Mondale and Gary Hart, but ahead of John Glenn and all other likely contenders. Other polls found that a Jack-son candidacy would draw, just to start with, about 5 percent from Mon-dale's vote in the primaries. Mondale, who was the more traditional liberal among the serious competitors for the nomination, "started talking about how even the idea of a black running for president was significantly going to hurt his prospects," relates Richard Hatcher. "Which was kind of a weird notion, that we had an obligation not to run because it might hurt him." But before long, Jackson's voter-registration campaign through the South had assumed such import that Mondale entreated the Democratic National Committee to mount one of its own, addressed to blacks, His-panics, women, the young, and the elderly, for which he pledged to raise $1 million himself. At the same time, Mondale aides began meeting with Jackson, ostensibly to entertain his suggestions about what should be the Democrats' agenda in the 1984 race against Reagan—as did, shortly, Gary Hart and John Glenn. Jackson at least assured the party's stewards that, contrary to his preachments in the seventies, he would not be taking his building multitude of voters outside the party into an independent candi-dacy; while that might have seemed his most natural course given his past, he recognized it would virtually ensure Reagan's reelection. Besides, ani-mating his effort was the thrilling prospect of at last coming in out of the cold—with one great stroke and on the largest scale—as a Democratic presidential candidate.

As it happened, also taking place during Jackson's voter-registration ral-lies across the South that summer was a series of private conferences of the nation's black leadership—elected officials, civil rights figures, academics, business magnates, collectively referred to as "the Family"—a floating core group of around fourteen with usually up to twenty or so local leaders who gathered in airport hotel suites in a succession of cities to try to con-struct some comprehensive design for coping with that new, grimmer time of Reagan. Hatcher, who was at almost all of those sessions, calls them a continuum of "that history going back to at least 1857 of African-Americans having conferences and conventions in which there's been a kind of two-track theme—one that actually probably started from the day the first two slaves were brought to this country—and that is: what's our best strategy, integration or separate empowerment?" In this instance, that old question had come to pertain to politics. The conclusion had been forming for some while, says Hatcher, that the classic kinds of protest of King's day, "civil rights marching and demonstrating . . . weren't going to get it done any longer. With the kind of problems the black community was facing now, we had to become more active politically, running for office, getting elected, becoming a part of government." Initially, though, "the meetings were meant to go about what blacks had always done historically, which was develop the set of issues for the next election and then sort of pick out the candidate to support on the basis of, Will he support these issues?" But the discussions rapidly evolved from that essentially integrationist matter of which white candidate to support to the separate-empowerment consideration of an actual black presidential candidacy. "The real question all along in that," says Hatcher, "was *who*, to be honest." And at that point, with the atmosphere that Jackson had concurrently produced for these deliberations with his rousing voter-registration crusade through the South, a pronounced division set in over Jackson himself. Joseph Lowery, who was now president of SCLC, would grump afterward, "The process was stampeded by Jesse's campaign."

The furor thus provoked traveled from meeting to meeting. Advocates for his making the run included Hatcher, Washington mayor Marion Barry, and New York political dons Percy Sutton and Basil Patterson. "Those who were resisting it," says Hatcher, "were in fact the majority," among them Detroit mayor Coleman Young, Birmingham mayor Richard Arrington, Los Angeles mayor Tom Bradley, the NAACP's Benjamin Hooks. "The older, more established national leaders had this thing of, 'Look, we're practical politicians, we don't run around on theories. And you guys are gonna find yourselves out in the cold. The black community is going to be out in the cold.' " But beyond that general uneasiness, Jackson particularly vexed them: "Here's this young, untutored person," as Hatcher explains their consternation, "who's walking around talking about 'Up with hope and down with dope,' you know. The very idea of Jesse not seeming intimidated about running for president, that just struck some people as, Who does he think he is? Oh, gosh, he was perceived as arrogant. How could he even think about being a presidential candidate, he hadn't even been elected dogcatcher—it was going to be a joke."

But Andrew Young also termed a Jackson candidacy "extremely dangerous," contending it would divert support from the likely Democratic nominee, Mondale, to the benefit of Reagan. When journalist Ken Bode asked Young during this period why, after he had campaigned so heartily among blacks for Carter in 1972, he should now be squeamish about an outright black candidate like Jackson, Young insisted, "We can't afford to play black games this year." Coretta King was, if anything, even more sternly opposed, remembers Hatcher, "a lot of it going back to when Dr. King was killed and Jesse's actions then, and still some resentment about his leaving Breadbasket and setting up his own organization. A lot of criticism of Jesse came from those sources in Atlanta."

Along with all the other protests, there were, not negligibly, the same misgivings of those student militants in Greensboro years before as they had deliberated bringing Jackson into the demonstrations there, several now in these black summit conclaves warning, "Jesse's gonna go off and do his own thing. He's not gonna sit down and talk to advisers like us." At one preliminary meeting of local leaders in Chicago, according to one of Jackson's clerical supporters, "you started hearing insinuations from some that, if we decide on this, guess who's going to run it all. Some of them didn't even want him at that meeting, because they were sure he'd take it over. Because when he walks into a room, you know, he owns it. But lo and behold, he showed up at the meeting, and there was a different air immediately. He said after a while, 'We've got to think in terms of, whoever wants to run, they've got to be able to do several things. They've got to be able to command the media, they've got to be able to raise money, they've got to be able to call the people forward—' And as he went on down the line, you looked around that room and there was no one else who could meet all these criteria Jesse was listing, except Jesse." Publisher John Johnson notes that "he has a way of moving in and taking over so smoothly that even the people that he's taking over from are not completely aware of what he's doing."

Still, all through those debates among the Family about a black presidential candidate, Jackson himself was not as yet altogether certain that he should be that figure. In his hesitation to give himself over finally to that gathering dynamic which he had so vigorously cultivated—as if by this point he were most at home dwelling simply in possibility, uneasy about being captured in any actual consummation of that possibility—he even began urging others to make the run, among them Atlanta mayor Maynard Jackson, even Andrew Young. "I mean, he asked *me* to run," says Hatcher. "But it was something, interestingly enough, that people were not knocking each other down wanting to do. They saw it as placing themselves at great risk, financially, politically with the party, lot of reservations."

Jackson himself was at the Family's last meeting—"the last," says Hatcher, "because as a consequence of the decision that was made there, some were not speaking to each other afterward"—which was held in Chicago, in a conference room at the O'Hare Airport Hilton. Hatcher recounts, "The debate had just gone on and on, and it was obvious that people were dancing around a decision. The majority were still against Jesse," but he had with his southern sweep of rallies placed them "in a position where it was very hard for them to simply say no. So I said, 'Look, why don't we just go around the table and ask each one of us, Do you want to be a candidate for president, so we can get past all this ducking and dodging.' And as we went around the table, every person said, 'No, I don't want to,' or 'I'm not sure this is the time.' " Before this sounding had begun, Jackson had moved to stand a short space back from the table, looming over the proceeding, as it were, while "it went around to everybody else who was seated there at the table before it got to him. So his was the last turn, and when it came to him, it was clear that nobody else was prepared to say they'd make the effort. And he said then, 'Well, if nobody else wants to run . . . I'm willing.' "

A compromise resolution finally issued from the meeting, agonizingly euphemistic in formulation, which only endorsed a black candidacy while remaining noncommittal on Jackson. "I remember how carefully it was worded," says Hatcher. "Anyone who chooses to become a candidate for president should feel free to do so, and anyone in that meeting who chooses to support that person is free to do so." But at the least, "it was sort of like giving permission, you know? It was clear that most of the people in that meeting were not going to help him, did not think it was a great idea. But we thought an implicit part of the resolution was, even if you don't agree with it, you're not going to publicly criticize the decision. Big mistake. *Big* mistake. Over the following months, every time things seemed to get going, here would come a statement from Atlanta, from Andy or Joe Lowery or Mrs. King, 'We don't think this is a good idea at all.' "

When the meeting had finished, Jackson turned immediately to Hatcher and three or four others and briskly said, "C'mon, I want to talk." This small cluster, Hatcher remembers, followed Jackson down the hotel corridor to his room, and sprawling wearily in chairs and on the bed and on the floor, "we started talking right away about how we were going to organize this thing."

"Duality Without Contradiction"

BUT FOR JACKSON, all of these developments combined into what was still only an awesome possibility. The truth is, he was proceeding in that provisional fashion by which he had negotiated his course through most of his life, all the way to what would be his elaborate computations in 1995 on whether to make at last an independent presidential run. It was a pattern of operating that his former adviser Mark Steitz describes as "duality without contradiction"—a polyality, really, of simultaneous purposes, a kind of "massive parallel processing," in Steitz's words, in which "he has an ability to engage in not only seventy-five thoughts and conversations but courses of action at exactly the same time." In that procedural complexity, he pursues a plot for himself that is like an intricately interlooped cat's cradle of contingencies. And he will delay until the very last necessary instant excluding any active possibility, partly out of a vigilance that "just about anything can happen at any given point to completely change your thinking about a situation," but also from a sense that such deferral only quickens the pulse of all his other conditional concomitant possibilities until the right one comes into certain definition. When several years later he would long and publicly ponder running for mayor of Washington before finally concluding the office would be a hopeless cul-de-sac, "a lot of people in the media became disenchanted," says Bert Lance, " 'cause they thought he'd been sort of teasing, showing a lot of leg, you know, and then drawing it back. But he just isn't gonna preempt anything—as we say in the South, ain't gonna cull *nothin'*—until he absolutely has to." As a result, he tactically acts in a manner that often resembles his own personal version of Brownian Movement, or the Uncertainty Principle.

Now, even with all the auspicious circumstances that had accumulated for his committing to a presidential run, what finally most lured Jackson about the prospect was the larger, parallel purpose that it might serve. In perhaps the most ambitious "duality without contradiction" he would ever essay, a presidential campaign could—quite apart from any serious considerations of actually winning, lacking the great moral drama of King's time—become the means to make a quantum leap into a magnitude of his own, through a political succession to King as a national apostle of conscience: as a presidential candidate, he might at last come into his fulfillment. His former theology professor Alvin Pitcher would later concur that "in running for president, Jesse for the first time had a role that was commensurate with the size of his being. He was a big fish in a big enough pond now, and it freed him. Really freed him." If nothing else, a presidential campaign would afford him splendidly enhanced acoustics for amplifying his social witness. "I was bringing into it all the passion and ideology I'd always had," he contends now, "but by making this tactical move, I could gain an access that I couldn't have had on the outside. I'd be up there on the stage with the other candidates, and therefore the issues I raised could no longer be ignored. I could begin to *expa-a-a-and* the system, so it'd have to adjust to my ideas. When you can't get the media to come to where the problems are, you take the problems to a higher plateau as a presidential candidate. *Then* you can take the media to the inner city—they'll go. Or to Appalachia—they'll go."

Still, Jackson waited until all seven of the other Democratic candidates had declared. Jackie relates, "Strangely enough, my husband always shares with me the most serious things while he's putting on his socks in the morning. We'd been talking about it, of course, but it wasn't until this one morning when he was pulling on his socks that he said, 'Jackie? I'm going to run for president of these United States of America.' I said, 'Hot dog! Way to go, Jesse!' We had our little pep rally right there, you know. 'Yes! I *am* somebody! Keep hope alive!'" Finally, with a mention first to Mike Wallace in another 60 *Minutes* profile, then with a three-hour rally at the Convention Center in Washington, he announced that he was entering the race for president.

And with his resort to that expedient, the mischievous equation was laid.

XIII
The Dilemma of Soul Politics

HIS HIGHER MISSION in a presidential campaign, Jackson always insisted, was "to transcend society, to make America better, in a way that is still the movement, more spiritual and less concrete than usual politics. You don't strive for love between institutions; you strive for love between individuals and justice between institutions." It would be a kind of prophetic political ministry, as he once posed it, "to help lift the veil from the face of the multitude and open up their vision to what's really possible."

Any number of others besides Jackson, of course, ranging from the rankly bogus to the devoutly delusional, have presumed to take on the character of some sort of prophet-hero. But what had always been singularly interesting about that aspiration in Jackson was that he actually seemed to have the wherewithal for it. At the least, for all his plentiful vagaries, he struck more than a few observers as, if still only potentially, the genuine article. "Lord knows he certainly screws up enough," says one longtime pastoral acquaintance. "But I think God chooses some people *no matter*, and I think Jesse is chosen." His former campaign consultant Mark Steitz acknowledges, "There was a quietness that came to any of us who spent much time around this question of what's going on with Jesse, a quietness out of respect for the fact that it was evident something meaningful and bigger than us was at work there. For one thing, you're not finally getting him if you discount his own religiousness. I mean, he's just all the time *praying*—every day, and every day *lots*. What other people would say is thinking he calls praying. 'Have to pray on that. Give me a little bit. This is serious, have to pray on it.' For myself, I call it grazing, when I'd wake up in my hotel room in the morning, and just sort of lying there, thinking, letting the muses come. Then I'd come down for breakfast, and he'd say, 'Here's Steitz, comes downstairs in the morning after he's had visions. People been talking to him up there.' Now, I don't think of it as a state of prayer or hearing voices, but he does. And that difference might lead to a lot better ideas for him. It's earnest thinking, but it's also passive thinking, God is speaking to him, he's receiving, he's not forcing—you know, 'I heard a voice last night, said, Here's how to deal with this thing.' He's saying it with a certain playful panache, but he's also quite serious."

Whatever, since the sixties, he had continued to live fundamentally from the memory of King, endlessly referring to him, as if feeling himself somehow still in King's presence. He seemed to be performing his own sort of continuation of King, still surpassingly acting from King's operational dynamic of, as he once postulated it, "make it tense, but not ugly. From creative tension, new life comes." More, his whole sense of his ministry remained a direct projection of King's moral metaphysic, even now into his extension into a presidential contest. "For instance, Martin on Vietnam did not win in Congress, but he raised the right concerns, and those concerns did finally win. Like he used to say, if it's morally right, it'll eventually become politically right. Because the universe has a moral center. And what I'm saying is, we in the *heart* of that center."

Indeed, in his anticipations of how he would fare in his presidential adventure, Jackson was counting on the workings of a semimystical physics he called "the force of the moral center. It's the great gravitational center, it can't be—it's *irresistible*. Like the sun. Once you get to that center of the morality of a given situation, that becomes the point where all books close, all arguments end, all extremes are reconciled, all politics come together. Now in moving things toward that center, there's oftentimes a troubled transition period of tensions—sometimes have to sort of *revolve* toward that center. But you got to know that's where you headed, and as long as you have that fix, everything else sooner or later falls into place; if you don't have that fix, nothing does, nothing lasts very long. So you have to keep refining the argument until it gets to that center, which is the point where people have to back away, can't challenge. Because when you get there, everybody inside recognizes it innately, it's an awareness built into us. Like it's structured into nature. For a tyrant, finally even his children's innocence confronts and accuses him. That's why the only way somebody can beat you is to move you away from that center. Because the moral center leaves your enemy defense*less*."

He expatiated further on this one morning, some five years later, in Luanda, as he was waiting to pay a call on Angolan president dos Santos. He was asked, if his principle of moral physics was true—that the moral will eventually become the political reality—would that not mean a yet better world would be constantly aborning? "Well, in many ways, it *is*," he muttered back. "An old world is passing away before our eyes, a new world is being born, and we're now in the morning of that new day. There are more free people today than at any time in the history of the world. There are more forces in motion today to fight poverty and famine than ever before. Feudalism's gone, colonialism's fundamentally gone, fascism's on its way out, all forms of totalitarianism, going. [This happened to be some months before the release of Nelson Mandela and the disassembling of apartheid in South Africa, and before the epochal developments at the end of 1989— the dissolution of the Soviet empire, the fall of the Berlin Wall.] You *got* to say the world is getting better. So it does prove if something is morally right, it will eventually be politically valid. Now it may take an awfully long time, like with the Portuguese here in Angola—" He was sitting on the back patio of the former colonial governor's villa, on a bluff overlooking the far shine of the South Atlantic, with a rooster strutting about under an acacia tree of flame-red blossoms. "But this morning, we sit here on the former governor's back porch. He is *gone*. The last Portuguese governor will *not* return. Because he did not represent moral truth. And it's the yard boy who grew up around here who's in charge of this place now. You know, there's a Scripture, I think in Isaiah, says, And you'll grow up and you'll have your inheritance, world that you didn't build, you'll inhabit houses and inherit kingdoms you didn't build. That's got some interesting applications, you know?"

On the whole, Jackson operated from a moral vision that did seem arrestingly original. It was as if he proceeded not only by spying gaps in the prevailing political ecologies around him, but more, in the common moral perceptions of matters, moving in to create previously unremarked associations, new connective patterns—new moral synapses, as it were. Remaking thinking in that way, he proposed, could remake reality. "Part of the reconstruction of our society is allowing people to see and feel anew. Get people seeing the whole of where equality and justice are, and are not, in their environment—and history's gonna *move*." Some years later, to a dinner of government officials in Zimbabwe, he would propound, "The reality here was, this would always be Rhodesia. Reality was, Ian Smith couldn't lose. Reality was, he had the tradition, the institutions, the technology, the equipment, the media—" Yet again one wondered, was he also talking in another of his paralleling self-parables? "That was the reality of things as they were. But then that reality came into confrontation with a dream. Dreams are elusive, because they're spiritual. But that dream left the reality on the junk heap of history. You either keep dreaming, or they decay on you and turn into nightmare."

In regard to Jackson's own particular lifelong dream, it's likely that no aspiring social prophet has ever been so elaborately, analytically, volubly aware of himself as such, has so consciously crafted himself to become that, and has been so noticing of his effects in that effort. He would expound in almost obsessive detail on the nature of the authentic moral hero. "Need ego, to a degree. No one should be trusted to lead a people who's got a ego deficiency. Ain't nothing wrong with bein' average, 'cause you got a lot of company, but you sho cannot be average *and* great. It's like, if you a sergeant and you got an army, you soon reduce it to a platoon, but if you a general and got a platoon, pretty soon you turn it into an army. Things ultimately fit the size of a leader's mind, what I'm sayin'." But it's seldom, he went on, that a moral hero "can survive the system, because it's really geared now to producing nonraces among packaged candidates"—this being one of his unlikelier, though not insignificant, synaptic snaps, from the heroic to the political. "Authentic involves more risks, less immediate rewards, more daring, more long suffering. But these TV-packaged leaders now, they give three sentences and then check with their aides to see how it might read tomorrow morning, sound on TV. They try to make up for their emptiness with commercials. That's a very different something going on there."

By way of explaining his sense of the heroic quality in a figure, Jackson recounted how King, speaking once in a Chicago church, began to ruminate aloud about the likelihood that he would be slain, would someday never return home to his family, "and there was a stillness all over that sanctuary," says Jackson. "Some people began to cry. Then a few weeks later, a local preacher was addressing a ministers' conference, and you know how preachers'll pick up from other preachers what they think's effective . . . this local guy, he says"—and Jackson's voice rose to a wavering, mincing mimic—" 'Sometimes when I get up in the morning and I leave home with my wife and children still asleep, I feel sometimes I won't ever get back home again.' Somebody sittin' beside me says, 'What, he think he's gonna get hit by a damn train or something?' I mean, it was so empty, wadn't nobody worried about *him* not coming back home. But when Martin said the same words, it was authentic. Touched you. You only know that thing, that authentic force, when you feel it. Ain't nothing you can prove or explain. But when that something happens, it's what people call charisma, the spirit of God moving through people, a wave from person to person, making them one with what the speaker's saying. It's not something you can really be appointed to, or inherit, or be assigned, or elected to, either. There's a long history of the power of conscience and truth through the unelected individual being an activator of profound change. Elected officials wouldn't've initiated a drive for public accommodations, elected officials didn't lead the drive for the right to vote, for open housing, to end the war in Vietnam, for arms reduction. Jesus wasn't elected. Paul wasn't elected. Frederick Douglass wasn't elected. Gandhi wasn't elected. Dr. King wasn't elected." As King's old associate C. T. Vivian posits it, "Martin King decided law in this nation without ever holding political office, because of a moral and spiritual presence reaching the conscience of America. That's the higher calling, raising those great religious questions, which politics then tries to solve. So the question is, was this the movement of Jesse as politician, or as a prophet that speaks to the political structures?"

But that seemed to be precisely the paradox of Jackson's fancy now to make a presidential run. The noted gospel-existentialist, circuit-riding Tennessee minister Will D. Campbell submits, "Prophets never *are* elected to office. Never have been, never will be if they're gonna stay prophets. They preach and witness *to* the offices of authority. How can you become a part of what you suppose to be prophesying to?" But Jackson now risked entering into a kind of implicitly sabotaging contract. A presidential campaign may have tempted as merely a means for enlarging his social evangelism, but in making the crossing between those two essentially antithetical realms of interests—from moral apostleship into politics—the danger, particularly for someone of Jackson's vast pride and vast wants, was of being subverted and finally claimed by what one initially thought only to use.

However provisionally at first, Jackson was passing into a reality with its own considerably less than visionary judgments. The most commonly heard question about Jackson before long was "What does Jesse really want?" and the stock answer became "Respect"—but it was as much his probably misbegotten hope to bring that respect to his message, to his preachments, through a presidential candidacy. So consummate a political maestro as Bert Lance concedes, "A lot of things about politics are mean, are nasty. It's ugly, it's nonredemptive. But Jesse decided that was the avenue for him to go, to get to his larger business. That he could never achieve those larger things he wanted if he stayed simply a black preacher extolling his ideas at Operation PUSH." The inherent disjunction in that recourse, though, as Jackson's friend from his seminary days in Chicago, Henry Hardy, presents it, was "Jesse, carrying the burden of his own destiny with him, was let down into an area where other people don't always see that you're talking as a spiritual man, that you're engaging in that way, that it's *that* that's driving you—that to you, in a way, you *are* John the Baptist crying in the wilderness, you *are* Isaiah saying, 'Here am I, Lord, send me.' You're Ezekiel in the valley of the dry bones—that's what he envisions himself as, that kind of a spiritual anatomist to put together those bones and give them body, and make them move and breathe. But he was carried by the movement of history into the political arena, and there's always going to be a dialectical tension there. Because Jesse is primarily a spiritual visionary. But you talk God language or spiritual communication there, it sounds to them like you're talking some mystical mumbo-jumbo, and they say, 'You have no business here, you're not playing by the established rules of the game.' " Another longtime intimate insists, "You would have to kill Jackson to get the Jesse Jackson out of him and make him something that people expect in presidents."

Andrew Young encountered much the same difficulty after Carter appointed him ambassador to the U.N. "I told Vance and Carter that I was only in that post in the first place because of Martin Luther King," says Young, "which happened to be true for Carter, too. And that I thought Martin was killed in part because he insisted on our talking to the North Vietnamese during that war, and that I was not going to go to the U.N. and snub people." But it was not only in his unauthorized meeting then with PLO representatives that Young outraged all the orthodox political respectabilities; he also once observed that the Ayatollah Khomeini was really not that different from Georgia's own religiously fundamentalist segregationist governor in the sixties, Lester Maddox, and another time he offered that the British had one of the most racist histories among the Western democracies. His liability in all this was that he was not so much performing diplomacy as acting as an extension of the movement's moral vision into the processes of power. "And that became Jesse's problem, too," Young concedes. "We're part of the same legacy."

King himself, for that matter, when he had proposed that Red China be admitted to the U.N., and declared there would be no civic peace in the United States until there was peace in Vietnam, had set off furors similar to those that finally forced Young to resign his U.N. post. Accordingly, Jackson now, in what constituted his platform for his first presidential exertion, called for an immediate suspension of America's nuclear arms buildup; a 20 percent decrease in overall defense spending and a commensurate increase in allocations for public works projects, jobs retraining, and education; a more rigorous supervision of corporate behavior; more restraint in foreign interventions; a halt to all aid to South Africa's apartheid society; support for the ultimate creation of an independent Palestinian state; and an official recognition of Cuba. The critical squall provoked by these notions was hardly mitigated by the oratory accompanying them: U.S. suzerainty over the Panama Canal, Jackson averred, had cost the Panamanians "shame, hurt, pain, denial, disgrace, and economic exploitation . . . the worst dimension of American segregation and South African apartheid," and about Fidel Castro, he pronounced, "He's in the Third World, and I have a Third World experience in suffering and exploitation right here in America. I'm a Third World person, I grew up in an occupied zone, and had to negotiate with the colonial power." In fact, it was as if, to Jackson, what was taking place all over the rest of the globe were merely a repetition of his own experiences in Greenville, writ large. But "most people in the world today are yellow, brown, black, and red," he insisted. "We must join the *real* world order." One way to begin, he suggested, was "to be more patient of Third World nations in their transitions toward development." But that sentiment sometimes took on a fervor that produced more dubious propositions: about the Irish Republican Army, he opined, "I would tend not to identify with violence, but I would not confuse the tactic with the mission. I feel an identity with the mission of a struggle of anticolonialist forces"; and even more dubiously, about the stories of savage repression out of Cambodia and Vietnam, he could only bring himself to remark, "Unfortunate. Sometimes people struggling for freedom lose their way. Sometimes the best of people do become cruel and repressive."

Carrying such perspectives now into a presidential campaign, Jackson was soon being decried as, at best, the proponent of a "radical idealism," but more frequently as "hysterical and inflammatory; many of his words are just plain claptrap," as it was put by *The New Republic*, which was to prove one of his most assiduously vituperative critics, with its repentant, postliberal mentality. One among its commentators would eventually declare, "Face it, America's interests would not be safe with this man in power. Fundamentally, he does not believe in the moral superiority of Western values."

The Media Backfire

GIVEN SUCH PRESS reactions to his candidacy, it now seems almost poignant that Jackson went into his presidential undertaking still enthralled with the media's potential for giving back to him affirming reflections of his significance. After an appearance or address, he would linger amid a clump of reporters, no matter how far behind schedule he was, to engage in prolonged play with their questions. "I just want to ask one more thing," a reporter would say, and Jackson would hoot, not ungladly, "Yeah, I know, and so would he"—pointing to others around him, almost as if prompting them, too—"and he would, and she would, and he would, but this is my last, I got to go—" Yet he would dangle on among them for twenty more minutes, before cheerfully calling out at last, "Now, I really, I can't, I really got to go, friends," tossing high an open palm to everyone in happy benediction: "Okay? Goin' bye-bye now." Beyond that, he was constantly attempting amiable little appropriate blandishments. Once, at the end of a day of rallies in New York, just before he ducked into Bill Cosby's East Side town house for a few hours, Jackson ambled back to the press car pulled up behind him and, leaning down to its back window, told a woman reporter for a network, who had covered him often before, to call him later that evening at the Plaza. When she finally reached him there, it was only to be informed by Jackson that he had found her questions that day to be unusually sharp, and, furthermore, he liked very much the outfit she'd had on. Occasionally, he would make an attempt to conscript a reporter outright. As he was about to depart from the airport in Luanda, he suddenly dragooned a *New York Times* correspondent into putting together a press contingent to accompany him on an excursion to the Cabinda oil fields when he returned to Angola in a few days. With one hand clapped on the correspondent's shoulder, turning to an Angolan official, he said, "Now, who will be his contact person in your office?" and then to the reporter, "You two exchange numbers now, and work it out. I'll call you from Zambia, okay?"

For one particular importunate ploy Jackson was to come by a certain fame—or infamy—among journalists: at some unspeakable hour of the night, a reporter's phone would suddenly ring, and when the receiver was fumbled to the ear, there would be Jackson's voice, drawling low and thick, "Hey. 'S yo brothuh . . ." After Ben Bradlee's marriage to Sally Quinn, "Jackson would call well after midnight," Bradlee recounts, "and he'd say, 'Ben? . . .' with this lowered, slightly leering quality in his voice, 'Ben? Is that good-lookin' woman Mizz Sally lyin' next to you right now?' " Besides Bradlee, who was then editor of *The Washington Post*, and Don Hewitt, executive producer of *60 Minutes*, other recipients of these late-night greetings included, over time, Dan Rather and Tom Brokaw—all of whom Jackson would proceed to ask for counsel as a way of sort of implicitly enlisting them in the course of his career. "But you know, I was quite surprised that he really did finally run for president," says Bradlee. "I'd thought it would be no more than a threat, a gambit. Of course, you were always aware of his capacity to fuck things over for everybody else, or to make people deal with him. Yet that was his attractive quality, too. By the force of his personality, of his sheer gall, he probably achieved a lot more than he would have without it." Bradlee recalls, not without some fondness now, "I talked to him, must've been, two or three times a week for eight years. I guess we all felt we had a special relationship with him, though it wasn't as if you didn't know what he was doing. He'd ask for advice on something, but then generally tune out what I had to say. It was mostly to explain how there was something going on in America, generally involving him, that *The Washington Post* and the rest of the press was not paying sufficient attention to. Yeah, I was extremely useful to him, he thought. He called me once from the office of the president of some African country, said, 'Ben, I want you to talk to President So-and-so here.' I said, '*What for?*' Obviously, Jesse had told him, I know that editor of *The Washington Post*, shit, he'll do what I tell him, see, I'll call him right now and show you. But if he was trying to enhance his importance with that, in the eyes of a really smart African president, the editor of *The Washington Post* has got to be way down on his list.

"He was filled with these exaggerated gestures," Bradlee goes on. He and Sally once happened to be in Paris on Sally's birthday, "and I took my birthday wife to Maxim's for a big, fat dinner and dancing and all that. All of a sudden there's this big stir. Waiters are breaking down tables and shoving them together. I said to Sally, 'You watch, there's some big sheik about to come in.' But then, in walks Jesse. With his wife, Jackie, maybe two of their children. And Jesse comes over to our table, and the next thing is, two dozen long-stemmed roses arrive from him. And then the goddamned orchestra starts playing 'Happy Birthday.' The whole room now is riveted by this scene. Then, of course, he comes over and asks Sally to dance. Sally and I had been trying to have our own evening, but he just intruded himself into it, and soon we were just part of his evening. I said to Sally, 'Can you *believe* this son of a bitch?' He'd go back and sit down, then here he's coming over again."

Bradlee cackles. "But once I ceased to be editor of the paper, I ceased to be of any interest to him. I knew exactly what it was, I didn't deceive myself about that. Still, I'm pissed at him now because he dropped me like a hot goddamned potato as soon as I left the editor's chair—I mean, *the day*. No more calls. I went to some big dinner not long ago, and he was there, and he got down on one knee in front of me, before five hundred people, saying, 'The great Bradlee!' I said, 'You son of a bitch, you haven't talked to me for two years. . . .' But we got along well. I like rogues anyway, I like bullshitters. Maybe it takes one to appreciate a master at it."

In all of his eager cultivations of journalists, though, Jackson's ultimate hope was to induct them into his own excitements about what seemed to him his momentous political apostleship. His somewhat naive assumption persisted that journalism's main purpose was a didactic, instructive one, answering to the prior interest of some cause. Largely for that reason, he insisted black journalists should keep faith with a "Black Code," in which serving the interest of their common racial condition in America transcended any merely reportorial considerations. He once upbraided a black reporter for personal queries into his life, "No white reporter tells it all, and neither should you. You just don't tell it all." And after one conference session of black journalists in Los Angeles, he collected a number of them in a corner to admonish them, "Black journalists and white journalists ain't the same, but black journalists and black politicians *are*. We are in the same situation, the same predicament. Just look in the mirror. You got an inherent problem if you assume we are in different positions." But with journalism in general, whether *Ebony* or *The New York Times*, he seemed oblivious to the principle that there should be a distinction between an advocate and a reporter, that the impulse should be one of simple, detached, disinterested curiosity: "Media's not just a transmitter," is how he stated it once, "it's s'pose to be an *interpreter*."

Nevertheless, Jackson was not long in discovering that those who seek to prosper by the media can quickly perish by the media, when all his efforts to assimilate reporters into his enthusiasms almost invariably ended in rude disappointment. To be sure, he was to become the subject of some unusually aspish-humored journalism. Besides *The New Republic*, especially persistent in his ammonial scorns would be columnist George Will, who, questioning Jackson once on television, "in the spirit of old crackers giving voting quizzes to blacks when they tried to register," as Garry Wills later observed, "asked Jackson, 'As president, would you support measures such as the G-7 measures [*sic*] and the Louvre Accords? [*sic*]' Like the red-neck quizzers, Will got the trick question slightly wrong—the Louvre Accord *was* a G-7 measure for the international market." Jackson would begin grumbling about "reporters trying to make a living off of asking you a question that frustrates you, so they can go back and say, 'Hah, hah, hah.' I've not sat down with any big-time reporter who hasn't stayed up the night before thinking up questions to embarrass me. Though they haven't been very successful so far, I'd say." But the media's failure to become enchanted by his candidacy seemed to leave Jackson authentically baffled. Whenever his campaign appeared to be gaining an unexpected vitality, Jackson complained, "You'd think that would be a right amazing thing, but the major press, they'll never write it down, never report that—just say, it's unreal, it's bullshit. 'Cause it's out of their accustomed thought processes. Never write an article about how this movement of Jackson's is expanding." It was suggested to him then that part of the reason might be that, in his evocations of a populist Blessed Community, he struck some journalists, as one termed it, as "a candidate more of poetry than prose," with a campaign composed of wishful sentimentalisms belonging more to folk-song lyrics than to the national realpolitik. "Just the opposite," Jackson snapped. "It *is* real. Gonna be a hit song, too."

The media's refusal to recognize that, Jackson finally ascribed to its being "enmeshed in that whole system" of power in the country that had perversely continued to discount him. "The media's never really understood what I'm about" was his conclusion. "So many of 'em moral midgets, want to know the truth. I mean, may sound a little egotistical to say that what I'm about is larger than they capable of graspin', but in a lot of cases, dammit, it's *true*. May not even be so much racial as they just can't make the cultural and sociological adjustment in their head." But that disregard Jackson clearly considered *was* essentially racial. "They got this attitude, they'll tell me, 'You say these things about issues, and people respond 'cause you got a . . . a *fol-low-ing*. You be a good talker, and they are reacting, and neither one of yawl making a lot of sense. They just caught up in the thing.' So their coverage is all about bright lights and showtime and diversion. All about jive. No appreciation of the people or me intellectually. Ain't that I'm thinking and they thinking—we not cogitating, we just rappin'. You know, *In reality, he don't understand the real facts of life, the big stuff*. Just, 'You talk 'cause you a parrot.'"

What made these complaints of Jackson's rather difficult to dismiss as mere peevish sulking was that no slight strain of truth ran through them. But basically, what confronted Jackson now in his press coverage was something like the fume and static resulting from an effort that resembled less an exercise of moral physics than a kind of alchemy—a labor to merge two naturally adverse elements. And he met with a carbolic cynicism not only about his message when he shifted it into a presidential competition—one newsmagazine columnist later insisting that "his thinking on most major issues still isn't much deeper than his rhymes and riffs"—but about him personally, as well, the same columnist adding that "far more serious than Jackson's Mother Goose populism is the lingering sense that this man is something of a hustler." It was also quickly apparent that he could no longer expect the tolerant inattentions allowed to certain untidy matters in his past, when he had been careering about in the looser and more private latitudes of an entrepreneurial activist. Consequently, all the mystery of his hugely mixed and contradictory nature now fell under a critical squint. But few of us are accustomed to understanding character in such a myriad sense, let alone the quick, everyday curiosities of the journalistic reality. The hazard now to the larger meaning that had always obsessed Jackson was that he was pursuing that meaning in a dimension where he would begin to be defined precisely by that smaller-gauge register of fractional perceptions.

"It'd drive him crazy," says Bert Lance, "and he kept trying to fight it. He'd call up somebody and say, 'Look, you don't know what you're talking about.' I tried to tell him, 'You got to put your head above all that. Stick to the message. Because this kind of criticism is just always gonna be there. You're not gonna remove it. It's just part of the price.' But he never could really accept that. Never could stop hoping."

A Sterner Auditing

THE GAUNTLET OF scrutiny now facing Jackson included not only questions about the void of any governmental experience in his past, which was cited to discount the validity of his political professions now—even Andrew Young volunteered, "Only in America can someone who could not be elected mayor or governor run for president"—but queries soon arose about exactly how he had subsidized himself all that time as a free-form social evangel. Ben Bradlee still exclaims, "*God knows* how he's gotten along. I would ask him, 'How the hell do you support yourself and your operation?' He'd just say, 'The Rainbow! The Rainbow!' "

The truth is, Jackson has always seemed genuinely muzzy about the specifics of how he's actually been carried, proceeding in broad strokes as he does. "You can't be superintendent of education and bookkeeper, custodian at the same time" is how he cast it once. But the flares of media inquiry now gradually exposed a complex of arrangements as varied and intricate as some Mesopotamian irrigation system—an informal, ad hoc, almost measurelessly diffuse network of funding, improvised in the disorderly fashion of virtually all past movement operations, including King's own SCLC.

He had continued to derive substantial support from his personal "people always take care of those who serve them" principle, and from the beneficiaries of the corporate compacts he had negotiated for black businessmen through the past fifteen years. "My strongest relationships have been with those people I gave service to," he would concede. "Interesting leverage in that relationship. Kind of like the one a mother has over you. She's given you more than you can ever give her." As for himself, though, he stipulated, "I never once took one of those franchises or dealerships, and I *could* have. But I always felt, if ever I traded off what I was doing for a dealership, I would give up the moral authority I had. That's hard sometimes for people to grasp. Like when I went to the Middle East in 1979 to try breaking that invisible barrier on the Palestinian question, met with Arafat, met with Assad. When I got back, got a call from the Onassis people, Christina and her advisers, to meet them in New York at their downtown offices. I went there, ships and all these emblems of their empire all over the place. When we sat down, all they wanted to talk about was oil shipments to the Middle East. It was inconceivable to them that I had gone over there and taken all that political heat and risk, and it was not in exchange for some oil deal with the Arabs. They simply could not imagine it on any other basis." Such protestations did not dispel suspicions, though.

But among the extensive and diverse array of other private patrons he had accumulated over time—Bill Cosby, Donald Trump, Quincy Jones, Hugh Hefner, Berry Gordy, Norman Lear, even, at times, Ross Perot—was a Los Angeles real estate investor named A. Bruce Rozet, who would give the birthday party for Jackson at his Brentwood Hills home near the close of the 1988 campaign; in 1989, when Rozet was to land in difficulties over reported slum conditions in some of his HUD-funded properties, Jackson sought to intercede for him with Housing Secretary Jack Kemp—with little success.

Yet larger troubles awaited him now from the means he had contrived to fund his virtuoso social ministry. Jackson had also assembled a complementary community of patrons abroad, among business figures in countries—Nigeria, for one—he'd visited. It emerged that some governments overseas had directed disbursements into his operations, including two donations to PUSH-Excel from Syria through the Arab League that totaled $200,000, and a $10,000 gift to PUSH from a Libyan diplomat in 1979. Jackson had apparently not hesitated to apply to Arab eminences a version of the same leverage he had exercised with corporations in his economic campaigns: he was quoted by *The Washington Post* in 1979 as averring, "There will be no black leader left willing to come to the aid of the Palestinian cause if there is not an immediate infusion of funds into the black community from Arab states. We will all learn to recite the alphabet without three letters—P-L-O." To the subsequent outcry about his accepting assistance from such sources, Jackson retorted, "If the Arab League can contribute to Harvard and Georgetown and other institutions of higher learning, can they not contribute to the PUSH foundation?"

For that matter, not only the Ford Foundation but CBS and Merrill Lynch had also relayed monies to PUSH. Over its twelve years of operation, in fact, subsidies received from private and corporate contributions and federal grants had totaled some $17 million. U.S. government agencies alone had supplied PUSH-Excel over $6 million in grants and contracts for its programs in the black community—funds so haphazardly accounted for, though, the organization was eventually obliged to pay a $500,000 fine, exacted by the Reagan administration, to settle a claim of $1.4 million. Jackson called it merely "a dispute between accountants and auditors." *Time* would later report, "Many news organizations, including *Time*, have dug through the well-worn Government audits of Jackson's PUSH-Excel program, only to conclude, as have federal authorities, that the group's handling of federal funds was sloppy and incompetent but not illegal." It still constituted, though, a compromising circumstance.

Further support came from various extramonetary considerations, such as provisions of personnel and services from labor and trade unions, and accommodations from foreign governments during Jackson's travels abroad. Meanwhile, Jackson himself had steadily gathered increasingly plump fees from his ceaseless round of speeches. Also, one of his ministerial acquaintances relates, "Jesse will call me about three times a year, usually on a Saturday night before our Sunday services, and say, 'I'm speaking for you tomorrow.' He'll do that sometimes when he's testing a new idea, but then he'll also always take up an offering from my people." Indeed, at the close of almost all his appearances before black groups and in black churches, he would ease into an appeal, "A movement like ours does not run on soul alone. It costs. It takes *coal* to keep the freedom train rollin'. Now, those of you out there can give a thousand dollars to help us carry on this work, please stand. Please stand. Will you stand and come down front here? . . ." and so make his way on down declining denominations until he had reached the ten-dollar level, at which point he would sigh into the microphone, "Now, don't make me beg here. I can beg if I have to, but please don't make me have to do that. Just ten dollars for this movement. Will you please stand? . . ." To some, this seemed close to grotesque mendicancy. And that was without virtually anyone noting that, as he tracked back and forth about the country, people would occasionally slip up to him in hotel and airport lobbies and extend an envelope: "Should I give this to you, or should I mail it?" with Jackson intoning, "Awww, thank you, friend, I'll take it, thank you so much, buddy, ain't this wonderful!"

For all the random and obscure workings of this financial support system evolved by Jackson over the years, it had sustained him comfortably enough—his income, by the mid-eighties, having reached over $200,000 a year. Jackson once asserted that he could allot himself far more if he chose, and that his income was far less anyway than what heads of comparable organizations and foundations received. But he also acquired such assets as an interest, under Jackie's name, in the privately held company Inner City Broadcasting, an interest that would be worth over $1 million by 1988, as estimated then by the company's former chairman and old Jackson compatriot, Percy Sutton. Nevertheless, maintains Jackson's longtime associate at PUSH, Willie Barrow, "Jesse may have made some money, but he doesn't really love money. It's never interested him that much. Jesse just loves power and big results." John White, the former Democratic national chairman, observed in 1994, "Jesse's lived well. But not nearly as well as he could have if he had been in it all just for the money."

But if Jackson was hardly a simple profiteer, he kept himself in circumstances that did seem exceptionally ample for a purported populist apostle—almost always flying first class, sometimes occupying two hotel suites. "When he was in New York," recalls his editor at Viking, Rich Barber, "he stayed at the Plaza or the Park Lane—always the top-rate hotels," and another editor who visited him in one of those suites still remembers, "He had on this exquisite wafer-thin watch—the kind, you know, if you turned it sideways, you couldn't see it." Many were the stories like the one related by a former aide of an instance in the mid-eighties when, with his organization's finances again so bitten that most of the staff had gone unpaid for three weeks, Jackson nevertheless elected to fly back from a tour of Europe on the Concorde, along with four of his children and several assistants, at a cost of more than $2,000 each. When the aide suggested afterward that this might have been a slightly intemperate indulgence, Jackson's incensed rejoinder was "You're trying to sabotage my spirit."

It may have been, as C. T. Vivian contends, that in all these self-provisionings "Jesse was getting what was right done, and he was building the means to get more that was right done. The more you envision is possible, the more you have to build a base to make it possible." When all these aspects of how he had financed himself emerged in the glare attending his presidential enterprise, they would considerably complicate his image as a supposed successor to King who was continuing King's moral vision in the life of the nation.

The Ladies Problem

BUT THERE WAS another liability left from his freestyle past that had also been a concern debated through those hotel-room sessions of the Family— what some would come in time to call, after the mishap that would befall another presidential contender four years later, Jackson's "Hart problem": the widely distributed stories of his exuberant romantic corsairing. "Maybe it was that he was just trying to be like King in too many ways," one journalist suggested. But as early as his years with Breadbasket, Jackson himself was not abashed about advertising, "I don't need nobody to give me no plaque, 'Here is a man who can walk by a swimming pool full of women and never look up.' No, that ain't no plaque for me. When I see a beautiful woman with a miniskirt on, my eyes get big as teacups. Oh, yeah, I ain't gonna be lyin'. They swell up because I'm young and I'm healthy!" One of his editors at Viking states, "You'd go up to his room for a meeting or something, and a young lady would walk out as you were walking in. And I mean, there were some real honeys. Nothing was ever really said. It was like she'd come up for an autograph or something like that—but the ultimate autograph, you might say. If you were, as I was then, a fairly young and active guy yourself, it wasn't hard to figure out." Jackson will still allow himself the occasional waggery on the matter. When a reporter, after complaining about Jackson's eighteen-hour-a-day pace, ruefully philosophized, "Well, guess man cannot live by sleep alone," Jackson flipped back, "Man cannot live *sleepin'* alone."

Reports had him more seriously involved, at various times, with singers Nancy Wilson and Aretha Franklin, and around 1973, there was a conspicuous and, by all signs, humid relationship with Roberta Flack, the two of them seen much and raptly in each other's company—the assumptions about that attachment hardly discouraged when she produced a breathy love ballad titled "Jesse," which she performed on two network shows. Asked about the song, Jackson merely said, "I'm flattered by the thought." Other queries about their connection he would rebuff as "inappropriate" and tending "to reduce the question of moral tone to just sexuality." But he did add, "Until such time as I'm ready to concede some formal relationship, I refuse to deny it. Roberta is a close personal relationship, and I refuse to have it muddied. She has her own spirituality." Besides, he declared, "I have a very enviable home situation. Jackie has made me secure in many ways. Our marriage is private and it's stable, and I need not comment on the quality of it. Jackie understands me. She gives me rope, but I haven't hung myself." Even so, some found the understandings all around passing into the baroque when Jackson's daughter Santita wound up singing in Roberta's backup group.

David Wallace now cites as one of his reasons for leaving PUSH "all the adulteries. Many of us, really, but with Jesse, it was so *open*. One of them was actually traveling with him, and expected him to leave his house and break up his family. Earlier, during the Poor People's Campaign, I had one woman come to me saying, 'Jesse's told me we're getting married as soon as he can get free, but he hasn't told me when yet. Has he told you?' It really started bothering me." By 1984, though, however spirited his past disportings, Jackson had apparently become somewhat more subdued and circumspect. Richard Hatcher contends, "We spent an awful lot of time together—late at night, in hotel suites all over the country—and during all that time I never saw anything. And that kind of thing is pretty hard to conceal, you know, you'll suddenly see a strange face show up." Hatcher then suggests, "Let me tell you why I think there wasn't anything. I have almost never heard Jesse, at any time, engage in anything you would call small talk. He's just always on the case, always talking about big matters and issues and strategies—you know, what do you think is really going on in the Middle East, what do you think we ought to do about this policy of the administration, that sort of stuff. But never, like . . . now, that's an attractive woman." Ben Bradlee is actually inclined to the same notion: "He's always played it flirtatious with Sally, but hell, so do a lot of people. He seemed to me almost more interested in talking politics than screwing. I've come across people like that before."

Still, it's remained a vulnerability that Jackson has hardly been unaware of, and in heavier ways than many may suspect, particularly in its cross-racial aspects: "Any black man who's attractive to white women," he once dolorously mused, "his days gonna be short and full of trouble." One morning in 1989, while walking toward a flight gate at the Los Angeles airport, Jackson began reflecting, though somewhat obliquely, on the amatory notoriety in his past. "Like Dr. King, for example, said, 'We should have peace in Vietnam.' Opponents said, 'Yes, but you love wimmin.' 'But peace in Vietnam.' 'Yes, but we sent Mrs. King the tapes.' That's always the tactic, to distract and discredit and destroy." Asked about the possibility that he could face the discomfort of similar disclosures, Jackson said, "Well, when all that stuff came out about Dr. King, some in the press asked me, 'What about all this? What, what you say about—' and I told 'em, 'Look. Dr. King gave us the public accommodations bill. He gave us voting rights. He was a husband to his wife. He was a father to his children. Case closed'"—this perhaps a wishfully dismissive reference. But Jackson insisted, "The point is, one of the things the oppressor can never let the oppressed be, and that is a moral agent who represents the moral center. Conscience threatens the status quo. That's why anybody who occupies that position must either be accommodated or eliminated in some way, because people don't like the nonnegotiable discomforts of conscience. So those who fight you must use ways, whatever the pretext, to prove you have no right to be in the moral center. 'You may be right, but reason you not in the moral center, you went to jail one time a long time ago, or you stole an examination when you were ten years old.' Mean, it's all a way of separating and isolating you from the moral center, by making you out to be less than honest, as immoral-like."

Another time he offered, "We don't just live by the law of nature, we also have ethical standards as human beings that are not in concert with nature. You can't just . . . nature may say, *An attractive woman! Grab her!*— but no, our code of ethics says, you can't do that. That you must," he specified with no apparent sense of wryness, "first establish an acquaintanceship. Or you're married," he thought to add, "and therefore you shouldn't." But the actuality is, he went on, "of course as human beings, we've all strayed from the moral center. That's why people name schools and roads after great people after they've died. Because the saintly status can be put in concrete then, when you *under* the concrete. But all of us have sinned and fallen short of the glory of God"—this was one of his fondest and most frequent scriptural invocations—"we *all* fall short of it. But the struggle! *The struggle*. Sometimes when I preach about these things," he later acknowledged on a flight over the Atlantic, "I sometimes convict my own self. Conscience. Will not sleep, will not go away, lingers, lingers. Conscience—'Mama, I bought you a fur coat for Christmas, I'm gonna buy you some earrings.' 'Yes, but how you gettin' along with your wife now?' Her instinct made her ask that question, she knows the pull of your soul. Sometimes, you know, your wife comes back at you, *And you call yourself a preacher?* Ain't no answerin' that, how you argue against that? *You call yourself a preacher?*" And he bent his brow prayerlike into a cupped hand, with a moan, "Oh, *maaann.*"

Nevertheless, while noting that "all men have missed, and your enemies try to use your misses as the basis to do their hitting," he could not refrain from the wistful plaint, "People want high ethical standards, and yet they don't want it if *they* got to be judged by it. People have a kind of double mind about that—mean, for human being–type politicians, there's a reasonable expectation as to their public service record, but it's so hypocritical to begin to use standards not called for by the Constitution, people's daily behavior." He happened to be delivering these ruminations at the time of the debate over the personal indiscretions of former senator John Tower after he was nominated for defense secretary, and Jackson had some reason to sympathize with Tower's duress. During one television panel discussion about Tower's alleged romantic roosterings, an eagerness to pounce elsewhere on that count was evidenced by a crack from the squintily choleric Pillsbury Doughboy of rightist polemics, Pat Buchanan: "What about Jesse Jackson?" But as Jackson saw it, "If John Tower had been in some compromising relationship with respect to national security, that's one issue. But when you start looking through every detail of his private past—that's imposing some *extra*." As to what attitude he would hope might be taken toward trespasses in his own past, Jackson proposed, "Just as they say in the gospel, that you would forgive as you'd expect to be forgiven. Because no one really has the moral authority *not* to forgive, because no one is free enough of sin to not forgive."

Besides, he then submitted, "when the Bible says Jesus went about doing good, didn't say *being* good. Said *doing* good."

ALL THIS PROBLEMATIC baggage from his rise over the past two decades Jackson, whether or not suspecting its hazards, hauled on with him into his presidential enterprise. But as it would develop, he was carrying a yet more profound vulnerability in his endeavor to move King's apostolic vision into the nation's highest political tournament for power.

In any case, after announcing his candidacy in Washington, Jackson flew back to Chicago. He had called Hermene Hartman the night before to tell her, she recounts, " 'It's different now, Hermene. It's different.' I said, 'What do you mean?' Talk to me. *Talk to me.*' He just said, 'It's different. Be ready.' "

His arrival back in Chicago was "a day I'll never forget in my whole life," says Hartman. "We were to receive him in a holding room at the airport before he proceeded out into the public. When Jesse came in, he reached out for me and I reached for him. But all these Secret Service guys now were around him, and one knocked me back with his elbow against the wall. I was stunned. He had hit me so hard, I started crying, tears coming down. Jesse came over, and I said, 'Jesse, what *is* this? He *hurt* me.' He said, 'Just sit over here and let's talk a second.' I tried to lock arms with him, but hit something hard with my elbow. I said, 'What do you have on?' Well, it was a vest shield. I thought, *Oh, my God.* He sat me down and said, 'That's what I was trying to tell you—it's different. It's another ball game now. I've got all these people around me now who are strangers. But I need you. You gotta help me. Don't leave me. Not now. I really need yawl now.' "

Despite that, says Hermene, "We all kind of started looking at Jesse Jackson as, he's not our Jesse anymore." There was a rally that night, after which everyone gathered as usual at Jackson's home. Only now a Secret Service trailer had been installed in the backyard. "Jackie and I were at the kitchen window, looking out at that trailer. And I can remember, we just hugged each other for a moment. There were no words. When we got ready to leave, about twenty of us, we were in the foyer and Jesse said, 'Let's hold hands.' We held hands, and we knelt and we prayed. But then we had to get up and leave. It was the Secret Service saying, 'All right, everybody move out now.' "

XIV
The Guerrilla Candidacy

EARLY THAT FALL, before announcing his candidacy, Jackson had performed the obligatory trip abroad, making a swing through Europe that went mostly unregarded by state figures there. One who did accord him a meeting, Queen Beatrix of the Netherlands, was left appalled when, after their private talk, he quoted her as regretting the deployment of additional American missiles on the Continent. More unpropitiously for the campaign ahead, before the tour was over Jackson and his party discovered they had exhausted all their traveling funds, and he was forced to phone one of his benefactors in Chicago, a car dealer, with a plea to cable enough money for them to get back to the States.

Jackson had proclaimed at one point that, as projected by Frank Watkins in his 1982 memo, some forty thousand black churches would be contributing $250 apiece for his presidential run, which would have meant an awesome $10 million treasury, surpassing the combined campaign capital of Walter Mondale and John Glenn. That never came to pass, not least owing to the irritated intervention of the conservative leader of the National Baptist Convention, the Reverend T. J. Jemison, who still entertained an old pre-King mistrust of employing churches in political action. Consequently, simply to get the campaign in motion, Jackson's staff had to send out an emergency solicitation letter to some two thousand names on a mailing list hastily scraped together by various supporters.

In about the same frenetic fashion, Jackson at last set forth. "It started out as four people in an office on M Street in Washington—that was our national headquarters," says one staffer in that campaign, Eric Easter. "Four people and one phone. A lot of it had to do with, How much can you do with nothing? We were so completely disorganized that when the press asked, 'What kind of campaign *is* this you're running?' we'd say, 'Well, this isn't a campaign, this is a *movement*.' That was our excuse." In effect, Jackson simply phased his voter-registration evangelism through the

South into a guerrilla foray into the Democratic presidential primaries, continuing to live mostly off the land as he went, his scanty financing coming principally from collections taken up in black churches along the way—"which was about the only thing that made that campaign even possible," says Richard Hatcher—while being transported from appearance to appearance in old church buses and sometimes the Cadillacs and Lincolns of local preachers and funeral parlor owners, and now and then availing himself of a ramshackle turboprop plane. For the most part, Jackson recounts, "I stayed in the homes of farmers and fruitpickers and people in the projects." Jackson initially had so little success in tempting anyone to even consider managing this campaign that he actually showed up once at Ken Bode's house to appeal to him; with some discomfort at the request, Bode declined, too. One who finally agreed was a black political broker in Ohio named Arnold Pinkney, and he would later recall that, when watching the campaign troupe tumbling into a Columbus motel well after midnight, he groaned to himself, "Oh, my God, what a mess."

Not unpredictably, the wider reaction to Jackson's undertaking was generally one of lightly amused incredulity. Jackson himself, for that matter, had long held, under all his bravado, a lurking uncertainty. Roger Wilkins remembers that "we were at a reception at some embassy here in Washington when he first came up to tell me he was going to run for president. I said, 'I agree with that.' But he kept on talking, kept on selling, until finally I said, 'Will you just shut up and listen? I said I'm for you, I'm going to work for you!' And he stared at me in absolute astonishment." Once it was actually under way, even his own enthusiasts seemed sometimes befuddled by the development. At one rally in a tiny church in East Texas, local supporters slipped up to a Jackson aide to complain that the Secret Service had obviously shuffled off on Jackson their lowest-grade, defective agents: "Look at 'em. They all wearing hearing aids." It became Hermene Hartman's lot, she says, "for about a week to try to acclimate the Secret Service to black folk. They were trying to keep all these people away, and I saw some old ladies grab them and say, 'Look, sonny. Who do you think you're talking to?'" The constant presence now of the Secret Service around Jackson occasioned more bumpiness than that. Several among them, says Easter, "had a problem with seeing so many black folks every day telling them what to do, while none of us had ever really personally dealt with the Secret Service before. I mean, there were actual fistfights between staff people and a couple of the Secret Service people on a couple of trips. For them, to live your whole life protecting presidents, and then you have to guard some black guy and spend your days in black churches, with poor black folks kind of shouting, it was just a complete shock to a lot of the Secret Service. And they to us. It *was* strange to be walking out of Jackson's hotel room and see Uzis leaning against the wall out there. And there was this feeling that they might as well be the FBI, that they were really there to listen to the Reverend's phone calls. There was just a real distrust of the government being that close. And if he got shot, it was probably going to be one of them."

For all the apparent implausibility of his campaign, though, Jackson had already begun operating outside the scan of general notice, or "under the screen," as he termed it: "What he'd do," says one assistant, "is, starting at six o'clock every morning, he'd conduct these phone interviews with black radio stations all over the country. Nobody understood that about the time they were waking up every morning, Jackson had already talked to twenty states on black radio call-ins and black radio networks and one-minute spots. He didn't have any money, but he's talking to them out there."

The general scripture-text for his candidacy was a call for "a new covenant" for a democratic renewal of the nation's power arrangements—a fuller, more authentically proportional representation of "all the elements in our rainbow coalition," blacks, Hispanics, women, in the governing of the country, in the Democratic party's leadership and candidates, in labor organizations, in "corporate America." But to a considerable extent, the agenda of specific issues developed more or less simultaneously with the course of the campaign itself, taking shape, as one commentator observed, "in existential motion from speech to speech," in a strategy that seemed to answer simply to the old movement impulse "to go where the spirit says go." It was, indeed, finally a campaign more of spirit, of symbol and allegory, than of program. Through those first several weeks, it seemed an exertion of little more than Jackson's audacity of imagination, the sheer flash and flair of his public presence. Few supposed it could ever count for much beyond that.

But some two months into this rambling makeshift enterprise, it was suddenly vivified by a lightning stroke of fortune—an unexpected, delayed return from Jackson's encounters with Yasser Arafat and Syria's president Assad during his passage through the Middle East in 1979.

The Damascus Intercession

THE UNITED STATES, that winter of 1983, still had a marine outpost in Beirut, and on December 4, two Navy AE-6 Intruder jets were shot down over Syrian positions in eastern Lebanon; the bombardier-navigator of one—Lieutenant Robert O. Goodman, Jr., who was black—was captured by the Syrians and taken to a military prison in Damascus. The Syrian government declared that he would be held there until the United States removed its marines from Beirut.

On December 19, at a conference of black ministers at a Holiday Inn in Memphis, with a snowstorm blowing outside, Jackson mulled aloud to a large gathering in his twelfth-floor suite, "You know, there's a black navy flier who's a prisoner of war over there in Syria, and the United States has forgotten him." In fact, it had been reported that special Mideast envoy Donald Rumsfeld had recently met twice with Syria's foreign secretary without once mentioning Goodman's name. Jackson had already sent a cable to Assad asking for Goodman's release as a humanitarian act during that Christmas season. Then, on Christmas Eve, back in Chicago, the Reverend Addie Wyatt was cooking the next day's dinner in her kitchen when the phone rang: "It was Jesse, and he said, 'I need yawl to come over here, I got a decision to make.' And I took off my apron, and my husband and I drove straight over to his house. He was lying up there in that bed, and we all talked and prayed together until late that night, and then we came back home. It must have been four in the morning when I finished up doing the cooking." Jackson's wife, Jackie, who was herself about to set out on a trip to Nicaragua with a women's peace group, remembers that after they awoke the next morning, Jackson—again, as he was sitting on the edge of the bed pulling on his socks—announced to her, "I'm gonna go get that boy."

He asked a former King aide, the Reverend Wyatt Tee Walker, pastor of Harlem's Canaan Baptist Church of Christ, to accompany him as his chief assistant, while advising him, "We don't, of course, know whether they'll actually turn him loose if we go over there." Walker, a thin, tensely wired, goateed man, told him, "If you knew that before you went, then they can send him parcel post, you don't need to go. I don't know whether you'll ever be a presidential candidate again, but you're always going to be an ordained preacher. You need to do what's right. And sometimes you just have to make a leap of faith."

On Christmas Day, Jackson proclaimed that he was flying to Damascus on a "rescue mission" to bring Goodman out of his Syrian jail. There followed an instant outcry from the Reagan administration and press critics that, out of his prima-donna ambitions, he was recklessly complicating U.S. foreign policy in a sensitive situation with a jackleg stunt that was blunderously headlong and naive. "But there were a lot of things I already *knew*," says Jackson, explaining his elaborate computations beforehand. "There was another one of those big gaps here. First, Reagan wasn't gonna say I couldn't go, he'd be too exposed to criticism himself, 'cause he had failed to get Goodman out. Same time, he couldn't very well lead any strong effort himself, 'cause he'd already said there'd been too much emphasis on the Iranian hostages. So he was paralyzed. All he was using his power for was to scheme without substance or strategy. In effect, Reagan's policy was just to leave Goodman there to rot. He wouldn't even return my calls before I left. Now on the other hand, the Syrians, they couldn't very well keep holding Goodman and have black Americans and Middle East peace activists attacking them on that basis. So had an impasse—a gap, a vacuum—and all it'd take was a leader stepping into it. And I'd called for a peace breakthrough between Israel and the Palestinians, for the U.S. and Syria to have better relations. So they had to see me in Damascus as not hostile to them, and my being there would make it difficult for them to fundamentally say no to me.

"But then," Jackson continues, "the navy called Goodman's parents and tried to undercut us. Told 'em, 'If you support Jesse Jackson's goin' over, you'll jeopardize your son's life.' Pentagon, administration, they couldn't get him out, so didn't want anybody else to, either. But Goodman's mother said, 'I trust Reverend Jackson.' Which was key. If she had been attacking me for not knowing what I was doing and endangering her son's life, we simply couldn't've gone. But she saw us off at the airport."

Jackson happened to go into this exposition years later by way of refuting still-prevalent suggestions that he proceeds, especially in the international extensions of his gospel populism, with bombastically simplistic moral romanticisms. "See, I know how to put the pieces together. I'm a quarterback, I can set up plays. Actually, I was serene about what I was doing. The pieces of the equation were still not complete, but at some point you have to take a leap of faith. Something journalists find hard to understand, 'cause they can't analyze it by their usual working terms. But my sense was, the gap was there, I had the moral authority, and if I could just *get* to Assad, I could make the case and get him offa dead center."

Jackson landed in Damascus on a clear desert night. With him was a rather populous retinue, many of whom had had to pay their own way: some nine staff members, about a dozen journalists, his two older sons, his personal doctor, a Secret Service contingent, and an ecumenical collection of clerics that included—felicitously, as it would turn out—Chicago's high minister of the Nation of Islam, Louis Farrakhan. Settled into the Sheraton-Damascus, Jackson proceeded through three days of preliminary discussions with various wary Syrian officials, who kept maintaining that releasing Goodman would seriously demoralize Syrian troops who had been the target of his bombing flights. Indeed, on the night of Jackson's arrival, a conclave of Syria's high military chiefs had determined that Goodman should remain imprisoned no matter what appeals Jackson made. The stiff and balky process of Jackson's exchanges with Syrian authorities was not a little eased, however, when Farrakhan opened several sessions by singing, in Arabic, prayers from the Koran. Jackson also visited a refugee camp of Syrians dislodged from the Golan Heights in the Six-Day War with Israel seventeen years before, and in his customary fashion he waded through shoals of children with swooping hugs, "Bless you, honey, *love* you, now," and then boomed out to the crowd packed around him in the dust and smoke, "You may have been born in a slum, but the slum wasn't born in you," leading them finally in his "I am somebody" responsive chorus.

On the afternoon of New Year's Eve, Jackson was allowed to take his doctor and a few journalists to visit Goodman in his cell in a military compound, where he gave him a letter from his mother, and when he asked if anyone had a Bible to leave with Goodman, the only one at hand was offered forth by none other than Farrakhan. That evening, Jackson and his troupe dropped by a reception at the residence of the U.S. ambassador, who had appeared markedly glum at their arrival at the Damascus airport and now had withdrawn to his bed with a politic case of the flu, leaving his wife to host the affair. Jackson shortly left to visit another holiday party under way nearby, held by the embassy's marine guard, which he soon turned into a prayer service.

But he had yet to see Assad himself. The next day, close to midnight, he met in his suite at the Sheraton with a leader of the PLO faction in Damascus, which subsequently urged the Syrian government to release Goodman to Jackson. At last, a little past noon of the following day, he was summoned to meet with Assad, and set out in a caravan of cars for the president's villa about a half hour north of Damascus.

Assad, when he appeared to greet Jackson, looked a trifle frail under his high bulbed forehead, but with a brisk cordiality he conducted Jackson and several of his staff into a study just off the patio. Jackson advised him that he was there not as a diplomat or lawyer but, in that immemorial sly opening feint of the southern style, "just a simple country preacher." Jackson would later relate to the others back at the hotel, "He told me he hoped we were going to have a successful meeting, and I told him, 'Presidents and pastors are very much alike—they have very few unsuccessful meetings,' and we did a lot of backslapping and hee-hawing like colored folks do." But Jackson then quickly swung into his appeal.

As he would later reconstruct it, "I told him, yes, it was a war situation, but even in war, there must be some attempt at redemption, some move toward trust. I didn't come here to argue the rightness or wrongness of American policy. I'm in Syria on a mission seeking mercy. What I'm asking is one brave act of mercy that can lower the temperature of tensions. *Somebody* has to break the cycle of pain and wrath. Somebody has to take the risk for peace." Jackson then made one of his acrobatic symbolic associations, between the illumination that struck Paul on the road to Damascus and "this great new light that can come again from Damascus two thousand years later. . . . Besides," Jackson went on, "what're your alternatives? The question is the worth of Goodman to you and what you call your military staff's pride, against the possible consequences of diplomatic estrangement and even military rescue efforts. You can't just keep him for war-bait like this." He finally managed to draw Assad off into in a corner, where he leaned over him in Lyndon Johnson's manner of exhortation by progressive personal envelopment ("You heard about the old half-Johnson and the full-Johnson," says Mark Steitz, "and exactly the same way with Jackson, you can measure the distance between his face and yours until the actual conversation becomes almost irrelevant"), and he pressed on, "You say you almost persuaded, but almost isn't enough. You *can't* let me go back home empty-handed. If I do, people will say the humanitarian approach just doesn't work with you. But I think it does. Return that boy to his family, and you'll leave a surprising good taste in the mouth of the American people." Assad indicated he would have to counsel with his staff, and Jackson told him, "I'll trust in that. If I had to pick just one lawyer in Syria to plead my case, Mr. President, it'd be you. From what I've heard, you can make a pretty compelling case, people usually have a way of coming around to your view of things."

In all, Jackson would afterward explain, with both governments immobilized in a gridlock of "horizontal" confrontation, "we made a vertical appeal—a moral appeal from God to man—to try breaking it open." For whatever may have been Assad's own more temporal calculations, he decided to turn Goodman over to Jackson—though notification did not come until the next morning, in a last meeting at the foreign secretary's office: "President Assad has asked me to inform you that on the basis of your moral appeal . . ." And with the finish of the interpreter's sentence, Jackson vaulted to his feet, stood blankly for an instant, then clutched the foreign secretary and bussed him lavishly on both cheeks, hugged a member of his party with such might it cracked three of his ribs, and then collected everyone in a circle of joined hands for a brief thanksgiving prayer.

Earlier that morning, Jackson still recounts deliciously, when he had been hurrying through the Sheraton lobby for the ride to the foreign secretary's office, he had noticed one television correspondent "standing down there saying his little piece to the camera about how it looked like we had failed." On the whole, Jackson says, "I'd had no way of knowing the kind of coverage the thing was receiving back home, no sense of that. All I knew was, I had never had this level of press around me before." But after the even sweeter gratification of flying back with Goodman in the Air Force VC-137 once assigned to Henry Kissinger, Jackson's elation swiftly evaporated on landing just before dawn at Washington's Andrews Air Force Base: "Never forget, after flying all that night across the water, comin' off that plane about five-thirty in the morning, still dark, cold as hell, and going into this building with the press, first big question a national journalist asks about it all is, 'Who paid the hotel bill?' That's right. Not how did you feel when the prison doors opened for Goodman, what'd you say to Assad, how did the dynamics go? Just, 'Who paid the hotel bill?' Mean, going over there and getting Goodman out of a Syrian jail, like the first, the most important, what the whole thing came down to for them was 'Who paid the hotel bill?' " (As it turned out, one of Jackson's private benefactors, a North Carolina businessman, did.)

In general, Jackson returned with Goodman to a fusillade of reproaches from the press. *The New York Times*, for one, in an editorial titled "Have Carpetbag, Will Travel," characterized the whole mission as "superfluous" and "contemptible," declaring, in what was becoming the increasingly familiar cynicism, "Mr. Jackson is a skillful self-promoter," who had embarked on "a shallow venture mainly because it is a chance to stir a lot of televised commotion." Altogether, it was a reaction that he would encounter again some six years later after traveling to Baghdad to seek the release of foreign nationals held captive by Saddam Hussein, and that would rankle forever after. One morning in 1989, after breakfast in a government guesthouse in Lagos, he was still fretting, "It all reminded me of when Jesus healed a blind man, and people came flockin' from everywhere, 'That the guy who can see now?' 'Yeah, that's him, that's the one.' But didn't ask the man, how does it feel to see light, to see colors? Instead went straight and asked Jesus, 'Lookahere, now, by what authority did you do this? And why'd you do it on Sunday, that's breakin' the law, outside policy. This whole thing ain't *regular*.' Meanwhile, blind man, he's headin' on down the road, he wadn't about to get in no debate about his sight— they might of voted him back in*to* blindness. He's way on down the road when they finally catch up with him. 'Blind man! What actually happened here?' 'Don't know what happened.' 'Why'd he do this on Sunday? Ain't legal.' 'Don't know nothing about that.' 'Well, why'd he *really* do this? What were Jesus' political motives?' 'Don't know that, either. Don't know what his politics are. Don't know nothing else, I ain't articulate, ain't no

public analyst or explainer. All I know is: as once I was blind, now I *see*!' "
And Jackson gave one of his deep belly-chuckles. " 'All I know, was blind,
now see.' Goodman, was captive, now free."

More specifically, there were strenuous complaints—also to be repeated
after his Baghdad journey—that he had simply lent himself to being used
to embarrass the U.S. government. One White House consultant remarked, "I don't think it takes a very sophisticated citizen to figure out that
it was kind of a free shot for the Syrians to try and embarrass Reagan." Jackson now reflects, "That was the naive factor again. But my feeling is, every
American patriot ought to want to be used for peace and freedom. Not
being used is to be useless, to have no role or purpose. Only issue is *mutual*
use, mutually beneficial. But all those journalists worrying about me acting naively . . . the biggest threat is not the appearance of naïveté in those
daring something creative, but the extent to which journalists themselves
will accept it when they given a left leg, like Reagan getting a question he
can't answer, don't have the faintest idea what it's about, and saying"—and
Jackson's voice bottoms into a heavy-toned mimic—" 'Well, some things
we can't tell yuh. Can't discuss that, it's classified.' Lettin' him get away
with that, I mean, complicity in allowing ignorance to be classified? Classified ignorance is a very dangerous business."

As it developed, Jackson says, his success in Damascus "set up a whole
wave of people trying to duplicate what we did" with the hostages in
Lebanon, a shadowy scramble of entrepreneurial diplomacy that "had a
success rate of zero, zero, zero. They did not realize the moral dynamics
that had to be involved. They wanted to reduce all what happened to luck.
You know, why couldn't *they* buy some of it? The government finally got
into the business itself, like McFarlane and North slippin' over to Iran,
what all led eventually to the whole Iran-contra thing." Jackson acknowledges he later ventured approaches in Beirut, sponsored by Ross Perot, on
behalf of the hostages there. "The government-to-government contact was
even more uncertain than with Syria, and with Iran it was actually more
hostile. So needed somebody who could be a bridge. We sent out messages
on the radio over there, TV public service tapes, took out ads in the newspapers and knew the captors were reading them. We were making pene-
trations, no question about it, we were beginning to get some response,
when all of a sudden, the doors just closed. I didn't quite understand
what'd happened at first. Then I learned they had what they thought was a
better contact—they had the White House directly, and were getting
money and arms. That totally foreclosed our humanitarian appeal. That
was the administration's chicanery, to discredit us using the humanitarian
argument and placing us in the position of intruding on government business. Their method was illegal and, of course, ultimately unproductive—

in fact disastrous. And in this instance, your own government could've well been the most dangerous force in the equation, to the extent they might've *actively* tried to intercept an effort. Least, you leave on that mission and something happens like with Terry Waite, government's not gonna do much to pull you out. That situation in Beirut, you'd be goin' into a fire without a hosepipe." Even so, in a later book about Oliver North, Ben Bradlee, Jr., reported that Jackson had exercised a crucial influence in the eventual release of hostage Jeremy Levin in 1986.

DESPITE THE DISCOMFORTS of press commentators and the administration over Jackson's extemporaneous intercession in Damascus, he and Goodman were accorded a reception by Reagan in the Rose Garden—Reagan dutifully genial, allowing, "You don't quarrel with success," and Jackson barely able to contain his exhilaration, at one point directing Reagan on where to stand before the banked cameras, and then, says one who was there, "he literally took the microphone from Reagan, who had not intended for him to say anything, took the microphone away from him and spoke."

On the whole, the coup he had pulled off in Damascus, Jackson relates, "changed things, man. Sho did." Alan Cranston's campaign manager conceded that Jackson's Damascus success "is going to be the equivalent in media attention to someone winning a big primary," and a Republican strategist agreed, not uncheerfully, that "right now Jesse Jackson is totally dominating his own party, and everybody has got to me-too Jesse and praise Jesse." All at once, he had relegated to bystanders, however momentarily, all seven of the other contenders for the nomination, including Mondale, while electrifying his potentially enormous constituency in black America. Jackie remembers that "the first I knew what had happened was, all of a sudden calls started bombarding into the house, some from people I hardly knew or hadn't heard from in years—'We got that boy out! We got that boy out!'" One Democratic savant told *The New York Times*, "He is now without question the most formidable black leader in America." Before long, says Eric Easter, "many of the folks flocking to the campaign were old movement folks. There was a sense that this was an opportunity to rekindle the movement. That whole twenty-year span between the late sixties and this campaign was kind of a lost period, you know. Folks who had become accountants or store owners or lawyers were finding this was a way to get back into that old sense of struggle, to get that energy of their young years again."

Though his campaign remained a mostly helter-skelter operation, it no longer seemed quite so quaint a fringe exercise; indeed, it now began to ramify wider than the capacity of its skimpy organization to keep up with it. One poll sounding in New Hampshire around mid-January discovered that, in a population only 1 percent black, Jackson was likely to attract up to 16 percent of the vote in the primary there in about a month—placing him third in the field of eight, just behind Mondale and John Glenn.

Already, a pronounced modulation of Jackson's personal style had been remarked upon by one of his high school teachers when Jackson returned once to Greenville: "There in the seventies, he was wearing those dashikis with his hair way out to here, you know, but then when he started running for president, he came by here to see me, and he was dressed in a real sharp dark-blue suit and a nice tie, blue shirt. I told him, 'Well, I'm glad to see you out of that black radical uniform now and back into a regular American man's uniform.' " (Some ten years later, Jim Brown, the former Cleveland fullback, happened to run into Jackson in the lobby of a Los Angeles hotel one morning, and chortled to him, "Man, you *still* in those suits and ties? You used to *never* wear those ties. When'd you start that?" and Jackson muttered, a little apologetically, " 'Bout ten years ago, but still ain't used to them, still feel too tight.")

And now, in somewhat the same way, with his campaign unexpectedly assuming a heavier national caliber after his Syrian exploit, it was noted, as one journalist phrased it, "Jackson is taking great pains to avoid shrillness and ultimatums." In his television debates with his seven competitors for the nomination—Mondale, Glenn, Hart, California senator Alan Cranston, Florida governor Reuben Askew, South Carolina senator Ernest Hollings, and George McGovern—Jackson was strikingly composed and knowledgeable, almost *presidential* in demeanor. The night before the first debate, in New Hampshire, he called his old mentor at A & T in Greensboro, Dr. Samuel Proctor, to ask, "Doc, what must I do?" and Proctor told him, "They're gonna be nitpickin', Jesse, they're gonna be playing with each other about small points. But you're not in this, you won't be there for that. You're there to call the attention of the American people to *big* matters. So every time they put the microphone in front of your mouth, you climb to the highest ground you can find . . . and stay there. Call people to great things. Don't fool around in little eddies and little shallow waters. Take them out into the *deep*. 'Cause you know how to do that. *Take 'em out into the deep*. . . ." Subsequently, when more than once the other candidates would pitch into blusterous tiffs, Jackson would serenely admonish them that a contestant for the presidency should comport himself "in a serious vein." The impression he began making in these debates may have been relative to anticipations from past characterizations, but he improbably emerged as an almost magisterial presence among the company of contenders.

In all this, though, while Jackson may have still considered his own presidential candidacy just a means to another, transpolitical end, he had in fact crossed over a subtle but significant threshold. From having acted principally up to now as an evangel to the nation's system of power, he had suddenly come to count seriously as a player in that system himself—and with that, became subject, wittingly or not, to scrutinies far more rigorous than any he had ever experienced before. The consequences were not long in ambushing him.

"Like an Atom Bomb in the Middle of Our Campaign"

ONLY THREE WEEKS after bringing off the sensation of Goodman's release, he was chatting with two black reporters in a cafeteria at Washington's National Airport about the New York primary ahead in April, when he shifted to a more confidential tone—"Let's talk black talk"—and in a casual patter about New York City's Jewish constituency, used the terms "Hymie" and "Hymie-town." Nineteen days passed before those references appeared, almost incidentally, thirty-seven paragraphs deep in an analytical piece by one of the reporters, Milton Coleman of *The Washington Post*. But when plucked forth for an incensed editorial a few days later, "it was like somebody dropped an atomic bomb right in the middle of our campaign," says Richard Hatcher. The compressions for that detonation had collected and been waiting, of course, ever since Jackson's 1979 jaunt through the Middle East and his photographed embrace of Arafat. His quoted asides now set loose a furor that rapidly engulfed his campaign, turning the happy effects of his Damascus feat inside out. The uproar seemed to leave him at first in a haze of pained bafflement. The word "Hymie" had long been in the sort of light and occasional colloquial usage in both the black and white South that *shvartzer* was commonly in the Jewish community, and was at any rate considerably more innocuous than any number of other slang epithets. At least, its mention by Jackson seemed clearly less a matter of malice than, as *Newsweek* observed, a thoughtless insensitivity. Ben Bradlee, editor of the *Post* at the time, accedes, "You know, having listened to politicians tell dirty jokes and listened to them call a fellow politician an asshole, and having gone bail for them anyway, 'What the fuck, I'm not going to—' I've often wondered if we should have put that in. I mean, it's haunted him a lot." But in interviews immediately afterward, Jackson, with his characteristic flinch when uncomfortably challenged of giving a little twist of his head as if to loosen his neck in his collar, bumblingly denied he had ever uttered the words, then claimed, "I have no recollection of it."

But what was particularly nightmarish for him, as he watched his grand movement into a presidential campaign apparently collapsing around him, was that it was happening on the most squalid moral count: his own purported racism. It became both a political and a personal misery. His wife, Jackie, would later recall with a still-radiant resentment, "My husband pined over this particular situation—it hurt him deeply. When he's misunderstood, it's painful for him. It was a bad joke, but are we to die for it?" Jackson convened a meeting of his PUSH staff in Chicago, and after citing to them King's line in his Washington March speech about judging men "on the content of their character," he asked them, "Tell me the truth, please, honestly: what do yawl think about the content of *my* character?"

At the same time, though, he began to brood that he had been blindsided—that because of a carelessly coarse utterance, he was subject now to something like an ongoing mass public mugging. "It was a stupid, dumb, wrong thing to say," says Roger Wilkins. "It was wrong to think. But people did come down on him awfully hard . . . and Jesse's a proud man, a stubborn man. I felt that he had to do something about it fast, say I'm sorry, it was a mistake, I was wrong. But he couldn't do it at first. He said, 'I'm not going to have anybody wrestle me to the ground on this.' And a lot of people around him were saying, 'Oh, no, don't let them tell you what to do.'" Most of his advisers, indeed, were exhorting him, as one of them relates, "No matter what you do, no matter how you reach out, they're gonna keep attacking you. *Fuck 'em.* It won't make any difference, 'Hymie-town' will just keep right on following you." Richard Hatcher argued that "if he made a public apology, it wouldn't be enough. There'd be a demand, now we want you to say this, now we want you to say that. I just saw no end to it."

Finally, though, over the protests of these supporters, none of them more spirited than Jackie's, he undertook to explain and to entreat forgiveness in a couple of appearances before Jewish gatherings. But even while he was waiting with aides in the small office of a synagogue in Manchester to address an assembly there, on a Sunday night just two days away from the New Hampshire primary, "the debate went on around him, and it was furious," recalls one in the room, Herb Daughtry. "He was at a desk writing, making notes on his speech, but when the arguing reached a high pitch just before he was supposed to go out, he looked up from his writing and said, 'Listen. It's the thing to do. My instincts tell me this is the thing to do, and I'm going to do it.'" The fracas had been so fierce, the female staffer typing the additions to his speech suddenly broke into tears. When she finished her typing Jackson yanked the sheet out and swept on out of the room.

Standing before the synagogue's congregation, he looked, to one journalist who was there, to be vaguely ill. Mentioning the circumstances in which he had made his comment, Jackson said, "However innocent and unintended, it was wrong. I deeply regret any pain I might have caused at any time. In private talks, we sometimes let our guard down and we become thoughtless. It was not in a spirit of meaness [but] an off-color remark having no bearing on religion or politics. . . . I categorically deny allegations that there is anything in my personal attitude or my public career, behavior, or record that lends itself to that interpretation. In fact, the record is the exact opposite."

After this public profession of remorse at last, Jackson and his party traveled through a snowstorm on up to the northern tip of New Hampshire, from which, early the next morning, they were to begin campaigning back down through the state. But first, says Daughtry, "my concern was to make calls to leadership across the country about his statement, so everybody would know what to expect." At five that next morning, however, he found that Jackson had stayed up through most of the night making those calls himself. They then set out on their tour down the length of the state, and "what shocked him," says Daughtry, "was that the first horde of the media we met, they started asking him, 'Well, Jesse, are you prepared to withdraw from the race now?' And they didn't let up—everywhere we stopped, all day long, the only question they'd raise was 'Hymie-town,' and are you ready to withdraw. And the reports that were coming back from Jewish leaders, they were not impressed. It really shook him. If ever there was a time in my experience that he came close to being disoriented, it was that time. He was beginning to bob and weave a bit—you know, how a person who has the utmost confidence in himself, when that confidence is shaken—and he told me later, 'My head was dancing all over the place, I didn't know if I was going to make it or not through that day.' That was probably the lowest I've ever seen him—the first time, and probably the only time, he'd ever expressed any real sincere self-doubt. Because he had misread it. Had misread this one, and it was a crucial one. People were still coming at him. He had gone out on a limb, and about ninety-seven percent of the people I knew felt that he shouldn't have apologized, but he had taken this leap—and for what? You know? For what?"

Richard Hatcher recalls, "The character of the campaign really did change after that. A lot of blacks who wanted to be very supportive of Jesse, it gave them pause, they were just not as enthusiastic as they'd been before. And of course, it did not end the attacks at all. They did, in fact, escalate—

well, he didn't apologize in the right way, he didn't say the right things, and we don't believe him anyway, we don't think he is really sorry. And it's continued to just go on and on and on ever since, really. He's never been able to free himself from it. It was his 'Chappaquiddick."

THE MELANCHOLY ASPECT of the whole affair, Jackson said, was that "something so small has become so large that it threatens the fabric of relations long in the making." A while later, he would assert, "Marriages aren't like that. You don't just find one 'gotcha' after twenty years and end it."

The truth was, Jackson over the past had engaged in periodic attempts to reconcile the discords developing in the traditional political alliance between blacks and Jews—tensions, as that relationship carried into the postmovement moral complexities of the seventies, over such matters as affirmative action, the drastic economic disparity between the two communities, the growing identification of many black militants with the Palestinian movement as another Third World liberation struggle. In 1974, he had called a conference of Jewish leaders, where he declared that blacks and Jews "share a common mandate" and were "necessary to each other," and urged that both "rise above the rhetoric of the past few years, which has too often been abrasive and tended to divide us, and share a common vision for social change in this country." (Some at that conference might have questioned why it was to them that his appeal was addressed.) But he had also, on occasion, committed himself to more personal extensions: he had once brought his family along with him to join Jewish demonstrators protesting a march by neo-Nazis in the mostly Jewish community of Skokie, Illinois. And in 1974, after the chairman of the Joint Chiefs of Staff, General George S. Brown, averred in an address at Duke University that Jews "own, you know, the banks in the country, the newspapers—just look at where Jewish money is," Jackson dispatched a letter of rebuke to him for that "canard": "As we all know, this kind of distortion of economic reality was widely used by Hitler's propaganda machine to produce Fascism . . . Given your position of authority, and the access you have to public media, to be careless in your public pronouncements is to be irresponsible . . . really to spread ignorance."

Yet there also seemed, in Jackson's turbulently mixed nature, something still clumsily and rudely callous, which disquieted not only many Jewish leaders but a number of others generally sympathetic to him. Revived now in the outrage over his "Hymie-town" remarks were memories, from Jackson's years as a freebooting social militant, of complaints about "Jewish slumlords" and "Jewish fight promoters," and his denunciation of Andrew Young's forced resignation from his U.N. ambassadorship, after Young's informal meeting with a PLO representative, as a "capitulation" to Jewish pressure. He had once termed Zionist nationalism "a poisonous weed," explaining, "Zionism is not a religion, it's a political philosophy. Judaism is built upon faith and forgiveness." He struck many observers as, at the very least, unsettlingly ambiguous in his sentiments. Privately, he could lapse into disconcertingly boorish moments. After a wholly innocuous incident at a dinner one evening in 1990, in which a Jewish member of his party had introduced a black member to a visitor by the wrong name, Jackson was riding in an elevator back up to his room when he abruptly offered, "You know, Jews can just be so insensitive sometimes and not even know it"—a remark whose own gratuitous insensitivity he seemed as oblivious of. Another time, while he was waiting in his hotel suite in Los Angeles to address a convocation of Jewish leaders, someone remarked that the Jews had long seemed to hold some extra richness of humanity that made them in all a special people, and Jackson barked, "No people are special. Irish not special. Jews not special. Japanese not special. *Everybody* is special. Trouble exactly comes from a people thinking they special. What happened in Germany—the chosen people came up against the master race. And the master race won that one, buddy, that was the horror of that special-people collision." (About that particular quip, a magazine editor in New York proposed, "What gets Jackson in trouble is, against what may be all its larger implications, he just can't resist a tripping phrase. His ebullience for the snappy epigram can be his undoing.")

But with far more energy Jackson would also assert, as he did once in an airport lobby disquisition on the unanswerable force of moral right, "Like the argument in '48, 'Jews need a state in Israel.' 'But, man, that'll cost a lot of money to support. And you gonna upset the Arabs, what about the Palestinians there?' 'Yeah, but people need a home. Have to work it out with the Arabs, something fair for the Palestinians. But thing is, Jews need a home. Been homeless two thousand years, suffered, been persecuted—they ought to have a *home*. 'Cause that's what's *right*.' Keep arguin' the moral right of a case, it becomes irresistible, it's the drops of water that break apart those ole rocks of adamancy." But he added, " 'Course, it's just as true now for the Palestinians, they got to have a homeland, too. If those two moral rights are not reconciled somehow, *nobody*, including Israel, is gonna be secure. I remember Martin telling me before he died, that was gonna be the next big new tension in the world, about the Palestinians."

At the same time, though, it had done little to dispel Jewish misgivings about Jackson that, on his stop in Israel in 1979, he was reported to have bustled through the Yad Vashem Holocaust memorial with a cursory impatience, and was quoted as telling the publisher of *Israel Today*, "It's about time American Jews stopped putting Americans on a guilt trip about the Holocaust." He reportedly went on to observe that Yad Vashem had given him a fuller appreciation of why Jews had "a persecution complex" that "almost invariably makes them overreact to their own suffering, because it was so great. The suffering was atrocious, but really not unique in history," noting that "sixty million blacks" had been exterminated over the four centuries of slavery in the Americas. It was almost as if to Jackson there were some running competition between blacks and Jews for primacy among the historically abused. In fact, he regularly elected to employ the long ordeal of blacks from slavery through segregation as "our one trump card," as he expounded one morning in 1989 while riding through the Armenian countryside, "the card that has no toppers. I mean, nobody has experienced *that* within our history—no ethnic group that migrated, whether because of war, famine, persecution, pestilence, can match that experience. Of course, the Jews argue that the Holocaust was not only tragic but unique—they argue *both*. But we've argued neither, we don't" —and he gave a thin little incredulous laugh—"we don't argue the tragedy *or* the uniqueness of our situation. But how can we sit at the table and not play our heaviest card?"

Finally, then, though his 1979 trip to the Middle East had largely been an endeavor to persuade Arafat to abandon terrorist violence and accept the reality of Israel so negotiations of some peace arrangement might begin at last, when he was photographed in Beirut affably embracing Arafat, it constituted for many of his already plentiful Jewish critics his conclusive outrage, and the image of that embrace was to hang ever after at the center of Jewish suspicions about him. Thus, if that sojourn eventually produced, in his negotiation of Goodman's release, the highest lift of his 1984 campaign, it now also unloaded heavily into its lowest moment. And all his explanations and apologies to mollify the fury about his "Hymie" comments availed him little. "There's an irony with 'Hymie,' " Nathan Perlmutter of the Anti-Defamation League declared afterward. "On the scale of insults, 'Hymie' isn't a yellow star pinned on your sleeve. [But] it's what opened up [the chance] for somebody like myself to be heard on a dimension of Jesse Jackson's character. He could light candles every Friday night, and grow side curls, and it still wouldn't matter. He's still a whore."

But of course, the scandal had unsettled not only Jews but many other citizens. And despite a poll projection back in January, shortly after his return from Syria with Goodman, that had Jackson making a 16 percent showing in the New Hampshire primary, he wound up, after his "Hymie-town" imbroglio, with only a little over 5 percent of the vote. Jackson himself continued to seem abstracted, morose, fitful of temper. "I remember him a couple of times coming in and blowing up at his staff," says Eric Easter, and for that matter, through that time "fights were breaking out, I mean literally fist-fights, among staffers in the campaign office." But the more embattled Jackson felt, the more testily defensive he seemed to become, which only had a way, in turn, of provoking a higher pitch of censure.

Nevertheless, it's not inconceivable that the tumult over his "Hymie" remarks might have receded in time, as did the commotion over Jimmy Carter's "ethnic purity" comment during the 1976 presidential race, if Jackson's deepening sense of desperate besiegement had not finally led him to take shelter in the eagerly vituperative defenses of the incendiary high messenger of the Nation of Islam, Louis Farrakhan.

Then, the Farrakhan Trap

WELL BEFORE FARRAKHAN had lent his facilitations to Jackson's sessions with the Syrians, a kind of informal accord had evolved between the two men in Chicago's black community, climaxed by an agreement worked out at Jackson's dining room table on Thanksgiving night of 1983. Farrakhan supplied bodyguards to Jackson from his black-suited Fruit of Islam stalwarts, up until Jackson was assigned Secret Service protection, and he would occasionally serve as introductory speaker at Jackson's appearances before black audiences. Then, when Jackson announced his presidential candidacy, Farrakhan, despite the Muslim doctrine of total separation from the nation's political order, registered to vote for the first time in his life, and urged his followers to do the same. Jackson, for his part, was much taken with how Farrakhan's Muslims, with their austere ethic of discipline and pride and their abjuration of drugs, were countering the depredations in the black community. For most blacks, in fact, says Eric Easter, "Farrakhan and the Muslims represented these folks knocking on your door and selling fish and bean pies, and standing very upright. There was a respect people had for them, that here were these guys who were much cleaner and much neater and much more moral than you. It was kind of looking at yourself in the mirror of what you should be." It occurred to Ken Bode during that time that "this guy's message was so close to what Jesse had been saying to his own people that it was going to be very hard for him to divorce himself from it, in spite of the attendant baggage of black nationalism that message carried."

But Farrakhan himself, with his flash-grin over his bow tie while delivering his viperish invective, had long been regarded as a malignant figure, not only by Jews, whose faith he termed a "gutter religion" while advertising his admiration for Hitler's leadership qualities, but by whites generally, whom he described as "dirty" and "a degenerate race." Some reporters who had covered him suggested that he may not have been, in actual quieter practice, quite the malevolent specter that his polemics indicated. Jackson, while insisting that "no man can tell a man who is hurting how to holler," once characterized Farrakhan as "naive"—with the implication that, like Malcolm X before him, he represented both a casualty of and a judgment on America's racist history, its own tormented creation, one of those unnerving figures who have periodically glared up before the eyes of white society as a kind of lurid reflection of its own long systematic dehumanizations, in that way that great crimes tend to leave an imprint of their viciousness in the nature of their victims.

But in his beleaguerment after his "Hymie" remarks, Jackson seemed to fall into a curious, passively acceptive thrall, a kind of compliant captivity, to Farrakhan's shrill defenses of him. At one Chicago assembly of Farrakhan's faithful, Jackson stood mutely beside him, listening solemnly as Farrakhan delivered a notice to all accusers, "If you harm this brother, I warn you in the name of Allah this will be the last one you harm." Unusually subdued, Jackson indicated no demurral from this pronouncement. A short while afterward, Farrakhan vowed to "make an example" of Milton Coleman, the black journalist who had first reported Jackson's remarks: "One day soon, we will punish you with death! . . . This is a fitting punishment for such dogs," adding that Coleman's wife in the bargain would "go to hell . . . the same punishment that's due that no-good, filthy traitor." Beset then by a storm of questions from journalists about Farrakhan's threats in his behalf, Jackson responded, "I discourage violence or intimidation or threats or the implication of it anywhere, anytime." But he still declined to denounce Farrakhan directly. Ben Bradlee admits, "I was upset, yeah. We had to hire a guard for Coleman. We didn't talk much for a while after that. It made him a lot more difficult friend to have."

In the end, Jackson's dogged reluctance to disconnect himself from Farrakhan probably compromised him even more devastatingly than his "Hymie" quips. For much of the Jewish community and many other observers, it seemed the climactic confirmation of a covert and unregenerate anti-Semitism in him, Farrakhan having made manifest and incarnate that dark inner disposition of Jackson's.

Jackson at length stirred himself to declare that, while he deplored the intemperance of Farrakhan's message, he would not allow himself to be harried into an outright condemnation of Farrakhan personally. "My whole life is about redemption," he insisted. "I can't change that now." He then proffered some analogies that could not have greatly charmed Farrakhan himself: in the past, he said, "I have reached out to George Wallace, even though some people got killed because of him. I've reached out to some of the lowest-down bastards you can imagine," and besides, "Jesus repudiated the politics of assassination, but he did not repudiate Judas. . . . I don't have the moral power to condemn a whore. The action, yes; the person, no." In the same way, in the early seventies, he had declined to join the general cry against the Black Panthers, whom he described as "the logical result of the white man's brutalization of blacks," even while he condemned their more violent tactics and Marxist-guerrilla dogma. As early as 1969, actually, he was maintaining, "Some of my brothers can't accept a nonviolent approach because it was the white man who shot Dr. King. But the common enemy is not the murderer, but murder; the answer is not to hate, but to end hate; and we must not resent the liar, but the lie itself."

In any event, Andrew Young, by now mayor of Atlanta, pointed out, "Jesse's campaigning is the first thing that has moved [Farrakhan] toward the mainstream of American politics. Jesse's reluctant to just dump him back." At the same time, though, Farrakhan had more than intimated that he was entertaining his own designs. He announced to one Chicago audience, "You're not ready for Farrakhan, so God gives you one that you like, that's closer to you. My job takes off where Jesse's leaves off. That's why he and I are together." The tempest resulting from that association, attests Bradlee, "put Farrakhan on the map. He wasn't much on my screen before that—I mean, he was like the guys in the red bow ties at Fourteenth and Pennsylvania selling *Muhammad Speaks*. But that sure put him on the screen all right." His industriousness in leaping vociferously to Jackson's defense did not go unremarked by some of Jackson's aides, like Eric Easter, who recalls one meeting in a room at the Howard Inn in Washington "in which Jesse and Farrakhan and some of their staffs were going to discuss this away from everyone. Farrakhan had some of his bodyguards standing around while this was going on. And it was quite contentious. We all came out of that meeting angry, it bothered a lot of us. We thought this was something Farrakhan was doing to kind of push himself. It seemed he had much more of an interest in advancing his name, and using the campaign as a step up for the Nation of Islam, than in rallying people to vote for Jesse. It became somewhat clear that it wasn't as much an innocent support of the Jackson campaign, and that the attention he was getting was not just originating in the press, but also Farrakhan's own attention to the press, calling press conferences where for the last twenty years he'd been relatively silent. And I think that was a big disappointment for Jesse, I think he was really surprised. And as it went on, the relationship got a little strange."

Jackson was still publicly asserting, "Black people are not gonna bury [Farrakhan] because white people overreact to him," but privately, says Easter, "I don't think he really knew how to deal with it." Richard Hatcher says, "How do you go to a person who himself is a leader of thousands of people, and say, 'I think you ought to stop what you're doing because it's hurting me'? He really agonized over the principle of that." In fact, Jackson's hesitation to repudiate Farrakhan was also owing to the circumstance that, behind Farrakhan, there happened to repose an immense population, extending well beyond his own Islamic fellowship, of the angry and alienated, whom Jackson hoped to embrace in his candidacy. Wyatt Tee Walker avers, "Most black people live just two steps this side of rage. They're mad as hell with white folks. And when Farrakhan comes to town, they plunk down twenty-five dollars to go hear him cuss Whitey." But Walker also felt that "it was sociological masturbation, didn't mean anything, and everybody would then go back to business as usual." Richard Hatcher contends, though, "Jesse saw Farrakhan as sort of this generation's Malcolm, someone who had the courage to speak out and who had a tremendous attraction for the black community. Even to this day, I can think of only one black leader who could call a meeting almost anywhere in the country, and ten, twenty, thirty thousand people would show up— and that's Farrakhan. Even Jesse couldn't do that. It's incredible. And those people are certainly not all Muslims." Jackson's unwillingness to anathematize Farrakhan was actually shared by many black ministers. "I cannot disown him, because he is a black brother," announced the Reverend T. J. Jemison, president of the National Baptist Convention, U.S.A., Inc.; and the head of the Congress of National Black Churches, African Methodist Episcopal bishop John Hurst Adams, declared, "Farrakhan is tapping deep feelings based on four hundred years of racism, and speaks for many more blacks than just his followers." Robert Borosage, a white Jackson adviser distressed by the woe that the connection was visiting on the campaign, admits, "I found out there was a totally different reality in the black community about Farrakhan from that in the liberal white community. Somebody told me, 'This is not as easy as everybody thinks. You have to understand that Farrakhan just gave the keynote address last week to the Organization of Black Political Leaders.' I said, 'What?'" Ken Bode, who was then NBC's principal political correspondent, covered a convention in Kansas City of the National Association of Black Mayors, where "Farrakhan had been invited to address one of their prayer breakfasts," he relates. "There were roughly 435 black mayors at that time, and probably 310 of them were

Baptist ministers—mayors of small to medium-sized southern towns, right? So Farrakhan comes and gives them this 'up by your own bootstraps' speech. And those black preacher-mayors were on their feet roaring for Farrakhan . . . just *roaring*." Yet most of white America remained wholly unsuspecting of that rapport, Bode goes on, and "NBC killed the piece, said it wasn't consistent with what their sources were telling them about Farrakhan. *Their sources.* The only black who was around the *Nightly News* operation was an intern, who told them that Louis Farrakhan was not a major factor among people she talked to. And who had asked her about that? A white Irish-Catholic woman. It was a scandal."

Jackson once offered, as to why he still would not renounce Farrakhan, "My purpose is to bring blacks into the system, not drive them away." But the tribulation now besetting him was like a punishing toll exacted by his dependence on the single, critical resource—mass black support—that had given him an entry into a presidential candidacy in the first place, and his reluctance to risk any possible disaffection among that constituency. And a cost, as well, of his old fixation, abiding from Greenville, of belonging most of all to his own people's experience, his passionate fidelity to that racial identification which had brought him their prodigious support. "If I give up my slave tradition," he later explained, "I have no integrity, I have no character. *White* people, let alone blacks, will not respect you any more than you respect yourself." Bert Lance reports that "we had conversations about that, where I'd say, look, there's going to be a certain cost to you in doing this, you could take another position that might get you two percent more of the white vote. But that it was very little to gain and a lot to lose, you know." Years later, when Andrew Young was defeated in his gubernatorial race in Georgia, Jackson attributed it to Young's inattentions to the black community to avoid offending white sensibilities: "Expansion's one thing, but crossover is cross-out. You lose both ways. You don't win respect by ignoring your own people." But how to keep the trust of his first constituency, without alienating the potentially larger one in that national and transracial coalition to which he aspired, has always been "exactly the dilemma," he confesses. And in that dilemma were intimations of the possibly fatal paradox in his greater ambition: what had made his pursuit of that ambition possible to begin with could also ensure its final failure. As one analyst pronounced after the Farrakhan affair, "Jackson has so far failed to transcend the politics of race: he is still identified primarily as a *black* candidate, not just a candidate. . . ."

Bert Lance now reflects, "Take a Bill Clinton or a Dukakis or Jimmy Carter, their best political interest and that of their core constituency primarily remain the same, so they don't have a lot of soul-searching they have to go through. Jesse's best interest, in the broader scope of things politically, and the best interest of his constituency, are often not the same. Sometimes totally opposite. But to his great credit, he has always come down on the side of his constituency—I don't think there's ever been anybody in politics who felt a stronger commitment to his constituency than Jesse has to his. Therefore, he's taken a different approach than the ordinary political figure. Where it was obvious that certain decisions wouldn't be to his best political interest, he'd still come down on the side of something that was unpopular with eighty percent of the American people but was totally popular with his own constituency. That's where he'll always show up, he's not going to leave his constituency, whatever the cost. And don't think he didn't understand the cost." To the extent that his faithfulness to that constituency has acted finally as a barrier to his passing into any larger national relevance, says Lance, "it is tragic. Because he *is* an extraordinary figure, really, in what he could do."

In time, though, Hatcher reports, Jackson "saw the damage that was being done to the campaign" by Farrakhan, "and there were a number of contacts between their emissaries, where essentially Farrakhan agreed not to be close to him or seen to be associated with him. The idea Jesse put to him was, I'm running for president and I'm serious, this is not just a gesture. And Farrakhan understood that."

Traveling for Absolution

THE OUTCRY, HOWEVER, did not appreciably relent, and as if simply to flee it, Jackson set off in the summer on a six-day expedition through Central America and then to Cuba, in pursuit of another feat of mediation that might repeat in some form the marvel he had pulled off in Syria, and so perhaps provide a deus ex machina stroke of deliverance out of the lasting torments of his "Hymie"-Farrakhan ordeal. He hopefully styled it "a moral offensive," proclaiming that "our Rainbow Coalition must function beyond conventional politics." Even so, with an entourage of sixty-three journalists and TV technicians, some thirty Secret Service agents, along with a dozen aides, it was an exercise of intercession in the region's Cold War conflicts, in the old spirit of the movement, that seemed an eccentric outing for a presidential candidate. In Panama City, he met in his Hilton suite for four hours with leaders of the guerrilla insurgency in El Salvador, then took their negotiation proposals to El Salvador, delivering them to Salvadoran president José Napoleón Duarte—all of this coming to little more than a kind of histrionic recycling of the intransigencies of both sides. But then, arriving in Cuba, he encountered in Fidel Castro a figure of not dissimilar size and energies and audacities as a folk tribune, and to all appearances, the two of them got along rousingly. They talked for more than eight hours altogether, and Fidel at last agreed to release forty-nine prisoners to Jackson—twenty-two Americans being held on drug charges and twenty-seven Cubans imprisoned for political activities. At the Havana airport just before his departure, Jackson was presented a long Cohiba cigar by Fidel, which he first tried to light from the wrong end until Fidel plucked it from his mouth, lighted the proper end, and returned it to Jackson, whereupon Jackson rolled it between his fingers and then chugged on it with an adolescent's exaggerated relish.

Jackson's success in Cuba was of an even larger measure, in a way, than his Syrian achievement, but the reaction turned out much the same. *New York Times* columnist James Reston chided, with his parched Presbyterian propriety, that Jackson was "interfering with the constitutional rights of the President and Congress to conduct foreign policy" and might be in "violation of the Logan Act," while Secretary of State George Shultz termed it all "disruptive" and "scandalous" and a mere "propaganda victory." But more desolating to Jackson, what he had accomplished in Havana was instantly lost in the continuing furor about Farrakhan. When he returned with the released prisoners to a mobbed terminal at Dulles International Airport—a setting, it was to prove years later when he returned from a similar mission to Iraq, never kind to him on such occasions—"the first questions he was asked," recounts Eric Easter, "were about Farrakhan. I remember standing next to Kenneth Walker, the ABC correspondent who had covered the trip for *Nightline,* and he was arguing on the phone with the *Nightline* producer, I mean just yelling, about how important the Cuban thing was, but all they wanted him to ask Jackson was about Farrakhan. I was amazed."

While Jackson was in Havana, reports had reached him of yet further utterances by Farrakhan, including his reference to Judaism as a "dirty religion." Actually, as Richard Hatcher reprises it now, "we were under the impression that he was making one speech after another saying these things, and I got a little angry—how could he do this, going out every night, it seemed, making another speech with more statements that were just creating all kinds of problems for us? Then we found out that these quotes were all part of one speech. They were simply coming out like time-release capsules, you know, a little this week, a little next week." Nevertheless, Jackson felt compelled to approve, from Havana, a statement produced by his office that at last denounced Farrakhan's fulminations as "reprehensible and morally indefensible."

But by that point, his long equivocation on Farrakhan left him seeming capable of an astonishing moral myopia and insensitivity, an impression from which he has never completely recovered. The whole "Hymie"-Farrakhan episode was to trail him through the following years as the great nemesis of his career.

XV
An Uncontainable Force

NEVERTHELESS, JACKSON MANAGED to brawl on through the primaries with a power of effect that startled all the given political wisdoms. For one thing, both black registration and actual voting continued to mount beyond any past measure, especially in the South. In eleven states there, black registration expanded from its 1982 level by nearly 30 percent, to 5.5 million—in nine of those states, double the number of new white voters. And throughout the primaries, the percentage of registered blacks voting actually exceeded that of whites, though, as some pointed out, this new surge of black voting activity aroused by Jackson was commonly countered by increases in white registration as well: in five southern states where some 400,000 new black voters had registered, it had stirred a rise of 1.2 million in white registration. For that reason, political analyst William Schneider of the American Enterprise Institute termed Jackson "a poisonous influence to the Democratic party. He turns an awful lot of whites off. . . ." He never drew more than 9 percent of the white vote in any primary. Still, the gap between black and white in eligible voters who were now registered had at least almost closed, at about 66 percent for both.

But finally most striking was how that expansion of the black electorate articulated into Jackson's showing in the primaries against the assumed nominee, Walter Mondale, and Gary Hart and the five other contenders. In Virginia and South Carolina, Jackson outpolled all of them, and finished second in five other southern states. At one point, recalls Ken Bode, when Jackson was addressing a rally in a Detroit church, "two very close Mondale people slipped in, thinking they'd be observed by the press paying a courtesy call and it would make a column in the papers. They were decent enough guys, and they thought that Mondale's civil rights record was strong, that black leaders would get as close as they could to the eventual nominee as soon as they could, like they always had. You know, 'Don't worry about this guy, the *real* black leaders will understand they're impor-

tant to us only if they get with us early.' Well, Jesse delivered one of his typical church-rally speeches—and they were absolutely blown away. They
told me, 'This is a hell of a lot more powerful than anything we'd anticipated.' "

In New York State, where Jackson held rallies in, at times, five churches
a day and then led the congregations in mass marches to nearby polling
places to register for the April primary, some 270,000 blacks voted, more
than ever before in the state, which, along with about a fourth of the Hispanic vote, gave him 26 percent of the statewide total, his strongest performance in any primary up to that point, and only one point behind the
second-place finisher, Hart. In New Jersey, he won 24 percent of the vote,
and in California 19 percent. In all, he carried forty-one congressional districts and seven major cities, and was to arrive at the convention in San
Francisco with 3.5 million votes, 21 percent of the total in the primaries
and caucuses, and with 384 delegates—a distant third behind Mondale
and Hart but astounding all the initial assumptions about the whimsicality
of his venture. At that stage, he was asked by one reporter, "You don't
really think you have a chance to be elected president, do you?" and Jackson retorted, "Well, there's at least five white guys now who think so."

Well before the convention, actually, a certain uneasiness had begun
eddying through the upper reaches of the Democratic party, and the Mondale campaign in particular, about the hobgoblin of Jackson's unforeseen
vitality, and that alarm shortly precipitated a series of delicately tense
meetings with Jackson and his staffers to explore the possibility now of
some operating accord. The tension in those encounters, as Vernon Jordan observed at the time, was precisely that Jackson's candidacy had,
amazingly, turned out to be "real. It is exciting, it is powerful, it is having
a lasting impact on the American political process. The best thing about it
is that it is a *fact*. The worst thing is the inability of white America to deal
with that kind of audacity." At the least, it confronted Mondale and the
party now with the utterly unaccustomed reality of an assertive black political force that could no longer be presumed to be a Democratic property
free of any real expense.

In his sessions with party officials, Jackson began introducing particular
demands—for a more democratic loosening of the procedures for fashion-
ing the party's platform; for an abolishment of runoff elections in state and
local primaries, which tended toward the total elimination of minority
candidates. But he insisted with special heat that admission of delegates to
the convention be more proportional to a candidate's popular vote in the
primaries. Under the party rules at the time, though he had won 24 percent of the vote in the New Jersey primary, he was allotted only eight, or a

little over 7 percent, of its 112 delegates. The party's general stipulation that a candidate had to win at least 20 percent of a primary or caucus vote to be accorded any delegates at all, with sparse graduations up from that, would mean that at the convention, despite his 21 percent of the primary vote total, the delegates allocated to him would amount to only about 11 percent of the total number.

"There was no question but that Jesse was right about that one," says Bert Lance. "The rules *had* been fixed so that the nominee in '84 had to be either Ted Kennedy or Fritz Mondale. They sat down and figured out how to make the results consistent with what they wanted." It was during this period of the party's gingerly negotiations with a suddenly unignorable Jackson that he happened to enter into his improbably close camaraderie with Lance, then Georgia's Democratic state chairman, a shambling heap of a figure with an amiable coonhound's face masking a vast country-boy cunning. "People got to calling us the odd couple of American politics," Lance recounts. "The first time I ever saw Jesse," he says, "I'm sort of like Maurice Chevalier, I remember it well. He'd come to do a rally in Savannah in '84. And when he started his 'I am somebody' thing, you could just feel the pride, hope, aspiration flowing from those people there: 'We never thought we'd even be able ever to be free, much less have here one of us who is now running for the presidency of the United States.' " (In the same way, the national Democratic chairman under Carter, John White, found himself surprisingly moved when "I was with Jesse early one morning to talk to him, and I saw the cleanup people in the building we entered, all of them black, actually cheer him when they saw him. I'd never seen anything like that before. It was like he represented to them a dream that they never thought any black could achieve.") Lance, who later served as Jimmy Carter's director of the Office of Management and Budget, had been obliged to leave Washington and return to his spacious country spread a few miles out of the small north-Georgia town of Calhoun after a congressional investigation into his somewhat informal practices as a banker there. He had subsequently come into such a warm personal concord with Jackson that, he says, "somebody once let him use a bus to take his family from a Rainbow convention in Memphis down to Hilton Head. One afternoon, I looked down at the bottom of the hill, and saw this Greyhound bus pulling up in front of the house. I knew I'd become sort of famous, but I couldn't remember tour buses having this much interest in Lance, so I went down to see what was going on. Jesse Jackson gets off and says, 'We're just in time for supper!' He had his grandmama and his mother and the whole family, along with a few other folks, in there." In 1984, Lance was a Mondale operative, but he nevertheless assembled thirteen other southern state party chairmen for a breakfast with Jackson to discuss the party's 20 percent primary-vote "threshold" rule for awarding delegates. "Now, these were all white males, understand, southerners," says Lance, "and Jesse was late as usual, about thirty minutes, and they were muttering, 'Why should we sit here waiting for this third-rate candidate?' But then Jesse comes in, and I introduce him around, and he addresses each of them by their first name. And he sits down and says, 'Look, let me tell you about the rules of the Democratic party. You remember the story of the blind man and the Pharisees and Jesus—?'" Jackson commenced to unscroll that story again, "and, man, got about as eloquent as you ever heard anybody. Here's a black man who'd been in the area of protest, saying things that probably most of that group didn't atall agree with. Told them, 'It was not only against the rules but against the law to heal somebody on the Sabbath. But Jesus didn't pay any attention to the rules, because they were unfair. He gave the blind man his sight back because that was the right thing to do. And you know the only person not bitchin' about the rules? Fella who got his sight back.' Then Jesse said, 'The Democratic committee are the Pharisees in this situation. The rules are wrong. They ought to be *changed*.' Well, I mean"—and Lance claps his hands—"people in that room who ordinarily would have been Jesse's biggest critics . . . standing ovation."

But it proved another case of his gospel politics coming up against the workings of a ruder actuality. At stake for Mondale, with Hart persevering up to the end of the race with his dry-ice burn of purpose, was a first-ballot victory at the convention, without which it could well break loose from him. And if the party had consented to Jackson's demand for a share of delegates closer to his portion of the primary vote—an additional four hundred, Jackson claimed—it would have dissolved Mondale's already uncertain margin, and almost certainly have thrown the convention into a free-for-all between the Hart and Mondale forces. But in his own private conferences with Jackson to arrive at some détente with him and the new electoral energy he represented, Mondale's exquisite dilemma was that, in whatever accommodations they reached, he felt he could not be perceived as beholden to Jackson in any important way, so politically gamy a figure did he still seem. This obsession was to recur with Dukakis and again, most grimly, with Bill Clinton. One Mondale adviser confided to a reporter, "We wouldn't mind a few fights over some of Jesse's more ridiculous notions, like supporting a PLO homeland. It would look like we weren't caving in just for the sake of getting black votes"—a ruse that, eight years later, Clinton was to perform with a robust implacability.

Bob Beckel, Mondale's campaign manager, in his own initial talks with Jackson, found him "an extremely big, imposing guy—that's one intimidating aspect of Jackson. The other thing is you probably get in one word for fifty of his. I'd sit down with him and say, 'Hello, Reverend,' and didn't speak my next word for forty minutes. He was still a preacher, and you needed to let him give his sermon, and if you try to interrupt that, you're not going to get anywhere, because he *is* going to finish. So you might as well sit back and listen." Beckel admits that "there were many times when I could have strangled him. His impatience, his lack of understanding of the other guy's situation, a sense he could never be wrong about anything. And it could take days or months to get a closure on something, and some- times you never did." Mondale himself was to later protest, "He wants you to keep offering things like a smorgasbord. He wants to test you and see what the outer limits are." But Beckel's principal frustration as a harried in- termediary between Jackson and the Mondale campaign was "trying to translate back Jacksonian speech and explain its importance without being seen as a sucker by a bunch of white guys who resented the hell out of him."

Lance, who was also acting as an arbiter, declares, "They never really understood him." Before Mondale's first concerted session with Jackson, recounts Lance, "Fritz called me in, with some of his other advisers sitting there, and asked me, 'What should I talk to Jesse about?' He had this legal pad, you know, and I said, 'Well, Fritz, first thing, you can put away that legal pad, 'cause you ain't gonna talk to him about anything; you're going to listen. If yawl think for a minute you're gonna go over point A, point B, point C, yawl just out of your minds. You've invited him, but this is gonna be Jesse's meeting. And the first thing he's gonna tell you about will be a grape and a raisin.' Mondale says, 'Grape and a raisin? What're you talking about?' I said, 'Just be prepared. First thing he's gonna say to you is that what you're doing to the Democratic party, you're taking a grape and squeezing all the juice out of it and turning it into a raisin, and you can't ever turn a raisin back into a grape. Now,' I said, 'is this gonna be a high- level political conversation or *not?*' . . . So when the two of them got through talking and came out for a press conference, I looked at Mondale, and he smiles and says, 'Got to give you credit. I now know just about all there is to know about grapes and raisins.' "

But in a more profound way, Mondale—though long a worthy liberal regular in the zesty Minnesota tradition of Hubert Humphrey, whose po- litical protégé he had been—still seemed uncomprehending of Jackson's candidacy as a political extension of the moral mission of the movement. "Just never had any understanding of him," says Lance, "except that he saw him as a major threat to his ability to get nominated." Beckel acknowl- edges, "Mondale was from the old school of politics. You sit down, 'Here's where you are, here's where I am, let's cut a deal.' But he said about Jackson, 'I don't understand this guy; I can't seem to get to him. All he ever does is preach to me.' Mondale'd always go back to, 'I've done everything for the civil rights movement, this, this, and this—' And he had. And he'd say, 'I could deal with Martin, I can deal with John Lewis. But Jesse, I just can't seem to get through.' Also, Mondale had spent years in the trenches, and he sort of saw Jackson as coming in and stealing the thunder, not having put that much time in it." Too, Jackson's dramatic public presence, says Beckel, "Mondale kind of resented, I think. Because Fritz had a very difficult time with television"—as one political consultant recalls it, "every time he looked in the television camera, it looked like he was staring into his tackle box." But on the whole, says Beckel, "Mondale took a great deal of pride in what he had done for the black community, and he didn't think that Jackson appreciated that." Mondale would later complain, "I recognized that he was the first significant black candidate for president, and I thought he had to be dealt with with dignity and respect, and I did. But that was not reciprocated."

In fact, Jackson had once grumped, "Mondale acts like he's got a Ph.D. in blackness," and during the primaries, he had declared, "They say I'm in Mondale's way. Without Mondale, I'd have won Georgia, South Carolina, and Alabama. I'd say that he's in *my* way." He also now carried into their discussions an old smolder of indignation about Mondale's endorsement of Mayor Daley's son Richard, an opponent of Harold Washington in the 1983 Chicago mayor's race. Most of all, though, Beckel recalls of their exchanges, "Jesse believed, going back to his '83 registration drive, that nobody appreciated how much he had done with that. I certainly did, because I saw the numbers—it was significant—and he had a legitimate case to be made. But the problem was, Jesse never understood how much he scared people in the white community, and in the Jewish community particularly."

But Jackson did detect, in the course of his encounters with Mondale, that this probable presidential nominee of the Democratic party was afraid of him, according to several who were there. Jackson once allowed, "I can look into a person's eyes and tell what he's really up to"—and Mondale's seemed unusually elusive, by some accounts, his speech hasty and scattered. Lance declares, "Jesse's very aware of people's reactions to him. Whether it's hate or love or fear or something in between those emotions, he knows. Like blacks instinctively and viscerally understand feelings toward them because of their circumstances in growing up in a mostly white America, Jesse can sense right off the bat whether you are condescending or respect him or are afraid of him. That's his great strength as a negotiator, actually." In Jackson's sessions now with Mondale, recounts

Lance, "Mondale's nose would go like a rabbit's nose, you know, every time Jesse got close. I mean, the fear was so thick you could slice it. Scared that any sort of agreement with Jesse, didn't matter whether it was right or wrong, would go against his core support. Scared of his ability to talk, of the *way* he talked. The way he carried himself. Scared of just about everything about him." Furthermore, when they emerged for a press conference after their first meeting, "you would have thought Jesse was the nominee, and Mondale was the fella who was just standing by. Jesse dominated the news conference. Of course, all the Mondale folks got terriby upset, they said, 'Jesse's taking control.'"

"He Had Arrived"

THE SKIRMISHING OF negotiation continued all the way to the convention in San Francisco, only by that point, says Beckel, "Jesse himself would hardly ever appear for the detailed discussions about when he was going to speak or what the platform language ought to be. He was a big-picture man now, there was no doubt about that." He had advanced far enough by that time to determine, as he apprised John White, "I don't want to be the guy who goes to the meetings. I want to be the guy who sends the people to the meetings." Even if the meetings were conducted mostly through emissaries, the row over Jackson's insistence he be apportioned more delegates to reflect his actual share of the popular vote, which would have mortally imperiled Mondale's still tenuous hold on a first-ballot victory, grew especially vehement. "He wanted that rule change because he was going to run again," says Beckel. "I never spent a nanosecond questioning that. He was running again, and so a lot of what he was doing was to position himself for 1988." The party at last agreed to lower, but not until after 1984, the "threshold" requirement for being allotted delegates, from 20 to 15 percent of primary or caucus votes. "But I also had terrible battles with people internally over whether he should get prime time to speak," says Beckel. "To me, it was inconceivable that it would be anything otherwise. But when we finalized the details of that in a scheduling meeting, a guy in the Mondale campaign got up and slammed his book down and said, 'I hope you're fucking happy, you've given this character the biggest audience he's ever had.' The guy starts to walk out of the room, and then turns around and says, 'And he better not fuck us!'"

Beckel now reflects wryly, "Some of the Clinton people have since said to me, 'Why did you guys give so much to Jackson? You shouldn't've got pushed around like that.' I told them, 'That's easy for you fellows to say. He didn't have a single delegate at your convention.' Also, they misunderstand that when you think you've got Jackson cornered, you don't win that way with him. You're dealing with someone who knows how to get out of corners and end run you better than you'd ever believe. And there was always the underriding fear that if he and his people got mad enough, you could have rump caucuses getting up and walking out. It was very delicate."

In fact, most of Jackson's other concerns—for the elimination of runoff elections, which would have ended the ensured domination of white majorities in primary outcomes, and for including in the platform a call for a one-fourth reduction in the military budget and a renunciation of any nuclear first strike—were all finally rejected, and it left Jackson's delegates infuriated. "There were people ready to go to war," says Herb Daughtry. "They were saying we ought to walk out of the convention. Had Jesse given the word, it would have been pandemonium, a revolution within the Democratic party." But once again, Jackson's inherently conservative inclinations swung in to deflect that possibility: "I have never walked out of a Democratic convention," he proclaimed. "I've always fought to get *in*." Even so, the party cadre around Mondale contemplated with trepidation what might be Jackson's humor in his impending address to the convention. "Before I gave that speech," Jackson recollects, "people were saying, 'When he gets up on that stage, when he gets that big of a platform, *my God*, he's liable to— We don't have any influence on him, he's unrestrained, what's gonna happen?' Waitin' for the monkey show, you know, 'Never know what he's gonna do.' " It was, of course, a continuation of Jackson's art for deploying simultaneous possibilities and uncertainties in a kind of dynamic suspension so that, up to the very last instant, they would not know what he'd be saying.

"While I knew he would be giving a magnificent speech," says Beckel, "I didn't know the content of it, didn't know what he'd say about Mondale, didn't know any of it. But I do remember I didn't particularly want to be on the floor while he was giving it." About two hours before Jackson was to speak to the convention, Beckel visited him in his suite at the Hyatt on Union Square, and from the balcony the two of them looked out over the steep slopes of San Francisco in the late-afternoon light, with fog already spilling like heavy smoke through the far hills across the bay. As Beckel relates it, "He said after a moment, 'Yeah, well, Beckel, tonight you're either gonna be a champ or a chump.' And I said, 'Well, Reverend, let it be a champ, will you, please? I know you're going to do well, but this is really important for all of us.' And he just looked at me with that sort of a smile that he has." Beckel says now, "I resented it a little bit. I could understand that he considered he got there by winning a lot of delegates, more than anybody had imagined he would. And he did do that. But I don't think he ever understood what I went through. I think he saw me as just a kind of staff guy that he could always use as a go-between. I remember when I walked out of there, I thought to myself, 'You know, I don't think this guy has ever once said thank you.' Though that was all right. That's Jesse."

But Beckel also recalls, with a livelier warmth, a ceremonial meeting on the eve of the convention of Mondale, Hart, and Jackson, convened by House Speaker Tip O'Neill, that was "sort of the final big-guys' summit meeting, you know, with the feeling, 'Okay, we've all worked it out, now let's get together and show some unity.' " It took place in a majestic penthouse suite at the Fairmont Hotel, "a just unbelievable suite," says Beckel, with vaulted ceilings and ornately tiled floors, its tall windows thrown open to the blue summer evening. "That meeting was a very important moment for Jackson," says Beckel. "He came in his motorcade, you know, the other two came in their motorcades." Hart and Mondale had already arrived and were standing together, their aides clustered along the walls around them, when Jackson entered the room with a powerful and lordly assurance. Actually, says Richard Hatcher, who had accompanied Jackson to the Fairmont, "there'd been a lot of negotiations regarding whether he should be in that meeting at all. There're two worlds in this country, and one almost does not have a clue as to what's going on in the other. For a lot of those in that room, it was probably their first realization: boy, this guy has really got something. It was like Columbus discovering America: he just happened to be a little behind everybody already there." At any rate, says Beckel, "people in that room who'd never dealt with Jackson directly, people in our campaign who had wanted to just roll over him and could never understand and kept screaming at me, 'Why do you keep coming back and trying to work something out with Jackson?' . . . when Jackson came in with that tremendous presence of his, I looked at those people, who'd only seen him on TV up to then, and I got a sense of vindication. Because they were looking at him in total awe. And they walked across the room kind of meekly to shake his hand. I could almost hear them saying in their minds, 'Jeez, now I understand what Beckel's had to deal with here.' And," says Beckel, "Jackson seemed to me to sense, at that particular moment when he walked in, that he had arrived. And he knew that people in that room sensed he had arrived. He has the best sense of theater of anybody I've ever come across in politics."

At the least, it was a moment fabulously far from his beginnings on Haynie Street. . . . He talked to Mondale and Hart with an easy, magisterial, courtly expansiveness. "Jackson can be very, very good, a very charming guy, when he wants to be," says Beckel, "and he considered that with

Hart and Mondale he was with his peers now. But he was smart enough to realize that Mondale kind of represented the old Democratic party, that he was the last of the old liberals and he wasn't going to win, and Jackson, in his view, stood to inherit a lot of what Mondale had. So Mondale wasn't going to be around, but Hart was. And he watched Hart very carefully, listened to him very intently. It's often hard to keep Jesse's attention, but when he does listen, he picks up everything like a vacuum cleaner. That's what he'd turn on Hart every time he spoke." In all, it seemed to Beckel that the occasion of these last three Democratic candidates of 1984 gathering in that suite at the Fairmont that evening "was a kind of changing of the guard in Jackson's mind."

Advent

AFTER NEW YORK governor Mario Cuomo had opened the convention with a lyric address of his own, Jackson took the podium on Tuesday evening, a darkly glimmering figure in the sun-bright blaze of the stage lights, with more people across the country now watching on television than at any point of the convention. "There is a proper season for everything," he began. "There is a time to sow and a time to reap. There is a time to compete and a time to cooperate. I ask for your vote on the first ballot as a vote for a new direction for this party. . . . But I will be proud to support the nominee of this convention." At this indication finally of the course Jackson would be taking that evening, the flush of relief among the party stewards collected offscreen was almost palpable. "We must turn to each other and not on each other, and choose higher ground," Jackson rolled on, in what quickly took on the steam and smack of a populist tent-revival sermon. "Our flag is red, white, and blue, but our nation is a rainbow— red, yellow, brown, black, and white, we are *awlll* precious in God's sight! . . . All of us count and all of us fit somewhere. We have proven that we can survive without each other, but we have not proven we can win and progress without each other. We must come together! . . . We are much too intelligent; much too bound by our Judeo-Christian heritage; much too victimized by racism, sexism, militarism, and anti-Semitism; much too threatened as historical scapegoats, to go on divided from one another. . . . We *must* come together!"

He soon had the hall aroar with successive, exploding ovations. "Throughout this campaign, I've tried to offer leadership to the Democratic party and the nation. If, in my high moments, I have done some good, offered some service, shed some light, healed some wounds, rekindled some hope, or stirred someone from apathy and indifference, or in any way along the way helped somebody, then this campaign has not been in vain." In obvious reference then to the "Hymie"-Farrakhan affair, he continued, "If, in my low moments, in word, deed, or attitude, through some error of temper, taste, or tone, I have caused anyone discomfort, created pain, or revived someone's fears, that was not my truest self."

It was another of those moments in which Jackson uncannily seemed to become suddenly bigger than himself—and it brought an answering expansion now of the spirit of his audience. One black delegate from Mississippi would later relate, "Gradually I'm realizing that white people around me are crying. I mean the men. I'm not talking about no lightweight little white girls. I'm talking about we're-going-to-fight-you-nigger-till-you're-gone white folks. They were sitting there in tears." One white woman in his state's delegation clutched his hand, he reported. "I mean, we don't touch each other," but "I'm standing there next to this white lady from Mississippi who's there in tears on my shoulder. I realized, 'My God, I'm part of something very important.'"

Jackson pealed on for some fifty minutes, as applause kept whelming over the hall. "When I see a missing door, that's the slummy side. Train some youth to become a carpenter, that's the sunny side. When I see the vulgar words and hieroglyphics of destitution on the walls, that's the slummy side. Train some youth to be a painter and artist, that's the sunny side. . . . Our time has come. Our faith, hope, and dreams have prevailed. Our time has come. Weeping has endured for nights, but joy cometh in the morning. Our time has come. No grave can hold our body down. Our time has come! No lie can live forever. Our time has come! We must leave the racial battleground and come to the economic common ground and the moral higher ground. America, our time has come! . . ." And at one point, he cried out, "I am not a perfect servant. I am a public servant doing my best against the odds. As I develop and serve, be patient. *God is not finished with me yet! . . .*"

IMMEDIATELY AFTER JACKSON'S address, Florida governor Bob Graham declared, "If you are a human being and weren't affected by what you just heard, you may be beyond redemption." Some commentators proposed that it may have been the greatest oration delivered at a presidential nominating convention since William Jennings Bryan's in 1896. What's more, subsequent tabulations found that, astonishingly, the television audience had kept increasing as Jackson spoke, ultimately reaching 33 million.

With that oration, he had passed through a kind of star-gate into an incomparably wider popular magnitude, had come into his apotheosis at last after all his feverish strivings through the years since King's death. In that respect at least, his stratagem of entering a presidential race to magnify the range for his movement ministry had actually worked.

Still, his speech had irked no small number of his supporters as, in an after-flare of their reaction to his address in the Manchester synagogue, "too conciliatory, too apologetic," says Herb Daughtry. Richard Hatcher considered it "to some degree motivated by a fantasy": incredibly, according to Hatcher, Jackson had already passed from his initial political purpose of a moral social evangelist into "the fantasy that somehow Mondale would select him as his vice presidential nominee. Which we all knew wasn't going to happen." Jackson professed gratification that Mondale at least selected a woman—Geraldine Ferraro. "But at that point," contends an old PUSH associate, Robert Starks, "he should have organized a solid force to regenerate the Democratic party, or formed his own independent party. For about two months there after the convention, you were ahead of the game, you could still set the agenda, and he could have put something together that could have made a great difference in this country." But because of his abiding wistfulness, despite everything, to come in from the outside, to be admitted into the party's inner pavilions of importance, "none of that happened," says Starks. "And the window of opportunity was lost as soon as Mondale was defeated. The impetus was gone. It allowed the Reagan-Bush people to take the momentum on issues, because you're now just reacting to somebody else's agenda. And it also allowed the Democratic party internally to adjust to this new thrust of leadership that Jesse had created, to reorganize and come back and cut him out. 'Eighty-four was a great missed opportunity."

Instead, Jackson, after meeting with Mondale at his Minnesota home in August, went on to campaign for the ticket, traveling more miles finally than either Mondale or Ferraro themselves. Mostly because of that, the huge rise in black voting activity that had accompanied his own candidacy in the primaries transferred on into the general election—in which more blacks, 10 million, cast ballots than in any previous presidential contest—and it exerted a telling impact as well on local elections. California's Willie Brown called Jackson "the Jackie Robinson of American politics," who was sure to "spawn a whole lot of Little Leaguers in many cities and counties that you and I will never hear about," and Jackson himself had promised, "My running will stimulate thousands to run, and millions to register. If you can get your share of legislators, mayors, sheriffs, school-board members, tax assessors, and dogcatchers, you can live with whoever is in the White House." He did largely catalyze the emergence of a substantial new black leadership community across the nation; the 1984 election producing the heaviest increase in black mayors in a single year since 1970.

Beyond that, as Jackson continued his voter-registration revivals into the 1986 interim elections, it came to be generally conceded that his efforts mainly accounted for the Democrats' regaining their majority in the Senate that year. What Alabama senator Howell Heflin termed all these "new votuhs" materializing out of Jackson's campaigns furnished the decisive margins in the elections of John Breaux in Louisiana, Wyche Fowler, Jr., in Georgia, Terry Sanford in North Carolina, Alan Cranston in California, and Richard Shelby in Alabama—all of whom drew only a minority of the white vote—and figured crucially as well in the elections of Barbara Mikulski in Maryland, Bob Graham in Florida, Tim Wirth in Colorado, and Tom Daschle in South Dakota. Despite that, Bob Beckel points out, the party's "white male establishment never did get it that the Senate came into Democratic hands only because of Jackson's voter-registration drives in the South, but I know that to be true." Even Lee Atwater, the mongoose-shrewd genie of electoral strategy for both the Reagan and Bush White House, acknowledged, "Jackson and his coalition gave the Senate back to the Democrats in 1986 and made possible a new liberal politics in the dying years of the Reagan administration." Among the results of that was the Senate's denial of a seat on the Supreme Court to the orthodox conservative ideologue nominated by Reagan, Robert Bork. As Jackson himself had formulated it, in what was a forecast of how the black vote could become the activating agent for the re-creation of a comprehensive liberal coalition that not only might reorder the country's politics but provide a far wider constituency for another presidential campaign in 1988, "If blacks vote in great numbers, progressive whites win. It is the only way progressive whites win. If blacks vote in great numbers, Hispanics win. When blacks, Hispanics, and progressive whites win, workers win, and women win."

But Jackson had already accumulated, with the sizable new black electorate he had built, impressive capital for the future. Along with that, says Richard Hatcher, "just the idea that you could have a black making a serious run for the presidency of the United States, to me that was absolutely thrilling. But the thing that excited me almost as much was that finally we were going to build a cadre of people in the black community who knew what running a presidential campaign was all about. We'd never had that before."

IN ANY EVENT, after Jackson's address to the San Francisco convention, Michigan congressman John Conyers, Jr., pronounced, "He is to blacks what JFK was to Catholics." When he appeared at black gatherings now, he would be introduced as *"our* president . . . this great prince of black America . . . the *mighty* Jesse Jackson!" In truth, to great masses in the black community, he had become something like America's black political Prometheus, to the degree that his voter-registration crusades and then his presidential candidacy had brought to them a liberating fire of pride and hope, a sensation of genuine power. He gave them a sense, as well, that they had an authentic tribune representing them in the high keeps of the nation's white custodial estate. Percy Sutton still likes to tell of "this old woman in Harlem who said, 'What you mean, Jesse Jackson can't win?' We be winnin' every time I see him on television 'batin' with them other people runnin' for president and lookin' good. Knowin' what he's talkin' 'bout, up there tellin' those white folks what is what, that be *winnin'.* And every time some colored boy or girl see him on TV and there is no basketball in his hands and he is runnin' for president, Jesse be winnin' and *we* be winnin'.' " After 1984, James Baldwin measured Jackson's gift to black America: "Nothing will ever again be what it was before. It changes the way the boy on the street and the boy on Death Row and his mother and his father and his sweetheart and his sister think about themselves. It indicates that one is not entirely at the mercy of the assumptions of this Republic, of what they have said you are, that this is not necessarily who and what you are. And no one will ever forget this moment, no matter what happens now."

There were some demurrals from this enthusiasm, misgivings that "his power is more personal than political," as one observer wrote in *Commonweal,* and that his force of personality had preempted any deeper impulse in the black community for true systemic change, that he was a kind of spectacular distraction. Former movement partisan and black scholar Julius Lester proposed that, though "not even King galvanized black America the way Jesse Jackson has," his constituency "has become obsessed by the politics of the messiah" and was not "committed to something other than one man." The peril in that, as James Wall of *The Christian Century* posited, was that "opponents can resist an entire cause by resisting him."

But of surpassing meaning now for Jackson himself, he was at last being hailed almost unanimously in the black community as the manifest successor to King. One black minister introduced him to a convocation in Flint, Michigan, with the cry, "Martin! The problem of the poor and hungry and homeless is still being addressed, Martin. There's a young man still doing those things you died for, Martin. Martin! . . . *Jesse* is still on the case!" And soon, his long estrangement from most in King's old circle, which had endured ever since Memphis, began finally to wane into a warming amity. At the San Francisco convention, when Andrew Young and Coretta King appeared before a black caucus, they were roundly hooted at by Jackson delegates for their resistance to Jackson's candidacy, until Jackson himself hurriedly arrived and, reproving the hecklers with the remembrance, "When I think about the roads I've walked with Andy, and the leadership of Mrs. King, her home bombed, her husband assassinated, her children raised by a widow," he insisted they be shown honor; everyone onstage then linked arms and sang "We Shall Overcome." Not long afterward, when Jackson was again in San Francisco and delivered one of his gospel-populist exhortations to an assembly of Democratic officials, a note was delivered to him in his hotel room from Young: "You make me proud and humble when I hear you speak. Martin would be proud, too. You have my full endorsement as the moral voice of our time." Jackson would still occasionally grumble about the remnants of King's company "down there in Atlanta, they think they're the center of the universe," but he derived immeasurable gratification from the signals of approval and acceptance now from King's old aides and from Coretta, their invitations to him to preside at ceremonies of remembrance for King, "as this thing's come full circle," he privately rejoiced, "from being rejected by all of them, you know." It was like the pronouncement of a final benediction when, one Sunday morning during his second campaign, after Jackson had delivered the sermon at King's Ebenezer Baptist Church in Atlanta, Coretta stood beside him during a commemoration service as he placed a wreath at King's tomb. Before the eighties were out, she would declare him "the conscience of America during this difficult decade." Jackson now proudly reports, "She calls me 'my son.' That's right. 'My son.'"

But even more widely did it seem that, with the San Francisco convention, he had come into his advent at last. Some of his most diligent press critics would acknowledge him to be, as one wrote, "a symbol who has . . . transformed American politics," and Norman Mailer would eventually propound that "the problem beneath other problems is that the gulf between blacks and whites has not begun to close," and while "Jesse Jackson is not perfect . . . [he] offers a cogent sense of sympathy for human suffering," and "speaks to our powerful passion for human promise and improvement," and "could illuminate our lives and give us dignity again as Americans. I want to believe in that. I am tired of living in the miasma of our indefinable and ongoing national shame." Finally, a generation that had never known King had now grown up glimpsing Jackson's recurrently reappearing figure on television, and the sensation of his convention address, like a clap of electricity flashing through that collective familiarity, had produced a kind of supernova burst delivering him into a national pop-mythic celebrity—"with the exception of Ronald Reagan and possibly Ted Kennedy," Roger Simon of the *Baltimore Sun* would later observe, "the only true political celebrity in America." He came to move now among a constellation of the miscellaneously famed: Hollywood luminaries, entertainers like Willie Nelson, sports-team owners, financiers like Donald Trump. Says Richard Hatcher, "You hung around him long enough, anybody that you ever wanted to meet, you were going to meet them." He eventually even showed up as host on *Saturday Night Live*.

A more arresting testimonial, though, to the singular public figure he had become was presented by a scenario running through several days early in 1985. As recounted by Herb Daughtry, who accompanied him through it all, it began with a huge antiapartheid rally one February afternoon in Central Park, Jackson, at the end of his address, announcing to the throng, "Now I'm going up to Sylvia's Restaurant and have me a big chicken dinner," in effect inviting the entire host to follow him up to the place, a classic soul-food emporium on Lenox Avenue in Harlem. When he climbed out of his car there, several derelicts slumped against a building front squalled out to him, "Hey, Jesse! Jesse, what's happenin', man?" and he squatted on the sidewalk for a lingering chat with them in the cold winter dusk—"just sittin' down and breakin' bread with folks on the street," says Daughtry, "people with wine bottles, some of 'em weaving from drugs." By now, the enormous crowd that had followed him from Central Park was so thickly collected around Sylvia's, "we could barely get in," says Daughtry, and while Jackson sat making his way through his chicken dinner, "everybody gathers around him, all kinds of people from all over the country." From that chaotically mobbed dinner Jackson rode to JFK and took an overnight flight to Rome to meet with the pope. Arriving at the Vatican the next day, proceeding past Swiss Guards to a reception chamber, "we were told the pope would be meeting with us for only about fifteen minutes, I think it was," says Daughtry. They were presently conducted into Pope John Paul's office, where Jackson, "in his way of being totally not awed by anybody," says Daughtry, seated himself "very close beside the pope. And Jesse began to urge the pope, politely but with his persuasive intenseness, that it would be helpful if the pope would be more outspoken on the antiapartheid question. The pope said something like, 'We have been addressing that question,' but he seemed kind of reserved, quiet, almost like withdrawn into a shell. So Jackson kept pushing him for a more vigorous position from the Vatican—might say, kind of gently *teaching* him. And this is *the pope*! It was incredible. Whatever time we had been allotted, we went *way* over it, man, about double." From this session with John Paul at the Vatican, Jackson went on to pay a call on Italy's prime minister—"the same attitude and manner of, I'm here because I'm supposed to be here, this is what I'm supposed to be doing"—and from there, he flew to London to meet with the archbishop of Canterbury. Before boarding that flight, though, Jackson made phone calls and tarried so long to talk with passing travelers who recognized him, that the Pan Am attendant assigned to them, says Daughtry, "began turning sweaty and red in the face, finally coming to me and pleading, 'Can't you get him to move?' I said, 'Look, you might as well calm down, because there's absolutely nothing you can do that's gonna make him move until he wants to.' Jesse, you know, he always moves in his *own* time."

The plane had to be held several minutes, and when they were finally settled aboard, says Daughtry, "he started taking his nap. Then all of a sudden he jumped up, said, 'Where's my pencil, where's my paper?' and he started making notes for the meeting with the archbishop of Canterbury." From London they flew to Canterbury, where Jackson held an extended palaver with the archbishop. On the flight back to London, their small plane hit a buffeting snowstorm, "and the pilot wasn't sure whether he shouldn't go back to Canterbury, but when he radioed them, the airport there was closed. So he said, 'Well, guess we'll see if we can make it to London.' " The plane reeled on through the blizzard, and managed to make the landing in London. Where, says Daughtry, "we stayed a little longer than anticipated," while Jackson pitched into a series of secret negotiations with Iranian officials and several Arab representatives in various hotel rooms and other obscure locations, appealing for the release of the American hostages held in Beirut. "He was at it day and night," says Daughtry, "trying to work through that thing. It wasn't successful, but man, did he try. Finally, we flew on back to Washington.

"But what I'm saying is," concludes Daughtry, "I can't think of anybody else in the world who could do all that, all in a straight streak of about four days. . . ." In a way, it was as if the reminiscence of his old neighbor in Greenville, Barbara Mitchell—"I'd look out the window around suppertime, and see him coming down the street by himself, just good ole little Jesse swinging along the street in the dark, happy, master of his kingdom, prince of the neighborhood"—had all these years later come to describe his buoyant amblings about the whole world.

Two weeks after landing back in the United States from that quick circuit about Europe, Jackson was leading a demonstration by steelworkers in Pittsburgh protesting the dismantling of a steel mill; then a demonstration by 1,000 farmers in Plattsburg, Missouri, protesting the foreclosure on a seventy-three-year-old man's farm; then toward the end of that year, he was leading an antiapartheid march of 100,000 people in London; and then, at a superpower summit in Geneva, accosting Soviet leader Mikhail Gorbachev about the tribulations still imposed on Soviet Jews.

The Faustian Temptation

THAT PERIOD FOLLOWING the San Francisco convention was the spring of Jackson's political fortunes. But in retrospect, it appears a kind of illusionary spring he had entered into, an increasingly eager absorption in the unanticipated flourishing of what was originally to be only a means to a more exalted mission. During his early days at PUSH, some had already spied a certain elemental contradiction in Jackson's readiness, out of his old outsider's urge to belong, to use the system of power itself as the medium for his realization as a social prophet. Chicago's veteran militant Robert Lucas submits, "You know, I lived through the civil rights movement, and what I'm going to say here may be cutting down on the people who'll be attending my funeral. Nor is it easy for me to be saying this—I mean, Jesse certainly cares and is eloquent, he's brought tears to my own eyes with his speaking. But I think the reason Jesse has never achieved real greatness . . . I think what was missing . . . was courage. It's been his reluctance to really confront the system in any fundamental way. I think he felt that he could achieve greatness if the Democratic party had to negotiate with him as the spokesman in the country for the black community. But that need to be accepted and to work within the system, that's why I feel he has missed real greatness, I really do."

In fact, it had all along seemed that the tensions of Jackson's position as an outsider had essentially energized his rise, had most defined him, and undertaking now to enter the system in this large way could mean losing that distinctive power and meaning, and, in that sense, losing himself. Jackson himself stoutly contended, "Yes, you end up with a kind of hybrid, conventional politics plus movement, and that *is* a difference. But what I've done, in addition to that background in the moral struggles of the movement, is gone on to the stage where the mass media has to come to grips with that moral vision within the context of conventional politics—and then with that, to get actual *votes*, man!" He would even come to enthuse to reporters, "There's been nothing like this in history! This has been the greatest social movement ever. It's gone beyond King. King tried to plow the ground, but the ground was too hard. But this is the direction he was heading." Nevertheless, according to one of his pastoral counselors, Dr. William Howard, "Jesse Jackson privately wrestles with the two roles constantly. He will often say that Martin never ran for president, but he had an impact on presidents." When asked himself if King would ever have carried his apostleship for social redemption into any actual competitions for offices of authority, Jackson said, "Well, whether or not he would have formally turned support for his mission into a political bloc, I don't know. But he, in *effect*, did that, in how he impinged on the political life of the nation." In going about that, Jackson added, "Dr. King was tactician enough to move in ways that kept his base covered while pushing the system back, opening it wider."

But the difference was that Jackson was endeavoring to transfer his base *into* the system. And the initial success of that gambit, surprising even Jackson, disclosed to him the bewitching possibility of accomplishing his own apostolic fulfillment, unlike King, inside rather than outside America's system of rule—and so, at the same time, belonging in a dizzily fuller measure than he'd ever imagined, even if it should wind up only a vice presidential nomination. Thus, in contrast to King, who always seemed wary about being captured in the baser traffics of power, Jackson became progressively beguiled by—instead of acting simply as a prophet to power—becoming a player in it. The result, contends Larry Shaw, has been that "while he was ahead of his time, it's stunted him. The role of president is not big enough for what he could be. All of politics narrows him."

It's impossible to determine exactly at what point, and to what extent, Jackson made the crossing in his spirit from pure social evangelism into this political appetite—likely Jackson himself is still not certain where he floats between the two. But he admits he has long been caught in an "inner-outer struggle," as he describes it, "between condition and position. It's spirit against flesh. It's moral authority over against just having power. And you can't let that outer win. Since my birth, seems, it's always been an effort to keep running away from superficial pleasures unto death." He once mused of a young black activist with a promise apparently not unlike his own as a youth, "His image of authority and respect are ministers as social leaders like Adam Clayton Powell, Dr. King, like myself—he wants that flair and command. But you got to have some meat beneath that gravy, that flair and command is just the part that people see, and it can become dangerous in itself. Of all the gifts that a prodigy can have, the most dangerous are the most powerful gifts. The gifts of tongue—you can talk your way out of anything, or into anything and then back out of it, because the gift has that kind of power. And like an extremely gifted young singer, for instance, there's so much power in singing, it attracts exploiters and crowds, all these people screaming, coming after you wanting some attention, some sex, some money, some glory . . . they want some of all that comes from your gift." In the same way, he said, "it's very difficult now to be in the traditional political scene where people always wantin' these unholy trade-offs."

But more than that, the enthrallments of political fame and consequence—"You speak, it's in all the papers; you act, it's on national TV; you move, thousands jump"—were the siren musics he had to battle against, he claimed. John White relates, "I was to introduce him once as the keynote speaker at a Democratic convention in Texas. He was supposed to speak at eight o'clock that night, and everybody was there—few liberals from Austin, but most were courthouse operators from East Texas and West Texas. Nine o'clock, Jesse was still in his hotel room, and everybody was tired of waiting, getting mad as hell. I called him and told him if he wasn't there right away, I was leaving. He just barely got there in time for me to introduce him. And he started out. And I want to tell you, within less than ten minutes he had those ole West Texas and East Texas boys—and these were *not* Jesse's people—had them standing on their chairs, waving their straw hats and cheering. I'd seen some of the best political speakers in this country, Hubert Humphrey, Everett Dirksen, but I've never seen anybody take a basically hostile crowd like that and get the cheers that he got . . . it was phenomenal. I told him afterward, backstage in a corner, 'Listen, you've got a gift that very few people have in this world. You take care of it.' And he says, 'Brother, I understand what you're saying.'"

Jackson now offers, "Dr. King, you know, struggled hard, with all the headiness, to stay unpretentious. And it is *such* a struggle, striving to stay what my mama would call 'humble in thy service.' It's Jesus saying, 'He who would follow me must first deny himself.' Gandhi talked about denial. Leaders must constantly go through an inner purification. Because look how many leaders been brought down by the old classic temptations of the spirit—greed, sex, power, egomania. It's what the guy talks about in that song, praying to God to help him not become drunk with the wine of this world. But you must know it will always be a struggle. *Constant* war inside you against your baser nature."

Despite such earnest professions, though, it is also one of Jackson's many dualities of nature that, like a kind of ritual calisthenic of inverted tension, he seems always to be supplying himself the worldly lures for that never-ending struggle. "When someone asked me if he was going to run for president the second time," says Calvin Morris, "I said, '*Of course* he's going to run.' They said, 'Why? Can't win.' I said, 'He doesn't have to win. For a person like Jesse, being in the kind of situation where you have people, all three networks, continuously covering you—your every step, your every moment, somebody has got a camera on you—that is as close to heaven as you ever want to be.'" And well before his 1984 primary campaign had ended, he had arrived at the exuberant recognition that, along with all the material mannas from that natural contract of service, "service makes *power* . . . service *is* power. In the order of nature, the only protection against elimination is to remain necessary, and those who offer the most vital services are gonna be rewarded in the social and political order. That's why Jesus said, 'He who would be greatest among you must be a servant.' If you a servant, people will pay you homage. Other hand, arrogance and pretentiousness is exactly the way *not* to get power, and if you get it, the way to lose it real quick. But when you serve with authenticity, the power is even stronger than officials of government. Service! Homeboy, it really does *work*. We do not seek to be powerful, we seek to be good—because if we are good, we'll be powerful enough. Power—you realize that service is the way *to* it. It's the keys to the kingdom!"

XVI
A Campaign of Democratic Poetries

MONTHS BEFORE THE 1988 presidential campaign began stirring to life, polls were indicating that Jackson had already become, at least in popular regard, a leading prospect for the nomination. By the spring of 1987, a sounding by *The New York Times* found him placing first, six points ahead of Massachusetts governor Michael Dukakis, among a field of eight possible Democratic candidates, and he mostly held that front position in national polls running on into December, when the final cast of candidates had taken form—besides Jackson and Dukakis, Missouri congressman Richard Gephardt, former Arizona governor Bruce Babbitt, and Senators Albert Gore, Jr., of Tennessee and Paul Simon of Illinois. One party notable conceded, "Contrary to the old adage that a soufflé doesn't rise twice, Jesse has the potential to be a bigger factor in '88 than in '84." More than that, promised a past political director of the party, Ann Lewis, who was now a close Jackson adviser: " 'Eighty-four was a crusade. This is a *real* campaign."

Actually, Jackson had never really paused after the 1984 convention, still swarming through twenty-hour days, often returning with his aides to his hotel well after midnight to find, arrayed in his suite by local church-women, a spread of dishes like an indoor dinner-on-the-grounds: fried chicken, collard greens, potato salad, peach pie, lemonade. But unlike his 1984 folk crusade, when a rickety turboprop had intermittently lugged him from locale to locale, he was now equipped with a DC-9. His organization, too, had become notably more cosmopolitan and professional. Besides Ann Lewis, he was directly attended now by Bert Lance: "I told everybody, look, I'm for Jesse—he's got a contribution to make to the Democratic party, and you'd better keep him positive, 'cause he can create enough mischief." Among others with whom he had come to frequently commune was Manhattan's high curate of financial polity, Felix Rohatyn.

It was also then that Mark Steitz had come to him, out of the tabloid flameout of Gary Hart's candidacy in May of 1987; as deputy policy director and senior economist to Hart, Steitz had constructed for him an alternative federal budget, and fearing that Dukakis, with his technocrat's heatless calibrations, might turn out the nominee with Hart gone, "it occurred to me one morning, while I was floating in the pool at my apartment in Denver, to give the budget to Jackson. It was just sort of whimsy." Steitz confesses that, at that point, "I still had all the disrespect for Jackson that anybody who gets their opinions of him out of a newspaper has—flamboyant, shallow, unfocused, self-centered, kind of a burlesque figure. I didn't really want to work for him because I was afraid my reputation would be hurt." But he sent the budget to Jackson nonetheless, and "I get a call the next day. 'Hello. This's Jesse Jackson.' I can barely understand a word he's saying, except, 'Can you fly to Chicago tomorrow? Let's talk, this is interesting.' So I fly to Chicago, go to his house. Totally discombobulating. People are walking in and out, sort of peering at me, telephones ringing everywhere, and I'm sitting there in the living room waiting, and waiting, and waiting. Finally Jackie walks in. 'Oh! Who are you? What do you do?' I say, 'Well, actually, I'm unemployed at the moment.' She throws herself into a big overstuffed chair and says, 'Oh, shit. I so hoped you were some rich young white boy here to bail us out.' " Jackson himself at last strolled in, casually dressed, says Steitz, "and we sit and talk for a while. Then right in the middle of the conversation, he said, 'Hold that thought, put a pin in it, I'll be back in a second—' and vanishes. Comes back a moment later in a suit and tie, says, 'You're coming with me to the airport.' " At the airport then, says Steitz, "walking through Midway, watching people react to him was just astounding to me. I'd had no idea from the press of just the emotional . . . I mean, people coming up to him, these toughs who would ordinarily frighten anybody, you know, but almost whispering, *Reverend Jackson! Reverend Jackson!* I fly back to Denver like in a daze: what is this going on?"

The mathematics of his prospects remained daunting. Some surveys showed that 23 percent of the white electorate was still intransigently adverse to any presidential candidate who was black, which meant that Jackson would have to draw over 60 percent of the rest of the white vote to even stand a chance of gaining a majority in the general election. As for the Democratic primaries themselves, despite the lowering of the party's vote-percentage requirements for being accorded delegates that Jackson had won in 1984, forecasts of the number of delegates he could still expect to bring to the convention in Atlanta ranged not much beyond seven hundred.

Nevertheless, his support in the black community had become well-nigh monolithic. Most of those black leaders who had been queasy about his 1984 adventure now found themselves compelled to gather behind him. "It was like moths to the light," says Richard Hatcher, who was vice-chairman of the 1988 campaign. "People were coming out of the woodwork: 'I'm willing to work for you, you're gonna need some real professional help for this campaign.' "

But from this formidable black base, Jackson undertook to fashion a wider constituency reaching across the whole span of American society— farmers, white union members, women's rights advocates, Hispanics, students, environmentalists: a true, omnibus, populist mass coalition. For years, Jackson contended, the standing Democratic proprietorship, intimidated by defeats running from Nixon's politics of the Silent Majority to the neo-McKinley homiletics of Ronald Reagan, had been occupied in a labor to blandish back into the party some lost Main Street America by simply offering a modified version of the same political mentality. But, Jackson maintained, recent presidential-election outcomes had been configured and defined simply by the character of the choices finally presented to the American populace. And reconstituting the party now in the image of his proposed new populist coalition could revive it much in the way that the Republican party managed to regenerate itself only when, beginning with Goldwater, it proceeded to shift from merely a more circumspect reflection of the Democrats' Rooseveltian liberalism to a distinctive conservative alternative: it would be, for the Democrats, a liberal turn on the old Goldwater battle cry, "A choice, not an echo." He insisted, "Don't nobody get moved by any milder, modified version of anything. People rather have fire in their face than just warm spit down their back. If people have to choose between the authentic and an imitation, they'll choose the authentic every time."

SINCE THE 1984 convention, then, he had coursed over the country preaching his own political gospel—decrying the "economic violence" visited on people's lives by "the merger maniacs and corporate barracudas" and particularly the "American multinationals firing free labor at home to hire repressed labor abroad," which was becoming a global version of how northern industry had once transferred their factories to the nonunionized South, leaving behind them in the North wasted communities; and sounding alarms, too, on the decay of urban America, the absence of a national system of health insurance, the deterioration of public schools—while endeavoring with this message to enclose in his tribuneship now white coal miners in Kentucky, striking airline employees, angry and despairing workers like those long on strike at a Hormel meatpacking plant in Minnesota, others battling for union rights in Maine. He pitched into environmental confrontations in New Hampshire, assisted union leaders in Wisconsin in arranging a settlement with Chrysler before it pulled one of its plants out of the state, renegotiated loans for struggling farmers in Iowa and Missouri. After leading one demonstration of beleaguered farmers, he flew to Kansas City, Missouri, still clad in coveralls over his basketball sneakers, to be greeted by a throng of more farmers chanting, "Jes-see! Jes-see!" He led them then on to a local black church holding some two thousand of his enthusiasts for a common mass meeting, which presented a classic vision out of the original populist dream of an alliance of all society's discounted and discarded, black and white, from the cities and the farmland. At the same time, in these rallies, more than one reporter noted that Jackson seemed to have a capacity for an instant, deep connection to the lowly and desperate and afraid before him, whether black or white—including white workers outside a General Electric plant in Cicero that was about to close, the streets of that Chicago suburban neighborhood, over twenty years since King's open-housing marches, now clamoring with cheers of "Win, Jesse, win!"

What Robert Borosage saw at work in all this was that "Jackson simply has a minister's belief in the word, that the word can lift people out of that moment in their small lives and into their better selves, into a larger reality." Borosage recounts one occasion when Jackson addressed an audience of three hundred white machinists in Rome, New York, who'd been on strike for some two years. "These guys are going to lose, they're losing their jobs, they're peeling off one by one, they just can't sustain it. Jackson tells them, 'I know this struggle of yours has been very long. But this is an important struggle. It's against what's happening in the world economy, what corporations are doing to a lot more people like you. So when you fight here, you fight not just for yourselves, you're fighting for working folks all across this country.' Well, these people are now in tears. Because he's taken their struggle and put it in a historical and moral context that's bigger than themselves, and given it nobility. He makes it somehow worth it that they've gone through all this, that they're part of a struggle that will keep on. They were just reduced to tears by somebody giving it, giving *them*, that great dignity."

Jackson ranged on into reaches of the American experience where no important presidential candidate before him had ever seriously ventured. Stanley Crouch reported an instance in which Jackson appeared before a congregation of over five thousand in Milwaukee's Mecca Arena and "challenged his audience by going on at length about his participation in the Gay Rights march. He knew that most of them did not want to hear about that. When he talked of embracing homosexuals who were dying, revulsion was in the air. But he persisted. It is not right, he said, it is not right. . . . It was an act of true courage by a man determined to push his constituency beyond provincialism."

Ultimately, his campaign embraced a sense of the American family more comprehensive than any tried perhaps since Robert Kennedy. After spending a night in a housing project in Watts, he met the next morning with gang chieftains who, as related by Garry Wills, told him, "If you talk long enough and strong enough about black folks, they gonna kill you." Jackson replied, "I don't worry 'bout what *they* gonna do, don't yawl be worryin' 'bout *them*. I don't want *yawl* to kill me. If you do that, I die twice. You already killin' me every time you sell drugs, buy weapons, shoot each other. You stoppin' everything I'm tryin' to do. You in a muddy hole, and nobody can get you out but yourselves. Not even Jesse Jackson. I been in a muddy hole, and I know the way out and I can help you. But only you can do it. I can get you jobs, but only you can show up on time, not drunk, not high." At their insistence then, he took them downtown to ask then mayor Tom Bradley for a job-training program in their ghetto. "Few leaders, black or white, could go into Watts and talk to gang leaders the way Jackson did," Wills later wrote, "and then take those gang leaders down to city hall to talk with the mayor. As he can represent black car dealers with the Ford corporation—or as he can take Fidel Castro to church."

Somehow even more improbably, he got a standing ovation when he addressed the Montana state legislature. And in one of his early, singularly lonesome excursions into Iowa, a state with a population almost 99 percent white, he was scheduled to speak at the United Methodist Church in the little country town of Greenfield on the evening, it was belatedly realized, of the Super Bowl game. Though his staff urged him to cancel the appearance, he made the drive from Des Moines anyway, with the temperature around fifteen degrees, and entering Greenfield he noticed, still a mile from the church, a line of cars parked along the side of the road, and when he reached the church, discovered some eight hundred townsfolk waiting for him. He was so transported by this that he decreed Greenfield would be the center for his statewide presidential effort. By the summer of 1987, he was running second to Richard Gephardt, from neighboring Missouri, in preference polls among Iowa's Democratic voters.

At Rainbow Coalition conferences, there began appearing not only large delegations of farmers but destitute oil workers from Texas and Oklahoma, labor leaders like William Winpisinger of the International Association of Machinists and Aerospace Workers. After being endorsed at one Teamsters' meeting in Atlanta by a behemoth-sized wrestler called "Silo Sam," who honked to the assembly, "I love this man, and you oughta listen to him," Jackson jubilantly hauled him along for the rest of his campaign stops that day, advertising him as one exhibit of the support coming to him from "ordinary people." Indeed, it seemed at times as if he were aspiring to become a kind of populist Noah, urging every reachable species of constituent aboard the homemade ark of his Rainbow Coalition.

"Jackson is mobilizing a constituency," political essayist Henry Fairlie observed at the time, "which neither the other black leaders nor white Democratic candidates have thought or been able to mobilize on a national scale with such energy." But the stupendous difficulty in trying to birth a new popular political phenomenon—and consciousness—of such dimension, says adviser Robert Borosage, was that "you were bringing people together who had never been together before. And all against the established powers and money of the Democratic party, and the encrusted leadership of each of those constituencies, which was with whoever's the anointed one. There wasn't any inheritance. So you had to do it almost literally union hall by union hall; in each state, Jackson had to construct the coalition when he got there almost by hand, because it wasn't natural, it hadn't existed before. He was the only civil rights leader trying to make a link between African-Americans and the white working people in the country, whereas most of the civil rights connection had been between the affluent liberal white community and the impoverished in the black community. And most in that coalition—the black unionists, progressive white unions, the peace community—had never been collectively electoral. But what Jackson did in '88 was reveal people to one another. So they could see themselves in their true strength together, with their shared interests, a much greater strength than they'd ever imagined. If they had just known that ahead of time, they could have actually nominated the son of a bitch."

In the course of this effort, adds Borosage, "what he was also doing, and few people saw it unless they were watching closely, was he was bringing a lot of the Reagan Democrat working class into this very progressive political movement." Jackson himself later claimed, "You had these very basic West Virginia, Wyoming, Georgia folks reaching out to me to protect their interests, many of whom may have voted for Reagan either because of the promise of economic security or because of racial insecurity. Reagan, you know, promised 'em no more welfare queens. Well, he sho performed on that, but at the same time, he was union bustin'. Same time, no health insurance. Same time, people losin' their jobs, goin' homeless. Reagan did not deliver on that economic security, so they were willin' to say, 'We been had.' And they began turnin' to me everywhere I went. Union hall, Chattanooga, unemployed Du Pont construction workers, and their leader gets up and says, 'Now I know you fellas may have a lot of trouble with Jesse, but I just want yawl to listen to him and ask yourselves, which would yawl rather have: a black friend or a white enemy?' "

Beyond that, as Henry Fairlie reported, Jackson was "bringing into the political mainstream a crucial number of American citizens who seemed to have permanently abandoned any hope or belief that they might one day find a place within it." That was all along the X factor in projections of how Jackson's candidacy might fare, the huge unknown of that population of the previously indifferent and detached—"whole body of people that nobody has ever even counted," as Jackson described them, "who haven't voted for anybody because they saw no difference in 'em, no hope in voting"—but who might materialize heavily in this election in response to Jackson's message, somewhat in the way George Wallace's candidacy two decades earlier had discovered a popular potential unsuspected up to that point, an enormous submerged expanse of discontent and alienation in the American commonry that was subsequently pursued, in varying manners, by presidential candidates from Nixon to Carter to Reagan. At any rate, reporters began finding, among the crowds at Jackson's rallies, significant numbers of citizens who had long felt utterly estranged from the combine of interests presiding over the country, and who, if they had ever voted, had most recently voted for Reagan, and some even for Wallace in 1968.

As it happened, Jackson had twice visited Wallace in Montgomery, encounters that had a certain ghostly, if not macabre, irony about them—the first time in 1983, when Wallace, much dimmed since his crippling in an assassination attempt during his last presidential foray, had mumbled, "Jesse, you're running for president, hunh? It's a real tough thing, running for president," and then had imparted to him the counsel, "Keep the hay down where the goats can get at it," which Jackson in his customary way could not refrain from enlarging on, "Yeah, can't have no goats jumpin' up in the air after that hay." In 1988 he called on him again, Wallace aging and gnarled and reportedly given to moments of remorseful weeping over his blusterous racial rancors in the sixties, with Jackson now swallowing up his lumpy little paw of a hand in his own capacious grip and conducting a prayer for his "healing and health," and Wallace blurting out, "Jesse, thank you for coming. And I love you. . . ."

For that matter, some even thought they discerned in Jackson similarities to Ronald Reagan, too, another national political celebrity who was mostly an exhorter, a myth giver, "a spirit and symbol, but not terribly attentive to particulars," as one observer put it. Each, Garry Wills noted, was "a master at wrapping a deeply felt conviction inside a one-liner" in "reaching toward a larger audience using traditional appeals," though both, *Newsweek* columnist Meg Greenfield wrote, had "started out with the contempt of the moderate centrist establishment, being ridiculed and/or anathematized as a dangerous, marginal, radical, troublemaking, sectarian . . . *kook*." In its own less than affectionate comparison, *The New Republic* had stated that "like Reagan's, [Jackson's] are the extremely effective politics of resentment, long on grievances, short on decent alternatives," and Reagan, too, had "struck many as a skilled manipulator of public emotions with only the vaguest understanding of public policy; a dangerous sloganeer; a man whose political views consisted of simpleminded bromides, whose attempts to present himself as reassuringly mainstream were belied by his past record. . . ."

ACTUALLY, JACKSON BROUGHT into his more ambitious 1988 presidential enterprise many of his pentecostalisms from 1984. Besides his inveighings against the social depredations of goliath corporate enterprise — "Capital does not follow conscience, and it needs constraints" — he continued to deplore U.S. complicity in the perpetuation of whatever repressive and autocratic regimes abroad were perceived as congenial to U.S. interests in the ongoing global competition of the Cold War: "Reagan says the last forty years have not been good for the West. What Reagan means is that all these nonaligned nations in the U.N. have been beating up on us for forty years — beating up on *us*, Batista, *us*, Diem, *us*, Pinochet, *us*, the Shah, *us*, Somoza, *us*, Marcos. Might be 'bout time to start thinking about redefining 'us.' " He also called again for a hold in the nuclear arms race with the Soviet Union, for appreciable reductions in the military budget, a graduated troop withdrawal from Europe, and the closing down of such weapons projects as the MX, cruise, Midgetman, and Trident D-5 missiles, along with Reagan's Strategic Defense Initiative (SDI) program. At his rallies, he would ask those who owned a stereo or television set made in Japan to raise their hands, then those who happened to have acquired an intercontinental missile to lift their hands: "Well. Looks like we been makin' what ain't nobody buyin'."

In place of the continuing colossal escalation of military spending, he proposed, along with beginning conversions to peacetime industry, a massive project of domestic reconstruction of virtually New Deal scale — a concerted national endeavor of "research, reinvestment, retraining, and reindustrialization to rebuild America, to restore the nation's transit system, create affordable mass housing, which would generate thousands and thousands of new jobs." While he would have reinstated the top tax rate for the wealthiest private incomes and the largest corporate profits, he contended that this prodigious undertaking of internal reconstruction could be principally financed by federally guaranteed allocations, in the form of bonds, from 10 percent of the nation's vast pension fund reserve.

That was a new proposition of his in 1988. Also added now to his 1984 battery of issues was an appeal for a comprehensive offensive against the American blight of drugs—trade sanctions against those countries indulgent of their export; harsh actions against banks implicated in processing money from the commerce; and a mobilization of the Coast Guard, the U.S. Customs Service, and the U.S. Navy to intercept shipments. But he stipulated that those measures would be at best only supplementary to the central responsibility of youths themselves to refuse to use drugs. The old, inherently conservative moral message of his PUSH-Excel mission was discovered anew, as he declared to audiences in America's great continental megasuburbia, from Long Island to the San Fernando Valley, that no president could, himself alone, by sheer presidential decree, abolish drug use or sexual promiscuity or the violence and ennui in the nation's schools, nor create there a sense of commitment to one's community; this was a transformation that finally fell to personal will and initiative. One of Jackson's more chronic press critics, Joe Klein, allowed, "It remains a wonderment that Jesse Jackson is the *only* Democrat talking about crime and morality and family values this year."

It had been partly to try exorcising the lingering onus of Jewish antipathies that, in 1985, when Reagan paid his visit to the cemetery in Bitburg, Germany, holding Nazi war dead, Jackson made his own countervisit to the site of a concentration camp in Alsace, and went on to his confrontation with Gorbachev at the summit in Geneva. During a small ceremonial meeting in which Gorbachev had intended to pass only a few minutes chatting with Jackson and several peace activists with him, Jackson suddenly told him, "There is a great anxiety among the American people about the plight of Soviet Jews." Gorbachev, insisting it was a "so-called problem" without real substance, made to talk about other matters, but Jackson pressed on, and it wound up a forty-five-minute exchange, which Moscow television news gave seven minutes to reporting, only two less than its coverage of the summit itself.

On the whole, with the wider reach he was attempting this time, his manner and rhetoric seemed to many markedly more subdued and tempered than in 1984, with the prevailing racial motif of that campaign now modulated and subsumed in a broader collection of concerns. Jackson himself once offered that, while the party had its conservative and progressive wings, "it needs two wings to fly." He was soon accused by, dependably, one of *The New Republic*'s polemical clerks of the reformed liberal respectability of "succeeding in spreading amnesia about his sympathy for radical liberation movements." Actually, he was still calling for some provision for a Palestinian homeland, but that sentiment had already become by now far less scandalous, indeed "unexceptional," as one commentator remarked. And some of the more febrile spirits on the left were incensed by what they detected as his new circumspection on the PLO itself. In response to a query on *Meet the Press* if he would sit down to parley with Arafat, Jackson had replied, "I would not. It is not necessary to . . . equate Arafat and the PLO with a sovereign people, the Palestinian people," and Alexander Cockburn bristled in *The Nation*, "If Jackson ends up talking like a *New York Times* editorial, then what is the point of the Jackson campaign?"

Nevertheless, Jackson was sounding over the land in 1988 "the single most identifiable and attractive message," declared Mario Cuomo, to be heard issuing from any of the candidates. *The Washington Post*'s Paul Taylor, in his perceptive account of the campaign, *See How They Run*, cites a national survey conducted for the World Policy Institute, in which a prospective platform was posed: "Spending $200 billion a year more on research and technology, job training, rebuilding roads and railways, cleaning up toxic and nuclear waste dumps, investing in education, building low-income housing to reduce homelessness, fighting drugs and expanding care for the elderly. Cutting $125 billion a year from the military budget by turning over to Europe and Japan greater responsibility for their own defense. Raising $125 billion a year in new taxes on upper income households (over $80,000 a year) and corporations." That entire program of profound reorderings of policy turned out to be supported by 81 percent of the voters polled, and Taylor points out, "[I]n case anyone missed it, there *was* a candidate in 1988 who advocated this platform: Jesse Jackson." One white tavern owner in the Midwest told *Newsweek*, "He's the only one who's saying anything. The rest of them put you to sleep." In fact, it wasn't long before selections from his message, especially its elements of economic populism, began to be mimed, to his exasperation but also delight, by Jackson's opponents.

In his subsequent series of debates with those opponents as the campaign got under way, Jackson now carried, from his passage through the 1984 debates, something of the sangfroid of an experienced senior performer, an aplomb that also owed to the fact, he claimed, that "I've dealt with more world leaders than any of 'em. Take all the Democratic candidates, blindfold us, drop us anywhere in the world with a dollar in our pockets, and who do you think would lead the others out?" Robert Borosage reports that "most of the other candidates would drop out for two or three days before a debate with their issues advisers, every aspiring future assistant secretary, and their briefing books, to prepare themselves. Jackson would take, at best, two hours before a debate to get what we called 'briefed.' It was a joke. Phones ringing, he's talking to other people, he's reading other stuff. We would sort of just throw our notes into this maelstrom." Then, says campaign aide Carolyn Kazdin, "he would get up and go into his bedroom and go to sleep." While those other candidates would arrive early to meticulously prepare themselves before each telecast debate, Jackson often showed up only a few minutes before airtime, and then he would visit each of the other candidates in their respective stalls, where they were having makeup applied while listening to a final briefing. He would tarry just long enough with each "to play games with them," says Mark Steitz. "He'd wish one luck, knowing it would unnerve him. Another, he'd say, why don't I just accuse you of this or that tonight? Sometimes he'd pump one of them up—if Gephardt had become a problem in the campaign, pump up Dukakis. He understood that, right before going out to contend before TV cameras, everybody was nervous and trying to memorize their notes, and that his strength was that he was more relaxed and happy about it all than the rest of them." Paul Simon, in particular, was given to studiously reviewing his precisely arranged packet of note cards, and before one debate Jackson snatched the packet from him and scrambled the cards; another time, only moments before the cameras blinked on, he sauntered over to Simon, plucked one of his cards from him, and kept it tucked in his coat pocket for the duration of the broadcast.

For his part, he would more or less freely surf his way through each debate. "There was one wonderful moment," says Borosage, "where Gephardt was going on about trade policy, Dukakis was going on about taxes, Gore was going on about nuclear weapons, and Jackson says, 'Well, he wants to be secretary of commerce, he wants to be the IRS guy, he wants to be secretary of state. I want to be your president. Let me talk to you about America.' " Jackson still relates with glee how he once managed to "snooker" Gephardt and Dukakis into avowing support for the African National Congress (ANC), then still an underground resistance in South Africa that was suspected by many of Marxist inclinations. "That night I kept pushing the South Africa issue, and finally I asked Gephardt, 'Well, would you supply arms to the freedom fighters of the ANC?' Gephardt came back, 'Based

upon certain principles, *yes*, as we do other freedom fighters.' And his people"—Jackson gave a grunting snicker—"they like to leaped out from behind that curtain offstage. He didn't know what he had just— He just heard
'freedom fighters': '*Of course!*' So then Dukakis was trapped, couldn't seem
to be to the right of Gephardt on the South African question. And he *agreed*
with Gephardt on the ANC—" Jackson clapped his hands, happily
whooped. "That was the *best* damn— And another time, asked Dukakis,
'Would you support the frontline states in southern Africa, like Mozambique, getting weapons to defend themselves against South Africa?' Dukakis
then"—and Jackson's voice fell to a deep, round-toned imitation—" 'No,
now, uh, we must exhaust other means.' I said, 'Well, Reagan and Thatcher
offer arms to Mozambique. You mean you to the right of Reagan and
Thatcher?' Dukakis, 'Well, uh, see, what we tryin' is, maybe if—' and his
people off-camera are goin' like—" Jackson grimaced antically while fanning his hands in X-crossings in front of his face. "Godamighty, he was 'bout
to do it *again*! . . ."

His Sun at the Highest

IN THE OPENING contests, in Iowa and New Hampshire—both states
where blacks made up barely 1 percent of the electorate—Jackson drew
about 10 percent of the vote. In New Hampshire, he defeated both Bruce
Babbitt, who now dropped out of the running, and Albert Gore, who had ex-
pended over $250,000 in his effort there. Up to that January, in fact, Jackson
had spent only $100,000 on television ads to Gore's $3 million and Dukakis's
$2 million, and less than a fourth of Dukakis's total $11 million outlay. "We
had no money for media, had no money for polling," says Borosage. "No internal polling whatever. Our polls were the USA *Today* polls." Then in Minnesota, whose population was less than 2 percent black, Jackson came in
second with 20 percent of the vote. In Maine and Vermont, states with even
more microscopic black populations, he won 30 percent of the vote, finishing second in Maine and actually winning Vermont. He was now only a
week away from the giant, multistate, single-day tournament of primaries,
centered in the South, that was being called Super Tuesday.

But no matter how more impressive his campaign this time, Jackson had
remained, to the Democratic party proprietors, more or less a rogue phenomenon, a radical privateer who could ultimately work nothing but bedlam in the party's fortunes. Accordingly, they found his advancing prospects
progressively unsettling: "People are beginning to talk about it in whispers
late at night," Bob Beckel reported at the time. Even nominally liberal

commentators like Anthony Lewis and Hodding Carter III began serving up reminders that, for all his gifts, Jackson was entirely too inexperienced, after all, and really too garish a leftist to be considered for the presidency, and *The New Republic*, of course, warned, "Were Jackson to win a place on the Democratic ticket, the result would be certain and apocalyptic defeat." As it was, not a single Democratic governor or state chairman had endorsed him. But the consternation of the party's curators, as one state chairman explained it plaintively, was a repetition of Mondale's dilemma, only on a larger scale now: "We can't win with him, and we can't win without him." One party official wistfully suggested, "I think he'd be happier on the outside, in a role that is more consistent with his temperament and background." In fact, that was exactly where—on the outside—the party had been strenuously maneuvering to keep him since the 1984 campaign. Jackson, while riding around Washington one afternoon with Ann Lewis, began anguishing over the humiliation of having been excluded from a party dinner to which all other past and potential Democratic presidential candidates had been invited, despite the legions of new voters he had registered who had returned the Senate to the Democrats in 1986 and had revived the party electorally over much of the country. Lewis tried to reassure him, "They are not the party. We are. The reason there's a Democratic Senate is not six guys in a room in Washington in bow ties. If you give them the power to shut you out, you're giving them a power they don't have."

Another Jackson supporter publicly advised the party's leadership, "Somebody better figure out a way very soon to deal with Jesse as an adult. Otherwise, there'll be hell to pay when the klieg lights are burning in Atlanta." But their main way of dealing with him continued to be a preoccupation with keeping him outside, isolated, and quarantined, and by means that extended considerably beyond exiling him from party banquets. As a final, emergency barricade against his ever actually advancing to the unthinkable at the convention, party officials had created a bloc of 645 unpledged "superdelegates," made up mostly of party operatives and members of Congress, all of whom could be counted on to collect behind almost anyone other than Jackson at that stage.

But well before he would reach that point, the megaprimary of Super Tuesday in the South, which now lay immediately ahead of him, had been contrived as a baffle to filter out any liberal candidacy like Jackson's should it still be in the field, and to ensure that the candidates coming out of it would be of a conservative disposition reflecting the supposed political temperament of that region—and, not incidentally, the temperament of the inner fraternity of similarly cautious-spirited party figures making up the Democratic Leadership Council, who had largely invented the strategy. "Chuck Robb, Bill Clinton were part of that group," says Hatcher, "they worked like mad on that thing. They saw Super Tuesday as Jesse's Waterloo. Because you've got all these southern states voting on the same day, see, this is like a huge barrier, erected on this road to catch Jesse."

But to all these designs gathering against his campaign, Jackson posed his own relatively primitive, existential computation: "When all's said and done, it's still the people who decide." That endured for him as the original, primary pulse of all power in politics, the energy that all its accessory engines and attendants existed to create in the first place. "I've always gotten my votes, not from the pundits and party leaders, but from the people. *That's* where the life is." In this instance, what the party's inner management had seemed to forget in their ornate calculations for Super Tuesday was that Jackson had finished first or second in the primaries of seven of those southern states in 1984. "All these very seasoned veteran politicians," says Hatcher, "somehow failed to realize, when this idea probably first popped into their minds, that many of those southern states had a significantly greater number of African Americans on the voter rolls now because of Jesse's voter-registration drives." As a result, one Jackson organizer not unmerrily observed, "they set up Super Tuesday to maximize the conservatives' say in the process, and what they're going to get is the maximization of a lot of blacks voting for Jesse."

There were actually twenty-one primaries and caucuses altogether on that day, March 8. Jackson ran first or second in sixteen of them. In the South, he finished first in five states and second in nine others, winning 27 percent of the popular vote, more than anyone else, and claiming almost a third of the region's delegates. In fact, when the day was over, Jackson had actually become the overall leader in popular votes in the Democratic presidential primary campaign. One journalist who was visiting friends in Jamaica would later relate that, while they were all watching coverage of the returns, the family's thirteen-year-old son at one point turned to ask if there were actually more black people in America than he'd somehow been informed. For Jackson's staff, remembers one of its logisticians, the giddy exhilaration of Super Tuesday "was that it said to us, you really can do it, because here are the numbers. Almost for the first time, we felt we had a chance to actually *win* this thing." The day left it essentially a three-man contest, among Jackson and Dukakis and Gore—though Gore, who had anticipated that all those primaries taking place at once across his home ground would provide the making of his campaign at last, was instead effectively demolished there.

From Super Tuesday Jackson moved into the Michigan caucuses, where he won a stunning 55 percent of the vote. That included 20 percent of the white vote, four times what he had drawn there in 1984. Dukakis, who had unloaded almost $1.5 million into his Michigan campaign, trailed some twenty-seven percentage points behind Jackson. "Oh, there was magic in that evening," says Mark Steitz. Jackson phoned Bert Lance that night, "just amazed at what he'd done," says Lance, "totally astounded and excited. I told him, 'Our worst fears may be coming true, you know— you may get the nomination. Then what're we gonna do?' " After thirty-one primaries and caucuses, Jackson was not only still ahead in the popular vote but, according to the Associated Press, was about even in delegates won—and suddenly, after Michigan, for the duration of at least one delirious week, he was widely regarded as, phantasmagorically, the leading candidate for the nomination. *Time* placed him on its cover, with the single, bannered word: "Jesse!?"

Within the party itself, one Democratic national committeeman confessed, Jackson's Michigan victory produced "absolute panic." Roger Wilkins recalls that, right after the outcome in Michigan, "I was on an airplane, and happened to be sitting in the aisle seat beside this Democratic operative who had been involved with Humphrey, and across the aisle from me is a guy who used to work for Kennedy. Now, I was no whiter that day than I am today, I was no less visible than I am now, I mean, you could not look through me and see something over there on the other side, but those two guys looked right past me anyway, talking to each other, 'This Michigan thing, what is this? What is this Jackson thing? What are we going to do?' Their distress over Jackson was such that they were expressing their dismay right through me about this black guy forging out ahead. But it was the whole party, I mean, it was thrown into a perfect whip-snitch." Jackie herself recollects with a throaty chuckle, "I guess we scared the hell out of them, you know? It was kind of amusing to me. You wonder, What are they making so much of this for? We're just people running like anybody else."

In fact, Michigan quickly occasioned a breakfast meeting, arranged through Lance and John White, between Jackson and the party's elder druids—including Clark Clifford, figures from past campaigns like Frank Mankiewicz and John Kenneth Galbraith, some thirty-two attendees in all—held at the Jefferson Hotel in Washington. "It didn't make any difference if anybody else was there or not, actually," White later observed. "If Clark Clifford was there, it was an important meeting." On the whole, though, said White, "Jesse got basically nonquestions from nearly everybody. It was a polite session. Not an endorsement, just sort of a tentative blessing." Borosage remembers, "We did have people standing up saying, 'We'd like to be of help.' " Clifford himself remarked to the group that Jackson could "bring a new innovation into our political process," and could be expected if president to assemble "the best brains the party and the country have to offer"; he afterward pronounced the session "an extraordinary event." For his part, Jackson, after his exclusion from such similar party conclaves in the past, seemed determined not to appear especially awed by this one he had finally compelled. Having characterized it beforehand as an instance of "old wineskins expanding to make room for new wine," he now quipped to the room, "Sometimes you can make energy out of trash." Everyone scrupulously avoided betraying any umbrage at that. But however slightly strained the affair, it was, in a way, an even more auspicious moment for Jackson than that penthouse meeting in San Francisco in 1984: this breakfast gathering a kind of high political sacrament of recognition at last. And Jackson negotiated it with the same proud, commanding bearing. White would afterward relate that he wound up patiently holding a glass of orange juice, which Jackson had asked him to bring to him, until Jackson completed one of his perorations: "My definition of a leader is someone who can make you fetch. I haven't done that for anyone since LBJ. But first thing I knew, the son of a bitch had made a fetcher out of me, just like Lyndon Johnson. . . ." (As it would turn out, when White died in 1995, Jackson, as White had requested but over the obstreperous objections of some of his friends, was to deliver the oration at the memorial service for him, "a black man in a white robe," says Lance, "standing in the rotunda of the Texas state capitol.")

Throughout that euphoric week after Michigan, Jackson swirled over Wisconsin, a state whose population was only 2 percent black, but he boomed away to enormous throngs at every stop. With white parents holding up their small children to see him, Jackson exulted to the thousands stretching before him, "Dr. King's heart is rejoicing right now!" Each of these rallies ending in billowing roars of "Win, Jesse, win!" "He was higher than a kite," Borosage declares. "At that point, he was about to be the nominee. Dukakis was looking terrible. And those *crowds* . . . they kept getting bigger and bigger and bigger. There's no question he felt he was finally breaking through. That people were hearing him who had never been able to hear him before." Lance says, "He was doing better than he'd ever hoped, he had moved into new ground now," and as if for some reassurance in this sudden, unfamiliar environment of import he had entered, he began phoning Lance "ten, twelve times a day," Lance reports. "He'd say, 'Look, something is happening up here, and I'm not quite sure what it is. But this outpouring of affection wherever I go, it's for real—it's *real*, I'm telling you, it's *there*, I *know* when it's there.' "

He even began to ponder on his cabinet and ambassadorial appointments, and somberly notified his staff, "We're living now in a very expanded fishbowl, because we will be viewed as possibly running the Western world. From now on, staff members can have no personal life. You're going to start being looked at as the White House staff, and you might want to start thinking about behaving like that." Mark Steitz admits, "There *was* something frightening about being taken seriously at that level."

For that matter, privately, "it frightened *Jesse*," according to Frank Watkins. It was as if he uncomfortably began to sense himself now about to be captured, in his outsider's exploit, in far heavier gravities of consequence than he had ever really reckoned on. Robert Borosage acknowledges, "He was scared to death by it, in some sense"—one not negligible aspect of that personal trepidation, adds Borosage, being that he was "scared to death almost literally." In his admonitions to his staff to comport themselves more carefully now, he had happened to mention, "People will be assigned to destroy us character-wise—before they try to physically."

THE POSSIBILITY OF being suddenly ambushed by the same sort of annihilating blow of violence that had stricken King was a worry that had shadowed Jackson throughout the years. An actual plot to assassinate him had been discovered as early as 1969, and another in 1974, and his progress had always been accompanied by a low flickering side-glare of other death threats. With his first presidential effort in 1984, those threats multiplied by the hundreds. Ken Bode recalls that, after one rally in Illinois, "I got into the car to ride with him, and his raincoat was as thick as a bread plate. And he began telling me about the seriousness of the threats against him." Jackson's youngest son, Yusef, then seventeen, had demanded of him, "What happens to us if something happens to you?" and Jackie had for a time ferociously opposed his ever running again. His family's fears had given him pause, but he finally elected to press on in defiance, he said, of the "dreambusters" at large in America. In 1988, he moved through his second campaign frequently garbed in a bulletproof blue raincoat, with the Secret Service contingent around him conspicuously more numerous and heavily armed than those around the other candidates. That spring, police had arrested a Missouri couple, linked to a white supremacist sect, for threats to kill him. Even a planned side visit to Bert Lance's country place outside Calhoun, Georgia, had to be canceled when, Lance says, "the Secret Service called and said one of their informants had overheard somebody talking in a bar. They actually took somebody into custody."

Bode tells of "one experience I'll never forget from '88, when he was going to give a speech at the Capitol, and I went with him into a sort of back room in the Capitol building where a bunch of Democratic senators were waiting for him, including Cranston and Hollings. He takes off his coat while he's talking to them about the campaign, and starts strapping on a bulletproof vest. I couldn't believe what I was feeling—watching this man having to put on a bulletproof vest to go out and give a speech from the steps of the Capitol of my country. And Fritz Hollings and Alan Cranston too—both these guys had run for president in 1984, and never incited any enthusiasm or rancor or any other feeling to ever have to do what this guy who'd beaten them both was now having to do in front of them—and I could see on their faces the same feeling I had: What the hell are we watching? This man putting on a bulletproof vest to speak at the Capitol of the United States? But Jesse never said a word about what he was doing, just went on talking about his hopes for the country and the campaign while he was strapping the thing on absolutely matter of course."

It was only seldom that Jackson would evince any uneasiness about the specter of fatal danger constantly hanging after his movements. At the end of one brutally long day of campaigning in Texarkana, Texas, for other Democratic candidates, when Secret Service protection was no longer around him, he emerged after his last rally from the back door of a church to head for the cars waiting in the rear driveway, immediately alongside a stand of deep woods into which the full blackness of night seemed already to have collected; and Jackson, as he plunged hastily into the front car, growled to an aide, "Right next to these trees! *Damn.* Who was the genius that figured this out?"

In the spring of 1995, he journeyed to Atlanta to lead a march, protesting Republican contractions of social programs, that was to wind through Newt Gingrich's district in Cobb County, just north of Atlanta—a kind of outer-suburban-gothic territory of the rawer New South. Its terrain of jack pines and broomsage and red dirt was still in somewhat uneven transition, high-tech industrial parks and shopping malls having only recently finished pushing out the mules and moonshiners and palmists, with a still-fresh past of rabid Klan nests and occult rightist sects led by local urologists. The night before the march, in his hotel room in Atlanta, Jackson sagged heavily back in a couch, his tie off and shirt unbuttoned down to his stomach, rubbing his eyes wearily in the lamplight. "Nothing can ever save you from ambush if somebody's gonna do it," he murmured thickly. "Never know when it might come, and nothin' you can do about it when it does. Coward dies a thousand deaths. I'd of already died a million times by now if I thought like that. Thing is, don't be careful, be prayerful. But if tomorrow should be my day, it won't find me over in some corner cowerin'. If tomorrow *is* my day, will find me still out there carryin' on the work I have all my life. Be out there *marchin'*."

Recoil and Judgment

FOR WHATEVER MIXTURE of reasons—whether sensing that with his Michigan win he had reached a height at last intolerable to hidden lethal animosities, or disquieted about finding himself suddenly spirited into that utterly new and unknown dimension of potential power, or in a swim of simple heedless celebration because of that—Jackson through that last week of campaigning in Wisconsin seemed curiously to enter into a kind of hectic and reeling recklessness, in which he largely returned, as if for the reassuring familiarity of the nature and spirit of the beginning of all this, to the guerrilla style of his 1984 effort. An episode that shortly ensued looked to many suspiciously like a politically suicidal impulse to escape his now fearsomely mounting prospects. Without consulting anyone, Jackson lurched into the bizarre flourish of international stuntsmanship of writing a letter to General Manuel Noriega, the tin-pot El Jefe of Panama who had been recently indicted in Florida on drug-trafficking charges, pontifically adjuring him to resign. "That Noriega pen-pal relationship," says Lance, "I still don't know what that was all about." Borosage says, "I was in theory his foreign policy adviser, and I never heard of this thing until National Public Radio called me to ask, 'Is it true?' It was a classic screwup, just unbelievable."

At the same time, if Jackson appeared atilt in backwinds of uncertainty, it was a misgiving answered, it would seem, by a developing mood among the Wisconsin citizenry as well. E. J. Dionne would elegize in *The New York Times*, "Let it be recorded that for at least one week in American history, in a middle-sized Midwestern state, a broad range of white voters took the Presidential candidacy of a black man with the utmost seriousness." But that may have also finally been its undoing. It was as if the implications of his startling showing in Michigan had set off, under all the effervescence of the crowds in Wisconsin, more widely and deeply a gradual recoil of graver second thoughts; thus, his candidacy, in passing into the realm of serious presidential possibility, at that moment may also have doomed itself. "As long as people could vote for him as sending a message to Democrats saying we support this kind of economic populism and moral voice, they were anxious to vote for him," says Borosage. "But as soon as he got close to actually winning the nomination, I think people just said, 'Whoa. We're never going to do *this*,' " and Bert Lance suggests, "The fear factor took over. There were people saying, 'Oh, my goodness, Jesse Jackson has a chance to gain the Democratic nomination, what's this going to do to my seat in Congress, to my race for county commissioner, to the mayor's race?' None of us wants to be a racist, so we look to see if some other circumstance can allow us to say to ourselves, 'Well, I'm not doing this because he is black, but because of these other circumstances'—and we cleanse ourselves and we're free to go ahead. And God knows, Jesse gave them a lot of opportunities to do that."

In any event, Jackson lost Wisconsin to Dukakis, by a margin of 48 to 28 percent of the vote. Lance believes that "in his heart of hearts, it was some blow to his confidence. 'Well, perhaps I'm not as good as I thought at being able to tell what's going on.' " For many others, though, it comfortably restored some measure of reality to the race.

Yet "we were still up," insists Borosage. "We had run very well. Jackson was still actually out in the lead. So we head for New York." In their anticipations, says Hatcher, "we saw the road stretching out after New York on to the Atlanta convention, and it would be ours." Hatcher continues, "We started in the western part of the state, and the rallies were big, and overwhelmingly white. I was really encouraged, I felt we had dodged a bullet in Wisconsin and still had a chance to do it. But then, the closer we got to New York City, I couldn't understand what was happening, because we'd had this great success upstate, but the change, the coldness, the meanness, was as perceptible almost as if someone had drawn a line across the sky. It became clear that Ed Koch was absolutely doing a job in New York City."

EDWARD I. KOCH, the jauntily obstreperous mayor of New York, was a creature of insuppressible combativeness—in contrast to the Manhattan Democratic tradition of suave silk-stocking liberalism, he was something of a cotton-sock, pavement populist. Tall, with an ungainly bulkiness, long-legged and high-paunched and gantry-armed, with crisping gray hair around his bald pate and a sly little smirk of a grin, he rather suggested some manic and obscurely disreputable bachelor uncle long a source of vague discomfiture and nervous edginess to the rest of his family. In a way the consummate New York commoner, he governed his fractious, insular subnation of a city principally through a politics of wisecrack and chipper insult, delivered in a quacking voice whose sound was once compared to that of Ping-Pong balls panging off tin. His vision of humankind tended not to be the most elevated. He had already once professed, "My experience with blacks is that they're basically anti-Semitic," adding, "I think whites are basically antiblack," and then submitted, "It's not possible to remake the world."

Now, despite all of Jackson's labors since 1984 to redeem himself from the acrimonies over his "Hymie-town"–Farrakhan episode, it was all clamorously reinvoked and loosed again by Koch, who proclaimed himself the "Paul Revere" to alert New York and the nation to Jackson's true menace. Having decided that he would endorse Albert Gore, who was making his last, wanly frantic primary stand in New York, Koch announced that Jews "would be crazy to vote for Jackson," repeatedly citing not only his "Hymie" remark but his embrace by Arafat in 1979. Gore, now enclosed in the dubious embrace of Koch, correspondingly belabored Jackson for his sympathies for the Palestinians and his offenses to Jewish sensitivities. In fact, all the cargo of liabilities from Jackson's past that he had carried into his presidential enterprise seemed now to come toppling down on him. Koch even recycled the old accusations about Jackson's behavior after King was shot in Memphis, charging him with "lying under stress." Along with that, Gore kept pointing out that Jackson had a "complete and total lack of experience in national government." Finally, the fundamental ambiguity of Jackson's very attempt to translate his movement gospel into a presidential competition came into an open and direct challenge. "We're not choosing a preacher," declaimed Gore, "we're choosing a president. The Oval Office is a whole lot more than a pulpit."

In all, New York turned out to be, for Jackson, a political abattoir, "a gang war," says Borosage, that was loudly abetted by the media—"Everyplace he goes, it's anti-Semitism and Hymie-town, as if no other issues mattered." Steitz reflects, "Because he had done so well with Jewish groups since '84 and it seemed so much progress had been made, he really thought he was past things that he wasn't, and here he was getting into that ugliness again." Under the barrage from Koch, whenever it began to seem that Jackson in a speech might be sagging toward answering the mayor in kind—"there *is* a part of Jesse that wants to get into a pissing match," says Borosage—his staff would mutely signal him from the back of the crowd, with lifting motions of both hands, to recover his moral altitude. In an address to the New York Economic Club, he appealed for an elevation of the campaign above its rancorous distractions. But at the same time, purportedly to avoid incendiary confrontations, he chose to appear before no Jewish groups, and even declined to walk in the Salute to Israel Day parade along Fifth Avenue.

In the last days of the New York campaign, says Borosage, "we were going around the clock, had no sleep," and Steitz could plainly tell that Jackson "was at ill sorts politically. When he's not exactly clear about how to handle something, he moves faster and faster, diving around trying to find the footing, the way to talk, what to say. And he will drive himself to distraction and sickness doing that. He did in fact get sick. He was in very bad shape. His face puffed up. He looked awful. He physically displays, a lot of times, you know, what's going on in his spirit like that."

The beneficiary of all the cacophonous mayhem of the New York primary campaign was Michael Dukakis, who succeeded in keeping himself primly apart from most of it. He subsequently wound up with 51 percent of the vote—Jackson drawing a still respectable 37 percent, but Gore only 10 percent from Koch's raucous services to him, and finally disappearing from the race. Jackson, as it happened, won New York City itself, with 98 percent of the black vote and 63 percent of the Hispanic, providing the precept for David Dinkins's defeat of Koch one year later in the Democratic mayoral primary, before going on to become New York City's first black mayor.

Nevertheless, there seemed little likelihood now of Jackson being able to battle Dukakis on to even a standoff at the Atlanta convention. After New York, in the words of one aide, Jackson was "battered and almost wiped out." Roger Wilkins confesses that it was the most desolated he had ever seen him. "I knew New York was going to be a crash after the high reach of Michigan. What he did in New York anyway I think was a political miracle. There would not have been a Mayor Dinkins had it not been for what Jackson put together there in '88. But when he lost and saw everything slipping away, that was the moment I saw him most dispirited. The rest of us could say that it was all a great civics lesson, had paved the way for a future black presidential bid that would succeed, had encouraged black youngsters all over the country that they are really a part of this country. But if you're Jesse, in the middle of the thing and you've got Secret Service and your airplane and then you get into the lead and all of a sudden these people are running around *believing*, then *you* can start believing, you think your dreams of the Oval Office could just possibly come true. . . ."

Somewhat short of that ultimate fancy, though, Jackson's campaign had flourished not a little, while there was still a multiplicity of other contenders in the field, from what was like a political adaptation of the principle of his economic campaigns—the disproportionate effect of a concentrated minority force applied to the fractions of decisive margin in an otherwise impossibly larger equation. New York, however, had ended even that possibility, by reducing the situation to the elemental terms of mere majority preponderance. "We'd done well in part," acknowledges Hatcher, "because there were at least three or four other serious candidates still in the race. But by the time we got to New York, Gore was the only one left besides Dukakis." But then, says Hatcher, "Koch killed Gore off. When we lost Gore, we knew we were in trouble, because then it became just a head-on race between Dukakis and Jesse, and in that kind of head-to-head situation, that's when majority factors, including race, are really going to kick in. So Dukakis didn't have to say much about anything from that point on—he had clear sailing." It also meant, as Bert Lance observed at the time, that with Gore gone, "Jesse gives Dukakis great cover" for appearing a moderate merely by contrast. "The moment New York left it so there weren't going to be two white guys and Jesse heading into California," says Steitz, "it became harder to come up with any plausible scenario."

STILL, JACKSON PUSHED on grimly. "His feeling was," says Bert Lance, "there's a different standard being put on me. In 1980, when Kennedy was running against Carter, nobody called for *him* to make a contribution to the party by doing the right thing and stepping out. Yet they want me to do this." At one rally of two thousand supporters, he testily notified a troupe of reporters, after referring to them as "barracudas," "Let me make this clear. We are running right through June seventh. Write that down. We intend to set the agenda for the national campaign. . . . We will keep setting the moral tone of the campaign. Write that down. We intend to get our share of the delegates based on popular votes. Write that down." But his whole endeavor now unmistakably shifted from an actual campaign back once more to a crusade. "We were committed to going all the way," says Hatcher, "but winning was not the only thing it was about." That's why, when the campaign manager Jackson had taken on the previous November—an Ohio political consultant named Gerald Austin, who had twice conducted Richard Celeste into the governorship of that state—happened to mention to the press that the main hope left to Jackson's campaign now was the vice presidential nomination, Jackson and the rest of his staff were appalled, and Austin was shortly dispatched back to Ohio. "Sure, we're not going to win at that point," says Borosage, "but we're still building this new coalition, still spreading this new movement, trying to get all these communities—urban people, ministers, politicians, progressive whites—to get them all together for the first time." All the while, though, Hatcher admits, "it never left our minds that lightning might strike, that somehow, some way, despite everything, we might actually wind up in a position to gain the nomination anyway."

But Dukakis went on, with heavy wins in Pennsylvania, New Jersey, California, to collect more than enough delegates to ensure him the nomination. Even so, at the conclusion of the primaries, out of the original gallery of six candidates, Jackson had finished second with 7 million votes—29 percent of the total cast, and about equal, actually, to Mondale's count in 1984.

Moreover, some 2 million of those votes had come this time from whites, almost as many as had gone to Gore, Gephardt, and Babbitt put together. Afterward, Jackson would gleefully bugle, "No black has ever gotten more white votes *ever*. In the history of the *earth!*" In all, he had placed first or second in forty-six primaries and caucuses. And he was headed now for the convention in Atlanta with more than twelve hundred delegates, eight hundred short of the majority needed for nomination, but almost a third of the total.

And at this auspicious moment, the old urgency, lasting since Greenville, which had always been the more questionable part of his temptation to move his social apostleship into a contest for the highest political consequence, at last blurted forth in fullness—the hope and hunger to come in from the outside: to belong.

XVII
The Desperation After Coming This Far

JACKSON DECLARED HIS eagerness for the vice presidential nomination far more baldly this time than in 1984. "For some people," he announced, "who have come by way of the stars and have had silver spoons in their mouths and many job options—shall they run their father's ranch, shall they run his plantation, shall they run the family corporation?—maybe vice president is a step down for them. But do you understand my background? The vice presidency is not quite the top, but it's a long way from where I started. . . . One heartbeat away from the leadership of the free world and of Western civilization is not an unimportant job."

Jackson was still clinging to the inspiritment of a poll conducted three days before the Wisconsin primary for *U.S. News & World Report*, which indicated that a Dukakis-Jackson ticket would defeat the presumptive Republican nominee, George Bush, by 47 percent to 42 percent, while "Mr. Dukakis without Mr. Jackson would lose by 44 percent to 43 percent." And *Time* now commented that "anyone else with [Jackson's] impressive series of wins and shows would have a clear claim" to the vice presidential spot. Jackson himself contended, "I certainly will have earned serious consideration because of what I bring to the ticket. It's an option that my constituency has earned." And he stipulated that "consideration means *offered*. It does not mean just in passing."

The probability of that ever transpiring, however, seemed to virtually everyone else hardly much higher than it was in 1984, for about the same array of reasons—cultural, social, political, personal. Now, what quickly came to be perceived as the rank desperation of his pursuit of a vain political want was finally to sabotage almost irreparably that original, vaster aspiration of his: to make himself into a moral heroic protagonist like King in the life of the country. He had, to be sure, wandered a long way from the exaltation of his epiphany that hot afternoon in front of the polio hospital back during the Greensboro demonstrations. In his struggle now to be named the vice presidential nominee, warned the old movement re-doubtable John Lewis, who had since become a congressman from At-lanta, "Jesse must be willing to see that what's going on is not the civil rights movement. This is not the March from Selma to Montgomery." But Jackson's furious grappling for the vice presidential post, while refusing to concede to or to endorse Dukakis, was to leave a conclusive impression confirming all the years of skepticisms and suspicions of him as simply an inveterate self-prospector, insatiable of ego, graceless and petulant—a "big talker" merely "seen as a symbol and spoiler" given to "rant," in the reprise of his character furnished by *New York Times* columnist Maureen Dowd as late as the autumn of 1995, one who "thrives on disorder" and whose "idea of fun is jumping in front of cameras."

Immediately after the final primary in California, Jackson had retreated to La Costa, the patrician resort in the hills north of San Diego, where he passed two days deliberating with aides on how he could compel Dukakis to name him his vice presidential selection, convinced that Dukakis would finally have no choice but to offer it to him. But Jackson's almost frantic longing for that, a passion now welling up out of his self-mythic sense of the progress of his life against adversity and denial, seemed to leave him oblivious to the obvious fact that for Dukakis it was inconceivable.

For one thing, with Jackson's outsized public presence and unconfinable assertiveness, it was hardly lost on Dukakis's staff, if not Dukakis himself, that if Jackson were his running mate, as Ben Bradlee for one declares, "Jeez, he would have eaten Dukakis alive." Neither did it especially commend Jackson's case that one poll of registered voters had found that 66 percent of them regarded him as an "exciting" candidate, as against only 34 percent for Dukakis. In general, says Borosage, "Dukakis didn't even like to be around Jackson. Because he was a little guy, you know, and every time they're together, Jackson lifts his arm up, right? . . . and virtually lifts him off the ground." At one joint appearance before the Congressional Black Caucus, Jackson for a while watched with fascination the discreet gymnastics of the moderator to smuggle a small platform up to the microphone each time Dukakis moved forward to answer a question, and he finally stepped atop the platform himself before it could be withdrawn again, and from that exaggeratedly lofty height, intoned, "I've waited years for equal standing. . . ." Indeed, he was never unmindful of the difference in public effect between himself and Dukakis, and could not resist occasional little delicious notations of it. Aboard his plane one night during the general election campaign, a reporter clicked on a miniature handheld television and happened to pick up Dukakis broadcasting one of his appeals to the nation; at one point, the small screen blanked into static, and Jackson swung around in his seat to call to the reporter, "What hap'n, Dukakis just deliver one of his punch lines?" then turned back around with a low chortle.

But more than a chariness about comparisons to Jackson's overlarge public persona was on the mind of Dukakis's people. Increasingly sensitive to being styled as radical liberals by Bush's forces, they became implacably averse to any detectable associations whatever with Jackson's neo-populist political community. New York governor Mario Cuomo had cautioned them that Jackson "is not like other defeated candidates. Nobody has an influence with seven million voters like his influence with his people. Why must Dukakis treat him differently? Dukakis doesn't have to—unless he wants to win. Without Jackson's vote, there is no victory." But, says Bert Lance, "I met with them a few times, and it was obvious they had no real understanding of Jesse at all. They kept wanting to talk about, how do we *handle* Jesse Jackson? I told them they reminded me of Mondale's questions about Jesse earlier. That if you had to ask that question, you'd never be able to deal with him because it showed an absolute lack of understanding. But they really didn't *want* to understand." Instead, Dukakis's simple preoccupation was a repeat of Mondale's before him, and would be repeated again by Clinton after him: fatal it would be to seem too closely connected to Jackson, with the task then becoming merely to try mollifying him somehow to avoid alienating his great following, while still, in more important deference to all those white voters supposedly offended by him, rigorously sustaining the appearance of being detached and unbeholden to him. Dukakis adviser John Sasso would later explain the calculation that was also to be precisely the obsession of Bill Clinton's campaign four years later: "If the presidential candidate disagrees with the party's most influential black leader, the candidate must . . . break out of his political fright and disagree. In some ways, voters seem to judge the strength and skill and character of the Democratic candidate on how effectively he gets along or copes with Jackson. It becomes an unending litmus test."

After the New York primary, Dukakis allowed himself only a few perfunctory meetings with Jackson, almost always with staff present. With his technician's passion for efficiency, Dukakis's mode for contending with Jackson was, says one observer, "to stick to the conventional, and say little, say little, say little." Before long, Jackson was widely protesting, "He won't talk to me. He just won't talk to me alone."

With the Atlanta convention approaching, Jackson convened a council of some twenty-five of his close advisers in a hotel in Chicago, Lance among them, and Lance shortly called John White: "You got to get involved in this, because Jesse is about to get steered the wrong way by some barn burners here." White later recollected, "For sure Jesse had a lot of delegates, and the question of how he used those delegates could determine the course of the campaign and the party, not to mention Jesse's own future. Now people in that meeting were advising him to make an independent run for the presidency, telling him, 'You ought to be on the ticket, you've earned the right.'" Lance recalls, "They were firmly convinced that Jesse was a viable vice presidential candidate, and John and I made the point, look, this talk doesn't make any sense, this is just stuff that there's no way it's gonna happen, they're not gonna put you on the ticket. Dukakis, unless he was operating outside his own mental abilities, wouldn't have ever done anything like that. So I told Jesse, 'Don't get yourself in a position where you have to be turned down.'" Nevertheless, it was clear to White that "Jesse still hoped he *would* be chosen. No question about it."

One reason why, White continued, was perversely that "Dukakis's people kind of led Jesse on"—no doubt essaying thereby to keep him contained for as long as possible. White attended one of their sessions with Jackson, ostensibly among their series with other possible nominees, that was conducted at the Grand Hyatt in Washington by two chief Dukakis advisers, Paul Brountas one of them, and White reported, still incredulous, years later, "I sat in that room as they actually interviewed him about the vice presidency." Despite suggestions beforehand to Jackson that such interviews were most often mere ceremonious pleasantries, White was surprised by how "this interview was in such detail, an extensive, lawyer-type interview. It went into a lot of personal things, you know," inquiries into his fabled past amatory capering, and asked him "about his health reports. As I remember, he wouldn't submit his health report because, he said, Dukakis hadn't submitted his." White chuckled, "Yeah, Jesse's always negotiating." But White's discomfort was, "I didn't think it was serious. And I thought they were making a mistake. I really didn't understand why they didn't be more direct with him from the beginning, say, 'No, Jesse, we're not going to do it, we're going with somebody else.' But Jesse asked them, 'Am I seriously being considered?' and they said, 'Yes, you are.'" As a result, for White, it wasn't hard to understand why Jackson's vice presidential illusions continued to be excited when "somebody seriously talks to you about it who has the power to do it."

For all their ruses to restrain him, though, by early July, Jackson still had neither conceded nor endorsed Dukakis nor actually ceased his barnstorming about the country, in which he was getting twice the coverage accorded to the party's certain nominee. Dukakis became so vexed by Jackson's intimations of pitched battles on the convention floor over his platform propositions—for denouncing corporate "economic violence," for a domestic Marshall Plan, for a further democratization of voter registration—that he finally barked at a press conference, "Jesse Jackson can do what he wants." Nevertheless, only a little over two weeks before the convention, Dukakis was persuaded to at least perform the gesture of inviting Jackson and his wife to his home in Brookline, Massachusetts, for a Fourth of July dinner and then a fireworks concert by the Boston Pops. Borosage attests that "Jackson expected something serious to happen"—in fact, he supposed it was all meant to offer him the vice presidential spot at last—"but Dukakis expected to just socialize, and that it would be a big thing for Jesse. You know, 'I've brought you into Brookline, what more could you want?' "

When Jackson and Jackie landed at the Boston airport, no one was there to pick them up, and though Jackson assumed his people had apprised Dukakis's staff that he could not eat milk products, almost the entire menu was to consist of milk-based dishes, New England clam chowder and poached salmon in cream sauce and ice cream. Nevertheless, the occasion did not turn out to be quite the wholesale disaster that was afterward generally reported: to Jackie at least, the evening seemed to ripple along fairly amiably. She and Jackson arrived at the Dukakis home around six o'clock to find a considerable crowd collected outside, with both Dukakis and Kitty at the front door to greet them. Inside, the rooms were filled with freshly cut flowers, Jackie noted, "which reflected the time taken with them," and she and Jackson, directed to a place on a sofa, were asked what they'd like to drink. Jackson, explaining that he did not partake of spirits, requested a Coke, but both Jackie and Kitty had rum libations.

The conversation moved into a patter about their children, and after some minutes of this, Dukakis mentioned the immense changes that had taken place in America since all four of them had been children. Kitty, herself Jewish, remarked that she had received only one anti-Semitic letter during the campaign, declaring her wonder at how America had grown. Jackie mused to herself, "She has to be lying," and Jackson cited the death threats he had received. Dukakis asked if they were as plentiful as during his last campaign, and Jackson reported there were more—though, he added, his two campaigns had finally constrained the country to deal with the full, diverse racial composition of American society. From that, he went on to the actual racial complexion of the world. . . . During these mostly meandering exchanges, Jackie had time to note that Dukakis, when he crossed one leg over the other, displayed an unusually large shoe for so diminutive a man. It also appeared to her that "Kitty has a great deal of influence over him," which moved her to the meditation that "in a white woman's world, they control their man. Black women don't."

The dinner itself impressed her, whatever its milk constituents, as "a hearty meal." With all but Jackson sipping white wine, they discussed the Middle East, Nicaragua's Daniel Ortega, and Castro's situation in Cuba, those in Latin America who in another time and with different U.S. administrations would probably have been natural friends—and in this colloquy, it seemed to Jackie that Jackson and Dukakis "agreed on nearly everything. One would have thought they were twins."

They all then repaired to another room for what Jackson now trusted would be the more pertinent conversation, and finally, as Jackie remembered it, came "the great question." Dukakis said to Jackson, "If I offered you the vice president spot, would you accept?"

Jackson speedily and flatly replied, "Yes." He then could not refrain from pressing, "Why do you ask?"

Dukakis merely responded that he was still talking to others about it, and that he would "have to get back" to him. He asked Jackie how she felt about it. At about that moment one of the Dukakis daughters terminated the discussion by coming into the room to tell them dessert was ready.

They proceeded on to the concert along the banks of the Charles River, where Irving Berlin melodies ascended to spatterings of fireworks across the summer night sky, all of which Jackie thought "spectacular." At its finish, Dukakis professed to be sleepy, and asked Jackson to phone him the next morning.

On the whole, it had seemed, by Jackie's testimony, more or less like some quiet, pleasant, casual evening with political neighbors from just around the corner. But it also left her with a faint, less pleasant sensation of having been elaborately patronized, that Dukakis had all along "led us to believe he was asking questions he did not know." One detail in particular, she noticed, "was quite interesting. Much of the conversation, when Dukakis initiated it, was directed to me," not to Jackson himself.

As for Jackson, according to some accounts, he left enraged. One friend averred, "He felt he'd been treated like a nigger."

The End in Atlanta

AFTER THAT VISIT to Brookline, and just two weeks now before the convention was to open in Atlanta, Jackson—who still had not conceded, deploying his usual complex suspense of multiple unforeclosed possibilities—set out on a seven-day blitz of rallies through nine major cities across the nation, delivering an average of four speeches at each stop. Dukakis's people at last concluded that it was bootless to delay any longer apprising Jackson he would not be offered the vice presidential nomination, and Brountas called him in to make that plain to him. Jackson, his face a mask of impassive gravity, informed Brountas that he expected at least to be spared the humiliation of learning of the choice through the press. That wound up, however, to be precisely how the word came to him that Dukakis had selected Texas senator Lloyd Bentsen. But again, when he received this news, however clobbering an interior hit, he remained uncustomarily quiet and still. "Whenever you see him like that," says one intimate, "that's when he's most dangerous."

Jackson shortly came up with the stroke of existential guerrilla theater of setting out from Chicago for the convention in Atlanta in a cavalcade of seven buses called the Rainbow Express, announcing, "You got to keep up the street-heat to get what you want." This caravan—laden with Jackson partisans and some 165 reporters and photographers, Jackson riding in the front bus in a white safari shirt—advanced for three days like a kind of motorized militant mass meeting with Jackson discharging phosphorescent shells at rallies along the way, in Indianapolis, Louisville, Nashville, Chattanooga: "I cannot be asked to go out into the field, pick up voters, bale them up, and deliver them to the big house where policy is made and not be a part of the equation. We want partnership, equity, and shared responsibility." With the vice presidential possibility now irrecoverably lost, this had become Jackson's final, fierce struggle to claim the acceptance within the system that he felt he had earned after a lifetime's exclusion—to at least make his long and unceasing campaign over the past six years an integral element of the Democratic party. His bus caravan paused at the Holiday Inn on Interstate 75 just outside Calhoun to pick up Bert Lance, along with Dan Rather. Lance recalls, "By that point, it was taking on all these different aspects of: what was he gonna do when he got to Atlanta?" Besides the harrowing possibility for the party of a turmoil of walkouts and even some rump convention in the street outside the convention hall, "Jackson's got twelve hundred delegates," says Robert Borosage, "who'd be quite happy to break out into a demonstration to keep Mike Dukakis off the stage the day he's nominated."

But in the meantime, Dukakis had gone into something like a lock of outraged intractability about engaging with Jackson at all, "refusing to talk to him," says Borosage. "Cuomo, Gephardt, all of them are calling Dukakis, pleading with him. Cuomo tells him, 'Are you crazy? *Call the guy.* Make a deal.' But Dukakis thinks, I won the nomination, it's mine, why do I have to deal with this guy? Why is he causing trouble? He should just shut up. Dukakis seemed to have no real grasp of what was at stake. He just says, 'Well, what does he want? He want money or something?' It was really quite clear that what Jackson wanted was to show that his seven million votes were part of this party, and that it would be together that they'd make the national campaign. But Dukakis and his people wanted nothing to do with that. They either thought he was trying to hold them up for money, or they just wanted no part of the other thing." Much reinforcing that adamancy was the old neurosis about the question now once more being widely dinned around them: "The press kept building it up," says Borosage. *"Is Dukakis going to cave to Jesse?"*

Jackson's cavalcade of buses finally, late on the Saturday afternoon before the convention's opening on Monday, pulled into Atlanta, where thousands of supporters were massed waiting for him in a midtown park, and Lance remembers that "it was this triumphal entry almost like, you know, Palm Sunday, Jesus coming into Jerusalem." But according to Borosage, "Those ten thousand people in that park were ready to march on the Democratic convention, burn something down. All they want is marching orders." When Jackson addressed them, he urged on them instead the ordered discipline of a patient and steady hope, "talking to them about all they'd built together," says Borosage, "how far they'd come but the long way they had to go yet. We don't have to march to protest outside the conventional hall, we have seats inside now. We've earned our way inside the convention. We're here now to build from the inside out, rather than sack the place from the outside in. It was an enormously responsible speech."

Afterward, Jackson tried making another call to Dukakis, and this time managed to reach him. As Borosage relates it, he told Dukakis, "Look, this thing's gonna blow apart. I can't keep holding it together. You've got to meet with me, we've got to get an agreement—" advising Dukakis then with a peculiar solicitude, "You can't give me anything, because the press will burn you. So we just have to have a peace agreement." It was again, of course, that deftness Jackson had employed ever since the Greensboro demonstrations for developing a situation's barometric pressure to a point of emergency, which he would then offer to step into to ease.

When Jackson was settled into his suite at the Marriott Marquis, just across the street behind the Hyatt Regency where Dukakis was installed, Borosage late that night brought in Harold Ickes, who had managed Ted Kennedy's convention challenge of Carter and would go on to join the Clinton campaign in 1992, winding up as one of Clinton's chief White House deputies. When they found themselves finally alone with Jackson, Borosage told him, "Harold here knows these kinds of conventions, and I just wanted him to run through your alternatives. We're not trying to push anything, it's just that he can give you a kind of sense of things." Jackson sleepily mumbled, "Okay, then," and as Borosage tells it, "Harold gets this glint in his eye, he's crazy as a loon but a genius, and he says, 'Reverend Jackson, this time on Thursday you could either be seconding the nomination of Michael Dukakis to be president of the United States . . . or twelve hundred delegates could be blowing whistles and keeping him from speaking on prime time.' Well, Jackson's eyes go wide. He says, 'Oh-oh. You two white guys are trying to get this little black guy in trouble.' And he walks out of the room. It was very clear that he knew exactly what he could do, but he wasn't about to do it." Despite all that had happened to him up to now, Jackson resolutely persevered as, in a way, "the most loyal Democrat of them all," Borosage says. Not only because of his abiding compulsion to belong, but from the historical nostalgia that "the Democratic party had been the vehicle by which civil rights had taken place, the party of working people and the poor."

Around midnight on Sunday, Dukakis at last phoned Jackson, reaching him backstage at the Fox Theater, where, a half century after the premiere there of *Gone With the Wind*, a gospel music gala in tribute to Jackson's candidacy was in progress, and Dukakis invited him to a breakfast meeting the next morning in his suite. Even so, Dukakis still contrived to avoid having to face Jackson alone, arranging for Paul Brountas to be there and, to complement him, Ron Brown, who had become Jackson's convention manager. The discussion lasted some three hours, a carefully courteous affair. Jackson would later relate, "When Dukakis hadn't even called to tell me about his vice presidential pick, well, I intercepted that pass and held that moral advantage until I thought it appropriate to give it back at the convention. Then, in the name of party unity and creating a basis for future relationships, I stepped back from a confrontation." But the agreement that would emerge after their meeting was to prove only a marginal and ephemeral return on Jackson's last battle for at least some impingement on the party's prevailing structures. It provided for the inclusion of some Jackson staffers in the Dukakis campaign organization and the Democratic National Committee, the eventual reduction by half of the 645 super-delegates (who predictably were to vote almost in toto against Jackson in Atlanta), the furnishing of a small jet for Jackson's use in campaigning for the ticket—but little more than that, and little of any of it lasting. Even at that, it was an arrangement actually mostly worked out before that Monday-morning encounter, so that in their meeting "Jackson has to ask Dukakis for nothing," says Borosage, "absolutely zero." Instead, it became mainly a matter of, at first, their exchanging their respective irritations over commentary and conduct toward each other over the past weeks, with Dukakis then reviewing the logistics and technicalities for a united campaign operation, while Jackson kept undertaking deep-fathom soundings of Dukakis's true soul.

But after their meeting, Borosage says, "the headlines are great for Dukakis: 'Dukakis Faces Down Jackson,' 'Dukakis Gives Jackson Nothing'—headlines that, of course, Jackson arranged to help him get, right? To give some lift to this Democratic nominee who's got to take on the Republicans. But after the convention, they try to isolate Jackson from the campaign, while Dukakis proceeds to piss away a seventeen-point lead over Bush, and then they try to rewrite the history of it all by saying, 'The reason we lost was because Jesse Jackson had such a huge effect in Atlanta, because the Democratic party looked like it was Jesse Jackson's party.' Amazing." After the election, Dukakis's campaign manager, John Sasso, did, in fact, present exactly that explanation in parsing for reporters why Dukakis was defeated by Bush.

As it was, immediately after Jackson's session with Dukakis, one Democratic regular groused to *Esquire* writer Peter Davis, "This isn't going to play well across the country. Jackson's presence is dominating this convention, and he hasn't even spoken yet." When he did, on Tuesday evening, he produced again a mighty oration in which, one journalist remarked, "Cheers erupted almost whenever he took a breath"—some fifty-five interrupting swells of shouting applause altogether, with eighteen standing ovations. Though Walter Cronkite, long the electronic high vicar of the nation's centrist civic propriety, afterward ruminated on Jackson's dangerous potential for demagoguery, Jackson's oratorical poetries were again compared, this time by Frank Mankiewicz, once press secretary to Robert Kennedy, to Bryan's "Cross of Gold" speech in 1896.

Toward the end of the convention, Jackson, chatting with an assembly of his delegates while sitting on the edge of a table with his tie loosened, tried to enhearten them with the assurance, as he had admonished those in the park on his arrival, "If there's some hurt here today, try Atlantic City, 1964 convention. We couldn't even get into the hall then. We've come too far to turn back now. So let's keep going. . . ."

Indian Summer

BUT WITH THE conclusion of the convention in Atlanta, Jackson seemed to sense that his own high political season, six years now since its beginnings in his voter-registration evangelisms through the South, might have finally come to its finish. Through the following days, he affected a brave buoyancy—asked by aides, "How you doing, Reverend?" he would ring out, "God's been good to me, been good to me." But all the loud multitudes, the trampling gangs of reporters and camera crews, the Secret Service agents swimming around him, all had abruptly vanished like an uproarious mirage. When Jackson returned for a few days to La Costa, the villa beside his, where a Secret Service detachment had always been quartered, was, this time, dark and empty, and "it was a little weird," recalls Eric Easter. "All of a sudden, we had to start watching out after all our own things, and he was a lot more tense about how organized things were—'Do we have the plane tickets?' He was nervous about people getting close, and we would always try to close the elevator doors before anybody else could get in."

One among the old faithful at PUSH who had journeyed down to Atlanta to assist Jackson remembers, "That was one time I really saw him at his top, at the pinnacle. And that excitement, with just everything happening everywhere, had been going on for him for months and months, you know. But then all of a sudden"—and she snaps her fingers—"it's over." When Jackson at last came back home to Chicago, she says, he passed several days simply sitting in the living room by himself "not talking at all. As if he was thinking, 'Where did it all go?' Like, you almost had it in your hand and now it's gone." Whenever the phone rang, "he'd grab it up himself. I think he really wanted to talk to somebody, to people out there. . . ."

But for weeks, few, if any, of those calls came from anyone with the Dukakis campaign. With a fixation still about not disquieting the white Reagan Democrats whom he hoped to beguile back into the party, Dukakis diligently continued to keep Jackson at an inconspicuous distance, until his political technician's strategy of nonideological competence finally appeared to be fatally foundering. John White would recount being summoned by Lance to yet another conclave of Jackson and his major supporters in Chicago, "in which the barn burners now were all out for attacking Dukakis. That was a hot meeting. Jesse was saying he wasn't going to take the treatment they were giving him, and I remember somebody telling him, 'Yeah, this suit don't fit you.' And right about then, Sasso called into the meeting for Jesse—just at that moment, it just happened somehow. Maybe they'd gotten word some way that Jesse was terribly pissed and was in this meeting. But Sasso talked to Jesse and asked him to come to New York to meet with him. And they worked out a program there for him."

Once called, however belatedly, full force into the campaign, Jackson whaled away at it heartily, and was able, by its end, to authentically claim,

"I've traveled more miles for this ticket, spoken to more people, than Dukakis and Bentsen have. Worked harder for them than they've worked for themselves. Yeah. S'pose either one of them would have done that for me?" By mid-September, according to one poll, black support for Dukakis over Bush had lifted from 51 percent to 81 percent. Another, earlier poll by the Joint Center for Political Studies, before Jackson had been summoned into the field, found that the black vote was likely to drop significantly from its high in 1984 and, what's more, black support for Bush was nearly double what it had been for Reagan. But on the day of the election, both the turnout of blacks and their vote for Dukakis wound up about what they had been for Mondale in 1984.

BUT EVEN WHILE he was swooping about the country for the Dukakis-Bentsen ticket those last fall weeks of 1988, Jackson could not abstain from long broodings. Despite his entente cordiale with the Dukakis campaign now, he complained that it had discarded his own organizers and, along with them, the mass constituency he had built, especially in the inner cities. "That crowd around Dukakis, they still just don't understand the whole of this country. They got about the same picture of it that Bush's folks do, that's been their problem. They don't know where all the bodies really are. I can't remember seeing a one of their ads that's reflected the diversity of America." On the day of the election itself, while flying to Milwaukee in response to a last-hour entreaty from Dukakis's headquarters, he sat in a kind of peaceful suspension high in the fading afternoon and began reflecting, with obvious gratification, to the cluster of reporters around him, "If I can help by making this appearance in Milwaukee, I will help. I made myself available to help in Atlanta, and I've done the best I could. We always had the numbers to win. I was not in charge of prioritizing those numbers, but I've done my best to arouse them where I could. Thing about America's cities, it's all races and classes, a mass multiethnic base. It's the true Democratic base. In a macrosense, it's the base we *should* have launched from, now calling on us at the last minute here, trying to crash-land at."

He went on then wistfully to propose that he could have been "just as effective an X factor in this election for the Democrats as Reagan's been for the Republicans. But our X factor was not projected." One reporter suggested that this comparison might be a touch overweening, Reagan being the president and he not, and Jackson snapped back that official position wasn't the point, but the sort of popular mobilizing power "that's resulted in my registering more new voters than any other Democrat in history. Congressional races of 1986, Reagan hit the field for Republican candidates, I hit the field for our candidates, and we won—kept our majority in the House and won back the Senate. In this campaign, I have consistently drawn bigger crowds than Reagan has. The coverage just hasn't been equal. Networks ought to have made a better judgment there."

That old aggrievement about how the media had disregarded him was one of the scenarios from his past efforts that he kept replaying, as, through those few weeks he seemed to be passing through a strange sort of apparitional Indian summer of his own national campaigns. "Receptions by white farmers, for instance, though I probably couldn't of seemed more distant from them at first, in their minds the profile of a friend began to emerge, and they started responding everywhere. But media never did notice that something important was happenin' here. . . ." He now happened to be riding with a small party of journalists through a cold and overcast Iowa countryside, in a mammoth $72,000 Winnebago Itasca Windcruiser, like a floating motel lobby inside, which the driver, one of Jackson's white supporters, had acquired after winning the Iowa lottery. Just as Jackson had been finishing a speech a half hour before at a courthouse rally, the Winnebago had come looming around the square with the abrupt fabulous improbability of some strayed steamboat, its two-horn synthesizer lustily tootling out "Happy Days Are Here Again." It was now bearing Jackson to the Des Moines airport with its owner, a man rather of the proportions of a compacted bale of hay, settled behind the wheel at perfect peace with the world, the two-horn synthesizer blasting out Sousa marches over the wide, drab fields. Jackson, perched sideways in the elevated swivel seat beside the driver, was wearing a natty gray-plaid suit with a green feed-company hat clamped on his head. But even though this was near the very last day of the general election campaign, Jackson was still fretting to this final straggle of reporters scattered over the sofas behind him about how slightingly he'd been covered back during the primaries. "Tip-off should've been when I could get the votes in Iowa in '88 that Hart got in '84, with all the baggage that I carry, stereotype of my background as an urban black male. I mean, for me to even come *close* to getting double digits here in Iowa, better than Gore or Babbitt, against my sociological odds, is a bigger statement than just *numbers*. But in the television reports through that whole night, we got only 'bout fifteen seconds, 'Oh, yeah, by the way, Jackson—'" He kept impatiently snatching his trouser cuffs up almost to his knees to tautly tug up his high socks. "I mean, Super Tuesday, popular vote, hell, we *won*. Even *with* that afterthought kind of coverage. We had a whole planeload of reporters, but the story just wasn't breaking through. If there had been a respect based on substance and the implications of this dynamic, we'd be in an entirely different kind of situation riding along here right now—understand what I'm sayin'?"

Still, on the day of Dukakis's defeat, Jackson was already proclaiming, with deathless hopefulness, "The new political season starts tomorrow, and I will continue to serve. The full scope of my leadership has yet to blossom and flourish."

What He Availed Anyway

THE EXPANDING POLITICAL assertion with which Jackson seemed to have become entranced over the previous six years may not have been what in his beginning, from Greenville through Greensboro to his time with King, he had actually meant to do, meant to be. But even if his two presidential exertions had amounted to grand digressions from his original prophetic impulse, they had nevertheless, in the assessment of many, worked their own not inconsiderable effects.

"Jesse paid a very high price in those campaigns," Andrew Young submits, "but I think he may have well saved the country with them, at that critical time during Reagan. He restored a mass focus on black concerns, on poverty and other conditions holding a real danger of social eruption if left ignored. He inspired great hope in the black community. And his voter-registration efforts brought a liberalization of the makeup of Congress— it was how we got forty blacks in the House, how we got those Democratic victories in the Senate. In fact, those voter-registration campaigns of his were ultimately how we got Clinton elected, want to know the truth." It would also come to be generally acknowledged that it was Jackson's expansion of the black electorate that eventually supplied the margin to repulse the reach for the Louisiana governorship by Ku Klux Klan leader David Duke, who had actually drawn the majority of the white vote in that election.

At the least, Jackson became for a time the sole national protagonist offering any prospect for a survival of the traditional liberal conscience in the country's political life. "Look, when it's all written down," asserts Bert Lance, "who's the fella who really raised the question of health care in this country? Jesse Jackson raised health care in a manner that came *home*, talking about those women who remove bedpans from a hospital room they can't even get a bed in when *they're* sick; let me tell you, Ted Kennedy ain't never talked about nobody with a bedpan. And the first time the number of thirty-seven million people who don't have health care was ever raised was by Jesse Jackson in his '88 presidential campaign, which is the forum, a presidential campaign, in which it had to be raised. Just was nobody in those races like him. South Africa. Who was the fella who ultimately called attention in a large way to the plight of Mandela? Jesse Jackson was talking about Mandela and South Africa way back there in those '84 debates, when almost nobody outside the black community knew who Mandela was or what was going on over there."

Mark Steitz recollects, "Taxing the rich was the type of thing that, when Jackson said it in '88, he took huge heat for—oh, there the radical goes again. The notion of restraining defense spending—oh, back to the old Democrats. Having an aggressive investment program in education and rebuilding America—oh, more big spending. But that radical set of ideas was exactly what won Clinton the presidency, whatever he's done with them since." Another former Jackson adviser maintains, "When Clinton was looking for a central theme to run on, he came up with 'putting people first'—remarkable echoes of Jackson, right down to the phrasing." When he was once again campaigning for the Democratic nominee, this time Clinton, through the autumn of 1992, Jackson, after an early-evening appearance in Odessa, Texas, mused aloud when back in the dark of his van, "Yeah, reinvest in America, convert defense industry to peaceful enterprise, all those themes . . . it's like Little Richard and Pat Boone. Little Richard wrote all those songs that Pat Boone then took, whitened 'em up, and made millions. But that's all right. Give me anybody to train for a while, I'll be his Little Richard, and he can take off."

Simply the popular span achieved by Jackson's populist apostleship was, Andrew Kopkind wrote, "of historic proportions. He traversed lines of class and race—African-Americans, Native Americans, Arab-Americans, field workers, white displaced farm and factory families, the underclass and the working poor—to create a genuine populist force that played serious politics in the highest national arena." At the same time, while his two campaigns could not be taken, with all the doubts raised about Jackson personally, as a final measure of how much the nation remained a racially fissured society, yet his candidacy was no insignificant reconnaissance into that more momentous question: To what extent does racial schism endure as the old, inherent, fundamental American malady? On that count, the specific results were at best ambivalent. He did wind up faring far more strongly among white voters than almost anyone had initially anticipated, and especially with his Super Tuesday showing, Garry Wills remarked, he "began to make it seem possible for Democrats to cooperate with blacks without losing all the whites who have defected in the South since the sixties." Yet Jackson never approached anything like a majority of the white vote, and, by many reports, prompted about as much antipathy as support in the white community.

In the end, figures like Jackson "rarely win elections," Paul Taylor observed in his chronicle of the 1988 campaign, but they "invent new possibilities." Jackson himself would once declare while campaigning for Clinton in 1992, "You can't lose when you run, because you make things happen." To be sure, blacks were carried in the tides of his two campaigns more deeply and extensively into America's political life than ever before. Jackson's first pastoral supporter in Chicago, Clay Evans, declares, "He didn't make it to president, but all his campaigning helped many mayors get elected, many aldermen, and other people like governors, senators. *Because of him.* Some black, some white, but all the recipient of Jesse Louis Jackson. Because Jesse was going all over the country to register people" — and Evans begins punctuating a rising incantation by slapping his hands together—"and waking people up," *slap*, "that you can do it," *slap*, *slap*, "and we can do it," *slap!* "He helped build up hope," *slap*, "here," *slap*, "there," *slap*, "everywhere!" *Slap!* "Can't take that away from 'im. He's been shakin' the tree for a lot of 'em, and the fruit falls and they get it and make themselves jam and jelly. And then he never gets any of it, because they'll never give him credit. That's sad." Asked if there were any intimations in that of Jackson's winding up a tragic figure, Evans merely grunts. "I don't wanna talk about that."

More, there's little question that Jackson himself made the initial breach through that old barrier in the general mind to any serious consideration of a presidential candidacy by a black—leaving open a possibility through which, it appeared for a while in 1995, Colin Powell could well pass. Richard Hatcher suggests that Jackson had become something like a political version of King in that, "like Moses, he's been allowed to see the Promised Land but will never be able to get there himself. He cannot be Joshua, going on over with the people into Canaan. Ironically, that could be some person very different from Jesse, who, in what he represents and wants to do, will irritate fewer whites, will be more acceptable to them, because they will see him as more like themselves—'Okay, I think I can get past the color thing and vote for him, because I know in my heart that in his heart he's just like me. He's proven that.'" The question would then become what has actually been gained, says Hatcher, "what difference does it make that the color of their skin happens to be like mine if, in fact, they are not sensitive to the problems African Americans face in this country, if they have in fact spent their careers and will spend their entire tenure in office running away from that?" But whoever it might be, says Hatcher, "while Jesse has hastened the day when there will be a black president, Jesse himself will never become president. In a way, there's a sadness in that."

XVIII
Taking Gospel Populism Abroad

EVEN BEFORE THE end of Jackson's 1988 primary effort, David Halberstam proposed, "Jesse Jackson isn't going to get to be in this system what he might think he wants to be. But he could be something actually more important. He has become America's media black man in the world media age." Indeed, in his expeditions abroad, there increasingly seemed intimations that Jackson could actually find his largest realization as a kind of global gospel-populist tribune. Television's gradual forming of a new, planetary consciousness means the beginning of a new global conscience; Jackson himself suggested during a 1989 jaunt overseas: "All our yards much closer to each other now, which expands the compass of the golden rule about loving your neighbor as yourself." He cited, as one instance of how direct popular witness through television can act to overwhelm government policy, the vast spontaneous mobilization of aid to Ethiopia during the famine there in the mid-eighties "despite Reagan arguin' those people were starving because of Marxism, not drought. Some things you just can't stop anymore, with all the world connected and watching now like it is." For the same reason, he contended, it had become enormously more difficult to conduct massive and systematic crimes such as slavery or the Holocaust, because evils of that dimension depend on being generally unwitnessed. "Of all the forces on this planet right now, none is more momentous than world television. It's producing a whole new order of world awareness and world politics, and with that, a new sort of world leader, world figure."

To a degree, Jackson became part of that phenomenon. A former associate at PUSH, Robert Starks, remembers that "his 1984 campaign was a benchmark in terms of international coverage of a political event in America, because it was the first time they had the big satellite stuff. So there was a global audience. And Jesse became an instant worldwide personality." After his 1988 campaign, as Jackson was touring a hospital in Moscow one murky winter morning, tramping along sallow corridors past ticking radiators, nurses and orderlies collected around, one of them exclaiming to a member of Jackson's group, "We watched him in your election, we were very much for him, and now to see him here among us, it is unreal for us!" Then, at a dinner given for him by government officials one evening in Yerevan, the republic's Communist party chairman announced, "We watched on television here many of your presidential campaign speeches, you know. Especially your speech to the Democratic convention. Here in Yerevan, I have recorded what you said in that speech, yes. From time to time, I play it again. That was a great speech in politics. In my opinion, Mr. Jackson, whether you accept it or not"—and the chairman, a stout man, now rather ruddy from multiple toasts of Armenian brandy, bustled upward in his chair as if preparing to vault across the table—"I'll tell you, that was the greatest political speech, second to none! A speaker like that I have never seen in my life! Here in the Soviet Union," the chairman went on, "we have such a thing in our standards committees which is called the quality sign. You, Reverend Jesse Jackson, have the quality sign. My son, I will tell you, who is in second year at the university, when he talks about America, he has three figures he respects most: Frank Roosevelt, Jack Kennedy, and Jesse Jackson, you yourself!"

The same enthusiasms gather around him in even the most obscure back reaches of the countries he visits, his passage through those remote parts turning into uncanny reflections of his popular processionals back in the States, with the same sort of instant folk communion, ranging from the pandemonious to, in some situations, the almost reverential. When Jackson journeyed to the Soviet Union in 1989 to discuss a relief program for victims of the earthquake in Armenia, he traveled one iron-cold afternoon through the snow-spattered ruins of Leninakan, where some 14,000 people had perished, to a hospital that was caring for some of the injured children. And as he made his way on through the stark rooms of women grouped at the bedsides of their maimed children, he drew the women into enveloping hugs, muttering, "Love you very much. Just hold on. God's gonna take care of you, got you in the palm of his hand now," and some of them, along with the nurses and other doctors, followed him back outside to the courtyard, where a huge throng was now collected. After he had stepped up into the bus, they all crowded against its side, looking up at him through the window, and he finally climbed down again, once more taking them one by one into smothering hugs. Later that afternoon, when he arrived at the town of Spitak, where only 2,000 out of its pre-earthquake population of 20,000 were left alive, people began sifting out of the chaos to form a dense multitude around him in the bitingly cold dusk.

Jackson cried out hoarsely, "I know it's hard now, know you're hurtin', know you're grievin'—know it's lookin' awfully *dark* now. But mornin' *is* comin'. *You are not alone.* So keep on holdin' on." Then, as he was forging through the crowd with double-seizing handshakes, there suddenly sounded a cry of "King!" Jackson, startled, looked around. A squat, thick man, grinning at him through a grime of unshaven beard, called out again, "King! Martin Luther King, you!" Jackson turned to murmur in amazement to one of his party, "Hear that? Even way back out here—you hear that?"

Developing from global television is what Jackson describes as "a global congregation. . . . A few in that congregation are seen as its elders, but none is seen as its pastor. Political leaders are not pastors. Their service is legitimate, but there's nothing about a deacon or treasurer or usher that makes you, for *awlll* the people, the presenter of their case on Sunday morning. When you pastor of the *big* church you must see the needs of all within that congregation. But those in authority so far aren't answering that." That could offer, with Jackson's instinct for detecting and moving into openings in the ecology of situations around him, the largest gap of all in which to make himself through forming new connective synapses. "The Bible says, if those who should speak out don't speak out, the very rocks will cry out. Well, if nobody else will speak out for the moral case in situations over the whole world, and if you then stand up and testify, the congregation will say *Amen* and bless you. And you become its leader, the pastor of the congregation."

Actually, Jackson sets out on his ministerial tours abroad with more or less the view that the rest of the world is merely a duplication, on a larger scale, of the experiences of his own origins. "It's the same dynamics everywhere, whether it's Greenville or Jerusalem, Chicago or Soviet Union. Same hopes and paradoxes. When I was in South Africa, it was incredible how the exploitation I saw there was so parallel with home. Fact, there were some white people there who'd grown up and worked in textile plants around Greenville, over in South Africa now working in the same kind of system I'd come from. And yet, within those systems, you also always find those few good people, those few honest and righteous. It's like it all has to be played out again and again, over all the world. But that's why the simple moral truths of Haynie Street and Long Branch Baptist Church are just as real whether behind Kremlin walls or in the Middle East or South Africa—or the White House, I might add. Those truths work wherever human beings are."

Even so, while he may consider all the world just an expanded version of neighborhoods back home, he forges about those distant locales with an almost boyish ebullience of tall adventure. In Lagos, he had passed a long morning soliloquizing over the remains of breakfast while waiting for air clearance for his flight down to Angola, during the war there. After Luanda at last confirmed clearance, and as Jackson's plane was lifting from the Lagos airport, he let out a happy yawp, "Awright! Goin' down into the *country* now. Goin' into *deep* country, yawl!" He will ceaselessly excite himself in this manner about the novelty and high drama, as he imagines it, of what he is embarked on in foreign countries. After discussions with Angola's president dos Santos about a then pending peace accord for the region, Jackson, while striding back to his car, could not resist shouting, "Man, something's goin' on in the world—and we *right in the middle of it!*"

JACKSON'S JOURNEYINGS FROM capital to capital are generally accompanied by official receptions of considerable high protocol, he being greeted by government delegations and brigades of local dignitaries as if he were some curious sort of itinerant minister without portfolio. In some locations, the welcoming ceremonies have been somewhat whimsical. On landing in Lagos once, he was carried directly from the airport north into the Nigerian interior, where he was to be formally received by a Yoruba king, called the Oba, at his palace compound in a small community named Oyo. On the way there, Jackson's motorcade was preceded by an escort of police cars and motorcycles, provided by then president Ibrahim Babangida, that careened wildly, to clear the road immediately ahead— one man riding double on a motorcycle stretching out in midair delivering ferocious whacks with long clubs on the fenders and doors of balky vehicles, pursuing them off the road and into ditches. "Could use those guys during rush hour in New York," said someone in Jackson's car, and Jackson said, "They Babangida's special guys. They actually *trained* to drive that way, you know?" Outside the king's compound in Oyo, Jackson was greeted, amid a great dinning of drums and flat clanging of bells, by a deputation of the king's eunuchs, bald men as slight and wiry and gray as skinned squirrels, clad in simple homespun drapery. With a flutter of syllables they ushered Jackson—who was still attired, in the hot blaze of the morning, in one of his elegant banker's suits—into the king's enclave of bare, earthen dwellings, where Jackson's appearance was accompanied by a pulsing, two-tone blast from a thinly attenuated trumpet like a medieval herald's. The king's long, low lodge of a court looked as if it had been furnished with remnants from an early-sixties Holiday Inn: a nubbly gold carpet on the ground, the walls covered in wood veneer, and, reposing at the end of the room as a throne, a giant-sized wine-colored velour chair.

The king himself then appeared through a creaking side door—a small, plump, cinnamon-brown man with darkly wistful eyes, outfitted in a voluminous turquoise gown and a kind of winged cap, a bulky gold watch drooping from one wrist. Jackson was seated beside the king with the eunuchs squatting in a cluster at the king's feet, listening with meek kittenish stirrings, while a servant whisked a wide feather fan over the king's enormous chair. His company of gowned advisers were now ranged down the length of the room, settled in two facing rows of only slightly less capacious gold-colored velour easy chairs. The discourse between Jackson and the Oba before this audience had a certain drowsily wandering pleasantness. "How far back you trace your history?" Jackson asked, and the king replied, in a low croon, "To the Sudan." Referring to the king's gallery of advisers before them—one of whom had dozed off in the heat with one barefooted leg comfortably stretched out across the rug—Jackson said, "And how large is your cabinet here?"

"Cabinet? Ah, my cabinet . . ."

"The size."

"Ah. The size . . ."

Their talk eddied on in this fashion, to the slow swipes of the fan. At length, the king seemed to determine that the occasion had arrived at its proper climax. Declaring to Jackson, "You are a man among men," he thereupon decreed him a high chief of the tribe, with the name now of Atun-ayese, and presented him a brightly beaded walking stick, a dashiki embroidered in harlequined patterns of soft blues and greens—which Jackson promptly pulled on over his shirt and tie—and a winged cap like the king's own, all of which gave Jackson rather the look of a tropical Robin Hood. Afterward, on the drive back to Lagos, Jackson was informed by his Nigerian host, "The new name that the Oba gave you, it means, 'To better mankind over the world.' That is your title, and now you have to do it. It means you cannot bow to anyone, people must now bow to you." Jackson grunted. "Well, we need to get that word out real quick if we can, to let 'em know back in Washington 'fore I get back."

While in Moscow in 1989, Jackson had been invited to drop by the office of Vitaly Korotich, then the editor of the liberal journal *Ogonyok* and one of the most spirited early advocates of democratic reform. A profusely cordial man with the rosy face of a middle-aged leprechaun, Korotich enthused to Jackson in his merrily burbling approximation of English, "It's really great that you are here, one of the most important politicians of the globe, really. Great! And it's right thrilling for us that we are sitting here with leading American and one of greatest outside politicians." At that moment, a note was brought in to Korotich, and after glancing at it, he an-

nounced, "Our common friend want to contact you, Georgy Arbatov"—
who, as director of the U.S.A. and Canada Institute, had long been the Soviets' principal Americanologist—"I'll now try to call him for you," and
Korotich directed an assistant to put through the call. "While you are here,
he want to meet real American force for—" Korotich was notified the call
was ready, and he picked up the receiver of a phone beside him and
handed it to Jackson, who, lounging sideways in his chair, bayed out,
"Hey, man! . . . That right? You really glad to hear me? . . . I been tryin' to
catch you all day, buddy. Where can I reach you about six-thirty? . . . Just
one second, let me get that number, just a moment"—and he handed the
phone to Korotich to hold while he scuffled in his coat for a pen. Instead,
Korotich hung up the phone. Jackson sputtered, "Wai-wai-wai-, naw,
naw!" and Korotich said, "Ah, excuse me, please. We will call him back.
But these Kissingers, our great political leaders, they are not waiting on the
phone usually." Right then, Arbatov's office rang back, and Korotich himself took the number, then said to Jackson after hanging up the phone
again, "Please, everybody wants to see you, I don't know, for me is hard to
handle so many people knowing great politician and really great friend sitting here."

On the whole, it often appears that Jackson is taken with rather more seriousness abroad than back in the United States. And he does not hesitate
to assume a correspondingly magisterial mien. When Korotich finally had
to leave to close that week's issue of his magazine, Jackson simply appropriated his office for a discussion with three young democratic militants
just arrived to see him, seating himself in Korotich's vacated place at the
head of the table and calling out over the rising chatter, "Hey, hey, folks!
We movin' into another meetin' here." After his talks with presidents and
premiers in countries he visits, he will conduct press conferences before
waiting hosts of reporters with all the assured amplitude of some at-large
secretary of state. Once, after a private session with President François
Mitterrand, he held forth on the steps of the Elysée Palace, his voice
whomping over the gravel courtyard as he propounded on the international tensions he had just discussed. His manner with those heads of state
tends toward a gustily expansive bonhomie. At the conclusion of his talk
with Mitterrand, he had one of the president's aides bring an American
journalist waiting downstairs up the grand staircase to the drawing room
where he and Mitterrand were still standing together. Jackson announced,
"President Mitterrand here says I'm a mystery to him," and then turned to
Mitterrand, "Go ahead, Mr. President, tell him what you were telling me
about bein' a mystery to you," impressing Mitterrand into performing, with
a perceptible absence of pleasure, the exercise of repeating to this Ameri-

can reporter, through an interpreter, his observations to Jackson about how unusual it was for "a man of ideas" to rise so high in American politics. And at the completion of his recital, Mitterrand abruptly pronounced, "*Au revoir*," pivoted around, and departed the room.

For his part, Jackson will unfurl the most florid tapestries of acclaim to every eminence he visits. While in Zimbabwe, he called on President Robert Mugabe one morning at his government residence in Harare, the two of them sitting side by side in a large bright room with white-jacketed waiters soundlessly floating about with trays of tea and small sandwiches. Mugabe, once a Jesuit seminarian before turning Marxist bush guerrilla in the struggle against the old white Rhodesian regime, chatted with Jackson with a certain taut fastidious comportment, a strange professional delicacy to find in one formerly so fierce a guerrilla commander. Wearing fine gold-frame glasses, he was swankily appareled in a deep-blue suit, the toe of one lacquered black shoe flexing against the rug as he spoke in crisply donnish inflections. "May I congratulate you," he said to Jackson, "on your campaigns in America. A *job well done*. Wonderful performance," and he lightly clapped his hands, then briskly beat them on the arms of his chair, "Well done!" But Jackson then startled Mugabe by proposing that he make a Jackson-style popular campaign tour of his own across the United States. "I think a new relationship between America and Africa must be asserted by *you*," Jackson proclaimed. Mugabe seemed at first not entirely certain Jackson was serious. But to his indications of deep skepticism about the plausibility of such an expedition, Jackson assured him with his customary sweeping gusto, "Mr. President, by making Zimbabwe a united nonracist society, you have become the center of hope for reconciliation around the world. You don't have any idea how popular you are in America." Mugabe, dubious yet a bit dazzled by this revelation, piped, "Well, well, well," and tilted slightly forward to wipe his napkin in tight circles on the tray table before him: "Amongst whom?"

"Whole *reservoir* of people," declaimed Jackson, and as he went on, Mugabe seemed, despite himself, to be caught up in the notion. He did mention an uneasiness that he might find himself, as on an earlier visit to the United States, confined by certain demeaning constrictions of protocol. Jackson sighed, "Mr. President, Mr. President. The risk of humiliation is really very remote. If you allow yourself to get trapped in worries about protocol, you've let them put you in a box. It's too late for you to be gettin' conservative about these things now. Every time I look in the pages of history, change was never initiated through protocol, it was initiated by *dreamers*." Jackson waxed more animated in his exhortations, spanking the arm of Mugabe's chair, his voice swelling to pulpiteering resonations, until Mugabe, in a kind of vertigo, finally exclaimed, "Well, well, well! Good show! Most persuasive! Good show!"

Afterward, riding through the quiet small-town streets of Harare, Jackson shook his head. "All hung up on that protocol question. Ain't that something? So sensitive about being shown the proper respect now he's president. It's a long way from when he was fighting out in the countryside, tell you that. That protocol thing gets 'em all once they get in office. But I still try to communicate with these heads of state on the common human denominators," Jackson went on, "try to relate to them as just another human being who's got needs, blind spots, vanities, instead of within the trappings of protocol and did I cross my legs right. Most Americans who meet with these leaders talk conservative protocol to conservative protocol, always operate within that rigid set of boundaries around a policy. But that ain't my way. What can really come out of that, that hadn't already been scripted from a distance, out of contact?" When meeting in 1984 with Castro, said Jackson, instead of addressing him within the constraints of protocol formalities, "I dealt with him horizontally, and gave his humanity as much of a chance as I'd want people to give mine. Argued back and forth like two grown people. About what *made sense.*" The efficacy of such diplomacy through informal, personal engagement, Jackson suggested, was memorably demonstrated "with Reagan and Gorbachev. I mean, Reagan had these big speeches hard-grounded in ideology—Russia an evil empire, all that, arousin' our fears—but then one day, like the virgin, he went and messed around and had himself a relationship. Would *not* be stopped from going to Russia, and all of a sudden he's huggin' Gorbachev, talkin' about 'my buddy.' He concluded that Russians are human beings, too—lost twenty-two million people in World War Two, understand death pretty good, too, cherish life right much, too. So what happened was, Reagan engaged Gorbachev, they did the most basic thing in diplomacy, they *talked,* and that hasn't stopped affecting history ever since."

BUT IN JACKSON'S own rangings about the world as a sort of alter statesman unto himself, the importance accorded him by the governments of countries he passed through occasioned no little irritable befuddlement among U.S. embassy officials along the way. "Just what are we supposed to do with this guy?" complained one as he stood watching from the edges of a Jackson press conference in Lagos. "Exactly who is he representing? What's he supposed to be?" At a gathering one evening with several U.S. envoys, Jackson was recounting his trip to Cuba to talk with Castro, when one of them interrupted to ask, "But you went down there as what? In what capacity do you make these foreign calls?" "As me," said Jackson. "*Me.* A citizen of the world." Not all U.S. embassy staffers regarded his progress through their capitals with exasperation, though. During Jackson's long morning of discoursing in the dining room of the guesthouse in Lagos, a question arose as to exactly what term might describe what had occupied him through these years, and a U.S. embassy officer sitting at the far end of the table, who'd been listening to Jackson expound for about three hours, suddenly spoke out, "Prophecy. I mean, it's sort of Old Testament prophesying, isn't it?"

Jackson himself almost always makes a point, in casual chats with U.S. diplomatic personnel along his itineraries, of amicably reassuring them, in what they might feel is their remote and marginal isolation, "Up to me, if I could wave some revolutionary wand, I'd take the whole State Department and send it to the field, and send all o' yawl to Washington to run our foreign policy." This commonly stirs forth little coughs of tentative, appreciative laughter. "That's right. Workers in the field get out, rassle among the people. Those in the field know the possibilities in a country. It's the guy on the ground who's really looking internationally, 'cause he's out there where it's real, while those in Washington mostly looking nationally. This thing gets *narrower*, don't get broader, as it goes on up. Understanding narrows as you go up the ranks, like a pyramid, until with some of 'em, like Reagan, when it reached him, it passed the vanishing point."

He put this proposition to a pair of U.S. envoys in Harare during a late dinner in a hotel restaurant, with a piano across the room cascading through cocktail-lounge melodies, and one of them lamented, "But yet you have to go up the levels. There's no way to shuck the organization. You can try, but that means you get thrown out of paradise, and there's no way back in." This profession had come after Jackson had delivered to the envoys some of his extended reflections on the spiritual character of leadership, a disquisition in which they'd quickly become swept up, one finally declaring, "But our political system does not tend to reward heroes. Period. You've gone through that yourself." When Jackson left to take a call from *The Michael Jackson Show*, a radio talk program broadcast from Los Angeles—proceeding through an interview from the telephone by the restaurant's cash register—one of the envoys remarked, "Extraordinary. You just don't hear politicians using terms like that, heroes and authenticity and moral center."

When Jackson returned to the table, the envoy continued, in a tone almost of appeal, "Those of us in the trenches, we see the moral inconsistencies and complications, and we keep reporting, 'This is the way it is.' But in the end, we can't put things in terms of right and wrong, because if we do, people kick us in the pants." Jackson and the two embassy officers were now leaning, almost conspiratorially, together in the ruby glow of the tiny lantern on the table, as the piano in the background was now surging through theme melodies from *The King and I.* The first envoy confessed, "For us, it's a question of your job. Jesse Helms, if we go up against him, we wind up getting smacked around, and then when we come up for an ambassadorship, we don't get promoted."

The second envoy added, "One of the problems, Jesse Helms's views have been built in over all his years in the Senate—"

"Man, Jesse Helms's views on Africa have been built in *all* his years," expostulated Jackson, "and the ones on Charlotte and Asheville, too. Mean, if you can't call *him* a racist, you don't have the capacity to understand the term. His reactions are that, his sympathies are that, his record is that. If you don't see in him fascism, you might as well stop reading books. Guys like Helms making these big foreign policy decisions about Africa, their basic perspective is someplace between a Tarzan movie and how they reacted to the civil rights movement."

The first envoy then volunteered the rather remarkable sentiment for a foreign service officer, "But America has always played out its delusions and fantasies, and masqueraded it as foreign policy."

This prompted Jackson to begin dissertating on the United States's long shunning of Castro. "We have the capacity, by our sheer physical proximity and size, to have an overwhelming influence on Cuba. Through a constructive engagement, we could divide Cuba simply by expanding its options, could have Castro before long almost completely dependent on us. But we got such a *thing* about the guy, he bearded us right in our face, you know, and we got such an ego hangup about Castro that—"

"It's not ego," said the first envoy. "It comes from the unconscious."

"Well, now," drawled Jackson, "you a little *heavier* than I am, see, I dropped out of school finally, missed some things, never did learn all about this unconscious business. But it seems awfully conscious to me, very carefully designed policy. And I'll tell you, my friend, that no-engagement, no-talk foreign policy toward Castro, PLO, other adversaries like that, which was originally ill conceived by Kissinger and signed off on by succeeding administrations, it never *did* make sense, never did work. Instead, kept conflicts going and resulted in many people getting killed that did not have to die. We can't let men like Kissinger represent genius to us."

The first envoy was inspired to offer another philosophical riff, "But there's an ideology of institutions. Kissinger is a power politician, and that means Kissinger thinks of himself as speaking as an institution, not as an individual. But if you don't speak as an individual, you can't speak to other individuals," and the envoy then produced the eminently un-State-Department-like proclamation, "If you run away from your heart all the time, you can't speak to the heart of anyone else."

Having gradually disclosed himself, over the course of the dinner, to be close to Jackson's own political sensibilities, the envoy at last confided, "By the way, I voted for you, you know."

Jackson cackled. "Awright, now, now we gettin' down to it." Jackson hunched farther over the table to propose, "If anybody knows, you guys should know that the world community is such, our foreign policy's gonna jeopardize the strength of our country in a significant way if we don't have leadership equal to the task of a liberal new world order. Which is emerging. Gonna be emerging everywhere you turn around over the next few years. It's just something loose in the air now. Cannot be held back."

When Jackson propounded this, the disassembling of apartheid in South Africa, the fall of the Berlin Wall, the dissolution of the Soviet empire were still many months away.

His Movement Apostleship to the Soviets

MORE THAN ANYTHING else, Jackson has set out on his foreign treks—to southern Africa, to Latin America, to the then Soviet Union, to the Middle East in 1994—as an apostle for the expansion of King's moral vision over the rest of the globe. During his visit to the Soviet Union in 1989, in discussions with Soviet authorities and democratic militants alike, Jackson took to expatiating on the struggle of perestroika, or democratic restructuring, in which they were all then caught up, by casting it, in one of his large historical synapses, as a kind of extension of the civil rights movement in the South during the sixties. Indeed, a case could be made that the process which was to climax there in about two years—when the putsch attempt of the old Soviet totalitarian guard was confounded by popular resistance that soon ramified into the collapse of the Soviet state—had actually begun some thirty years earlier in Mississippi and Alabama. Those rousing mass meetings in black churches, and the marches moving with a mighty clapping and singing toward city halls and courthouse squares where deputies and state troopers waited with billy clubs and dogs and paddy wagons, produced confrontations that were like great shouts across the South of the human spirit freeing itself. And the phenomenon continued, in a sporadic and uneven but amplifying historical dynamic, called by the movement "people power," on into the demonstrations against the Vietnam War, and eventually protests in South Africa, the confrontations in

Prague in the spring of 1968, arcing on over the decades to the Solidarity movement in Poland, the popular overthrow of Marcos in the Philippines, then to Tiananmen Square, then to Eastern Europe, where, in the squares of its capitals, demonstrators were heard singing, like some grand echo crossing time, the anthem "We Shall Overcome," until it reached at last into the streets of Moscow and Leningrad. "In a certain real sense," Jackson maintained then, "it's all been a projection of the soul-force of the movement struggle back in the sixties."

While in the Soviet Union, Jackson missed encountering the figure who might have been considered his natural political counterpart, Boris Yeltsin—though Yeltsin, at that time, still seemed more a buffoonish eccentric galumphing toward self-calamity. But as Jackson swept from meeting to meeting, he was filled with exhilaration about what he construed as the immense existential adventure on which the whole country was embarked. "You know, we already got all this experience in democratization, but the people here . . . they're restructuring *their whole thinking.* Imagine it! Party official been around like forever, he comes up to me, says, 'If you'd told me a year ago some of the things happening now, I would never have believed it. And now it's day to day, we don't really know what's coming next.' Man, I'm sayin' that's gettin' *real,* that's fermentation, that's things *comin' to life!*"

Accordingly, when government and party figures would confess to him their tribulations in laboring to reinvent their society, Jackson would counter, "Exciting!" He would then go into his own exposition on the nature of their undertaking that not a little anticipated the convulsive crisis to come some two short years later. It was a kind of millennial populist vision he put to them: "I mean, the bus drivers in Moscow and the bus drivers in Washington are not angry with each other. The maids in Leningrad and the maids in Chicago are not angry with each other. The students in Armenia and the students in Alabama are not angry with each other. So all these factions must come together and form the fundamental infrastructure of an entirely new transcultural relationship. We must create a new collective soul!" he jubilantly expounded to one panel of somewhat agog deputies, "with new joint ventures, school-to-school relations" —he spiraled on into this prospect of some transcendent social marriage between the two countries— "new church-to-church relations, hospital-to-hospital relations, sharing mass media events together"—so enlarging the implications of perestroika to virtually a superhistorical dimension, stripping the gears of an already radical domestic initiative by escalating it into an international epic— "reduce Third World debt together, peace corps with the U.S. and Soviet Union going together to less developed parts of the world, end regional conflicts together. It's a concept that needs to be applied all over the world!"

This particular peroration had come during Jackson's first session with the Armenian Communist party chairman and sundry colleagues at the party's palatial headquarters in Yerevan. In a vast chamber under majestic chandeliers, yet another collection of thickish senior apparatchiks was plunked in a row across the table from him with the look of a battery of pipe fitters sacked in gray gabardine, with black-frame glasses and oil-combed hair, lumpish hands clumped together before them, tiny gold glints in the back-crannies of their grins. The chairman, a thirty-year party veteran, had the same squat chunkiness of his cohorts but was rather more suavely preened, his silvering hair carefully combed straight back, and a slightly imperious stare in his frost-blue eyes. He responded a little anticli-mactically to Jackson's astral extrapolations of perestroika's meaning by cit-ing his own more prosaic travails with the disruptions it was occasioning. "Only a few years ago, it was much easier to govern, to regulate. I can tell you with no doubt that glasnost and perestroika is making the life of polit-ical and party organization in the Soviet Union much more difficult."

"That's good," said Jackson. "Way it's s'pose to be. This process of de-mocratization you're engaging in is very deep in nature." He once again struck one of his long historical synaptic associations. "I am a personal ex-ample of it happening in America. When I was growing up, my parents did not have the right to vote—we came from a minority community locked out of the system. I've engaged in demonstrations and protests in my own country, I might point out, and been jailed for it. But now I have the right to run as a serious candidate for president, which attests, I think, to the greatness of our country. But it also shows how perestroika can work among the common people. That's because it honors the natural law of self-determination. So democratization," he advised them, "is going to re-lease a new energy through this society. Gonna release energies people never really used before, never even really realized they had. You've set something loose, Mr. Chairman, can't be controlled or revoked, you know. A state simply cannot contain the natural urges of its people to move into a freer arrangement. Fact, perestroika and glasnost couldn't't've come a moment too *soon* for this system. But it'll be challenging! Be ex-citing!" He then added eagerly, "Govern-, govern-, government of the peo-ple, by the people, for the people, is a retirement plan for stagnant leaders. Yeah. Leaders got to keep up with the course of this process—or they have a Siberia in their future. Right?"

This brought an awkward clatter of short laughs from the other side of the table. The chairman then leaned forward on his elbows and declared, with a certain irritated clang in his tone, "But each state, each society, has laws, which nobody has the right to violate." The general affability in the room had rapidly waned. The chairman went on brusquely, "We have the same laws that you have. I must tell you, seriously and directly, you should be aware that we have been very patient with the antisocialist manifestations of certain people for a very long time." The chairman grew more exercised, speaking with emphatically whacking gestures. "Certain people have tried to destabilize the situation in our republic, to put us into anarchy," he said, glaring around for affirmation from his colleagues. "I have told these people, 'You are violating public order. This is not acceptable!' There is a Russian expression which says, 'To put sticks in the wheel.' In all civilized societies, there are certain laws about having meetings and demonstrations. . . ." It was, in all, a reflex almost spookily reminiscent of the refrains from courthouse officials over the South during the demonstrations of the sixties, and Jackson would comment afterward, "Didn't want to be disrespectful by saying it, but America called Dr. King subversive to law and order, too, called us rabble-rousers, radicals. I am not unaccustomed to the state coming down with those terms."

But he merely replied now, "One of the real points made by Mr. Gorbachev has been about human rights. You going through a process here, and you got to keep that process going to keep hope alive."

"No question about it!" declared the chairman. He then submitted, "I would like you, Mr. Jackson, to be aware that we are living through a very difficult time for our society. The political activism of the people which is happening now is something which doesn't have any precedent in our history—"

"That's what I know. That's just the thing."

"And perestroika covers all areas of human life in this country, so we don't conceal any defects which we have in all these fields. So we are not afraid of criticism!"

"Well, that's hopeful to hear," said Jackson. "Because a lot of creative energy comes out of that criticizing process. In the long run, it makes leaders better, because it makes them broader. Why that's crucial," he again undertook to apprise them, "is because what you guys are facing now is, from my own experience, only a little thing compared to what'll be coming down the road, as this process you've started really opens on up."

Later that evening, at the dinner for Jackson, the chairman had altogether recovered his conviviality, not negligibly assisted by the repeated toasts of high-octane Armenian cognac. He began enthusing to Jackson that he had projected the implications of perestroika into a magnitude that had not yet quite occurred even to its own authors. "To hear that analytical speech of yours this afternoon about glasnost and perestroika, I told them in Moscow that Mr. Jackson was talking about perestroika better than we do. Is true!"

"Well," Jackson further surprised them by casually announcing, "my understandings of perestroika and glasnost come out of my understandings of the New Testament." In fact, considerable stretches of all of Jackson's sessions with Soviet officials had been given over to impromptu religious promotionals. Earlier, during his afternoon exchange with the chairman, Jackson had eased into a first preacherly pass by suggesting, "Freedom of worship becomes a great measurement of a society. Many people will take their signal from the church here as to whether perestroika is working or not." The chairman had rejoined that, if anyone had previously told him that the Catholics, the high patriarch of the Armenian church, would one day become a deputy in the Supreme Soviet, "I would have said it would be like thunder in a clear light!"

"That's God speakin', you know," said Jackson. "Thunder and lightnin'."

"No, but five years ago," the chairman said, "could you imagine me going over to talk with the Catholics about this and that like I do now?"

"Don't watch out," Jackson returned, "you gonna mess around and catch religion runnin' back and forth over there."

Now at dinner, Jackson proceeded to deliver, to the tableful of briny and carbuncular provincial commissars, one of his gospel-populist explications on how Jesus was actually the primary precedent for what they were all essaying in the Soviet Union. "Great societies are built from the bottom up. When Jesus was born, there was this great concentration of royal power in Rome. But Jesus' position was, *everybody* had royal blood, and we should be judged by our service, not on our social standing." It sounded like he was patiently leading them through a Sunday school lesson. "So Jesus fought for reform. He kicked the money changers out of the temple to stop corruption in the church. He reached out to people who'd been abandoned. Jesus one day came across this woman being punished, all these men throwing rocks at her—they accused her of being a prostitute. But they didn't look for the men that she had engaged in sex with. Jesus' point to them was, she couldn't be a prostitute by herself—"

This prompted a bawl of laughter from the chairman. "You're right! You're right!"

Jackson solemnly went on, "So Jesus wanted to bring in a new morality—wanted to ... to ... to *restructure* the society, open up the arrangement for everybody. His point was, everybody had a right to the tree of life. So the idea that somebody born in a stable could become a powerful enough leader to actually transform the society he was so humbly born into was in a real sense a fundamental kind of perestroika." The party officials had so far responded with politely approbative nods to this Bible homily of Jackson's. "But eventually the government turned on Jesus. The old leaders who'd adjusted to the society as it was, they didn't like him, began plotting to destroy him. That risk is always part of the struggle for perestroika, too, you ought to know." This now put somewhat ambivalent expressions on the faces across the table. "Those who wanted to keep society closed and undemocratic, protect their positions and privileges, they finally managed to kill him. So there's always gonna be a reaction, it's inevitable. But as you develop perestroika to open up the society to make room for the worth and the will of the common people, I'm sayin' this is an idea, a tradition, that's really very deep in my faith—goes all the way back to its source. Whether you're religious or not, it's the same thing. You should feed the hungry. You should house the homeless. You should comfort the sufferin', and set at liberty them that are in bondage. That's what Jesus was about. *Deep* perestroika, two thousand years ago. . . ."

Even in his later conversation with Vitaly Korotich, Jackson could not refrain from a turn of sermonizing. "Now in our society, as we moved from a very closed society to our own glasnost and perestroika, it was much church-driven. Abolishing slavery, ending our own apartheid of segregation, right to vote, withdrawal from Vietnam, movement to stop the arms race—in each instance, it was very much the church that mobilized the people, always driving the state to be moral. The church was the source of prophetic pressure on our government. What I'm wonderin', would that type pressure on the Kremlin be tolerated here?"

Korotich responded a bit obliquely, "Depends on if president or politician who believe in something better and stronger than his own being. He is not so dangerous a politician than one who believe that all is finished with him. Because when you can push button and stop the life on earth, you must believe in something more, not to push this button so easily. Not to be Nero in fire in his Rome and playing music—"

"But what I'm getting at," Jackson persisted, "in this new arrangement here, if a politician, say, opened up one of his speeches with a prayer, how do you think that would be taken?"

"It means," said Korotich, with an elfin flicker of a smile, "he want to divide the responsibility between him and somebody else."

There was a burst of laughter from everyone in the room, except for Jackson. "Well, I'm convinced that in the days ahead," he pressed on, "there is inherent in perestroika a theology that won't be able to be avoided now this dynamic's been set going. It's a theology that assumes something larger about man—the definition of generic man. So I think that in this development, there must be a theological discussion of some depth as well."

One sometimes suspected that, in his insistent scriptural exegeses to Soviet authorities, Jackson actually half entertained the ambition, as he indicated once, "At what point can you, in fact, convert? Your proselytizing is your interest." After his talk with Aleksandr Yakovlev, one of the master architects of perestroika and head of a Politburo commission overseeing Soviet international policy, Jackson reported that he had posed to him "how there was something in openness, democratization, restructuring, that is in the natural order. He said, 'Natural order. I like that.' But the thing about that natural-order business, I told him, next step beyond that is, there's something or somebody that *controls* it." Jackson then speculated, "These guys start thinking in those terms, it's bound to lead to what we call back home something bigger than you and I—" and he suddenly gave a high, Halloween-wavering wail, as if before some approaching mysterious immensity. "Sooner or later, they got to start dealing with he who controls nature, who parts the waters and has bedecked the heavens with stars. Something *else* going on here, too, besides systems of governing people."

BUT JUST AS Jackson went about exhorting Soviet officials from his own experience in the movement, so he exhorted democratic militants who were often ranged against those authorities in perestroika's stormy evolution. After he had commandeered Korotich's office for his meeting with the three young liberal activists, they were introduced to him, by a *Manchester Guardian* correspondent who had accompanied them there, as "the SNCC of the Soviet Union"—a bespectacled delegation in baggy corduroys who, indeed, had something of the fervid earnestness of those northern youths who had come down to Mississippi during the Freedom Summer of 1964. One of them explained that they were "representatives of the new wave of democratic movement here, informal movement. These different, informal groups, they are playing the role of the alarm clocks for the purpose of awakening the civil population."

"Yeah, I thought there was something familiar-lookin' about you guys," said Jackson. Leaning back in Korotich's chair, he then commenced to pass on to the group counsel from his movement days during the sixties. "There're so many parallels with our struggle for our own form of perestroika," he told them. "Dr. King and others of us who went to jail, we said if we have the right to use restaurants and hotels like everybody else, if the right to vote is supposed to be real for everybody, let's *test* it. We all equal? Well, then, let's run for mayor and Congress, let's even run for president.

So if you have five thousand people marchin' down the streets of, say, Leningrad, demanding a certain adjustment, if they are then arrested and beaten, then you've proven limits, but if they're not, then you've expanded realities. I mean, have to *define* it, then *test* it. Get what I'm sayin'?"

But the three young militants seemed more impatient to present to him their elaborately fretful pessimisms about the whole outlook for perestroika, and Jackson grew steadily more nettled to find them dissenting from what he felt was the momentous excitement of that development. He asked briskly, "But is this society *more* or *less* open today than three years ago?"

More open, they hesitantly agreed, but with qualifications about which all three then fell to vigorously disputing. One finally declared to Jackson that his particular reformist group had written "an entire collection of articles criticizing the monetarist policy of our economic reform—"

Jackson blinked. "Criticizing the what?"

"Monetarist policy guiding our economic reform. And we sent these articles to almost all the major publications—"

"Say did."

"Yes, and none, *none*, agreed to publish. Not one! Those words were never published! Because they were against the line which is now adopted."

"Well, now, lemme, lemme, lemme just suggest this for a minute," Jackson retorted, "mean, we can write some articles to *The New York Times* won't get printed, too. *Washington Post, Boston Globe*—some of 'em get through, but they don't just run every one of my thoughts and sayings, either. You know? You thinkers and theorists, you sort of got to separate some personal disappointment from what's the general condition. Not gettin' something of yours published don't prove glasnost and perestroika is all false. Uh, mean, just 'cause you have a car wreck, you can't assume all cars wreck. What I'm sayin', if there is more openness and more potential openness than there was a few years ago, you must not convince yourself it ain't actually more open because you couldn't get a committee article on monetary policy published—might've been very important, but also just mighta been *dull*, not sayin' it was, understand. But if you admit that things *are* more open, then you must . . . *keep* . . . *pushing* . . . *it* . . . *open*. And not just be"—he dropped his voice gently—"*complainin'*."

He went on cautioning them to resist bitterness over disappointments. "Point you make that people'll meet and protest, and still nothing happens—that's always gonna be true no matter what the social order. Parallel at home is, we're a fairly open society, but I've seen countless numbers of farmers, union folk, unemployed, and homeless, all marching in big protests, who either get completely ignored or get only meager victories. So you can conceivably demonstrate in great numbers and not change much at first. But in time, *in time*, the movement of that number of people *will* begin to make something happen, it's too many people not to be dealt with after a while.

"Just the right alone to protest," Jackson concluded, "holds its own kind of promise—if you just *hold on* and don't give up when the counterforce comes. Which it will, sooner or later. In this new arrangement here, those in power are still gonna try to stack the deck against you to assure their own survival. Some of them I've talked to, I can guarantee you that. But that's natural, that would happen anywhere—it's built into the system everywhere. But so often, the great-idea people, like you guys, have a tendency to give up when the counterforce comes. And I want to stress again, that counterforce *is going to come.* So when that happens, what you guys here in Moscow and in Leningrad, and all those provincial towns you've talked about, what yawl got to do is *hold on.* Like the old movement song, keep yo' eyes on the prize—hold on! 'Cause yawl are, after all, representing something in nature and the moral universe ultimately *stronger* than that counterforce. That's what yawl must never forget as this thing plays itself on out. That's what 'Keep hope alive' really means."

Return of the Dreamer to Jerusalem

LONG AFTER THE turmoils that subsequently dissolved the Soviet Union, leaving Yeltsin clumsily ruling over a kind of roisterous Yukon Territory democracy beset by demons loosed out of the Russian past, Jackson was still at his international apostleship, journeying to Israel and the West Bank in the spring of 1994 to try transferring the movement's principle of nonviolent moral witness onto the region's old furies. Some considered it a little late in the game to be introducing such a proposition into that long conflict. But after attending the signing of the initial accord by Arafat and Rabin on the White House lawn, Jackson had arrived in Israel just when the first slow and gingerly constructions of a possible peace from that accord had been critically jolted by, first, the slaughter of Muslim worshipers at a Hebron mosque by an American Jewish settler and then the explosion of a terrorist bomb on a civilian bus in the northern Israeli town of Afula. In addresses to both Israeli and Palestinian audiences, Jackson appealed, "A massacre in Hebron, a bombing in Afula. Innocent people killed and hurt on both sides—the same old cycle of pain and outrage and grief. But we cannot go on here just swappin' pain for pain. Not when we got this chance to end that tragic cycle at last." After making visits to the sites of both attacks, he told a collection of Palestinian community leaders at a hotel banquet in east Jerusalem, "In Hebron and Afula, I saw even more clearly that those who are frightened by peace, who oppose any change in the old impasse of mutual violence, have time on their side. Each horror creates more hatred and more fear, which then creates yet another horror. A momentum has to be sustained in this peace process that cannot be dissipated by sabotages of violence like these two acts. Peace is not some gift comin' down out of the sky, my good friends, it is a struggle right here where you are on the ground, that in many ways is more difficult than war. Leaders like you on both sides must not allow this process now to die through a return to mutual recrimination and retaliation."

Throughout his six days there, Jackson was constantly on the phone with Arafat, then still in Tunis, and with Foreign Minister Shimon Peres, along with Prime Minister Yitzhak Rabin occasionally, relaying messages back and forth among them. On a visit one morning by Jackson to Jerusalem's mayor, Ehud Olmert, a member of the Likud party, which had already pitted itself against Rabin's initiative, Olmert energetically protested to Jackson Arafat's apparent reluctance to deplore the Afula bombing as openly and unequivocally as the Israeli government had denounced the Hebron massacre. Jackson suggested to him, "Clearly, if anyone were *here* and actually saw the burnt faces of those babies and people's bandaged bodies, something a little stronger perhaps would be coming out. In spite of that, I would hope we could get beyond who has the most eloquent apology, and back into getting on with the peace process. The saboteurs of the peace possibility take nothing but delight in our fighting now about apologies and eulogies." Even so, when he was beckoned from a luncheon at a Palestinian hospital near Bethlehem and shown into the administrator's empty office to take a call from Arafat, he blared into the phone, "Hey, my brother, how you doin', buddy? Just wanted to tell you, within the country here the Afula bombing is creating very strong feeling. Some tryin' to use it against you and the whole peace process. Look, you got to morally rise above that thing, not just react to reactions to it. I wish you'd make a stronger statement, you really ought to—expressing real sympathy for the families and regret for the incident. Say it was just *wrong*—was bad, wrong, harmful—and offer your prayers for the families. Do that? . . . Naw, you don't have to check with nobody else, if you feel it, do it! *You* the leader. Something else I want you to know," Jackson continued. "Since we talked last night, I've talked to the prime minister, and he's agreed yawl should meet soon as possible face-to-face. . . . That's right, said he'd be willin' to do that. Because these outstanding problems about Jericho and Gaza should be dealt with immediately. Yawl got to accelerate the timetable, which will also accelerate the world's timetable of support, know what I mean. But if there's delay, it's simply gonna allow more of these acts of violence to occur. Right? So the timing is in your hands. What? . . . Well, I suggest you call and seek to meet with him *immediately*. He said he was willin'. . . . Don't *worry* 'bout that checkin' with all your fellas. Comes a time when the leader himself has to take over and *lead*, ole buddy. And I do not think you can try to micromanage this thing through by telephone from Tunis. Soon as you can, you got to manage it on the ground *here*. . . . What? Naw, I'm tryin' to tell you, you can call him *today—right now*. Or tomorrow if you want, but he can be reached today or tomorrow by *you*. . . . That's right, what he said. He's waiting on your call. So *call 'im*. Let's get these details on Jericho and Gaza behind us— we 'bout to start refightin' a war that's over. To get caught up in a lot of minutiae now would just allow the opponents on both sides to dig in and undercut you and set off more Afulas and Hebrons. Ain't that right? . . . Okay. He's waitin' to hear from you now, okay? Hey, buddy—main thing to keep in mind. You on your way back *home*."

JACKSON HAD MADE this intercessory jaunt to Israel at coinciding invitations, as it happened, from Palestinian leaders there and the Israeli government, which he elected to combine and accept as one joint invitation, and Foreign Minister Peres, at his dinner for Jackson at the King David Hotel, noted in his toast, "A year ago, this would have been impossible— invited by the Palestinians, invited by the Israelis." Jackson was even afforded the previously unimaginable gratification of hearing Israel's chief rabbi, Meir Lau, pronounce upon him the blessing "You can be a messenger of God." At the least, the visit turned out to be a kind of denouement of his own long adversity through the past over the Israeli-Palestinian matter. His wife, Jackie, who had accompanied him, observed to one gathering of Palestinian notables, "This situation has been so heavy on our lives for the past fifteen years. We've suffered much because of it, it has taken an incredible toll on us." Jackson himself would remind Palestinians he met, "A handful of us had to take the weight of shaking your hand and affirming your personhood. When I left here in 1979 and went to Lebanon to see Arafat, then went back to the States to make the case for mutual recognition and mutual security and respect, for a let's-talk policy rather than a no-talk policy, I was roundly dismissed. That picture of me and Arafat embracing in Lebanon, they tried to make that *the death knell* of me. But what I was advocating made just as much sense then as it makes now." Neither did he neglect to cite this irony of time's passage to Israelis as well, remarking to one audience assembled in a sunny lecture room at the Truman Institute of Hebrew University, "When we were here many years ago, that for which we were then attacked and misunderstood is now center stage. The powers that be have caught up with that view." He made a point of reporting to them now, "I made the case to Arafat in 1979, 'Drop *any suggestion* of driving Jews into the sea—inciting their fears is not any key to peace. Just state clearly what you actually want.' He said, 'West Bank and Gaza.' I said, 'Well, *say* that.' And I took this back to Washington, but our government couldn't respond, because it wouldn't *talk*. Now that there's this new framework for peace, I do find joy in that. What was not so politically fashionable yesterday is now politically respectable. But it was always *right*."

As a result, he declared to a large convocation of Palestinians in Hebron, "We've tried to live and work and talk and walk in such a way, we can talk to both sides now, and be a bridge to help end this conflict finally." Specifically, what Jackson now heartily applied himself to, in this return to Israel at that critically tenuous moment right after Hebron and Afula, was an evangelism urging both Palestinians and Israelis to free themselves of the dark undertow of their common violent past, "the perpetual recyclings of your pain and despair and rancor. People have sometimes been living so long in the emotion of fighting, they can't even recognize peace when it actually offers itself. But it's not enough to live from your experience. There must be a leap of faith. That's what the ancient visionaries knew. The Bible puts it this way: we shall all be transformed by a renewal of our minds."

Accordingly, to a small gathering in a bare and frowsy classroom of a Palestinian university in Hebron, he proposed, "Palestinian youths and Israeli youths must do something that their parents have not learned to do: live together. That means an adjustment in how we see each other. Because maybe the ultimate crime of war is that we're taught to dehumanize each other, which then allows us to kill each other. But the fact always is, the opposition *is* human—Israelis have their pain and fears, as you have your pain and fears." At the same time, he insisted in his sessions with various Israeli figures, including the leader of the Likud party, Benjamin Netanyahu, "You have pulled off the miracle of, out of many, becoming one, bound together by a common religion and heritage. Now, there's the challenge to live with the neighbor next door. We have to do something very difficult now. We have to unlearn some old lessons. We've got to exalt some downtrodden people. We've got to recondition some spirits. And this country has such an awesome record for educating its own and other peoples, if it *wills* to do so. The future of our children depends on their being taught what their parents didn't learn: how to rehumanize each other."

To that end, Jackson spent much of his time in his talks with Israelis and Palestinians laboring to explain the psyche of each to the other, equally putting to both, "Why *are* Israelis afraid? Well, if you have dismissed their humanity, it does not *matter* why they're afraid. Why are Palestinians in so much pain? If you have discounted their humanity, it makes no difference why they're hurtin'—or even that they're *capable* of hurtin'. You get my drift?" Even at Afula, after he had gone from room to room in a hospital visiting and praying with casualties of the bus bombing, he risked trying to impart some sense of the Palestinian ordeal, too, the craze out of which this particular barbarity had come: "They have been bearing this struggle for so long, there're so many damaged spirits, they've witnessed the burial of so many relatives, they're just full of so much old hurt and fear and desperation." At a breakfast meeting with Uri Savir, the chunky, boyish-faced, formidably brilliant Foreign Ministry official who had negotiated the beginning of the peace initiative with PLO deputies in Oslo, he reported the deepening dismay of Palestinians that, while awaiting determinations on the status of Jerusalem, "you're still moving their people out and moving your people in. It's like, from their point of view, by the time it gets to negotiations, it's *over*." Jackson also passed on to him the distress of Palestinian leaders about the abrupt cancellation of a conference in an East Jerusalem hotel, which Israeli troops had surrounded during a banquet the night before: "It was so raw; I mean, 'The *army*'s outside!' And with no intermediary contact to resolve the problem. Those people were humiliated. They were *humiliated*. And they weren't youths throwing rocks. They were the professional and intellectual elite of the Palestinian community." Savir conceded in a slow, measured, quiet voice, "It's a very, very complex tension. We have public opinion, too. I would just caution you that the Palestinians are still committing a mistake that we did for many years. They make certain propaganda, and then they start believing it. We did this for many, many years. I think we have maybe a generation to go before people will learn to trust each other. But you've come here, Reverend, at the most apt time ever, this time of transition when all of this is new to us."

Jackson later met with Likud leader Netanyahu at the King David Hotel in a small room off the lobby, with dark paneling and a colored-glass window. Netanyahu, a hefty man with a boisterous self-assurance, gave his own burly reiteration of the old suspicions and adamancies of his Likud predecessors, Menachem Begin and Yitzhak Shamir, about an accommodation with the Palestinians and the PLO especially. With the agreement between Arafat and Rabin now, he maintained, "there is a sense of insecurity to a level in this country that I don't remember since I was born, except for the wars. Arafat promised to annul the Palestinian charter calling for our destruction as a precondition for this whole thing. Promised to condemn terrorism *personally*. Promised to act against recalcitrant groups within the PLO. Hasn't done any of it. *Nothing*. At the same time, a spectacular growth in terror. What do you think the broad masses of Israelis are saying? *This is no peace.*"

"Well," Jackson said softly, "you know, we've been talking to the Palestinians, the PLO, quite a bit since we've been here. You have to understand, most of them, all they've ever known has been war." And then, to Netanyahu's bluff mistrust of the whole peace overture to the PLO, Jackson put the quaint proposition, "You may have to help them learn to be secure. You gonna have to relieve them of their pain. As you impose this peace plan on the situation now, I think you'll produce a sea change of hope among them. And as their hope and sense of self rises, they may redirect their energies and relieve you of some of *your* fears." Netanyahu merely stared at Jackson with a little askew smile, not quite masking his stupefaction at the credulous naïveté of this suggestion. But in his address at Hebrew University, Jackson submitted that Israel actually had a vital interest in enhancing Arafat's position, by not only initiating substantial and conspicuous troop withdrawals from the West Bank but by assisting him in a program of civic renewal there, constructing schools and hospitals and housing, even in developing a system of self-government. "The quicker that Palestinians can see him achieving these things, his support will go up. And as his support goes up, so does Israel's security."

For the most part, the Israelis seemed agreeably receptive to his appeals about escaping the imprisonments of past aggrievements and personalizing their old adversaries. He had a rather more difficult time of it, however, with the Palestinians.

Their sessions with him were largely taken up in recitals of old indignations and impatient doubts about Israeli intentions now. But he urged them, in turn, to try to understand the Israeli dilemma: "The kind of heat the Afula bombing is placing on Peres and Rabin, the kind of heat Netanyahu is putting on them—they can stay only about a step ahead of their own people's politics, the base of which is still full of fear. So to expect them to push out a further step is just unrealistic. It could well give you Netanyahu to deal with." In a long afternoon meeting with a panel of PLO officials in Jerusalem, he further undertook to convey to them some realization of the interior damage worked on the Israelis themselves by the occupation, and so to give this enduring enemy of theirs a tragic human dimension for them, too: "I mean, this occupation business destroys the *soul* of the occupier. You've got to almost *die* to adjust to steppin' on people's throats. I mean, the occupier . . . the *occupier* hurts. Some of the most gripping stories to me that have come out of this situation are not Palestinian stories, interestingly enough, but young Israeli soldiers talking about the pain they suffer learning how to be an occupier. The way they're required to act, for many of them, their insides just blow up 'cause it's so contradictory to their sense of social justice and what they thought Israel meant."

But if, as he observed to the evening banquet of Palestinian worthies in the East Jerusalem hotel, "I appreciate the unique opportunity to talk to the Israelis about you, and to talk with you about them, with a degree of integrity possible with both of you," that had not exactly been what they themselves had been hoping of him in his visit there; they wanted him simply to tell the Israelis about them. He was repeatedly confronted with such insistent expectations from them as, "Are you going to say something to the Israeli leaders that will help reduce some of our sufferings?" At a kind of Palestinian town hall meeting in a civic center in Hebron, tumultuously crowded, windows open to the hot morning, he was introduced with the announcement, "We hope Reverend Jackson will be with us in our stand to have the settlers removed from this city." What they were not particularly in a mood to be told was, as Jackson nevertheless told them, "As I listen to my friends here, you relate your pain. As I talk with many Israelis, they relate their fears. On both sides, fear and pain." In his suggestions to the Palestinian leaders at the hotel banquet to at least consider that dual dimension of the conflict, Jackson afterward confessed to Uri Savir, "they just barely tolerated me." But he pressed on anyway in his address at the banquet to ask them to understand that, in this mission there, "I cannot be more Palestinian than you. Or more Israeli than Peres, for that matter." He tried to reassure them by reporting that, in his sessions with Israelis, "I've talked about the urgency of your predicament on a level of frankness and friendliness with people who got the power to *do something* about it. I can't be just *fussin'* at 'em. But when I meet with Peres and Rabin"—he was reduced to entreating them—"*trust me*. Trust me to argue with integrity. Because *somebody* has got to try building bridges here."

Yet it seemed an oddly morose and testy humor he was contending against now that they had moved to the edge of a peace and possible nationhood at last. In all his appearances before Palestinian groups, he kept imploring them to abjure the pessimisms and abnegations of those still locked in the past. "You cannot withdraw into cynicism, as if that's even an option in this situation. To say it can't happen, that's no great thought process, that's no revolutionary position"—as, for that matter, he had admonished Netanyahu, "It doesn't take much wisdom and leadership to prove something can't happen 'cause it ain't happened yet." The danger in that was, as he told both sides, "if leaders get to convincin' themselves and then each other that they have *not* made progress, then the people might start believin' 'em, and it can all quickly return to that futile cycle of violence answerin' violence, that brute dialogue of killin'." He thus strove mightily to cheer his Palestinian audiences out of what increasingly seemed to him their obdurate bitterness. "You need to know that you are *winning*," he cried out to the throng packed in the Hebron civic hall. "Even as we talk, the Israeli occupation is on the way out of Gaza, on the way out of Jericho. Palestinians are on their way *in* to join and protect other Palestinians. Some who have been jailed are on their way back home to begin to re-build the Palestinian people and a new nation." After having long resisted a campaign "to dehumanize you out of the conversation, out of human recognition," he declared, "there's now a rehumanizing process going on. Isn't this what all we been after? You should be rejoicin' today!"

Nevertheless, he continued to be answered mostly with extensive reprises of the old outrages. One Palestinian dignitary, speaking at a luncheon near Bethlehem, made mention of Jackson's earlier visit to victims of the bus bombing in Afula and then embarked on a protracted comparative evalua-tion of violences that Palestinians had borne, as if it were all a competition of suffering. Perhaps in exasperation after how much his efforts to get the Palestinians to this point had cost him over the past, Jackson finally even complained to Savir, with a surprising harshness, about "this cycle of whin-ing. You just hear no sense of their winning. Many of them are very en-lightened people, but they just keep themselves on the defensive."

Over the decades they may simply have come to be instinctively afraid of believing in any hope involving the Israelis. But in his conference with the PLO eminences in Jerusalem, after listening with deepening despair to their intricately proliferating description of all the checkpoints and al-ternative routes the Israelis forced them to take to various destinations, Jackson at last burst out, "I got to say this, yawl" — and he bowed his head wearily, rubbing his brow with one hand while beginning in a low, slug-gish groan — "Yawl might run me out of here for saying this. But what you just told me is something a cabdriver needs. I mean, it's *sad*, but it doesn't help very much. It is not *enough* to keep on everlastingly about how they do what all they do to you. Occupiers *do things* like that, they put elbows in people's eyes . . . I mean, they just *do* all these little bitty mean things. If I'd started analyzing the way our white folks did things in America, I'd of stayed busy just watching the way they go about doing the things they do. Question becomes, what is your moral offensive against all that? If I'm standing still, they can keep on doing their things to me. But if I'm on the moral offensive and they're reacting, they can't do a lot of those little funny things."

Instead, Jackson had been urging all the Palestinians he met, rather than still trusting to violent street protest during this critical period, to "give real consideration to taking into account, at this stage of your struggle, the power of massive, disciplined, nonviolent witness." Propounding this now to the PLO officials across from him, he suddenly smacked the table with a fist, his coffee cup clattering. "There's a more powerful weapon than throwing rocks. That ain't a smart way to fight. They got more guns than you got rocks. Neither is blowing each other up in cars and buses the way to do it—if it were, troops woulda been out long time ago. Your strongest suit, since you not known for havin' a lot of airplanes and tanks and missiles, is the *rightness* of your cause. And if you're going to use moral rightness, the weapon must correspond with the cause. Don't discount how heavy was our occupation. I was raised on the West Bank in America. Many of us, whether it was the black struggle in the South, or the Indian struggle or the brown struggle, we understand West Banks. I've known nights in jail, I've known degradation, I *understand*. But in our struggle, when it was guns versus morality and we'd move by the thousands, we'd almost always win. We *beat* the guns. Now en-vision . . . to have ten, fifteen thousand Palestinians just marchin' down the road for the *moral rightness* of your cause—without rocks! facing guns!—those *without* the guns will *win*! A serious nonviolent mass witness . . . it's Gandhi's march to the sea, it's King marchin' from Selma to Montgomery."

It was a prospect he kept arraying for the contemplation of Palestinians wherever he spoke. "Now if five thousand youths march down the road, each with a gun in their hand, saying, 'I demand justice,' there is a jail cell or a graveyard waiting for them. But I can assure you that if those same five thousand youths march down that road *without* guns or rocks, armed with prayer books and moral authority, demanding the decencies of life—edu-cation, hospitals, job training, equal protection under the law, human rights—that will have infinitely more power than five thousand rocks hurtling through space. The occupiers are not prepared to fight that kind of soul power. Five thousand youths, and their mothers and fathers, and their sisters and brothers and aunts and uncles, walking down a dusty West Bank road to Bethlehem or Ramallah, saying, 'I simply want to breathe free,' the occupier's army is more prepared to deal with rocks than that kind of witness by a people whose humanity will just not give up. When you step into the *moral* range, you move into a domain that armed might is not comfortable with." Indeed, Shimon Peres privately conceded, near the close of his dinner for Jackson, that had the Palestinians initially em-ployed the nonviolent mass resistance of the movement in the States, "there would have been nothing we could do to counter it. Nothing in the end. And we would have reached this point long ago—with so much less killing, and so much less of the hatred that's making it so difficult now."

To a vast late-afternoon audience at a Palestinian university in East Jerusalem, Jackson expounded on how nonviolent struggle itself can become a transfiguring, re-creating force. "There are those of you who have been immersed in the struggle all of your lives. But now the accords offer a chance to change that struggle, of moving from endless confrontation to governing, to rebuild a people long dispersed, to build new institutions; many of you have been without equal protection of the law so long, even learning how to demand that law be honored becomes a new experience. And as you move into that new struggle, Tolstoy, Gandhi, Dr. King found that creative nonviolence has redemptive power. It builds the conscience of the people and the soul of the nation. It changes the terms of conflict from condemnation to conciliation, from funerals for our youth to futures for our youth."

But the difficulty in this attempt of Jackson's to translate King's nonviolent moral dynamic, even at this advanced point, into the swelter of old animosities here was that to the Palestinians it seemed precisely the violence of the Intifadeh that had finally compelled the Israelis into beginning negotiations in the first place, that had gotten them to this point where Gaza and Jericho were about to be returned to them. In other words, the past had worked for them. For that reason, there persisted a more or less total disconnect between Jackson's message and the mentality of his Palestinian audiences—evidenced not always in decorous blank silences. After his address at the civic hall in Hebron, he wound up in the middle of a march that was supposedly to seek admittance for a small Palestinian delegation into the mosque beside Abraham's tomb that had been closed since the massacre there over a month earlier. In a rapidly growing boil of youths, Jackson was lifted to a high terrace along the street, from which he shouted out, "This is a chance to build! To build families! To build schools! To build housing! A chance to stop the violence—so we can lay stones for foundations, not throw them. So let us be disciplined." Each one of these phrases—translated to the crowd by a long-gowned mullah beside him, a member of Hamas, an organization belonging more to the apocalyptic Iranian mentality on the situation (not least of the marvels worked by the peace initiative was that it had transformed the PLO into the establishment of the Palestinian community)— was mightily cheered, but a PLO official watching with the rest of Jackson's party, including Jackie, from the shelter of the bus that had transported them down from Jerusalem, suddenly wailed, "They are not translating what he is saying! They are translating the opposite!" Jackson then tried leading the seethe of youths in his chant of "Keep hope alive," which they at first haltingly chorused after him, but it was shortly engulfed in a roar of *Allahu Akbar!* as Jackson was hefted up on the shoulders of several of them and delivered back to the bus. "I don't even want to see this," said Jackie, already with foreboding. After depositing Jackson back in the bus, the crowd then started sweeping down toward the Israeli troops clustered at the bottom of the street. The confrontation was joined like a strangely ritualized familiar choreography—stones began to loop through the air, answered by flat bangs of gas grenades from the troops. The driver of the bus, with a wordless frantic concentration, began wheeling it cumbersomely back around, but managed only to get it trapped against a barricade, exactly in the middle of the clash, great blams of concussion grenades blasting out around it, its sides thumped by rocks and rubber bullets, whiffs of tear gas infiltrating its now-closed windows. Someone called to Jackson that they could not remain simply sitting there, and he looked around with a heavy glare and snapped, "Well, what you want *me* to do about it?" Someone else proposed that he step back down into the street "to calm this crowd," and Jackie instantly shouted to him, "Don't you dare even *think* about getting out of this bus!"

A way was finally cleared for the bus to leave, but afterward, Jackie, having already grown bluntly impatient with the interminable Palestinian cataloguing of past grievances ("They like adolescent boys who won't grow up"), was furious that their PLO escort had allowed the Hebron trip to so break loose from them. Though the incident seemed principally the handiwork of Hamas, then still engaged in a contest of militancy with the PLO, she tartly upbraided the gallery of PLO officials at the meeting later in Jerusalem for what had happened. As for Jackson, it had not failed to occur to him that he and his visit to Hebron had been craftily appropriated simply for a more publicized replay of the old brutal scenario, and he angrily told the PLO officials, "As I watched those kids march down that street and get into that rock-throwing thing, I thought how much more powerful they could be with the training to do mass nonviolent demonstrations instead. But they kinda been led to think their *rocks* are more powerful—you know. 'That's the only way you can fight. Uncle got killed, you got hurt yesterday, therefore got a right to throw rocks.' Well, might be understandable. But whatever we said today down in Hebron about the peace process and the chance to build a nation now, all that will be lost in the reports tonight about the rocks. And if leadership doesn't say anything about that, then it means it consents to it. So much of your good story is lost in the stereotype of rocks and bombs and—"

"Terrorists!" snapped Jackie.

"*That!* It plays into that stereotype. The Palestinian story must not get bogged down in a tactic in the short term gratifying, but does not move the world community. Your real story is lost in those rocks."

IN HIS APPEARANCE at Hebrew University, after Jackson had urged the Israelis to consider the trauma behind all the years of Palestinian rage, even at its most berserk, and to try humanizing their old enemy, one young scholar stood and declared, with shrill anger in his voice, "These same Palestinians who you say we should walk hand in hand with as brothers, they were on their rooftops *dancing* as the Iraqi Scuds came into Tel Aviv. And you want us now to believe that we should be *brothers* with them?" and he pronounced then, with disgust, "I think you are a dreamer."

"Well, I *am* a dreamer," Jackson said. "And I intend to keep on working to see my dreams realized, and not my nightmares. Because I have both. I have both. . . ."

In between his sessions with Palestinian groups, Jackson had made a return visit to Yad Vashem, the Holocaust memorial—this time with a somewhat more deliberative focus than his pass through it in 1979, moving slowly past its glimpses into the deeps of both human malignance and human endurance. At one point, he came across the famous photograph, enlarged to mural size, of phantomlike faces staring out from bunks in a concentration camp barracks, and he was told by his guide that one of them was Elie Wiesel—with whom Jackson periodically conferred back in the United States.

"What? Elie? Where?"

Wiesel was pointed out to him, and Jackson peered in closer. He pointed and asked, "This? This one?" He leaned down yet closer, his face almost touching the barbed wire that was strung across the mural, staring into Wiesel's face. "Goodgodamighty. And these other . . . where—?" The guard told them, "This was the liberation of Buchenwald." Jackson kept gazing at Wiesel's spectral young face. "*Elie!*" he murmured. It was almost as if it were the first time he had truly realized what had happened to him. (Immediately on returning to his hotel that evening, Jackson phoned Wiesel in New York to report with wonder that he had seen him in the camp photo.)

A few moments later, he paused again before another famed photograph, that of a rank of captured female camp guards, a pale-eyed look on their plain faces of the beast going back, it seemed, half a million years. Jackson commented in a whisper, "People infinitely capable of being either high or low. You know? In fascism, racism, anti-Semitism, left unleashed and unchecked, there're no limits to the depths of the demonic spirit in man's nature. Only those better angels that are in us too can save and lift us up from"—he nodded at the photograph—"from that."

Finally, on his last afternoon in Israel, Jackson met with a small group of Israeli and Palestinian youths assembled by Peace Now, the reconciliation movement in Israel, in a whitewashed basement room in a quiet

Jerusalem neighborhood. Addressing the Palestinian youths, who had managed to make their way there through roadblocks thrown up after the Afula bombing, he said, "You have as much right and reason to visit Yad Vashem and see what the Holocaust did to its victims as anybody else does. You really *need* to do that, in fact." Then, to the Israeli youths, he said, "For that matter, you got as much reason to know the West Bank story, from the view of those who've endured it, as anybody else does. When both of yawl begin to share some of those feelings and rehumanize each other that way, then you'll start looking out for each other, which is the surest way of looking out for your own people, too, by making sure that none of that stuff ever happens to each other . . . *to each other* . . . again. Because this is your world now."

But at length, a Palestinian girl ventured, in a thin and faltering voice, "You're saying all these beautiful things to do, and like, all right, we will try that. Because we *do* want peace. I mean, we want it . . . *so much*. But it's . . . it's *so difficult*." She began weeping before him.

It was plain that she had socked Jackson's heart. His voice abruptly much thicker, he said, "It *is* difficult. I know that violence abounds. It's *not* easy. It's more difficult than war is. And when you commit to nonviolent witness for resolving conflicts, you'll be discounted and ridiculed as crazy: 'They just don't understand reality.' But the reality is, in our movement it *did* work, because we appealed to people's conscience and sense of humanity. That's why a creative minority in the moral right—and it's almost always a minority—has the power to transform a society. Here now in your land, as these agreements keep coming, just as now there're military soldiers, there'll be *peace* soldiers, too—*soldiers* to keep the peace. Then at last life instead of death will begin—*this's gonna happen!*—and those beautiful things we been talkin' about will start taking place. I know it's hard not to be downhearted here at times, but those beautiful things are not naive, they're *real*, and they're coming just as sure as every night must end and morning rise into the sky. You must trust in that, and be proud, all of yawl, that you're working for that right now."

Before leaving, he had them stand and sing with him, arms intertwined, "We Shall Overcome," adding a verse beginning, "Palestinian and Jew together. . . ."

Then he cried out, with a clap, "Awright, yawl. Got to move on now."

One People Who Embraced Him As a Prophet

IN HIS TOAST to Jackson at the dinner at the King David Hotel, Foreign Minister Peres had acclaimed him as having become in America's history "the strongest voice of the black community, after King." But in all his extensions of his movement apostleship abroad, it has been his underrunning aspiration—as it has always been back in the United States—to deliver himself beyond the perception that his significance is solely that of a racial figure. Jackson had apprised *The Washington Post* in 1976 that he carried "a tension in my own mind about the place I'm assigned to and the place I deserve to be. That's why I resist the press calling me a black leader. I'm a *moral* leader who just happens to be black." Accordingly, during his 1989 visit to the Soviet Union, he was visibly gratified to hear *Ogonyok* editor Vitaly Korotich, when asked what exactly people made of Jackson there, effuse that "this man was all the time counted here as serious political figure, but level of political specialist. Now is really interesting, he's known politician that people don't ask if he Afro-American or European American. We start to understand that American politician can be popular not only in Harlem and in South, but yes, for first time I believe, man being Afro-American can be popular in rest of America and be president. And it changed feeling also toward America, make America better in our eyes."

Nevertheless, almost all the encomiums bestowed on Jackson by foreign officials seemed sooner or later to end up lauding him as a specialized, black leader. Even Korotich eventually warbled, in precisely the sort of confining sentimental identification Jackson hoped to range beyond, "I feel you are most popular Afro-American politician here after Paul Robeson. From the beginning of our country, we have such a nice, soft, and loving story about Afro-American people." While he was in the Soviet Union, the one high official who had not yet received him was Gorbachev himself. But in his repeated requests for a meeting, Jackson finally foundered against the Soviets' unsentimental, elemental computation of where the true stores of power lay.

IN HIS JOURNEY a few months earlier through southern Africa, Jackson had found himself, there at least, recognized and acclaimed in full measure to those huge old yearnings for greatness. In his appearances at conferences and state dinners, spotlights would seek him out at the head table. He was hailed by Zimbabwe's president Mugabe with a tribute heard again and again from other presidents, council ministers, foreign secretaries: "Were it not for race, we are sure you would be in the White House now. You would have won!" In his tours into the countryside, he met with an adulation approaching the demireligious, multitudes greeting him at every stop in barrages of drums and gales of high glad choiring, a great cry always rising around him of *Jes-see! Jes-see! Jes-see!* And as in his campaign processionals in the United States, Jackson seemed to be trying exultantly to merge himself, lose himself, in the throngs—once undertaking to dance with a circle of befeathered young women, executing vaguely discolike tilts until he was hastily advised they were maidens undergoing initiation into womanhood and "they can be touched by no man, please, Reverend Jackson," with which he passed a paternal palm over their heads, singing out, "Yawl be good, now!"

In all, he passed through a celebration in southern Africa that was like a rhyming completion of the largest circle of all in those "poetries of time" he is so obsessively fond of noting. About one hymn he heard in Zambia, he enthused, "I suddenly recognized it as what we sang as 'Come by Here, My Lord.' As I sat there listening, it was like I was back in Long Branch Baptist before we got the piano." More, he maintained he detected everywhere around him assonances of common ways of experiencing. "Live, *passionate* feelings, I'm talkin' 'bout. Live colors, movement, a certain *flair*—almost as if it's a congenital character trait. Shows up even in the style of African-American leaders like Adam Powell, certain consistency of flair." He further liked to suppose that he spied resemblances between black members of his entourage and various African citizens, and his middle son, Jonathan, who was with him on the trip, eventually came to be taken up in this excitement. Emerging from one meeting in Luanda, Jonathan began exclaiming in a low, urgent voice, as if he had just realized he was discovering who would have been his people in another lifetime, "I see people who look like, I mean, me *personally*! The vibes here! That girl—" He nodded toward an Angolan television reporter, a tall and willowy young woman. "I could have actually courted her once! We only talked for a few minutes, me from the States, her growing up here, but it was like, man, I *knew her* in this strange way."

The particular inspiration that had launched Jackson off on this tour of southern Africa was the possibility of a major U.S. engagement with the continent to help develop its incalculable natural promise, and he had reflected on the flight over, "The paradox of it would be almost biblical, you know? Like Joseph, sold into slavery in Egypt by his brothers. But in time, he found favor in the belly of the Egyptian giant, rose to become its prime minister. Then, during a time of famine, he became the savior of both Egypt *and* his brothers, when those brothers appeared before him one day pleading for food to take back to their people. Same way, we were not just *stolen from* Africa but were *sold by* Africans. We were taken to a foreign land, survived two centuries of slavery. But now we operate as full citizens in that land. America cannot dismiss us. We are in the central nervous system of the most powerful nation on earth, in its culture, its politics. We hang close to America's heart. And our ability to point America toward good has become central to America's story." Indeed, Jackson has hardly ever been insensitive to the proposition that America had abducted violently into its midst, into a condition of subjugation, a people who would come in time to constitute the sustaining marrow of humanity in the white bones of a coldly systematic and acquisitive society: because they had been left for centuries with nothing to own and cherish and cultivate other than their own humanity, they had come to know more thoroughly, had become more accomplished in, hope, gladness, lonesomeness, grief, forgiveness, compassion, endurance, love, than most of the rest of the society around them. At the same time, despite their experience, or perhaps because of it, probably no other people had come to believe in the American democratic promise more transcendingly—a bondage people who had become America's soul, and the keepers of its conscience. Jackson had preached more than once in the past, "The oppressor is confused. He thought he'd brought us here to be his slaves. But God sent us here *to save him*, and possibly, along with him, the human race itself." Now on his way to Africa with his notion of a great geoeconomic alliance with the United States, Jackson speculated, "We who went through that whole long process of slavery, we could become the emancipators of both America *and* Africa. Could complete our Joseph story. Like other struggling peoples over the earth, Africa looks to America in awe, admires its prosperity, identifies with its democratic values, and we could provide them now their economic salvation."

While he was in Nigeria, his host was a combination business magnate and putative chief named Harry Akande, a tubby, unremittingly amicable man who proved close to manically euphoric to have Jackson briefly in his keeping. After his own induction as a chief at the king's compound in Oyo, Jackson set out with Chief Harry on a ride to his home for a dinner with a selection of other Nigerian gentlemen of substance. After a while, Jackson grumbled, "Chief, how much farther away *is* your house, anyway? Said was just down the road a piece from the king's. Since I landed in Lagos, you had me in this car with you now goin' on most the day, hadn't you?" Chief Harry giggled. "Next exit. Next exit." Another considerable stretch of time passed. Jackson asked again, "You say, what, Chief, five more minutes to your house?" Chief Harry assured him, "Next exit." Jackson snuffled, "*Damn*, now, Chief, that's what you said half an hour ago. You have gone and *hijacked* me here." The car at last turned off onto a skinny potholed road that trailed into a hilly little town, finally pulling up at a multitiered, cement-walled house suggestive of a small-scale citadel. Jackson entered the house ahead of Chief Harry, to find congregated in the main parlor a company of local notables in voluminous ornate gowns—two judges, four other nominal chiefs, several lawyers—who greeted Jackson with a profusion of courtesies. In the mezzanine dining area, everyone seated himself at a long table covered with a brocade cloth. The king himself presently arrived from his palace in Oyo, a trifle late, and he was afforded a seat at one end of the table, where he immediately applied himself to the meal, undistracted by the ensuing discussion.

From the other end of the table, Jackson, still wearing his chief's vestments, proceeded to invoke, for these soberly attentive civic worthies in this obscure Nigerian town, the epochal vision of, as Jackson presented it, "a Marshall Plan for Africa, an initiative for African development mounted by the efforts of African-Americans. The reality is, no other region has the natural constituency in America—thirty million of us—that Africa has. They are a natural, waiting, ready, massive lobby to argue this case for you."

"Yes, but you see," interjected a barrister, with a gently obstinate disputatiousness, "have not American blacks themselves abandoned any wishes to be separated from the rest of America by identification with Africa? Have they not become so *Americanized*?" This skepticism touched off a clamorous agreement from others around the table, from which the lawyer derived more vigor as he continued, "The very moment you start letting the American authorities see there is—"

"A bloc!" someone cried.

"Yes, a bloc," another burst out.

"That the whole business is from—"

"They will," this in passionate dismay, "*denounce* you!"

"Yes, *denounce* you!"

Jackson tried to intervene by flurrying, "Well, I'm gon— I'm, I'm gonna tell you, wait a second—"

"They won't *give up*!"

"Well, wait, now, listen. The reason they'll change is that it's now to America's distinct interest to have Africa within our sphere of influence. . . ."

To this there came from the contentious barrister, surprisingly, a yelp of "*Right!*" One suddenly sensed that they all actually wanted to believe this stupendous prospect posed by Jackson of an American-African symbiosis, but, almost angrily, didn't dare.

"And in our development and maturity as African-Americans," Jackson continued, "with congresspeople, mayors, our ability to make and break presidents and all that, this demand now for a relationship between you in Africa and us in America cannot be denied. What's more, I'm sayin' there's come to be an appreciation of the *value of it*."

Some began now to allow themselves, tentatively, to admit to the possibility in concert with Jackson, "The whole idea, yes—the value— They *know* it! They *know* it!"

But the barrister, with a pugnacious tugboat bulge to his jaw, was not yet disposed to be so openly convinced. "But to identify yourselves as one set within American society having a bloc. . . . They want to show the outside world a common face, to say, 'We are all Americans, whether black, brown, green, or whatever.' So they will now say, '*Ohhh*, so you want to call yourself an African-American?' Then they start to say, 'Ah-*hah!* Ah-*hah-hah-hah!*' Is so?"

"But again I assert," rejoined Jackson, "reason why this thing can happen is they can't stop us from identifying Africa as our home. It's . . . it's *unstoppable*."

This produced bellings of laughter around the table. It was as if they were all pulling for Jackson in his argument against their pessimism about this heady prospect. "Tell us what you mean!" one exclaimed.

"I mean unstoppable in a cultural sense, but beyond cultural, trade and business and development connections. Say, 'It's all right for Tenneco and Conoco to get some of our oil, but we also have a right to buy into some refineries, get a guaranteed market.' "

This was answered by a loud commotion of approval.

"But let me just inject one thing," the lawyer kept on. "I think that willingness for political sharing is one thing, but economic sharing is another. We know the Americans for what they are!"

"But what I'm tryin' to get across to you, man," said Jackson, "America isn't isolated anymore. In today's international financial environment, even Wall Street is beginning to fight for debt relief in Africa, in Latin America. Because so long as yawl in debt and can't grow, then America can't grow. *Because it ain't got no new markets.* Simple as that. That's why some of these old frames of reference"—by which he plainly meant the doubts of these respectable Nigerian burghers as to what attentions they might expect from the United States—"those old perspectives don't apply to this new situation. So yawl take heart. Go to work on this new arrangement. It's a different day."

He had by now inspirited them to the point that they all, including at last the barrister, gave him a flourish of applause.

BUT MOST OF all, Jackson's journey across southern Africa became a traveling jubilee of reunion, a reembrace over immense intervening reaches of history and space—in a way the largest synapse of all, this personal one of his. One evening in Gabon, just a few days after Christmas, he dropped in on a worship service in a tiny plank church, perched along a hilly back lane in Libreville, which had been established in the 1840s by Boston abolitionist missionaries. It was packed this hot night with a congregation all dressed in starched white, who, as Jackson entered, were clapping and singing, with a glad, full-lung blare, "Allelujah! Allelujah! . . ." The sanctuary, plain and clean and austere, was filled with palm fronds for the evening's service, with twinklings of blue and silver tinsel. When Jackson at length took the pulpit, he began, "I feel great joy to be here with you tonight in the house of the Lord—" and his voice rolled on between translations. "Many years ago, nearly twelve million people were taken from here in Gabon and all over this coast of West Africa, and shipped to South and North America. Many died along the voyage, yet that terrible passage could not separate us from each other. Not all the years of slavery could separate us from each other, and could separate neither of us from the love of God, a God who *controls* the long arc of history. . . ." It could have been one of those mass meetings in a clapboard tabernacle in the backcountry of Mississippi during the sixties, or one of his voter-registration revival rallies in those same churches in the eighties, and under the surging of his voice an answering hum and sibilation of exultation gradually gathered from the rows of rapt faces. "Tonight, three hundred and fifty years later, we don't talk alike. But we still *look* alike, we *feel* alike, we *sing* alike. Because we *are* alike!" This released an ovation that sounded too huge somehow to be issuing from the congregation in that small chapel.

"This *is* our motherland," he continued a few days later in Lagos, speaking to a reception of assorted Nigerian civic leaders and their wives, assembled by Chief Harry in a hotel suite high above the wide dull sheen of the city's smoggy bay. Chief Harry, shining with sweat, had first read an introduction from crumpled notes, his voice and his hands shaking, and when Jackson, still wearing his chieftain's raiment, had taken the microphone from him and begun speaking, two women standing in the crowd had suddenly begun soundlessly weeping, as if at the sheer resonance of his voice pealing over the room. "Some of us may be in America, or South America, or the Caribbean, or Paris and London. We may now speak the language of our captors. Languages and waters may now divide us. But they are not as strong as the blood that still binds us." At that, two more women in their elegant Nigerian drapery, along with Chief Harry himself, went into tears. "But this can be the beginning of a new day, reconnecting Africans in our own diaspora over the face of the earth. Other immigrants came to America of their own volition, to rid themselves of chains. African-Americans were hauled there *in* chains. But now, my friends, across those waters"—and he motioned toward the bay sprawled below them—"out there, not far from you, are twenty million African-Americans, members of your family. Not far from you. Now mayors, state legislators, twenty-four African-American congresspeople who can shape U.S. foreign policy. Your own people. *Not far from you.* Let us all now come back together again. And wipe out poverty together, wipe out illiteracy and disease and hunger—together, wipe out all those forces that would make us less than we really are."

However messianically hopeful this proposition, it became Jackson's recurrent sermon in a series of triumphant visitations, from Nigeria to Zambia, that lasted for sixteen days. And it was at least evident that, if not quite in America or anywhere else, he had arrived here as that moral-heroic figure he had so long hungered to become.

Late on New Year's night in Lagos, Jackson, after watching a pro football game by satellite relay at the residence of the U.S. chargé d'affaires, returned to the somewhat seedy government guesthouse where he and his party were installed, its enormous rooms scantily furnished with a faded decor suggestive of some fifties Las Vegas hotel. And as he was preparing to go to bed, he glanced up to discover, immediately outside the opened double doors of his suite, the house's ancient and lanky steward in the process of bowing to him in his long gown, repeatedly and deeply, almost horizontal to the floor, with one dusty-ankled leg stretched out long and straight behind him, while whooping, with each swoop downward, "Long may you live! Long may you live!" To each of these hosannas Jackson, who was sitting on his bed waiting for a call to go through to his mother's home in Greenville, answered with a loud honk, "Love yuh! Hear me? *Luuuv* yuh!" The steward stumbled off back down the hall, muttering, "Dot mon. Dot mon. I do love dot man so much!"

Meanwhile, Jackson's phone connection to Greenville had finally struggled through. "Who is this?" he bellowed. "G'mama?" Sitting on the edge of the bed in a white V-necked undershirt and Jockey shorts as he talked to his grandmother, he had the curious look of some hugely overgrown schoolboy about to turn in at bedtime. "G'mama? Know where I am? I'm callin' you right from where your people come from. Hear me? That's right. Talkin' to you from where all yo' people *first came from.* . . ."

Several days later, when he was at last on his way back to the United States, he bounded out of his seat as the Gulfstream jet provided him by Gabon's president headed on out over the Atlantic, and happily hollered down the aisle, "Hey, man! From Greenville to Gabon! From Haynie Street to Harare! Sump'm, hunh? . . . ." Awakening an hour or so before landing in Chicago, he immediately mentioned, almost offhandedly, "Gallup poll, top ten most admired men in the world—recently heard I been on it for apparently some amazing number of years, something like seven or eight. In the top three, too, along with the pope. Carter was on there when he was president, but he's off now. Kissinger was on it for a number of years, now he's fallen off. Yeah. But I been constant in the top three. Me 'n' the pope." And he gave a long, lionlike yawn of drowsily luxurious satisfaction.

XIX
Coming Back Home

SHORTLY AFTER I had arrived in Greenville, that weekend after the 1988 election, to join Jackson for the community commemoration of his mother's birthday, I first took a walk along Greenville's main street, and found that, no doubt in answer to the competition of outlying shopping malls, it had been converted into a studiously picturesque promenade like a Disneyworld replica of small-town Middle America. A more surreal indication, though, of the tonnages of time that had trucked by since Jackson's beginnings there was displayed with a shrinelike reverence in a showcase window: two painted portraits, somewhat crudely but vividly done, one of Elvis Presley and one of Jackson.

Still, the aboriginal racial partitions of the town discreetly abided. When I had checked into a hotel along the downtown plaza—its lobby a modified suburban version of the Hanging Gardens of Babylon—no one at the desk seemed quite certain of the location of Haynie Street, though it could have been no more than a few blocks away. "It's around where Jesse Jackson grew up," I said.

"Oh, is that right?" chirped the young woman behind the registration counter. "I just wouldn't have any idea about that part of town."

Returning from my room to the lobby a few minutes later, I asked a young white bellman at the front entrance if he knew where Haynie Street was—he did, it turned out—and I then asked him if it was within strolling distance. "It's not that far," he pleasantly offered, "but I certainly wouldn't recommend walking around over in that area. Let me call a cab for you." When the cab appeared, I was not entirely surprised to see that its driver was black. As we pulled away from the hotel, I told him why I was looking for that particular street, and he said, "Man, anything you want to see havin' to do with Jesse, I'll *show* you. I know all them places where he grew up. That what you want to see, won't even charge you for it." The ride from the hotel to Jackson's old neighborhood took only about two minutes—that close but still that isolated remained the town's two zones of habitation.

Later, after I met Jackson at Greenville's small airport, we set out on his wandering tour, in that long amber Saturday afternoon, back through the locales of his boyhood. A little after sundown we came to a corner that had a dumpy honky-tonk look instantly familiar to me from the black sections of countless other small southern towns in the fifties and sixties, the sort of abbreviated little strip which, on ripe summer nights, would be alive with a carnival tumult, music whomping from jukeboxes through the opened doors of cafés, a clattering of pool balls, while under gaudy guttering neons a continuous romping flirtation proceeded with glad-eyed women in fluorescent dresses. "Oh, man," murmured Jackson, "did I spend a lot of time on this corner." Now, in this chill blue November dusk, as Jackson directed the driver to pull up in front of a pool hall, it had the forsaken look of some ghost-set from a long-forgotten movie, wholly vacant of sound or motion. Even so, as soon as Jackson climbed out of the car, several people stirred into view—old cohorts and schoolmates of his, they proved to be—not unlike apparitional figures emerging out of the deeps of his past. They collected around him on the sidewalk, gaping at his uncanny materialization before them, out of his remote glories of television fame and throngs in convention halls, a mystically transfigured form of the youth they had once known.

He was surrounded by their delighted cackling, "It's *Jesse.* . . . Aw*right* now, what's happenin'? . . . What's up, man, what you doin' here?" The men were wearing shabby synthetic slacks of faded Crayola colors, the women wrapped in scrappy sweaters, all their eyes slightly muddy, a sweet tinge of alcohol hanging about them. One woman crooned, as if his appearance here were simply something she'd long been expecting, "*Therrre* you *arrre,*" and she curled up against him with thin little cat-meowings, "You awright, Jesse?" He replied, "Just fine, how you doin', baby?" It became a small, baroque kind of inter-hymning. . . .

"Jesse Jackson!"

"How you been, honey?"

"Lookin' *good.*"

"Hey, my man!"

"What's up, man, what you doin' here?"

"Something for Mama over at the Ramada Inn tonight. Yawl doin' awright?" He turned then to tell me, "These all my classmates. Used to help me do my homework all the time."

A thin, leathery man who was the owner of the pool hall, named James Blasingame, shouted, "Thass right! I gave 'im everything he know!"

Jackson broke out into a bay of laughter. "That's all too true."

Everyone then followed him in a great gleeful hubbub as he wandered on into the pool hall, a quiet clacking of balls echoing over its cement floor. One man, glancing up to discover him, missed his shot, and Jackson hooted, " 'Bout the same as ever, hunh, Wilbur? Still can't sink nothin'." The man yelled, "Where you come from?" Jackson called out, "Somebody give me a stick." One was handed to him, and as he leaned with it over the table, the man declared, "Watch 'im, he can't shoot. Go ahead, shoot, Bo." Jackson stroked the eight-ball into a corner pocket, and stood back up and let loose another bay of laughter. "Just as good as ever, Wilbur. Still couldn't beat me."

They all then followed him back outside, ganging around him on the sidewalk. Jackson yelled, "Hey, Wilbur? Where you at? C'mere . . ." The man slipped up beside Jackson, and Jackson threw an arm around his shoulders: "Wilbur here, we were playin' football one day, and he was runnin' out for a pass—and ran straight into a tree!" Everyone guffawed with Jackson, including Wilbur. Jackson gave his shoulders a couple of hugshakes. "Ran *smack into* a tree. 'Member that, Wilbur? Maybe you don't, hit that tree so hard."

With that, he turned back toward his car, "Got to go, yawl, got to go." They called after him in the dusk, "Awright, bye, Jesse. When we gonna see you again, Jesse?" He threw them a high wave as he opened the door, "Back soon, yawl."

Jackson sat very quiet and still for several blocks as he left behind that pool-hall corner on which, like some cul-de-sac in fate, the friends of his youth had remained stranded. Finally he murmured, "Those guys, love 'em so much, we all grew up together. One thing I always remember when I come back home is how ambitious they were back then, how many of them now on that corner were so brilliant when we were in school—academically much smarter than I was. Guys like Blasingame, for instance, if they could've gone to Furman, would've been very different people now. But back then, wadn't much to lift us beyond our situation, still seemed closed in on all sides. Blasingame dropped out of high school around the tenth grade—the corner got him. On that corner, they all learned to settle for so much less. To just exist. And they still on that corner." He went on in the same barely audible voice, sitting in the front seat by the driver and staring straight out the windshield into the gathering dark, as if he were recollecting all this more to himself, musing on how that corner was, in fact, an image of the condition of millions of black youths over the nation. "Trapped forever in that corner culture. The low expectations, the drinking, the hanging out . . . flash your clothes, show off how well you doin'.

Go into the army, come back home, head right back to that corner. Sooner or later, little time in jail—'He's gone, he'll be out in six months.' But come right *back* to that corner. Never get far away too long from that corner."

He shook his head, still looking out through the windshield. "Now, I was *on* the corner, but for some reason never really *in* that corner culture. Seemed there was this expectation for me even among those guys. After I left for college, I came back home to have some knee surgery, and dropped back by that corner once. They said, 'What you doin' here? Gotta have surgery? Ain't they got no doctors up there at that school you been at? Why you got to come back here?' Like there was this *resistance*, you know, to seeing me back on that corner. Like they were trying to warn me, to shoo me away from it." Now, with a generation of other black males like those old friends of his behind him still caught in the grim gravities of such blind-end street corners, "Wherever I speak now, like that address to the Democratic convention in Atlanta last summer, somehow in the back of my mind I'm always seeing those guys back there we just left."

LATER THAT EVENING, the birthday banquet at the Ramada Inn to honor Jackson's mother brought out a large and festive host of citizens. They crowded in through the lobby—where a small combo of saxophone, drums, and keyboard synthesizer was ladling out such purling melodies as "The Shadow of Your Smile"—and milled on into a banquet room festooned with clusters of red and white balloons. Among those there was Jackson's seventh-grade teacher, Sarah Shelton, who in 1984, the year of Jackson's first presidential run, had herself been elected to the state legislature, and served two terms. Also showing up was a respectable deputation of Greenville's white townsfolk, including a past South Carolina governor, Richard Riley, later to become Clinton's secretary of education, along with the state's current lieutenant governor and the president of the county's Democratic women's association. Greenville's mayor, while not putting in an appearance himself, had nevertheless decreed that Saturday to be "Helen Jackson Day." Jackson at last arrived with his mother, leading her through the lobby on his arm—she smiling a bit glassily, attired in a rich-red spangling gown. It was forty-seven years now since her son's birth in that flimsy board house in Greenville's black quarter, but her round soft face still had a girlish brightness, her skin still the hue of honey, with dark-glowing eyes.

Seated then behind the table on the podium, she received through the evening, from a succession of friends and various dignitaries of

Greenville's black community, homages of a somewhat semireligious lambency altogether: "I'm reminded of the story of Hannah, the prophet Samuel's mother, who said, 'Lord, if you give me a child, I promise I'll give it back to you.' . . . Helen Jackson, God raised you up out of the dust, and we celebrate the miracle of your motherhood. . . . Hail, Helen, blessed art thou among women, blessed is the fruit of thy womb. . . ." When her turn came to respond to these tributes, she stood a little stiffly behind the lectern, and read with a precise deliberation from carefully crafted remarks of slightly ornate locution, "I am humbled by this magnanimous gesture . . . such an unparalleled honor . . . this banquet extraordinary," praising the speakers before her as "the vivacious . . . the dynamic . . ." She also tendered a "thank-you to my son, who interrupted his busy schedule to be at my side at this time."

In fact, after getting his mother settled at the podium table, Jackson had expeditiously returned to the lobby, where, as the program proceeded in the banquet room, he stood off in an alcove amid a covey of local reporters, not a little relishing their vibrant interest on his return to his hometown as a two-time presidential candidate, eagerly discoursing about the general election a few days earlier. "It actually showed broad-based support for the basic thrust of the Democratic party—"

"Are you going to run for president in '92?"

"Well, it's completely premature to be talking about that, but—"

"Just a matter of finding the right candidate for it?"

"Just a matter of time, matter of time."

"You gonna be the man for that time?"

"Well, I already told you a second ago"— and he then smuggled them a coy smirk— "Yawl tryin' to be so *tricky.*"

But he managed to get back to seat himself beside his mother in time for the even more voluptuous gratification of hearing—here in this community where, over thirty years before, he'd grown up a poor and illegitimate black youth—former governor Richard Riley, a member of an old family of Greenville's white gentry and himself a graduate of Furman University, now claim to the gathering that "our two families have been friends for years," and yet further range into an enthusiastic comparison of Jackson to an Old Testament prophet: "Jeremiah took his people when they were down, said, 'Got to help each other.' He was a fighting preacher, an insurgent. He spoke forth even when it hurt. Talked to the church in tough terms. He was a *fighting* prophet. . . ."

It had turned out to be, of course, as much a celebration of Jackson as of his mother, climaxing his long afternoon's passage back through the settings of his beginnings.

The House on Arbutus Trail

WHEN THE DINNER ended, we rode to his mother's house, where she and Jackson's grandmother, Tibby, had been living alone since Charles Jackson's death in 1979—a small but handsome split-level residence of yellow wood siding and dark brick, set on a steeply sloping lawn along a twining little road named Arbutus Trail, in a tranquil and heavily wooded neighborhood, fairly integrated, of similar spruce brick homes: it seemed another country and century away from the dingy warren of her own and her son's origins. Her old friend Vivian Taylor would later remark, "She was pulled out of her environment, which was among the indigent, and over into that neighborhood which is very well-to-do, and she always felt a little isolated over there. She'd call me sometimes and say, 'I wonder why I'm over here all by myself.' " Two mortar lions flanked the short driveway up to the house, which had a tall skylight over the front door, a parlor furnished with a certain formal lavishness—lampshades dangling strands of crystal beads, a gilt coffee table, brass urns in the corners holding copious green plants, all resting upon plush expanses of pale carpeting amid a profusion of birthday flowers. She sat for a while on a stool in the corner of her kitchen, still in her deep-red gown, a woman still possessed of her church-choir soloist's meticulous decorum, and politely worried, "Do you think everything went all right tonight? I just couldn't tell, but I hope it all went nicely."

Jackson's grandmother had no doubts whatever about the success of the entire evening. Now in her eighties, a sprightly cricket of a woman, Tibby seemed ready to continue the conviviality on through the night. Before they had left for the affair at the Ramada Inn, the house had been moiling with people—neighbors, old friends, local and state politicians, miscellaneous women who seemed not particularly attached to anyone, Jackson's own sizable entourage. Arrayed across the dining room table for all these callers was a bountiful buffet of fried chicken, ham, macaroni and cheese, rice and gravy, soft heapings of green beans simmered in fatback, a sweet-potato casserole under a crust of toasted marshmallows. From this cycloramic southern spread, Jackson and I had laden our plates high and taken them into the relative quiet of the kitchen, where, on a small television set on the counter, a football game was in progress. Tibby shortly followed us into the kitchen to watch us as we ate. She had proudly proclaimed to me earlier that Jackson had been born in her bed, and "when he came, he looked 'bout as big as he is now." All his present expansive effects and circumstances, including the retinues of strangers he periodically trailed into the house, were clearly still a thing of wonderment and fascination to her.

Jackson was expounding on the implications of the presidential election that past Tuesday when Tibby interrupted to ask me, "And where *you* from?"

"What I'm saying is," Jackson kept on, trying to ignore this diversion, "after the convention the party ran away from the issues and coalition that could have kept that seventeen-point lead of Dukakis's. Blowin' that lead was what that 'not ideology but competence' stuff got them. Got a southerner on the ticket, but wouldn't have *me* on the ticket. Understand what I'm sayin'?"

Tibby thereupon asked me, "You gettin' enough to eat? We got lots more food out there."

"Mean, it was like," Jackson pressed ahead, "you had a weak team falling behind in a game, and got this versatile player can throw things open but you don't—"

Tibby broke in again to inquire, "And how many chil'run you got?"

"Where's Mama?" Jackson now asked her a bit curtly. "Hadn't you better be gettin' yourself something to eat?"

She replied, "I ain't got the *ti-i-ime*," singing the word. And did not budge. Finally Jackson, as he reported that there was to be a gathering of Democratic stewards in Phoenix that weekend to which he did not expect to be invited either, "be just the state chairs there, others in the, you know, the political family," abruptly got up from the table to rinse out his glass rather overvigorously under the sink faucet.

Now back at the house after the Ramada Inn event, when Jackson indicated he was about ready to turn in—"Gotta leave early in the morning, gonna be on *Face the Nation*"—Tibby nestled herself under his arm and chirruped, "Got to go when?" patting his now rather ample midriff and singing in her sighing drawl, "You not gonna *go-o-o* again?" She then happily informed the others in the room, in what seemed also a kind of general marvelment over the miraculous turns of fate in life, "Never know about Jesse, can't keep up with him."

Absent that evening, and only glancingly mentioned, had been Jackson's half brother Charles Jr., Helen's son by Jackson's stepfather. He had been located now for some years in Los Angeles, where he made a living for a time in the nebulous shimmers of the music and entertainment business, then operated a small soul-food restaurant not far from the Los Angeles airport. A slight, quiet man, he tagged along after his famed half brother on one of his stops in L.A. for an evening visit to Lionel Ritchie's home, and then afterward, asked not Jackson but a young photographer with Jackson's group, "Wonder if you could give me a call later and let me know what he'll be doing tomorrow."

Neither one of her sons, Helen Jackson would sometimes gently fret, did she herself regularly hear from very much. "But I don't want to bother them about me," she said, "don't want them to think they have to watch out for their mother. For those things I can't do to help myself, I have others around, my neighbors, some of the people at church." Since her retirement as a beautician and her husband's death, she had mostly passed her days reading her Bible in the early mornings, occupying herself occasionally in incidental church work, now and then taking fishing trips with her friend Vivian Taylor. In deference to Jackson, she would dutifully make efforts to appear at most local Democratic functions, "but she never spoke up," says the president of the party's county women's association, Joanne Montague. "She's not an issues-oriented person. She's very private. She's mostly kept to herself."

Helen herself stipulates, "I've striven to walk circumspectly." Occasionally, she reports, strangers will approach her "and ask, 'Do you know Jesse Jackson?' I say, 'Well, I *think* I do. You know, I'm his mother.'" But that the extraordinary figure Jackson became over the years happened, amazingly, to have been born to her was, she will insist, "only an accident." Once, in one of her infrequent ventures out of Greenville to join Jackson, she heard him preach at a church in south-central Los Angeles: seated in the front row, luminous in a snowy white fur stole and white dress and turban, she gazed up at him in the pulpit with a blissful raptness on her face as he recited once more how "some of us were born in places like the stall in which Jesus was born, grew up in the *lowly* places, doing without, struggling. But if God could reach down and touch Mary and Joseph, he can reach down and touch and lift up you and me. . . ." But while rooms are filled with memorabilia from her son's progress over the years—awards, honorific certificates, framed photographs of him everywhere on the walls—she has remained at a final remoteness from the sweep and flare of his life. It has not always been necessarily at her own election. Vivian Taylor says, "She would complain that because he'd become a national figure, she could hardly get fifteen minutes with him." Only a day or two before the Democratic convention in Atlanta, she phoned the county party chairman to inquire, "Do you know anything about any arrangements for me? Am I supposed to be there with Jesse? I haven't heard anything from him, and I don't know whether he wants me there or not. Could you find out for me? And if he does, could I ride over there with you all?" Only when Jackson's staff was then contacted were provisions hurriedly improvised for her inclusion in his party.

For the most part, she says, "I see him on television. And when he's on television, quite a few people will call me. It's a great joy." At times, she will go down to the large den in her basement and put into the VCR a cassette of his speeches at the two Democratic conventions, replaying them again as "I sit there by myself, and I look and I say, *Well!* I wonder to myself, how can he think on every level almost that I have ever heard of whenever he speaks?" She was watching him from her basement den as he delivered his address at the 1992 Democratic convention in New York, and she placed her hand on the TV and prayed for God's spirit to fill him.

But in this remove from him now, "she is often very frightened, because she figures that he will have to be a martyr," says Vivian Taylor. "She has lived with the fact that someone will try to take his life. She figures that martyrdom is near whenever he pushes as fast as he does. With all the strides he has made, running for president and everything, it doesn't always please her. I wish he'd calm down some, because it keeps her so tense. When he made his jump to run for president, this was her greatest fear—'They killed the Kennedys, you know. Killed them boys.' She just wishes he would stop now." Helen herself concedes, "You don't know when, you don't know where. You know, he's out there like he is, in so many places, under so many abnormal conditions. He's flying while most people are asleep. I just talk to the Lord, I say, 'Lord, build a hedge around him. Take care of him. Take care of the power that's driving the plane. Take care of the people that he's around.'" The few times she has been with him on trips, she says, "Some of the young men with him, he'll up and go over to get a paper, and they'll say, 'We want you with us right here, not over there like that.' But Jesse will just walk on, and I say, 'I wonder why he won't listen to them.' But maybe he's in another world."

After mentioning that she mostly sees Jackson now only on television, she suddenly added, despite her professed resolve not to concern him about her state, "I want you to know this about when I see Jesse because this includes him knowing it, too, that he knows I'm here alone." On the whole, as she once confided to Joanne Montague, "people assume I'm very busy, but I'm not. I'm really a very lonely woman." At moments when "I get a little lonesome," she says, "I start saying Bible verses. You know, like, 'Fear not, for I am with you. Be you not dismayed, for I am your God, and I will help you and strengthen you, I will uphold you with my right hand.'" Nevertheless, she admits, at times "I could just say, 'Oh, Lord, send me somebody in here. I just want *to be with somebody.*'..."

ONE SPRING MORNING in 1995, she sat in her front parlor and reflected, "You know, just recently one of my cousins told me, said, 'Helen, would you think back and realize? You never lived a life of your own.' I said, 'I hadn't thought about that. It's true.'" When she was growing up, she recounts, "I couldn't get very far out of Mama's sight at all," and these many years later, according to one longtime friend, "Helen would sometimes complain about how her mother still insisted on going everywhere with her." But then, about two years after that evening of Helen's birthday commemoration, Tibby had been felled by a succession of strokes that left her only a faintly conscious effigy of who she had always been. For several years after, Helen had consigned herself to a virtual captivity in the house to tend to her. "We don't have anyone else in the world now but each other," she maintained, "and she gave me so much, I owe this to her. She was my mother and my father and my sister, my brother. She was much stronger than I am. What she had, you didn't get in school. I had to put her first now. I had no way out." At last, though, Helen agreed to release her into the care of a nursing home a short drive from the house. Jackson periodically came down to see her. Helen would visit there regularly, sitting for hours by the bed in which Tibby lay inert, combing her hair, patiently plaiting it into short braids, kneading her hands, calling to her, "Mama? Mama? Bo's coming! Jesse's gonna be here again. Jesse's coming, Mama!" And at that, Tibby's eyes would falteringly open, staring blearily about the room for a brief instant before closing again.

THAT SATURDAY IN November of 1988 when Jackson had returned to Greenville for the community observance of his mother's birthday, she allowed when back at the house, "Whenever he's here, he's always so busy, going on with his work, making calls, seeing people, never still, that I'm hardly able to spend any real *quality* time with him at all. But that's all right. I'm happy just to stand back and watch him with the people." But for all the testimonials that he had heard from his hometown's citizens that evening, despite all that had transpired since he had slung with a centrifugal force out into the world, the whole long arc from his advent under King to his expanding national fame, his two presidential campaigns, his missions abroad, all of it, in what should have been his night of fulfilling and affirming return to where he began, he seemed left still with some flat, vague, fretful, distracted discontent. Before the house had quite emptied of the guests who had followed him from the Ramada Inn, Jackson had retired to a bedroom only to reappear at its door a moment later, his tie off, his shirt unbuttoned over the sag of his paunch. He called, "Mama. *Mama!*" She came out into the hall from the kitchen. He barked, "Why is the air conditioner on?" She said, "Well, 'cause of all the cooking today, it was still a little warm in here. I'll turn it off, I'll turn it off, you just go on back to bed." With only a last mopish look, he did.

PART

THREE

ADRIFT

X X
A Battle Against Invisibility

AFTER THE HUGE exertions of his presidential ventures, Jackson now seemed strangely adrift in a limbo of unengagement, with no real fix yet on what might be his next moment of truth, whether a third presidential campaign or some other appropriately large manifestation. Indeed, it was as if his passage as a gospel-populist evangel through the roar and blaze of those presidential contests had left him in a curious dislocation, hung between his old movement mission and a lingering political thrall, no longer quite belonging in either world, and somehow misfitted to both.

IN THE SUMMER of 1989, he left PUSH altogether in Chicago to move to Washington, "to be closer to the center of where things are happening." Instead, in that clamorous capital of ego and ambition, he seemed merely to recede further into incidentalness. The problem, says Richard Hatcher, was that "everybody in Washington is or thinks they are important. *Everybody.* They wouldn't be in Washington otherwise."

Actually, after his arrival, Jackson soon found himself being widely solicited to run for mayor of the city, to replace Marion Barry, who was then already beset with allegations of drug use. As Bert Lance, for one, encouraged him, "It would have removed the question that always came up in '84 and '88 that 'you never have really run anything, you haven't really ever been elected to anything.' " But no one urged him to take on the mayorship any more energetically than *Washington Post* editor Ben Bradlee. "Totally unlike me," Bradlee says. "I never tell anybody to do anything. In my years with Jack Kennedy, I never gave him a single fucking piece of advice. But I said to Jackson, 'Why don't you come over for breakfast and let's really talk?' The case I made was this. 'You're not going to be elected president of the United States anytime soon. You just aren't. The reason is because you're black. We can bemoan it and everything else, but that's just a fact. An additional reason is that you haven't done anything. You're all talk.

Nobody knows what the Rainbow Coalition really is. So if you could show that you could do some almost impossible job like being mayor of this city, show you can attract blacks and whites into a coalition of responsibility here, can get somebody besides an asshole to run the health and housing situations, get rid of all this boarded-up housing while people are home-less, if you could pull it off, it would eliminate all the bullshit that you've never done anything.' " Beyond that, says Bradlee, "I thought he had a great secret weapon. He could go up to the Hill and frag those bastards into giving more money for this city, 'cause they never have paid enough. Without saying it specifically, pass 'em the message, 'I'm gonna throw your white ass out of Congress if you don't come along.' He had tremendous power, you know, to go out and make a speech against some senator or congressman who was holding up something." If he committed himself to serve as Washington's mayor until 1998, Bradlee told him, "then he could be out of there, and with this fantastic record, run for president in 2000, saying, 'I am the candidate for the millennium.' He liked that. He defi-nitely liked that."

Bradlee admits, "I'm not that sure he would have been a great mayor, you know. Because if he dallied with it and ran off to Rwanda every twenty minutes . . . it would have taken him necessarily keeping his mind to it, not commenting on everything else." But if that sort of sedulous applica-tion and restraint seemed wholly against Jackson's nature, says Bradlee, "my theory was he wasn't going very far *with* his nature. Besides, he could have been a Pied Piper. He could have walked through the city block by block and picked up all the support he needed, and then *hired* some son of a bitch to fix the sewers. And another thing, I told him, 'Jeez, you could drive the White House crazy if you were the mayor. Any visiting dignitary that comes to town, you're out there on the tarmac elbowing the president aside. They send out the vice president or the chief of protocol, you come out there as Jesse. Tower over 'em all.' " But in the end, Bradlee claims with a scampish grin, "I just thought it was a great story, you know? That was my real interest in it. It would have been a great story if he ran."

Under an agreeable siege of blandishments from many other quarters, including some eager conjecturing in the national media, Jackson long deferred indicating his inclinations, while privately contemplating with delight "the commotion" provoked by the prospect, in that way he always likes to step back and relish the effects he sets off: "For somebody from that old neighborhood in Greenville to take a no-comment position about a mayor's race, and it captures the political dialogue in this country. Affects the Democrats, affects the Republican response to the Democrats, affects the whole landscape. Understand what I'm saying? . . . *somebody from*

Haynie Street!" But at the same time, he was not unaware that much of the enthusiasm for him to assume Washington's mayorship was an enthusiasm to have him thus removed from the Democratic party's field of vision for 1992 and confined in the entanglements of an almost impossible responsibility that could then furnish rich occasion to belabor him for failure. "My mama didn't raise no fool," he said. "They want me in that job so they can pile up rocks on my head."

In fact, it had always seemed an unlikely bit of casting. "You've got to worry about potholes and picking up garbage and that sort of thing, which I don't think have ever appealed to Jesse Jackson," concedes Lance. As for the embattled Mayor Barry, he once remarked during all the spirited speculation about Jackson, "Jesse don't wanna run anything but his mouth." Jackson's former aide Eric Easter, a Washington resident, further suggests, "I think folks on the street respect him as Jesse—but Jesse in all his glory. People here expect the mayor to be hanging out at the clubs with them, doing all that kind of stuff, and they don't really think Jesse cares about whether the trash gets picked up or if there's a new stop sign." For that reason, there was actually some substantial doubt that he could have won. His old college chaplain, A. Knighton Stanley, who was now pastoring a church in Washington, observes, "The community has good sense, and they knew that being mayor of the city was not exactly Jesse's thing. I asked a friend of mine here, 'If Jesse had been elected mayor, could he have run the city?' My friend looked at me and smiled, and said, 'Yeah. If he had had the greatest experts in city management that you could ever find, he could have run the city for maybe three hours.'"

Jackson's own final view of the matter was, "My destiny's larger than that." Nevertheless, when he announced at last that he was abstaining from the race, he was stunned by the blast of scorn it produced—yet another after-flare of the liability of his having entered into the political theater of power to begin with. George Will, not unpredictably, cited his demurral as "part of his descent into triviality," and David Broder wrote in *The Washington Post*, "What is disturbing . . . is his readiness to deny himself a challenge from which he would have learned much. . . . My guess is he'll never be taken as seriously again." It was an impression hardly repaired by his subsequent election to the mostly token position of shadow senator from the District, technically a post simply to lobby for statehood. Should that have ever come to pass, it would have almost certainly given Jackson a seat in the Senate. But more realistically, Bradlee bluntly declared, "This is a dogshit position he's got here. A nonpaying job to get statehood for the District, which is a lost cause. Why does he want to do that?"

Back at PUSH:
What Once Was but Is No More

BACK IN CHICAGO, Jackson's departure had left PUSH trying to sustain a faltering boycott against Nike while more generally struggling not to dematerialize completely. Jackson had resigned its nominal leadership in 1984 to set out on his first presidential effort, and through the ensuing four years, "while Jesse was flying around the country," one PUSH official lamented, "things in Chicago were in absolute chaos. We stumbled from one crisis to another." Now, one of PUSH's original stalwarts, Alyce Tregay, wistfully submitted, "We don't have the people that we used to have with Reverend Jackson, 'cause he's a charismatic man," and another of those early regulars, Lucille Loman, said with a sigh, "PUSH just kind of diminished after he ran for president." Asked about the outlook for it now, she hesitated just an instant, then offered with a thin chipperness, "Well, we're plodding along." It was reduced to surviving mostly on periodic fund-raisers and lonely little promotional booths at various civic festivals around Chicago. At one, says Aileen Walker, "we were calling out, 'Join PUSH today,' but people kept walking on by. Then we took out a Jesse Jackson picture—it was about ten years old, from the 1984 convention, which we've still got tens of thousands of copies of—and as soon as we started sticking that in PUSH envelopes and saying, 'Here's some literature on PUSH, get a free picture of Jesse Jackson,' then they came from everywhere, we couldn't hand them out fast enough."

But a profusion of old photographs is about all they have left of him and the elations of those past years. They still dwell in reminiscences of how he once so fabulously enlarged their lives: "Over twenty years we were going around with him," says Aileen Walker. "Running around this country with him wherever he went. And thousands of people wherever he'd go, masses of people that would listen to him. Like all the nation was listening to him." Jackson had perhaps no more intrepidly loyal believer, right up to her death in 1995, than Esther Thompson, the fiercely doughty woman with the winsome resemblance to Yoda, and sitting in a back office at PUSH one afternoon, she recalled the wonders of following after Jackson in his presidential campaigns. "The Secret Service, I could never do nothing in life but every Secret Service man would be taking notes on me. All the Secret Service people now know me all around the country. I'd go to where his headquarters was and be waiting to go up in the elevator, and this fella would say, 'Are you Esther Thompson?' And I, you know, 'Who the hell are you?' and 'How do you know me?' He said, 'We know. I'm one of the Secret Service with Reverend Jackson.' I mean, they got my history and life, they know Leroy and everybody else in my family's life. So I'd go on up to the penthouse where Jesse'd be, I didn't have any problem. Once in New York, I got separated from him a little 'cause so many people were crowding around, and I didn't know where the hell I was at, didn't have no money with me, all the money was up ahead of me. So I went up to one of the Secret Service agents and said, 'I got to get to Jesse, you can't leave me behind along the way!' He said, 'You better keep up then,' and I said, 'But I'm a *short person here*! If people keep pushing me back, what am I supposed to do?' So he made sure I kept up with Jesse. And I'd go everywhere he was going. I've gone on private planes. He'd have a couple of fellas to drive us when we landed. Went to Iowa. We stayed in people's homes—people'd go out at night and just leave the house to us. They'd just do it! In Iowa! I'd sit with the caucus folks out there at their meetings. Once the fella kept counting and every time he'd say, 'I've got one too many.' They couldn't figure out why they kept coming up with one person more than they'd come with. I wasn't telling them nothing—I'll vote for Jesse anytime I get a chance, myself. But they finally worked it out, I guess 'cause I was the only black person in the room."

Even though those sweeping, windy times were over now, Esther's fidelity to Jackson remained undaunted. "People get such bad, irreverent thoughts. But to anyone that brings up a discussion about how much they disagree with him, I want to know from them: do you have anyone in your family can do what this man's done? Do you have anyone that can speak like he can? He will not fall on his face as long as *I'm* living. You hurt Jesse, I'll hurt you! Anything about him I don't like, I tell him personally, okay? I don't discuss it with nobody. It's not America's business. I just tell him." Besides, she grimly maintained, "He has not really left PUSH whatsoever. He isn't gone. He's in and out, but he never *will* be gone."

A Pass into the Television Void

STILL, PUSH HAD been about his only palpable creation; beyond that, one critic pronounced, "the only other thing he's ever accomplished is running for president." A particular peril for Jackson by this point was a growing suspicion of a certain evanescent helium quotient in the long pageantry of his career, a kind of booming insubstantiality. Now, in this indefinite hiatus before another possible presidential assertion in 1992, Jackson found himself having to battle against his own disappearance.

For a while, he even pondered an invitation from the NAACP to assume its chairmanship, until it occurred to the board that it would almost certainly mean their own submergence in his presence, and they turned instead, haplessly as it developed, to Ben Chavis. "Jesse was hurt by that NAACP thing, though," says Percy Sutton. "Afterward, he said to me, 'Homeboy, they did it to us, didn't they? Doesn't look good for homeboy now.'"

In 1990, he tried a mutation into a television personality, as the host of his own discussion program, syndicated by Time Warner and produced by Quincy Jones. From the outset there lurked a fundamental misrhyme in the attempt to transfer Jackson's congenital didacticism into the glib composures of a TV moderator. Several months into the project, he still had not been able to divest himself of his morally pedagogical deportment. During a story conference about a program on the hidden messages of comedy, he kept fretting, "But I mean, what is this show *about*? I'm not clear on yet what exactly is the *point* of it. What is the *redeeming social value* of this show?"

At the same time, reported his son Jonathan with despair, "he just won't focus. He's got his mind on two dozen other things, too, all these other things up in the air. Keeps vacillating on this presidential thing. He'll call the office and get news that puts him in a bad mood the rest of the day."

The taping of one program, a discussion on the homeless, turned out cumbrously sententious and stilted. Over the weeks, both Jonathan and Jesse Jr. had repeatedly implored their father to be less preacherly of tone, to follow more closely what his guests were saying; "But he won't *listen*," said Jesse Jr. "We keep telling him, Why won't you listen to us? We don't want anything from you, we don't have any hidden agenda, we not gonna be trying to trick you or anything. You *can trust us*. But now he's gotten this news about McDonald's and Pepsi-Cola signing on as sponsors, so he's gonna say, See there?—he's been doing everything just right." During a break in the taping, Jesse Jr. abruptly declared, about his long and dutiful toilings to assist his father's fortunes, "I've given it over six years of my life. Now I'm gonna go off and prepare myself for my own life. I got to, it's time. Then I can come to him, you know, from a foundation of my own, and maybe then he'll listen to me." At that point he saw Jackson striding toward him down the studio's corridor, and he muttered, "Oh, man, here he comes now, he's gonna think we talkin' about him. Just tell him we been making up jokes for him for this next show."

Actually, the program on the unspoken sentiments camouflaged in comedy somehow went far more friskily than anyone had dared hope. "Your best yet," Jackson was congratulated by the executive producer afterward. "It came alive." Nevertheless, the program continued to flounder in the bottom reaches of the ratings. In the end, its central difficulty was that Jackson seemed to be locked in some ongoing battle with the very nature of television itself. For one thing, he was discovering the radical difference, in television's peculiar field of reality, between acting as the subject observed and presiding as the observing agent. Jackson's essential quality had always been the spontaneous, assertive vitality of a protagonist, and in his effort to pass from that into the role of moderating his own program, he became oddly compressed, gawkily confined in the rituals of manner and bearing imposed by the medium's technology, with which he seemed in constant warfare. "Why can't I just get up and go into the audience when the spirit moves?" he protested to his producers. " 'Stead, I got all these damn wires plugged into me, earplug in here, microphone here. Once had *two* of those things in my ear—on one of 'em, somebody telling me to do one thing, on the other, somebody telling me to do the exact opposite." After one especially calamitous taping had bumbled to its finish, Jackson gathered his staff around him in a back room and, in a barely contained rage, plucked out his earpiece through which directions from the control room had been transmitted; fingering it like some toxic pellet, he railed, "Could hear everything they were saying up in that booth. Even them talking just to each other, cussin' and all. Tell you, it's a *nightmare*."

Jackson finally retreated to La Costa, the resort near San Diego, for several days to confer with his fleet of producers. They undertook to tone him more to the nuances of the television form by showing him cassettes of Phil Donahue, Ted Koppel, Oprah Winfrey, Barbara Walters, tutoring him in their varieties of hand gestures, postures, attitudes in questioning. "But the thing is," Jackson interjected, "whenever we doin' a show, I got all these different things in my mind. There's the audience I'm talkin' to. Then all the critics—"

"*Forget* the critics," cried one producer. "*Fuck* the critics—uh, 'scuse me, Reverend—"

"Just be in the moment," said another. "Occupy the moment!"

Getting up from his chair once to stand off by himself, he confessed in a low, dull voice, "Sump'n might surprise yawl to hear. But sometimes still, when I see that camera comin' straight in toward me, I get a little frozen. Don't know what I'm gonna say. I ain't always as sure as I might seem to be."

But his producers were now having to contend with a more deeply gathering uncertainty in Jackson about what he had undertaken. During one session in his suite, he slumped lower and lower on a sofa until he was almost horizontal, and at last blurted out, "See, see, the problem is, there's the me that's *me*, and then there's the me that's *TV*."

In fact, it was as if the bright electronic mirror of television, with all the inner machineries of its alter reality of sheer appearance and impression, held a hazard of immobilizing and blighting something elemental in Jackson. One morning in Burbank, he was taping a series of promotional spots for the local news shows of stations carrying his program, inserting in each repeat of his lines the name of that particular locale and finishing with a flat little grin to the camera that, as he flicked it on after each delivery, began to look like some ticlike rictus. As he paced through these recitations, the next location to be named would be called out from a list by a young assistant in the rear of the studio, and she once hesitated: "Birming . . . Birmingha . . . Is that with an 'n' or an 'm'?" Jackson stared out into the gloom from which her question had come, as if suddenly startled at discovering himself in a region this distant from even a memory of the sites of those tidal dramas of the sixties. "I know what it is," he finally mumbled. "Let's go on."

In the summer of 1991, after a run of about six months, Time Warner canceled the show. But by that point Jackson had already begun negotiating with CNN to conduct a discussion program there. It was one of several converging indications that he might not make a presidential effort in 1992.

Yet the Political Thrall Lingers

ACTUALLY, POLLS THROUGH the spring of 1991 had found sizable popular support for him as the next Democratic candidate; he and Mario Cuomo led by an appreciable margin the long train of other prospects, and one Times-Mirror poll even showed him leading Cuomo by ten points. He was so positioned that "politically he could have done almost anything," Richard Hatcher is convinced. "He was on a roll from 1988." As his former adviser Robert Borosage cases his potential at that point, "In '88, Jackson had shown that progressives could well be a majority of the party. A huge number of people who believed in everything Jackson was saying went with Dukakis because they thought Jackson couldn't win. But the populist activist unions, the public interest community, the Democratic liberal activists, the whole white progressive community, adding to that the African-American community mobilized in the primaries—that's probably a majority. Which a lot of people didn't want to recognize. But he had a real future. He was actually building a progressive movement, and '92 would have been a great moment for him to run. As long as you're getting bigger, which he surely was coming out of '88, you can keep running, and when

you run you build even more connections, until you have a coalition inside the Democratic party that can take it over. It would have been vicious,
because the money was still massed on the other side. But he could have
done it—basically, by white working-class people joining with black working-class people and a smattering of progressives to create a socially progressive Democratic party."

While Jackson himself approached the quickening of the next presidential campaign season still slung in an abeyant uncertainty, it was at
least the wide assumption that he would sally forth once again. As one analyst confidently posited in *The New Republic*, "Jesse Jackson says he has
'not yet made the decision to run for President in 1992,' which is like the
sun saying it has not yet made the decision to rise tomorrow."

And in truth—even if Jackson now seemed to have somehow lost his
gravities, to be afloat in some middle indeterminate zone between two
alien purposes—he was still dazed by how he had actually fared in those
ventures. "This country has seen me as a fighter, one who argues for the
disinherited," he proposed to Roger Simon of the *Baltimore Sun*. "But the
country has not seen me operate in an official capacity. . . . And in 1992
clearly the nomination will be in reach." During one of his flights abroad
in 1989, he ebulliently contended, "We must not allow history to hold us
back, to tell us what can*not* happen, what we can*not* be. Just think about
where I come from. And when I can come so close, virtually within a
stone's throw, of the White House, there can be no more impossible
dreams!" Indeed, says another of his past advisers, Mark Steitz, "You look
at the distances he has traveled in his life, and it's not that hard to understand how any distances from here forward will all seem tantalizingly
small to him." As Jackson posed it to Simon, "I am down on the five-yard
line and it gets rough. But look back at the ninety-five yards I have come."
Nevertheless, many considered any progress he would make toward closing that final five yards a political version of the old theorem about how a
cricket can forever jump half the distance to a doorsill without ever getting
across.

If nothing else, there endured the intractable resistance of the party's
inner company of regulars. Even before the Dukakis campaign had
lurched to its finish, a member of the Democratic National Committee
was warning, "If Jesse Jackson takes over the Democratic party, the party as
we know it will be destroyed," and calls began arising from other party figures for "major surgery," as one expressed it, to excise from their midst
Jackson's constituency of believers. The Democratic Leadership Council,
the consortium of self-styled moderates formed after Mondale's defeat in
1984 to rehabilitate the party from its liberal tradition—those New

Democrats who had contrived the Super Tuesday primary in the South in 1988 to edit Jackson out of the running—now in 1990 convened in New Orleans to pointedly deplore any wayward liberal urges as fatal to the party's future. The DLC's own operating costs, as it happened, depended almost entirely on subsidies from Fortune 500 corporations, and at the New Orleans convention, Arkansas governor Bill Clinton, already a prospective candidate, declared, "We don't think the party should lead with class warfare"—while, as reported by Margaret Carlson in *Time,* "being whisked off in a limousine in the evening to Antoine's by lobbyists for RJR Nabisco." For his part, Jackson termed the DLC "Democrats for the Leisure Class," and once described them as "Democrats who comb their hair to the left like Kennedy while moving their minds to the right like Reagan." It was an elementary antagonism—almost as much one of sensibility, of personal manner, of outlook, as of ideology—that was to come to a climactic heat-flash in 1992.

In the meantime, when a scatter of regional elections in 1989 had lifted a number of black Democrats into office—including David Dinkins as New York City's first black mayor and L. Douglas Wilder as governor of Virginia, the first elected African-American governor in the nation's history—they were somewhat wishfully hailed by DLC eminences, along with a plentiful chorus of commentators, as a "post-Jackson" order of temperate, "mainstream" black politicians who, in contrast to Jackson, had diligently earned their way up through the infrastructures of government, and whose victories had relegated Jackson to the windblown political margins. Columnist Richard Cohen of *The Washington Post* opined that Jackson stood now to "get supplanted in the affections of black Americans (and others) by such pragmatists" as Wilder. In fact, those newly elected black Democrats were largely beneficiaries of Jackson's own national campaigns and the vast black voter registrations he had galvanized—not least among them Wilder, whose state Jackson had swept in the 1988 presidential primary. Even so, Wilder—already with brave, if ultimately faery, presidential visions of his own—made to discount Jackson as any factor in his fortunes, declaring that it was "the same thing as saying I'm indebted to P. B. S. Pinchback," an allusion to a freed slave installed as governor of Louisiana for one month during Reconstruction.

Jackson had little doubt that, behind much of the celebration of the Dinkins and Wilder elections, the same mentality was at work in which an uneasiness about him had acted to enhance other black figures in the party: "Congressmen, party leaders, some journalists, they all arguing now quite vocally, 'We got to find some alternative to Jesse Jackson. We got to project another black. We want, for instance, Bill Gray [the Pennsylvania congressman recently elected House Democratic whip].' Well"—and Jackson gave a muffled half-snort—"never wanted any African-American before. Hunh? Am I right? Now all of a sudden, others saying, 'If Ron Brown [named by Jackson his campaign manager for the Atlanta convention] becomes Democratic party chairman, Jesse Jackson'll be neutralized. Be less likely to split the party.' So for all kinds of cynical reasons, they saying, 'Let's make Bill Gray number four guy in the party, let's elect Ron Brown chairman.' All just for somebody other than Jesse Jackson. They become the party's ABJ black stars now—'Anybody but Jackson.' "

In fact, Brown campaigned for the party's chairmanship in 1989 generally on the premise that he would be able to contain Jackson and, specifically, could restrain him from galloping into the 1992 race. One Democratic operative commended him as someone who "can stand up to Jesse without being race-baited," and Brown himself once complained of some hesitation of support from a number "who praised me for finally signing on with Jesse last May because they said I would be a calm, stabilizing presence." Once elected DNC chairman, Brown then set about mitigating many of the rules changes Jackson had won for opening up delegate qualifications for the convention, and strenuously discouraged Jackson from entering the 1992 campaign. Bert Lance would later observe, "Jesse has found out that putting your friends in a position of being able to capture higher positions doesn't help him any. I mean, Jesse Jackson is the one fella responsible for Ron having been chairman of the DNC. And then Ron, you know . . . very quick, very smart and agile in those days." Whatever proved his services in deflecting Jackson from figuring importantly in the 1992 Democratic presidential contest, Brown was subsequently presented with the commerce secretary post in Clinton's cabinet.

Through that interval of unfocused suspension between 1988 and 1992, Jackson came to feel himself, despite his significant performances in the past two campaigns, steadily more isolated from the nominal powers in the party. In a reference once to Ralph Ellison's novel, he protested, "It's like they're trying to turn me into 'The Invisible Man' all over again." Shortly after the conclave of state party chairmen in Phoenix following the 1988 election, Jackson angrily reported to a private strategy session of the Rainbow Coalition, "A fundamental decision was made to lock us out. All the speakers were white. It was an all-white analysis of the party's future. That was an unrepresentative meeting of what's happening in America." Beyond that, he dourly warned his staffers that "there's a body of those who would take the party to the right in a way that further isolates us. Once you get as organized as we have the potential to become now, organizations are infiltrated and there're moves to discredit and disrupt from within. We must have enough good sense to recognize that we are fighting the power system for change, and they fight back—with money, infiltration, and guns, and other kind of schemes."

In that closed conference, Jackson went on to note, "Fact is, most of the candidates we supported who won didn't get elected because the party supported them. They won *without* it. The problem with party support is, when you win that way and then play by its rules, you've given up the right to determine what winning means." Some months later, as he was riding one afternoon through south-central Los Angeles, he abruptly declared that he no longer felt any need for the approval or acceptance of the party's proprietorship. "I've paid those dues, see? I've graduated from that school. We at a new stage of development now. The test of a relationship is reciprocity. And I've traveled more miles and registered more voters than any other Democrat in history. I've done more for the party than the party's ever done for me. The party did not help me get my seven million votes, but in '86 I helped the party keep the Congress and regain the Senate, by their own admission. The law of reciprocity ought to apply. The Democratic leaders from those states and congressional districts I went into and won during our campaigns are indebted to me for registering all those new voters that got them elected. I'm not indebted to them for going against the will of their people by not supporting me, even though I won their districts and states. Damn *right*, I've got a lot of reciprocity coming. But the party needs me more than I need it. I have no need for however the party might treat me, but they do have a need for my kind of treatment of them, for the kind of gifts I can bring them."

No doubt inevitably, Jackson soon began pondering the possibility, as he had briefly in the early seventies and as he would once again in 1995, of simply running as an independent, which would at least be an eloquently pure expression of his fundamental and abiding condition as the outsider, the loner. "Everybody's so interested in watching the front door," he said, "might not even be coming in that way. Might be coming around on them from another way nobody's even watching." His deliberations then were much the same as those he would entertain in 1995: "So often our parties come together in a common front, coequal in their blindness. There must be some force outside of that. Like I've said before, I rather be a fly in the eye than a gold tooth in the mouth. Gold tooth has great market value, shiny and all that, but once the mouth it's in is closed, it's gone, imprisoned, invisible. But the fly . . . the fly *moves*. The fly's value is its freedom." To be sure, Jackson had always seemed, in virtually all his computations, possessed still by his aboriginal aversion to being captured within anyone else's constructions—political, institutional, even perceptual.

But one sensed that Jackson was growing increasingly ambivalent about launching out at all this time. The zestful speculation about his political obsolescence goaded him once to vow, "They keep on sayin' I've become irrelevant, that's just what *will* make me run. I'll jump in there faster'n they can turn around." In particular, he could not hide his disgruntlement about the generally cordial press notice being accorded to the presidential inclinations of Governor Wilder. After doing one radio phone-in talk program, he happily relayed the comment of a black caller about Wilder: "Guy said he'd been raised on a farm, and he'd been taught never to eat anything that'd grown up overnight." But in April of 1991, after he had led a rousing mass rally in downtown Los Angeles for a national reform of police conduct, he mulled aloud on the drive back to his hotel about "how much more authentic" such popular demonstrations were than the "pseudo-reality" of the official political estate. Elective office, he went on, could in fact work "to separate you from the people," and he then suggested he might be more effective operating outside the system: "That way, I got access to both—to the people like those back there at that rally, and because of that connection, to the people in the system, too. Move between 'em both. That's something sort of special, after all."

Most arrestingly, though, Jackson began evidencing that he had at last begun to be overtaken by doubts about his resort to the political process to find his realization as a social apostle, a restiveness about that compact into which he had entered some seven years earlier.

ON A MILD evening one weekend in September of 1991, only a few days before Jackson was supposed to announce his decision on a third presidential campaign, I sat with him on the back patio of his home in Washington while he continued to travail over what that decision would be. Wearing a black warm-up jacket and tilting back in a wrought-iron chair, he said, "I'm just tired, you know? After all these years, I'm just tired physically, mentally, spiritually. I got to have a breather here. I need some time to regather my inner energies. Fact is, it could actually leave me stronger for '96. But then, on the other hand, there's this empty opening out there now. . . ."

As he went on arguing with himself in this fashion, traffic charged loudly back and forth in the street immediately alongside the yard fence, with a repeated shrilling of nearby sirens and police helicopters battering by overhead. "We *in* the neighborhood now, man," Jackson paused at one point to remark. It was his and Jackie's second residence in Washington, and they'd been occupying it for only about three months—a three-story brick house that Jackie had found derelict, a roost for drifters and junkies, on a corner of a somewhat ragged neighborhood near Howard University. Jackie's inspiration was to restore the house and, thereby, prompt a restoration of the whole area into a handsomeness more befitting its proximity to the Howard campus. But after Jackson had taken his first look at the place, he had phoned Jackie from a small grocery across the street, his first words being, "You completely out of your mind?" After three months the house still had a chaotically unfinished look that could have been a metaphor for the hectic uncertainty of Jackson's own life at that moment. The small front yard was still lumpily unsodded, and the rooms seemed in a state of arrested upheaval, with boxes heaped everywhere, bedcovers thrown over miscellaneous furnishings stacked atop beds, sheets covering the windows and cardboard spread over the floors.

Now this autumn evening, while Jackie sat inside with some half-dozen visitors finishing a late dinner of take-out fried fish, out on the patio Jackson pressed on through a recital of reasons for not running again, as if to convince himself by simply sounding all the factors once more. There was his commitment to CNN for a weekly talk program, an arrangement he was reluctant to disengage from, even if temporarily, since it had been put together by his old patron Percy Sutton. Too, he was still laden with an oppressive debt from his 1988 campaign—around $600,000—which would considerably cramp his ability to call on the sources he would need to subsidize another national effort. Beyond that, he said, "there're all these cultural forces still arrayed against me," including, he contended, "sanctions against me in the white press and major media, all the high pundits and analysts." Along with that, he had remained a party outcast: "Last three Jefferson-Jackson Day dinners, you know they didn't invite me to a one of 'em?" One thing that enduring party antipathy meant, he said, was that instead of having available to him the "forests of organizational support" the party could provide other Democratic prospects, he would forever be in a position of "having to win tree by tree."

But a more personal consideration, he said, was that his children had only recently disclosed to him fully the ordeals visited on them through his past two campaigns, not the least of which were more threats of violence to his family than were directed toward all other candidates combined—by one report, some three hundred bomb threats alone. Jackie herself was now ferociously set against his trying another run. At one point, she came out to sit on the patio, and remarked, "Why should he do it again? What for? What difference did the last two times make? What's it gotten us except a lot of grief? They'll never accept him. *Never*. I just don't have the spirit to go through all that ugliness again. I can't even sing 'We Shall Overcome' anymore, it fills my heart with such pain."

But after Jackson had reviewed these other reasons for forgoing the race this time, he suddenly leaned forward and confided the most striking uneasiness of them all: a misgiving about his whole effort since 1984 to transfer the movement's moral vision into a presidential campaign. "It's been dealing with the Devil, to an extent. Secret of that is, don't give away any more than you can get back by sundown. But after a while, get to wonderin' if you can tell all the time. Way I feel now is like what Martin said the night before he died: I just wanna do God's will. I don't want to live to do the will of the Democratic party. Don't want to live to do the will of Congress or the White House or the media. Just wanna do *God's* will." And taking himself out of the contest for the presidency, he said, should remove from his continuing political ministry the suspicion of a mere personal ambition. "It's a way to protect my authenticity. If I don't have that, I don't have anything else. I still got what I treasure most—my freedom. People say, 'He got seven million votes. Not looking for some sort of high official position? What *does* he want?' Well, one thing I know is that by operating without formal trappings and encumbrances, I can feel *truly* free. To keep on movin'."

Barely fifteen minutes later, though, he proposed, "But you know, just to get the *vice presidential* nomination—*just the nomination*—that would be an incredible victory, wouldn't it?"

XXI
The Clinton Tribulation

THE TANTALIZATION OF plunging again into the contest he could not bring himself to relinquish for another month—right up to the last feasible instant of possibility. But in November of 1991, he finally announced that he would not be taking to the field this time. Instead, he declared, he would set about organizing "a new, independent democratic majority" to open up the nation's political life from its domination by what had become "the one party with two names." He continued to make mutterings of some "alternate route 92," and intimated that he would begin consolidating newly registered voters in the South—"like we did in '84"—into a force that "they'll have to take into account as this presidential process goes along." He expected resistance from the party hierarchy in that, though. "All those new voters makes the Democrats stronger, but a lot of those guys in the party rather *not* be stronger if it means we stronger, too."

Still, it was as if, having once passed through the mighty gravitational pull of presidential politics, he simply could not disengage his psyche from it. A few days after his withdrawal from the race, he admitted in a late-night phone call, "I have so much mixed emotions. You know, maybe what I've done is just shift from being chas*er* to chas*ee*. Hunh? Now they gonna have to come to us. I'm positioned so there can be no serious discussion about vice president without our being right at the center of it."

That wistful conjecture, still lingering despite everything from as early as 1984, was even more vaporous this time, considering who was to emerge as 1992's Democratic candidate.

AS HE WATCHED with a deepening restlessness the 1992 presidential primary campaign proceeding to unfold without him, and Bill Clinton taking on definition as the likely Democratic nominee, Jackson began to fret to a number of confidants that he had made a mistake in withdrawing. One among his past advisers, Robert Borosage, is convinced that if Jackson had run, "Clinton would not have been the nominee, because he wouldn't have gotten out of the South. He only survived what happened to him in New Hampshire because of the South. From losing in New Hampshire, he loses in Maryland, and he's only saved by Georgia. He wouldn't have had that win if Jackson had been in the race, because the black vote was Jackson's base. And the South would have gone to Jackson." As it developed, with Jackson out of the running, the black turnout in the southern primaries was to sag hugely from the level reached in 1988—by 41 percent in Georgia, from 265,000 to 99,000 in Louisiana, and from 165,000 to 81,000 in Mississippi.

At the same time, though, Clinton conducted a campaign, for all his DLC cautions, that was not a little patterned after Jackson's own populist gospel in 1988, as a number of analysts afterward pointed out. "He says, 'I'm going to put $50 billion a year and reinvest in America,'" one notes, "and 'I'm putting $20 billion a year into the cities. I'm going to cut defense, going to build roads, rehabilitate education, democratize health care.' Very populist agenda. He saw how it had worked before for Jackson, understood that and went with it and left the DLC stuff behind for the time being. And did as well as he did in the primaries because of that kind of populist message—who can really question that?"

But any surviving vice presidential whimsies of Jackson's vanished as Clinton continued to thrive in the primaries. A tension already glowered from Clinton's time with the Democratic Leadership Council, and its efforts, including the contrivance of Super Tuesday in 1988, to impose what it considered more sensible modulations on the old liberal exuberances, particularly Jackson's, of the Democratic past. Consequently, a testiness bristled between them almost from the outset of the primary contests. While Clinton was campaigning in Georgia, he suddenly began fulminating to reporters, during a pause in a television interview, that Jackson had betrayed an initial promise to him of neutrality—"He has gushed to me about trust and trust and trust"—by accompanying one liberal opponent of his, Iowa senator Tom Harkin, in his rounds about South Carolina. "It's an outrage. It's a dirty, double-crossing, back-stabbing thing to do. . . . an act of absolute dishonor!"

But there had occurred at least one other instance of dissonance between them, not as public, even before that. In January, just as Clinton's flourishing campaign in New Hampshire had been thrown into havoc by allegations of a long dalliance with a blond Arkansas lounge siren named Gennifer Flowers, he was also confronted with the decision of whether to allow the execution of a black convict named Rickey Ray Rector, who had been condemned for the slaying of an Arkansas policeman over ten years earlier. Immediately after that killing, Rector had shot himself through the temple, which had left him effectively lobotomized, with about the understanding of a five-year-old. Nevertheless, Clinton had come by a profound appreciation, through the vicissitudes of his political career in Arkansas, of the doom of ever venturing too far beyond the apparent common popular mood, and he was hardly unaware of polls showing a nearly 80 percent citizen approval of capital punishment. While several of his primary opponents had also avowed support for the death penalty, Clinton, as governor of Arkansas, happened to be the only one in a position to incontestably demonstrate his support by actually applying it. During that week of the Gennifer Flowers furor, one of the other questions being raised about Clinton's political validity was, as *Time* put it, "Suppose Clinton does sew up the nomination by mid-March and the Republicans discover a Willie Horton . . . in his background?" And the director of the University of Arkansas's governmental studies institute commented to *The New York Times*, "The death penalty is about as good a way to get Willie-Hortoned as there is." Even though Clinton was not statutorily obliged to be in Arkansas at all on the day of an execution, he flew back there anyway, out of his Gennifer Flowers duress in New Hampshire, to immediately preside over this particular one. The *Houston Chronicle* later remarked, "Never—or at least in the recent history of Presidential campaigns—has a contender for the nation's highest elective office stepped off the campaign trail to ensure the killing of a prisoner." But, another journalist observed, "Clinton's political salvation meant that Rickey Ray Rector was going to have to die for Willie Horton's sins."

Soon after Clinton's return to Little Rock, he received a call from Jackson. Jackson urged him—"Now, Bill, just on a moral, humanitarian basis"—to stay the execution the next morning of Rector, a man already blasted to a dim simplicity comparable to that of Lenny in *Of Mice and Men*. As Jackson afterward reported the exchange, "I told him Rector obviously was going to be harmless and institutionalized for the rest of his life, and to kill him anyway would serve no defensible purpose," and, in addition, that "we should always be mindful of the biblical injunction against harshly punishing our fellow human beings, that more blessed is mercy." Clinton's response, according to Jackson, was that "he'd been researching various ways to get around it, but it just couldn't be done. That there were doctors who'd testified for the prosecution that Rector was competent. Said he'd be praying about it, though. I said, well, I did hope he would keep on *at* his praying, and get on through to God on the thing." Nevertheless, the execution of Rector duly proceeded the next morning, and Clinton flew out of Little Rock to resume his campaign. After his nomination, it would come to be considered that his decision on Rector, as one Democratic operative then asserted, "completely undermines" all attempts "to define Bill Clinton . . . as out of touch with the mainstream public and even mainstream Democrats." New York's seasoned political impresario David Garth stated it more simply: "He had someone put to death who had only part of a brain. You can't find them any tougher than that."

In his determination to define himself as a new edition of Democrat free of the party's past liberal sentimentalisms, Clinton also applied himself with much more vigor than had Mondale or Dukakis to the presumed imperative of separating himself from Jackson, and to do it in some conclusive public way. In the summer of 1992, shortly before the Democratic convention in New York, Clinton decided to appear at a Rainbow Coalition conference in Washington, which Jackson meant to be an occasion of at least political, if not personal, conciliation and concord. "The whole idea of it," says Robert Borosage, "was to have this substantive meeting of the Rainbow endorse Clinton, so that we're not heading into New York with this 'What does Jesse want now?' kind of thing, to have all that behind us and let Clinton have a unified party." In fact, Borosage had arranged a meeting the evening before, between Jackson and Clinton, along with a few Clinton advisers, including George Stephanopoulos, to discuss the next day's program, during which, Borosage recalls, "Clinton was just as nervous as he could be, wanting to please." It had already been made fairly clear to Jackson that he was not in consideration for the vice presidential post. As Clinton was to tell him, according to campaign adviser Paul Begala, he, Clinton, had too much respect for him "to put him through the agony that Dukakis and Mondale did." One explanation presented to Jackson, says Begala, was that "Clinton's father died at twenty-nine, and he knew you can be gone young. So he wanted somebody just like him in case he didn't make it." Still, says Borosage, after the meeting he got a midnight call from Stephanopoulos "to make sure everything was on board for the next day, that Jackson was not going to be upset that he wasn't going to be offered the vice presidency. He was still worried about that."

Among others attending the conference, as it happened, was a young rap performer named Sister Souljah, who, after the Los Angeles riots following the first-trial acquittal of the policemen who had beaten Rodney King, had produced a bitter swagger of rhetoric that was at least partly a coarse attempt at a kind of Swiftian "Modest Proposal": "If black people kill black people every day, why not have a week and kill white people? You understand what I'm saying? . . . If you're a gang member and you would normally be killing somebody, why not kill a white person?" The callow brutishness of such rancor had, in fact, dismayed a number around Jackson, which was mainly why she had been invited to the Rainbow's conference. Says Borosage, "Jackson was trying to keep her from getting more crazed." The night before Clinton was to speak, Jesse Jr. had talked with her for several intense hours in the spirit of his father's ministry to bring the wrathful and estranged in out of their nihilistic abnegation and into enough hope and realism to at least try working inside the system.

But Clinton had been alerted that she was at the conference, and the media were subsequently alerted to be on hand for his address. "They had already briefed the press corps that something was going to happen," says Borosage, "that they were going to do something to Jesse at this meeting, press people told me afterward. That they were going to come in straight on Jackson." Without any word to Jackson beforehand about the denunciation he would be articulating, Clinton, in his address, noting that Sister Souljah had spoken to the gathering the day before, and citing her outburst after the L.A. riots, declared that Jackson "was wrong in not condemning such hateful comments from Sister Souljah, and the Rainbow Coalition is doubly wrong for giving her a national platform." Among those in the audience was Esther Thompson, perhaps the most redoubtable of Jackson's following at PUSH, and she was still incensed two years later: "Clinton was into his speech, and all of a sudden, without any type of warning, he just jumped on Sister Souljah and attacked Reverend Jackson—at his *own conference*. Everybody just froze. *What is he doing?* Like Reverend Jackson had something to do with it. I was ready to kick his butt. Trying to be slick and sly when Jesse was trying to make it comfortable for him to come in there and be welcomed. Without those black voters Jesse registered, wouldn't be a lot of white folks in office, including like him. I'm gonna tell you something—*God don't love ugly.*"

Mary Matalin, a director of Bush's reelection campaign, would later remark, "We wondered from the beginning how they were going to deal with the Jesse Jackson factor, and they did it in one fell swoop. Not only did they not kowtow to him, they publicly humiliated him"—a stunt in which "they never frontally assaulted Jesse," but "picked the vehicle of this clearly radical-looking, radical-sounding crackpot. . . ." Whether or not Clinton had in mind turning Sister Souljah into something like Jackson's Farrakhan for 1992, his industrious condemnation did have the effect of inflating her, however momentarily, into a far more famed figure than she otherwise could ever have hoped to become. Begala remembers hearing Jackson protest afterward, "Man, I was *reaching* her. How could yawl *be* so stupid." But it was instantly clear that, as John White later stated, "Jesse was used." Borosage admits, "It was quite well done. Just pure vicious race-based outrage, and they did it quite consciously. But it was very effective." Jackson himself seemed at first strangely stunned, as if he could not yet fully register what Clinton had done to him. In a private meeting with Clinton afterward, despite the evident understanding confirmed in conversations the day before, some of Clinton's people claimed that Jackson had applied for the vice presidential post by submitting a ten-page, single-spaced memorandum on the electoral power he could bring to the ticket, and was summarily rebuffed by Clinton. Jackson flatly denies that account, and Borosage calls it "total bullshit. If anything, it was just a political strategy memo on vote potentials that Frank Watkins had gotten up for Jesse to give as a favor to Clinton."

In any case, when Jackson came to realize the ploy Clinton had executed, it left him infuriated. He described it to R. W. Apple, Jr., of *The New York Times* as "a Machiavellian maneuver," designed "purely to appeal to conservative whites by containing Jackson and isolating Jackson," but which had "again exposed a character flaw" in Clinton. Roger Wilkins remembers how Jackson privately anguished and raged over the incident. "After Clinton had done his nasty thing with the open mike about Jesse, you know, they had struck a deal. But then he comes to Jesse's convention and does this little cheap, scummy trick. When people do things like that to him, Jesse first gets hurt, and then he gets angry. When he gets sucker-punched the way Clinton sucker-punched him, you have to sit with him while he just goes over it and over it, keeps talking about it and you talk about it back to him. But it's like he has to purge it out of him. It's almost like, you know, when somebody dies, and you have to keep talking about it—'I saw him just before he went, I thought he was fine.' . . ."

A Ghost Campaign

NEVERTHELESS, IN THE fall, when the by now customary requests arose once more, Jackson could not resist setting out yet again on another auxiliary campaign for yet another Democratic presidential candidate, even if this time it was Clinton. At one outdoor rally in Washington State, someone called to him from the crowd, "Is Clinton for real?" and Jackson turned toward where the voice had come from, "Well, the *heat's* gonna mature him." In a conference with black ministers in San Antonio, he was asked, "Can we trust Clinton?" and Jackson offered a recountal of Clinton's support "for universal day care, adequate minimum wage, wealthy paying their fair share of taxes, national service back in the neighborhoods." But, he added, "It's not Clinton or Jackson now. It's whether we gonna choose Clinton over Bush. Let's keep this thing in perspective." Accordingly, as he swooped from rally to rally across far reaches of the country, he again, as in 1988, boomed away at Bush and, particularly, Dan Quayle, with no perceptible diminishment of zest: "Oh, the *arrogance* of some rich young ruler preachin' down to us about family values. My mama went to work with runs in her stockin' so my brother and I could go to school with matchin' socks and not be laughed at. *She* knew about family values! But Bush and Quayle never had to shop for socks. They never had to shop for groceries—that's why Danny can't spell potato, that's why Bush don't know about scanners in checkout lines. They've never known struggle. They were already born to prenatal care, born to day care, nurses, butlers, cooks, chauffeurs. And they talkin' to us about family values? Who've never known sufferin', never had to make choices about how to survive? They've always had a tailwind, never a head wind. They *can't* understand."

He could not refrain from intimating now and then that perhaps Clinton, too, did not entirely understand. "Everybody emphasizin' the middle class now. Well, that's good, that's right, they *are* hurtin'. But the state of the union is measured by how we treat the least of these among us. What about those hurtin' on the bottom? The jobless, the homeless? If your caring is large enough to reach to those least of us, it's surely gonna also cover the middle class of us." But he mostly reserved his gusto for commentaries on the nation's lot under the Bush administration, including its economy: "We still givin' away jobs to countries like Japan in return for VCRs and video games. You can't keep exporting what is essential to get back what is irrelevant." Of Bush's recent visit to Japan with a group of corporate chairmen, including the heads of Ford, Chrysler, and General Motors, to seek a loosening of Japanese trade regulations, Jackson declared, "Here're the strongest symbols of American manhood, goin' over there beggin' for a break. Askin' for *corporate* affirmative action. Understand what I'm sayin'?"

But as in 1988, his campaigning for Clinton was as much an alter campaign of his own to continue his national gospel-populist ministry. He even paused, after a rally in Tacoma, Washington, to negotiate what had become an acrimoniously protracted labor dispute between the mayor and city workers, taking everybody into a dreary little office of the city's recreation center, where the rally had been held, and shouting back over his shoulder to an aide who told him there was a phone call for him, "Can't take it right now, got to save the city here!" With the mayor, several council members, and union leaders all crowded around him in the small office, Jackson admonished the union officials to publicly repudiate the

personal harassment by some of their members, urged everyone collectively to move beyond their individual animosities and to "find that common ground that's waiting in this situation for the sake of all Tacoma," and
then had them join hands as he led them in a prayer: "Father, protect
these leaders of this city, build around them a fence of your care, as you
lead them on now in the love and understanding of your presence to work
this thing out. . . ." As it turned out, a tentative settlement was reached a
day or so later, "in large part," said one city official, "thanks to the spirit of
Reverend Jackson's visit. It changed the atmosphere of the whole thing."

In all, he bravely advertised through the final weeks of the 1992 campaign, "There'll be another struggle beginning November fourth. It'll be
about the priorities of this administration. Our struggle continues. We winnin' every day!" But it somehow had the sound this time of a slightly forlorn bravado. (When he spoke at one rally in a far corner of Washington
State, in a fresh-washed sunshine after heavy morning showers, a *New York
Times* reporter even set the whole event in "a howling rainstorm," as if to
evoke Lear railing on the heath as an image of Jackson's exile from any national consequence.)

Nevertheless, the crowds he addressed seemed, amazingly, about as
large as they had been in 1988. Some six thousand people turned out to
hear him on a dusty-gold October afternoon on the campus of the University of Oregon, "the largest assembly we've seen," said one school official,
"since the last time Jackson was here." At another rally inside an enclosed
Fort Worth shopping center, Jackson's voice rang over the fifteen hundred
people collected among the potted greenery, "Oh, if only Dr. King could
be here today and see your faces, what a *joy* it would be to him!" at which
a young black mother standing at the edge of the crowd was asked by her
small son, "Who's that? Who's that?" and she leaned down to tell him,
"That's *the* president, baby." After making a late-afternoon appearance at a
voter-registration center in the Cotton Exchange Building in Houston,
Jackson paused outside to take a call on his cellular phone. Leaning one
elbow atop his Lincoln while his eyes swept happily over the loudly
mobbed sidewalks around him, he tilted the phone away for a moment to
remark, "Ain't this *sweet!*"

YET IT ALL had a peculiar ghostlike quality. And after one rally, just at
sundown, under the magnolias on the front lawn of the county courthouse in Beaumont, Texas, with a Gulf wind softly blowing under a clear
sky, Jackson suddenly flung himself into leading a popular ruction when
a number of blacks from the crowd were denied admittance to the courthouse's voter-registration office a minute or two after its official closing for

the day—a somewhat exorbitant uproar, actually, greatly discomfiting the local congressman, Jack Brooks, a reedy old political rooster tracing back to Lyndon Johnson, who had introduced him at the rally. But it seemed as much an abrupt lunge by Jackson to rouse a last reinvocation of the splendid old turbulent confrontations of his movement days, before he had ever passed into any political candidacy. Someone in the crowd had cried to him, "We were within a hundred feet when they shut the doors," and with everyone then sweeping after him, Jackson stalked off toward the registrar's office, hauling Brooks along with him with one hand clamped on his arm, while baying out, "People got the right to vote! This's dishonest! People in there got the obligation to open those doors!" Brooks, with no choice for the moment but to trundle along in Jackson's clasp, tried pleading in a low furtive rasp, "Jesse, it's after hours, they can't let all these folks in now." To that, Jackson blared loud enough for everyone to hear, "People here bein' disenfranchised because of a technicality. They don't *want* these people to vote." Brooks muttered imploringly, plaintively, "Jesse. Jesse . . ." But they had all swirled now on through the lobby up to the locked glass doors of the registrar's office, with the clerks still inside staring out stunned at Jackson and the crowd churning around him, and Brooks elected at this point to make a kind of sideways sidle out of the commotion, out of the lobby altogether. Jackson bellowed to the crowd, "We must protest to the Justice Department immediately! This is a racist act, this is indefensible! This is a throwback in time!" Brooks then reappeared at his side, after an apparent hurried consultation somewhere close by, and tugged at Jackson's arm, whispering, "Jesse, Jesse, come on with me just a second, let's see if we can't work this out." Jackson allowed himself to be led by Brooks out into a side parking lot, where several local officials were standing beside cars with the doors opened, motors rumbling. Brooks said, "Here, Jesse, let's go talk about this in my office, c'mon, you can ride with me. We afraid for your safety here—" Jackson recognized then the maneuver Brooks was essaying, and barked, "I'm not *about* to leave," swinging around and heading back for the lobby, at which Brooks and the others simply piled into the cars and swiftly removed themselves from the site. Jackson's return to the lobby was greeted with a bedlam of cheering. "What do we do?" someone yelled, and another called out, "Hush, lis'en, lis'en here to Jesse!" Jackson shouted, "We got to file a complaint. We got to start marchin' here. We must turn this into an even *bigger* voter-registration drive. All this shows is that the struggle continues. Let us join hands and raise our voices in prayer. . . ." Yet it seemed he had come back from the parking lot to a strange sudden emptiness, the fading of a heat that had only briefly glared, and as his prayer echoed in the lobby, there sounded from a near distance the long, tapering hoots of a Texas-twilight train.

"He Could Not Stop Wanting"

BUT EVEN WHILE Jackson had trooped about the country through those weeks of the 1992 campaign with a sturdy doughtiness, he continued to carry in him a cold rage from the Sister Souljah incident and a virtual chemical loathing of Clinton. On the last afternoon before Election Day, he remarked, in a quiet, even, flat voice, "I can maybe work with him, but I know now who he is, what he is. There's *nothin'* he won't do. He's immune to shame. Move past all the nice posturing and get really down there in him, you find absolutely nothing . . . nothing but an appetite."

Despite that bitterness, he bizarrely entertained the improbable speculation, which he began enthusiastically unfurling one late afternoon as he paced about the tarmac of a little windy airport while waiting to fly to his next campaign stop, that he might actually be appointed by Clinton ambassador to the U.N. "It's just something I *feel*, you know? Everywhere I'd go then, would be with this portfolio. And, man, all those Third World countries, Africa, Latin America, they'd be comin' straight to *me* with their concerns." He seemed unaccountably, almost pathetically oblivious to the fact that such a prospect was precisely why the Clinton administration would never come anywhere close to considering the idea.

For that matter, during his campaigning for Clinton he was privately bewailing the far less imaginary happenstance that "they keep trying to *isolate* me. All my life I've had to battle against being isolated. Clinton now, he just sees no place for equals that includes the Rainbow Coalition. He still sees us more as an enemy than an asset." And he was still complaining about a year after Clinton's inauguration, "He spent his campaign distancing himself from me. Now that he's president, he's trying to dismiss me." As he told Michael Kramer of *Time*, "He's trying to prop up other black leaders. It's not working. Look at the polls, walk the streets. The other guys don't have the juice." With Clinton's subsequent circumspect equivocations on the populist intonations of his campaign, "what we have now is the Bush program we thought we'd defeated," Jackson went on. "Our quarterback has joined the other team." Jackson then darkly observed, "He thinks we'll have nowhere to go except with him in '96. Well, that's what other Democrats thought when they talked the talk but then didn't deliver."

Thus, once again, he began contemplating an independent presidential run. Jackie herself averred, "You have not seen the last of him. Some more excitement's coming. There're some questions that he has raised about this country's course, and they *will* be answered, and we are going to give the American people the opportunity, as many times as is necessary, to make the decision for themselves as to their leadership." His own musings were not a little energized by a CNN/*Time* poll in February of 1994, which disclosed that Jackson was not only still regarded by 86 percent of black Americans as their most important leader but was their overwhelming choice for president as well, even if he ran as an independent—about ten points ahead of Clinton and, at that time, almost forty points ahead of Colin Powell. Several months later, Bert Lance appraised the potential indicated by that poll: "For the first time, there's no compelling reason for Jesse to remain a Democrat. The Democrats haven't done anything for him, they've only ridiculed him, talked about the baggage he brought to the party. But Ross Perot proved one thing beyond any doubt whatsoever: that you can gain ballot access without being a Democrat or Republican. Jesse can go straight to the general election campaign without having to go through the primaries, because he can gain ballot access with very little money, very little effort or organization—none of which he's ever had before anyway. For Clinton, this is serious. I mean, it directly affects his lease on the White House. If Clinton were a sixty percent president, it might not. But Bill Clinton is a forty-three percent president." And the votes that Jackson would draw from Clinton with an independent candidacy in the 1996 general election, Lance maintained, would almost surely be mortal to Clinton's prospects for a second term. "Quite simply, Jesse holds the fate of Bill Clinton's presidency in the palm of his hands."

The lavish irony of that now, Lance pointed out, "is the Sister Souljah thing. Clinton handled the Jackson factor extremely well. Mondale never handled it, Dukakis never handled it, but Clinton did—in a way that infuriated Jesse. But while it probably helped elect him, now Bill Clinton has to pay the price for Sister Souljah. He's faced with, How do I go back and put together a ruptured relationship? Got to reverse that relationship to keep it. As a result, Jesse is going to be courted in a way that he's never been courted before—more than Mondale and Dukakis ever did put together. And it's with a fella who is the best in the world at extracting something. But what can Clinton really give Jesse that Jesse wants or needs right now? In Jesse's greatest dreams, what would come anywhere near this? Having Clinton now come to him hat in hand, and saying, 'Jesse, anything you want? Anywhere you'd like to go, for instance?' "

No doubt for that reason, when Jackson returned from his 1994 trip to the Middle East, Clinton had him come by the White House, and asked him to head the official U.S. delegation that would be dispatched to South

Africa to observe the election between Frederik de Klerk and Nelson Mandela. And astonishingly, for all his past resentments and execrations of Clinton, Jackson confided after this invitation, "You know, it would be *disrespectful* to the man to say no. So I guess I'll be going."

If there was some murmur of desperation in his quick readiness for almost any honoring recognition, even from Clinton, it intimated just how astray and unsure Jackson had come to feel as a movement evangel since his passage through the power field of a presidential campaign. But he could not stop wanting—"wanting everything," reflected his old friend Roger Wilkins, shaking his head with a rueful, wry smile. "Now, say, I slam the Clinton administration and say these terrible things about the man, I do not expect them to invite me to *nothin'*. But Jesse wants to be able to say those things, and still have entrée to sit at the big tables in the White House at the same time. That's what vexes me about Jesse. The administration sent a later delegation, led by Mrs. Clinton and the Vice President, over to Mandela's inauguration in South Africa—and Jesse was *delighted* to be on that delegation, too. They asked my friend Harry Belafonte to go, and he said no, he wasn't going to be on any delegation representing any president who was dumping Haitians at that moment back into Haiti to get killed. But Jesse? He just *wanted to go*." In all, Wilkins allowed, Jackson remained bewitched by the notion of using political currency to enhance his original, larger, movement ministry, but "there's a trick to that. And sometimes he wins the trick, and sometimes they win the trick." Jackson had a particular vulnerability in that game, though, Wilkins added: "I just wish sometimes that he would not need recognition as much as he does."

XXII

"The Way You Begin Is the Way You End"

A DAY OR two after the 1994 congressional elections, which had suddenly lofted Newt Gingrich and his dry-cleaned legion of cyber-conservatives into dominion in Washington, Jackson proposed in another of his late-night phone calls, "It's *movement* time again." Indeed, one of King's old horsemen, C. T. Vivian, propounds, "Every thirty years in this country during this century, there's been a people's movement that's made further gains in defining what it means to be human. First part of this century, it was a poor white people's movement. Thirty years later, the labor movement and FDR. Thirty years after that, here comes Martin King and the civil rights movement, peace movement, women's movement. This has been the Humanizing-of-American-Life Century. Now, time has come again for a new movement. But these forces on the right are working as never before to cut it off, go back to pre-FDR. It would stop the natural play of the century. So we approach this next century ready for a whole new struggle. And here's Jesse. At a time like this, someone who can reach out and mobilize as he can to renew our social vision and Martin's dream, to take this nation on to the fulfilling of the Humanizing Century, that person becomes ten times more important than he would be otherwise."

But it had become a season—what with Gingrich's new technotronic Republican order having apparently inherited the political play of the land, even if it happened to be a revolution by only a 19-percent-of-the-electorate mandate; and then Louis Farrakhan's own Washington march the next year, followed by the at least implicitly countering phenomenon of the national excitement about Colin Powell—in which Jackson seemed even more to have receded to a marginal figure.

Jackson's fundamental plight remained that against which he had been struggling ever since his days with King—the absence of any distinct social front of crisis to engage that would match his King-scale aspirations: as if someone of potentially heroic proportions had misoccurred in a mundane and bleary middle period in which he could only conjure on his own some fittingly dramatic moral situation in which to act. "The world is hungry for a vision of where we should go in the twenty-first century," says Andy Young, "but nobody's found it yet, and that's certainly the problem with Jesse—he can't really get a hold on the right issue." Now, from 1994 into 1995, as he seemed to be passing deeper into a media eclipse, he skirmished against suspicions of an impending invisibility with a yet more frenetic scatter of exertions: pitching himself into what he termed "moral witnessing" against racial discriminations in baseball, in the media's operations, against the NAFTA agreement, as well as such momentary obsessions as his public appeals that the South Carolina mother convicted of drowning her two sons be spared execution herself, which one of his most devoutly durable and cheerfully sensible aides, Eddie Wong, characterized as "one of his twenty-four-hour-virus things." "Every time he goes out on a new crusade," says 60 *Minutes* producer Don Hewitt, "he calls and says, 'You guys want to cover this story, you want to go with me?' But after a while, it's gotten to be like a vaudeville act. Every question you ask him, you get the patter, that singsong, like a guy on a Broadway stage."

For a time, he gave himself over more meaningfully to an evangelism against the degradation of the pop culture of black youth, and particularly the pandemic violence consuming a generation of young blacks in the inner cities, as if that were what King's dream had somehow tragically devolved to. He declared at one point, "There is nothing more painful to me at this stage in my life than to walk down the street and hear footsteps and then look around and see someone white and feel relieved." He could not stop publicly anguishing over this matter even while in Israel, telling audiences there, "Within our own struggle in the States, we're suffering in the African-American community from a kind of internal destructive syndrome, a pattern of despair and hopelessness that's driving us into killing each other in record numbers. And instead of a push toward more schooling and jobs and family-support care, the cry now is for more jails and more electrocutions." His moral witnessing on this particular point happened to occasion some consternation in the black community. After one Rainbow Coalition conference on black crime, reports Roger Wilkins, "People started jumping me in the halls: 'What's he doing this for? Why's he talking about violence? That's what white people are all the time doing.' "

On the whole, he seemed to be trying to navigate his way through this prolonged and weightless interval with fitful attentions, but "to go to Iraq and do something with a weight of world importance," says Eric Easter, "and then to come back and address a baseball strike, it just doesn't seem to match. The public loses a real sense of what he's about because he is up to so much." That dismayed even some of his fondest supporters. His old Chicago patron Cirilo McSween observed, "If you look at Martin, you know, Martin settled big matters. Public accommodations—settled. Voting rights—settled. And they remain settled. Jesse does still have that potential, ain't no question about that. But it would take a . . . ah, let us say . . . a *oneness* of purpose." Jackson did briefly consider, after the ascension of Gingrich's Republicans, what might have been a truly defining fulfillment for him at last—reviving King's great unfinished business of the Poor People's Campaign. But it was mostly now a repeat of the reflex that Mark Steitz had noticed during the ordeal of the 1988 New York primary: "When he's not exactly clear what he's doing, when he's confused, he moves faster and faster, diving around trying to find a footing." Brooklyn pastor Herb Daughtry submits, "All of us who feel greatly for him have expressed the concern that sometimes you can be more effective if you just drop out for a while and let people wonder where you are, what you're doing. Sometimes you need to kind of not be *quite* so visible." Jackson himself insisted once toward the end of 1994, "It's just that I sit here and these things keep coming up." In fact, says one of his former PUSH associates, Robert Starks, "He'll hit on something"—Starks claps his hands—"and it's amazing, I mean this guy has come up in the last half of the twentieth century with a good ten or twenty just absolutely brilliant ideas, but which were never followed up, never developed. An international bureau, for instance, for African development and trade with African Americans. And on and on, one after another. You look back and say, 'God, what a window of opportunity, if he had just followed on through with this and that idea.'" Instead, as he continued to lurch from impulse to impulse through the nineties, the impression only widened that he simply amounted to a kind of peripatetic Catherine wheel of flamboyant inspirations—his domestic Marshall Plan to restore America's infrastructure from the reservoir of pension funds, his program for a wholesale renaissance of America's schools—the only problem being that few of those Roman-candle notions ever settled to earth and formed into actuality.

ONLY IN HIS mid-fifties in 1995, Jackson was, of course, still very much an unfinished man, his still an unfinished life. And it has been part of the rampant energies of his originality, which have already carried him this far from that glum black quarter of Greenville, that he has so regularly surprised surrounding assumptions about his prospects. "He is constantly pronounced dead and gone," says Robert Borosage, "but he's like a phoenix:

he always rises again. He's always moving, always out there. He outworks, outthinks, outcares anybody else that's around." Jackson's mentor while he was a student at A & T in North Carolina, Dr. Samuel Proctor, proposes, "You know, I'm a great believer that novel situations occur, and I look for something novel to take place in his life. Because it always has before. I don't know what it'll be, how it'll break forth. But he's like a broken-field runner. Where other people would just stumble and get tackled, he sees light here, light there . . . goes right for it."

But after the 1988 campaign, it was already evident enough that Jackson had been left profoundly displaced and directionless. At a conference of the African-American Institute in Lusaka, Zambia, the following January, where he delivered an address, Charlayne Hunter-Gault had posed to *New York Times* columnist Flora Lewis, albeit a touch patronizing in its distress, the question, "What are we going to *do* with Jesse?" To the degree he has always bulked as an oddly unclassifiable figure, though, he has seemed un-placeable in any role he has not custom-made for himself. Nevertheless, Stanley Crouch, for one, declared in 1988, "If America cannot use this man in some way, by fusing his colossal ambition with his ability to inspire involvement in the democratic process . . . then there is a problem of po-litical immaturity in our time much greater than any we have admitted to thus far." Mark Steitz suggests, "There may be some tragedy in that, not just for him but the world, that we haven't used him better. But the tragedy question is not for anybody to answer yet. Not until he's dead, because he's done extraordinary things up to now." It was at least Bert Lance's inspira-tion once to try persuading the Bush administration to have Jackson ap-pointed U.N. high commissioner for human rights: "It would've gone right to his strengths, to his very nature. Would've been the smartest thing they ever did. But Bush's people heehawed it." Richard Hatcher considers it Jackson's inveterate difficulty in such prospects that "he has a tendency to simply overshadow anybody. Few presidents can handle the idea of some-body towering over them like that. Yet it's such a waste. Such a waste."

Whatever else might develop with Jackson, though, by 1995 one was be-ginning to hear appraisals of him like the surprising pronouncement even of Ben Bradlee: "He *is* the heir to Dr. King, there's nobody else who comes close. In the last analysis, he remains a marvelously interesting cosmic man. I mean, a big figure in this century. He's going to disappoint, because he probably couldn't have lived up to the promise that he inspired. But *goddamn*, he had a good whack at it!" Over the years, declares Samuel Proctor, who was a classmate and later counselor to King, "Jesse has been one of the agents in our time who reminds us of that wide, deep channel of moral goodness in the world that is so little explored and so little traveled that, when you do travel it, you become unique. But when there's been a big moral vacuum, by God he's found it can be occupied, and he's moved right into it. Over and over again." In his own original moral-apostolic aspirations, Jackson may have always struggled against adversities not only outward but, perhaps even more, inward. But Dr. Alvin Pitcher, who taught Jackson theology in Chicago, asserts that "human beings are mysteries. Now, I don't know what it really was in Jesse's experience that made him what he became. You can of course interpret it as, somewhere, someone got the word of God to him, it came and hit him and stayed. But it's an ambiguous reality. These characters are created by mysteries. They're miracles. It's something you can't predict or contain in analysis. They're just unbelievable gifts."

Even so, there are some melancholies among his early enthusiasts about what has happened with him. Jackson's original ministerial sponsor in Chicago, the Reverend Clay Evans, who in 1994 was still pastoring his Fellowship Missionary Baptist Church deep in the city's West Side ghetto, sat in his study there on a late afternoon and proudly acknowledged, "Now, I have received an awful lot of honor because of Jesse. I know you wouldn't even be here talking to me if it weren't for Jesse . . . naw, naw, wouldn't of happened. I have met all kinda people and been accepted by them because of Jesse Jackson. Unh-hunh. And everywhere he'd go, he tell people, 'That's my pastor.' My name jumped all over the country, you know? On television, everywhere. And that's meant an awful lot to me, just being related to somebody who's great—and he *is* great." But Evans then gently offered a more disquieting reflection: "He is mixed, yeah. He does have some ego problem. Ain't nothin' *condemning* about that, but he does have multiple natures in him. One of them is, Jesse has really been called and anointed of God to preach God's word. But what has grieved me is I've felt like he has pushed his spiritual nature on the back burner, as he became overinvolved in the political arena. He's neglected that spiritual part of his life, his relationship to God. As a minister myself, I think that the greatest calling one can have is to be a prophet. He's already run for president twice, which was just fantastic, we never had anybody to make the mark that he's made. But the political can overwhelm and be a distraction. That's the danger of it. That's why I always wanted Jesse to *pastor*, shepherding the sheep, like King also did. But he never wanted to just settle for that. Never wanted to. I was grieved about that, because I felt so close to him."

Jackson's fellow seminary student from those Chicago days, Henry Hardy, agrees that "some have said that that's where the real tension in him lies, in that you're a preacher, a prophet, and the prophet is one who looks at things from the outside and speaks to them. Whereas politics is where it's compromised. So some see a disjuncture. That Jesse moved into, quote, 'the palace,' as opposed to standing outside the palace and prophesying to it." A much harsher judgment, though, was pronounced by his old and now disaffected friend, David Wallace, about Jackson's subsequent passage into politics: "He hankers so after the approval of those people, who are the most bankrupt folks that ever existed. Why does he want that? Who needs that? Why's he want to go with that? There was such a greater way he could have sustained his ministry without going that route. Where he would not have sold his soul."

Jackson himself had come to seem uneasy at times that, in his political beguilements, he might have somehow lost his way. While touring Yad Vashem on his visit to Israel in 1994, he had just entered into a tunnellike passageway when his guide happened to refer to him as "a politician," and Jackson halted, curtly notified him, "That's not what I am. I'm not a politician. I'm a public servant, just trying to serve God. Maybe sometimes politics is *a method*, but that's not what I'm driven by." "I'm sure," the guide said apologetically.

Now, in what seemed the equally dim tunnel into which his meaning and prospects had wandered by the end of 1995, he still had not lost his old impulsion to realize himself as some form of prophet-hero of his time. What mainly occupies him, he avowed, "is to keep the plumb line of justice holding down steady in it all. When the curtain finally falls on me, all I want is for history to say, 'He was a part of the conscience of his age.' I'll rest then." As his former aide Eric Easter assays it, "He's still searching for a place in history beyond the presidential thing. To wage the first legitimate big presidential campaign by a black, and to lay claim to opening up the democratic process, that's one thing, but it was just one path. That wasn't finally enough for him. I've always felt that's why he keeps jumping from issue to issue. Every issue that comes up, he feels maybe this could be the one, this might be *the* issue to do it. But," Easter then suggests, "those folks who are our heroes, a lot of what happened with them happened by accident. They may have always been prepared for it, but something then took place that did it. Jesse, though, *seeks* it. He really seeks it. He wants his works to be recognized, and I think that's part of the reason why they never get that recognition. I was taught growing up that if you do a good job, that's all that matters, and if you do it good enough, eventually people will notice and talk about it. You know, you build, and it comes. But when you seek others' approval for the good works you do, then you'll always be disappointed."

Richard Hatcher remarks, "We all want to be respected, and for most of us it's enough to be respected in your family or in your town. But for some people, they're not going to be satisfied unless they have the respect of the whole world. And maybe not even then. That's Jesse." As early as Jackson's days at the seminary in Chicago, one of his fellow students remembers that he detected some bottomless need in him: "The pattern of his life has been such that I would think it would be difficult for him to ever really sense that he's arrived. That he's found his place."

Jackie herself will sometimes simply cite a pronouncement her mother made years ago: "The way you begin is the way you end."

SO IT COULD come, ultimately, to a parable of a prodigiously gifted outsider who, precisely because of his enduring sense of not belonging despite all his huge gifts, simply tried too much, asserted himself too urgently and extravagantly, to be accepted as wholly genuine by that general American community to which he had hoped histrionically to belong by becoming a moral-heroic figure in its life. In that sense, finally, he would be defeated by his very obsession with his apartness. And that fate could not then be separated, because his lot as an outsider has mostly owed to his being black, from a larger and bleaker irony of American racism itself: that all it has taken, in audacity and grandiosity of ambition, for Jackson to have made his way as far as he has from so far outside—compulsions, however excessive, that were probably the only way an illegitimate black youth from the poorest black quarter of a little South Carolina town could have come so near realizing such oversized dreams—would also finally deny him the great dream most driving him: to belong by making himself into a moral hero of his time. And in the circular, bitter calculus of that irony— that he could lose, in the wider society, because of what it's taken, exactly because he is black, to win as much as he has—would lie a more particularly bitter question: to what degree, in presenting himself as a contender for a leadership role, did he seem too arrant, too irregular and theatrical, also simply because he is black?

Jackson himself, while addressing a convocation of Los Angeles black ministers in 1995, at one point wandered into the sardonic reverie, "Yawl know who my *real* hero is? 'Course, there's King out there, he has his place. And Gandhi, him, too. But my real hero is Albert Gore. That's right, Al Gore. Father a senator—mine a janitor. He went to Harvard—I went to a little black college in North Carolina, A & T. Albert was elected to the U.S. Senate—I was just in the movement, worked with Breadbasket and PUSH in Chicago. Then, in 1988, I beat him in Iowa, a state ninety-eight percent white. He said it was 'cause of liberals and farmers. So I beat him in New Hampshire; he said it was 'cause he was off campaigning in the South. So I beat him in the South on Super Tuesday. He said Dukakis had split his support. I beat him then in Illinois, in Michigan; he said he wasn't really tryin'. I beat him then in New York; said he ran out of money. But now, here I am this afternoon, talkin' to yawl in this church in south-central L.A.—and he's Vice President of the United States. How'd he manage to do that? *Amazin'*. Al Gore's my real hero, bein' able to do something like that. They attackin' affirmative action now 'cause of what they call racial preferences. Preferences? Racial preference? Don't be comin' to *me* talkin' about racial preference."

Roger Wilkins proposes, "There are professional football players who can play with more pain than other players can, you know. And there are people who can absorb more psychic shocks than other people can. Jesse can absorb more psychic shocks than anybody else I know. The guy is never going to give up, not as long as there's breath in him." Despite his sense of confinement in a lasting racial exile, that fall evening in 1991 as Jackson sat on the back patio of his Washington home obsessing over whether to withdraw from a presidential contention, he suddenly snapped forward and declared, with a dour round-eyed glower, "They may think it'll mean they got me out of their hair if I don't run. But I'm *never* gonna get out of their hair. They didn't put me in their hair in the first place, and they can't get me out of it now. I'm unwashable, I'm unremovable. I'm gonna be in their hair as long as I live—be even more in their hair after I die."

But regardless of whatever shifts might transpire in the exterior circumstances around him, it may be that Jackson is caught up in the performing of a self-saga of interior conflicts that will, in fact, never arrive at a culmination. Instead, he could wind up, like a kind of apostolic Flying Dutchman, forever roaming about in public life, looming imposingly from one tension after another in endless pursuit of his ultimate hour, that promise he has sensed ever since his youth. Only, with a deepening discomfort that his life might come in the end merely to a sum of brilliant approaches to a greatness into which he is never finally to be delivered.

"My own sense of Jackson," says Robert Borosage, "is that one big thing that haunts him is, he's now outlived King by many years. And for all he's done, he hasn't been slain. So, have you been working hard enough to be slain? You must not have been out there enough putting it on the line. Which drives you to go harder to expose yourself." But in Martin Luther King's social ministry, Andrew Young observes, "King was fortunate in that he had the Kennedy administration and then Lyndon Johnson who knew that what Martin was suggesting was mostly right. What we forget is that Jesse has had to deal with the likes of Reagan and Nixon and Bush." Beyond that, says the Reverend Samuel Kyles, who was with King on the motel balcony when he was shot, "People wear leaders out. If you do fifteen years, you're doing good. I tell you, if Martin had lived to be sixty-five, there'd never have been a holiday in his honor, because we would've used him up. Had he lived, he'd walk into a room now and we'd say, 'Oh, there's Dr. King. Hey, Martin, have a seat.' 'Cause life is like that. And it's started with Jesse now. 'Oh, there's Jesse again. What does he want now?'" The author and book editor Michael Korda, one of the long succession of editors who have labored to get an autobiography out of Jackson, suggests that the primary disparity between Jackson and Martin Luther King may be simply that King had the terrible exaltation of a violent martyrdom, "of passing on before the disillusionment could set in"—a historical editing, just at a point where he seemed sinking into decline, that spared him from what could well have become a progressive tiresomeness and marginality and compromise of his image.

Eric Easter claims that Jackson has even become a mostly irrelevant relic to the latest generation of black youths. In that emerging generation, Easter says, "I don't know that people are looking for a spiritual leadership anymore. They're looking for a guide to good living. So whatever he meant in '84 and '88 has just completely gone out the window. They don't really know who he is, except they've seen him in their history books and things like that, maybe they know he ran for president once. But the way he communicates, it's a language that no longer connects, it's not what they're used to now. He might as well be the school principal." One reason for that, says Easter, is "the information that's reaching them, by TV and cable and all that, is just moving too quickly. It's a kind of anesthetic of the past." Thus can the sort of media being that Jackson sought to become— to find in the absence of any great theater of moral conflict like that in which King acted a compensating definition—also soon expire in the media's electronic evanescence.

Nevertheless, Jackson stoutly professes, "The harvesting in my kind of work doesn't come as a massive personal payday. I don't think that's why you sow. The results are never spectacular and obvious to everybody. If you can just see now and then things growing that you've sowed over the years, you get as much of a return. It's a psychic income." In any case, he insists, "Leader, when he gets disappointed or frustrated, can't start spreading misery, talking cynical, hoping somebody will feel sorry for you. They may feel sorry for you, but that's *all* they'll feel. They won't follow you." So he heaves on, with the old barging urgency that has already carried him such far distances, as if almost for its own sake now, whatever the growing risks of futility and derision. "Though your enemy seeks to humiliate you— 'What's Jesse Jackson after? What's *he* know about anything? What's he ever *really* done? Why won't he just quit?'—you can't be deterred by that threat of humiliation. We may indeed be rejected, and that *is* humiliating. But the risk of humiliation and ridicule is one of those crosses you got to keep on bearing."

Robert Borosage contends, "To get up in front of a crowd that is struggling for their jobs, has been on strike for six months and increasingly knows that it's a hopeless strike, to get up in front of those audiences and inspire them, give them hope and energy, and do that again and again and again, it's enormously difficult. You should try it. Now you can call it just giving a speech, but it's a lot more than a speech. What Jackson has been straining to build over the years is a movement, a spirit, a moral voice and moral vision. And as long as he continues to do that and people continue to have their spirits and hope lifted by him, his time will not have passed."

Nevertheless, back in Greenville, one of the neighbors who watched him grow up, Barbara Mitchell, after reminiscing one June morning in 1994 about his engaging ebullience in those days, paused, took a deep breath, released it in a long sigh, and said, "But he's not happy like that any longer. He's not as happy as he was when he first started out in college and then with Dr. King in Chicago, and even that first presidential campaign of his. You can tell his heart is heavy now. He's taking situations too heavily. He still tries to put on that little boy's smile of his, but he's been hurt and disappointed so much, it's not so good a smile anymore. You can see it—least, *I* can see it. . . . And I wish sometimes I could just grab him and run somewhere with him and hide him away for long while. So he could rest, you know? Because I can tell he's tired. His body, his spirit . . . he's just so *tired*."

In fact, Jackson, as he moved on through the nineties, seemed increasingly given to stray, darkening ruminations. Speaking to an assembly of civic leaders in Chicago, he suddenly called out, "Where we think we are and where we going, it can be so different from what may actually be. It's almost like, what's the point? Just this talking here is so temporary. So much of what we see now as acting in the main events of our day is really, in history, just a comma, a parenthesis. And it can be that at our strongest moments—in the twinkling of an eye, there's no more. *Twinkling of an eye.* And we gone."

He was in Havana through the Christmas week of 1993 for discussions with Fidel Castro, in which he hoped to persuade that aging revolutionary to make some concessionary moves that might open a possibility for a minimal rapprochement with the United States. After one long session of listening to Fidel declaim, like a grand haunted ruin of a colossus, about how he'd felt himself outrageously bullied by what the United States had done to him and his revolution over the past three decades, Jackson returned to his guesthouse, remarking on the way that it was hard not to feel a certain warmth for Castro, since "they've treated him like a nigger, want to know the truth." He sat up late that night in a rocker in a far corner of the living room, rummaging through a Bible, and finally, abruptly looked up and murmured, "Trying to battle cynicism over what's happened to you in order to keep hope alive for others . . . I know what that battle's like. That's the most terrible battle of all—against cynicism. Been tempted myself at times to give in to it, you know? Feel like just giving it all up. I mean, just wanna *die*. Have it all over with, all the hurt and trying. Get some *peace* at last."

THE IRAQ CODA

THE IRAQ 1004

JACKSON'S JOURNEY TO Iraq, in the early weeks of the Gulf crisis in August of 1990, to try to persuade Saddam Hussein to release the foreign nationals he was holding hostage, was an episode that turned into something like a coda of Jackson's whole life. Through those several days, all his mixed compulsions and meanings, what was both extraordinary and most woefully petty about him, as well as the media and government's disregard that had so long tormented him, seemed to come into a fever-bright focus.

In the first days after Saddam's invasion of Kuwait, Jackson surprised many by endorsing a military reply. Addressing a conference of black journalists in Los Angeles, he robustly recommended, "Unilaterally or multilaterally, send military troops in and get Hussein's ass *out* of Kuwait." Then, after Saddam announced that he was detaining foreign citizens, mostly Westerners, and intended to distribute them to potential military-strike targets around Iraq, Jackson became intrigued with the possibilities of another personal intercession that might repeat, on a much larger scale, his journey to Syria in 1984. He detected, he claimed, a certain expectancy in the air. After speaking to a labor convention in Washington, he strolled past six white union members talking together off along a wall, he reported, "and they said, 'C'mere a minute.' Said, 'You goin' over there and clear up all that shit? Gonna get them hostages?' See, it was on their minds already, that's what they'd been over there talking about." After mulling it over for a few days, he decided to try it, and obtained a letter of invitation from the Iraqi embassy.

He was then in the final plottings for his first television talk show, and his initial notion was simply to have its producers, Time Warner and Quincy Jones, subsidize the expedition as the subject of the first broadcast. That way, he could also comply with recently imposed U.S. restrictions on contacts with Iraq by going over as a journalist. It was a guise, though, which brought from almost everyone else muted struggles not to betray amusement. To doubting queries from a group of reporters, Jackson solemnly maintained, "Well, I *am* a journalist. After all, got my own television program, discussin' issues. What I'm doing is movin' into a gap here. Nobody's talking directly to each other, they just observin' the other side talkin'. So journalists are filling that gap, the diplomatic gap, like Koppel and Rather. Like journalists have done before—Cronkite, Walters, back when Sadat and Begin wouldn't talk to each other."

In fact, though only a few weeks had passed since Saddam's seizure of Kuwait and it would be five more months before the launching of Desert Storm, a certainty of war was already gathering. Jackson passed much of one morning talking with Colin Powell, then chairman of the Joint Chiefs of Staff, who advised him that the administration was not exactly enchanted with the idea of his mission, "but I can't really tell you not to go." He also had a chat with Secretary of State James Baker. But meanwhile, Time Warner was developing a pronounced queasiness about the project, and heavy second thoughts had also apparently befallen Quincy Jones. A mild frenzy spread through the show's production offices in Washington, and at one point Jackson sauntered in and wandered among the agitation with a casual bemusement, then gathered some of his staff into a side office to case the situation, not unlike a quarterback trying to rally the confidence of a team unsure of whether the game is being played anywhere but in the quarterback's head: he posed the options as "a one-stage rocket and a two-stage rocket. First-stage rocket, we just go ahead and *go*. Second-stage, we wait, and say the government has closed us out from going. Then see what reaction that produces. Might be enough to finally make that first-stage one lift on off, you know? . . ."

But apparently, concerted heat from the White House was now coming down upon the corporate brow of Time Warner. "Seems like, at some point, the yellow light from the White House went to a firm and positive red," said one staffer. One had the sense that Jackson had mostly been occupied in furious applications of artificial respiration to an already hopelessly moribund proposition. Quincy Jones and Time Warner chairman Steve Ross had finally placed themselves beyond the reach of Jackson's ceaseless telephone importunings by taking off for a fishing trip on the coast of Scotland. All three of the major networks and a few other news services also declined to sponsor the expedition. It appeared the whole venture was terminally off. At that point, Jackson's middle son, Jonathan, took to the phone himself and, in just a few minutes, managed to put together an arrangement with KingWorld Productions, which would fund the trip and, from the footage brought back, air several pieces on its weeknight telecast of *Inside Edition*.

Late on a Sunday afternoon, a call came to me at my home in Los Angeles: " 'S's yo' brother. Jesse Jackson from Greenville, South Carolina. Catch a red-eye tonight. We goin'."

The next evening, we all, including a television crew and two producers, boarded a TWA flight at Washington National Airport for connection with a Royal Jordanian flight at Kennedy Airport in New York. But thunderstorms hanging over JFK had stopped all traffic there, and Jackson's plane remained stranded far down a line of others on the runway. He presently ambled up and leaned in the door of the cockpit, casually mentioning to the crew where he was headed and why. A few moments later, the captain, after radioing TWA supervisors and the control tower, was cleared to ease his way up to the front of the line, "thanks," as he reported on the passenger-address system, "to a little political influence we have aboard." Again, one was awed at the enchanted realm one seemed to enter when traveling with Jackson: his planes transferred to the front of stalled lines, columns of cars awaiting with police escorts outside his hotel lobbies at the direction of governments, sirens parting thronged traffic like the Red Sea ahead of him. . . .

In the TWA terminal at Kennedy the plane's captain pushed his way through the crowd to shake Jackson's hand emphatically, telling him, "I just hope you get those people out, is all I can say." This caught the attention of an elderly white matron sitting nearby with arms folded firmly across her middle, and squinting up at Jackson, she said, "Where you going?" He bent with a quick little eager dip down to her, and said, "Goin' to Iraq." Unlike the captain, she failed to be stirred whatever by this revelation, merely replying with a flat "*Umh*" —a grunt that seemed to bespeak all the popular dubiousness about any Jesse Jackson jaunt to Iraq that had hoodooed Time Warner.

But as we stood waiting for our baggage to be collected and transferred to the Royal Jordanian flight, Jackson, with most of his party of fifteen clustered around him, commenced to declaim, in what was like an impromptu, mini–prayer meeting there in the gate lobby, "Now, if the Lord be with us—the *Lord* be with us—who can be against us? The *Lord* is our strength, of whom should we be afraid. We settin' out on the Lord's work here, everybody. That right? Say, Amen, then!"

We were conducted at last to the Royal Jordanian plane, proceeding through dark back-mazes of JFK, plunging through empty lobbies and deserted baggage areas. Jackson commandeered a policeman who showed up along the way, "Stay with us, hunh?" taking him by the arm. Before long, little flockings of press folk began to appear unaccountably at various turns, as if signaled by some frequency beyond ordinary human hearing—

"Why are you going, Reverend Jackson?" "Will you meet with Hussein?" "What do you hope to do?"

When we entered the muggily packed cabin of the Jordanian plane, Jackson's appearance produced a burst of applause up and down the aisles, and he hiked up his thumb, with its ibex-horn back curve, before settling himself beside Jonathan in the first-class section. After liftoff, a young Jordanian businessman seated beside me began enthusing, "Everybody has much hope for this trip of the Reverend Jackson to Iraq. He is a man we know is maybe only person can maybe make peace now. Everybody believes very much in the Reverend Jesse Jackson, yes!" It was as if Jackson, on entering the plane, had stepped immediately into an entirely different, more warmly hospitable climate of perceptions.

Through the long hours as the plane beat through the night toward Amman, Jackson dozed under a thin blanket. On his tray-table rested a small book with waxy yellow covers, *The Complete Sayings of Jesus*, as annotated by, of all metaphysicists, Norman Vincent Peale—one of those inexpensive little inspirational volumes with rainbow-hued illustrations that one might find in the Sunday school supplies section of a fundamentalist Christian bookstore. It seemed somehow the most quaintly improbable primer for the endeavor into which he was heading.

LANDING IN AMMAN around midafternoon, into a small blizzard of press and cameras, Jackson was driven by the U.S. ambassador to the royal guesthouse where Jackson's party would be installed overnight. On the way there, the ambassador delicately undertook to inquire, "I just wonder—of course, you'll be getting a lot of questions as to whether this is an official mission, and, that is, what are you going to represent as your . . ." Jackson promptly assured him that he would be explaining that he had come over simply as a journalist, to the ambassador's perceptible relief.

That evening in Amman, after a dinner with Jordan's Crown Prince Hassan, Jackson returned to the guesthouse and retreated to his suite. Scheduled to fly on to Baghdad the next morning, he sprawled on the enormous bed in the enormous and imperially lush bedchamber as he reviewed the situation with Jonathan. Now and then he took a small sip from a glass of red wine, and with his other hand scrawled occasional notes on a yellow legal pad—all the while listening, as invariably in his treks abroad, to Ray Charles tapes, Charles's Georgia-summer-night voice husking over the regally draped expanses of this room in Amman.

Waiting at the Amman airport the next morning, isolated off to one side of the field, was an Iraqi Air 747 jetliner, glinting white and Kelly green in the sunshine. When we got on, we found it full of passengers, and once again, at Jackson's entry into the cabin, applause broke out along the aisles. But the flight itself was strangely quiet and unexpectedly brief. Baghdad's airport, as the plane slowly lumbered toward a gate, had a curiously abandoned and derelict look, and the glassily futuristic concourses and lobbies inside were ringingly empty, their arcades of shops locked shut. We made our way through this peculiar vast hush in a small, momentary, self-contained furor. Government cars were aligned along the curb outside to drive us into Baghdad and the Al Rashid Hotel—a ride through a yawning pale beige plain as relentlessly level as the Mississippi Delta, with a look of unexpected familiarity from childhood history books of primeval Mesopotamia, plush plumes of solitary date palms scattered across its wide distances—all this in breath-stunning heat. As we rode into the center of Baghdad, there seemed a sun-dazed stillness everywhere about us, the streets only incidentally inhabited. But once inside the Al Rashid's marble-and-mahogany swankiness, about the only traces of the embargo clamped on Iraq was that at breakfast each morning in the dining room, the apricot juice seemed cut just a bit thinner with water.

Late in the afternoon, Jackson called at the U.S. embassy, which bulked like a military compound in the middle of a short side street with Iraqi sentry posts at both ends. As soon as the cars bearing Jackson and his television crew pulled up outside the embassy's wall, it quickly became evident that the determination inside was indeed to take him absolutely as simply a journalistic figure: waiting at the gate was an embassy press officer, who shouted as Jackson and his party emerged from their cars, "No filming here! No filming, no exceptions! You're journalists just like all the others." He led us inside, through a warren of low rooms and angling passageways that had the distinct feeling of a bunker, past youths lounging in civilian clothes but who all had harsh haircuts that could have come from an Oklahoma Saturday-afternoon barbershop, and then up a short rise of stairs to a relatively spacious office. There, Jackson was greeted by the chargé d'affaires, Joseph C. Wilson IV, who had taken over for the ambassador, April Glaspie, after she was left stranded abroad by Saddam's invasion of Kuwait. Wilson, a hefty, somewhat rumpled and harried-looking young man, but with a carefully measured manner, at first formally assumed the official attitude about Jackson's presence: "These are the rules for journalists. . . . This is on background for you as journalists. . . . If you wish to use the phone in the embassy here to file your reports. . . ." But Jackson quickly moved to talking to Wilson from an implicit position as a potential mediator, and Wilson, with no further pretense otherwise, as quickly followed. He apprised Jackson that, despite Saddam's proclamation just the day before that foreign women and children would be allowed to leave Iraq, "a headline was all it was," and that Iraqi officials had simply introduced endlessly changing procedural complications that left all detainees effectively still hostages. "We're completely stymied," Wilson told Jackson. "So anything you can do . . ." and his voice tapered off into an unuttered plea.

On the drive back to the hotel, Jackson kept turning to peer at the ubiquitous billboard portraits of Saddam towering about Baghdad with a stupendous redundancy matched then in perhaps no other state on earth save Kim Il-Sung's North Korea—his mustached visage inescapable, and his wardrobe seemingly infinite, from business suits to military greens to Arab desert drapery to even Babylonian garb. "Homeboy sho likes his picture took, don't he?" Jackson finally murmured. "Just in case you maybe forgotten about him after going two blocks." Turning in at the hotel past yet another grand-opera portrait, Jackson shook his head, "There he is, done changed his clothes again." But even inside the hotel, Saddam's shade lurked everywhere one turned: about every third man one glimpsed, from the hotel desk clerks to plainclothes security men to waiters, wore the same harsh black mustache and eyebrows, like endless replications of their ruler.

During dinner, as we were awaiting word as to whether the original himself might see Jackson that night, Jackson began twitting an American journalist at the table who, a resident of Washington, had been greatly disapproving of Jackson's decision not to run for mayor of the city. "Now if I'd run, I might've got to be mayor," Jackson submitted, "but I would hardly be sitting here right now on this mission to Saddam Hussein, would I? You neither, I might add."

"But we just wanted a good mayor," said the journalist.

"Fine," said Jackson. "Find you one. Need a president, too. This one we got now has brought us to the verge of war."

As the talk rippled on among the others around the table, Jackson fell quiet for a moment, and then, as if having privately reviewed once more exactly what he was doing here in Baghdad, he pronounced, "Well, we're here tonight on principle. Against great odds, opposition. But this is the right place to be. I feel good about it. Feel good about it. . . ."

Early the next morning, a call came from the Iraqi Foreign Ministry, inviting Jackson to a session with Foreign Minister Tariq Aziz. Before dressing to leave, Jackson threw himself into an accelerated sequence of his usual morning exercises, vigorously pumping away at pull-ups, push-ups, beside his bed. Arriving some thirty minutes later at the Foreign Ministry, Jackson was immediately enclosed by a contingent of functionaries and hastily escorted up to Aziz's office. The two of them, after a short interchange of pleasantries, seated themselves in easy chairs, at slight outward angles to each other. Aziz, a portly man in heavy black-rimmed glasses, with a bristly patch of a mustache, was attired for this conversation not in his customary diplomat's dark business suit but in a somewhat snug deep-green Ba'athist party uniform with epaulettes, the shirt opened at his dewlapped throat. Below his trouser cuffs, his short socks showed several inches of pale shin. After smoothing back his silver hair with the heel of his hand, he lighted a mammoth cigar and began the discussion.

After all the oblique and fretful circlings over the last several days to this moment, Jackson swung into his presentation with a booming vibrancy, all for obvious relay later to Saddam himself. "We rassled to come here against all kinds of resistance, we were under embargoes not to come. The feeling among those who resisted was that it was not journalistic," he said deadpan, "but diplomatic." Beneath Aziz's mustache fluttered the faintest smile. "But even though I *am* here as a journalist, we feel a keen sense of obligation. We want to give the conflict a broader perspective. War," Jackson went on reverberantly, "is intellectual and moral failure. But if preconditions for talks are too high, war is inevitable. The time has come to start trying to reason together. Can't have babies at certain times of months," he offered, recycling one of his fondest little metaphors, "but now it's pregnancy time."

Jackson advised Aziz, though, "If hostages, detainees, guests, whatever, are kept, I think Bush and that group will *level* this place. The power is in the hands of President Hussein," he declared. "There must be some pictures of people coming *back*, by bus, boats, planes. Think it needs to be more than women and children, too. Send 'em out on Iraqi Air, if you want. But bold steps like that would have a neutralizing impact, might even have a *reversing* impact, on this blind rush now to war." Referring then to the U.S. embassy in Kuwait City, which Iraqi forces had isolated in a kind of retaliatory, miniature siege-embargo of their own, Jackson added gravely, "This business of cuttin' wires at embassies, cuttin' off water, stuff like that, doesn't really *do* anything, what I'm tryin' to say." Over his own career as a negotiator in civil rights confrontations, he mentioned, "I've found that such tit-for-tat struggles are distracting, diversionary. . . ."

As Jackson talked on, with Aziz periodically making notes on a large pad, Jonathan, slumped on the end of a sofa beside his father, was locked in a soundless battle to keep from slipping into sleep, and losing, intermittently nodding off in the wash of voices and the cool breathing of the air-conditioning. "These are good ideas," Aziz finally responded, as he refired his cigar. "If they're put on the table, they will be considered." He then felt obligated to remark that much of the tension between the United States and Iraq owed to "misunderstandings of the American press" because

"Zionist circles are so powerful in your country, they want to burn bridges between us." At this, Jackson, though refraining from comment, gave a noticeably impatient twist in his chair.

He listened as Aziz proceeded to style the Kuwaiti royal house of the Al-Sabahs, with a snort of disgust, as "those crooks," a near-illiterate riffraff, sort of oil-sheik Snopeses, by his progressively hotter account, who had not even had the temerity themselves to take on the title of king, "even they were ashamed to call themselves king in front of everybody."

"That may all well be the case," said Jackson. "But I ain't exactly over here on their behalf, you understand."

Toward the end of the meeting, Aziz told Jackson, "As a prominent American politician, we know your role in your own country. You are not yet in power, but we hope you will be one time—we'll negotiate a lot more agreements." But it had also become clear, from Aziz's commentary, that the Iraqis were having difficulty computing Jackson's appearance there as that of a journalist. Aziz referred once to Jackson's traveling to Iraq as "a statesman," and Jackson retorted, perhaps a touch too playfully, "Journalist, Mr. Minister!" Aziz grunted. "Journalist, then. Whatever you want to call yourself." (That the Iraqi government might even suspect he was an unofficial emissary from the White House, Jackson later suggested, "might not be that bad a thing, if they thinking that. Know what I mean?") Jackson now began pressing Aziz about an interview with Saddam, and Aziz, still with an air of vague uncertainty as to whether Jackson was serious, replied, "Well, this is, after all, a matter of chemistry between you and my president—between two leaders. He knows just Jackson the politician, he did not know about the journalistic connection. Just use on him your chemistry about that."

LATE THAT AFTERNOON, back at the Al Rashid, Jackson was abruptly summoned to the presidential palace for at least a first talk with Saddam. Rushing out of the hotel, he managed to snatch along only a few of his aides. By their reports, after it was made plain on Jackson's arrival that there would be only discussion and no interview at this encounter, Jackson swiftly assumed a manner of actually ministering to Saddam, this enigmatic figure widely regarded as a cold predatory felon. Addressing him as "Brother Saddam," Jackson assured him, through an interpreter, "I do not underestimate your anguish. I know you feel isolated, ignored." He even once invoked Jesus, as a figure who demonstrated the essential difference between right and might—and how much more powerful was right, in the end, against temporal forces. Jackson went on to propose that, though Saddam may have been for years a man "ignored" (Jackson afterward explained, "Seemed sort of better to use 'ignored' instead of 'despised,' you know"), he now had a chance to capture the world's attention. "The wisest among us must change the course of events," Jackson said. "Don't wait for what Bush is gonna do. The world is waiting for *you* to make a bold new move."

Altogether, his exhortations to Saddam in this meeting, as recounted afterward by those who were there, largely repeated what Jackson had put earlier to Aziz: "The substance of your case is getting lost in the cutting of wires at embassies in Kuwait. It's being lost in hostages, detainees. And this idea of annexing Kuwait, recovering lost territories and all that . . . Syria could annex Jordan because of history, Israel says the Bible gives it the West Bank. Even your allies feel threatened by this annexation thing. The question now is whether we can do a harder thing than fight, and that's *think*. Iraq has finally got center stage to make its case about all its grievances against Kuwait, the stolen oil fields you say, the undercutting in oil prices, all that. But what's your case right now? You saying, 'My case is, we'll close the embassies, hold 'em prisoner.' Saying, 'My case is, we'll hold the people against gettin' bombed.' There's a great danger of losing your real case, because you not arguin' it with things like that. Mean, holdin' *the sick and old*. What I guess *I'm* arguin' for—without government portfolio—is that you have the power now to redefine the reality of the moment. You have the power to avert a war. And I think you should be secure enough in your real case to make the first move, daring moves that will, in fact, cost you nothing. Say, three or four planes of people coming out of here. Releasing a thousand people, to start with, will cost you nothing. It could, in fact, shift the agenda." With Saddam now and then taking notes with a fountain pen, Jackson suggested that he could condition a withdrawal from Kuwait on the formulation of a new international aid plan for all the Middle East, whereby its oil-rich principalities and the West would commit themselves to developing the poorer nations to regenerate the entire region. "Now the world will identify with *that* vision," said Jackson.

To all this, though, Saddam reportedly responded with a glumly ritualistic formality—at the least, he did not seem perceptibly moved, whatever points Jackson may have dropped like depth charges in his mood and mind for later effect. Saddam did mention that, since a visit by the U.S. ambassador back in April, no one else from the United States, "not one, has come to me to talk," and he thanked Jackson for making the trip over to do that. He announced that he now felt there was "a human bridge" between himself and Jackson, whom he decreed to be unlike most American politicians, who "refuse to show what they believe inside as human beings." But then, he appropriated Jackson's earlier reference to Jesus as, bizarrely, an emblem of himself and his own situation now in the world community: "At the time of his death, he had eleven disciples," as Saddam recollected the count, "and was betrayed by one of them. But ultimately, he had millions of followers." As Saddam expanded on this conceit, he seemed to be suggesting that he meant to take on himself all the centuries of abuse and vilification of the Arabs by the West, to present himself as a sacrifice in a great apocalyptic firestorm of war in which he would, as it were, be immolated into immortality among the Arab people. This indication of a kind of holy, Götterdämmerung bunker mentality may have been calculated for transmission by Jackson to the Bush White House, especially if Saddam supposed Jackson might be an informal, exploratory emissary from the administration. But it cast a chill on those sitting with Jackson.

It was also a measure of how unlikely Jackson's putative journalistic incarnation remained to the Iraqis that Jackson had so terrific a struggle persuading Saddam to even consider a television interview: as Jackson put it on his return to the hotel, "I just about had to get down on my knees and go into my Greenville beg: 'Please, Mr. President, you can't do this to me.' " Even so, he left with no final commitment on an interview. But he did manage to come away with one important achievement—permission, and the provision of an Iraqi plane, to fly down to Kuwait City the next morning, which would be the first visit there by any outside observers since Iraq had seized the country. "Make do with that for now," said Jackson.

That night, he decided to drop in on a party of U.S. embassy personnel at the home of Joe Wilson, the chargé d'affaires. When we arrived, we found also collected there some who had just escaped from the U.S. embassy in Kuwait City. Still a bit benumbed from their four-hundred-mile drive up to Baghdad, they described the destitution they had left behind them—improvised toilets dug on the embassy grounds, water distilled from the swimming pool, an unremitting violent heat. The mobbed rooms around them now were filled with a steady roar of voices and shouting laughter, two men behind a bar splashing together drinks without pause and people socking them down one after another, a faintly berserk festiveness to it all. Jackson circulated through the crowd, but, in this token extension of the United States once again, only as a kind of exotic and slightly questionable presence to most there—which he soon seemed to sense, and he shortly departed.

EARLY THE NEXT morning, as we assembled by a line of cars outside the hotel lobby, preparing to set out for Kuwait, three reporters appeared, including one for *The New York Times*, who had learned of the trip from someone who'd been at the party the night before. Once told by Jackson there was room for him and the others to come along, he then began to fret exceedingly, despite all Jackson's reassurances, as to whether his tagging along might offend Iraqi officials. Finally, Jackson, with some exasperation at finding himself having to act as a liaison for the reporter, went over to one of the Iraqi escorts and had him affirm there was no problem. But the reporter began querying Jackson about exactly who had cleared him for the trip, and started over to ask the Iraqi escort himself. "*Wait, now, man,*" Jackson hissed, "you keep on askin', they gonna finally say no. It's all right, I'm tellin' you, just *c'mon.*"

The motorcade departed for the in-town airport, a special field surrounded by military security forces, where an Iraqi Air 727 was waiting. During the one-hour flight down to Kuwait City, while we were high over the thin, glinting, convoluted twining of the Tigris River, Jackson pulled himself out of his seat near the front and ambled back to sit across the aisle from the Washington journalist who had been critical of Jackson's declining to run for mayor of the city. Jackson leaned over and remarked to him, in an amiably confidential tone, "Know what I was doin' last night? Kept worryin' about the slow ambulance service in Ward Six. Spent the night worryin' about them flooded basements in Ward Eight. Couldn't hardly sleep, all those problems. . . ."

When the 727 eased to a stop on the runway at the Kuwait City airport, we emerged from the cabin into a blasting heat, a wastescape of empty runways and terminal gates across which nothing was moving but a hot wind. Jackson was met at the foot of the plane's stairs by a small Iraqi deputation, headed by a balding man in a limp, snuff-brown, synthetic leisure shirt, who presented himself as the chief protocol officer there, but who had a somewhat extradiplomatic, nine-millimeter automatic pistol stuffed in the belt of his drooping trousers. Kuwait had been occupied by Iraqi forces for almost a month now, but the airport's interior was still totally forsaken, and we were led through it, past motionless luggage conveyors, and then out into the slamming heat again, where a motley agglomeration of cars was ranged along the curb, all obviously of recent annexation themselves and already with a look of slight dilapidation, beside which waited men with AK-47s, a soot of beard on their jaws. The car I got into was a red Toyota whose ignition the Iraqi driver started with the blade of a knife. On the way into Kuwait City, the road on both sides was scattered with the scorched and crumpled hulks of cars, with tanks squatting out in bare sweeps of tan sand, encircled by scribblings of barbed wire, and occasional tatters of black smoke blowing across the highway. We finally pulled up at the Kuwait International Hotel, which was right across the street from the wall enclosing the U.S. embassy, and rode an escalator up to the main, mezzanine lobby, a sprawling affair with much gilt and smoked mirrors, where the hotel's manager, a spiffily tailored and resolutely perky Austrian not without his own mordant wryness, threw wide his arms and tootled, "Welcome to paradise!"

The lobby's marbled expanses were patrolled by Iraqi soldiers and security men wearing loose-hanging sport shirts and holding AK-47s at a low dangle against their slacks. Jackson's party now began scampering about with a certain high skittering excitement at simply being here, the first Western observers allowed into Kuwait since the invasion, the reporters and TV crew for Jackson's show circling for some starting locus for their coverage. Jackson finally called out, "Everybody! We gonna have a staff meeting right now. Little staff meeting, everybody come up close here." When his group was gathered around him, he said softly, "Now, look. We runnin' around in this place like blind dogs in a slaughterhouse. We kind of getting out of control. We actin' like American brats or something. We not in Six Flags or Rockefeller Center here, you know. And *those* guys"— he nodded toward the Iraqi security men deployed over the lobby—"they not too sure what they doin', either. They not in complete control of this situation themselves. We don't want to be havin' any incidents or misunderstandings. So let's just stay cool and disciplined. Only one person in control of us in this thing, and that's *me.*" It served to remarkably recompose his party.

For the next several hours, Jackson applied himself to a phone on the counter of the reception desk, talking to the deputy chief of mission, Barbara Bodine, in the U.S. embassy across the street, and trying to arrange some means of seeing those confined within its walls. The Iraqis had forbidden anyone to enter the embassy, and those inside were refusing to leave its grounds. Jackson's phone negotiations on this double-lock impediment continued through the morning and on into the afternoon. Between calls once, Jackson settled himself low in a stuffed chair, and napped.

Eventually, the hotel's management took Jackson, accompanied by his entourage and several Iraqi guards, up a Piranesian labyrinth of back passageways that opened finally into sunglare on the hotel's flat graveled roof, which, we saw when we wandered to its edge, overlooked the embassy's sprawling grounds by the sea. The walled enclave below us, all its water and electricity and food deliveries cut off, looked oddly remote and dreamlike in the afternoon sunshine, as if it were in some other dimension. A few tiny figures were stirring under the edge of an awning alongside a long swimming pool, another minute figure jogging alone on a pathway off in a back section of the grounds. A call from the lobby phone downstairs had informed the embassy that Jackson would presently be on the hotel roof, and as he now began waving his arms in high sweeps, far below several figures trickled out from under the poolside awning and, from what seemed that strangely distant and unreachable remove of their captivity, gave barely perceptible waves back.

Down in the lobby again, Jackson at last concluded by phone an arrangement to walk across the street to the embassy, with an escort of four Iraqi security police, and to talk, through the locked front gate, with Bodine and the ambassador, W. Nathaniel Howell III. As it happened, Jackson had visited the embassy once before, back in November 1987, and he now said to Howell, as they clasped hands through the bars of the gate, "Good to see you again." Howell, tall and bearish, with a grizzled beard, and wearing a pale-blue T-shirt and orange gym shorts and sockless loafers, had a certain haggard sag to his big body and a bruiselike shadowing under his eyes. Bodine was a trim and energetic woman in a yellow sundress, with her dark hair pulled tightly back from her taut face. They hurriedly reported to Jackson their most critical needs at the moment—evacuation of the women and children among the eight staff members and forty-two civilians pent inside the compound, as well as the several elderly or sick Americans who had taken refuge there from places out in the city, and delivery of bottled water and diesel fuel for their generators, their only source of electricity. Jackson promised them he would confront Saddam with those concerns when, as he hoped, he met with him the following day. Before leaving, Jackson reached for their hands again through the gate, and said a prayer: "We know peace will come. Bless our nation. Bless its people. And bless our world. . . ."

Later, on the flight back to Baghdad, he reflected, "Least, if there's nothing else gonna happen, least there's been this. Given those folks their first live contact with somebody from the States since they been shut up in there. That's *something.*"

ONLY A SHORT while after arriving back at the Al Rashid, just before sundown, Jackson was called to the office of the culture and information minister, Latif Nusayif Jassem, to work out particulars for a possible television interview with Saddam the next day. "Hardly time to catch m'breath," Jackson mumbled. "But no choice but to go, if this thing's gonna come off. Ought not to take long."

Jassem was waiting, virtually alone in his ministry offices at that late hour, in his forest-green Ba'ath uniform—a stocky man with a shaggy, graying sheaf of hair and dark, dewy, almost spaniel-sweet eyes. As he and Jackson began talking in a corner of Jassem's commodious private office, which resembled an airline VIP lounge, Jassem appeared somewhat abstracted, and was damp with sweat. Jackson proceeded to unfold his appeal once more for a release of the hostages, going into it now with all the fullness and elaboration as if the decision were actually up to Jassem.

The dusk's last light dimmed in the room's windows. It was Friday—the Muslim day of withdrawal from the world's clamors into rest and solitude and prayer. Suddenly, while Jackson was in the middle of an exchange with Jassem, there sounded from somewhere close outside a muezzin's long languishing wail, announcing the close of this Muslim sabbath. A moment later, just as Jackson was moving into a spirited exposition on why it would be particularly meaningful if Saddam himself could appear for any hostage release, an aide brought in, with a rapid noiseless tred, a note for Jassem. As Jackson orated on, Jassem read the note closely, and then interrupted Jackson to announce, "Now we will take the tour."

Jackson's momentary stare of puzzlement quickly regathered into a bland expression of expectant suspicion as he stood with Jassem to leave.

Outside the ministry's entrance, our drivers had been replaced, we noticed in the darkness, by sprucely uniformed soldiers with a martinet's bearing. But for a long while, we only rode in interminable turnings through the nighttime streets of Baghdad, now loudly milling in release from Friday's sober pieties, repeatedly crossing bridges spanning the Tigris, once or twice even doubling back on our course. After about an hour of this meandering about the city, we swung onto a long wide boulevard and approached the barricades of a military sentry post, pausing there momentarily, and then passed on through a succession of giant iron-grille gates into a kind of fortress-park of immense lawns beneath softly underlit palms and eucalyptus trees, turning at last into a drive vast enough to be a cargo-plane landing strip that swooped up to the floodlit facade of a colossal building that resembled some grand Mediterranean casino-hotel—the palace of Saddam Hussein.

Inside, everything was constructed on an Ozymandian scale, megalithic columns and great, ringing, high-vaulted corridors of sandstone and marble, a giganticism not unbefitting the sort of personality who could cover his country with operatic circus-poster images of himself, the very architecture of megalomania. On stepping into it, one had a sensation of having instantly shrunk to miniature size. The news months later, when the bombing began, that this palace had been reduced to rubble was dumbfounding; it looked, that night, to be of a monumentality that could withstand a meteor collision.

Jackson was shortly beckoned away, his figure dwindling off across a far rotunda. After waiting for a while in a side drawing room, the rest of us were then conducted out across the same yawning distances of marble, to a relatively compact but resplendently chandeliered chamber, where Jackson was standing with Saddam.

Saddam struck me, as he went through the introductory handshakes, as, despite the grandiosity he had surrounded himself with, a surprisingly middling figure altogether. Like his handshake, he seemed oddly unvital—a formal, darkish man, in a graphite-blue suit, a shirt of powdery whiteness, and light-blue floral tie, who had the bleakly careful reserve of some Albanian funeral director. After we were all seated, he and Jackson resumed their conversation, Saddam once interrupting to command a military officer standing nearby, in a low rasping, to adjust the air-conditioning to a slightly cooler tinge. His face was rather baggy, with two small polyp bumps on his lower right cheek, and the pallor of his skin gave an almost vicious blackness to his heavy eyebrows and mustache and hair, which looked dyed with ink. His expression remained virtually changeless, that of a faintly vexed patience, with a narrow black depthless peer that somehow brought to mind all the methodical slaughterings he had administered over his long career. He addressed Jackson, through the interpreter, in a voice that had the peculiar dead, harsh quality of burned cordite. There was about him, in all, a certain dull, heatless, machinelike deliberation, his gestures infrequent and exactly measured, and executed with a gawky looseness of wrist—the movements of a man who somehow did not appear wholly at home in nature. His hands, speckled on the back with age-freckles, were almost completely hairless, with a paleness as if from excessive washing, the fingers pinkish on the ends like shrimp buds, and he kept them alternately clapped clumsily together, folded below his chin as if in prayer, or simply dropped straight down from the arms of his chair with fingers closely packed straight together. Even while aware it was probably an absurdly hyperbolic and melodramatic fancy, I could not help feeling, as I sat watching the two of them, that Jackson had happened to come into confrontation now, whether conscious of it or not, with at least one instance of the mystery of evil on this earth, even beyond what he had experienced growing up in the segregationist order of Greenville.

Jackson, perhaps a bit overbuoyant now that he had apparently arrived at the decisive encounter with Saddam, brought up again the matter of the hostages. Saddam interjected an irritable mention that the American nationals among them still showed a great mistrust of him, many now keeping their whereabouts secret. Jackson told him, "The women and children are afraid. That's why they are hiding underground."

"This is Bush!" Hussein retorted, in a voice like the swipe of a rake through cinders. "Because he keeps threatening war."

"Let me say it another way, Mr. President," Jackson said. "Fear makes people irrational."

Hussein's reply was ominous: "After a while, we will have to say that any adults still hiding themselves will be regarded as spies."

He did not seem, on the whole, in the most promising of humors. Jackson pressed on nevertheless about possible arrangements for a release, until Hussein asserted, "We are not in the custom of having the head of state discuss details like this," which, despite its nettled tone, was yet the first intimation that he might already have come to some larger decision. In any event, it was clear that at least the television interview was on for that evening. Saddam finally allowed himself the drollery that, while he very much liked Jackson the politician, "let us see how we are going to like him as a journalist."

We shortly trailed back out into his palace's titanic spaces to another chamber—this one like a Congress of Vienna ballroom, where there was already arranged, with a dainty preciseness, cameras and lights and two facing chairs. Jackson and Saddam took their appointed seats, and Saddam could not resist quipping once more, "So now we're sitting with Jesse Jackson the journalist."

The interview turned out a dismally heavy-slogging affair. Jackson repeatedly endeavored rigorous, journalistically respectable questions, but Saddam responded to each one with extended trudging marches over measureless salt flats of pontification about historical honor and his indifference to all the West's wrath and might now massing against him. It was a kind of sullenly resigned intractability, no matter what fearful clobberings might be awaiting him, that would also seem his lumpishly submissive fatalism toward the ruin descending on his boasts and, more unhappily, on his country some five months later. At any rate, after persistent attempts to somehow hot-wire this hortatory address of Saddam's into a conversation, Jackson began to glance around him in a furtive dismay. But he toiled on. Saddam, during a camera break, wiped his face with a tissue, which came away smudged dusty orange with makeup. He then lifted his hand to look at his watch: "We had agreed to sit together for one hour, but as you see, we have been together for two hours and a quarter now. I am not annoyed at this," he stipulated. "I respect you as a man. The most important, I respect you as a human being. It is on this basis that I can relate to you, regardless of positions or posts or influence or power."

Perhaps encouraged by this, Jackson again undertook to query Saddam again about the hostages, though it was coming close to hectoring by this stage—"Let me ask you this last set of questions. There are some pressure points that can be relieved. . . . What steps are you willing to take now to release persons who are designated as a guest against their will, within the next twenty-four to forty-eight hours?" Saddam shifted forward, flapped his hands open, and replied, stonily, "This is a matter that I have addressed. I have made the position clear on that matter, and there's nothing more to add as regards my position in the coming forty-eight hours"—a time frame that Jackson seemed to have especially irked Saddam by specifying. Despite that, Jackson bluntly persisted, "You've announced your willingness to release women and children and those who are sick. Is there a plan in place to collect them and to evacuate them?"

Hussein replied, if anything more crustily, "I have answered this question—" and again, in apparent testiness over Jackson's deadline, "I have nothing to say about the forty-eight hours to come."

Jackson seemed to assume that was that. The interview ended, and they both stood and shook hands.

Then, despite the unalleviated aridness of the preceding few hours, Saddam, still in a voice with all the warmth of asbestos, proclaimed himself to feel that "it has been a good evening. And a deep human exchange." He continued, "And in honor of every American who looks at the Arabs and the legitimate rights of people in the way that they deserve, so we shall transfer the hospitality," which in this context, according to the translator, could also mean the care and keeping, "of four of them who are allegedly sick to join you on your plane to the United States."

Jackson, standing very still now in front of Saddam, with his hands poised together at his waist in a cage of lightly touching fingertips, blinked. So four, at least, he would be getting out. Had Saddam simply been cat-pawing him on this through the whole night's session? Jackson said, "Let me express my thanks to you for that, Mr. President." Then, with only the slightest hang of a pause, he decided to try further, "And about the women and children . . . could they, is it possible they could be included in this?"

Saddam's voice rose a bit. "The women and children wanting to leave Iraq? You want to take them tomorrow?"

For some reason, Jackson appeared momentarily stunned. He glanced over Saddam's shoulder to where I was standing, just a few feet behind Saddam, and without thinking I nodded with an overemphatic vigor. Saddam had begun to turn to see where Jackson was staring when Jackson said, quietly, "Yes."

"You want to take them with you?" Saddam repeated, in a cawing shout. More resonantly, Jackson declared, "Yes. Yes, I do."

"Yes, then!" exclaimed Saddam, and the translation now began scurrying along after his voice, "Yes, all right! You will take them with you on the Iraqi plane to—" And, showing more animation than he had the entire evening, he made several rapid upward flings of both hands as if he were throwing birds into the air, tossing the whole matter to the heavens. A thought flickered: was it possible he had been moved himself by this generosity elicited in him by Jackson? Could that principle, often propounded by Jackson, that we feel a special affection for those who allow us to feel we are good, actually be at work now even in Saddam Hussein? Whatever the case, he fairly bubbled on, "Take the women, the women who are allowed to leave, and the children, yes, and the four men who appear to be sick—" It grew giddy. "We will send them on the Iraqi aircraft that will take you to the United States. They will take you to Amman and from there to Washington—or wherever!"

Jackson gazed down at Saddam, his face impassive, completely composed, attentive, waiting, as Saddam went on, "This is in your honor. I'm doing this for you—not Bush! I have no respect for Bush. But for you!"

Jackson then gently proceeded, "Kuwait as well as Baghdad."

In fact, he had him. A small snag-hold at least. Saddam had finally, in this sudden access of sentiment, tipped just far enough forward from the rigid posture he had maintained all evening to give Jackson for the first time a clasp on him. Quite likely, Saddam had been prepared from the start to grant some releases; Jackson, as an unofficial intermediary of nevertheless considerable standing in the United States, presented to Saddam a means to begin relieving himself of an increasingly unprofitable and cumbersome liability without seeming to capitulate to the demands of the U.S. and other Western governments. But in the high spirits now of his doing that, Jackson was swiftly expanding the transaction beyond what Saddam had likely reckoned on, especially with the inclusion of the people in Kuwait—pushing Saddam's consent as wide, as fast, as he could get Saddam to go. What it had become, in the few minutes they were standing there in the middle of the room after the interview, was a kind of bazaar-booth haggling, only this merchandise being the number of lives to be freed—from four, quickly now to hundreds. "Kuwait, too?" cried Hussein. And then, "If you have a list . . ."

It ended in a noisy exhilaration and repeated handshakes between Jackson and Saddam, who appeared improbably close to bouncy, between Jackson's party and Saddam's own retinue, including even the palace photographer. Then, abruptly, Saddam pivoted around and left the room, his heels clacking across the empty immensity of a rotunda, something in his brusque departure suggesting an ambush of embarrassment at his feelings. It was the last we were to see of him. The suspense left hanging over the rest of our hours in Iraq was whether, like Pharaoh, he would come to resent his concession and move to retract it.

Back in his suite at the Al Rashid, Jackson quickly changed into khaki shorts and a black T-shirt for the business that still lay ahead that night. Logistics began to be worked out in a salvo of telephone calls. The U.S. embassy was notified, then Deputy Secretary of State Lawrence Eagleburger in Washington. Saddam's secretary called once to insist to a Jackson aide that only four of the five men listed as ill on the embassy roster supplied to Jackson could be permitted to leave, "so will you pick who those four will be, and call us back?" Apprised of this, Jackson said, "No way we gonna get into making decisions like that. That's actin' God." He called Saddam's secretary back. "Mr. Secretary? 'S Jesse Jackson. Now, look—" and went into a murmurous disquisition for about a minute. When he hung up, he said simply, "All five." The actual count of those to be taken out, from both Baghdad and Kuwait City, and already ranging now from Americans to other nationals, began to blur in the tumble of phone negotiations going on through the night: all that was clear was that the number was still expanding.

At one point, Sadun Zubaydi, Saddam's translator, appeared in Jackson's suite. Zubaydi had come by a brief notoriety at the outset of the Gulf crisis as the unctuous interpreter in television broadcasts of Saddam's memorably grotesque chat with children of English hostages, including a conspicuously uncomfortable five-year-old named Stuart Lockwood. With his arrival in Jackson's rooms, Sadun—a slender, youngish man with silvering hair and heavy foxlike eyebrows arching behind delicate aviator glasses, and the crisp fastidiousness of some overrarefied junior professor in a Kingsley Amis novel—was shortly caught up in the effervescence of the developments, and it became evident that he was considerably more than a translator in his authority. Making several calls from Jackson's phone, he concisely dispatched a series of complications, including provisions for a flight first down to Kuwait City to pick up those released there. In the course of contributing these services, he quickly acquired a kind of tentatively reckless vivaciousness: he seemed, more than anything else, profoundly relieved. He once merrily sang out, "You people think you have problems? Imagine *my* job," and went on to confide that he had been the author of the term "guest" for the hostages: "How do you find a word to reconcile enforced hospitality? Not easy, I tell you!" Jackson presently contrived to put him on the phone with Eagleburger in Washington, on the pretext of confirming arrangements for landing rights in Paris and London and finally Dulles: when Jackson held out the phone to him, with Eagleburger on the other end of the line, Sadun hesitated with a shrilly skittish alarm, "No, no, no, it's not necessary, you must understand, I can't—" until Jackson hooted, "C'mon, just *speak* to the man, he's got to check his information with you." Sadun then took the phone in a gingerly finger-hold, and rather tonelessly exchanged perfunctory remarks with Eagleburger, while Jackson leaned back in a chair, listening, turning once to mutter with a wink, "Probably first contact since the invasion. No tellin' how you might get a dialogue started."

A few minutes later, Joe Wilson, the embassy's chargé d'affaires, entered the room, perspiring and a little disheveled, but radiantly convivial, saying to Jackson, "Congratulations are in order. Good work." He turned then to Sadun with a carefully tempered mien of mildly regretful affability: "Good to see you again. It's been some while." Sadun flushed in apparent deep distraction, but he was also obviously pleased to see Wilson: one distinctly sensed he was not at all at ease in the heavy direness of the national confrontation in which he now found himself caught. Even so, after a few moments, he departed, but not before submitting, with an unrestrained grin, to snapshots of himself and Wilson held in shoulder-hugs by Jackson, after which Wilson reached to shake Sadun's hand once more: "Good-bye, now. Take care. Hope to see you again soon when things are a little more pleasant." Sadun bolted out of the room.

Wilson slapped Jackson on the back, and said again, "You've done good work tonight."

"Ain't over with yet," said Jackson.

He stayed up—playing his Ray Charles tapes again—while he kept on making calls, pacing, assessing, scrawling notes, on through the night until dawn.

AN HOUR OR so later, around seven, Jackson presented himself in the lobby, looking a touch weary but barrelingly eager and spankingly arrayed in a double-breasted gray houndstooth-checked suit with a Rainbow Coalition button in his lapel. "When you talk, you act, and when you act, you change things," he jubilantly announced, and then, unable to abstain from a scriptural citation, he bugled out to everyone, "Settin' out to free the captives! What it's about." Sadun was also in the lobby, having decided to come along with us as a general facilitator. On the flight back down to Kuwait City, he seemed barely able to contain his festiveness. Bobbing down the aisle once to retrieve his coat from a back seat, where it lay stuffed with official papers, he fetched it up, piping, "So many secrets! So many secrets!"

The plan was to quickly pick up the evacuees collected at the embassy in Kuwait City, more having been called in from the city overnight, then fly back with them by early afternoon to pick up the some three hundred other evacuees waiting at Baghdad's airport, and finally fly on out with them all before sundown. But by the time we pulled up again at the International Hotel across from the embassy—only twenty-four hours since we were last there, yet seeming now a week ago—indications reached us that Jackson's agreement with Saddam the night before had set loose the beginnings of an even larger evacuation. More flights were now being organized in Baghdad to fly out with us, in what was turning into something of a hectic mass exodus. Partly for that reason, the wait in the International's now oppressively familiar lobby, like a back-lapse in time, stretched on into the afternoon.

Meanwhile, the embassy across the street continued to transmit additional names to Jackson to negotiate for inclusion on the list, with Sadun's plucky assistance. Not a little enjoying this business, Sadun at one point warbled, "More names? You have *more* names? You people!" But he acted with an awesomely nimble decisiveness in winning, one after another, further clearances from Baghdad, as the morning passed on into afternoon. With Sadun's aid, Jackson managed, from the lobby of the International, to enlarge the list of those to be taken out of Kuwait City, both Americans and other foreign nationals, from the original twenty-one agreed upon the night before to about double that number.

Then, late in the afternoon—when most of those to be freed had been assembled at the embassy across the street, and at the Kuwait City and Baghdad airports—Jackson waved me over to where he was sitting with Sadun. Motioning me to lean down, he whispered behind his hand, "Somebody told me just a bit ago, there's this lady up on the third floor here, wants to leave with us. Room number is 306. Says she has an American passport. Slip up there quiet as you can and check. Room 306. If she's got her passport, tell her she can come with us."

Joining me at the elevator to ride up to the room was a veteran aide of Jackson's named Jeff Griffiths. A long, lean, surpassingly gentle and soft-spoken man, with a gnarled right hand mangled in a long-ago machine-shop accident, Griffiths was a black radio journalist who had been attending to audio transcriptions for Jackson for years. With Iraqi security police thick around the lobby, Griffiths and I eased into an elevator as unobtrusively as possible and rode up to the third floor. The corridors there were empty, soundless. We found Room 306 at the end of one short hallway, and Griffiths tapped on the door. After a long moment, it swung open—a handsome woman in her early forties, with meltingly dark eyes and black hair, and wearing a grass-green pants suit, stood peering at us with uncertain alarm. Behind her, the room was filled with stacked boxes, closed suitcases. I told her who we were, and asked if she had an American passport.

"Yes. Yes." Her face took on a stare of disbelief. "You mean I can leave? You mean, *right now?*"

"Right now," I said. She threw her arms around me and pressed her head against my chest, holding to me with a fierce tightness and crying, "Thank God, thank God, thank God. . . ." We all moved into the room, shutting the door noiselessly, and the woman sank down on a small couch, still gazing in astonishment at us. An American of Arabic descent, she had a home in Gainesville, Florida, where her daughter was living. She had been working as an assistant manager at the hotel when the Iraqis invaded, and had been hiding in this small room at the end of the corridor throughout the four weeks of the occupation, hearing all the reports of random abductions, street executions, tortures, rapes, disappearances. Sitting now on the edge of the couch among her packed belongings, she began trembling. "But what about the Iraqis?" she said. "Have the Iraqis given their permission?"

Her hands were twisting together in her lap in a terror that was almost childlike, and somehow shocking to see—this mature, agreeable-looking, and no doubt pleasantly sensible woman reduced to a wild abject dread. It was, in its own way, the most monstrous testimonial to what had been the nature of the Iraqis' rule here. She was obviously still too frightened to move from the room, and leaving Griffiths to keep her company, I went back downstairs to get Jackson.

He was still sitting with Sadun. When I told him the woman was in a panic about the Iraqis, he turned to Sadun and explained the situation, concluding, "She has her passport. President has said women and children can go. So no problem in her coming with us, is there?"

Sadun, in this instance, turned markedly less jaunty. "But why has she hidden?" he said thinly. "Why has she not come forward before now?"

Jackson said, "Like I been trying to explain to yawl, man, people are *afraid.*"

Sadun gave a large sigh, and shrugged. "Well, yes, all right. We are bending the rules, but we have been bending the rules everywhere today."

Jackson then said, "And I want you to come up with me to tell her, all right, buddy? Just to reassure her."

About this, Sadun had even more painfully pronounced reservations: after allowing Jackson to hustle him as far as the elevator, he stopped and held up the palms of both hands, "No, no, actually, better you go up first. I'll wait here, you can send for me if you need."

This time, just before the elevator doors closed, a young plainclothes security operative quickly stepped in with us. He was short, compact, darkly sun-scorched, and he said absolutely nothing, did not look at us—not even when Jackson said, "How y'doin'?"—as the elevator rose back toward the third floor. When Jackson and I got out, he followed us down the hall to the room, and leaned back against the wall outside as we went in.

When the woman, who was still sitting on the edge of the couch, saw Jackson come looming into the room, her expression was as if she were beholding some supernatural manifestation. She slowly stood, dazed, as he moved to her and enclosed her in an immense hug: "We gonna take you home, honey. You ready to go? You comin' with us."

But even with Jackson's appearance before her now, which must not have seemed completely real to her, she could not yet quite free herself from her terror over the past weeks about the Iraqis. "Have they given their permission? I mean about *me*? If they find I have been hiding up here, they will take me out and—" It was as if her fear were paralyzing her in place at the very moment deliverance had opened for her.

Jackson, studiously making no mention of the security agent who had followed us down the hall, asked me to return to the lobby and bring Sadun on up. When I left the room, the agent was still leaning against the wall of the corridor.

When I arrived back at the lobby, the elevator doors parted to disclose Sadun in a spirited discussion with three burly men who, despite their casual civilian attire, were obviously security officers. When I walked over, Sadun said in a distressed squeal, "It is impossible. They say they have known about this woman up in the room all this time. She should not have hidden. It is very, very bad. She cannot leave today." Sadun's authority, impressive as it had proved up to now, was superseded here in Kuwait, it appeared, by that of the military, since it was territory under military occupation. I told him, "Well, why don't you come on up and explain that to the Reverend. He wants to see you upstairs." He relayed this to the three security men in Arabic, in which I detected a decidedly apologetic strain, and as we headed for the elevator, two of them followed and got on with us.

It was almost certain that they belonged to the *mukhabarat*, Iraq's famously barbarous secret police. Both of them had a tankish girth, with a dingy smudge of beard on their jowls, and that universal thickish look of their kind of being matter-of-factly acquainted with performances of savage mayhem on countless subjects in countless dim anonymous rooms— in fact, they immediately reminded me of sheriffs and deputies I had encountered in country courthouses across the American South during the gothic summers of the sixties.

When the woman saw the two of them piling into the room with us— she was still sitting on the couch, Jackson standing over her—the look on her face was one of blank doom. Sadun took a chair beside her, the two *mukhabarat* agents hulking behind him, and the woman began shaking. Sadun started questioning her in a querulous voice: "Why did you not come forward? What were you afraid of? We are not animals, you know." The woman—as if in a stupor of hopelessness, still shivering in little spasms, her hands twisting together on her knees—merely whispered, "I know you're not, I know you're not." But Sadun, perhaps sensing that he himself was under the surveillance of the agents standing right behind him, kept on at the woman in a scolding tenor, "Why have you not been open with us? There are procedures you must go through to leave. Why did you think you were an exception?"

"I didn't, I'm not an exception," she murmured in a dwindled voice, sounding as if she had somehow inwardly retreated to being a small girl again.

"Where is your passport, for instance?" said Sadun. He then plucked it from her fumbling fingers and handed it to the police agents behind him. Both their heads bent together over a rapid ruffle through its pages. They began imparting guttural phrases to Sadun for translation to the woman, not realizing yet that she also spoke Arabic. She thus knew, even more than was evident to the rest of us, that she was in the darkest trouble.

Jackson had been watching all this silently, standing motionless over the woman, his hands loosely folded together at his waist, his face completely expressionless. Then, as the voices of Sadun and the two agents began racketing away more loudly at the woman, like dogs baying a rabbit, while she seemed to be trying to huddle smaller into herself on the couch, Jackson suddenly spoke into the rising clamor, quietly and simply, "Let her go."

There was an immediate hush. Sadun and the two police agents stared at him.

"Let her go," he repeated gently, almost breathing the words. He then placed one hand lightly on the woman's shoulder beneath him. "She just told me a minute ago she has cancer. She just wants to go home to be with her daughter. Let her go." It became like a soft incantation—"She's no threat to the state. You can let her go"—with the lilt and tempo of one of his campaign-rally orations, and it sent a kind of thrill through the room. Sadun noticeably gulped. The woman looked up at Jackson with tears filling her eyes. "Just wants to go on back home now," he said, his hand still on her shoulder. "Let her go."

Sadun was blinking very rapidly behind his glasses. One of the police agents, apparently sensing a change in the emotional barometrics in the room and wanting to know what was going on, rattled something in Arabic to Sadun. He answered in Arabic, but plainly losing something of the full register of Jackson's appeal in translation—it produced only a glower on the faces of the two agents. The one evidently in charge spoke another short gargle of gutturals to Sadun, and Sadun said to Jackson, "The problem, you see, they say she has broken the law." He then suggested, almost as a plea, "Let us go downstairs for now, where we can discuss it further."

As we turned to leave the room, the woman lurched to her feet, as if in a pang of panic at being left alone there. Jackson said, "Can't she come with us?" When Sadun translated this to the senior officer, who was holding the woman's passport, he shook his head and waved a hand back and forth. Jackson said to the woman, "Don't worry, honey. We'll be back." Nevertheless, she trailed after us as we filed out of the room, and at the door made several weak lunges against the restraining hands of the policemen to follow us. At this, Jeff Griffiths, for all his customary unassertive mildness, wheeled on the Iraqi police agents, "Now wait a minute, she's an American and *I'm* an American, and—"

Jackson quickly called back to him, "Just come on now, Jeff."

As we headed down the corridor toward the elevator, Jackson abruptly muttered, "Yeah. The one lost sheep." In the midst of this grim little development, he had been moved to another of his gospel evocations—this from the parable of the shepherd who left the ninety-nine of his flock in the fold at evening to go out seeking, in the dark, the one still missing. "Others already gathered in, you know? Waitin' over there at the embassy, at the airport in Baghdad. They all right, they bein' cared for. But there's this one still lost."

Back downstairs in the lobby, Sadun insisted to Jackson, "If it were only up to me, I assure you, there would be no problem, I hope you understand." Jackson replied, a little tartly, "Well, see what you can do about it, then."

Sadun took the two police agents into a small glass-front office adjacent to the reception counter, and began placing calls to Baghdad in between lively exchanges with the two agents. Jackson, allowing them to argue the matter among themselves for a while, nevertheless made a point of stalking conspicuously back and forth right outside the glass wall as they conferred, pausing now and then simply to hang ponderously in the doorway. Sadun would intermittently come out to report to Jackson that it looked hopeless—for one thing, most government offices in Baghdad were now closed for the day.

"What about the president?" Jackson said. "You got his number, I'd imagine." Sadun insisted that would be the most impossible thing of all. In fact, the affair of the woman up in Room 306 had by now taken up almost three hours. With everyone collected in the embassy across the street and hundreds of other evacuees waiting at airports here and in Baghdad, inevitably a tension began forming as to whether the whole undertaking was being jeopardized for this one case.

Jackson finally called Sadun and the two police agents out of the office. Leaning back against a pillar with his hands clasped behind him, he casually observed to them, "You know, I just, I'm afraid I'm not going to be able to leave here until that lady's turned loose. I just can't really do that. Translate that to these guys for me, will you please, Sadun? I'm gonna have to stay here in Kuwait City until she's free to go with us." He was, in effect, now placing himself hostage, too, for the sake of getting this last one out. He did not neglect to add—"Tell 'em this, too, Sadun"—that his having to remain in Kuwait because of their reluctance to give up this one ill woman might prove somewhat irksome to their president, after such a productive meeting the night before and the president's own goodwill announcement that all women, children, and the sick were free to return to their countries. "She qualifies twice. She's a woman, and she's ill. You don't want to be embarrassin' your president 'cause you got some little technical legal problem here, do you?"

With that, all four of them—Jackson, Sadun, and the two police agents—returned to the office, where, between more phone calls to Baghdad, Jackson proceeded to exhort them at full throttle. Word of what was happening had spread through the lobby, and soon a sizable gallery was collected outside the office, at a circumspect remove—hotel clerks and their supervisors, other journalists who had come down with Jackson, curious Iraqi security personnel, assorted other onlookers—watching Jackson operate behind the glass wall: gesturing in his most urgently flourishing pulpit manner, leaning from his chair to clap his hand on nearby knees, periodically heaving himself to his feet to pounce about. Then, after a last phone call by Sadun, he talking briefly and then handing the phone to the senior police agent who, after listening a moment, handed it back to Sadun to hang up, those watching from the lobby saw them all stand and shake hands. Jackson came striding out with both arms flung high, thumbs hooked backward. Flashing a grin, he declared, "She's comin'."

The two *mukhabarat* agents came shambling up beside Jackson, and when he impulsively gave them both vigorous shoulder hugs, it actually jostled forth small smiles on their faces. We all then crowded into an elevator—the two police agents, Sadun, Jackson, Jeff Griffiths, myself—and rose in a kind of welling euphoria back up to the third floor, an exhilaration in none of us likely more novel a sensation than in the two agents.

When we entered the room again, the woman, sitting in the same spot on the very edge of the couch, gazed at us dully. Sadun told her she was free to leave. But she seemed lost in some far trance—it was the second time that afternoon she had been told this. She only moved to stand when the senior police agent brought over her passport to her. Sadun, for his part, seemed in a veritable vertigo of relief. "What do you wish to take?" he cried out.

"What?" she said. "To take? Oh—" She absently motioned toward two suitcases. Sadun glanced at her other belongings stacked about the room. "You mean, you are leaving all this?" he said,

"Leaving? Oh—" She mumbled something about sending for the rest of her things later. Then she said, "Is this really true? Is it really happening?"

Sadun happily crowed, "Yes! Yes! *Yes!* You can go now!"

She said, "My God." And simply headed straight for the door.

"Wait," said Sadun, "we must wait for the Reverend Jackson." With his five-hour negotiation at last ended, Jackson had, as soon as we came through the door, availed himself of this opportunity to repair to the bathroom. Sadun noticed a basket of candy atop one of the packed cartons, and he lifted from it a large, striped lollipop. "May I have this?" he cheerfully inquired.

The woman stared at him. She was in a suppressed torment to get out of the room. She murmured, "Of course. It was to be for my daughter, but of course, please." Sadun grinned. "Well, then," he said, and tucked the lollipop into the inside pocket of his coat. "It will be a gift from your daughter to my little girl!"

Jackson reappeared, and the entire motley procession surged on down the corridor to the elevator and a moment later tumbled out into the lobby—to an outburst of applause from the small throng waiting there. Enlarged by those in the lobby now to a kind of general extemporaneous parade, the procession spilled out into the hot night and swept across the street to the embassy. There, Jackson stood by the barred gate and greeted the hostages as, one by one, they straggled out, unsteady and blinking, into the flare of television lights. With this finish to his efforts over the past days, Jackson's eyes welled with tears. Indeed, more than one of the journalists, watching all this after the small saga of the woman in the room at the hotel, experienced a brief blur of their own vision.

The two police agents came along as vans carried us to the airport, where more freed hostages were waiting, and even tagged after us all the way into the plane, crowding close to Jackson in the aisle, all for no apparent reason except just to stay a part of the remarkable spirit of this happening for as long as they could. Once everyone had been settled, Jackson turned to the senior agent and gave him an Arab multikiss embrace, then hugged his heavy round balding head to his chest. The man emerged from

Jackson's hug momentarily off-balance, again with an unaccustomed little lopsided smile—but clearly moved: it was not the least of the wonders worked by Jackson over the past few days that he had managed to stir some dull glow of human warmth, some vague memory of mercy, in this thuggish *mukhabarat* agent. It wasn't until the last instant before the cabin doors were closed that he and the other agent slumped back up the aisle, with obvious reluctance, to get off the plane; he actually gave a wobbling wave of general farewell to the cabin, and to the woman of Room 306 in particular, who, nestled against a window, could only muster in reply a faint semblance of a smile.

While the plane sat poised on the runway before takeoff, I turned to talk with a woman behind me, who had sitting beside her a small girl, perhaps nine, whose ill mother was somewhere in the back of the plane. At one point, I happened to push up the shade on the window beside me, and the girl immediately shrilled, *"Don't open the window!"* I asked her why not, and she said, "Because the Iraqis said not to!" The woman merely shook her head with a look of pity: the terror of their weeks of confinement by the Iraqis still held the small girl imprisoned. I pushed the shade back down. But as I continued talking to the woman, the girl, after a minute or two, reached toward the closed shade beside her own seat and slowly nudged it up a tentative inch or so, then leaned her head close to peer out that merest slit for a long moment, in which one could almost see forming in her a first realization of release and freedom. And she then shoved the shade all the way up to the top with a triumphant slam. Even so, when the plane finally began moving down the runway and then lifting with a huge slowness into the air, the girl began sobbing, "I don't want to leave my daddy"—her father, the woman explained, was among those still hiding in Kuwait City. The girl was soon close to hysterics—not, actually, out of all the terror yet—screeching, plunging about in the arms of the woman until someone found a sedative to give her.

Others were later to relate horrific tales—families trying to escape Kuwait by car over the desert who were apprehended short of the Saudi border by Iraqi patrols, the men pulled out into the sand and shot, the women raped. An electronics engineer from El Paso, Lloyd Culbertson, who was in his seventies, with a scrappy white furze of beard, recounted what those in the embassy, whom we had glimpsed from the hotel roof only two afternoons ago, had been living through down there for the past weeks with water and electricity cut off—the unrelenting heat, decayed food having to be burned, but most of all the degradation of being held helplessly subject to a capriciously brutish force. "It began after a while to make you feel less than human," Culbertson said. He once interrupted his recountal to ask apologetically, in a strangely touching little courteous worry given all he had endured through the past month, "Uh, I hope I don't smell bad, do I?"

WHEN WE LANDED at the Baghdad airport, the released hostages assembled there had been waiting by now for over six hours, with little knowledge of what was taking place down in Kuwait City. Two other aircraft filled with freed hostages had already taken off. As Jackson was boarding the Iraqi Air 747 that was to take us all out of the country, one woman snapped at him, "We've been waiting on you since one o'clock this afternoon. Now, when are you going to go back down there and get my husband out?" This seemed to hit Jackson like a torpedo. He stammered some explanation of what had taken him so long in Kuwait City, but as he made his way on to his seat in the upper-deck section of the plane, he was sunk in a sudden huge gloom. Already, this quickly, a brackish tinge had fallen on what had seemed to him the overwhelming sweetness of the outcome of his labors here. And not for the first time in his life—one was reminded of the querulousness he had met with on his return from Syria with Goodman and from his similar success in Havana. Already he seemed contracting into a defensive umbrage. After we had lifted off, on our way to our first stop in Paris, Jackson leaned over in his seat to remark, "You know, I been thinking. About when Jesus went up on the mountaintop, had his transfiguration experience. When he came back down, everybody started picking at him, picking at his robe, fussin' and complainin', 'Do this for me; do that for me.' " He leaned back in his seat. "Just been thinkin' about that last few minutes."

But later that night, somewhere high over the Mediterranean, he climbed down to the darkened main cabin, which was packed with some three hundred people, French and British as well as American, and he took a long walk up and down the aisles in something like a solitary rejoicing survey of what he had done: almost all of them were now sleeping under lightly draped blankets, children curled against their mothers, including Stuart Lockwood, who had been the uneasy subject of Saddam's televised dotings; the woman from Room 306 settled in a window seat at almost the exact position of the one she had taken on the plane from Kuwait City—rows after rows of them, delivered out of captivity and being transported as they slept back to the freedoms of home. All the sheep now gathered in. Jackson returned then to the upper compartment, and fell at last into a deep doze himself, his first sleep since that initial morning flight down to Kuwait City, some thirty-six hours ago.

Nevertheless, as the plane proceeded westward, for Jackson it was as if he were flying from the great exaltations of what had taken place the last

few days, back into a drearily familiar cold front of disdain. We landed at
Heathrow, in London, just before dawn, and the instant the cabin door
was opened, a British official pushed in with a bustling imperiousness. Ignoring Jackson standing beside him, he snatched a bullhorn and blared
over the cabin, "Where are the Brits? All right, all you Brits . . . let's let the
VIPs get off first, and then we can welcome you home." It was a stunning
rudeness, and when Jackson gamely reached out anyway to shake the official's hand, the official clipped, "Oh, yes. Hello."

We lifted off from London in a pale dawn, heading at last for Washington, and as daylight began to fill the cabin, one sensed that the entire situation was going irretrievably flat for Jackson. After everything he had
brought to pass in Baghdad and Kuwait City, the subsequent accumulation of slights and discountings along this return journey had thrown him
back into old, bitter broodings. A few hours before we were scheduled to
land at Dulles, he returned to the lower cabin to sit for a while with the
group he had brought out of Kuwait, answering questions and sketching
out for them just what he had done to get them out. Most of them were
only learning this fully now for the first time, and they expressed effusive
gratitude, several of them with tears. Though the State Department would
not be paying their airfares in the United States, Jackson assured them
that, after arrival in Washington, if they were short of funds for flights on
back to their respective homes, his Rainbow Coalition would take care of
their tickets. It seemed, on the whole, the warmest of sessions. But back in
his seat upstairs, he remarked with an abrupt, morose detachment, "All of
'em were praying for a savior to come and get 'em out, and when he shows
up, he's black. Like they hadn't quite got used to that. Just can't quite accept that yet." He seemed to have retreated so completely into his old,
pained fixation of racial aggrievement that it now included even the profusely appreciative folks downstairs whom he had rescued.

Indeed, after his no doubt exorbitant anticipations of a flight back in triumph and glory, the progressive dismissals of his achievement that he had
met with instead, starting with the woman's complaint when he first
stepped onto the plane in Baghdad, had all left him hurt, furious, and now
dourly projecting what reception likely awaited him in Washington—
while also desperately determined that the meaning of what he had done
should not be completely stolen from him. This obsession of his somehow
reminded me of Hemingway's old fisherman who, after going out far beyond any sight of shore, then battles to make it through the sharks back to
harbor with at least some vestige of his big fish left. But it was not a good
omen for what lay ahead that, about an hour out of Washington, Jackson
sat off by himself intently making notes on a legal pad for pronouncements

to be delivered on arrival. I once suggested, perhaps a bit too playfully, about the image of his Iraqi mission that might emerge in the press, "But we're not concerned about how things look, are we?" and he shot back, not at all playfully, "That's why we got eyes—to look."

The arrival at Dulles turned out, not unpredictably, to be an appalling affair. Jackson quickly rummaged together as many of the released hostages as he could retrieve from the militantly efficient custody of U.S. officials—it was no more than five or six—and brought them to stand beside him before the bank of media folk mobbed behind a rope just outside the arrival gate. While he had someone search for his legal pad on which he had so carefully compiled notes for his comments, the small cluster of freed hostages dangled there beside him, glazed with weariness and stumblingly replying to questions swarming at them from the reporters. Jackson was at last handed his notepad, and from it he proceeded to expound on his visit to Iraq and his proposals for averting a conflict, with the returned hostages still agreeably standing beside him, two or three of them, though, tottering now just slightly. But as Jackson perorated on, one, then two, turned to slip away, including at last the woman from Room 306. None of this served much to mellow the humor of the journalists—Jackson refused to resign himself to the clear fact that they wanted to hear not from him but from the freed hostages—and sure enough, their questions shortly came snicking at him like a scissors assault, just as they had when he returned from Syria with Goodman and from Cuba with the prisoners released by Castro: Who had sponsored his trip? Wasn't he interfering in U.S. conduct of foreign policy? Exactly what he had expected. When the few returned hostages still remaining beside him did at last step to the microphone to speak, one of them—Lloyd Culbertson, the seventy-six-year-old electronics engineer—had to be reminded by Jackson, leaning down to whisper, to make some acknowledging mention of his efforts. This, to be sure, Culbertson did readily and robustly enough: "But for the grace of God and Jesse Jackson, we wouldn't be here. I want everybody to know— God forgive me for saying it—that our State Department hasn't lifted a hand for us."

But, whether because of Jackson's sheer weariness, or his final despairing frustration at the curt receptions that had greeted him since Baghdad—or both, most probably—it was an altogether gruesome show. It left one with the most dismal melancholy that such an extraordinary performance over the past few days should have ended, in this concourse at Dulles, so crassly and basely. Later, at the curb outside the baggage area, as Jackson was about to get into a limousine to be taken to a church service in Washington, I declined his invitation to come along, and when we shook hands in parting, it was with, for the first time since I had begun tracking about with him almost two years before, an empty awkwardness of cold disconnection. For that matter, Jackson himself seemed to be dimly beginning to suspect the calamity of the scene up at the gate.

OVER THE FOLLOWING days, Jackson's journey to Baghdad and his part in setting into motion what turned out to be a continuing, wholesale release of hostages by Iraq—abetted by subsequent trips to Baghdad by such figures as Willy Brandt and John Connally—received only an incidental and cursory notice from Washington and the news media. The State Department dispensed one glancing acknowledgment of his services: "We understand that the departure of several individuals was facilitated by Rev. Jesse Jackson." But that was it. Rather, the suggestion that had been directed at him on his return from Syria with Goodman was most commonly recycled: that he had been manipulated by his vanity to serve, in this case, Saddam's own purposes. Jackson's rejoinder was, "Well, anytime anybody wants to use me in a way that gets hundreds of people out of bondage, I'll be used for that anytime." Saddam himself, at least, after the bombing onslaught had fallen around him, reportedly grumbled that he had permitted himself to be cozened by "hypocrites from the West" into turning loose the hostages and thereby clearing the field for the air assault. But what may well have amounted to the most remarkable feat Jackson had pulled off in his entire career had registered in the general mind only flickeringly, and rather tackily at that. And then disappeared with virtually no trace, no memory.

Part of the press's discountal of Jackson's achievement owed, no doubt, to that practically viral resistance to him that had set in over his many years of avidly grappling for their recognition—his eagerness for them to discover, to realize, what he felt was his special import. That urgency, says one of his former seminary classmates, "is so overwhelming in him that I don't think people see past it, to how deeply he really feels, for instance, about the suffering of the oppressed." One journalist remarked after Jackson's return from Iraq, "It was just Jackson showboating and grandstanding again." And the reporter for The New York Times who had been so anxious about having Jackson confirm for him Iraqi approval of his going along on the initial visit to Kuwait City—and who, on the return to Baghdad, had entreated one of Jackson's party that, if he should land in any trouble while in Iraq, "I sure hope I can count on Jackson to step in for me"—had afterward written of Jackson's hours in Kuwait City, "he acted more like a cross between his old political self and a film celebrity. He asked a few questions and mugged for the camera. . . ."

That Jackson had wound up in a kind of perpetual war with the medium in which it had been his original, and probably misbegotten, hope to find affirmation may have always owed as much to the difficulty for the quotidian attentions of most journalism to reflect fully a character of Jackson's scale of complications and aspirations. Mark Steitz maintains, "There are plenty of things that one can argue about in terms of his perfection, but not about the size of his spirit, his vision, his person, and his desire to be involved in real transformations—rather than just the daily stated news flow." But, says Robert Borosage, "the way the press covers things, you see this guy yelling on television for maybe ten seconds, and then you move on without ever having heard the real message." As a result, almost by the nature of the form, quotidian journalism must necessarily get him partially, and therefore superficially, and thus in caricature. Even well after Jackson's mission to Iraq, Joe Klein, then with *New York* magazine, posed the waggery in a television exchange with Jackson, "Well, Louis Farrakhan was there, Ramsey Clark was there. What's to stop Jim and Tammy Faye Bakker from going there if they want a little press?"

"Nothing," said Jackson, "except courage, and conviction."

"And maybe the money for a plane ticket," Klein cracked.

In any event, the general disregard of what he had done in Iraq seemed, in the following weeks, to have knocked the wind out of Jackson's spirit. He remained curiously silent about the whole business, as if even he had begun to wonder whether what had happened in Baghdad and Kuwait City had been wholly real. Or as if he had simply, summarily disengaged from it all, cast it behind him, after it had brought only the same disdain accorded similar efforts in his past. He once offered the hazy optimism— something of a misappropriation of a phrase of King's about social justice, to apply to his personal disappointment—"You know, though? Truth crushed to earth will rise again."

IT WAS ONLY some days after my own seeming dead-end disillusionment at his ghastly performance at Dulles that I happened to recall a moment back at the embassy in Kuwait City, that hot night after the hostages had shuffled out into the blaze of the television lights. Among them was a thin blond girl of about twelve, huddling against her mother. The two of them were led to the gate and presented to Jackson by the girl's father, who had to stay behind, with the words, "Take care of them for me, Reverend Jackson." The girl was stooped over, and shuddering convulsively, and Jackson took her hand, and then her mother's, into his hugely enveloping clasp. And it was then that he had begun to weep—possibly from a final immense exhaustion after the exertions and emotions of the past few days, but also, one could not avoid noting with a cold little nip of suspicion, in the brightly lit televised theater of this event. It was the same prick of uncertainty I had felt at certain other moments like this over the past, as when, in Soviet Armenia, he was photographed wet-eyed at the hospital for children injured in the earthquake. But on this evening in Kuwait City, when all the released hostages had emerged from the embassy and were making their way down the long walkway toward the hotel across the street where the vans were waiting to take them to the airport, surrounded now by journalists in a brilliant aura of camera lights, I suddenly realized that Jackson was nowhere among them.

I looked around and saw that he had hung back, and was following at a considerable, solitary distance behind them. And then I saw that—out of the glimpse of any camera, all by himself in the dark—he was still weeping. For what one could only surmise, but at least this once, manifestly not for any media witness. . . . Perhaps it was from the reeling moral dramaturgy of the past few days having reached this finish. It could have been, too, a remembrance of the long distances he had come from Haynie Street, from his time with King, to this moment, yet how close they all still actually were; but despite his long struggle to realize that moral heroic promise sensed in his youth, his abiding condition still as an outsider. Though he'd been able to make something like this happen when probably no one else could or would have even tried, yet this, too, would probably not be enough, would be dismissed. So perhaps it was for what he could be, and should be, but wasn't, and never would be.

But he was sobbing, soundlessly, so deeply and unstoppably that when I went back to congratulate him and asked him what might be the significance of how his whole endeavor here had turned out—the sort of question he usually could not resist expatiating on at length—he could not reply. Could not speak. He simply went on weeping while he followed the group of hostages whose release he had won, as they walked on ahead of him, silhouetted in a flaring white light, toward their freedom.

BIBLIOGRAPHY

BOOKS

Abernathy, Ralph David. *And the Walls Came Tumbling Down*. New York: Harper & Row, 1989.

Anderson, Alan B., and George W. Pickering. *Confronting the Color Line: The Broken Promise of the Civil Rights Movement in Chicago*. Athens, Ga.: The University of Georgia Press, 1986.

Branch, Taylor. *Parting the Waters: America in the King Years, 1954–63*. New York: Simon & Schuster, 1988.

Briggs, Bill. *Faith Through Works: Church Renewal Through Mission*. Franconia, N.H.: Thorn Books, 1983.

Califano, Joseph A., Jr. *Governing America: An Insider's Report from the White House and the Cabinet*. New York: Simon & Schuster, 1981.

Chafe, William H. *Civilities and Civil Rights: Greensboro, North Carolina, and the Black Struggle for Freedom*. New York: Oxford University Press, 1980.

Colton, Elizabeth O. *The Jackson Phenomenon: The Man, the Power, the Message*. New York: Doubleday, 1989.

Faw, Bob, and Nancy Skelton. *Thunder in America: The Improbable Presidential Campaign of Jesse Jackson*. Austin: Texas Monthly Press, 1986.

Fish, John Hall. *Black Power/White Control: The Struggle of the Woodlawn Organization in Chicago*. Princeton: Princeton University Press, 1973.

Frank, Gerold. *An American Death*. Garden City, N.Y.: Doubleday, 1972.

Garrow, David J. *Bearing the Cross: Martin Luther King, Jr., and the Southern Christian Leadership Conference*. New York: William Morrow, 1986.

Goldman, Peter, Tom Matthews, and the *Newsweek* Special Election Team. *Quest for the Presidency: The 1988 Campaign*. New York: Touchstone/Simon & Schuster, 1989.

King, Coretta Scott. *My Life with Martin Luther King, Jr.* New York: Holt, Rinehart, and Winston, 1969.

Matalin, Mary, and James Carville, with Peter Knobler. *All's Fair: Love, War, and Running for President.* New York: Random House, 1994.

Phillips, Kevin. *The Politics of Rich and Poor.* New York: Random House, 1990.

Ralph, James R., Jr. *Northern Protest: Martin Luther King, Jr., Chicago, and the Civil Rights Movement.* Cambridge, Mass.: Harvard University Press, 1993.

Reynolds, Barbara A. *Jesse Jackson: The Man, the Movement, the Myth.* Chicago: Nelson-Hall, 1975.

Simon, Roger. *Road Show.* New York: Farrar, Straus, and Giroux, 1990.

Taylor, Paul. *See How They Run: Electing the President in an Age of Mediaocracy.* New York: Alfred A. Knopf, 1990.

Walker, Wyatt Tee. *Road to Damascus: A Journey of Faith.* New York: Martin Luther King Fellows Press, 1985.

Weisberg, Harold. *Frame-Up: The Martin Luther King–James Earl Ray Case.* New York: Outerbridge & Dienstfrey, 1971.

Wills, Garry. *Under God: Religion and American Politics.* New York: Simon & Schuster, 1990.

ARTICLES

Adler, Jerry, and Sylvester Monroe. "Jackson's White Organizers." *Newsweek,* February 8, 1988, p. 26.

Adler, Renata. "Letter from Selma." *The New Yorker,* April 10, 1965, pp. 121–59.

"Again: Character Tests." *U.S. News & World Report,* October 19, 1987, p. 8.

Ajemian, Robert. "Respect and Respectability." *Time,* August 17, 1987, pp. 16–17.

Alter, Jonathan, with Monroe Anderson. "Taking on the Networks." *Newsweek,* March 31, 1986, p. 66.

Alter, Jonathan, with Sylvester Monroe. "Jackson's Arab Connection." *Newsweek,* February 13, 1984, p. 29.

Alter, Jonathan, with Sylvester Monroe. "The Great Unspeakable." *Newsweek,* May 30, 1988, p. 39.

Alter, Jonathan, with Howard Fineman and Sylvester Monroe. "Jackson's Message." *Newsweek*, March 21, 1988, pp. 23–24.

Alter, Jonathan, with Sylvester Monroe, Vern E. Smith, and Howard Fineman. "The Jackson Dilemma." *Newsweek*, July 23, 1984, p. 21.

Alter, Jonathan, with Vern E. Smith, Margaret Garrard Warner, and Nancy Cooper. "Now, 'the Jackson Reaction.' " *Newsweek*, April 30, 1984.

Andersen, Kurt. "Jackson Plays by the Rules." *Time*, November 5, 1984, p. 29.

Arlen, Michael J. "The Air: Life and Death in the Global Village." *The New Yorker*, April 13, 1968, pp. 157–59.

"Bad." *The New Republic*, April 18, 1988, pp. 7–9.

Baer, Donald, with Harrison Rainie and Sandra R. Gregg. "The New Age of Jackson." *U.S. News & World Report*, March 14, 1988, pp. 16–19.

Baker, James N., with Bob Cohn. "Trying to Stop, Jesse, Stop." *Newsweek*, July 17, 1989, p. 29.

Barnes, Fred. "Jackson Rules." *The New Republic*, May 1, 1989, pp. 14–15.

———. "Jesse Goes Country." *The New Republic*, August 3, 1987, pp. 15–20.

———. "The Jackson Tour." *The New Republic*, July 30, 1984, pp. 18–21.

Barrett, Laurence I. "Big Apple Showdown." *Time*, April 18, 1988, pp. 22–24.

———. "Marathon Man." *Time*, May 2, 1988, pp. 21–24.

———. "Ready to Play Ball?" *Time*, June 20, 1988.

"Belatedly, Jackson Comes Clean." *Time*, March 12, 1984, p. 27.

Bell, Pearl K. "Hit the Road, Jack." *The New Republic*, April 3, 1989, p. 4.

Birnbaum, Norman. "Jackson and Jews." *The Nation*, April 23, 1988, pp. 557–58.

"Black America 1970." *Time*, April 6, 1970, pp. 13–29.

"Black Pocketbook Power." *Time*, March 1, 1968, p. 17.

"Blacks Wrap Up Slice of Action at Food Chains." *Business Week*, April 26, 1969, pp. 162–64.

Borger, Gloria, with Kathryn Johnson. "Super Tuesday: A Day of Reckoning for Democrats?" *U.S. News & World Report*, April 20, 1987, p. 21.

Branch, Taylor. "Lessons from the Fringe." *The Washington Monthly*, February 1987, pp. 56–58.

Carlson, Margaret B. "More Than a Crusade." *Time*, March 7, 1988, pp. 16–17.

———. "Why Can't Jesse Be Nominated?" *Time*, March 21, 1988, p. 29.

Chaze, William L., with Jeannye Thornton, Kenneth T. Walsh, and Ronald A. Taylor. "A New Form of Black Politics." *U.S. News & World Report*, May 25, 1987, pp. 20–21.

"Chicago: Jackson's Expo." *Newsweek*, October 4, 1971, p. 24.

"Chicago: The Touchiest Target." *Newsweek*, August 15, 1966, p. 29.

Church, George J. "Closing in on the Prize." *Time*, May 14, 1984, pp. 16–18.

———. "Keeping the Faith." *Time*, August 18, 1986, pp. 14–16.

———. "What Does Jesse Really Want?" *Time*, April 16, 1984, pp. 15–16.

"Civil Rights: Search for a New Selma." *Newsweek*, December 10, 1965, pp. 29–30.

Cockburn, Alexander. "The Kiss of Death." *The Nation*, April 23, 1988, pp. 560–61.

Cole, Patrick E. "The New Black Power Behind Jesse Jackson." *Business Week*, June 6, 1988, pp. 33–34.

Colt, George Howe. "Jesse: A Rare Visit at Home with a Sudden Presidential Front-Runner." *Life*, July 1987, pp. 25–30.

Conconi, Charles, and Woody West. "Someone Had to Carry on for King." *The New Republic*, July 13, 1968, pp. 13–14.

Cooper, Nancy, with Sylvester Monroe. "Keeping His Eyes on the Next Prize." *Newsweek*, November 21, 1988, p. 22.

Corn, David, and Jefferson Morley. "Sing Along with Tipper." *The Nation*, April 23, 1988, p. 559.

"Could His Wife Keep Jackson Out?" *Newsweek*, August 3, 1987, p. 6.

Crouch, Stanley. "Beyond Good and Evil." *The New Republic*, June 20, 1988, pp. 20–23.

Davis, Peter. "When Atlanta Burned." *Esquire*, November 1988, pp. 126–31.

Deming, Angus, with Milan J. Kubic and Chris J. Harper. "Jackson! Arafat!" *Newsweek*, October 8, 1979, p. 50.

"Democrats' Long-Distance Runner." *U.S. News & World Report*, December 2, 1985, p. 13.

Doerner, William R. "A Long-Awaited 'Embrace.' " *Time*, September 10, 1984, pp. 12–13.

Duffy, Michael. "Frustrated." *Time*, July 18, 1988, p. 24.

Dunbar, Ernest. "Rev. Jesse Jackson: A New Kind of Black Cat." *Look*, October 5, 1971, pp. 17–20.

"Employment: Jesse Jackson's 13 New Targets." *Business Week*, October 7, 1972.

Fairlie, Henry. "Jackson's Moment." *The New Republic*, February 27, 1984, pp. 11–13.

Fineman, Howard. "Jackson's New Clout." *Newsweek*, December 14, 1987, pp. 50–51.

Fly, Richard. "Jesse Jackson: Even More of a Force to Reckon With in '88." *Business Week*, April 7, 1986, p. 45.

"Follow the Money." *The New Republic*, February 20, 1984, pp. 8–9.

Fox, William L. "Jesse Jackson's Kingdom Theology." *The Christian Century*, May 4, 1988, pp. 446–47.

Friedman, Robert. "The Spiritual Electricity of Jesse Jackson." *Esquire*, December 1979, pp. 80–94.

"Further Travels with Jesse." *Time*, October 15, 1979, p. 63.

Gillespie, Marcia Ann. "Something to Celebrate." *Ms.*, July 1988, pp. 22–23.

Gleckman, Howard, with James B. Treece. "The Fat Cats Adding to Jackson's Kitty." *Business Week*, April 25, 1988, p. 75.

Good, Paul. "Bossism, Racism and Dr. King." *The Nation*, September 19, 1966, pp. 237–42.

Green, Philip. "The Reality Beneath the Rainbow." *The Nation*, March 17, 1984, pp. 309–10.

Greene, Bob. "Getting Out of Town." *Esquire*, December 1988, pp. 59–61.

Greenfield, Meg. "A New Kind of Racial Put-Down." *Newsweek*, April 4, 1988, p. 80.

———. "Does Jackson Want the Job?" *Newsweek*, June 27, 1988, p. 72.

———. "Strange Bedfellows." *Newsweek*, October 17, 1983, p. 100.

Hackett, George, with Karen Springen, Eleanor Clift, and Vest Monroe. "The Private Jackson." *Newsweek*, April 25, 1988, p. 15.

Halberstam, David. "Notes from the Bottom of the Mountain." *Harper's Magazine*, June 1968, pp. 40–42.

———. "The Second Coming of Martin Luther King." *Harper's Magazine*, August 1967, pp. 39–51.

Hess, John L. "Confessions of a Greedy Geezer." *The Nation*, April 2, 1990.

Howard, Lucy. "A Pitch for Jesse." *Newsweek*, March 14, 1988, p. 4.

———. "Jesse's Last Stand." *Newsweek*, May 9, 1988, p. 7.

———. "The GOP's Plan for Jesse." *Newsweek*, February 13, 1989, p. 6.

Hoyt, Mary Finch. "Meet Politics' New Jackie." *Good Housekeeping*, August 1988, pp. 60–64.

"Invisible Man." *The Nation*, May 30, 1987, pp. 708–709.

Isaacson, Walter. "Seeking Votes and Clout." *Time*, August 22, 1983, pp. 20–31.

"Its Ugly Head." *The Nation*, July 4/11, 1987, p. 8.

Jackson, Jesse L. "Give the People a Vision." *The New York Times Magazine*, April 18, 1976, p. 13.

"Jackson Brothers." *The Nation*, March 10, 1984, pp. 275–76.

"Jackson Sets Up Shop." *Time*, September 7, 1987, p. 20.

"Jackson's Heat." *The Nation*, July 30/August 6, 1988, pp. 79–81.

"Jackson's Puzzling Quest." *Time*, July 2, 1984, p. 16.

"Jesse and George." *National Review*, June 29, 1984, p. 13.

"Jesse Comes Calling." *Time*, February 19, 1990, p. 44.

"Jesse Jackson: Dumping an Ally." *Newsweek*, June 9, 1986, p. 22.

"Jesse Jackson: Is He a Troubleshooting Man of God, or a Troublemaking Demagogue?" *People*, December 24, 1979.

"Jesse Jackson Is Too Much." *National Review*, September 26, 1986, pp. 16–17.

"Jesse Jackson Quits SCLC After Being Suspended." *The Christian Century*, December 22, 1971, pp. 1488–89.

"Jesse Jumps In." *Newsweek*, November 14, 1983, p. 43.

"Jesse Speaks." *The New Republic*, August 3, 1987, pp. 16–17.

" 'Jetstream Jesse' Flies High." *Newsweek*, April 11, 1983, p. 24.

Johnson, Terry E., with Sylvester Monroe. "Again, It's Run, Jesse, Run." *Newsweek*, May 5, 1986, pp. 28–29.

Jordan, Hamilton. "A Black Candidate in '84?" *Newsweek*, June 20, 1983.

Karlen, Neal, with Sylvester Monroe. "Jesse Jackson: Issue-Hopping." *Newsweek*, April 29, 1985, p. 37.

Kelly, James. "Looking for a Way Out." *Time*, January 16, 1984, pp. 10–13.

———. "When PUSH Gives a Shove." *Time*, April 14, 1986, p. 88.

Kempton, Murray. "The Dukakis Truce." *Newsday*, September 28, 1988, p. 84.

"King." *The New Yorker*, May 1, 1965, pp. 35–37.

"King Moves North." *Time*, April 30, 1965, pp. 32–33.

Klein, Joe. "At Play in the Fields of the Lord." *New York*, February 29, 1988, pp. 44–47.

———. "Dealing With Jesse." *New York*, March 21, 1988, pp. 16–19.

Knoll, Edwin. "Jesse Jackson's Claque." *The Progressive*, August 1984, p. 4.

Kondracke, Morton M. "Endless Quest." *The New Republic*, August 8/15, 1986, pp. 9–10.

———. "Jesse's World." *The New Republic*, April 25, 1988, pp. 11–14.

———. "The Jacksonian Persuasion." *The New Republic*, April 30, 1984, pp. 13–16.

Kopkind, Andrew. "A Populist Message Hits Home." *The Nation*, July 18/25, 1987, pp. 51–55.

———. "Flo Don't Know." *The Nation*, April 9, 1988, pp. 484–85.

———. "Is Jesse the Great White Hope?" *The Nation*, December 26, 1987/ January 2, 1988, pp. 789–91.

———. "Jesse's Movement." *The Nation*, April 2, 1988, pp. 448–49.

———. "Strategies for Now—And Next Time." *The Nation*, September 25, 1989, pp. 312–18.

Kramer, Michael. "Jesse Jackson's New Math." *New York*, October 24, 1983, pp. 36–39.

———. "Taking Jackson Seriously." *New York*, May 14, 1984, pp. 24–25.

———. "The Jackson Problem." *Time*, December 12, 1988, p. 29.

———. "What to Make of the 'New' Jesse." *U.S. News & World Report*, November 16, 1987, pp. 34–44.

Lamar, Jacob V. "Reaching Common Ground." *Time*, August 1, 1988, pp. 16–19.

"Learning to Excel in School." *Time*, July 10, 1978, pp. 45–46.

Leerhsen, Charles, with Sylvester Monroe, Diane Weathers, and Lucy Howard. "Special Coverage for Jesse?" *Newsweek*, April 9, 1984, p. 72.

Lester, Julius. "Man in the Mirror." *The New Republic*, May 23, 1988, pp. 20–21.

Levine, Richard. "Jesse Jackson: Heir to Dr. King?" *Harper's Magazine*, March 1969, pp. 58–70.

Magnuson, Ed. "Stirring Up New Storms." *Time*, July 9, 1984, pp. 8–11.

Martz, Larry, with Eleanor Clift, Howard Fineman, Mark Starr, and Sylvester Monroe. "The Democratic Battle: Can He Win?" *Newsweek*, April 11, 1988, pp. 22–26.

Martz, Larry, with Howard Fineman, Sylvester Monroe, Eleanor Clift, and Andrew Murr. "The Power Broker." *Newsweek*, March 21, 1988, pp. 18–22.

Martz, Larry, with Howard Fineman, Ginny Carroll, Lynda Wright, Sylvester Monroe, and Andrew Murr. "Day of the Preachers." *Newsweek*, March 7, 1988, pp. 44–46.

McCormick, John, with Howard Fineman. "Jackson Strikes Out." *Newsweek*, March 13, 1989, p. 24.

McLaughlin, John. "Watch Jesse Run." *National Review*, June 6, 1986, p. 24.

"Minorities: A Split in SCLC." *Newsweek*, December 20, 1971, pp. 27–28.

Monroe, Sylvester. "What Makes Jesse Tick?" *Newsweek*, October 31, 1983, pp. 32–33.

Monroe, Sylvester, with Howard Fineman. "Jackson for Vice President?" *Newsweek*, June 20, 1988, p. 29.

Monroe, Sylvester, with Howard Fineman and Jonathan Alter. "Let the Joy Bells Ring." *Newsweek*, July 30, 1984, p. 32.

Monroe, Sylvester, with Vern E. Smith. "Atlanta's Odd Couple." *Newsweek*, July 25, 1988, pp. 16–19.

Morganthau, Tom, with Sylvester Monroe. "Jesse Jackson's Troubles." *Newsweek*, July 20, 1981, p. 29.

Morganthau, Tom, with Sylvester Monroe. "Jesse's European Jet Stream." *Newsweek*, September 26, 1983, p. 34.

Morganthau, Tom, with Elizabeth O. Colton and Thomas M. DeFrank. "Appointment in Damascus." *Newsweek*, January 9, 1984.

Morganthau, Tom, with Elizabeth O. Colton, Nikki Finke Greenberg, Margaret Warner, and Thomas M. DeFrank. "Jesse Wins a 'Syria Primary.'" *Newsweek*, January 15, 1984, pp. 14–15.

Morganthau, Tom, with Sylvester Monroe, Gloria Borger, and Diane Camper. "A Black Candidate in '84?" *Newsweek*, June 6, 1983, pp. 36–37.

Morganthau, Tom, with Sylvester Monroe, Nikki Finke Greenberg, Margaret Garrard Warner, Howard Fineman, and Gloria Borger. "What Jesse Jackson Wants." *Newsweek*, May 7, 1984, pp. 40–44.

Morganthau, Tom, with Sylvester Monroe, Frank Maier, Renee Michael, Gloria Borger, Vern E. Smith, and David Gonzalez. "What Makes Jesse Run?" *Newsweek*, November 14, 1983, pp. 50–56.

Morganthau, Tom, with Sylvester Monroe, Diane Weathers, Frank Maier, and Vern E. Smith. "Jackson's Albatross?" *Newsweek*, April 23, 1984, pp. 31–32.

Morrow, Lance. "Gospel According to Jesse." *Horizon*, May 1978, pp. 60–63.

"Mr. Big." *National Review*, May 4, 1984, p. 17.

Nauer, Barbara. "Hats Off to Jesse Jackson." *National Review*, June 25, 1976, pp. 674–77.

"Noble Son." *Time*, August 6, 1979, p. 55.

Ostling, Richard N. "Jesse Takes Up the Collection." *Time*, February 6, 1984, p. 57.

Page, Clarence. "'I Am SOMEBODY!' . . . But Who?" *The Washington Monthly*, February 1980, pp. 26–36.

Pekkanen, John. "Black Hope White Hope." *Look*, November 21, 1969, pp. 67–74.

Peretz, Martin. "Cambridge Diarist." *The New Republic*, February 6, 1989, p. 43.

Poussaint, Alvin F. "A Dialogue." *Ebony*, August 1970, pp. 62–65.

"Poverty." *Time*, June 14, 1968.

Purnick, Joyce, and Michael Oreskes. "Jesse Jackson Aims for the Mainstream." *The New York Times Magazine*, November 29, 1987, p. 28.

"Races: Jackson PUSHes On." *Newsweek*, January 3, 1972, p. 30.

"Ray's New Ally." *Time*, August 21, 1978.

"Reflections on Jackson." *National Review*, November 25, 1983, pp. 1455–56.

Rogers, Cornish. "Martin Luther King and Jesse Jackson: Leaders to Match Mountains." *The Christian Century*, January 12, 1972, p. 29.

"'Run, Jesse, Run: A Crusade Is Launched.'" *Newsweek*, November/December 1984, pp. 49–52.

"Running in Place." *Time*, October 24, 1983, p. 28.

Saar, John, with Peter Younghusband. "Jesse Jackson Takes on Pretoria." *Newsweek*, August 13, 1979, p. 36.

Seligman, Daniel. "Jesse on the Couch." *Fortune,* September 26, 1988, pp. 209–10.

Serrin, William. "Jesse Jackson: 'I Am . . .' Audience: 'I Am . . .' Jesse: 'Somebody' Audience: 'Somebody.' " *The New York Times Magazine,* July 9, 1972, pp. 14–21.

Shapiro, Walter. "Jesse's Sideshow." *Time,* June 6, 1988, p. 20.

———. "Taking Jesse Seriously." *Time,* April 11, 1988, pp. 13–22.

———. " 'Win, Jesse, Win!' " *Time,* April 4, 1988, p. 21.

Shapiro, Walter, with Howard Fineman and Monroe Anderson. "Blacks: A House Divided?" *Newsweek,* February 25, 1985, p. 28.

Shapiro, Walter, with Howard Fineman and Sylvester Monroe. "Jackson: PUSH Comes to Shove." *Newsweek,* August 8, 1983, p. 24.

Shapiro, Walter, with Howard Fineman, Margaret Garrard Warner, and Sylvester Monroe. "Mondale Kicks Off the Race for No. 2." *Newsweek,* July 2, 1984, pp. 20–23.

Shapiro, Walter, with Howard Fineman, Margaret Garrard Warner, Stewart B. Copeland, and Sylvester Monroe. "And Now for the Hard Part." *Newsweek,* June 18, 1984, pp. 26–35.

Sheils, Merrill, with Sylvester Monroe. "Education: Preaching Pride." *Newsweek,* June 27, 1977, p. 64.

"Signs of Erosion." *Newsweek,* April 10, 1967, p. 32.

Sklar, Holly. "Rainbow Future." *The Nation,* January 30, 1989, pp. 113–14.

Sleeper, Jim. "He Is Somebody." *Commonweal,* November 7, 1986, pp. 590–94.

"St. Louis Dues." *Time,* August 23, 1982, p. 12.

Starr, Mark, with Sylvester Monroe. "And Now, Senator Jackson?" *Newsweek,* July 16, 1984, p. 23.

Starr, Mark, with Sylvester Monroe, Howard Fineman, John Harris, and Marie Adrine. "Jesse Jackson Goes to Cuba." *Newsweek,* July 9, 1984, pp. 16–17.

Stengel, Richard. "An Indelicate Balance." *Time,* July 25, 1988, pp. 20–21.

———. "Return of the Invisible Man." *Time,* October 31, 1988, p. 16.

"Storm Over Civil Rights." *Newsweek,* November 7, 1983, p. 19.

Strasser, Steven, with Sylvester Monroe and Vern E. Smith. "The Jackson Difference." *Newsweek,* March 26, 1984.

"The Democrats' Tar Baby." *National Review,* April 29, 1988, pp. 12–14.

"The Democrats' War with Jesse Jackson." *Business Week,* February 25, 1985, p. 119.

"The Jackson Factor." *The Nation,* April 14, 1984.

"The Meaning of Jesse." *National Review,* May 18, 1984, p. 16.

"The New Gospel According to PUSH." *Newsweek,* August 16, 1982, p. 52.

Thomas, Evan. "Last Call, and Out Reeling." *Time*, June 11, 1984, p. 26.

Tifft, Susan. "PUSH Toward the Presidency." *Time*, August 8, 1983, pp. 34–35.

Trillin, Calvin. "Journal: Resurrection City." *The New Yorker*, June 3, 1968, pp. 71–76.

Wall, James M. "The Political Downside of Jackson's Success." *The Christian Century*, August 3–10, 1988, pp. 691–92.

Wattenberg, Ben J. "The Curse of Jesse." *The New Republic*, December 5, 1988, pp. 20–21.

Weisberg, Jacob. "Rainbow Warrior." *The New Republic*, May 12, 1986, pp. 10–12.

———. "The Disorganization Man." *Newsweek*, August 17, 1987, p. 19.

West, Rebecca. "Reporter at Large: Opera in Greenville." *The New Yorker*, June 14, 1987, pp. 31–65.

"Which Way for the Negro?" *Newsweek*, May 15, 1967, pp. 27–34.

Wilkins, Roger. "On Being Uppity." *Mother Jones*, June 1990, pp. 6–8.

Wills, Garry. "Jesse Jackson: Newsmaker of the Year." *The Christian Century*, January 4–11, 1989, pp. 3–4.

———. "Making History with Silo Sam." *Time*, March 21, 1988, p. 31.

———. " 'New Votuhs.' " *The New York Review of Books*, August 18, 1988, pp. 3–5.

Woodward, Kenneth, with Sylvester Monroe. "Tough Rules of Brotherhood." *Newsweek*, July 15, 1984, p. 80.

Zoglin, Richard. "Keeping All Kinds of Hope Alive." *Time*, October 1, 1990, p. 82.

Zuckerman, Laurence. "Has He Got a Free Ride?" *Time*, April 18, 1988, p. 24.

INDEX

A B O U T   T H E   T Y P E

This book was set in Electra, a typeface designed for Linotype by W. A. Dwiggins, the renowned type designer (1880–1956). Electra is a fluid typeface, avoiding the contrasts of thick and thin strokes that are prevalent in most modern typefaces.